Communications in Computer and Information Science 951

Commenced Publication in 2007
Founding and Former Series Editors:
Phoebe Chen, Alfredo Cuzzocrea, Xiaoyong Du, Orhun Kara, Ting Liu,
Dominik Ślęzak, and Xiaokang Yang

More information about this series at http://www.springer.com/series/7899

Jianyong Qiao · Xinchao Zhao
Linqiang Pan · Xingquan Zuo
Xingyi Zhang · Qingfu Zhang
Shanguo Huang (Eds.)

Bio-inspired Computing: Theories and Applications

13th International Conference, BIC-TA 2018
Beijing, China, November 2–4, 2018
Proceedings, Part I

Editors
Jianyong Qiao
Beijing University of Posts
    and Telecommunications
Beijing
China

Xinchao Zhao (ID)
Beijing University of Posts
    and Telecommunications
Beijing
China

Linqiang Pan (ID)
Huazhong University of Science
    and Technology
Wuhan
China

Xingquan Zuo (ID)
Beijing University of Posts
    and Telecommunications
Beijing
China

Xingyi Zhang
Anhui University
Hefei
China

Qingfu Zhang
City University of Hong Kong
Kowloon
Hong Kong

Shanguo Huang
Beijing University of Posts
    and Telecommunications
Beijing
China

ISSN 1865-0929   ISSN 1865-0937   (electronic)
Communications in Computer and Information Science
ISBN 978-981-13-2825-1   ISBN 978-981-13-2826-8   (eBook)
https://doi.org/10.1007/978-981-13-2826-8

Library of Congress Control Number: 2018957098

This Springer imprint is published by the registered company Springer Nature Singapore Pte Ltd.
The registered company address is: 152 Beach Road, #21-01/04 Gateway East, Singapore 189721,
Singapore

Preface

Bio-inspired computing is a field of study that abstracts computing ideas (data structures, operations with data, ways to control operations, computing models, etc.) from living phenomena or biological systems such as evolution, cells, tissues, neural networks, immune system, and ant colonies. Bio-Inspired Computing: Theories and Applications (BIC-TA) is a series of conferences that aims to bring together researchers working in the main areas of natural computing inspired from biology, for presenting their recent results, exchanging ideas, and cooperating in a friendly framework.

Since 2006, the conference has taken place at Wuhan (2006), Zhengzhou (2007), Adelaide (2008), Beijing (2009), Liverpool and Changsha (2010), Penang (2011), Gwalior (2012), Huangshan (2013), Wuhan (2014), Hefei (2015), Xi'an (2016), and Harbin (2017). Following the success of previous editions, the 13th International Conference on Bio-Inspired Computing: Theories and Applications (BIC-TA 2018) was organized by Beijing University of Posts and Telecommunications, during November 2–4, 2018.

BIC-TA 2018 attracted a wide spectrum of interesting research papers on various aspects of bio-inspired computing with a diverse range of theories and applications. In all, 89 papers were selected for this volume of *Communications in Computer and Information Science*.

We gratefully thank Beijing University of Posts and Telecommunications, Huazhong University of Science and Technology, the Operation Research Society of China, and the Chinese Society of Optimization and Overall Planning and Economic Mathematics for extensive assistance in organizing the conference. We thank Tingfang Wu, Lianghao Li, Di Zhang, Taosheng Zhang, and Wenting Xu for their help in collecting the final files of the papers and editing the volume. We thank Xing Wan for his contribution in maintaining the website of BIC-TA 2018 (http://2018.bicta.org/). Many thanks are given to Hui Tong, Guangzhi Xu, Rui Li, Sai Guo, Min Chen, Jia Liu, Jiaqi Chen, Shuai Feng, and Qing Xiong for their work in organizing the conference. We also thank all the other volunteers, whose efforts ensured the smooth running of the conference.

The editors warmly thank the Program Committee members for their prompt and efficient support in reviewing and handling the papers. The warmest thanks should be given to all the authors for submitting their interesting research work.

Special thanks are due to Springer for their skilled cooperation in the timely production of these volumes.

August 2018

Jianyong Qiao
Xinchao Zhao
Linqiang Pan
Xingquan Zuo
Xingyi Zhang
Qingfu Zhang
Shanguo Huang

Organization

Steering Committee

Guangzhao Cui	Zhengzhou University of Light Industry, China
Kalyanmoy Deb	Indian Institute of Technology Kanpur, India
Miki Hirabayashi	National Institute of Information and Communications Technology (NICT), Japan
Joshua Knowles	University of Manchester, UK
Thom LaBean	North Carolina State University, USA
Jiuyong Li	University of South Australia, Australia
Kenli Li	University of Hunan, China
Giancarlo Mauri	Università di Milano-Bicocca, Italy
Yongli Mi	Hong Kong University of Science and Technology, SAR China
Atulya K. Nagar	Liverpool Hope University, UK
Linqiang Pan	Huazhong University of Science and Technology, China
Gheorghe Păun	Romanian Academy, Bucharest, Romania
Mario J. Pérez-Jiménez	University of Seville, Spain
K. G. Subramanian	Universiti Sains Malaysia, Malaysia
Robinson Thamburaj	Madras Christian College, India
Jin Xu	Peking University, China
Hao Yan	Arizona State University, USA

Program Committee

Muhammad Abulaish	South Asian University, India
Chang Wook Ahn	Gwangju Institute of Science and Technology, Republic of Korea
Adel Al-Jumaily	University of Technology Sydney, Australia
Junfeng Chen	Hohai University, China
Wei-Neng Chen	Sun Yat-Sen University, China
Tsung-Che Chiang	National Taiwan Normal University, China
Shi Cheng	Shaanxi Normal University, China
Bei Dong	Shaanxi Normal University, China
Xin Du	Fujian Normal University, China
Carlos Fernandez-Llatas	Universitat Politecnica de Valencia, Spain
Shangce Gao	University of Toyama, Japan
Wenyin Gong	China University of Geosciences, China
Shivaprasad Gundibail	Manipal Academy of Higher Education, India
Ping Guo	Beijing Normal University, China
Yi-Nan Guo	China University of Mining and Technology, China

Hui Wang	South China Agricultural University, China
Hui Wang	Nanchang Institute of Technology, China
Yong Wang	Central South University, China
Sudhir Warier	IIT Bombay, India
Slawomir T. Wierzchon	Polish Academy of Sciences, Poland
Xiuli Wu	University of Science and Technology Beijing, China
Zhou Wu	Chonqing University, China
Bin Xin	Beijing Institute of Technology, China
Gang Xu	Nanchang University, China
Yingjie Yang	De Montfort University, UK
Zhile Yang	Shenzhen Institute of Advanced Technology, Chinese Academy of Sciences, China
Kunjie Yu	Zhengzhou University, China
Defu Zhang	Xiamen University, China
Jie Zhang	Newcastle University, UK
Gexiang Zhang	Southwest Jiaotong University, China
Peng Zhang	Beijing University of Posts and Telecommunications, China
Xingyi Zhang	Anhui University, China
Yong Zhang	China University of Mining and Technology, China
Xinchao Zhao	Beijing University of Posts and Telecommunications, China
Yujun Zheng	Hangzhou Normal University, China
Aimin Zhou	East China Normal University, China
Shang-Ming Zhou	Swansea University, UK
Xinjian Zhuo	Beijing University of Posts and Telecommunications, China
Dexuan Zou	Jiangsu Normal University, China
Xingquan Zuo	Beijing University of Posts and Telecommunications, China

Contents – Part I

Research on Price Forecasting Method of China's Carbon Trading
Market Based on PSO-RBF Algorithm 1
    Yuansheng Huang and Hui Liu

An Efficient Restart-Enhanced Genetic Algorithm for the Coalition
Formation Problem 12
    Miao Guo, Bin Xin, Jie Chen, and Yipeng Wang

U-NSGA-III: An Improved Evolutionary Many-Objective
Optimization Algorithm 24
    *Rui Ding, Hongbin Dong, Jun He, Xianbin Feng, Xiaodong Yu,
    and Lijie Li*

Elman Neural Network Optimized by Firefly Algorithm
for Forecasting China's Carbon Dioxide Emissions 36
    Yuansheng Huang and Lei Shen

Research on "Near-Zero Emission" Technological Innovation Diffusion
Based on Co-evolutionary Game Approach 48
    Yuansheng Huang, Hongwei Wang, and Shijian Liu

Improved Clonal Selection Algorithm for Solving AVO Elastic
Parameter Inversion Problem 60
    Zheng Li, Xuesong Yan, Yuanyuan Fan, and Ke Tang

A Pests Image Classification Method Based on Improved Wolf Pack
Algorithm to Optimize Bayesian Network Structure Learning 70
    Lin Mei, Shengsheng Wang, and Jie Liu

Differential Grouping in Cooperative Co-evolution for Large-Scale
Global Optimization: The Experimental Study 82
    Heng Lei, Ming Yang, and Jing Guan

Spiking Neural P Systems with Anti-spikes Based on the
Min-Sequentiality Strategy 94
    Li Li and Keqin Jiang

Solving NP Hard Problems in the Framework of Gene Assembly
in Ciliates 107
    Ganbat Ganbaatar, Khuder Altangerel, and Tseren-Onolt Ishdorj

A Study of Industrial Structure Optimization Under Economy, Employment
and Environment Constraints Based on MOEA   120
   Ruozhu Zhang

DNA Strand Displacement Based on Nicking Enzyme for DNA
Logic Circuits   133
   Gaiying Wang, Zhiyu Wang, Xiaoshan Yan, and Xiangrong Liu

Motor Imaginary EEG Signals Classification Based on Deep Learning   142
   Haoran Wang and Wanying Mo

DNA Origami Based Computing Model for the Satisfiability Problem   151
   Zhenqin Yang, Zhixiang Yin, Jianzhong Cui, and Jing Yang

DNA 3D Self-assembly Algorithmic Model to Solve Maximum
Clique Problem   161
   Jingjing Ma and Wenbin Gao

Industrial Air Pollution Prediction Using Deep Neural Network   173
   Yu Pengfei, He Juanjuan, Liu Xiaoming, and Zhang Kai

An Efficient Genetic Algorithm for Solving Constraint Shortest
Path Problem Through Specified Vertices   186
   Zhang Kai, Shao Yunfeng, Zhang Zhaozong, and Hu Wei

An Attribute Reduction P System Based on Rough Set Theory   198
   Ping Guo and Junqi Xiang

Spatial-Temporal Analysis of Traffic Load Based on User Activity
Characteristics in Mobile Cellular Network   213
   Moqin Zhou, Xueli Wang, Xing Zhang, and Wenbo Wang

A Simulator for Cell-Like P System   223
   Ping Guo, Changsheng Quan, and Lian Ye

Dynamic Multimodal Optimization Using Brain Storm
Optimization Algorithms   236
   Shi Cheng, Hui Lu, Wu Song, Junfeng Chen, and Yuhui Shi

A Hybrid Replacement Strategy for MOEA/D   246
   Xiaoji Chen, Chuan Shi, Aimin Zhou, Siyong Xu, and Bin Wu

A Flexible Memristor-Based Neural Network   263
   Junwei Sun, Gaoyong Han, and Yanfeng Wang

A Biogeography-Based Memetic Algorithm for Job-Shop Scheduling   273
   Xue-Qin Lu, Yi-Chen Du, Xu-Hua Yang, and Yu-Jun Zheng

Analysing Parameters Leading to Chaotic Dynamics in a Novel
Chaotic System.   285
    Junwei Sun, Nan Li, and Yanfeng Wang

Enhanced Biogeography-Based Optimization for Flow-Shop Scheduling   295
    Yi-Chen Du, Min-Xia Zhang, Ci-Yun Cai, and Yu-Jun Zheng

A Weighted Bagging LightGBM Model for Potential lncRNA-Disease
Association Identification.   307
    Xin Chen and Xiangrong Liu

DroidGene: Detecting Android Malware Using Its Malicious Gene   315
    Yulong Wang and Hua Zong

Visualize and Compress Single Logo Recognition Neural Network   331
    Yulong Wang and Haoxin Zhang

Water Wave Optimization for Artificial Neural Network Parameter
and Structure Optimization.   343
    Xiao-Han Zhou, Zhi-Ge Xu, Min-Xia Zhang, and Yu-Jun Zheng

Adaptive Recombination Operator Selection in Push and Pull Search
for Solving Constrained Single-Objective Optimization Problems   355
    Zhun Fan, Zhaojun Wang, Yi Fang, Wenji Li, Yutong Yuan,
    and Xinchao Bian

DeepPort: Detect Low Speed Port Scan Using Convolutional
Neural Network   368
    Yulong Wang and Jiuchao Zhang

A Dual-Population-Based Local Search for Solving Multiobjective
Traveling Salesman Problem   380
    Mi Hu, Xinye Cai, and Zhun Fan

A Cone Decomposition Many-Objective Evolutionary Algorithm
with Adaptive Direction Penalized Distance   389
    Weiqin Ying, Yali Deng, Yu Wu, Yuehong Xie, Zhenyu Wang,
    and Zhiyi Lin

Origin Illusion, Elitist Selection and Contraction Guidance.   401
    Rui Li, Guangzhi Xu, Xinchao Zhao, and Dunwei Gong

A Multi Ant System Based Hybrid Heuristic Algorithm for Vehicle
Routing Problem with Service Time Customization.   411
    Yuan Wang and Lining Xing

Model Predictive Control of Data Center Temperature Based on CFD   423
    Gang Peng, Chenyang Zhou, and Siming Wang

Computer System for Designing Musical Expressiveness in an Automatic
Music Composition Process   434
  Michele Della Ventura

A Hybrid Dynamic Population Genetic Algorithm for Multi-satellite
and Multi-station Mission Planning System   444
  Yan-Jie Song, Xin Ma, Zhong-Shan Zhang, Li-Ning Xing,
  and Ying-Wu Chen

An 8 to 3 Priority Encoder Based on DNA Strand Displacement   454
  Mingliang Wang and Bo Bi

Multifunctional Biosensor Logic Gates Based on Graphene Oxide.   473
  Luhui Wang, Yingying Zhang, Yani Wei, and Yafei Dong

Medium and Long-Term Forecasting Method of China's Power Load
Based on SaDE-SVM Algorithm.   484
  Yuansheng Huang, Lijun Zhang, Mengshu Shi, Shijian Liu,
  and Siyuan Xu

Coupling PSO-GPR Based Medium and Long Term Load Forecasting
in Beijing.   496
  Yuansheng Huang, Jianjun Hu, Yaqian Cai, and Lei Yang

Nonlinear Finite-Element Analysis of Offshore Platform Impact Load
Based on Two-Stage PLS-RBF Neural Network   508
  Shibo Zhou and Wenjun Zhang

Author Index   519

Contents – Part II

Application of Artificial Fish Swarm Algorithm in Vehicle
Routing Problem...................................... 1
   Shiyu Jia, Kang Zhou, Yu Yang, Huaqing Qi, Yiting Zhen, Long Hu,
   Zhou Zhang, and Heping Zhang

Three-Input and Nine-Output Cubic Logical Circuit Based on DNA
Strand Displacement 13
   Yanfeng Wang, Meng Li, Junwei Sun, and Chun Huang

A Simulated Annealing for Multi-modal Team Orienteering Problem
with Time Windows 23
   Yalan Zhou, Chen Li, and Yanyue Li

Discrete Harmony Search Algorithm for Flexible Job-Shop
Scheduling Problems................................... 31
   Xiuli Wu and Jing Li

Barebones Particle Swarm Optimization with a Neighborhood Search
Strategy for Feature Selection........................... 42
   Chenye Qiu and Xingquan Zuo

The Chinese Postman Problem Based on the Probe Machine Model 55
   Jing Yang, Zhixiang Yin, Jianzhong Cui, Qiang Zhang, and Zhen Tang

Research on Pulse Classification Based on Multiple Factors 63
   Zhihua Chen, An Huang, and Xiaoli Qiang

Hybrid Invasive Weed Optimization and GA for Multiple
Sequence Alignment 72
   Chong Gao, Bin Wang, Changjun Zhou, Qiang Zhang, Zhixiang Yin,
   and Xianwen Fang

RNA Sequences Similarities Analysis by Cross-Correlation Function....... 83
   Shanshan Xing, Bin Wang, Xiaopeng Wei, Changjun Zhou,
   Qiang Zhang, and Zhonglong Zheng

Refrigerant Capacity Detection of Dehumidifier Based on Time Series
and Neural Networks................................... 95
   Gang Peng, Zuhuang Yang, and Min Wang

An Improved Artificial Bee Colony Algorithm and Its Taguchi Analysis 104
   Yudong Ni, Yuanyuan Li, and Yindong Shen

PLS-Based RBF Network Interpolation for Nonlinear FEM Analysis
of Dropped Drum in Offshore Platform Operations   118
 Hongwei Liu, Wenjun Zhang, Shuaichen Liu, and Yan Li

Logic Circuit Design of Sixteen-Input Encoder by DNA
Strand Displacement   129
 Yanfeng Wang, Aolong Lv, Chun Huang, and Junwei Sun

PLS-RBF Neural Network for Nonlinear FEM Analysis of Dropped
Container in Offshore Platform Operations   138
 Zehua Li, Wenjun Zhang, and Haibo Xie

A Multiobjective Genetic Algorithm Based Dynamic Bus Vehicle
Scheduling Approach   152
 Hongyi Shi, Chunlu Wang, Xingquan Zuo, and Xinchao Zhao

Research on the Addition, Subtraction, Multiplication and Division
Complex Logical Operations Based on the DNA Strand Displacement   162
 Chun Huang, Yanfeng Wang, and Qinglei Zhou

An Improved GMM-Based Moving Object Detection Method Under
Sudden Illumination Change   178
 Jian Cheng, Yusen Gang, Shuai Bai, Yi-nan Guo, and Dongwei Wang

A Method of Accurately Accepting Tasks for New Workers Incorporating
with Capacities and Competition Intensities   188
 Dunwei Gong, Chao Peng, Xinchao Zhao, and Qiuzhen Lin

Iteration-Related Various Learning Particle Swarm Optimization for Quay
Crane Scheduling Problem   201
 Mingzhu Yu, Xuwen Cong, Ben Niu, and Rong Qu

An Image Encryption Algorithm Based on Chaotic System Using DNA
Sequence Operations   213
 Xuncai Zhang, Zheng Zhou, Ying Niu, Yanfeng Wang, and Lingfei Wang

An Image Encryption Algorithm Based on Dynamic DNA Coding
and Hyper-chaotic Lorenz System   226
 Guangzhao Cui, Lingfei Wang, Xuncai Zhang, and Zheng Zhou

Application of BFO Based on Path Interaction in Yard Truck Scheduling
and Storage Allocation Problem   239
 Lei Liu, Lu Xiao, Lulu Zuo, Jia Liu, and Chen Yang

Research on Optimization of Warehouse Allocation Problem Based
on Improved Genetic Algorithm   252
 Ding Ning, Wang Li, Teng Wei, and Zhao Yue

An Expert System for Diagnosis and Treatment of Hypertension
Based on Ontology   264
   Wang Jie, Peng Yan, Ren Xiaoxiao, and Qiao Yixuan

A Three Input Look-Up-Table Design Based on Memristor-CMOS   275
   Junwei Sun, Xingtong Zhao, and Yanfeng Wang

Complex Logic Circuit of Three-Input and Nine-Output by DNA
Strand Displacement   287
   Yanfeng Wang, Guodong Yuan, Chun Huang, and Junwei Sun

Modified Mixed-Dimension Chaotic Particle Swarm Optimization
for Liner Route Planning with Empty Container Repositioning   296
   Mingzhu Yu, Zhichuan Chen, Li Chen, Rong Qu, and Ben Niu

A Wrapper Feature Selection Algorithm Based on Brain
Storm Optimization   308
   Xu-tao Zhang, Yong Zhang, Hai-rong Gao, and Chun-lin He

A Hybrid Model Based on K-EPF and DPIO for UAVs Target Detection . . .   316
   Jinsong Chen, Lu Xiao, Jun Wang, Huan Liu, and Qianying Liu

A Hybrid Data Clustering Approach Based on Hydrologic Cycle
Optimization and K-means   328
   Ben Niu, Huan Liu, Lei Liu, and Hong Wang

A Decomposition Based Multiobjective Evolutionary Algorithm
for Dynamic Overlapping Community Detection   338
   Xing Wan, Xingquan Zuo, and Feng Song

Research on Public Opinion Communication Mechanism Based
on Individual Behavior Model   351
   Weidong Huang and Yang Cui

A Comprehensive Evaluation: Water Cycle Algorithm and
Its Applications.   360
   Rana Muhammad Sohail Jafar, Shuang Geng, Wasim Ahmad,
   Safdar Hussain, and Hong Wang

A Bias Neural Network Based on Knowledge Distillation   377
   Yulong Wang, Zhi Wu, and Yifeng Huang

LSTM Encoder-Decoder with Adversarial Network for Text Generation
from Keyword   388
   Dongju Park and Chang Wook Ahn

Quantum Algorithm for Crowding Method.   397
   Jun Suk Kim and Chang Wook Ahn

Random Repeatable Network: Unsupervised Learning to Detect
Interest Point   405
   Pei Yan and Yihua Tan

An Orthogonal Genetic Algorithm with Multi-parent Multi-point Crossover
for Knapsack Problem   415
   Xinchao Zhao, Jiaqi Chen, Rui Li, Dunwei Gong, and Xingmei Li

Cooperative Co-evolution with Principal Component Analysis
for Large Scale Optimization   426
   Guangzhi Xu, Xinchao Zhao, and Rui Li

HCO-Based RFID Network Planning.   435
   Jun Wang, Jinsong Chen, Qianying Liu, and Jia Liu

Cuckoo Search Algorithm Based on Individual Knowledge Learning.   446
   Juan Li, Yuan-Xiang Li, and Jie Zou

An Improved DV-Hop Algorithm with Jaccard Coefficient Based
on Optimization of Distance Correction   457
   Wangsheng Fang, Geng Yang, and Zhongdong Hu

An Image Encryption Algorithm Based on Hyper-chaotic System
and Genetic Algorithm.   466
   Xuncai Zhang, Hangyu Zhou, Zheng Zhou, Lingfei Wang, and Chao Li

A Performance Comparison of Crossover Variations in Differential
Evolution for Training Multi-layer Perceptron Neural Networks   477
   Tae Jong Choi, Yun-Gyung Cheong, and Chang Wook Ahn

Author Index   489

Research on Price Forecasting Method of China's Carbon Trading Market Based on PSO-RBF Algorithm

Yuansheng Huang and Hui Liu[✉]

Department of Economics and Management,
North China Electric Power University,
Baoding 071003, Hebei, China
895983934@qq.com

Abstract. The forecasting of carbon emissions trading market price is the basis for improving risk management in the carbon trading market and strengthening the enthusiasm of market participants. This paper will apply machine learning methods to forecast the price of China's carbon trading market. Firstly, the daily average transaction prices of the carbon trading market in Hubei and Shenzhen are collected, and these data are preprocessed by PCAF approach. Secondly, a prediction model based on Radical Basis Function (RBF) neural network is established and it parameters are optimized by Particle Swarm Optimization (PSO). Finally, the PSO-RBF model is validated by actual data and proved that the PSO-RBF model has better prediction effect than BP or RBF neural network in China's carbon prices prediction, indicating that it has more significant rationality and applicability and deserves further popularization.

Keywords: China's carbon market · Prediction method
RBF neural network · PSO algorithm

1 Introduction

The establishment of a carbon emission trading system provides a market-oriented means for countries around the world to implement low-carbon development. China, as the world's largest carbon emission country, is curbing the greenhouse gas emissions with pragmatic actions. A carbon emissions trading market is an effective policy tool for the Chinese government to control carbon emissions. China launched carbon emissions trading pilot markets in seven provinces and cities, including Beijing, Shanghai, Guangdong, Shenzhen, Tianjin, Chongqing, and Hubei from 2011, and launched all online transactions in 2014. As of the end of 2017, China has fulfilled its emission reduction commitments to the international community and completed the overall design of the country's carbon emissions trading system. National unified carbon emissions

© Springer Nature Singapore Pte Ltd. 2018
J. Qiao et al. (Eds.): BIC-TA 2018, CCIS 951, pp. 1–11, 2018.
https://doi.org/10.1007/978-981-13-2826-8_1

trading market will gradually mature in the next few years and will play an increasingly important role as a national policy adjustment platform in the area of emission reduction in the next decade.

The key to building a carbon trading market is a scientific and reasonable carbon price mechanism. However, Chinese carbon emissions trading market has just been formed, resulting in unstable carbon price, irregular changes and the more prominent market risk. Therefore, research on the carbon price forecasting model will help reduce the risk of carbon price fluctuations and promote the construction of China's carbon trading market. It can better manage risk to play the pricing function of the market, that is able to increase investment expectations and reduce risks rationally. Improve the efficiency and liquidity of the carbon market to lead the healthy development of the market.

Machine learning technology is increasingly being cited in the nonlinear and non-stationary time series predictions. Zhu and Wei [1] constructed a carbon price forecasting based on integration of group method of data handing (GMDH), PSO and least squares support vector machines (LSSVM). Zhu [2] also proposed a multiscale ensemble model, which is composed of empirical mode decomposition (EMD), genetic algorithm (GA) and artificial neural network (ANN) to forecast carbon price in ECX. Gao and Li [3] set up an international carbon financial market price error correction prediction model based on EMD, PSO and SVM. Fan et al. [4] established a multi-layer perceptron neural network (MLP) forecasting model to study the carbon price of EU EST from the perspective of chaos. Jiang and Wu [5] built a model based on Support Vector Regression (SVR) algorithm to predict international carbon market price. Sun et al. [6] found that using variational mode decomposition (VMD) and spiking neural networks (SNNS) to forecast the ICE carbon price can obtain a better empirical test effect. Zhang et al. [7] advanced a hybrid approach integrating PSO and multioutput support vector regression (MSVR) to forecast carbon prices. Jiang and Peng [8] presented a carbon prices prediction model based on BP neural network optimized by Chaos Particle Swarm Optimization (CPSO) algorithm.

In summary, neural network theory has shown good prediction ability in carbon price forecasting. RBF is a kind of neural network which is better than traditional neural network in time series prediction in terms of approximation ability, classification ability and learning speed, etc. The structure of RBF is simpler, and its training success rate is higher. Gu et al. [9] trained historical electricity price by RBF neural network and hierarchical genetic algorithm (HGA), and the test results are satisfactory. Zhang et al. [10] established a model to forecast short-term load though combining the RBF neural network with the adaptive neural fuzzy inference system (ANFIS). Coelho and Santos [11] found RBF neural network model with GARCH errors can show good results in application to electricity price forecasting. Shen [12] chose RBF neural network optimized by the artificial fish swarm algorithm (AFSA) to forecast the stock indices. Cecati et al. [13] designed new algorithm called ErrCor in machine learning to train RBF for 24 h electric load prediction.

RBF neural network has been successfully applied to time series prediction and analysis. However due to the inherent characteristics of RBF neural network can easily cause itself to fall into a local optimum. Furthermore, the center number of RBF and the network's weights extremely need to rely on past experience. If some optimization algorithm are adopted to overcome these defects, the network performance will be further improved. Therefore, this paper uses PSO to optimize RBF neural network and applies it to China's carbon prices prediction for the first time. Compared with the traditional forecasting model, the PSO-RBF model is more suitable for China's carbon prices prediction, thus providing a simple, practical and accurate price prediction method for China's carbon trading market.

The rest of this paper is organized as follows: Sect. 2 describes the fundamentals of RBF and PSO, then elaborates on the PSO-RBF model, Sect. 3 presents the used dataset and obtained results, Sect. 4 concludes the study.

2   Methodology

2.1   RBF Neural Network

Radical Basis Function neural network (RBFNN) is a three-layer feedforward neural network, which proposed by Moody and Darken [14] in the 1980s. The input layer consists of the signal source nodes. The second layer is the hidden layer, and the number of hidden units depends on the needs of the described problem. The third layer is the output layer, which responds to the role of the input mode. The general structure of an RBFNN is shown in Fig. 1.

$X = (x_1, x_2, \ldots, x_m)$ is an m-dimensional vector and $W = (w_1, w_2, \ldots, w_n)$ is the weight of output layer. $g_i(X)$, $i = (1, 2, \ldots, n)$ is Gaussian function selected as activation function, where n means the number of neurons in hidden layer. In $g_i(X) = g_i(||X - C_i||)$, C_i is the center of ith activation function, and $|| * ||$ is Euclid norm.

The output of the ith neuron in hidden layer of RBFNN can be represented in the form.

$$q_i = g_i(||X - C_i||) = exp\left(-\frac{||X - C_i||^2}{2\sigma_i^2}\right) \tag{1}$$

σ_i is the width of the receptive field.

The activation of the output layer is linear combination of units on the hidden layer, which can be expressed as:

$$y = \sum_{i=1}^{n} w_i q_i \tag{2}$$

where w_i is the connecting weights from hidden layer to output layer.

When the center point of the RBF is determined, the mapping relationship is determined. The transformation from the input space to the hidden layer space is nonlinear, the mapping from the hidden layer to the output layer is linear. The output of the network is the linear weighted sum of the output of the hidden layer, where the weight here is the tunable parameter of network.

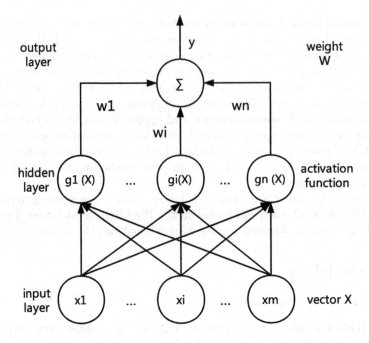

Fig. 1. General structure of the RBFNN

The theoretical basis of RBFNN is that radial basis exists as a hidden base to form the hidden layer space. So that the input vector can be directly mapped to the hidden space, does not need to connect through the weight. According to the Cover Theorem, the inseparable data in the low-dimensional space is more likely to become separable in high-dimensional space. In other words, the function of the hidden layer of the RBFNN is to map the input of the low-dimensional space to a high-dimensional space through a non-linear function, and then to fit the curve in this high-dimensional space. It is equivalent to finding a surface that best fits the training data in an implied high-dimensional space, so that the transition from the low dimension to the high dimension can be achieved. It can be easily solved problems which cannot be solved in the low dimension in the high-dimensional space.

2.2 PSO Algorithm

PSO is an evolutionary optimization algorithm, introduced by Kennedy and Eberhart [15] in 1995. Similar to GA, PSO is also belong to the population iteration. However, the particles of PSO follow its own optimal particle in the entire swarm to search the global optimum solution. Each particle keeps track of its own best position and velocity in the problem space, and its initial position and velocity are generated randomly. So PSO is an easy stochastic optimization technique because of a few parameters to adjust. For a complex nonlinear system, PSO is a better global optimization capability and high searching speed.

Let the position and velocity of the ith particle in the n-dimensional search space be respectively assumed as $P_i = [p_{i,1}, p_{i,2}, \ldots, p_{i,n}]$ and $V_i = [v_{i,1}, v_{i,2}, \ldots, v_{i,n}]$. According to a specific fitness function, the local best of the i th particle cloud be $P_i^l = p_{i,1}^l, p_{i,2}^l, \ldots, p_{i,n}^l$, and $P^g = p_1^g, p_2^g, \ldots, p_n^g$ is the global best found. The new positions and velocities of the particles will be updated at each iteration. This process follows the following two formulas.

$$P_i(k+1) = P_i(k) + V_i(k+1) \tag{3}$$

$$V_i(k+1) = V_i(k) + c_1 * r_1 * (P_i^l(k) - P_i(k) + c_2 * r_2 * (P^g - P_i(k)) \tag{4}$$

Where $i = 1, 2, \ldots, m$, m is the number of particles in a population. $P_i(k)$ and $P_i^l(k)$ are the position and the local best of ith particle at iteration k, respectively, P^g is the global best of all particles, $V_i(k)$ is the velocity of ith particle at iteration k. c_1 and c_2 are both acceleration coefficient, but one is the cognitive parameter and other is the social parameter. r_1 and r_2 are the random numbers between 0 and 1.

2.3 RBF Optimized by PSO

Predicting accuracy of the RBFNN lies on three parameters: output weights w_i, the hidden layer nodes widths σ_i, the data center of basis function C_i. The three parameters are updated by PSO, taking the place of the Gradient Descent method. In this paper, the number of hidden layer nodes of the RBFNN is 10, and the input data is normalization. The training error of RBFNN is taken as the fitness function of PSO, as shown in Eq. 5. The minimum value of the fitness function is get through the optimal particle positions calculated by the PSO algorithm, and the optimal value of each parameter of the RBFNN is obtained.

$$Fitness = \frac{1}{N} \sum_{i=1}^{N} \left(y_i - \sum_{j=1}^{M} w_j exp \left(-\frac{||X - C_j||^2}{2\sigma_j^2} \right) \right)^2 \tag{5}$$

The specific steps of adopting PSO to search the optimal values of the RBF network parameters are as followed and the flow chart of RBF optimized by PSO is demonstrated in Fig. 2.

Step 1. Define the number of particles, initialize their position and velocity.
Step 2. Calculate the fitness function to obtain the optimal value of each particle and the global optimal value.
Step 3. Update each particle's velocity and position.
Step 4. Recalculate its fitness and acquire the optimal value of each particle and the global optimum value again.
Step 5. Determine whether the fitness reaches the minimum value. If not, loop to step 3 until a criterion is met.

Finally, the optimal w_i, σ_i and C_i are get to form a trained RBFNN to predict the data of the testing set.

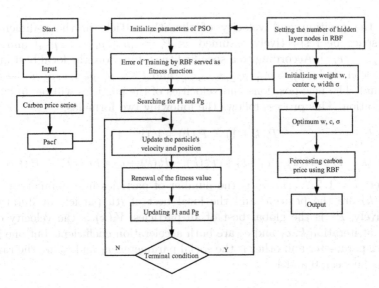

Fig. 2. The flow chart of RBF optimized by PSO

3   Simulation and Results

3.1   Data Preprocessing

This article mainly forecasts China's carbon market transaction prices. As shown in Fig. 3, Hubei's carbon trading volume is the largest among seven carbon emission trading pilot markets in China (we do not consider carbon market in Fujian), and its turnover is also the largest. The carbon trading pilot market in Shenzhen, as the earliest carbon markets in China, has a certain significance in research. Therefore, the daily average transaction prices (Data does not include holidays and no trading days.) of the carbon trading pilot market in Hubei and Shenzhen are selected as sample data, and details of samples are reported in Table 1. All the data comes from the Wind database.

Table 1. Samples of carbon prices.

Carbon price	Size	Date
Hubei	Sample set 980	28 April 2014–31 May 2018
	Training set 800	28 April 2014–30 August 2017
	Testing set 180	30 August 2017–31 May 2018
Shenzhen	Sample set 1090	5 August 2013–31 May 2018
	Training set 900	5 August 2013–29 June 2017
	Testing set 190	29 June 2017–31 May 2018

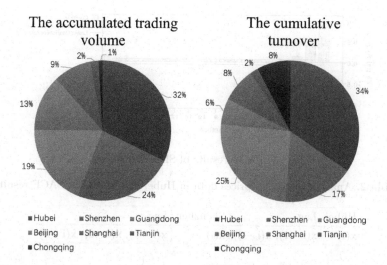

Fig. 3. The accumulated trading volume and turnover of carbon markets in China

In order to confirm the format of training data, PACF is selected to derive the autocorrelogram of data. Figures 4 and 5 respectively show the PACF results of Hubei and Shenzhen's data. Setting $x(i)$ as the output variable, if the partial autocorrelation at lag k is out of the 95% confidence interval, $x(i-k)$ can be one of the input variables. Table 2 shows input variables of carbon prices data in Hubei and Shenzhen obviously.

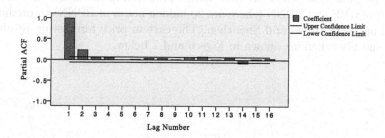

Fig. 4. PACF results of Hubei's data

As can be seen from Table 2, the carbon price of Hubei on the ith day is predicted by the carbon prices of the $(i-1)$th and $(i-2)$th days as the input variables of the model. Similarly, the carbon prices of the $(i-1)$th, $(i-2)$th and $(i-3)$th days are used as input variables to output the ith day's carbon price of Shenzhen.

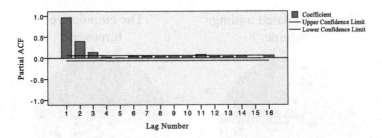

Fig. 5. PACF results of Shenzhen's data

Table 2. Analysis of carbon prices data in Hubei and Shenzhen PACF results.

Hubei	Lag	Shenzhen	Lag
x(i)	x(i − 1), x(i − 2)	x(i)	x(i − 1), x(i − 2), x(i − 3)

3.2   The Obtained Results of Forecasting Carbon Prices by PSO-RBF

Set up RBF parameters by PSO algorithm and use samples of carbon prices data to train the RBF network. In this research, Gaussian function is selected as the radial basis function, and the number of hidden layer nodes is set as 15. The input values are given by the data after dealing with by PACF. And the parameters of the PSO algorithm are as follows: the number of particles is 1000, and the learning factor is $c1 = c2 = 2$.

At the same time, the PSO-RBF model proposed in this article is compared with using RBF and BPNN (there are 20 hidden nodes in BPNN) to predict the carbon prices in Hubei and Shenzhen. The carbon price forecasting results for Hubei and Shenzhen are shown in Figs. 6 and 7 below.

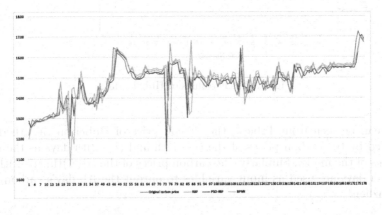

Fig. 6. Comparison of the Hubei's carbon prices forecasting results between PSO-RBF, RBF and BP

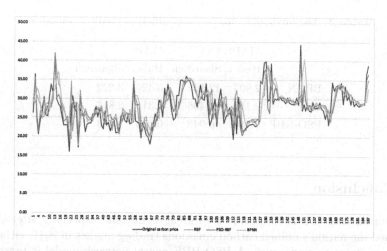

Fig. 7. Comparison of the Shenzhen's carbon prices forecasting results between PSO-RBF, RBF and BP

3.3   Comparison and Analysis

Figures 6 and 7 reveal the carbon price prediction results for Hubei and Shenzhen based on three different models, and it can be seen from the figures:

(a) Compared with a single model RBF or BPNN, the PSO-RBF model's carbon price prediction results are closest to the true value, and the forecasting results of RBF neural network is simultaneously better than BP neural network.

(b) There is a large deviation between the RBF model's individual prediction results and the PSO-RBF model's prediction results as well as the actual values, indicating that PSO plays a positive role in the parameter optimization of RBF.

The predicted value error of different prediction models is presented in Table 3, we also can be the same conclusion by comparing the size of the Mean Absolute Percentage Error (MAPE) and the Mean Absolute Error (MAE). From Table 3, the MAPE and the MAE of PSO-RBF model for the Hubei's carbon price forecasting are respectively 1.580% and 0.233, and the Shenzhen's are separately 6.942% and 1.863. These values are both smaller than the MAPE and MAE of RBF neural network and BP neural network. It is proved that the PSO-RBF model is superior to the BPNN model and RBFNN model in terms of prediction effect, prediction accuracy, etc. It also indicates the validity of the PSO-RBF model in Chinese carbon price prediction.

Table 3. The predicted value error of different prediction models.

	MAPE (%)		MAE	
	Hubei	Shenzhen	Hubei	Shenzhen
BPNN	2.907	12.102	0.420	3.222
RBF	2.175	10.405	0.316	2.817
PSO-RBF	1.580	6.942	0.233	1.863

4 Conclusion

Price forecasting of carbon market is of great significant, especially after China launched the nation's unified carbon emissions trading market in 2017, either for the government or companies. A PSO-RBF neural network model is presented and applied to prediction in this study. Set up a China's carbon prices forecasting model by comprehensive utilizing the self-learning ability of RBF network and the optimized advantages of PSO. As shown in this research by the results of an example of factual forecasting which is the prices of carbon market in Hubei and Shenzhen, this forecasting model can work effectively and enhance the predicting precision. Compared with RBF and BP neural network, the simulation results evidence that the PSO-RBF model has stronger approximation ability, faster convergence rate and higher forecasting accuracy.

As one of the largest suppliers of emission reduction markets, China's annual carbon trading volume will exceed 200 million tons in the next five years, and it is expected to become the world's largest market for carbon emissions trading. At the same time, China's carbon market transaction price may increase over time in the future. The proposed PSO-RBF method can be further extended to the future carbon price forecast for the nation's unified carbon emissions trading market in China.

References

1. Zhu, Z.B., Wei, Y.: Carbon price prediction based on integration of GMDH, particle swarm optimization and least squares support vector machines. Syst. Eng.-Theory Pract. **31**(12), 2264–2271 (2011)
2. Zhu, B.: A novel multiscale ensemble carbon price prediction model integrating empirical mode decomposition, genetic algorithm and artificial neural network. Energies **5**(2), 163–170 (2012)
3. Gao, Y., Li, J.: International carbon finance market price prediction based on EMD-PSO-SVM error correction model. China Popul. Resour. Environ. **24**, 163–170 (2014)
4. Fan, X., Li, S., Tian, L.: Chaotic Characteristic Identification for Carbon Price and an Multilayer Perceptron Network Prediction Model. Pergamon Press, Inc., Oxford (2015)

5. Jiang, L., Wu, P.: International carbon market price forecasting using an integration model based on SVR. In: International Conference on Engineering Management, Engineering Education and Information Technology (2015)
6. Sun, G., Chen, T., Wei, Z., Sun, Y., Zang, H., Chen, S.: A carbon price forecasting model based on variational mode decomposition and spiking neural networks. Energies **9**(1), 54 (2016)
7. Zhang, L., Zhang, J., Xiong, T., Su, C.: Interval forecasting of carbon futures prices using a novel hybrid approach with exogenous variables. Discrete Dyn. Nat. Soc. **2017**, 1–12 (2017)
8. Jiang, F., Peng, Z.J.: Forecasting of carbon price based on BP neural network optimized by chaotic PSO algorithm. Stat. Inf. Forum (2018)
9. Gu, Q., Chen, G., Zhu, L.L., Wu, Y.: Short-term marginal price forecasting based on genetic algorithm and radial basis function neural network. Power Syst. Technol. **30**(7), 18–22 (2006)
10. Zhang, Y., Zhou, Q., Sun, C., Lei, S., Liu, Y., Song, Y.: RBF neural network and ANFIS-based short-term load forecasting approach in real-time price environment. IEEE Trans. Power Syst. **23**(3), 853–858 (2008)
11. Coelho, L.D.S., Santos, A.A.P.: A RBF neural network model with GARCH errors: application to electricity price forecasting. Electr. Power Syst. Res. **81**(1), 74–83 (2011)
12. Shen, W., Guo, X., Wu, C., Wu, D.: Forecasting stock indices using radial basis function neural networks optimized by artificial fish swarm algorithm. Knowl.-Based Syst. **24**(3), 378–385 (2011)
13. Cecati, C., Kolbusz, J., Rozycki, P., Siano, P., Wilamowski, B.M.: A novel RBF training algorithm for short-term electric load forecasting and comparative studies. IEEE Trans. Ind. Electron. **62**(10), 6519–6529 (2015)
14. Moody, J., Darken, C.J.: Fast learning in networks of locally-tuned processing units. Neural Comput. **1**(2), 281–294 (2014)
15. Kennedy, J., Eberhart, R.: Particle swarm optimization. In: Proceedings of IEEE International Conference on Neural Networks, pp. 1942–1948. IEEE Press, New York (2002)

An Efficient Restart-Enhanced Genetic Algorithm for the Coalition Formation Problem

Miao Guo, Bin Xin$^{(\boxtimes)}$, Jie Chen, and Yipeng Wang

School of Automation,
State Key Laboratory of Intelligent Control and Decision of Complex Systems,
Beijing Advanced Innovation Center for Intelligent Robots and Systems,
Beijing Institute of Technology,
Beijing 100081, China
brucebin@bit.edu.cn

Abstract. In multi-agent system (MAS), the coalition formation (CF) is an important problem focusing on allocating agents to different tasks. In this paper, the single-task single-coalition (STSC) formation problem is considered. The mathematical model of the STSC problem is built with the objective of minimizing the total cost with the ability constraint. Besides, an efficient restart-enhanced genetic algorithm (REGA) is designed to solve the STSC problem. Furthermore, this paper constructs a comparison experiment, employing a random sampling method, an estimation of distribution algorithm and a genetic algorithm without restart strategy as competitors. The results of statistical analysis by the Wilcoxon's rank-sum test demonstrate that the designed REGA performs better than its competitors in solving the STSC cases of different scales.

Keywords: Genetic algorithm · Single-task single-coalition (STSC)
Minimizing the total cost · Ability constraint
Estimation of distribution algorithm

1 Introduction

Multi-Agent System (MAS) has become a hot research topic in artificial intelligence, control science and other fields. Because of good robustness and high efficiency, MAS has been widely applied to complex tasks such as multi-robot cooperation, distributed monitoring network, emergency disaster rescue, etc. [1–3]. In these complex missions, a single agent is obviously not enough to complete the task, and multiple agents are required to collaboratively perform the task. A group of agents with a common task is denoted by a coalition. How to select a group of agents to form a coalition is defined as the coalition formation (CF) problem which has become an important research in MAS and it was proved to be an NP-hard problem [4].

© Springer Nature Singapore Pte Ltd. 2018
J. Qiao et al. (Eds.): BIC-TA 2018, CCIS 951, pp. 12–23, 2018.
https://doi.org/10.1007/978-981-13-2826-8_2

Disaster relief is an example of multi-agent cooperation and coalition formation. Several capabilities are required to complete a rescue mission, including communication ability, mobility, load capacity, etc., when a rescue team is working. If no single agent is able to complete the given task, multiple agents need to cooperate and all work on the task at the same time. The total ability and the total cost of the coalition are the sums of these of the agents in the coalition, respectively. The total ability must meet the requirement of the task. The coalition formation problem can be viewed as a constrained optimization problem with the objective of minimizing the total cost for multiple agents that are heterogeneous both in their abilities and costs.

A coalition-related problem similar to the CF problem is the coalition structure generation (CSG) problem. In CSG, different coalition structures have different welfares. The objective of the CSG problem is to divide a group of agents into disjoint coalitions and identify coalition structures that maximize social welfare [5]. The CSG problem does not consider agent ability or task requirement constraint.

This paper mainly discusses the single-task single-coalition (STSC) formation problem. In many real-world situations, it needs to form a coalition to complete a task. For example, a target detection task in battle field may rely on a reconnaissance coalition composed of multiple units. Similarly, once a hostile target is detected, an attack coalition may be formed against the target.

Recently, more and more researchers focus on the CF problem and its solution. Guerrero et al. classified the coalition method into the following categories: centralized systems, self-organized approaches (swarm intelligence) and auction methods [6].

Qian et al. designed two bio-inspired algorithms: ant-colony algorithm and genetic algorithm for the CF problem and compared their performance [7]. However, they only took into account the number of the agents that the task requires and did not consider agent ability. Ye et al. put forward a self-adaptation-based dynamic coalition formation mechanism in distributed networks. Since the mechanism was based on negotiation, it was highly complex [8]. Smith et al. introduced three intuitive policies and solved the dynamic CF problem whose purpose is to minimize the expected delay between the arrival time of a task and its completion [9]. Lu et al. established a model of task-oriented collaborative abilities and proposed a coalition formation method with a stochastic mechanism to reduce excessive competitions. In addition, they proposed an artificial intelligent algorithm named cognitive compensation to compensate for the difference between the expected and actual task requirements [10].

According to the above research results, most scholars focus on distributed system in which a centralized decision maker does not exist. In contrast, the centralized decision maker can obtain global information to make a better decision. Therefore, a global algorithm is necessary for the STSC problem. In this paper, an efficient restart-enhanced genetic algorithm (REGA) is designed to solve the CF problem. REGA can search the solution space effectively and efficiently. The originality and contributions of this paper are summarized as follows.

According to the characteristics of the mathematical model, the constrained optimization problem is transformed into an unconstrained problem by using a penalty function method. Besides, this paper designs an efficient restart-enhanced genetic algorithm to solve the STSC problem by iterative sampling in the solution space.

The rest of this paper is organized as follows. Section 2 presents the mathematical programming model for the STSC problem. In Sect. 3, the designed genetic algorithm is described in detail. The experimental design, results and discussion are reported in Sect. 4. Section 5 concludes this paper.

2   Problem Formulation

In the STSC problem, because of task complexity and inadequate ability, a task is not completed by a single agent. Therefore, agents are demanded to form a coalition, and complete the mission together. Suppose that there is a set A of n heterogeneous agents, which are different from each other in ability value.

$$A = \{a_1, a_2, \ldots, a_n\} \tag{1}$$

where a_i ($i \in \{1, 2, \ldots, n\}$) represents the ith agent. Each agent a_i has r ability types that quantitatively describe the ability of the agent to accomplish a task, denoted by the ability set B_i. b_i^j represents the jth ability value of the agent a_i. $\forall\, a_i \in A,\ b_i^j \geq 0,\ j \in \{1, 2, \ldots, r\}$

$$B_i = \left\{ b_i^1, b_i^2, \ldots, b_i^r \right\}. \tag{2}$$

The task is denoted as T, which has an ability requirement set represented as

$$TB = \{tb^1, tb^2, \ldots, tb^r\} \tag{3}$$

where tb^j ($j \in \{1, 2, \ldots, r\}$) represents the value of each ability required to perform the task. According to the task requirement, a group of agents can be selected from the set A to form a coalition denoted by C ($C \subseteq A$). The decision variable vector is represented as

$$x = [x_1, x_2, \ldots, x_n] \tag{4}$$

where $x_i \in \{0, 1\}$, $x_i = 1$ means the agent a_i is selected to join the coalition C, otherwise the agent is not selected. The total ability of the coalition is the sum of the ability of the agents, denoted by CB.

$$CB = \{cb^1, cb^2, \ldots, cb^r\} \tag{5}$$

$$cb^j = \sum_{i=1}^{n} b_i^j \times x_i \tag{6}$$

where cb^j represents the jth ability value required to perform the task. The task can be completed, only if the total ability of the coalition is not less than the requirement of the task regarding each ability type. It can be described as

$$cb^j \geq tb^j, \; \forall \, j \in \{1, 2, \ldots, r\}. \tag{7}$$

Each agent $(a_i \in A)$ has a task cost $cost_i$ which the agent takes to perform the task. The set of the agent cost is represented by $Cost$.

$$Cost = \{cost_1, cost_2, \ldots, cost_n\}. \tag{8}$$

The objective of the STSC problem is minimizing the total cost to complete the task. Therefore, this paper employs the total cost as the objective function. It can be calculated by the sum of the agent cost in the coalition in Eq. (9).

$$f(\boldsymbol{x}) = \sum_{i=1}^{n} cost_i \times x_i \tag{9}$$

Optimization Model. The optimization model for the STSC problem can be formulated as follows:

$$min \; f(\boldsymbol{x}) = \sum_{i=1}^{n} cost_i \times x_i$$
$$s.t. \; cb^j \geq tb^j, \; \forall \, j = 1, 2, \ldots, r \tag{10}$$
$$x_i \in \{0, 1\}$$

3   A Restart-Enhanced Genetic Algorithm for the STSC Problem

Genetic algorithm (GA) was first proposed by John Holland in the 1960s [11]. GA is a global search algorithm which can search the solution space of the problem and generate useful solutions during the optimization process. As a result of good robustness in complex combinatorial optimization problems, GA has been extensively studied and widely applied to solve knapsack problem, vehicle routing problem and a lot of other problems [12–14].

As an iterative search algorithm, GA simulates the natural selection process and genetic principle. It simulates the reproduction of organisms in natural processes. New individuals are produced by a series of operations such as selection, crossover and mutation, and the individuals with high fitness are preserved to constitute new populations. This process is repeated, and the fitness of the population gradually converges to a higher level.

3.1   Solution Representation

According to the characteristics of the mathematical model, each solution will be represented by binary encoding (see Eq. (4)).

3.2   Objective Function

From the problem model (10), it can be seen that the objective function is the coalition cost. This problem is a constrained optimization problem. In order to solve the problem, a penalty function method is employed, which turns the original problem into an unconstrained problem. The method is described as follows.

$$rt^j = \begin{cases} \frac{tb^j - cb^j}{tb^j}, & if\ tb^j > cb^j; \\ 0, & else. \end{cases} \tag{11}$$

$$\alpha = \sum_{j=1}^{r} rt^j \tag{12}$$

$$f(x) = \begin{cases} \sum_{i=1}^{n} cost_i \times x_i, & if\ tb^j \leq \sum_{i=1}^{n} b_i^j \times x_i; \\ (1 + \alpha) \times (\sum_{i=1}^{n} cost_i), & else \end{cases} \tag{13}$$

where α represents the ratio of constraint violation. For example, the total ability vector of an infeasible solution is [200 150 160] and task ability requirement vector is [210 140 170]. Then, $\alpha = (210 - 200)/210 + 0 + (170 - 160)/170 = 0.106$.

Equation (13) represents the compilation method of the objective function. When the coalition abilities meet their corresponding task requirements, the objective function is the sum of the agents cost in the coalition; otherwise, the objective function is composed of two parts: the sum of all agent costs in the set *Cost* and the penalty part of dissatisfied requirement.

The penalty method can guarantee the function values of infeasible solutions are larger than those of feasible solutions, which means infeasible solutions are worse than feasible solutions. Besides, the infeasible solutions can also be distinguished from each other by the value of α in Eq. (12).

3.3   Selection

The selection operation will preserve individuals with higher fitness to produce new individuals, which imitates the survival of the fittest in nature. The individual fitness reflects its ability to survive in the natural environment. So far, scholars have summarized many selection operators, such as tournament selection, roulette selection, etc. [15].

The one to one tournament selection is adopted in this algorithm, which is easy to realize and has a good performance. Furthermore, it can keep a good balance between population diversity and convergence. Its operation process is described as follows. First, randomly select two individuals in the current population. Next, compare the objective function values of the two individuals and reserve the better individual. Since the problem is to minimize the value of the objective function, the better individual reserved is the one with a smaller value of the objective function. Repeat this selection operation N_p times to obtain a new population (N_p is the size of the population).

3.4 Crossover

Crossover is a very important operation that will happen at a certain probability denoted by P_c. For given parents, it will produce new individuals to search the solution space by means of crossover operation, which can reserve the parent genes and enhance population diversity.

The uniform crossover is employed in this algorithm. It exchanges each bit in the parent chromosomes with a probability of 0.5. For instance, two given parents are [1 0 1 1 0] and [0 1 0 0 1], respectively. And randomly create five values between 0 and 1, e.g. [0.2 0.7 0.8 0.1 0.3]. The new individuals are [1 1 0 1 0] and [0 0 1 0 1] by the uniform crossover, respectively.

3.5 Mutation

The mutation operation refers to changing one or more genes in individuals and simulates the mutation of chromosome genes in organisms. It can generate new individuals and enhance the diversity of the population. Although the probability of mutation operations is small, it can produce new individuals and deviate the algorithm from local optimum.

The uniform mutation is used. Each gene of each individual in population will change with a certain probability denoted by P_m. Each gene randomly generates a value μ between 0 and 1. If μ is not larger than the probability P_m, the gene will change. Since each gene can change with the probability P_m, an individual possibly becomes any individual by mutation. The probability of all genes changing in an individual is $(P_m)^n$ (n is the length of a chromosome).

3.6 Population Update

In each iteration, a new population will be produced by the above operations. All individuals in the parent population and the new population are sorted according to their objective values. A half of the individuals with smaller objective values will be reserved into the next generation.

3.7 Restart-Enhanced Genetic Algorithm

This paper designs a restart-enhanced GA based on the above operators for solving the STSC problem. The REGA is outlined as follows. In each iteration, it will implement selection, crossover and mutation operation for the population (Pop). Besides, a restart strategy is employed. Calculate the objective value of the new generation ($PopCost$) and the standard deviation of $PopCost$ ($PopStd$). When $PopStd$ is less than a constant σ, it will reinitialize the whole population in order to adjust population diversity and avoid wasting calculation cost. These operations will repeat until the maximum number of function evaluations (NFE_{max}) is reached.

Restart-Enhanced Genetic Algorithm

```
Input: A, B, TB, CB, Cost
Output: the best coalition and the corresponding objective value
Initialize the population Pop and calculate the objective value;
Set parameters Pc, Pm, Np;
repeat
  Tournament Selection(Pop);
  Uniform Crossover(Pop);
  Uniform Mutation(Pop);
  Calculate the objective value PopCost of the new generation;
  Calculate the standard deviation PopStd of PopCost;
  If PopStd is less than a constant;
    reinitialize the population and calculate the objective value;
  end
  Update the population Pop;
  gen = gen+1;
until NFE_max is reached
```

4   Experiments and Results

This section is devoted to the performance investigation of the designed algorithm. Firstly, an STSC test case generator is described to produce instances of different scales. Then, the algorithms for comparison and the parameter settings are briefly introduced. Finally, the experimental results and analysis are presented. In this paper, all experiments were carried out in MATLAB R2016b environment on a PC with Intel(R) Xeon(R) E5 @2.60 GHz and 32 GB RAM.

4.1   Test Case Generator

In order to test the performance of different algorithms in solving the STSC problems of different scales, this paper firstly generates a set of test cases. The sets B, TB and $Cost$ are included in each test case.

Generation of B and $Cost$: For each agent, its ability value B_i and $cost_i$ are both randomly generated in the range from 1 to 200.

Generation of TB: Each type of ability required for the task is produced to satisfy Eq. (14) to ensure the existence of feasible solutions.

$$\sum_{i=1}^{n} b_i^j \geq tb^j, \ \forall \ j = 1, 2, \ldots, r \tag{14}$$

4.2   Algorithms for Comparison

Genetic Algorithm (GA): The only difference between the GA and the designed REGA is that the former does not adopt the restart strategy.

Estimation of Distribution Algorithm (EDA): EDA is a relatively new optimization algorithm proposed in 1994 [16]. A population based incremental learning (PBIL) algorithm is employed for the discrete problem as a comparison. It first constructs a probabilistic model from a selected subpopulation which includes the excellent individuals in the current population. The size of the subpopulation is denoted by N_{sp}. Then, a new population is produced by sampling the constructed model. The learning rate in constructing the probabilistic model is defined as α. It will continue the modeling-sampling process until the termination criterion is satisfied. Furthermore, the same restart strategy is employed both in EDA and REGA.

Random Sampling (RS): RS is chosen as the other comparison algorithm [17]. It can be achieved by randomly selecting any agent to join the coalition. And the process will repeat until a feasible coalition is constructed.

4.3   Experiment Setup and Parameter Settings

In the experiments, 9 random test cases are generated including 3 different scales. The number of ability types r is set to 3. And the number of agents n in different cases is described in Table 1.

Table 1. Number of agents in different cases

No.	1	2	3	4	5	6	7	8	9
n	20	30	50	100	150	200	300	400	500

The designed REGA and three competitors will run 20 times for each case. In each run, the termination criterion is the accumulated number of function evaluations reaches NFE_{max}. All parameters settings of the comprehensive comparison experiment are shown in Table 2. Besides, the same calculation method of objective function is adopted by all algorithms.

Table 2. Parameter settings

Parameter	Value
Population size (N_p)	$2n$
Crossover probability in REGA (P_c)	0.9
Mutation probability in REGA (P_m)	0.001
Learning rate in EDA (α)	0.3
Subpopulation size in EDA (N_{sp})	$(2/3)N_p$
Maximum number of function evaluations (NFE_{max})	$2000n$

4.4 Results and Analysis

Experimental results of 9 test cases are shown in Table 3. The results represent the mean of the results of each algorithm in 20 runs in each case. In addition, the Wilcoxon's rank-sum test is used to analyze the results, which is shown in Table 4. Each row of Table 4 represents whether the results of REGA are different from those of the competitors when the significance level is 0.05. If the rank-sum test result is 0, it demonstrates the results of two algorithms are not different. Otherwise, if the rank-sum test result is 1, it demonstrates the REGA performs better; if it is −1, it demonstrates the REGA performs worse.

Table 3. Comparative experimental results

No.	RS	EDA	GA	REGA
1	863.45 ± 0.00	847.90 ± 4.02	903.10 ± 40.92	847.00 ± 0.00
2	928.50 ± 26.27	845.45 ± 11.39	880.65 ± 30.77	837.45 ± 2.01
3	1985.00 ± 54.12	1478.40 ± 7.47	1503.20 ± 32.59	1471.70 ± 2.90
4	3875.10 ± 36.96	2591.65 ± 7.51	2614.15 ± 20.27	2588.35 ± 7.53
5	7756.90 ± 98.40	4982.30 ± 11.71	4999.70 ± 27.95	4972.00 ± 6.46
6	8000.80 ± 104.73	4498.35 ± 11.97	4503.95 ± 15.76	4481.00 ± 4.46
7	13563.80 ± 193.46	7852.10 ± 16.62	7847.35 ± 19.05	7824.50 ± 4.98
8	15366.60 ± 164.54	7422.20 ± 10.15	7404.70 ± 6.31	7391.65 ± 3.00
9	23217.05 ± 224.81	11587.45 ± 8.99	11568.30 ± 6.63	11561.40 ± 2.74

Table 4. Wilcoxon's rank-sum test results

No.	1	2	3	4	5	6	7	8	9
REGA/GA	1	1	1	1	1	1	1	1	1
REGA/EDA	0	1	1	0	1	1	1	1	1
REGA/RS	1	1	1	1	1	1	1	1	1

Performance Comparison: In Tables 3 and 4, it can be seen that the designed REGA outperforms its competitors. Especially, the results of REGA are better than those of EDA in 7 of 9 test cases and better than RS and GA in all test cases.

Compared with GA, REGA performs better which confirms the effectiveness of the restart strategy. The restart strategy helps to keep a balance between population diversity and convergence speed and avoid population falling into local optimum.

In all cases, the mean objective values of REGA and EDA are better than RS. In the first two cases, the gap between RS and the other two algorithms is small. However, RS performs worse and worse as the scale of cases grows. This is because RS can not cover the whole solution space and does not utilize the information accumulated during the process of population generation.

Although EDA has a good performance to solve the STSC problem, REGA performs better than EDA in most cases. The outcome of EDA depends on the probabilistic model built. However, the solution space of the problem is too complex to construct an exact probabilistic model. Therefore, it may cause the population to evolve in the wrong direction or to fall into local optimum. In contrast, this situation does not exist in REGA because REGA generates new population by selection, crossover and mutation. What's more, these operators can make the algorithm find better solutions and jump out of local optima. In conclusion, REGA is superior to the other algorithms.

Convergence Analysis: The convergence curves of REGA and EDA in cases 2 and 6 are shown in Fig. 1. The horizontal axis and the vertical axis represent the number of evaluating objective function and the mean value of each algorithm in 20 runs, respectively. It can be drawn from the figure that REGA has faster convergence speed than EDA with the same number of objective function evaluations, especially in medium-scale and large-scale cases. This is because the probabilistic model of EDA is hard to capture the statistics of excellent solutions which makes it difficult to converge.

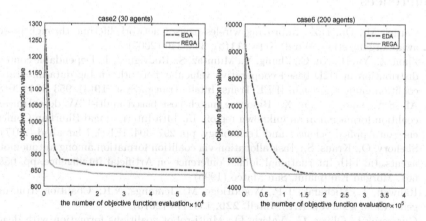

Fig. 1. Convergence Curves of REGA and EDA in cases 2 and 6

5 Conclusion

The coalition formation problem is a complex combinatorial optimization problem originating from multi-agent system. This paper mainly studies a single-task single-coalition formation problem. The mathematical model of this problem is constructed. In order to deal with this problem conveniently, the original problem is turned into an unconstrained problem by adopting a penalty function method. According to the characteristics of the model, this paper designs a restart-enhanced GA to solve this problem. The designed REGA employs tournament selection, uniform crossover and uniform mutation. Besides, the restart method is used to adjust the population diversity. Compared with EDA, the results of statistical analysis by the Wilcoxons rank-sum test demonstrates that REGA has a better performance in most test cases. Furthermore, compared with RS and GA, REGA performs better in all test cases. The REGA has a faster convergence speed than EDA for the STSC problem.

In the future, we will further study the STSC problem and improve the performance of the algorithm. For instance, priori knowledge and parameter optimization will be considered.

Acknowledgments. This work was supported in part by the NSFC-Zhejiang Joint Fund for the Integration of Industrialization and Informatization under Grant U1609214, in part by the National Natural Science Foundation of China under Grant 61673058, in part by the Foundation for Innovative Research Groups of the National Natural Science Foundation of China under Grant 61621063, in part by the Projects of Major International (Regional) Joint Research Program NSFC under Grant 61720106011.

References

1. Cardei, M., Du, D.Z.: Improving wireless sensor network lifetime through power aware organization. Wirel. Netw. **11**(3), 333–340 (2005)
2. Zhou, Z., Yu, H., Xu, C., Zhang, Y., Mumtaz, S., Rodriguez, J.: Dependable content distribution in D2D-based cooperative vehicular networks: a big data-integrated coalition game approach. IEEE Trans. Intell. Transp. Syst. **19**(3), 953–964 (2018)
3. Ali, S.A., Gao, X., Fu, X.: Resource match cost based multi-UAV decentralized coalition formation in an unknown region. In: 14th International Bhurban Conference on Applied Sciences and Technology, pp. 297–304. IEEE, Islamabad (2017)
4. Shehory, O., Kraus, S.: Task allocation via coalition formation among autonomous agents. In: 14th International Joint Conference on Artificial Intelligence, pp. 655–661. Morgan Kaufmann, San Mateo (1995)
5. Rahwan, T., Michalak, T.P., Wooldridge, M., Jennings, N.R.: Coalition structure generation: a survey. Artif. Intell. **229**, 139–174 (2015)
6. Guerrero, J., Oliver, G., Valero, O.: Multi-robot coalitions formation with deadlines: complexity analysis and solutions. PLoS One **12**(1), e0170659 (2017)
7. Qian, B., Cheng, H.H.: A bio-inspired mobile agent-based coalition formation system for multiple modular-robot systems. In: 10th IEEE/ASME International Conference on Mechatronic and Embedded Systems and Applications, pp. 1–6. IEEE, MESA (2014)
8. Ye, D., Zhang, M., Sutanto, D.: Self-adaptation-based dynamic coalition formation in a distributed agent network: a mechanism and a brief survey. IEEE Trans. Parallel Distrib. Syst. **24**(5), 1042–1051 (2013)
9. Smith, S.L., Bullo, F.: The dynamic team forming problem: throughput and delay for unbiased policies. Syst. Control Lett. **58**(10), 709–715 (2009)

10. Fang, H., Lu, S.L., Chen, J., Chen, W.J.: Coalition formation based on a task-oriented collaborative ability vector. Front. Inf. Technol. Electron. Eng. **18**(1), 139–148 (2017)

11. Holland, J.H.: Adaptation in Natural and Artificial Systems. MIT Press, Cambridge (1992)

12. Siva Sathya, S., Kuppuswami, S., Sendhil Kumar, S.: Gene silencing genetic algorithm for 0/1 Knapsack with object preferences. Int. J. Comput. Intell. Syst. **4**(5), 886–893 (2011)

13. Wang, S., Lu, Z., Wei, L., Yang, J., Yang, J.: Fitness-scaling adaptive genetic algorithm with local search for solving the multiple depot vehicle routing problem. Simulation **92**(7), 601–616 (2016)

14. Fatin, H.Z., Jamali, S., Fatin, G.Z.: Data replication in large scale content delivery networks: a genetic algorithm approach. J. Circ. Syst. Comput. **27**(12), 1850189 (2018)

15. Kaya, M.: The effects of a new selection operator on the performance of a genetic algorithm. Appl. Math. Comput. **217**(19), 7669–7678 (2011)

16. Mühlenbein, H., Paaß, G.: From recombination of genes to the estimation of distributions I. Binary parameters. In: Voigt, H.-M., Ebeling, W., Rechenberg, I., Schwefel, H.-P. (eds.) PPSN 1996. LNCS, vol. 1141, pp. 178–187. Springer, Heidelberg (1996). https://doi.org/10.1007/3-540-61723-X_982

17. Xin, B., Wang, Y.P., Chen, J.: An efficient marginal-return-based constructive heuristic to solve the sensor-weapon-target assignment problem. IEEE Trans. Syst. Man Cybern.: Syst. **PP**(99), 1–12 (2018)

U-NSGA-III: An Improved Evolutionary Many-Objective Optimization Algorithm

Rui Ding[1,2], Hongbin Dong[1(✉)], Jun He[3], Xianbin Feng[2], Xiaodong Yu[1], and Lijie Li[1]

[1] College of Computer Science and Technology, Harbin Engineering University, Harbin, China
donghongbin@hrbeu.edu.cn
[2] College of Computer Science and Information Technology, Mudanjiang Normal University, Mudanjiang, China
[3] School of Science and Technology, Nottingham Trent University, Nottingham, UK

Abstract. The Non-dominated Sorting Genetic Algorithm III (NSGA-III) uses a niche selection strategy based on reference points to maintain the population diversity. However, in an evolutionary process, areas near certain reference points which have no solution attached cannot be searched. To ensure the algorithm searching the entire solution space, and in particular, to avoid some areas not being explored due to no solution existing in the regions currently, we propose a uniform pool reservation strategy based on reference points in this paper. The strategy uses the individuals which are the closest to each reference point to guarantee population diversity. The improved algorithm is compared with classical algorithms based on decomposition and other improved algorithms based on NSGA-III respectively. The performance of each algorithm is evaluated by using inverted generational distance (IGD) and spread. The experimental results show the performance of the improved algorithm.

Keywords: Many-objective optimization algorithms · NSGA-III Reference points · Uniform pool

1 Introduction

Many problems in real life can be abstracted as multi-objective optimization problems. At present, an optimization problem with more than three objectives is called a many-objective optimization problem (MaOP) [1]. In recent years, MaOP has become a research hotspot due to its wide application in real world [2,3]. The goal of evolutionary many-objective optimization algorithms is to find a uniform solution set that is as close as possible to the solution set of the real Pareto Front [4]. Compared with a multi-objective optimization problem, it is much harder to select optimal solutions in many-objective optimization problems [5]. Another difficulty is that the number of solutions increases exponentially as the number of objectives increases [6]. These two difficulties present significant challenges for evolutionary many-objective optimization algorithms.

© Springer Nature Singapore Pte Ltd. 2018
J. Qiao et al. (Eds.): BIC-TA 2018, CCIS 951, pp. 24–35, 2018.
https://doi.org/10.1007/978-981-13-2826-8_3

At present, evolutionary many-objective optimization algorithms can be mainly divided into two categories [7]: one is based on a reference point set, the other is based on decomposition [8]. Still, relaxation domination, preference-based, indicator-based and dimension-based methods are also used in solving MaOPs [9,10].

Deb et al. [11] proposed the non-dominated sorting genetic algorithm II (NSGA-II), which uses a crowding distance to preserve the diversity of the population. NSGA-II can solve multi-objective problems effectively. However, the performance of NSGA-II is deteriorated in dealing with MaOPs because of the difficulty of evaluating the advantages and disadvantages of solutions under the current selection pressure. Deb and Jain [12] improved NSGA-II and proposed the algorithm NSGA-III in 2014 which is suitable for solving MaOPs. In NSGA-III, individuals are selected by a niche-based selection strategy to enter the next generation evolution.

In recent years, researchers have continued to improve NSGA-III by considering different methods to maintain the diversity and to increase the convergence rate. Ibrahim et al. [13] proposed Elite-NSGA-III in 2016. This algorithm preserves the individuals which are the closest to reference lines as elite individuals. The convergence rate is improved while maintaining the diversity. Bi and Wang [14] improved NSGA-III from a standpoint of individual selection. Instead of selecting individuals into next generation, they proposed an elimination operator. The worst individuals within the niche area of each reference point will be eliminated until the number of the remaining individuals reaches the size of the population. Zhang and Li [15] proposed a many-objective optimization algorithm based on decomposition (MOEA/D) in 2007. Combining mathematical programming with evolutionary algorithms, MOEA/D uses a decomposition strategy to solve MaOPs; Asafuddoula et al. [16] proposed an improved decomposition-based many-objective optimization algorithm in 2015, it is a variant of MOEA/D that solutions replace existing ones only if they are not dominated by any current solution. Khan et al. [17] combined the idea of MOEA/D with NSGA-III in 2016. The algorithm selects neighboring individuals for evolutionary operations under the framework of NSGA-III.

The current improvements of evolutionary many-objective optimization algorithms mainly focus on two aspects: firstly, ensure the population diversity, and consider whether an algorithm can search the entire solution space; Secondly, ensure an algorithm can quickly converge to the optimal solution set. From the point of view of maintaining population diversity, we propose a modified NSGA-III based on a uniform pool reservation strategy and reference points. The strategy aims to ensure the algorithm searching the entire target space.

The rest of this article is organized as follow: the second section introduces the related background knowledge. The third section explains the innovation and describes the complete algorithm. In the fourth section, we compare the proposed algorithm with some state-of-the-art algorithms. Finally, the fifth section gives the conclusion and future research direction.

2   Preliminary: NSGA-III

In this section, we briefly introduce the mechanism of NSGA-III, which is related to this paper.

NSGA-III is a evolutionary many-objective optimization algorithm proposed in 2014. Under the framework of NSGA-II, the algorithm proposed a niche selection strategy based on reference points to maintain population diversity. Compared with NSGA-II, NSGA-III initially defines a set of reference points within the solution space. When selecting individuals from the last acceptable layer F_l, individuals are selected by the niche selection strategy based on the reference points. The niche selection strategy first calculates the distance between each individual in set S_t (the current set of individuals which are selected for next generation) and each reference line (the line connecting ideal point and the reference point). Then, each individual can attach to a certain reference point with the smallest Euclidean distance to it. The number of attached individuals of each reference point is calculated, and a niche maintenance operator is used to select individuals from F_l to enter the next generation. Through a set of uniformly distributed reference points, NSGA-III decomposes the entire solution space into multiple search sub-spaces implicitly and searches these sub-spaces in parallel.

In the process of NSGA-III's reference-based niche selection, when the layer F_l is F_1, the algorithm would forget searching for areas near the reference points to which have no individuals attached. Therefore, no individual in the areas near these reference points is selected, and then, the above areas will not be searched. In extreme cases, the algorithm will only explore the regions near one or more reference points on which all the individuals are concentrated. Thus, the algorithm will be trapped into a local optimal searching and lose the diversity.

To overcome this shortcoming, we propose a uniform pool strategy based on reference points. This strategy enables the algorithm to search the entire solution space.

3   Proposed Algorithm: U-NSGA-III

To ensure the algorithm searching the entire solution space, and in particular, to avoid an area not being explored due to no solution existing in that area currently, a uniform pool strategy is proposed in this paper. The strategy is used to keep the individual which is the closest to each reference point participate in the evolution process. The strategy can guarantee population diversity.

3.1   The Idea of the Uniform Pool Strategy

The idea of the uniform pool strategy is as follows: calculate the distance between each individual and each reference point, put the individuals which are the closest to reference points in the uniform pool. If there are k reference points in the solution space, there are corresponding k individuals in the uniform pool. In the specific implementation of the algorithm, three cases are discussed.

- There have more than one individual attached to some certain reference points. The information obtained by NSGA-III is used to calculate the distances between these individuals and their attached reference points. Then the individual which is the closest to a certain reference point will be selected in the uniform pool.
- There has no individual attached to a reference point. Calculate the distances from the reference point to the individuals which attached to the neighbors. Select the nearest individual not in the uniform pool to join in the uniform pool to maximize the population diversity.
- When two or more individuals are at an equal distance from a reference point, the individual which is the closest to the ideal point is retained.

3.2 The Formula of Generating the Uniform Pool

Normalization. We standardize objective function values before calculating the distances between individuals and reference points. The standardized formula [18] is described as follows:

$$\overline{f}_i(x) = \frac{f_i(x) - Z_i^{min}}{Z_i^{max} - Z_i^{min}}. \tag{1}$$

Here, $f_i(x)$ represents the value of the ith objective, where $i = 1, 2, \ldots, m$, and m is the number of objective, $\overline{f}_i(x)$ is the value of $f_i(x)$ after normalization, Z_i^{min} is the minimum of the ith objective, and Z_i^{max} is the maximum of the ith objective.

Select Individuals for the Uniform Pool. The selection of individuals which remain in the uniform pool is formalized as Eq. 2.

$$u_k = argmin_{j=1}^{N}\|\overline{F}_j(X) - Z^k\|,$$
$$\overline{F}_i(X) = (\overline{f_1^i}(x), \overline{f_2^i}(x), \ldots, \overline{f_m^i}(x)), \tag{2}$$
$$U = \{u_1, u_2, \ldots u_k \ldots u_h\}.$$

u_k represents the elite individual corresponding to the kth reference point, and $\overline{F}_j(x)$ is the fitness value of the jth individual after normalized, where $j = 1, 2, \ldots, N$, and N is the number of attached individuals of the kth reference point. Z^k is the kth reference point. $\overline{f_m^i}(x)$ is the mth objective value of the ith individual after normalization. U is the set of individuals in the uniform pool, h is the number of reference points.

3.3 The Algorithm of Generating the Uniform Pool

In the iterative process, individuals in the uniform pool are constantly updated and participate in evolution. They generate offsprings with the same probability as other individuals. The algorithm of generating the uniform pool is described as follows:

Algorithm 1: Uniform Pool

```
Input
  P: a set of individuals as parent population;
  Z: a set of reference points on normalized hyper-plane;
Output:
  U : a set of individuals in the uniform pool;
  Ud: a set of distances between each reference point and
      uniform Pool individuals;
begin
  1  B = pdist2(Z,P);
  2  [Bdist,B] = sort(B,2);
  3  [Bline,Bnum]=size(B);
  4  While size(unique(B(:,1)),1)< Bline
  5    For i =1 to Bnum-1
  6      If ismember(B(i+1,1),B(1:i,1))
  7        B(i+1,1:Bline-1)=B(i+1,2:Bline);
  8        Bdist (i+1,1:Bline-1)=Bdist(i+1,2:Bline);
  9      EndIf
  10   EndFor
  11 EndWhile
  12 U= B(:,1);
  13 Ud=Bdist(:,1).
End.
```

In the algorithm of generating the uniform pool, U is a set of individuals in the uniform pool. Ud is a set of distances between each reference point and uniform pool individuals. Line 1 is used to calculate the distance between each member of P and each reference point of Z. The values of the distances will be sorted to select the nearest individual in line 2. Then, line 3 is used to calculate the number of columns($Bnum$) and rows($Bline$) of B for the following loop. The loop $while$(line 4–11) is used to delete repeat individuals and determine the uniform pool individual of each reference point. The if(line 6–9) is a certain process: if there has a duplicate individual, replace it with the suboptimal one.

3.4   The Framework of U-NSGA-III

Based on the framework of NSGA-III, U-NSGA-III uses a uniform pool to keep individuals which are the closest to reference points for maintaining population diversity. The proposed algorithm is described as Algorithm 2. Line 3 is used to generate the uniform pool. Individuals in the uniform pool will participate in the operation in line 8. And line 9 is used to update individuals of the uniform pool.

U-NSGA-III is an improved algorithm of NSGA-III. The computational complexity of NSGA-III is $\max\{O(N2\log M - 2N), O(N2M)\}$. For U-NSGA-III, individuals which are closest to reference points are retained in uniform pool. Calculating the distances from individuals to reference points requires $O(NH)$ steps, and selecting individuals in uniform pool requires $O(N\log H)$ steps. Due to

$O(N \log H) < O(NH) < O(N2M)$, the computational complexity of U-NSGA-III is still as same as that of NSGA-III.

Algorithm 2: U-NSGA-III

```
Input:
  H: the number of reference points;
  N: the number of individuals in the population;
Output:
  P_{t+1};
Var:
  maxgen=1;
  t=0;
Begin
  1  P_0=population initialization;
  2  Z=Generate-Reference-Points(H);
  3  [U_0,Ud_0]= Uniform pool(P_0, Z);
  4  Z_{min}= min(P_0.objs,[ ],1);
  5  While maxgen < 10000
  6    St=\phi;
  7    i=1;
  8    Q_t=Operator(P_t, U_t);
  9    [U_{t+1},Ud_{t+1}]=Uniform pool((Q_t, Z);
  10   R_t=P_t \cup Q_t;
  11   (F_1,F_2,...)=Non-dominated-sort(R_t);
  12     While |S_t|<N
  13       S_t=S_t\cup F_i;
  14       i=i+1;
  15     EndWhile
  16     If |S_t|=N
  17         P_{t+1}=S_t;
  18     else
  19         P_{t+1}=\cup^{l-1}_{j=1}F_i;
  20         P_n=Niching(N-|S_t|,Z,Z_{min},F_i,P_{t+1});
  21         P_{t+1}=S_{t} \cup P_n;
  22     EndIf
  23   Z_{min}= min(P_{t+1}.objs,[ ],1);
  24   t=t+1;
  25   maxgen=maxgen+1;
  26 EndWhile
End.
```

4   Experimental Study

Let's compare the proposed algorithm with six state-of-the-art algorithms: reference point-based algorithms of NSGA-III and Elite-NSGA-III, decomposition-based algorithms of MOEA/D-PBI and MOEA/DD. I-DBEA and θ-DEA are algorithms which combine reference points with decomposition.

Because of the scalable objective numbers, the Walking Fish Group (WFG) [19] standard test set is used to test these algorithms. The performance of each algorithm will be evaluated by IGD (inverted generational distance) [20] and $Spread$ [21]. IGD can evaluate convergence and diversity simultaneously, and $Spread$ is an indicator of diversity. The smaller $Spread$, the better the distribution diversity of algorithm.

4.1   Parameter Settings

We consider the number of objectives $m = \{3, 5, 8, 10, 12, 15\}$, and the corresponding number of decision variables is set to $n = \{12, 14, 17, 19, 21, 24\}$, respectively. The uniform population size of the algorithms is 100, and the maximum times of iteration are 10000. Simulated two-point crossover (SBX) operator and polynomial variation are used in NSGA-III and Elite-NSGA-III with the distribution index setting to 20. MOEA/D-PBI and I-DBEA use the aggregation function of Penalty-Based Boundary Intersection (PBI), and the neighborhood size T is set to 10. θ is set to 5 in θ-DEA. Each algorithm runs independently for 30 times on each test function with different number of objectives. The experiment runs on Windows (Intel (R) Xeon (R) CPU E5-2603 0 @ 1.80 GHz, 8.00 GBRAM) 64-bit operating system, matlab2016 is used for simulation verification. The comparison algorithms' code, except for Elite-NSGA-III, comes from Plat EMO [22].

4.2   Experiment Analysis

The advantage of U-NSGA-III is searching the entire solution space. The solutions obtained by this algorithm should have a significant advantage in distribution.

Table 1 shows the average values of $Spread$ on the test functions with different objective numbers. After these average $Spread$ values, ranks of these algorithms are given in square brackets. The optimal value of each line is highlighted with a gray background. As can be seen from Table 1, U-NSGA-III has a good distribution that obtains 25 times of the best value, accounting for 46.3%, while the distributions of the other six algorithms are poor. From the P-values, we can also learn the significant differences between the performance of each algorithm.

Further, we analyze the overall performance of these algorithms. Table 2 shows the average IGD values of each algorithm.

From Table 2, in the 54 tests of 9 functions, the algorithm proposed in this paper gets most of the best values, and the average rank is far higher than MOEA/DD, MOEA/D-PBI and I-DBEA, slightly higher than NSGA-III, Elite-NSGA-III and θ-DEA.

The P-values also show the significant differences between U-NSGA-III and MOEA/DD, MOEA/D-PBI and I-DBEA in IGD. For the other three algorithms

Table 1. Average *Spread* values for each algorithm with different objectives on WFGs

Problem	M	NSGA-III	Elite-NSGA-III	MOEA/D-PBI	MOEA/DD	θ-DEA	I-DBEA	U-NSGA-III
WFG1	3	7.4158E-1[4]	7.0610E-1[2]	8.6996E-1[6]	1.0597E+0[7]	8.5221E-1[5]	5.3242E-1[1]	7.3155E-1[3]
	5	7.5495E-1[3]	7.1572E-1[2]	9.9077E-1[6]	1.0409E+0[7]	8.4772E-1[5]	8.3093E-1[4]	7.1029E-1[1]
	8	9.7892E-1[3]	9.3722E-1[1]	1.0067E+0[4]	1.0573E+0[5]	1.3375E+0[7]	1.0829E+0[6]	9.6134E-1[2]
	10	1.0498E+0[5]	1.0450E+0[4]	1.0031E+0[1]	1.3827E+0[7]	1.3691E+0[6]	1.0178E+0[3]	1.0146E+0[2]
	12	1.0124E+0[4]	9.9113E-1[1]	1.0017E+0[2]	1.3664E+0[7]	1.2164E+0[6]	1.0311E+0[5]	1.0041E+0[3]
	15	1.0969E+0[4]	1.1529E+0[5]	1.0000E+0[1]	1.0016E+0[2]	1.2487E+0[7]	1.0072E+0[3]	1.1790E+0[6]
WFG2	3	3.4476E-1[3]	3.3461E-1[2]	5.4619E-1[7]	4.3322E-1[6]	3.5576E-1[5]	3.2892E-1[1]	3.4950E-1[4]
	5	5.8294E-1[1]	5.8656E-1[2]	9.2110E-1[7]	8.1457E-1[6]	7.8665E-1[5]	6.1714E-1[4]	5.9124E-1[3]
	8	9.6919E-1[2]	9.7666E-1[3]	1.0076E+0[6]	9.9782E-1[5]	9.8644E-1[4]	1.0169E+0[7]	9.4980E-1[1]
	10	9.3816E-1[1]	9.5539E-1[3]	1.0037E+0[6]	9.8096E-1[4]	1.0272E+0[7]	1.0025E+0[5]	9.5149E-1[2]
	12	9.7777E-1[3]	9.9315E-1[5]	1.0085E+0[7]	9.7686E-1[2]	9.9151E-1[4]	1.0056E+0[6]	9.7388E-1[1]
	15	1.0906E+0[7]	1.0724E+0[6]	1.0000E+0[1]	1.0015E+0[2]	1.0523E+0[4]	1.0050E+0[3]	1.0710E+0[5]
WFG3	3	6.7604E-1[3]	6.5719E-1[2]	8.0996E-1[4]	1.1546E+0[7]	9.1652E-1[6]	8.5717E-1[5]	6.3137E-1[1]
	5	6.5735E-1[2]	6.9345E-1[3]	8.4833E-1[4]	1.1766E+0[7]	9.2564E-1[6]	8.4962E-1[5]	6.2848E-1[1]
	8	7.9358E-1[2]	8.2121E-1[3]	1.0408E+0[6]	1.0440E+0[7]	1.0011E+0[5]	1.0001E+0[4]	7.7089E-1[1]
	10	7.9859E-1[2]	8.5882E-1[3]	1.0874E+0[7]	1.0464E+0[6]	1.0219E+0[5]	1.0000E+0[4]	7.7332E-1[1]
	12	7.7842E-1[2]	8.0823E-1[3]	1.0562E+0[7]	1.0026E+0[5]	1.0349E+0[6]	1.0000E+0[4]	7.6708E-1[1]
	15	1.2917E+0[6]	1.2317E+0[4]	1.1799E+0[2]	1.0687E+0[1]	1.2427E+0[5]	NaN	1.2129E+0[3]
WFG4	3	3.2182E-1[5]	3.2304E-1[6]	2.4097E-1[1]	3.0907E-1[3]	3.1639E-1[4]	2.8286E-1[2]	3.2811E-1[7]
	5	4.2728E-1[2]	4.2284E-1[1]	8.3469E-1[7]	6.8435E-1[6]	4.6533E-1[4]	5.1559E-1[5]	4.3034E-1[3]
	8	6.7524E-1[2]	7.1108E-1[3]	1.0833E+0[6]	1.2573E+0[7]	1.0284E+0[5]	1.0067E+0[4]	6.3938E-1[1]
	10	6.3432E-1[2]	6.4641E-1[3]	1.1470E+0[6]	1.2121E+0[7]	6.5852E-1[4]	1.0043E+0[5]	6.2694E-1[1]
	12	5.4554E-1[1]	5.6247E-1[3]	1.0886E+0[6]	3.1155E+0[7]	6.3241E-1[4]	1.0059E+0[5]	5.4705E-1[2]
	15	1.2619E+0[5]	1.2544E+0[4]	1.0437E+0[1]	1.1076E+0[2]	1.5537E+0[6]	NaN	1.1856E+0[3]
WFG5	3	3.3716E-1[4]	3.4024E-1[6]	2.8416E-1[1]	3.2991E-1[3]	3.4365E-1[7]	3.2553E-1[2]	3.3909E-1[5]
	5	4.9519E-1[1]	5.0513E-1[3]	9.4039E-1[7]	7.4998E-1[6]	5.5191E-1[4]	6.2623E-1[5]	5.0195E-1[2]
	8	8.9755E-1[2]	9.2721E-1[4]	1.0106E+0[5]	1.1480E+0[7]	9.2692E-1[3]	1.1471E+0[6]	8.2018E-1[1]
	10	6.9012E-1[2]	6.8943E-1[1]	1.1225E+0[7]	8.6880E-1[5]	7.3829E-1[4]	1.0000E+0[6]	6.9987E-1[3]
	12	6.6111E-1[2]	6.6356E-1[3]	1.0878E+0[7]	8.4204E-1[5]	7.1692E-1[4]	1.0001E+0[6]	6.4513E-1[1]
	15	1.4741E+0[6]	1.5014E+0[7]	1.0000E+0[1]	1.0270E+0[4]	1.3348E+0[4]	1.0000E+0[1]	1.4007E+0[5]
WFG6	3	3.4156E-1[4]	3.4658E-1[5]	2.6657E-1[1]	4.6676E-1[7]	3.2428E-1[3]	2.8919E-1[2]	3.4754E-1[6]
	5	4.8447E-1[2]	4.9844E-1[3]	8.6957E-1[7]	7.0752E-1[6]	5.2647E-1[4]	5.3803E-1[5]	4.8256E-1[1]
	8	9.7605E-1[2]	1.0396E+0[4]	1.0335E+0[3]	1.3236E+0[7]	1.2224E+0[6]	1.0879E+0[5]	9.7011E-1[1]
	10	8.0562E-1[3]	8.2955E-1[4]	1.0774E+0[7]	1.0192E+0[6]	7.7380E-1[1]	1.0031E+0[5]	7.9216E-1[2]
	12	7.3335E-1[3]	7.2383E-1[1]	1.0638E+0[6]	1.1898E+0[7]	7.5649E-1[4]	1.0046E+0[5]	7.2406E-1[2]
	15	1.2954E+0[3]	1.2851E+0[2]	1.0949E+0[1]	1.3058E+0[4]	1.7727E+0[6]	NaN	1.4054E+0[5]
WFG7	3	3.1958E-1[5]	3.1619E-1[4]	2.9347E-1[2]	3.2937E-1[7]	3.0699E-1[3]	2.8223E-1[1]	3.2040E-1[6]
	5	4.9573E-1[2]	4.9475E-1[1]	8.9586E-1[7]	7.5504E-1[6]	5.8015E-1[4]	6.2618E-1[5]	4.9914E-1[3]
	8	8.4860E-1[2]	8.8944E-1[3]	1.0199E+0[4]	1.2724E+0[7]	1.1048E+0[6]	1.0816E+0[5]	7.7899E-1[1]
	10	7.8722E-1[2]	7.9460E-1[3]	1.0723E+0[6]	1.4292E+0[7]	8.0849E-1[4]	1.0075E+0[5]	7.6533E-1[1]
	12	7.6643E-1[2]	7.8963E-1[3]	1.0569E+0[6]	1.3606E+0[7]	8.6020E-1[4]	1.0054E+0[5]	6.9759E-1[1]
	15	1.2288E+0[3]	1.4087E+0[5]	1.1063E+0[1]	1.4082E+0[4]	1.8985E+0[6]	NaN	1.1295E+0[2]
WFG8	3	4.1008E-1[4]	4.2457E-1[5]	3.2336E-1[2]	5.8425E-1[7]	4.2647E-1[6]	2.7325E-1[1]	3.9484E-1[3]
	5	4.4585E-1[2]	4.5706E-1[3]	8.7469E-1[7]	8.1399E-1[6]	4.9753E-1[4]	5.3651E-1[5]	4.4106E-1[1]
	8	8.6367E-1[2]	9.0960E-1[3]	1.2541E+0[6]	1.3987E+0[7]	1.1559E+0[5]	1.0017E+0[4]	8.4917E-1[1]
	10	8.7728E-1[4]	8.6397E-1[2]	1.2189E+0[6]	1.3254E+0[7]	8.7642E-1[3]	1.0023E+0[5]	8.3487E-1[1]
	12	7.9795E-1[2]	8.3299E-1[3]	1.1799E+0[6]	1.3597E+0[7]	9.5197E-1[4]	1.0022E+0[5]	7.5565E-1[1]
	15	1.2021E+0[4]	1.1930E+0[3]	1.0355E+0[2]	1.4287E+0[6]		1.0001E+0[1]	1.2418E+0[5]
WFG9	3	3.6828E-1[7]	3.4326E-1[2]	3.6268E-1[5]	3.5692E-1[4]	3.6818E-1[6]	3.3102E-1[1]	3.5516E-1[3]
	5	4.2187E-1[1]	4.2768E-1[3]	1.1653E+0[7]	7.3673E-1[6]	4.9287E-1[4]	6.7485E-1[5]	4.2665E-1[2]
	8	5.9993E-1[2]	6.1401E-1[3]	1.0417E+0[7]	9.9289E-1[6]	7.8074E-1[4]	9.2883E-1[5]	5.8372E-1[1]
	10	5.6060E-1[2]	5.8407E-1[3]	1.0847E+0[7]	9.8186E-1[5]	6.2050E-1[4]	1.0001E+0[6]	5.4831E-1[1]
	12	5.2263E-1[2]	5.5626E-1[3]	1.1067E+0[7]	9.5900E-1[5]	5.9248E-1[4]	1.0002E+0[6]	4.9986E-1[1]
	15	9.9767E-1[2]	1.0561E+0[5]	1.0257E+0[4]	1.0970E+0[6]	1.2556E+0[7]	1.0000E+0[3]	9.8120E-1[1]
average rank		2.93	3.22	4.74	5.59	4.80	4.14	2.35
count the best ranks		5	6	10	1	1	7	25
optimal rate		9.26%	11.11%	18.52%	1.85%	1.85%	12.96%	46.30%
P-value		0.002116018	1.6066E-05	5.08631E-07	2.42698E-10	1.48225E-10	1.55436E-05	

of NSGA-III, Elite-NSGA-III and θ-DEA, the advantage of U-NSGA-III in IGD is not apparent. In fact, NSGA-III and Elite-NSGA-III belong to the same framework as the proposed algorithm, and the first two algorithms have only 7 and 5 times of getting the best value, respectively, which are much lower than 21 times of U-NSGA-III. Although θ-DEA is not significantly different from U-NSGA-III in IGD, only one time of the best value is obtained in *Spread* index.

Analyze the tests in Table 2 which U-NSGA-III does not achieve the best IGD values. U-NSGA-III is not ideal for the functions of WFG1, WFG2, and WFG3, but works well on the other six functions, especially WFG4 and WFG5. We analyze the reason for different performance on different functions of U-NSGA-III. Since the Pareto Front of each function with 3 objectives can be displayed intuitively, the following Fig. 1 shows the real Pareto Fronts of test functions when $m = 3$, and the characteristics of these functions are analyzed.

Table 2. Average *IGD* values for algorithms with different objectives on WFGs

Problem	M	NSGA-III	Elite-NSGA-III	MOEA/D-PBI	MOEA/DD	θ-DEA	I-DBEA	U-NSGA-III
WFG1	3	1.1320E+0[4]	1.0872E+0[3]	7.9115E-1[1]	1.3872E+0[7]	1.0507E+0[2]	1.3350E+0[6]	1.2149E+0[5]
	5	1.7769E+0[4]	1.6507E+0[2]	2.1611E+0[7]	2.0119E+0[6]	1.3909E+0[1]	1.7375E+0[3]	1.8692E+0[5]
	8	2.7106E+0[4]	2.5159E+0[1]	3.3878E+0[7]	2.5605E+0[2]	2.9665E+0[6]	2.7536E+0[5]	2.6972E+0[3]
	10	3.1647E+0[2]	3.2385E+0[3]	3.9942E+0[6]	3.0811E+0[1]	3.4172E+0[5]	5.7230E+0[7]	3.3692E+0[4]
	12	3.7676E+0[3]	3.6957E+0[2]	4.5908E+0[7]	3.6948E+0[1]	3.8057E+0[4]	4.0854E+0[6]	3.8578E+0[5]
	15	4.8094E+0[3]	4.7745E+0[1]	5.4544E+0[6]	5.0492E+0[5]	4.9183E+0[4]	4.1458E+1[7]	4.7858E+0[2]
WFG2	3	1.9537E-1[2]	1.9380E-1[1]	3.8443E-1[6]	4.1181E-1[7]	1.9984E-1[4]	2.2586E-1[5]	1.9718E-1[3]
	5	8.2448E-1[2]	8.6579E-1[5]	1.9694E+0[6]	4.1736E+0[7]	8.2923E-1[3]	8.5870E-1[4]	8.1724E-1[1]
	8	2.8435E+0[1]	3.0340E+0[4]	5.2621E+0[5]	8.8937E+0[7]	2.9399E+0[2]	6.8231E+0[6]	2.9923E+0[3]
	10	5.7270E+0[1]	7.0601E+0[5]	5.9988E+0[2]	1.6315E+1[7]	6.5130E+0[3]	9.4215E+0[6]	7.0496E+0[4]
	12	7.6434E+0[4]	6.5872E+0[2]	5.6798E+0[1]	2.0364E+1[7]	7.3520E+0[3]	9.8527E+0[6]	7.9060E+0[5]
	15	8.9828E+0[3]	7.8452E+0[2]	7.1016E+0[1]	2.7723E+1[7]	7.7260E+0[1]	1.8783E+1[6]	9.0286E+0[4]
WFG3	3	1.5187E-1[3]	1.5043E-1[2]	8.5213E-2[1]	3.7377E-1[7]	1.5765E-1[4]	2.3812E-1[6]	1.6035E-1[5]
	5	7.6745E-1[3]	7.6375E-1[2]	8.5037E-1[6]	9.2720E-1[7]	6.6278E-1[1]	8.2094E-1[5]	7.7853E-1[4]
	8	1.2424E+0[3]	1.2366E+0[2]	2.2134E+0[5]	3.0054E+0[6]	1.6766E+0[4]	8.8364E+0[7]	1.1918E+0[1]
	10	1.9904E+0[4]	1.7656E+0[1]	2.7323E+0[5]	4.0740E+0[6]	1.9006E+0[3]	1.1169E+1[7]	1.8386E+0[2]
	12	2.1704E+0[4]	2.0901E+0[2]	3.5655E+0[5]	7.6552E+0[6]	1.9628E+0[1]	1.3418E+1[7]	2.1159E+0[3]
	15	5.5002E+0[3]	5.6731E+0[4]	3.0759E+0[1]	1.1195E+1[6]	5.3280E+0[2]	1.6962E+1[7]	5.6996E+0[5]
WFG4	3	2.3279E-1[3]	2.3289E-1[4]	3.0027E-1[7]	2.4641E-1[5]	2.2972E-1[1]	2.6856E-1[6]	2.3230E-1[2]
	5	1.3559E+0[2]	1.3735E+0[4]	3.0605E+0[7]	1.4702E+0[6]	1.3620E+0[3]	1.3976E+0[5]	1.3539E+0[1]
	8	3.9152E+0[3]	3.9086E+0[2]	8.8815E+0[6]	4.6833E+0[5]	4.2725E+0[4]	1.4118E+1[7]	3.8237E+0[1]
	10	5.7516E+0[2]	5.7983E+0[3]	1.3203E+1[6]	6.2607E+0[5]	5.8186E+0[4]	1.9112E+1[7]	5.7164E+0[1]
	12	7.0593E+0[3]	6.9964E+0[2]	1.6344E+1[6]	7.4679E+0[5]	7.1687E+0[4]	2.3117E+1[7]	6.9688E+0[1]
	15	1.2077E+1[2]	1.2101E+1[3]	2.3561E+1[6]	1.6126E+1[5]	1.3032E+1[4]	3.1160E+1[7]	1.1924E+1[1]
WFG5	3	2.3798E-1[2]	2.3800E-1[3]	2.8867E-1[7]	2.4902E-1[5]	2.3672E-1[1]	2.6770E-1[6]	2.3840E-1[4]
	5	1.3301E+0[2]	1.3332E+0[3]	3.1989E+0[7]	1.4483E+0[6]	1.3381E+0[4]	1.3665E+0[5]	1.3260E+0[1]
	8	3.9500E+0[2]	3.9937E+0[3]	8.2043E+0[6]	5.3107E+0[5]	4.2277E+0[4]	1.1882E+1[7]	3.9226E+0[1]
	10	5.7513E+0[3]	5.7381E+0[2]	1.1739E+1[6]	7.7704E+0[5]	5.8011E+0[4]	1.9316E+1[7]	5.7318E+0[1]
	12	7.1636E+0[3]	7.1629E+0[2]	1.6533E+1[6]	9.2850E+0[5]	7.2017E+0[4]	2.3921E+1[7]	7.1325E+0[1]
	15	1.2290E+1[2]	1.2319E+1[3]	2.5828E+1[6]	1.5764E+1[5]	1.2985E+1[4]	3.0963E+1[7]	1.2289E+1[1]
WFG6	3	2.7457E-1[2]	2.7650E-1[3]	3.1649E-1[5]	3.2778E-1[6]	2.6316E-1[1]	3.3947E-1[7]	2.7695E-1[4]
	5	1.3610E+0[1]	1.3620E+0[3]	3.2588E+0[7]	1.4548E+0[6]	1.3906E+0[4]	1.3906E+0[5]	1.3615E+0[2]
	8	4.1444E+0[3]	4.1202E+0[2]	8.4121E+0[6]	4.6119E+0[5]	4.2769E+0[4]	1.2732E+1[7]	4.0565E+0[1]
	10	6.2277E+0[3]	6.3391E+0[4]	1.2165E+1[6]	7.0161E+0[5]	5.9324E+0[1]	1.9124E+1[7]	6.0668E+0[2]
	12	7.4330E+0[3]	7.4014E+0[2]	1.5456E+1[6]	7.6977E+0[5]	7.3814E+0[1]	2.3287E+1[7]	7.4446E+0[4]
	15	1.2774E+1[1]	1.2958E+1[3]	2.4688E+1[6]	1.5150E+1[5]	1.3131E+1[4]	3.0610E+1[7]	1.2832E+1[2]
WFG7	3	2.3320E-1[4]	2.3307E-1[3]	2.9155E-1[6]	2.6260E-1[5]	2.2833E-1[1]	2.9951E-1[7]	2.3294E-1[2]
	5	1.3659E+0[1]	1.3734E+0[3]	3.2565E+0[7]	1.4822E+0[6]	1.3805E+0[4]	1.4026E+0[5]	1.3674E+0[2]
	8	3.9981E+0[2]	4.0336E+0[3]	8.2848E+0[6]	4.5672E+0[5]	4.3034E+0[4]	1.1672E+1[7]	3.9402E+0[1]
	10	5.7325E+0[3]	5.7294E+0[2]	1.2273E+1[6]	5.9302E+0[5]	5.8098E+0[4]	1.8469E+1[7]	5.6734E+0[1]
	12	7.1433E+0[2]	7.1776E+0[3]	1.6174E+1[6]	7.2537E+0[5]	7.2425E+0[4]	2.2734E+1[7]	7.0743E+0[1]
	15	1.2073E+1[3]	1.1876E+1[1]	2.4439E+1[6]	1.5362E+1[5]	1.2873E+1[4]	3.0892E+1[7]	1.1919E+1[2]
WFG8	3	3.2195E-1[3]	3.1891E-1[2]	3.7018E-1[6]	3.3137E-1[5]	3.1843E-1[1]	3.7177E-1[7]	3.2330E-1[4]
	5	1.3533E+0[2]	1.3612E+0[4]	3.3551E+0[7]	1.4566E+0[6]	1.3503E+0[1]	1.3797E+0[5]	1.3551E+0[3]
	8	3.9458E+0[2]	4.0010E+0[3]	9.3313E+0[6]	4.2606E+0[5]	4.0557E+0[4]	1.3821E+1[7]	3.8686E+0[1]
	10	6.2028E+0[5]	6.1323E+0[4]	1.2800E+1[6]	6.0475E+0[2]	5.6960E+0[1]	1.8641E+1[7]	6.1188E+0[3]
	12	7.4893E+0[2]	7.5608E+0[5]	1.6958E+1[6]	7.5264E+0[4]	7.4989E+0[3]	2.3301E+1[7]	7.3904E+0[1]
	15	1.2688E+1[1]	1.2830E+1[3]	2.4711E+1[6]	1.6710E+1[5]	1.2878E+1[4]	3.0603E+1[7]	1.2705E+1[2]
WFG9	3	2.4222E-1[4]	2.3950E-1[2]	3.0173E-1[7]	2.5342E-1[5]	2.3781E-1[1]	2.7977E-1[6]	2.4139E-1[3]
	5	1.2672E+0[1]	1.2766E+0[4]	3.0771E+0[7]	1.4334E+0[6]	1.2762E+0[3]	1.3158E+0[5]	1.2756E+0[2]
	8	3.6626E+0[2]	3.6733E+0[3]	8.5717E+0[6]	5.0020E+0[5]	3.9705E+0[4]	1.1811E+1[7]	3.6295E+0[1]
	10	5.4982E+0[3]	5.5030E+0[4]	1.2210E+1[6]	6.7927E+0[5]	5.4893E+0[2]	1.9311E+1[7]	5.4483E+0[1]
	12	7.1096E+0[4]	7.0738E+0[2]	1.6142E+1[6]	8.1728E+0[5]	6.9415E+0[1]	2.3896E+1[7]	7.0845E+0[3]
	15	1.1724E+1[3]	1.1704E+1[2]	2.2980E+1[6]	1.4680E+1[5]	1.2298E+1[4]	3.0966E+1[7]	1.1653E+1[1]
average rank		2.63	2.76	5.67	5.28	2.91	6.35	2.41
count the best ranks		7	5	4	2	15	0	21
optimal rate		12.96%	9.26%	7.41%	3.70%	27.78%	0.00%	38.89%
P-value		0.559321779	0.402978119	8.9327E-09	0.000158852	0.441738775	1.64812E-10	

For WFG1-3, the real Pareto Fronts are more concentrated than the others, especially for WFG3, which is concentrated in a very small rectangular area. The advantage of U-NSGA-III is searching the entire solution space evenly. From above tables and Fig. 1, we can see that U-NSGA-III has considerable benefits for the problems which real Pareto solution sets distribute wildly, while it has no advantage in the problems which solution sets are concentrated. However, when we solve problems in the real world, the real Pareto solution sets are unknown. Therefore, it is necessary to search for optimal solutions in entire solution space.

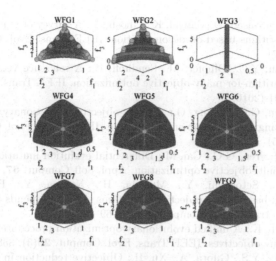

Fig. 1. The real Pareto Fronts of WFGs

5   Conclusion

This paper presents an improved algorithm, called U-NSGA-III, which uses a uniform pool reservation strategy based on reference points. The approach addresses the issue of NSGA-III abandoning searching areas around specific reference points where no dominant solution is nearby. U-NSGA-III maintains population diversity and ensures that the algorithm has the ability of searching the entire solution space. We compare the proposed algorithm with the other six optimization algorithms on WFG benchmark test set. The experimental results show that the proposed U-NSGA-III can deal well with most of the instances on WFGs. The obtained solution sets have outstanding diversity. In the future, we will further consider the problem of improving convergence when using the uniform pool reservation strategy.

Acknowledgments. We would like to acknowledge the support from the National Science Foundation of China (61472095), Heilongjiang Province Natural Science Foundation (F2016039) and Research Foundation of Education Department of Heilongjiang (1352MSYYB016). This paper is also funded by the International Exchange Program of Harbin Engineering University for Innovation oriented Talents Cultivation.

References

1. Raja, B.D., Jhala, R., Patel, V.: Many-objective optimization of shell and tube heat exchanger. Therm. Sci. Eng. Prog. **2**, 87–101 (2017)
2. Yuan, Y., Xu, H., Wang, B., Zhang, B., Yao, X.: Balancing convergence and diversity in decomposition-based many-objective optimizers. IEEE Trans. Evol. Comput. **20**(2), 180–198 (2016)

3. Trivedi, A., Srinivasan, D., Sanyal, K., Ghosh, A.: A survey of multiobjective evolutionary algorithms based on decomposition. IEEE Trans. Evol. Comput. **21**(3), 440–462 (2017)
4. Cheng, R., Jin, Y.C., Olhofer, M., Sendhoff, B.: A reference vector guided evolutionary algorithm for many-objective optimization. IEEE Trans. Evol. Comput. **20**(5), 773–791 (2016)
5. Cheng, J., Yen, G.G., Zhang, G.: A many-objective evolutionary algorithm with enhanced mating and environmental selections. IEEE Trans. Evol. Comput. **19**(4), 592–605 (2015)
6. Yu, X., Lu, Y., Yen, G.G., Cai, M.: Differential evolution mutation operators for constrained multi-objective optimization. Appl. Soft Comput. **67**, 452–466 (2018)
7. Ishibuchi, H., Setoguchi, Y., Masuda, H., Nojima, Y.: Performance of decomposition-based many-objective algorithms strongly depends on Pareto Front shapes. IEEE Trans. Evol. Comput. **21**(2), 169–190 (2017)
8. Seada, H., Deb, K.: A unified evolutionary optimization procedure for single, multiple, and many objectives. IEEE Trans. Evol. Comput. **20**(3), 358–369 (2016)
9. Yuan, Y., Ong, Y.S., Gupta, A., Xu, H.: Objective reduction in many-objective optimization: evolutionary multiobjective approaches and comprehensive analysis. IEEE Trans. Evol. Comput. **22**, 189–210 (2018)
10. Li, F., Cheng, R., Liu, J., Jin, Y.: A two-stage R2 indicator based evolutionary algorithm for many-objective optimization. Appl. Soft Comput. **67**, 245–260 (2018)
11. Deb, K., Pratap, A., Agarwal, S., Meyarivan, T.: A fast and elitist multiobjective genetic algorithm: NSGA-II. IEEE Trans. Evol. Comput. **6**(2), 182–197 (2002)
12. Deb, K., Jain, H.: An evolutionary many-objective optimization algorithm using reference-point-based nondominated sorting approach, part I: solving problems with box constraints. IEEE Trans. Evol. Comput. **18**(4), 577–601 (2014)
13. Ibrahim, A., Rahnamayan, S., Martin, M.V., Deb, K.: EliteNSGA-III: an improved evolutionary many-objective optimization algorithm. In: 2016 IEEE Congress on Evolutionary Computation, CEC, pp. 973–982. IEEE Press, New York (2016)
14. Bi, X., Wang, C.: An improved NSGA-III algorithm based on elimination operator for many-objective optimization. Memet. Comput. **9**(4), 361–383 (2017)
15. Zhang, Q., Li, H.: MOEA/D: a multiobjective evolutionary algorithm based on decomposition. IEEE Trans. Evol. Comput. **11**(6), 712–731 (2007)
16. Asafuddoula, M., Ray, T., Sarker, R.: A decomposition-based evolutionary algorithm for many objective optimization. IEEE Trans. Evol. Comput. **19**(3), 445–460 (2015)
17. Khan, B., Johnstone, M., Hanoun, S., Lim, C.P., Creighton, D., Nahavandi, S.: Improved NSGA-III using neighborhood information and scalarization. In: 2016 IEEE International Conference on Systems, Man, and Cybernetics, SMC, pp. 003033–003038. IEEE Press, New York (2016)
18. Carlos, A., Coello, A., Lamont, G.B., Van Veldhuizen, D.A.: Evolutionary Algorithms for Solving Multi-Objective Problems. Springer, New York (2007). https://doi.org/10.1007/978-0-387-36797-2
19. Huband, S., Hingston, P., Barone, L., While, L.: A review of multiobjective test problems and a scalable test problem toolkit. IEEE Trans. Evol. Comput. **10**(5), 477–506 (2006)
20. Sun, Y., Yen, G.G., Yi, Z.: IGD indicator-based evolutionary algorithm for many-objective optimization problems. IEEE Trans. Evol. Comput. (2018)

21. Zhou, A., Jin, Y., Zhang, Q., Sendhoff, B.: Combining model-based and genetics-based offspring generation for multi-objective optimization using a convergence criterion. In: IEEE Congress on Evolutionary Computation, CEC 2006, pp. 892–899. IEEE Press, New York (2006)
22. Tian, Y., Cheng, R., Zhang, X., Jin, Y.: PlatEMO: a MATLAB platform for evolutionary multi-objective optimization [educational forum]. IEEE Comput. Intell. Mag. **12**(4), 73–87 (2017)

Elman Neural Network Optimized by Firefly Algorithm for Forecasting China's Carbon Dioxide Emissions

Yuansheng Huang and Lei Shen[✉]

Department of Economics and Management,
North China Electric Power University, Baoding 071003, Hebei, China
1641297486@qq.com

Abstract. With the development of China's economy, more and more energy consumption has led to increasingly serious environmental problems. Faced with the enormous pressure of large amounts of carbon dioxide (CO_2) emissions, China is now actively implementing development strategy of low-carbon and emission reduction. Through the analysis of the influencing factors of CO_2 emissions in China, five key influencing factors are selected: urbanization level, gross domestic product (GDP) of secondary industry, thermal power generation, real GDP per capital and energy consumption per unit of GDP. This paper applies the Elman neural network optimized by the firefly algorithm (FA) to forecasting the CO_2 emissions in China. And the results show that the performance of the FA-Elman is better than the Elman and BPNN, verifying the effectiveness of the FA-Elman model for the CO_2 emissions prediction. Finally, we make some suggestions for low-carbon and emission reduction in China by analyzing key influencing factors and forecasting CO_2 emissions using FA-Elman from 2017 to 2020.

Keywords: Carbon dioxide emissions · Forecasting model
Elman neural network · Firefly algorithm

1 Introduction

Accompany with the rapid economic growth of China in the past three decades, Chinese energy consumption has occupied the top of the whole world in recent years. China is now one of the countries with the largest carbon emissions all over the world, and the CO_2 emissions have reached 103.57 million tons per year. In the 13th Five-Year Plan, the Chinese government proposed that by 2020, the per unit's GDP CO_2 emissions will be reduced by 18% compared to 2015, and the total amount of carbon emissions will be effectively controlled. This will promote CO_2 emissions of China to peak by around 2030 and China will strive to achieve the target at an even earlier date.

Many scholars have put forward a large number of studies on the prediction of CO_2 emissions. Ding et al. [1] developed a novel grey multivariable model

© Springer Nature Singapore Pte Ltd. 2018
J. Qiao et al. (Eds.): BIC-TA 2018, CCIS 951, pp. 36–47, 2018.
https://doi.org/10.1007/978-981-13-2826-8_4

to forecast Chinese CO_2 emissions from fuel combustion from 2014 to 2020. Meng et al. [2] proposed a hybrid forecasting equation combined by a nonhomogeneous exponential equation and a linear equation, and it has better performance on the prediction of CO_2 emissions than the traditional linear model and GM (grey model) (1, 1). Behrang et al. [3] employed bees algorithm and multi-layer perceptron neural network to predict the world CO_2 emission. Kone and Buke [4] applied trend analysis to forecast the top-25 emitting countries' CO_2 emissions from fuel combustion, and the calculated results showed that the projected CO_2 emissions under different scenarios are within the scope of the agreement. Auffhammer and Carson [5] exercised province-level information to predict CO_2 emissions of China, and we can get more CO_2 emissions information than national level time series. Zhao [6] predicted energy-related CO_2 emissions through using least squares support vector machine (LSSVM) optimized by the whale optimization algorithm. The effectiveness of this model was demonstrated by the prediction of CO_2 emissions in China.

Some literatures focus more on the innovation of forecasting methods, while some research consider the effects of known factors on CO_2 emissions and apply effective models to predict them. Pao et al. [7] found the predict effect of the nonlinear grey Bernoulli model in forecasting the CO_2 emissions, energy consumption and economic growth in China is better than GM and ARIMA. And we can know the CO_2 emissions, energy consumption and economic growth have long-run equilibrium relationship by the co-integration test. Wang and Ye [8] believed there is a nonlinear relationship between CO_2 emissions produced by fossil energy and GDP, and they used non-linear grey multivariable models to confirm this idea. Simultaneously, they also predicted Chinese carbon emissions from fossil energy consumption from 2014 to 2020. Zhou et al. [9] obtained driving factors of CO_2 emissions through decoupling analysis, include actual GDP, urbanization rate, industrial structure, population, energy structure, and electricity consumption. Then they advanced a hybrid model of grey neural network model based on GM and BP neural network to forecast CO_2 emissions. Sun et al. [10] extracted the potential factors of CO_2 emissions by factor analysis, then Extreme learning machine (ELM) optimized by PSO was proposed to forecast CO_2 emissions, finally analyzed some measures to control the growth of CO_2 emissions.

In summary, studying CO_2 emission prediction has certain practical significance. In this study, Elman neural network is used to forecast CO_2 emission of China. Elman neural network is one of the dynamic recurrent neural networks which has the function of mapping dynamic features by storing the internal state based on the basic structure of feedforward artificial neural network. So that the system has the ability to adapt to time-varying characteristics and temporal sequences modeling. Kelo and Dudul [11] developed a new recurrent neural network which integrated Elman neural network and wavelet to forecast short-term electrical power load the day before. Ding et al. [12] used genetic algorithm to optimize Elman networks processing non-linear complex data. Wang et al. [13] advanced a combination approach of empirical mode decomposition and Elman neural network that can accurately predict wind speed. Li et al. [14] created a hybrid quantized Elman neural network to obtain the short-term load forecasting. Liu et al. [15] improved the wind speed high-accuracy by bonding the secondary decomposition algorithm and the Elman neural networks.

Through the study of the above paper, it can be concluded that Elman neural network is very suitable for time series forecasting. However, because of its own drawbacks, such as the uncertain number of nodes, the problem of local minimum and so on, using Elman neural network to forecast time series is easy to make the prediction effect not perfect. Hence, in this paper, FA is applied to optimizing the weights, thresholds and numbers of hidden layer neurons of Elman neural network in order to improve training speed and generalization ability. And Chinese CO_2 emission and its influencing factors are selected as the input values, using the FA-Elman model to predict CO_2 emission of China and analyze the influencing factors which impact on CO_2 emission of China. The CO_2 emissions of Chinese history and its influencing factors as training data as input to the model, and using FA-Elman model to predict future CO_2 emissions in China. Finally, analyze the influencing factors which impact on China's CO_2 emission.

The remainder of this study is organized as follows: Sect. 2 introduces the FA, Elman and the FA-Elman model; Sect. 3 elaborates on the used data; Sect. 4 shows the experimental results and the conclusions are proved in Sect. 5.

2   Methodology

2.1   Firefly Algorithm

The optimization technique of bionic swarm intelligence is a hot issue studied by scholars at home and abroad in recent years. Its main idea is to construct the random search method by studying or simulating the social behavior of living creatures in the natural world. There are currently two kinds of algorithms studied more frequently: Ants Group Algorithm (ACO) and Particle Swarm Optimization (PSO).

Compared with other optimization algorithms, the firefly algorithm can not only optimize the unimodal function and multi-peak function, but also has strong local search ability. It can find the optimal solution of the region in a small area, which is easy to implement, and the parameters have less impact on the algorithm.

Firefly Algorithm (FA) is a bio-inspired metaheuristic algorithm inspired by the behavior of natural fireflies at night [16] and make use of the characteristics of fireflies' emitting light. Each firefly represents a candidate solution randomly generated in the search space. Fireflies can find out potential candidate solutions by moving toward other positions. In the process of moving, it will fulfill the iteration of the position to find the optimal position, so that the optimization process is completed.

The search pattern of FA is mainly determined by the attractions among fireflies, while the attractions is decided by the intensity of the emitted light.

For this reason, the search process of it is related to two important parameters: the light intensity I and the attractiveness β. The brighter the light means the better the position, and the brightest firefly represents the optimal solution in the search space. The brighter the firefly is, the more attractive it is to the surrounding fireflies. If their brightness is the same, then the fireflies move randomly or remain in its current position. These two important parameters are inversely proportional to the distance. The greater the distance, the smaller the attraction. Hence the light intensity of fireflies I can be defined by:

$$I = I_0 e^{-\gamma r_{ij}} \tag{1}$$

where I_0 is the intensity at r $= 0$, which is related to the value of the objective function, the better the objective function group, the higher the brightness of itself. γ indicates the light absorption coefficient that is set as a constant. When light passes through a medium with the light intensity in γ, I will decease with increasing distance. The distance between ith firefly and jth firefly is r_{ij}.

The attractiveness of these two fireflies $\beta(r_{ij})$ is calculated as Eq. (2), two fireflies x_i and x_j, they can be updated as Eq. (3).

$$\beta(r_{ij}) = \beta_0 e^{-\gamma r_{ij}^2} \tag{2}$$

$$x_i(t+1) = x_i(t) + \beta(x_j(t) - x_i(t)) + \alpha(rand - 1/2) \tag{3}$$

β_0 denotes the attractiveness at the source point, α is the step size and rand means a random value uniformly distributed on $[0, 1]$.

2.2 Elman Neural Network

Elman neural network is a typical local regression recurrent, first proposed by Elman [17] in 1990. It belongs to feedback neural network and is very similar to feedforward neural network. Elman-NN has yet stronger optimization calculation and associative memory function that can be viewed as a recursive neural network with local memory elements and local feedback connections.

The basic Elman neural network consists of an input layer, a hidden layer, a context layer, and an output layer, as shown in Fig. 1. Compared with BP network, Elman-NN has one more context layer for constructing local feedback. The context layer receives feedback signals from the hidden layer and each hidden layer node has a corresponding associated layer node connection. It can remember the past state and use the output value of the hidden unit in the previous time steps together with the current input value of the network as the input of the hidden layer at the next moment, which is seen as a step delay operator and equivalent to the state feedback.

Suppose the number of input and output neurons are respectively n and m, and the number of hidden and undertake neurons are r. The weight of input layer to hidden layer is $w1$, the weight of context layer to hidden layer is $w2$, the weight of hidden layer to output layer is $w3$. $u(k-1)$ is the input of neural work,

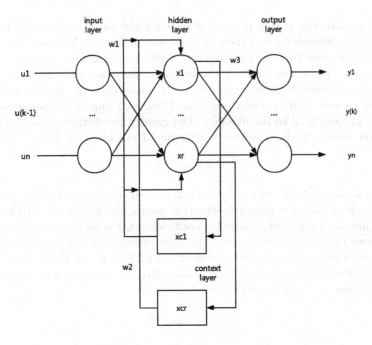

Fig. 1. The structure of Elman neural network

$x(k)$ is the output of hidden layer, $x_c(k)$ is the output of context layer, $y(k)$ is the output of neural network. The output of the hidden layer is as Eq. (4). The output of Elman is as Eq. (5).

$$x(k) = f(w_2 x_c(k) + w_1(u(k-1)))\qquad(4)$$

$$y(k) = g(w_3 x(k))\qquad(5)$$

$x_c(k) = x(k-1)$ and f means the hidden layer transfer function. g is the transfer function of output layer.

2.3   Elman Neural Network Optimized by FA

In this paper, we update the parameters $w1$, $w2$, $w3$ of Elman neural network through using FA to replace the back propagation algorithm. The step and the flow chart of FA-Elman model are displayed in Fig. 2.

Firstly, create the Elman neural network and initialize the parameters. The input data is dimensionless, the number of the Elman hidden layer nodes is set as 50 and the loss function is constructed by the mean squared error (MSE), as shown in Eq. 7. The MSE is shown in Eq. 6.

$$MSE = \frac{1}{N}\sum_{t=1}^{N}(y_t - x_t)^2\qquad(6)$$

$$LOSS = \frac{1}{N} \sum_{t=1}^{N} (y_t - (gw_3 f(w_1(u(k-1)) + w_2 x(k-1))))^2 \qquad (7)$$

Secondly, input the normalized training sample set into the Elman network for training to determine the Elman network's parameter. The determination process of the Elman network's parameter is the process of minimizing the loss function by FA. The algorithm can be summarized as follows: (a) initialize the parameters and the position of each firefly, select the loss function as an objective function; (b) calculate the attractiveness $\beta(r_{ij})$ between each pair of fireflies and select the direction of fireflies' movement based on relative brightness; (c) update the location of the fireflies in the entire population, recalculate the brightness of the fireflies; (d) terminate if a termination criterion is achieved, output the global extreme point and the best individual value; otherwise, return to step 2 to continue.

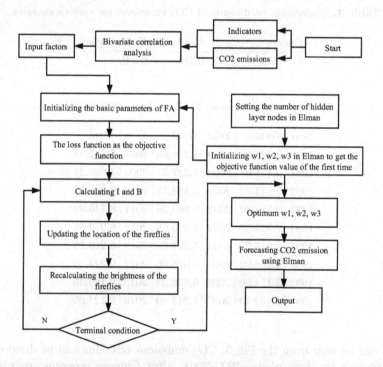

Fig. 2. The flow chart of FA-Elman model

Finally, the test sample will be brought into the network for testing, that is a training completed network model after getting the optimal $w1$, $w2$, $w3$ by the previous step. The output values are denormalized and we can obtain the final predicted value.

3   Data Analysis

3.1   Data Conversion

This paper selects data on Chinese CO_2 emissions and its influencers from 1990 to 2016, includes urbanization level, secondary industry GDP, thermal power generation, real GDP per capital and energy consumption per unit of GDP, of which the data from 1990 to 2011 is used as a training set, data from 2012 to 2016 as a test set. Since there is no public data of Chinese CO_2 emission, the carbon emission coefficient in the IPCC is used in this paper to calculate the CO_2 emissions in China. In the IPCC, the carbon emission conversion coefficient of coal, oil, and natural gas are shown in Table 1. CO_2 emissions of China from 1990 to 2016 are obtained by conversion coefficient, as displayed in Table 2 and Fig. 3.

Table 1. Conversion coefficients of CO_2 emissions for various energies.

Energy	Coal	Crude oil	Natural gas
Coefficient	0.747	0.585	0.448

Table 2. CO_2 emissions of China from 1990 to 2016.

Year	Total	Year	Total	Year	Total
1990	2,320.28	1999	3,278.65	2008	7,351.94
1991	2,451.97	2000	3,327.35	2009	7,695.21
1992	2,574.02	2001	3,486.15	2010	8,098.52
1993	2,782.36	2002	3,809.26	2011	8,746.92
1994	2,925.53	2003	4,495.68	2012	8,979.38
1995	3,015.77	2004	5,291.78	2013	9,218.75
1996	3,168.92	2005	6,058.26	2014	9,224.10
1997	3,154.00	2006	6,656.03	2015	9,164.45
1998	3,152.13	2007	7,211.09	2016	9,123.05

As can be seen from the Fig. 3, CO_2 emissions of China can be divided into three phases: the first phase, 1990–2001, after Chinese economic reform and open up, as the economy recovers, CO_2 emissions also slowly grow; the second phase, 2001–2011, following China's accession to the WTO in 2001, China's economy was in a high-speed development for a long time and CO_2 emissions also increased rapidly; the third phase, the growth rate of CO_2 emissions decreased in 2011–2016, and after 2013, CO_2 emissions decreased. This is due to the fact that China's economic growth rate has been declining in recent years. The Chinese government focus on environmental protection nowadays and it has carried out industrial upgrading to develop a low-carbon economy.

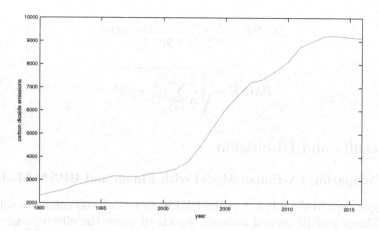

Fig. 3. CO$_2$ emissions of China from 1990 to 2016.

3.2 Bivariate Correlation Analysis

Bivariate correlation analysis is used to test the correlation between the selected influencing factors and CO$_2$ emissions. The results are shown in Table 3. The Pearson correlation in the Table 3 reflects the correlation between CO$_2$ emissions and different influencing factors. The values of urbanization, secondary industry GDP, thermal power generation, and per capita GDP are all greater than 0.95, indicating that these factors are highly correlated with CO$_2$ emissions. Energy consumption per unit of GDP is -0.729, manifesting that it is negatively correlated with CO$_2$ emissions. The five factors selected pass through the two-tailed significance test at the confidence level of 99% universally.

Table 3. Pearson correlation between different influencing factors and CO$_2$ emissions

Indicator	Pearson correlation
Urbanization	0.974**
Secondary industry GDP	0.967**
Thermal power generation	0.992**
Per capita GDP	0.952**
Energy consumption per unit of GDP	-0.729**

3.3 Model Performance Evaluation

In order to validate the prediction effect of model, it is necessary to select appropriate evaluation indicators. This paper selects mean absolute percentage error (MAPE) and root mean square error (RMSE) to evaluate the forecast results, and these formulas are as follows:

$$MAPE = \frac{1}{n} \sum_{i=1}^{n} \left| \frac{\widehat{y}_i - y_i}{y_i} \right| * 100\% \tag{8}$$

$$RMSE = \sqrt{\frac{1}{n} \sum_{i=1}^{n} (\widehat{y}_i - y_i)^2} \tag{9}$$

4   Results and Discussion

4.1   Comparing FA-Elman Model with Elman and BPNN Models

This paper uses MATLAB to test the FA-Elman model, and compares with the single Elman and BP neural network models to prove the effectiveness of the FA-Elman model.

The number of hidden layer nodes in the Elman neural network is 30. The parameters of the firefly algorithm are set as follows: the number of fireflies is 80, the maximum number of iterations is 1000, step factor (α) is 0.5, initial attractiveness (β) is 1.

As shown in Fig. 4, the FA-Elman model's forecasting results are closest to the true CO_2 emissions from 2012 to 2016, indicting the performance of FA-Elman model is obviously better than the single Elman and BPNN models. The single Elman model's prediction results are higher than the actual CO_2 emissions, however the prediction results after optimization are more in line with the actual CO_2 emissions. Table 3 gives the prediction errors of different prediction models. The FA-Elman model's MAPE and RMSE are the smallest among the three models, which are 0.64% and 68.60 respectively. While the BPNN model's MAPE and RMSE are larger than others. So, the FA-Elman model has the highest forecast accuracy, and BPNN is the worst model (Table 4).

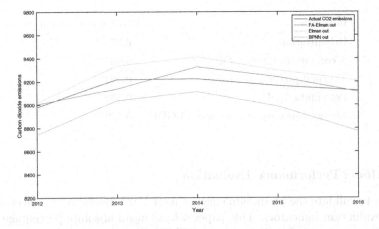

Fig. 4. The flow chart of FA-Elman model

Table 4. The prediction errors of different prediction models.

	FA-Elman	Elman	BPNN
RMSE	68.60	122.92	226.14
MAPE (%)	0.64	1.22	2.3

4.2 Using FA-Elman Model to Predict CO_2 Emissions in China by 2020

Through the use of Chinese CO_2 emissions from 1990–2016 and influencing factors as training data, CO_2 emissions of China from 2017 to 2020 are forecasted in Fig. 5.

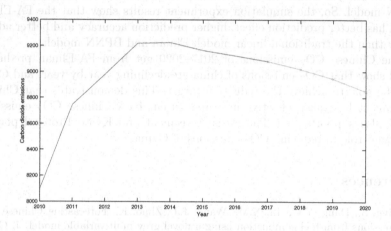

Fig. 5. Forecasting CO_2 emissions of China from 2017 to 2020

From Fig. 3, we can see that Chinese CO_2 emissions will decrease year by year in 2017–2020. This is because China attaches importance to energy conservation and emission reduction, reduces CO_2 emissions by vigorously developing the utilize of non-fossil energy, promoting the clean development of fossil energy, accelerating industrial restructuring and controlling industrial emissions. The government, moreover, actively builds and operates nationwide carbon emissions trading market. The China proposed in the UN Framework Convention on Climate Change in 2014 that China will control annual CO_2 emissions below 10 billion tons from 2016 to 2020. According to the current measures taken by the Chinese government to reduce CO_2 emissions, this goal can be successfully accomplished. The government also announced that the amount of carbon-dioxide emissions per unit of GDP in 2020 based on the 2015 will fall of 18%. According to Fig. 5, CO_2 emissions of China in 2020 is forecasted 8884.40 million tons. Calculated on the basis of China's GDP growth rate of 6.9%, we can get the amount of carbon-dioxide emissions per unit of GDP is 0.00895. Compared with emissions intensity of its economy of 0.0133 in 2015, the predicted value of 2020 cut by 32.7%, far exceeding the reduction target of 18%.

5   Conclusion

This paper mainly employs the FA-Elman model to predict CO_2 emissions in China. Firstly, five factors that are highly correlated with CO_2 emissions are selected through bivariate correlation analysis as input variables of Elman model. Then the Elman neural network is training by a training set, and its parameters are optimized by FA. Finally, apply a training completed Elman network model to predict Chinese CO_2 emissions for 2012–2020. The predictive values of 2012–2016 obtained by FA-Elman is closest to the true values, and the MAPE and RMSE of the FA-Elman model is smaller than those of the single Elman and BPNN model. So, the simulation experiment results show that the FA-Elman model has better prediction effect, higher prediction accuracy and better adaptability than the traditional linear model, Elman and BPNN model.

The Chinese CO_2 emissions of 2017–2020 get from FA-Elman prediction model show that CO_2 emissions of china are declining year by year, and China must be able to achieve the reduction target. This demonstrates that Chinese government has taken effective measures to cut back Chinese CO_2 emissions, and it also supports that The Paris Agreement and Kyoto Protocol play an important role in reducing CO_2 emissions of China.

References

1. Ding, S., Dang, Y.G., Li, X.M., Wang, J.J., Zhao, K.: Forecasting Chinese CO_2 emissions from fuel combustion using a novel grey multivariable model. J. Clean. Prod. **162**, 1527–1538 (2017)
2. Meng, M., Niu, D., Wei, S.: A small-sample hybrid model for forecasting energy-related CO_2 emissions. Energy **64**(1), 673–677 (2014)
3. Behrang, M.A., Assareh, E., Assari, M.R., Ghanbarzadeh, A.: Using bees algorithm and artificial neural network to forecast world carbon dioxide emission. Energy Sour. **33**(19), 1747–1759 (2011)
4. Kne, A., Bke, T.: Forecasting of CO_2 emissions from fuel combustion using trend analysis. Renew. Sustain. Energy Rev. **14**(9), 2906–2915 (2010)
5. Auffhammer, M., Carson, R.T.: Forecasting the path of China's CO_2 emissions using province-level information. J. Environ. Econ. Manag. **55**(3), 229–247 (2008)
6. Zhao, H., Guo, S., Zhao, H.: Energy-related CO_2 emissions forecasting using an improved LSSVM model optimized by whale optimization algorithm. Energies **10**(7), 874 (2017)
7. Pao, H.T., Fu, H.C., Tseng, C.L.: Forecasting of CO_2 emissions, energy consumption and economic growth in china using an improved grey model. Energy **40**(1), 400–409 (2012)
8. Wang, Z.X., Ye, D.J.: Forecasting Chinese carbon emissions from fossil energy consumption using non-linear grey multivariable models. J. Clean. Prod. **142**, 600–612 (2017)

9. Zhou, J., et al.: Prediction of CO_2 emissions based on the analysis and classification of decoupling. Pol. J. Environ. Stud. **26**(6), 2851–2860 (2017)

10. Sun, W., Wang, C., Zhang, C.: Factor analysis and forecasting of CO_2 emissions in hebei, using extreme learning machine based on particle swarm optimization. J. Clean. Prod. **162**, 1095–1101 (2017)

11. Kelo, S., Dudul, S.: A wavelet elman neural network for short-term electrical load prediction under the influence of temperature. Int. J. Electr. Power Energy Syst. **43**(1), 1063–1071 (2012)

12. Ding, S., Zhang, Y., Chen, J., Jia, W.: Research on using genetic algorithms to optimize elman neural networks. Neural Comput. Appl. **23**(2), 293–297 (2013)

13. Wang, J., Zhang, W., Li, Y., Wang, J., Dang, Z.: Forecasting wind speed using empirical mode decomposition and elman neural network. Appl. Soft Comput. J. **23**(5), 452–459 (2014)

14. Li, P., Li, Y., Xiong, Q., Chai, Y., Zhang, Y.: Application of a hybrid quantized elman neural network in short-term load forecasting. Int. J. Electr. Power Energy Syst. **55**(2), 749–759 (2014)

15. Liu, H., Tian, H.Q., Liang, X.F., Li, Y.F.: Wind speed forecasting approach using secondary decomposition algorithm and elman neural networks. Appl. Energy **157**, 183–194 (2015)

16. Albrecht, A., Steinhöfel, K.: Stochastic Algorithms: Foundations and Applications. Springer, Heidelberg (2005). https://doi.org/10.1007/11571155

17. Elman, L.: Finding structure in time. J. Cogn. Sci. **14**, 179–211 (1900)

Research on "Near-Zero Emission" Technological Innovation Diffusion Based on Co-evolutionary Game Approach

Yuansheng Huang, Hongwei Wang, and Shijian Liu[✉]

Department of Economics and Management,
North China Electric Power University, Baoding 071003, Hebei, China
liushijian1992@163.com

Abstract. As air pollution becomes increasingly critical, "near-zero emission" technological innovation in coal-fired plants are needed for the government and public consumers. The aim of this paper is to built the evolutionary game for analysing "near-zero emission" technological innovation diffusion in coal-fired plants. According to bionics research of evolution, this paper introduces the co-evolutionary algorithm to simulate the diffusion. By modeling the evolutionary gaming behavior of coal-fired plants, the simulation can capture the dynamics of coal-fired plants' strategy, which is adopting "near-zero emission" technological innovation or not. It is key to model the diffusion under electricity market and government regulation because it can provide some suggestions for promoting the diffusion. Simulations show that the coal-fired plant for most profit should adopt independent R&D for "near-zero emission" technology and increasing the subsidy intensity has a significant role in promoting the diffusion.

Keywords: Evolutionary game · Co-evolutionary algorithm
Technological innovation diffusion · "Near-zero emission" technology

1 Introduction

The energy consumption of our society is growing due to the ongoing development of the global economy. In order to fulfill the energy demands, the consumption of fossil fuels, such as coal and oil, is also increasing. It is able to result in excessive use of fossil energy, environmental issues, and increased health risks to the living creatures on earth. Therefore, how to achieve emission reduction of air pollutants has been considered as the important energy development issues in most countries and regions in the world [1,2].

At present, China has become the world's largest energy consumer [3]. With regard to China's primary energy consumption structure in 2016, coal consumption is accounted for 62%. It can demonstrate that coal has been the main

© Springer Nature Singapore Pte Ltd. 2018
J. Qiao et al. (Eds.): BIC-TA 2018, CCIS 951, pp. 48–59, 2018.
https://doi.org/10.1007/978-981-13-2826-8_5

component of China's primary energy. When it comes to the use of coal, there is no doubt in China that nearly half coal supply is used for power generation while more than 70% of electricity supply is produced from coal power plants. Owing to China's energy resource endowments, the prospective power production structure is dominated by coal power generation [4]. However, the use of coal as fuel for electricity production will inevitably release the dust, SO_2 and NO_x, which can cause air pollution issues. Thus, the technology for clean use of coal in coal-fired power generation is of particular policy importance to China's clean energy transition and China's air pollution emission decrease.

In terms of clean technology innovation for coal-fired power generation, Shenhua Group Corporation conducted a research on the "near-zero emission" technology for coal-fired plants in September 2012. The technology is being promoted in China, and the technology diffusion can result in significant reductions for the emission of the dust, SO_2 and NO_x. For example, after the technical innovation, it is demonstrated that the dust, SO_2 and NO_x concentration are lower than that emission limits for the gas turbine power plants with different loads in the long-term studied [5]. As the scholar Blaut [6] put forward, "The role of innovation diffusion is more important than innovation itself", only if the "near-zero emission" technology is adopted by most coal-fired plants can this technology reflect its economic and environmental value. Therefore, the aim of this paper is to explore the micro-interactive mechanism of the "near-zero emission" technological innovation diffusion, and propose some suggestions for promoting the diffusion of "near-zero emission" technology innovation.

It is considered in the innovation diffusion theory that innovation diffusion is a behavior that the potential adopters imitate the action of adopters. Scholars' research on the diffusion of technological innovation focuses on two aspects. The first is influencing factors concerning the diffusion of technological innovation. For example, Hu et al. [7] employed a stochastic evolutionary model to analyze the diffusion of alternative technologies, and the evolutionary characteristics of alternative technologies are obtained by computer simulations. Stephan et al. [8] pointed out that the department configuration in Japan Aluminium battery company has an important influence on the evolution of Japanese Aluminium battery technology. Eleftheriadis et al. [9] investigated the obstacles for the development of renewable energy in Greece, and furthermore analyzed wind power and photovoltaic power generation technology diffusion. On the other hand, government play a key role in the diffusion of technological innovation. For example, Tigabu et al. [10] presented the effect of official development assistance in the diffusion of renewable energy technologies in Africa. Cantono and Simona [11] proposed a network model for the diffusion of new technologies and explored the impact of limited subsidy policies on diffusion of new technologies. To promote the development of clean technologies, Foxon et al. [12] stimulated the development of a sustainable innovation policy regime, bringing together innovation and environmental policy regimes.

However, the diffusion model for technological innovation in the previous research did not consider the adaptive interaction between participants in the model. They failed to represent the process in which one player observes its opponents behavior, learns from these observations, and makes the best move in response to what it has learned. In this respect, the Evolutionary Game [13–15] derived from biological evolution can capture the dynamic adaptation of market participants better than the traditional model. This paper employs the evolutionary game theory to model "near-zero emission" technology innovation diffusion for coal-fired power plants. In reality, if a coal-fired power plant adopts "near-zero emission" technology, it's cost could be affected. Furthermore the competitiveness for coal-fired power plants in electricity markets could be changed. To estimate the economic value for "near-zero emission" technology, the coal-fired power plant can learn and modify it dynamically based on the behavior of rivals in electricity markets.

The evolutionary game theory is considered as a way of thinking about evolution at the phenotypic level when the fitness of particular phenotypes depend on their frequencies in the population. Hence, Co-evolutionary Algorithm is suitable to find the equilibrium point in the evolutionary game. Co-evolutionary Algorithm emphasizes the the interactive connection among the species. And each species will co-evolve with other species while seeking their own best propagation. It can be envisioned that co-evolutionary computation has great potential to analyze the diffusion of "near-zero emission" technology innovation in electricity markets by modeling coal-fired companies as the individual species.

In summary, this paper contributes in the following aspects:

1. By using the co-evolutionary game approach, this paper simulates the diffusion of "near-zero emission" technology innovation under electricity market and government regulation.
2. Some suggestions for promoting the diffusion of "near-zero emission" technology innovation is provided.

The rest of this paper is organized as follows. Section 2 introduces the evolutionary game theory and co-evolutionary computation utilized in this paper. Section 3 provides the sumualtion of "near-zero emission" technology innovation diffusion under electricity market and government regulation. Finally, Sect. 4 concludes the paper.

2   Method

2.1   Evolutionary Game Theory

Evolutionary game theory (EGT) [16] has been drawing more attention in the past several years. In comparison with the traditional game theory, EGT emphasizes the dynamics of strategy change more than the properties of strategy equilibria. EGT to some extent takes into account the personal knowledge, belief and risk preference of the agents. The equilibrium derived by the traditional game theory may not be realized in practice since participants have dynamic learning abilities. Nowadays, EGT is widely applied to analyze various gaming behavior such as firm and industry behavior, broader biological and dynamical systems, and economic growth theory [17,18].

Motivated by the evolutionary game theory, this paper does an analogous investigation to study diffusion of "near-zero emission" technology innovation. In order to achieve a higher profit, social competitiveness and other goals, coal-fired companies will develop "near-zero emission" technology, launch it into the market and spread it. However, when the original technology has occupied the most market share, it will resist "near-zero emission" technology innovation. On the one hand, the government regulations can gradually increase the efficiency of "near-zero emission" technology innovation diffusion, and eventually make the original technology forced out of the market. In addition, due to the original technology resistance, if the green innovation technology fails to produce more profits, coal-fired companies will abandon it and the diffusion for "near-zero emission" technology will stop.

This paper establishes the game model for the diffusion of "near-zero emission" technology innovation under market mechanism and government regulation. The coal-fired plant is concerned as participants in the game model. And each coal-fired plant has two strategies: adopting "near-zero emission" technology innovation and not adopting "near-zero emission" technology innovation.

Table 1. The evolutionary game model under market mechanism

| | | Coal-fired plant 2 | |
		Adopting	Not adopting
Coal-fired plant 1	Adopting	$\Pi(C_1 + I_1), \Pi(C_2 + I_2)$	$\Pi(C_1 + I_1), \Pi(C_2)$
	Not adopting	$\Pi(C_1), \Pi(C_2 + I_2)$	$\Pi(C_1), \Pi(C_2)$

Table 1 shows the evolutionary game model under market mechanism. Here are the payoff for each coal-fired power plant. When two sides of the game choose the strategy (adopt, adopt), the payoff for each coal-fired power plant is $\Pi(C_1 + I_1)$ and $\Pi(C_2 + I_2)$ respectively. C_i denotes all generation cost if the coal-fired power plant fail to adopt "near-zero emission" technology and I_i denotes the additional generation cost when the coal-fired power plant adopt "near-zero emission" technology. Moreover, I_i can be changed if the coal-fired power plant chooses independent R&D or introduction of the technology. In a word, $\Pi(C_i + I_i)$ denotes the profit that the coal-fired power plant gains by the cost $C_i + I_i$ in the electricity markets. When two sides of the game choose the strategy (adopt, not adopt), the payoff for coal-fired power plant 1 is still $\Pi(C_1 + I_1)$. However, coal-fired power plant 2 chooses the traditional power generation and the payoff is $\Pi(C_2)$. When two sides of the game choose the strategy (not adopt, adopt), coal-fired power plant 2 chooses the traditional power generation and the payoff is $\Pi(C_2)$. However, the payoff for coal-fired power plant 1 is still $\Pi(C_1 + I_1)$. When two sides of the game choose the strategy

Table 2. The evolutionary game model under government regulation

		Coal-fired plant 2	
		Adopting	Not adopting
Coal-fired plant 1	Adopting	$\Pi(C_1 + I_1 - a), \Pi(C_2 + I_2 - a)$	$\Pi(C_1 + I_1 - a), \Pi(C_2)$
	Not adopting	$\Pi(C_1), \Pi(C_2 + I_2 - a)$	$\Pi(C_1), \Pi(C_2)$

(adopt, adopt), both of them choose the traditional power generation and the payoff is $\Pi(C_1)$ and $\Pi(C_2)$ respectively.

Table 2 shows the evolutionary game model under government regulation. In order to develop clean technology for coal-fired power generation, the government must adopt macro-control measures to encourage and guide coal-fired power plants to adopt "near-zero emission" technology innovation. The government's regulation on the diffusion of "near-zero emission" technologies is price regulation. In terms of price regulation, the subsidy, which is denoted by a, is available for the coal-fired power plants adopting "near-zero emission" technology innovation.

2.2 Co-evolutionary Computation

The co-evolutionary algorithm introduces the concept of ecosystem based on the traditional evolutionary algorithm and maps the problem to be solved into an ecosystem composed of interacting and interacting species. The purpose of the problem is solved by the evolution of the ecosystem [19]. This paper combines evolutionary game theory and co-evolutionary algorithm to propose a co-evolutionary game algorithm to solve the model. Experimental results show that it has good performance.

In co-evolutionary game algorithms, coal-fired power plants are considered as individuals in the game. This paper assumes that coal-fired power plants belong to power generation companies and there are three different types of power generation companies that generate populations $P1$, $P2$, and $P3$, respectively. Power generation company 1 has independently developed "near-zero emission" technology. And some of the coal-fired power plants in power generation company 1 have adopt "near-zero emission" technologies. Hence, there are only two strategies for the other coal-fired power plants: adopting and not adopting "near-zero emission" technology. The power generation company 2 introduces the "near-zero emission" technology. The strategies for power generation company 2 is the same as power generation company 1. However, due to the cost of independent research and development and introduction of technology, I for power generation company 2 is larger. The power generation company 3 fails to research and develop independently or introduce the technology. Therefore, there are three strategies for power generation company 3: adopting the introduced technology introduced, adopting the technology for independent research and development and not adopting the technology.

Figure 1 shows the framework of a co-evolutionary game algorithm. In the process of cooperative evolutionary game, the three populations, i.e., the three coal-fired companies, separately perform standard genetic algorithm (GA) and constantly update their respective strategies until the optimal strategy or the number of iterations is maximized. For the calculation of fitness in GA, the profit of the coal-fired power plant in the electricity markets is used as fitness. The independent operators (ISO) in the electricity market calculate the on-grid power and market clearing prices of all coal-fired power plants based on the quotes of coal-fired power plants, and fed back to the coal-fired power plants.

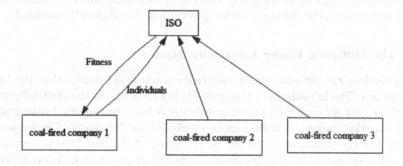

Fig. 1. The framework of a co-evolutionary game algorithm

To model the agents, we apply two agent rules that are based on the theory of individual choice:

1. Rational choice: Individuals decide which action is the best for them to take
2. Bounded rationality: Individuals reasoning is partially rational due to limited knowledge and abilities

The rational choices are demonstrated by coal-fired power plants' evaluating and choosing the representatives that have the best fitness values as the strategies. Meanwhile, the continuously updated estimation of the payoff for "near-zero emission" technology embodies the bounded rationality, which means coal-fired power plants have to estimate the payoff for "near-zero emission" technology because of lack of perfect information, and refine the strategies dynamically with the development of the game.

The solution steps for co-evolutionary computation are as follows.

Step 1: Input the original data and parameters, set the population distribution probability, randomly generate the initial population, and generate the initial feasible strategy combination.

Step 2: Simulate the market clearing process and yield profits for each individual in $P1$, $P2$, and $P3$.

Step 3: The power generation company 3 estimates the payoff for "near-zero emission" technology according to the profits of power generation company 1 and power generation company 2, and then changing their estimations.

Step 4: Evaluate the fitness for each individual in $P1$, $P2$, and $P3$.
Step 5: Three populations are selected, crossed and mutated to generate the next generation, respectively.
Step 6: Repeat steps 2–5 until the entire population reaches evolutionary stability or reaches the maximum evolution algebra.

3   Simulation Result and Discussion

To simulate the diffusion for "near-zero emission" technology innovation using co-evolutionary algorithm, we firstly analyse the diffusion under electricity markets. Furthermore, the diffusion under government regulations is modeled.

3.1   The Diffusion Under Electricity Markets

In this section, the diffusion under electricity markets is considered as the baseline scenario. The hypothesis of this scenario is as follows. In the electricity markets, if the cost for coal-fired power generation is low, the coal-fired power plant has the market power to obtain more market share for power. Consequently, the cost has the significant influence on the profit of the coal-fired power plant. It is assumed that C for the traditional generation cost is 0.40 Yuan/KWh, I for the additional generation cost by independent research for the technology is 0.0075 Yuan/KWh, I' for the additional generation cost by introduction of the technology is 0.0085 Yuan/KWh.

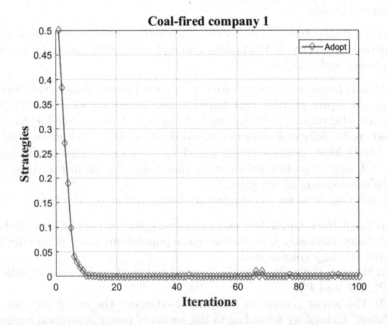

Fig. 2. Innovation diffusion for coal-fired company 1 under electricity markets

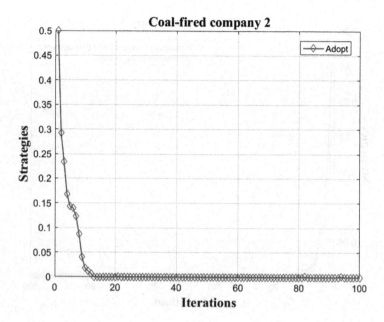

Fig. 3. Innovation diffusion for coal-fired company 2 under electricity markets

The Figs. 2, 3 and 4 shows the "near-zero emission" technology innovation diffusion for three coal-fired companies under electricity markets. The X-axis for the above figures means the iteration in co-evolutionary computation and the Y-axis denotes the strategy for adopting "near-zero emission" technology innovation or not. Besides, in The Fig. 4, the diamond curve means the probability for choosing independent R&D, and the square curve means the probability for choosing the introduction of the technology.

As the above figures indicate, coal-fired company 1 will not adopt "near-zero emission" technology innovation. the cost for coal-fired companies adopting "near-zero emission" technology innovation is lager than those not adopting "near-zero emission" technology innovation. Under the influence of economic interests, it is very likely that they will choose not to adopt the technology until the diffusion evolves to a steady state with a diffusion depth of zero. It is concluded that with no government regulations, "near-zero emission" technology innovation fails to be promoted.

3.2 The Diffusion Under Government Regulation

Based on the diffusion under electricity markets, this section considers the government's regulation, which is price regulation. When it comes to price regulation, the subsidy a is set as 0.006 Yuan/KWh, 0.008 Yuan/KWh, and 0.01 Yuan/KWh.

The Figs. 5, 6 and 7 shows the "near-zero emission" technology innovation diffusion for three coal-fired companies under government regulation. The X-axis

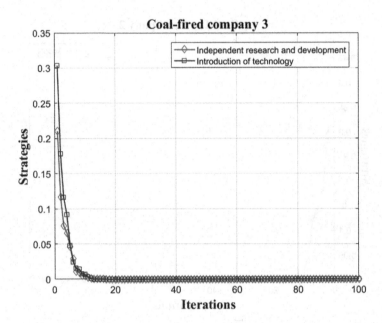

Fig. 4. Innovation diffusion for coal-fired company 3 under electricity markets

for the above figures means the iteration in co-evolutionary computation and the Y-axis denotes the strategy for adopting "near-zero emission" technology innovation or not. Besides, the diamond curve, the square curve and the star curve mean the subsidy as 0.006 Yuan/KWh, 0.008 Yuan/KWh, and 0.01 Yuan/KWh, respectively.

From Figs. 5, 6 and 7, it can be seen that if the subsidy a is 0.01 Yuan/KWh, the diffusion evolves to a steady state with a diffusion depth of one, which means coal-fired company 1 and coal-fired company 2 will adopt "near-zero emission" technology innovation. Furthermore, with regard to coal-fired company 3, it will adopt independent R&D for the technology. When it comes to subsidy a 0.008 Yuan/KWh, coal-fired company 1 and coal-fired company 3 will adopt independent R&D for the technology. However, coal-fired company 2 fails to adopt "near-zero emission" technology innovation. To carry out the subsidy a 0.006 Yuan/KWh, it is demonstrated that all coal-fired companies will not adopt the technology. It is concluded that increasing the subsidy intensity has a significant role in promoting the diffusion of "near-zero emission" technology innovation. Besides, independent R&D for the technology is more advantageous than introduction of the technology in the diffusion of "near-zero emission technology innovation.

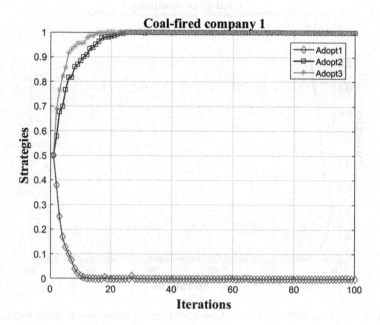

Fig. 5. Innovation diffusion for coal-fired company 1 under government regulation

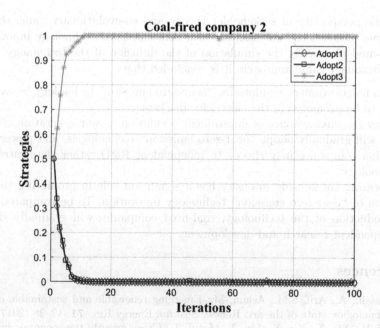

Fig. 6. Innovation diffusion for coal-fired company 2 under government regulation

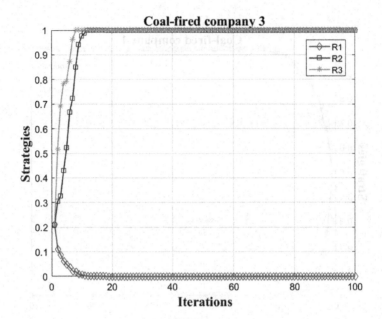

Fig. 7. Innovation diffusion for coal-fired company 3 under government regulation

4   Conclusion

From the perspective of stakeholder theory and co-evolutionary game theory, this paper analyzes the diffusion of "near-zero emission" technology innovation in coal-fired plants. By the simulation of the diffusion of the technology using Co-evolutionary game approach, it is concluded that:

1. With no government regulations, "near-zero emission" technology innovation fails to be promoted in the electricity markets.
2. Under the circumstance of government regulation, power generation companies will gradually adopt "near-zero emission" technologies, and power generation companies may choose to independent R&D rather than introduce technology.
3. Increasing the subsidy intensity has a significant role in promoting the diffusion of "near-zero emission" technology innovation. To be compared with introduction of the technology, coal-fired companies will gradually choose independent research and development.

References

1. Hussain, A., Arif, S.M., Aslam, M.: Emerging renewable and sustainable energy technologies: state of the art. Renew. Sustain. Energy Rev. **71**, 12–28 (2017)
2. Dai, H., Xie, X., Xie, Y., Liu, J., Masui, T.: Green growth: the economic impacts of large-scale renewable energy development in china. Appl. Energy **162**, 435–449 (2016)

3. Brockway, P.E., Steinberger, J.K., Barrett, J.R., Foxon, T.J.: Understanding chinas past and future energy demand: an exergy efficiency and decomposition analysis. Appl. Energy **155**, 892–903 (2015)
4. Yuan, J., et al.: Coal power overcapacity and investment bubble in china during 2015–2020. Energy Policy **97**, 136–144 (2016)
5. Wang, S., Liu, J., Energy, S.O.: Investigation of near-zero air pollutant emission characteristics from coal-fired power plants. Proc. CSEE **36**(22), 6140C6147 (2016)
6. Blaut, J.M.: Diffusionism: a uniformitarian critique. Ann. Assoc. Am. Geograph. **77**(1), 30–47 (1987)
7. Hu, B., Wang, L., Yu, X.: Stochastic diffusion models for substitutable technological innovations. Int. J. Technol. Manage. **28**(7–8), 654–666 (2004). (13)
8. Stephan, A., Schmidt, T.S., Bening, C.R., Hoffmann, V.H.: The sectoral configuration of technological innovation systems: patterns of knowledge development and diffusion in the lithium-ion battery technology in Japan. Res. Policy **46**(4), 709–723 (2017)
9. Eleftheriadis, I.M., Anagnostopoulou, E.G.: Identifying barriers in the diffusion of renewable energy sources. Energy Policy **80**, 153–164 (2015)
10. Tigabu, A., Berkhout, F., Beukering, P.V.: Development aid and the diffusion of technology: improved cookstoves in kenya and rwanda. Energy Policy **102**(102), 593–601 (2017)
11. Cantono, S.: A percolation model of eco-innovation diffusion: the relationship between diffusion, learning economies and subsidies. Technol. Forecast. Social Change **76**(4), 487–496 (2009)
12. Foxon, T., Pearson, P.: Overcoming barriers to innovation and diffusion of cleaner technologies: some features of a sustainable innovation policy regime. J. Cleaner Prod. **16**(1), S148–S161 (2008)
13. Wang, J., Zhi, Z., Botterud, A.: An evolutionary game approach to analyzing bidding strategies in electricity markets with elastic demand. Energy **36**(5), 3459–3467 (2011)
14. Browne, C., Maire, F.: Evolutionary game design. IEEE Trans. Comput. Intell. AI Games **2**(1), 1–16 (2010)
15. Smith, J.M.: Evolution and the Theory of Games. Cambridge University Press, Cambridge (1982)
16. Broom, M., Cannings, C.: Evolutionary Game Theory. MIT Press, Cambridge (2010)
17. Nelson, R.R., Winter, S.G.: Firm and industry response to changed market conditions: an evolutionary approach. Econ. Inq. **18**(2), 179–202 (1980)
18. David, P.A.: Clio and the economics of QWERTY. Am. Econ. Rev. **75**(2), 332–337 (1985)
19. Sim, K.B., Lee, D.W., Kim, J.Y.: Game theory based coevolutionary algorithm: a new computational coevolutionary approach. Int. J. Control Autom. Syst. **2**(4), 463–474 (2008)

Improved Clonal Selection Algorithm for Solving AVO Elastic Parameter Inversion Problem

Zheng Li[1], Xuesong Yan[1(✉)], Yuanyuan Fan[1], and Ke Tang[2]

[1] School of Computer Science, China University of Geosciences,
Wuhan 430074, China
yanxs@cug.edu.cn
[2] Department of Computer Science and Engineering,
Southern University of Science and Technology, Shenzhen 518055, China

Abstract. Amplitude Variation with Offset (AVO) elastic parameter inversion is a nonlinear optimization problem. When a linear or quasi-linear method is used to solve the problem, the inversion result will be unreliable or inaccurate. In this paper, the immune clonal selection algorithm is applied to the AVO elastic parameter inversion problem. The algorithm adopts the specific initialization strategy from Aki's and Rechard's approximation equation used in the elastic parameter inversion process to smooth the initialization parameter curve. Additionally, the genetic operation in the algorithm is accordingly improved. A large number of experiments show that this method can significantly improve inversion accuracy.

Keywords: Seismic exploration · Amplitude Variation with Offset
Elastic parameter inversion · Clonal selection algorithm

1 Introduction

Seismic exploration is a method of oil exploration using seismic information. As a part of seismic exploration, elastic wave theory-based Amplitude Variation with Offset (AVO) technology is used to study the variations of the seismic reflection amplitude with the distance between the gun point and the receiver (or incident angle). Based on elastic wave theory, AVO technology uses the gathered prestack seismic data's common depth point (CDP) to study and analyse the variations of the seismic reflection amplitude with offset. It then obtains the relationship between the reflection coefficient and the incident angle to analyse the lithological characteristics and physical parameters of upper and lower reflection interface. Finally, it predicts and determines the fluid properties and the lithology of oil and gas reservoirs [1]. Prestack seismic data contain abundant useful information for the prediction of underground oil and gas conditions [2]. The three elastic parameters of the P-wave velocity V_p, S-wave velocity V_s and density ρ are the key parameters. The three elastic parameters can reflect the lateral saturation of

© Springer Nature Singapore Pte Ltd. 2018
J. Qiao et al. (Eds.): BIC-TA 2018, CCIS 951, pp. 60–69, 2018.
https://doi.org/10.1007/978-981-13-2826-8_6

underground oil and gas [3,4]. The P-wave velocity V_p is nonlinear with the gas saturation, while density ρ is linear with the gas saturation. The S-wave velocity V_s can reflect some rock properties. Therefore, information on the variations of these three elastic parameters is needed to determine the saturation of underground oil and gas. The inversion of prestack AVO elastic parameters requires the construction of a suitable objective function, followed by the optimization of the objective, function which is generally non-linear. In particular, when solving nonlinear inversions with multi-parameter and multi-extremum characteristics, these linear inversion methods encounter bottlenecks. Thus, the inversion of the AVO elastic parameters is a nonlinear optimization problem. Therefore, if a nonlinear inversion method is used, the nature and state of the solution space are superior to the linear inversion method. However, the global optimal intelligent optimization algorithm has a strong local and global optimization ability, good convergence, and improved computational efficiency. It is suitable for non-linear, multi-parameter and multi-extremum geophysical inversion problems.

Since the mid-1980s, non-linear global intelligent optimization inversion technology has attracted the attention of experts and scholars in the field of geophysics. Nonlinear global intelligent optimization inversion technology has been widely used in various types of inversion problems, and has achieved a number of significant research results [5–18].

Although intelligent optimization algorithms have been widely used in geophysical inversion and can obtain good results, they still have some shortcomings in solving the nonlinear inversion of geophysics, such as premature convergence and lower convergence in later period. These defects of intelligent optimization algorithms restrict the progress of the inversion problem. Therefore, the algorithm needs to be improved so that an efficient solution can finally be proposed for the specific problem.

De Castro proposed a clonal selection algorithm (CSA) based on the principle of clonal selection. This algorithm simulates the response of the human immune system to antigens and has the characteristics of fast convergence and stronger global optimization ability. Therefore, this algorithm can be widely used in pattern recognition and optimization problems [19–26].

2 AVO Elastic Parameter Inversion Problem

The basic steps to solve the AVO elastic parameter inversion problem are as follows. First, three parameters are obtained through a series of operations. Then, the three parameters are substituted into the approximation equation to obtain the reflection coefficient. Next, the seismic data are obtained by the convolution of the reflection coefficient and the seismic wavelet. Finally, the seismic data are compared with the real seismic data. If the data are close to each other and the three parameters well fit the real three parameters, the inversion accuracy is high.

2.1 Inversion Model

The establishment of inverse convolution model is one of the main steps in the inversion of AVO elastic parameters. The establishment of the convolution model includes the following steps. First, calculate the reflection coefficient R_{pp}. In this paper, Aki's and Rechard's approximation equation [25] is used to calculate the reflection coefficient R_{pp}. Second, obtain the seismic wavelet. The seismic wavelet is another component of the seismic record convolution model. The seismic record data is obtained by the convolution of the wavelet and reflection coefficient. It is suitable for establishing the forward model and making the synthetic seismic trace record. In this paper, the Ricker wavelet, which is a zero-phase seismic wavelet, is used. Third, the reflection coefficient is convoluted with the Ricker wavelet.

2.2 Objective Function

In this paper, the AVO elastic parameter inversion problem is transformed into an optimization problem. Since the optimization algorithm evaluates the individual based on the fitness function transformed by the objective function, the advantages and disadvantages of the objective function constructed for the inversion problem are the main factors that affect the inversion effect of the prestack AVO elastic parameters. In this paper, the inversion objective function can be established as follows.

$$f(x) = \sqrt{\frac{\sum_{i=1}^{n} \sum_{j=1}^{m} (s(\theta_{i,j}) - s'(\theta_{i,j}))^2}{n * m}} \tag{1}$$

where $s(\theta_{i,j})$ is the forward seismic record and $s'(\theta_{i,j})$ is the inversion seismic record.

3   Improved Clonal Selection Algorithm

3.1 Improved Initialization Strategy

In the algorithm proposed in this paper, the individual is composed of elastic inversion parameters. For the actual logging curve model, each sampling point is a layer, which is one dimension. Since the three-parameter inversion is studied in this paper, the length of the individual is three times that of the sampling point. Assuming there are n sampling points and 3 * n solution model parameters, the corresponding individual coding mode is:

$$G_i = (V_{p1}, V_{s1}, \rho_1, \cdots, V_{pj}, V_{sj}, \rho_j, \cdots, V_{pn}, V_{sn}, \rho_n) \tag{2}$$

In population space of this paper, the population individuals (chromosomes) are designed by traditional real-number coding. The population individuals are initialized by random initialization within a certain range. Each chromosome consists of a set of real numbers. Suppose the population size is N, where V_{pj}, V_{sj}, ρ_j indicate the values of the three parameters corresponding to jth sampling point of the individual G_i, and the variation range is set according to the actual logging data.

Set the number of population individuals as N. Each individual is represented by a one-dimensional array. The array length is $3 * n$. The initial values of individuals are selected within the limited empirical range (bound function constraints). Then, each parameter is optimized by the genetic algorithm. An optimal individual is finally output as the optimal set of elastic parameter solutions. In this paper adopts the following strategy for initialization. The bound constraints for the first three parameters are shown in formula (3).

$$0.9 * V_{p1well} \leq V_{p1} \leq 1.1 * V_{p1well}$$
$$0.9 * V_{swell} \leq V_{s1} \leq 1.1 * V_{s1well} \tag{3}$$
$$0.95 * \rho_{well} \leq \rho_1 \leq 1.05 * \rho_{1well}$$

The bound constraints for the three parameters of the second to n groups are shown in formula (4).

$$\begin{cases} V_{pi+1} = V_{pi} + \Delta V_{pi} \\ V_{si+1} = V_{si} + \Delta V_{si} \\ \rho_{i+1} = \rho_i + \Delta \rho_i & i = 1, 2, \ldots, n-1 \\ 0.8 * (V_{pi+1well} - V_{piwell}) \leq \Delta V_{pi} \leq 1.2 * (V_{pi+1well} - V_{piwell}) \\ 0.8 * (V_{si+1well} - V_{siwell}) \leq \Delta V_{si} \leq 1.2 * (V_{si+1well} - V_{siwell}) \\ 0.9 * (\rho_{i+1well} - \rho_{iwell}) \leq \Delta \rho_i \leq 1.1 * (\rho_{i+1well} - \rho_{iwell}) \end{cases} \tag{4}$$

3.2   Clonal Selection Strategy

In the artificial immune system, the antigen generally refers to problem and its constraints. Specifically, it is the objective function of the problem, which is the problem to be solved. Antibodies generally refer to the candidate solutions for problems, which corresponds to the individual genes in an evolutionary algorithm. The collection of antibodies is called the antibody group. The antibody-antigen fitness reflects the degree of matching between antibodies and antigens, which corresponds to the objective function's value in the evolutionary algorithm.

Burnet et al. first proposed the theory of clonal selection in 1959. The core idea is that an antibody exists in the form of receptors on the cell surface, and the antigen can selectively react with it. The mutual stimulation between the antigen and corresponding antibody receptor can lead to the clonal proliferation of cells. Throughout the process, the human immune system activates, differentiates and proliferates the immune cells by virtue of cloning to increase the number of antibodies and thus eliminate the antigens in vivo. According to Burnet's theory of antibody clonal selection, De Castro simulated the mechanism of clonal selection of the biological antibodies described above and proposed the clonal selection algorithm. The clonal selection algorithm is used to clone and proliferate the dominant population. After the population proliferation, the genetic manipulation is performed to generate a new population, and the population after the genetic manipulation is subject to the selection operation to finally achieve the goal of optimization. The objective function's values differ between different antibodies (i.e., the fitness of antibody antigens differ). To make a larger clone size possible for superior antibodies, the population is ranked prior to cloning with the strategy proposed by De Castro in formula (5).

$$N_c = \sum_{i=1}^{n} round(\frac{\beta \cdot N}{i}) \qquad (5)$$

where N_c represents the total size of the clonal population, $round(\cdot)$ is the rounding function, N indicates the total number of antibodies, and β is the cloning coefficient used to control the size of the clones. As seen from the above equation, the i th antibody will clone $round(\frac{\beta \cdot N}{i})$ antibodies of the same type. In other words, better antibody fitness results in larger clone size. Thus, the excellent genes in a fit individual can be better preserved and developed. In this way, the purpose of optimization is achieved.

The cloned population is subject to genetic manipulation. Suppose the original population size is n, the population size after the cloning operation is m, and the size of the clonal population is still m after the genetic manipulation of the clonal population. The original population of size n is combined with the clonal population of genetically manipulated size m to select the next generation of population size n. The final population size remains n.

The clonal selection algorithm clones all antibodies and determines the number of clones of the antibody based on the location of different antibodies in the antibody group. The size of the clonal population N_c is also definitive, given the size of the antibody group N and the clonal coefficient β. For the inversion problem, the value of the cloning coefficient β is 0.9 in the experiment, and the value of the population size N is 40.

4   Experimental Simulation and Analysis

4.1   Algorithm Parameter Setting

To validate the effectiveness of our proposed algorithm (the improved clonal selection algorithm (CSA2)), we validate the algorithm using logging data and compare the inversion result with the genetic algorithm (GA), particle swarm optimization (PSO), the differential evolution algorithm (DE) and the Basic clonal selection algorithm (CSA1). In the experiment, the clonal selection algorithm parameters are set as shown in the Table 1 and the experimental environment parameters are shown in Table 2.

4.2   Experimental Results and Analysis

The logging curve data in the dataset is obtained from 241 sampling points, including the P-wave velocity V_p , the S-wave velocity V_s and the density ρ. Each

Table 1. The setting of the related parameters of the immune clonal selection algorithm

N	β	$Cross_p robability$	$Mutation\_probability$	$Max\_iteration$
40	0.9	0.7	0.05	5000

Table 2. The experimental environment parameters

Simulation environment	Parameter description
Java version	1.8.0_111-b14
Compiling environment	$eclipse - jee - luna - SR1a - win32 - x86\_64$
Processor	$Intel(R)Core(TM)i5 - 6500CPU@3.10\,GHZ$
$Random - accessmemory\,(RAM)$	8.00 GB
Operating system	$64 - bit$ operating system

sampling point corresponds to 8 different angles: [0°, 6°, 11°, 17°, 23°, 29°, 34°, and 40°]. Each dataset uses these eight angles. Aki's and Rechard's formula is used to calculate the theoretical logging curve model, the reflection coefficient is calculated by using the logging curve model, and then the reflection coefficient is convoluted with the wavelet. Since the relationship between the upper and lower group of sampling points is needed for the generation of the seismic records, the seismic record data contains 240 * 8 data points.

By using different intelligent optimization algorithms to solve this problem, the experimental results are obtained as shown in Figs. 1, 2, 3, 4 and 5, the blue is the original data and the red is the generated data by different intelligent optimization algorithms. It can be concluded from the comparison data in Figs. 1,

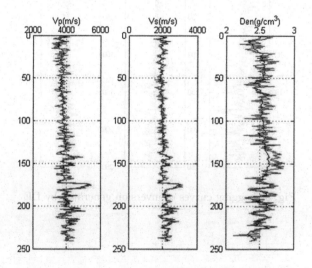

Fig. 1. Logging curves of inversion generated by GA

2, 3, 4 and 5 that the clonal selection method is obviously superior to the genetic algorithm, particle swarm optimization and the differential evolution algorithm. After being combined with the improvement initialization strategy, the effect is obviously better than the original algorithm.

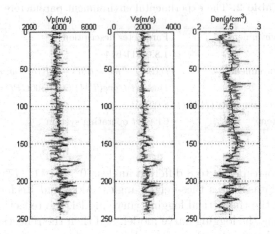

Fig. 2. Logging curves of inversion generated by PSO

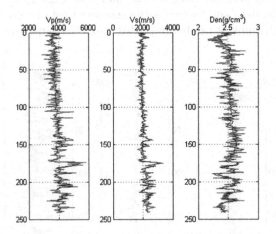

Fig. 3. Logging curves of inversion generated by DE

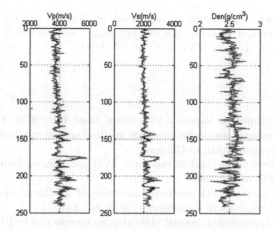

Fig. 4. Logging curves of inversion generated by CSA1

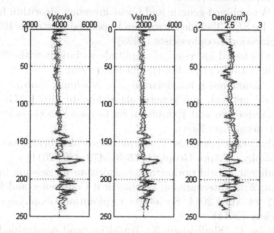

Fig. 5. Logging curves of inversion generated by CSA2

5   Conclusion

The AVO elastic parameter inversion is a nonlinear optimization problem. Therefore, if the nonlinear inversion method is used, the nature and state of the solution space are superior to the linear inversion method, while the global optimal intelligent optimization algorithm has strong local and global optimization ability that is very suitable for solving the problem. In this paper, a clonal selection optimization algorithm that is more suitable for solving the AVO elastic parameter inversion problem is proposed. The inversion is optimized by cloning the antibody group and improving the initialization strategy to improve the inversion accuracy. The experimental results show that the clonal selection algorithm can improve the inversion accuracy.

Acknowledgments. This paper is supported by Natural Science Foundation of China. (No. 61673354, 41404076), the Fundamental Research Funds for the Central Universities, China University of Geosciences (Wuhan).

References

1. Neidell, N.S.: Amplitude variation with offset. Lead. Edge **5**(3), 47–51 (1986)
2. Li, S.P.: AVO seismic parameter inversion method and its application. China University of Petroleum (2009, in Chinese)
3. Chen, J.J.: Inversion method of the three AVO parameters. China University of Petroleum (2007, in Chinese)
4. Wang, L.P.: Prestack AVO non-linear inversion of intelligent optimization algorithm. China University of Geosciences (2015, in Chinese)
5. Berg, E.: Simple convergent genetic algorithm for inversion of multiparameter data. In: SEG Technical Program Expanded Abstracts 1990, pp. 1126–1128. Society of Exploration Geophysicists (1990)
6. Porsani, M.J.: A combined genetic and linear inversion algorithm for seismic waveform inversion. In: SEG Technical Program Expanded Abstracts 1993, pp. 692–695. Society of Exploration Geophysicists (1993)
7. Mallick, S.: Model-based inversion of amplitude-variations-with-offset data using a genetic algorithm. J. Geophys. **60**(4), 939–954 (1995)
8. Priezzhev, I.I., Shmaryan, L.E., Bejarano, G.: Nonlinear multitrace seismic inversion using neural network and genetic algorithm. In: 3rd EAGE St. Petersburg International Conference and Exhibition on Geosciences-Geosciences: From New Ideas to New Discoveries (2008)
9. Soupios, P., Akca, I., Mpogiatzis, P.: Applications of hybrid genetic algorithms in seismic tomography. J. App. Geophys. **75**(3), 479–489 (2011)
10. Bai, J.Y.: Nonlinear hybrid optimization algorithm for seismic impedance inversion. In: Beijing 2014 International Geophysical Conference and Exposition, Beijing, China, 21–24 April 2014. Society of Exploration Geophysicists and Chinese Petroleum Society (2014)
11. Agarwal, A., Sain, K., Shalivahan, S.: Traveltime and constrained AVO inversion using FDR PSO. In: SEG Technical Program Expanded Abstracts 2016, pp. 577–581. Society of Exploration Geophysicists (2016)
12. Sun, S.Z.: PSO non-linear pre-stack inversion method and the application in reservoir prediction. In: SEG Technical Program Expanded Abstracts 2012, pp. 1–5. Society of Exploration Geophysicists (2012)
13. Sun, S.Z., Liu, L.: A numerical study on non-linear AVO inversion using chaotic quantum particle swarm optimization. J. Seismic Explor. **23**(4), 379–392 (2014)
14. Zhou, Y., Nie, Z., Jia, Z.: An improved differential evolution algorithm for nonlinear inversion of earthquake dislocation. J. Geodesy Geodyn. **5**(4), 49–56 (2014)
15. Gao, Z., Pan, Z., Gao, J.: Multimutation differential evolution algorithm and its application to seismic inversion. IEEE Trans. Geosci. Remote Sens. **54**(6), 3626–3636 (2016)
16. Yin, X.Y., Kong, S.S., Zhang, F.C.: Prestack AVO inversion based on differential evolution algorithm. Oil Geophys. Prospect. **48**(4), 591–596 (2013)
17. Wu, Q.H., Wang, L.P., Zhu, Z.X.: Research of pre-stack AVO elastic parameter inversion problem based on hybrid genetic algorithm. Cluster Comput. **20**(4), 3173–3783 (2017)

18. Wu, Q., Zhu, Z.X., Yan, X.S.: Research on the parameter inversion problem of prestack seismic data based on improved differential evolution algorithm. Cluster Comput. **20**(4), 2881–2890 (2017)
19. De Castro, L.N., Von Zuben, F.J.: Learning and optimization using the clonal selection principle. IEEE Trans. Evol. Comput. **6**(3), 239–251 (2002)
20. Gong, M., Jiao, L., Zhang, L.: Baldwinian learning in clonal selection algorithm for optimization. J. Inf. Sci. **180**(8), 1218–1236 (2010)
21. Feng, J., Jiao, L.C., Zhang, X.: Bag-of-visual-words based on clonal selection algorithm for SAR image classification. IEEE Geosci. Remote Sens. Lett. **8**(4), 691–695 (2011)
22. Karoum, B., Elbenani, Y.B.: A clonal selection algorithm for the generalized cell formation problem considering machine reliability and alternative routings. J. Prod. Eng. **2017**(15), 1–12 (2017)
23. Rao, B.S., Vaisakh, K.: Multi-objective adaptive clonal selection algorithm for solving optimal power flow problem with load uncertainty. Int. J. Bio-Inspir. Comput. **8**(2), 67 (2016)
24. Swain, R.K., Barisal, A.K., Hota, P.K.: Short-term hydrothermal scheduling using clonal selection algorithm. Int. J. Electr. Power Energy Syst. **33**(3), 647–656 (2011)
25. Chitsaz, H., Amjady, N., Zareipour, H.: Wind power forecast using wavelet neural network trained by improved Clonal selection algorithm. J. Energy Convers. Manage. **89**, 588–598 (2015)
26. Sindhuja, L.S., Padmavathi, G.: Replica node detection using enhanced single hop detection with clonal selection algorithm in mobile wireless sensor networks. Hindawi Publishing Corp (2016)

A Pests Image Classification Method Based on Improved Wolf Pack Algorithm to Optimize Bayesian Network Structure Learning

Lin Mei, Shengsheng Wang, and Jie Liu[✉]

College of Computer Science and Technology, Jilin University,
Changchun 130012, China
liu_jie@jlu.edu.cn

Abstract. The traditional pests image recognition technology is based on the point features and line features of the image. In the case of complex lighting conditions or changing camera angles, the classification recognition effect is inaccurate. This article proposes a pests image classification method based on improved Wolf Pack Algorithm (WPA) to optimize Bayesian Network (BN) structure learning. Firstly, We select a pre-trained Convolutional Neural Network (CNN) to extract the image features of data set. And then input the feature vectors and classification of images into BN. Secondly, improved the traditional Wolf Pack Algorithm and used as a search algorithm, Bayesian Information Criterion (BIC) as a scoring function to learn the structure of BN. Then the parameters of BN are learned by Maximum Likelihood (ML) algorithm to form a Bayesian Classifier. Compared with other pest classification method, this method has a certain extent improvement in the classification accuracy of pest image classification.

Keywords: Wolf pack algorithm · Bayesian network
Convolutional Neural Network · Bayesian information criterion
Maximum likelihood

1 Introduction

Crop diseases and insect pests are closely related to people's life and directly affect the development of agriculture. There are many kinds of pests, such as Psyllidae, Booklice, Psocoptera, leafhopper, Nilaparvata lugens, Ostrinia spp, Spodoptera litura, and so on. Traditional pest classification methods are classified by an expert based on the characteristics of pests. The accuracy of this method for pest image classification is related to the experience of experts, so this methods has limitation, labor intensity, time-consuming and laborious. Therefore, the classification and recognition of pests has become an imminent problem. Only accurate classification, can do to control crop diseases.

© Springer Nature Singapore Pte Ltd. 2018
J. Qiao et al. (Eds.): BIC-TA 2018, CCIS 951, pp. 70–81, 2018.
https://doi.org/10.1007/978-981-13-2826-8_7

There are many scholars have used various advanced technologies to propose many new methods for pest identification. The most effective one is the recognition of pest images. In order to identify red spider images, Li et al. [1] used the components A and B K-means of laboratory color model, and achieved good results. Wen et al. [2] tried to use the feature extraction method combining the global feature model with the local feature model to obtain the feature of the pest image. Liu et al. [3] realized the automatic counting and recognition of wheat aphids in the simple wheat field by extracting the HOG characteristics of the wheat aphid image and supporting the training of the vector machine. The above pests classification and recognition method is excellent in the data set set up in the laboratory controllable environment. However, in the uncontrollable environment of farmland, the image background, light environment, and pest attitude often have strong changes, and the accuracy and performance of the recognition method will decrease to a certain extent.

As one of the most representative network structures in depth learning, convolution neural network has been widely used in the field of machine vision and in Natural Language Processing field, and has achieved great success. Its main characteristics include weight number, local receptive field and convolution operation. The weight sharing mechanism of the convolution neural network greatly reduces the complexity of the network, and requires the training parameters to be reduced, especially in the processing of high dimensional data. Therefore, CNN has higher accuracy in image recognition. In October, 2012, Hinton applied deep convolutional neural network to research ImageNet and achieved the best result in the world, which made a great progress in image classification [4]. Sladojevic et al. [5] and Brahimi et al. [6], used CNN to identify plant leaf diseases, and good results have been achieved. CNN can effectively extract the feature vector of the image without complicated preprocessing work, but its classification work is entirely dependent on the full connection layer, Therefore, CNN is used only for image feature extraction, and the Bayesian Classifiers is used to classify.

At present, machine vision technology has great development prospects in the recognition technology of pests. As a machine learning, BN can not only display the structure of the problem directly in the language of graph theory, but also analyze and utilize the structure of the problem according to the principle of probability theory and reduce the complexity of reasoning. Therefore, the Bayesian classifier has a relatively stable classification effect compared to other classification algorithms. However, The learning of the structure of BN has always been a NP-hard problem. WPA as a population intelligent algorithm, is based on the characteristics of hunting and survival of wolves, through the initialization, walk, raid, siege behavior and winners as king, the survival mechanism of the strong person, complete the entire wolf group iterative optimization process. Compared with the traditional population intelligent algorithm has good optimization characteristics, but at the same time there are many limitations. At present, wolf group algorithm has been applied to many problems effectively, such as the multiple traveling salesmen problem, Three-dimensional unmanned aerial vehicle path planning and Hydropower station load optimization allocation.

So in this paper, we mainly propose an improved wolves algorithm is proposed to design the wolves update strategy to improve the accuracy of the learning algorithm so that it can be applied to learn the structure of BN. The process of learning the structure of BN is turned into the problem of finding the best wolf. After the structure of BN is determined, the parameters of BN are learned using the ML algorithm and a Bayesian Classifier is formed. Then we combine the unique advantages of CNN in feature extraction to identify pests image.

2   Bayesian Classifiers

The Bayesian classification method is a kind of probability classification method with a minimum error rate, which can be represented by the exact method of the mathematical formula and can be solved by a variety of probability theories. Its classification principle is to use the Bayesian formula when the prior probability of the object is known, to calculate the posterior probability of the object and select the class with the largest posterior probability as the class to which the object belongs. Bayesian Classifier learning is including the structure learning of BN and the parameter learning of BN. In this article, we mainly discuss structural learning. We improved the traditional Wolf Pack Algorithm (WPA) to learn the structure of BN.

2.1   Notation and Representation

In a structure of BN with n nodes, its structure can be simply represented by an n * n connectivity matrix, the elements in the matrix are given by the lower formula.

$$x_{ij} = \begin{cases} 1, & if\ i\ is\ a\ parent\ of\ j \\ 0, & otherwise \end{cases} \tag{1}$$

So we use string to represent a wolf's location code: $\{x_{11}, x_{12}, ..., x_{1n}, x_{21}, x_{22}, ..., x_{2n}, ..., x_{n1}, x_{n2}, ..., x_{nn}\}$.

2.2   Bayesian Network Structure Learning

Scoring Function. For a the structure of BN with n variables $X = \{X_1, X_2, ..., X_n\}$. Each variable X_i has i values $r = \{r_1, r_2, ..., r_i\}$, X_i's parent node $X_{pa(i)}$ can have qi values. The degree of matching between the structure of BN G and the data set Q can be measured using the Bayesian Information Criterion (BIC).

$$BIC(G|Q) = \sum_{i=1}^{n} \sum_{j=1}^{q_i} \sum_{k=1}^{r_i} m_{ijk} \lg \frac{m_{ijk}}{m_{ij}} - \sum_{i=1}^{n} \frac{q_i(r_i - 1)}{2} \lg m \tag{2}$$

The first item of the formula represents the degree of fit of the structure with the data, and the second item is about the complexity penalty of the model to avoid overfitting. The larger the score function value, the better the performance.

Search Procedure. The search algorithm is to search for possible DAGs. Each possible DAG represents a feasible BN structure. The possible the structure of BN with n nodes is represented by the following formula:

$$f(n) = \sum_{i=1}^{n} (-1)^{i+1} \binom{n}{i} 2^{i(n-i)} f(n-i), f(0) = f(1) = 1 \qquad (3)$$

Obviously, it is hard to find the optimal network structure in such a large search space. We usually use greedy algorithms to build networks. The greedy algorithm is to add edge to the search process, so that the current network quality has the greatest improvement until it is no longer possible to improve. Besides, Ant Colony Optimization [7], Genetic Algorithms [8], particle swarm optimization [9] and other optimization methods are also applied to BN structure learning. In this article, we propose an improved WPA as a search algorithm to search possible DAGs space.

In the next section, we will explain in detail the improved WPA.

2.3 Bayesian Network Parameter Learning

After determine the structure of BN, we must learn the parameters of BN. It is not the focus of this article. We use Maximum Likelihood (ML) to learn parameters. The ML estimation is based on traditional statistical analysis. He estimates the fit of the sample to the model based on the likelihood.

3 Wolf Pack Algorithm

3.1 The Original WPA

The WPA is based on the swarm intelligence of the wolf group, simulating the predator behavior and its prey distribution mode, abstracting the 3 kinds of intelligent behavior of walking, calling and siege, as well as the "winner's King" of the wolf generation rules and the "strong man survival" of the wolf group updating mechanism. And a new group intelligence algorithm is proposed. Those weaker wolves will be eliminated by the wolves. The concrete steps are as follows:

Step 1: Initialization. The position of wolf Xi and its number of N, the maximum number of iterations K_{max}, the scale factor of the safari wolf α, the maximum travel times T_{max}, the distance decision factor w, the step factor s, and the update ratio factor β.

Step 2: The safari process. Select the best artificial wolf as the leading wolf, the best n wolf outside the leading wolf as the safari wolf and execute the walk, until a wolf wolfi reconnaissance of the prey odor concentration Y_{wolfi} is greater than the leading wolf's prey odor concentration $Y_{wolflead}$ or the maximum travel times T_{max}, then turn step 3.

Step 3: The summon process. The fierce wolf attacks the prey. If the fierce wolf is on the way to the prey, the smell concentration Yi > Ylead, The fierce wolf replace the leading wolf and initiates the call behavior; if Yi < Ylead, the fierce wolf continues to attack until the dis ≤ dnear, and turn step 4.

Step 4: The Siege process. After the attacking fierce wolf is closer to the prey, the fierce wolf will jointly explore the wolf to closely siege the prey in order to capture it.

Step 5: Update operation of the wolves: According to the "winner is king" head wolf generation rule to update the position of the wolf; then follow the "strong survival" wolf group update mechanism for group update.

Step 6: Determine whether the optimization accuracy requirement or the maximum number of iterations K_{max} is reached. If it is reached, the position of the head wolf is output, that is, the optimal solution of the problem is sought, otherwise step 2 is performed.

3.2　The Improved WPA

Based on the references [10], the traditional WPA can be directly applied to continuous space optimization problems. The problem of the structure learning of BN is a 0–1 binary problem with complex conditions. So we need to improve the traditional WPA.

We propose an improved binary wolf pack algorithm. In the safari process of the Improved wolf pack algorithm, the reverse operator is proposed, which ensures the randomness of the wolf walk and effectively avoids the local optimal solution. In the summon process, the approximation operator is put forward to make each wolf approaches the best wolf at a certain rate which effectively ensures that the overall development direction changes toward the global optimal solution. In the siege process the interactive operator is propose deffectively ensures the interaction of information between wolves, so that wolves can gradually move to better positions. In the step of the renewal of the wolf pack, the chaotic mapping is put forward to generate new wolves. The way to generate new wolves to replace the eliminated wolves ensures the diversity of the population.

In this article, we propose an improved WPA named IWPA. The framework of IWPA is as follows:

Step 1: Set the initial parameters of the wolf pack:
Population quantity N; Maximum number of iterations K_{max}; Maximum number of safari T_{max}; The number of weak wolves Z; Safari step length $step_a$; approach step length $step_b$; Siege step length $step_c$; The number of search directions h; Random generation of initial group of wolves wolfi, i = 1, 2, 3..., n; Cost function f (wolfi);

Step 2: Calculate the concentration of quarries at the position of each wolf Y_{wolfi}, choose the best wolf as the leading wolf.

Step 3: Define the safari process in the IWPA

In the safari process of the Improved wolf pack algorithm, to ensures the randomness of the wolf walk and effectively avoids the local optimal solution, the reverse operator is proposed. The concrete steps are as follows:

Definition 1: reverse operator represented by the following formula.

$$\Theta = (X_{wolfi} random(step_a)) \tag{4}$$

In the formula, X_{wolfi} represents the location code of the safari wolf wolfi, random $(step_a)$ represents randomly select $step_a$ locations in the X_{wolfi} and reverse operator represents randomly select $step_a$ locations in the X_{wolfi} reverse the encoding.

Apart from the leading wolf, all the wolves are the safari wolves, and the walk behavior is performed. The wolf wolfi advance one step to the h directions, the safari step length is $step_a$, that is, to execute h times reverse operator for wolves, and after advance one step in each direction to record the concentration $Y_{wolfij}(j = 1, 2, ..., h)$ of quarries and the location code $X_{wolfij}(j = 1, 2, ..., h)$. Select the maximum value of Y_{wolfij} as Y_{max}, if $Y_{max} > Y_{wolfij}$, then Y_{max} corresponding the location code X_{wolfij} to replace the original location code X_{wolfi}, repeat the above safari behavior, until $Y_{wolfi} > Y_{wolflead}$ or the safari times to T_{max}. If $Y_{wolfi} > Y_{wolflead}$, the safari wolf instead of the leading wolf and initiates the summon behavior.

Step 4: Define the summon process in the IWPA

In the summon process, to effectively ensures that the overall development direction changes toward the global optimal solution, the approximation operator is put forward to make each wolf approaches the best wolf at a certain rate. The concrete steps are as follows:

Definition 2: Approximation operator represented by the following formula.

$$\Psi = (X_{wolflead}, X_{wolfi}, random(step_b)) \tag{5}$$

In the formula, $X_{wolflead}$ represents the leading wolf position code, X_{wolfi} represents the fierce wolf position code, and random $(step_b)$ represents randomly selecting a continuous location encoding with a length of $step_b$ in the leading wolf, and Approximation operator represents randomly selecting a continuous location encoding witn a length of $step_b$ in the leading wolf replacing the same location encoding in the fierce wolf. All the artificial wolves except the leading wolf are the fierce wolves. The leading Wolf summons the fierce wolf approach to the leader's position. The fierce wolf approach to the leading wolf with a larger approach step length $step_b$, that is to execute approximation operator for the fierce wolf. For example, $X_{wolflead}$(100101100) is the location code of the leading wolf, X_{wolfi}(100010101) is the location code of the fierce wolf, approach step length is 5, to select 2–6 location code in the leading wolf to replace the same location code in the fierce wolf, get the new location code $X_{wolfinew}$(100101101). Form the change reflects the global optimal solution for the influence of the individual and guidance. In the process of approaching the leading wolf, if $Y_{wolfi} > Y_{wolflead}$, the fierce wolf will be updated as the leading wolf and initiate a new summoning behavior. If $Y_{wolfi} <= Y_{wolflead}$, the fierce wolf wolfi will continue to approach the leading wolf, until the distance between the fierce wolf and the leading wolf is less than the decision distance d_{near}.

Step 5: Define the Siege process in the IWPA

In the siege process, to make wolves can gradually move to better positions, the interactive operator is proposed, effectively ensures the interaction of information between wolves. The concrete steps are as follows:

Definition 3: interactive operator represented by the following formula.

$$\Delta = (X_{wolgy}, Xwolfz, random(step_c)) \qquad (6)$$

In the formula, X_{wolfy} and X_{wolfz} represent two artificial wolves in the siege range, random $(step_c)$ represent randomly selecting a continuous location encoding with a length of $step_c$ in an artificial wolf, and interactive operator represents randomly selecting a continuous location encoding with a length of $step_c$ in an artificial wolf, replacing the same location encoding in another artificial wolf. Under the lead of the leading wolf, the wolves siege the quarries. We assume that the leading wolf's position $X_{wolflead}$, is the location of the quarries, and the distance between the wolves in the siege is very close. In order to catch the quarry as quickly as possible, it is necessary to perform an interactive operator to share information, Comparing the concentration $Y_{wolfnew}$ of quarries after change the position code and the concentration $Y_{wolfold}$ of quarries before change the position code. If $Y_{wolfnew} > Y_{wolfold}$, replace the previous position code with the changed position code, otherwise the wolf's position code is unchanged.

Step 6: Define the update operation of the wolves in the IWPA

In the step of the renewal of the wolf pack, to ensures the diversity of the population, the chaotic mapping is put forward to generate new wolves. The way to generate new wolves to replace the eliminated wolves. The concrete steps are as follows:

Chaos is the intrinsic randomness of the decisive system. In the prescribed range, all States are traversed without repetition according to their own "laws". The randomness of chaos will not decrease with the increase of the amount of information. Therefore, we use the way of chaotic mapping to generate new Z wolves to replace the weak wolves, make the new population do not appear duplicated individuals, thus increasing the diversity of the population. This renewal mechanism can keep the diversity of the population and effectively avoid the local optimal limit.

Step 7: When the results meet the requirements or achieve the maximum iteration number K_{max}, end the algorithm and output the leading wolf position. Otherwise, jump to step 2.

An improved wolf swarm algorithm flowchart as shown in Fig. 1.

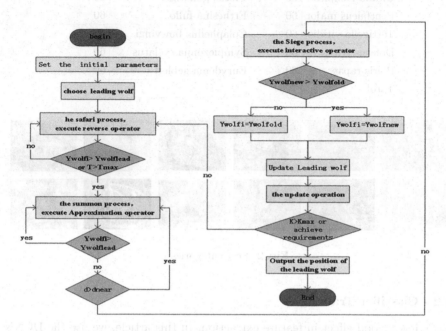

Fig. 1. An improved WPA flowchart.

4 Experiment and Analysis

4.1 Crop Pests Image Dataset

In the actual field environment, the images we obtain always have a complex background. Compared to the images with fixed background color samples, they have higher practical significance in complex backgrounds.

In order to meet the needs of pest image recognition, in 2015, Xie et al. collected pest images of several common crops such as corn, soybean, wheat, and rape, and listed 24 common crop pests [11]. In this paper we take 12 of these pests as research objects. In Table 1, we have reorganized the classification and number of images of the 12 pests selected. The appearance of each pest is shown in Fig. 2. In this experiment, we randomly selected 50 images of each pest as the training set and 10 images as the test set, and mirrored these images to double the amount of data to make full use of CNN.

Table 1. Comparison between our method and the other methods.

Name	Amount	Name	Amount
Aelia sibirica	60	Cnaphalocrocis medinalis	60
Cifuna locuples	60	Cletus punctiger	60
Pentfaleus major	60	Erthesina fullo	60
Tettigella viridis	60	Colaphellus bowvingi	60
Dolerus tritici	60	Sympiezomias velatus	60
Pieris rapae	60	Eurydema gebleri	60
Tatol	720		

Fig. 2. Pest categories.

4.2 Classifier Training

CNN has a good effect in feature extraction. In this article, we use the DCNN proposed in [12] as the pre-trained CNN, we removed the classification part after the full connection layer in the above CNN structure, and used only the first half part to extract the feature of pest image.

Firstly, the images of the training set and the test set are input into the pre-trained CNN to extract the feature vectors of the pest images. Then, the eigenvectors extracted from the training set and the corresponding classifications are input into the Bayesian network, and the Bayesian network that most closely matches the training data is trained by the above method. Then the eigenvectors and corresponding classifications extracted from the test set are input into the pre-trained Bayesian network for test and adjustment. The Bayesian classifier is finally generated. The training process of the classifier is shown in Fig. 3.

4.3 Comparison of Experimental Results

We compare our methods CNN+IWPA-BN with several recent advanced methods. Such as Deep Convolutional Neural Network (DCNN), Deep Residual Learning (DAL), and traditional CNN, Support Vector Machine (SVM) and BP Neural Networks.

In the same environment, We use data sets to test the above methods and the classification methods proposed in this paper 3000 times. The results of the

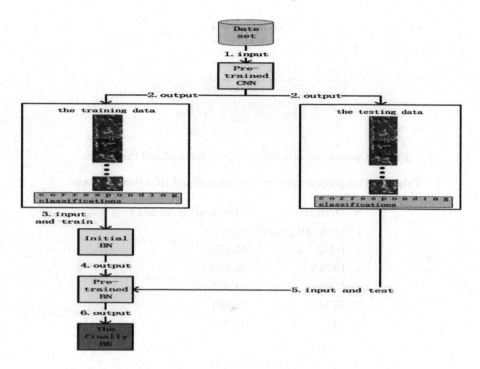

Fig. 3. The training process of the classifier.

experiment are shown in Fig. 4. All pest images have a complex background. In Table 2, we compare our method with the above methods after the convergence of the recognition accuracy rate. As can be seen from the data, the accuracy of BP, Support Vector Machine (SVM) and traditional CNN is low, Although DCNN and DAL have improved significantly compared with traditional methods, but the accuracy of the methods proposed in this paper in this paper is still slightly better than that of DCNN and DAL.

From the data in the chart, we can see that when the number of iterations is large enough, the accuracy of the method proposed in this paper has a certain degree of improvement compared with other methods. When the number of iterations reaches 3000, it can be seen that The accuracy of the proposed method has reached 96.23%. This shows that the method proposed in this paper has high reliability and practicability.

In order to verify that the method proposed in this paper still valid on other pest datasets, we conducted two experiments on the butterfly data set [13], which is shown in Fig. 5.

From Fig. 5, we can see that the pest identification method proposed in this paper still has higher accuracy than other methods on different pest datasets.

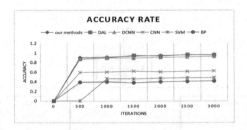

Fig. 4. Comparison of accuracy of our method and the others.

Table 2. Comparison between our method and the other methods.

N	Methods	Classification accuracy
1	CNN+IWPA-BN	96.23%
2	DAL	95.45%
3	DCNN	92.43%
4	CNN	62.26%
5	SVM	48.45%
6	BP	41.36%

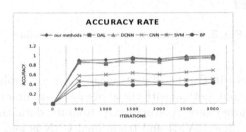

Fig. 5. Comparison of accuracy of our method and the others.

5   Conclusion

In this article, the pest image recognition method consists of three steps. Firstly, an improved wolf swarm algorithm, IWPA, is proposed. Secondly, IWPA is applied to Bayesian Classifier as a search algorithm of BN learning. Thirdly, combining the advantages of CNN in feature extraction, the pest image recognition is carried out effectively. The recognition accuracy of this method is much higher than that of support vector machine and other machine learning methods. Compared with the other methods, the recognition accuracy has been further improved.

Acknowledgments. This work is supported by the National Natural Science Foundation of China (61472161), Science & Technology Development Project of Jilin Province (20180101334JC), National Key Research and Development Project of China (2017YFB0102601).

References

1. Li, Z., Hong, T., Zeng, X., Zheng, J.: Citrus red mite image target identification based on k-means clustering. Trans. Chin. Soc. Agric. Eng. **28**(23), 147–153 (2012)
2. Wen, C., Guyer, D.: Image-based orchard insect automated identification and classification method. Elsevier Sci. Publ. B **89**, 110–115 (2012)
3. Liu, T., Chen, W., Wu, W., Sun, C., Guo, W., Zhu, X.: Detection of aphids in wheat fields using a computer vision technique. Biosyst. Eng. **141**, 82–93 (2016)
4. Krizhevsky, A., Sutskever, I., Hinton, G.E.: ImageNet classification with deep convolutional neural networks. In: International Conference on Neural Information Processing Systems, vol. 60, pp. 1097–1105. Curran Associates Inc. (2012)
5. Sladojevic, S., Marko, A., Andras, A., Dubravko, C., Darko, S.: Deep neural networks based recognition of plant diseases by leaf image classification. Comput. Intell. Neurosci. **2016**, 1–11 (2016)
6. Brahimi, M., Boukhalfa, K., Moussaoui, A.: Deep learning for tomato diseases: classification and symptoms visualization. Appl. Artif. Intell. **31**, 1–17 (2017)
7. Daly, R., Shen, Q.: Learning bayesian network equivalence classes with ant colony optimization. J. Artif. Intell. Res. **35**(1), 391–447 (2009)
8. Hsu, W.H., Guo, H., Perry, B.B., Stilson, J.A.: A permutation genetic algorithm for variable ordering in learning bayesian networks from data. In: Genetic and Evolutionary Computation Conference, pp. 383–390. Morgan Kaufmann Publishers Inc, New York (2002)
9. Xing-Chen, H., Zheng, Q., Lei, T., Shao, L.P.: Research on structure learning of dynamic bayesian networks by particle swarm optimization. In: Artificial Life, ALIFE 2007, pp. 85–91. IEEE, Honolulu (2007)
10. Wu, H.S., Zhang, F.M.: Wolf pack algorithm for unconstrained global optimization. Math. Probl. Eng. **2014**(1), 1–17 (2004)
11. Xie, C., Zhang, J., Li, R., Li, J., Hong, P., Xia, J.: Automatic classification for field crop insects via multiple-task sparse representation and multiple-kernel learning. Comput. Electron. Agric. **119**, 123–132 (2015)
12. Wang, R.J., Zhang, J., Dong, W., et al.: A crop pests image classification algorithm based on deep convolutional neural network. Telkomnika **15**(3), 1239–1246 (2017)
13. Xiao, B., Ma, J.F., Cui, J.T.: Combined blur, translation, scale and rotation invariant image recognition by radon and pseudo-fourier-mellin transforms. Pattern Recognit. **45**(1), 314–321 (2012)

Differential Grouping in Cooperative Co-evolution for Large-Scale Global Optimization: The Experimental Study

Heng Lei[1(✉)], Ming Yang[1], and Jing Guan[2]

[1] School of Computer Science, China University of Geosciences, Wuhan, China
leiheng94@gmail.com,yangming0702@gmail.com
[2] China Ship Development and Design Center, Wuhan, China
g_jing0414@163.com

Abstract. Cooperative co-evolution (CC) is a promising method for large-scale optimization problems. The performance of a CC framework is affected greatly by variable grouping. DG2 proposed by Omidvar et al. is accurate for variable grouping. DG2, which is a parameter-free differential grouping method, can distinguish overlapping components of decision variables of a function. In this paper, we test DG2 on high-dimensional functions with more than 1000 dimensions. We also test DG2 on the functions that it is highly imbalanced that the contribution of different components to the overall fitness. The experimental results show that the performance of DG2 is stable as the increase of the dimensionality of the functions, but the grouping accuracy of DG2 drops when the imbalance of contribution of different components to the overall fitness becomes greater and greater.

Keywords: Experimental study · Cooperative co-evolution
Large-scale optimization · Problem decomposition

1 Introduction

Evolutionary algorithms (EAs) are widely used to solve black-box optimization problems because they do not need to know their underlying structure in advance. However, EAs may lose their efficiency as the number of decision variables of problems increases greatly [1].

Cooperative co-evolution (CC) [2] is a promising framework of evolutionary algorithm to solve large-scale problems, which divides a problem into smaller subproblems (also known as variable grouping or decomposition) and solves the subproblems cooperatively. There are two issues in CC: how to divide the problem into subproblems and how to solve the subproblems one by one. The problem decomposition, i.e., grouping the decision variables of the problem into some subcomponents, affects the performance of CC [3]. If a variable grouping method can group decision variables into independent subcomponents, CC can solve the

© Springer Nature Singapore Pte Ltd. 2018
J. Qiao et al. (Eds.): BIC-TA 2018, CCIS 951, pp. 82–93, 2018.
https://doi.org/10.1007/978-981-13-2826-8_8

subproblems cooperatively. Theoretically, the higher variable grouping accuracy is, the better performance of CC is [3].

Omidvar et al. [4] proposed a parameter-free method, namely DG2, which is able to detect interaction between decision variables including the indirect and the overlapping interactions. The experimental results in [4] show that DG2 can correctly detect interaction between variables for 1000-dimensional problems. The subcomponents generated by the decomposition may have different magnitudes of influence on the function value [3]. In this paper, we test the effectiveness of DG2 when applying DG2 into the large-scale problems with more than 1000 dimensions and with subcomponents whose contributions to the overall fitness are imbalanced.

The remainder of the paper is organized as follows. Section 2 introduces the overview of CC and details of DG2. Section 3 presents the experimental studies. Section 4 concludes the paper.

2 Cooperative Co-evolution and Differential Grouping

CC employs the divide-and-conquer strategy to divide an optimization problem into some subproblems, which decreases the difficulty of solving large-scale problems. How to divide a problem into subproblems is the first issue CC needs to fix. After the problem is decomposed, CC can apply the conquer method to solve the subproblems cooperatively. DG2 [4] is a recently proposed decomposition method for CC. In this section, we review the CC algorithm and DG2 method.

2.1 Cooperative Co-evolution

The original CC, cooperative co-evolutionary genetic algorithm (CCGA), was proposed by Potter and Jong [2]. It divides a D-dimensional problem into D one-dimensional subproblems, then utilizes an evolutionary optimizer to solve the subproblems respectively (see Algorithm 1). Any evolutionary algorithm can be used to optimize the subproblems. The original CC only perform well on separable functions [2], and a function with n variables is separable when it can be rewritten as a sum of n functions with only one variable [5].

CCGA uses a round-robin method to select subcomponents to optimize. However, optimizing subcomponents equally is not the best strategy when dealing with a nonseparable problem. In a nonseparable problem, the contributions of the subcomponents to the improvement of the overall best function value are usually different [3]. Therefore, using a round-robin method to optimize subcomponents equally, without considering the unequal contributions of the subcomponents, results in waste of computational resources.

In order to overcome this problem, Omidvar et al. [6] proposed a contribution based cooperative co-evolution (CBCC). It optimizes the subcomponents based on their contributions to the improvement of the best global fitness, which considers the condition of the imbalanced contributions of the subcomponents and

---

Algorithm 1. CCGA [2]

---

for each subproblem S **do**
　Initialise a subpopulation $Pop(S)$;
　Calculate fitness of each member in $Pop(S)$;
end for
while termination criteria is not satisfied **do**
　for each subproblem S **do**
　　Apply genetic operators to $Pop(S)$;
　　Evaluate each individual in $Pop(S)$;
　end for
end while

---

makes the computational resources used more efficiently. However, the contributions in CBCC is counted from start to finish. As a result, it may assign too much computational resources to the subcomponent whose contribution is great at first but declines greatly after several generations.

Yang et al. [3] proposed a new CC framework (CCFR) which is able to intelligently allocate computational resources among subcomponents based on the dynamic contributions of subcomponents to the improvement of the best global fitness. CCFR can identify the stagnant subpopulations and stop the evolution of the stagnant subpopulations, which can save computational resources. The experimental results in [3] show that CCFR performs much better than other algorithms for the large-scale problem.

The accurate variable grouping is a prerequisite of CBCC and CCFR [3]. Only after variable grouping, the CC algorithms based on resource allocation, such as CBCC and CCFR, can start to allocate resources. The performance of a CC framework is affected significantly by the problem decomposition [7].

2.2 Differential Grouping

Many decomposition algorithms [8,9] would decompose a black-box problem into some smaller and fixed-size subproblems. In practice, we do not know the underlying structure of a problem. An automatic method is required to decompose the problem [10].

Chen et al. [11] proposed a cooperative co-evolution with variable interaction learning (CCVIL), which employs a two-stage approach (i.e., the learning stage and optimization stage). It detects the interaction between variables to finish the decomposition in the learning stage and optimizes the resultant subcomponents as the same as traditional CC in the optimization stages.

Tezuka et al. [12] proposed a linkage identification by nonlinearity check for real-coded GAs (LINC-R), which is accurate to recognize the linkage, which improves GA's search capability. Omidvar et al. [13] proposed a method to detect the interaction between variables based on LINC-R, namely differential grouping (DG). CC with DG performs well on a set of large-scale global problems with 1000 dimensions and outperforms CCVIL and LINC-R in term of grouping accuracy. The introduction of DG is as follows.

Theorem 1. [13] *Suppose $f(\boldsymbol{x})$ is an additively separable function. $\forall a, b_1 \neq b_2, \delta \in \mathbb{R}, \delta \neq 0$, if the following condition holds:*

$$\varDelta_{\delta,x_p}[f](\boldsymbol{x})|_{x_p=a,x_q=b_1} \neq \varDelta_{\delta,x_p}[f](\boldsymbol{x})|_{x_p=a,x_q=b_2} \tag{1}$$

then x_p and x_q are nonseparable, where

$$\varDelta_{\delta,x_p}[f](\boldsymbol{x}) = f(\ldots,x_p+\delta,\ldots) - f(\ldots,x_p,\ldots) \tag{2}$$

refers to the forward difference of f with respect to variable x_p with interval δ.

Theorem 1 indicates that if unequal results are calculated from Eq. (2), variables x_p and x_q interact. It is obvious that $\varDelta^{(1)} \neq \varDelta^{(2)} \iff |\varDelta^{(1)} - \varDelta^{(2)}| \neq 0$, where $\varDelta^{(1)}$ is the left hand side of Eq. (1) and $\varDelta^{(2)}$ is the right hand side. However, it is not practical to use the equality check on computers because precision of floating-point numbers is limited. Therefore, it is necessary to convert the equality check to an inequality check whose form is $\lambda = |\varDelta^{(1)} - \varDelta^{(2)}| > \epsilon$, where the parameter ϵ is able to control precision of detecting interactions.

Using Theorem 1, interactions between the first variable and all other variables are able to be checked. If an interaction between the first variable and any other variable is detected, the variable is excluded from the set of all variables and placed in a subcomponents. It repeats until all interactions between the first variable and all other variables are checked. Variables that interact with the first variable form the first subcomponent. If no interaction is detected, it is considered that the variable is separable. It repeats for the rest variables until no more variables left.

There are some major shortcomings of DG [13]. It requires the user to specify a control parameter ϵ which is related to the perform of DG significantly, and it is not accurate to detect variable interactions in overlapping functions [14], in which single variable is in multiple components simultaneously. In addition, it consumes high computational resource on fully separable functions and is sensitive to computational roundoff errors [15].

In order to overcome drawbacks mentioned above, Omidvar et al. [4] proposed DG2, an improved variant of DG. DG2 reduces the number of fitness evaluations significantly so that it is able to examine every possible interactions. That improves accuracy of detecting interactions between decision variables and makes DG2 is able to distinguish overlapping components of an objective function rather than exclude a variable from other groups when it is placed in one group.

In order to explain clearly DG2 how to reduce the number of fitness evaluations, it assumes that there is a function with 3 decision variables, i.e., $f(x_1, x_2, x_3)$. According to the Theorem 1, it is obvious that the number of fitness evaluations for $f(x_1, x_2, x_3)$ is $2n(n-1)|_{n=3} = 12$ if calculated one by one. But 5 objective functions are calculated repeatedly and only 7 objective functions need to calculate. So there is a matrix $\varLambda$ for saving the values of objective functions in advance. Inquiry the matrix Λ every time calculate the fitness. If the fitness we need does not exist in matrix Λ then calculate it and save the calculated result into the matrix Λ so that it is able to be taken out next time. If it exists in the matrix Λ then just take out the fitness directly. For this example, DG2 can save 5 fitness evaluations. Using the method of trading space for time and computational resource, the number of fitness evaluations is $\frac{n(n+1)}{2} + 1$ rather than $2n(n-1)$ originally for a function with n decision variables.

In order to get rid of the ill effect of computational roundoff errors as far as possible, DG2 introduces the greatest lower bound (e_{inf}) and the least upper bound (e_{sup}). Once the value of e_{inf} and e_{sup} are calculated, it is considered that variables x_i and x_j are separable if $\lambda < e_{inf}$ and nonseparable if $\lambda > e_{sup}$, where $\lambda = |\Delta^{(1)} - \Delta^{(2)}|$. e_{inf} and e_{sup} is calculated based on $f(x_1, \ldots, x_n), f(\ldots, x_i', \ldots), f(\ldots, x_j', \ldots)$ and $f(\ldots, x_i', \ldots, x_j', \ldots)$. In addition, the calculation of e_{inf} and e_{sup} considers the computational roundoff errors of the floating-point representation system according to the IEEE 754 standard [16].

After estimating e_{sup} and e_{inf}, reliable λ can be found and parameter ϵ can be defined dynamically:

$$\epsilon = \frac{\eta_0}{\eta_0 + \eta_1} e_{inf} + \frac{\eta_1}{\eta_0 + \eta_1} e_{sup} \qquad (3)$$

where η_0 is the number of element in the matrix Λ that $\lambda < e_{inf}$, η_1 is the number of element in the matrix Λ that $\lambda > e_{sup}$. That naturally makes DG2 does not require the user to specify any external parameter (a.k.a. parameter-free).

In summary, DG2 has four major improvements over DG:

- less computational resource consumption on fitness valuations.
- accuracy to detect variable interactions in overlapping functions.
- less affected by computational roundoff errors.
- parameter-free.

3   Experimental Studies

The dimensionality of CEC'2013 large-scale benchmark functions [17] is fixed, so we use the CEC'2010 benchmark functions [5] to test the effectiveness of DG2 on variable grouping. The CEC'2010 benchmark functions are classified into the following five categories:

1. separable functions $(f_1 - f_3)$;
2. single-group m-nonseparable functions $(f_4 - f_8)$;
3. $\frac{D}{2m}$-group m-nonseparable functions $(f_9 - f_{13})$;
4. $\frac{D}{m}$-group m-nonseparable functions $(f_{14} - f_{18})$;
5. nonseparable functions $(f_{19} - f_{20})$;

where D is the dimensionality of the problem and $D = \{100, 500, 1000, 2000, 3000, 4000, 5000\}$; m is the number of variables in each nonseparable subcomponent and $m = 50$, which is fixed in the definition of the CEC'2010 benchmark functions. Table 1 shows the underlying structure of the CEC'2010 functions with different dimensions. The number of variable groups varies with the value of dimensionality.

Table 1. The number of separable and nonseparable variable and the number of non-separable subcomponents.

F	D = 100			D = 500			D = 1000			D = 2000			D = 3000			D = 4000			D = 5000		
	Sep	Non-Sep		Sep	Non-Sep		Sep	Non-Sep		Sep	Non-Sep		Sep	Non-Sep		Sep	Non-Sep		Sep	Non-Sep	
	Vars	Vars	Groups	Vars	Vars	Groups	Vars	Vars	Groups	Vars	Vars	Groups	Vars	Vars	Groups	Vars	Vars	Groups	Vars	Vars	Groups
f_1	100	0	0	500	0	0	1000	0	0	2000	0	0	3000	0	0	4000	0	0	5000	0	0
f_2	100	0	0	500	0	0	1000	0	0	2000	0	0	3000	0	0	4000	0	0	5000	0	0
f_3	100	0	0	500	0	0	1000	0	0	2000	0	0	3000	0	0	4000	0	0	5000	0	0
f_4	50	50	1	450	50	1	950	50	1	1950	50	1	2950	50	1	3950	50	1	4950	50	1
f_5	50	50	1	450	50	1	950	50	1	1950	50	1	2950	50	1	3950	50	1	4950	50	1
f_6	50	50	1	450	50	1	950	50	1	1950	50	1	2950	50	1	3950	50	1	4950	50	1
f_7	50	50	1	450	50	1	950	50	1	1950	50	1	2950	50	1	3950	50	1	4950	50	1
f_8	50	50	1	450	50	1	950	50	1	1950	50	1	2950	50	1	3950	50	1	4950	50	1
f_9	50	50	1	250	250	5	500	500	10	1000	1000	20	1500	1500	30	2000	2000	40	2500	2500	50
f_{10}	50	50	1	250	250	5	500	500	10	1000	1000	20	1500	1500	30	2000	2000	40	2500	2500	50
f_{11}	50	50	1	250	250	5	500	500	10	1000	1000	20	1500	1500	30	2000	2000	40	2500	2500	50
f_{12}	50	50	1	250	250	5	500	500	10	1000	1000	20	1500	1500	30	2000	2000	40	2500	2500	50
f_{13}	50	50	1	250	250	5	500	500	10	1000	1000	20	1500	1500	30	2000	2000	40	2500	2500	50
f_{14}	0	100	2	0	500	10	0	1000	20	0	2000	40	0	3000	60	0	4000	80	0	5000	100
f_{15}	0	100	2	0	500	10	0	1000	20	0	2000	40	0	3000	60	0	4000	80	0	5000	100
f_{16}	0	100	2	0	500	10	0	1000	20	0	2000	40	0	3000	60	0	4000	80	0	5000	100
f_{17}	0	100	2	0	500	10	0	1000	20	0	2000	40	0	3000	60	0	4000	80	0	5000	100
f_{18}	0	100	2	0	500	10	0	1000	20	0	2000	40	0	3000	60	0	4000	80	0	5000	100
f_{19}	0	100	1	0	500	1	0	1000	1	0	2000	1	0	3000	1	0	4000	1	0	5000	1
f_{20}	0	100	1	0	500	1	0	1000	1	0	2000	1	0	3000	1	0	4000	1	0	5000	1

Table 2 summarizes the variable grouping accuracies of DG2 on the CEC'2010 benchmark functions. It can be seen in Table 2 that the variable grouping accuracies are 100% on the most functions with different dimensions, except on f_2, f_3, f_6, and f_{11}. Variable grouping accuracies on f_2 are almost 100% but it is 97.88% when dimensionality is 5000, which is caused by the rise of the dimensionality. Variable grouping accuracies on f_3, f_6 and f_{11} are almost 0%. The three functions are all instances of Ackley function [5]. DG2 may not deal with Ackley function well, but it performs well on f_{16} which is based on Ackley function and only has nonseparable subcomponents (see Table 1). Generally, DG2 performs well on most CEC'2010 functions, even on the functions with more than 1000 dimensions.

To further investigate the effect of imbalance, functions $f_9 - f_{18}$ can be modified in the following way:

$$f' = \sum_{k=1}^{G} w_k \times F_{nonsep} + F_{sep} \tag{4}$$

where G is the number of nonseparable subcomponents and

$$w_k = \begin{cases} \alpha^{\frac{k-1}{G-1}} & \text{if } G \geq 2 \\ 1 & \text{otherwise,} \end{cases} \tag{5}$$

Table 2. Grouping accuracy of DG2 on the CEC'2010 benchmark functions.

F	D=100		D=500		D=1000		D=2000		D=3000		D=4000		D=5000	
	sep	nonsep	sep	nonsep	sep	nonsep	sep	nonsep	sep	nonsep	sep	nonsep	sep	nonsep
f_1	100.00%	100.00%	98.20%	100.00%	100.00%	100.00%	100.00%	100.00%	100.00%	100.00%	100.00%	100.00%	100.00%	100.00%
f_2	100.00%	100.00%	94.40%	100.00%	100.00%	100.00%	100.00%	100.00%	100.00%	100.00%	100.00%	100.00%	97.88%	100.00%
f_3	0%	100.00%	0%	100.00%	0%	100.00%	0%	100.00%	0%	100.00%	0%	100.00%	0%	100.00%
f_4	100.00%	100.00%	100.00%	100.00%	100.00%	100.00%	100.00%	100.00%	100.00%	100.00%	100.00%	100.00%	100.00%	100.00%
f_5	100.00%	100.00%	100.00%	100.00%	100.00%	100.00%	100.00%	100.00%	100.00%	100.00%	100.00%	100.00%	100.00%	100.00%
f_6	0%	100.00%	0.44%	100.00%	8.63%	100.00%	22.10%	100.00%	8.27%	100.00%	15.75%	100.00%	25.92%	100.00%
f_7	100.00%	100.00%	100.00%	100.00%	100.00%	100.00%	100.00%	100.00%	100.00%	100.00%	100.00%	100.00%	100.00%	100.00%
f_8	100.00%	100.00%	100.00%	100.00%	100.00%	100.00%	100.00%	100.00%	100.00%	100.00%	100.00%	100.00%	100.00%	100.00%
f_9	100.00%	100.00%	100.00%	100.00%	100.00%	100.00%	100.00%	100.00%	100.00%	100.00%	100.00%	100.00%	100.00%	100.00%
f_{10}	100.00%	100.00%	100.00%	100.00%	100.00%	100.00%	100.00%	100.00%	100.00%	100.00%	100.00%	100.00%	100.00%	100.00%
f_{11}	0%	100.00%	0%	100.00%	0%	100.00%	0%	100.00%	0%	100.00%	0%	100.00%	0%	100.00%
f_{12}	100.00%	100.00%	100.00%	100.00%	100.00%	100.00%	100.00%	100.00%	100.00%	100.00%	100.00%	100.00%	100.00%	100.00%
f_{13}	100.00%	100.00%	100.00%	100.00%	100.00%	100.00%	100.00%	100.00%	100.00%	100.00%	100.00%	100.00%	100.00%	100.00%
f_{14}	100.00%	100.00%	100.00%	100.00%	100.00%	100.00%	100.00%	100.00%	100.00%	100.00%	100.00%	100.00%	100.00%	100.00%
f_{15}	100.00%	100.00%	100.00%	100.00%	100.00%	100.00%	100.00%	100.00%	100.00%	100.00%	100.00%	100.00%	100.00%	100.00%
f_{16}	100.00%	100.00%	100.00%	100.00%	100.00%	100.00%	100.00%	100.00%	100.00%	100.00%	100.00%	100.00%	100.00%	100.00%
f_{17}	100.00%	100.00%	100.00%	100.00%	100.00%	100.00%	100.00%	100.00%	100.00%	100.00%	100.00%	100.00%	100.00%	100.00%
f_{18}	100.00%	100.00%	100.00%	100.00%	100.00%	100.00%	100.00%	100.00%	100.00%	100.00%	100.00%	100.00%	100.00%	100.00%
f_{19}	100.00%	100.00%	100.00%	100.00%	100.00%	100.00%	100.00%	100.00%	100.00%	100.00%	100.00%	100.00%	100.00%	100.00%
f_{20}	100.00%	100.00%	100.00%	100.00%	100.00%	100.00%	100.00%	100.00%	100.00%	100.00%	100.00%	100.00%	100.00%	100.00%

where $\alpha = \{10^5, 10^{10}, 10^{15}, 10^{20}\}$. The overall structure of the functions is multiplied by a coefficient to create the imbalance effect. The larger value of α can cause a greater imbalance of contribution of nonseparable components to the overall fitness. The modified functions $f_9 - f_{18}$ are denoted as $f_9' - f_{18}'$.

$f_9' - f_{13}'$ have $\frac{D}{2m}$-group m-nonseparable variables and $f_{14}' - f_{18}'$ have $\frac{D}{m}$-group m-nonseparable variables (see Table 1). Figure 1 shows the grouping accuracies of DG2 for nonseparable variables on $f_9' - f_{18}'$. In the case that $\alpha = 1$, the functions are the original version of functions without the change by Eq. (4). It can be seen that the grouping accuracies of detecting nonseparable variables are all 100% on every imbalanced functions when $\alpha = 10^5$, which are the same with the case that $\alpha = 1$. The grouping accuracies of detecting nonseparable variables are 100% on almost every imbalanced function except on f_{13}' and f_{18}' when $\alpha = 10^{10}$. When $\alpha = 10^{15}$ and $\alpha = 10^{20}$, the grouping accuracies of detecting nonseparable variables decrease greatly. Figure 1 shows the downward trend of grouping accuracy as the increase of the value of α. The larger value of α is, the greater imbalance of contribution of nonseparable components to the overall fitness is. The results shown in Fig. 1 indicate that DG2 may lose its efficiency for the functions when the value of α is large.

DG2 check whether two variables are separable according to the difference of the function values [see Eq. (1)]. The function value enlarges as the value of α increases [see Eq. (4)], which results in a computational error in computing Eq. (1). The computational error may result in the error of DG2 for detecting the interactions between variables. In order to confirm whether the enlargement of the value of α results in the error of detecting the interactions, we set the value of α to $\alpha = \{10^{-5}, 10^{-10}, 10^{-15}, 10^{-20}\}$, which can decrease the function value. Figure 2 shows the grouping accuracies of DG2 for nonseparable variables on $f_9' - f_{18}'$. It can be seen that Fig. 2 shows the similar results to Fig. 1. DG2

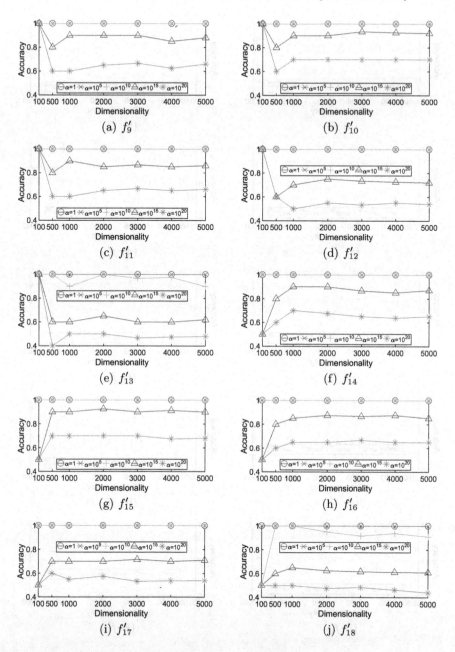

Fig. 1. Grouping accuracy of DG2 for nonseparable variables on $f'_9 - f'_{18}$.

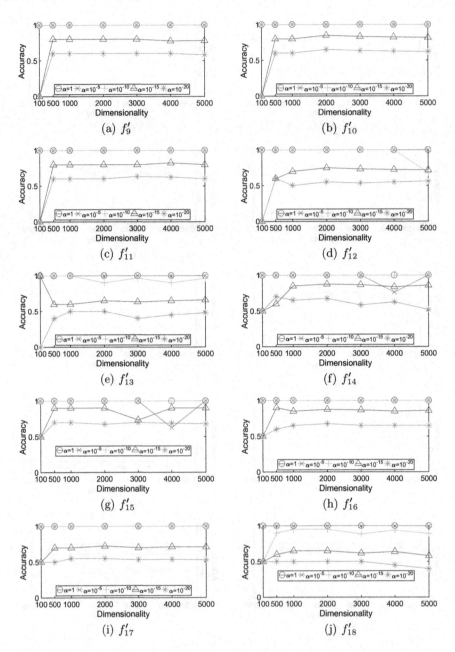

Fig. 2. Grouping accuracy of DG2 for nonseparable variables on $f'_9 - f'_{18}$.

may not be suited to detect the interactions between variables in the imbalanced functions.

Table 3. Grouping accuracy for separable variables on f'_{10}.

	$D = 100$	$D = 500$	$D = 1000$	$D = 2000$	$D = 3000$	$D = 4000$	$D = 5000$
$\alpha = 10^{20}$	100.00%	100.00%	100.00%	100.00%	100.00%	100.00%	100.00%
$\alpha = 10^{15}$	100.00%	100.00%	100.00%	100.00%	100.00%	100.00%	100.00%
$\alpha = 10^{10}$	100.00%	100.00%	100.00%	100.00%	100.00%	100.00%	100.00%
$\alpha = 10^{5}$	100.00%	100.00%	100.00%	100.00%	100.00%	100.00%	100.00%
$\alpha = 1$	100.00%	100.00%	100.00%	100.00%	100.00%	100.00%	100.00%
$\alpha = 10^{-5}$	100.00%	100.00%	100.00%	100.00%	100.00%	93.00%	96.32%
$\alpha = 10^{-10}$	100.00%	100.00%	100.00%	100.00%	100.00%	93.00%	96.32%
$\alpha = 10^{-15}$	100.00%	100.00%	100.00%	100.00%	100.00%	93.00%	96.32%
$\alpha = 10^{-20}$	100.00%	98.40%	100.00%	100.00%	100.00%	93.00%	96.32%

Table 4. Grouping accuracy for separable variables on f'_{11}.

	$D = 100$	$D = 500$	$D = 1000$	$D = 2000$	$D = 3000$	$D = 4000$	$D = 5000$
$\alpha = 10^{20}$	100.00%	100.00%	100.00%	100.00%	100.00%	100.00%	100.00%
$\alpha = 10^{15}$	100.00%	100.00%	100.00%	100.00%	100.00%	100.00%	100.00%
$\alpha = 10^{10}$	32.00%	100.00%	100.00%	100.00%	100.00%	100.00%	100.00%
$\alpha = 10^{5}$	0%	0%	0.20%	0.90%	1.73%	3.85%	5.36%
$\alpha = 1$	0%	0%	0%	0%	0%	0%	0%
$\alpha = 10^{-5}$	0%	0%	0%	0%	0%	0%	0%
$\alpha = 10^{-10}$	0%	0%	0%	0%	0%	0%	0%
$\alpha = 10^{-15}$	0%	0%	0%	0%	0%	0%	0%
$\alpha = 10^{-20}$	0%	0%	0%	0%	0%	0%	0%

The grouping accuracies for the separable variables are similar to the accuracies shown in Table 2, except on f'_{10} and f'_{11}. The grouping accuracies on f'_{10} and f'_{11} are shown in Tables 3 and 4. It can be seen in Tables 3 and 4 that the grouping accuracies for the separable variables decrease as the value of α decreases, which is contrary to the results of grouping the nonseparable variables. When the value of α is relatively large, comparing with the nonseparable variables, the separable variables affect relatively less the function value. For the separable variables, the difference of function value may not be identified by DG2. DG2 may deem the difference of function value is zero and consider the variables are separable. When the value of α is small, DG2 can identify the difference of function value. However, DG2 detects wrongly the separable variables of f'_{10} and f'_{11} in such case.

4 Conclusion

In this paper, DG2 was tested on the imbalanced functions with different dimensions. The experimental results indicate that when the dimensionality of the CEC'2010 functions becomes large, DG2 can also group the interacting variables well on these functions. For the imbalanced functions, DG2 can detect the interactions between variables well when the imbalance is not great. However, when the imbalance becomes greater and greater, the grouping accuracy of DG2 drops greatly. Besides for the nonseparable variables, which have interactions with other variables, the imbalance of contribution of different components to the overall fitness also affects DG2 identifying the separable variables, which have no interaction with other variables. DG2 may not be suited to group the nonseparable variables with great imbalance.

Acknowledgement. The work was supported by the National Natural Science Foundation of China (Grant No. 61305086), the Fundamental Research Funds for the Central Universities, China University of Geosciences (Wuhan) (Grant No. CUGL170412), and the Open Research Project of the Hubei Key Laboratory of Intelligent Geo-Information Processing (Grant No. KLIGIP201602).

References

1. Peng, X., Wu, Y.: Large-scale cooperative co-evolution using niching-based multi-modal optimization and adaptive fast clustering. Swarm Evol. Comput. **35**, 65–77 (2017)
2. Potter, M.A., De Jong, K.A.: A cooperative coevolutionary approach to function optimization. In: Davidor, Y., Schwefel, H.-P., Männer, R. (eds.) PPSN 1994. LNCS, vol. 866, pp. 249–257. Springer, Heidelberg (1994). https://doi.org/10.1007/3-540-58484-6_269
3. Yang, M., et al.: Efficient resource allocation in cooperative co-evolution for large-scale global optimization. IEEE Trans. Evol. Comput. **21**(4), 493–505 (2017)
4. Omidvar, M.N., Yang, M., Mei, Y., Li, X., Yao, X.: DG2: a faster and more accurate differential grouping for large-scale black-box optimization. IEEE Trans. Evol. Comput. **21**(6), 929–942 (2017)
5. Tang, K., Li, X., Suganthan, P.N., Yang, Z., Weise, T.: Benchmark functions for the CEC 2010 special session and competition on large-scale global optimization. Technical report, Nature Inspired Computation and Applications Laboratory, University of Science and Technology of China, Hefei, China (2009)
6. Omidvar, M.N., Li, X., Yao, X.: Smart use of computational resources based on contribution for cooperative co-evolutionary algorithms. In: Proceedings of the 13th Annual Conference on Genetic and Evolutionary Computation, GECCO 2011, pp. 1115–1122. ACM, New York (2011)
7. Salomon, R.: Re-evaluating genetic algorithm performance under coordinate rotation of benchmark functions. A survey of some theoretical and practical aspects of genetic algorithms. Biosystems **39**(3), 263–278 (1996)
8. Shi, Y., Teng, H., Li, Z.: Cooperative co-evolutionary differential evolution for function optimization. In: Wang, L., Chen, K., Ong, Y.S. (eds.) ICNC 2005. LNCS, vol. 3611, pp. 1080–1088. Springer, Heidelberg (2005). https://doi.org/10.1007/11539117_147

9. Yang, Z., Tang, K., Yao, X.: Large scale evolutionary optimization using cooperative coevolution. Inf. Sci. **178**(15), 2985–2999 (2008)

10. Weicker, K., Weicker, N.: On the improvement of coevolutionary optimizers by learning variable interdependencies. In: Proceedings of the 1999 Congress on Evolutionary Computation, CEC 1999, vol. 3, pp. 1627–1632. IEEE (1999)

11. Chen, W., Weise, T., Yang, Z., Tang, K.: Large-scale global optimization using cooperative coevolution with variable interaction learning. In: Schaefer, R., Cotta, C., Kołodziej, J., Rudolph, G. (eds.) PPSN 2010. LNCS, vol. 6239, pp. 300–309. Springer, Heidelberg (2010). https://doi.org/10.1007/978-3-642-15871-1_31

12. Tezuka, M., Munetomo, M., Akama, K.: Linkage identification by nonlinearity check for real-coded genetic algorithms. In: Deb, K. (ed.) GECCO 2004. LNCS, vol. 3103, pp. 222–233. Springer, Heidelberg (2004). https://doi.org/10.1007/978-3-540-24855-2_20

13. Omidvar, M.N., Li, X., Mei, Y., Yao, X.: Cooperative co-evolution with differential grouping for large scale optimization. IEEE Trans. Evol. Comput. **18**(3), 378–393 (2014)

14. Omidvar, M.N., Li, X., Tang, K.: Designing benchmark problems for large-scale continuous optimization. Inf. Sci. **316**, 419–436 (2015)

15. Mei, Y., Omidvar, M.N., Li, X., Yao, X.: A competitive divide-and-conquer algorithm for unconstrained large-scale black-box optimization. ACM Trans. Math. Softw. **42**(2), 13:1–13:24 (2016)

16. IEEE standard for floating-point arithmetic: IEEE Std 754–2008, 1–70 (2008)

17. Li, X., Tang, K., Omidvar, M.N., Yang, Z., Qin, K.: Benchmark functions for the CEC'2013 special session and competition on large-scale global optimization. Gene **7**(33), 8 (2013)

Spiking Neural P Systems with Anti-spikes Based on the Min-Sequentiality Strategy

Li Li[1] and Keqin Jiang[2(✉)]

[1] Anqing Radio and Television University,
Anqing 246003, Anhui, China
lily@aqtvu.cn
[2] School of Computer and Information, Anqing Normal University,
Anqing 246133, Anhui, China
jiangkq0519@163.com

Abstract. Membrane computing models based on cell structure and function have important applications in computer science and provide new theories and methods for modeling biological systems. The spiking neural P system based on the min-sequentiality strategy is a special kind of membrane computing model. Anti-spikes and inhibitory functions are introduced into spiking neural P systems based on the min-sequentiality strategy. We construct two sequential spiking neural P systems with anti-spikes in different ways. The corresponding modules of the two systems are designed separately. Finally, we prove that the two spiking neural P systems with anti-spikes based on the min-sequentiality strategy are universal as both number generators and acceptors.

Keywords: Membrane computing · Spiking neural P system
Anti-spike · Inhibitory synapse · Min-sequentiality · Register machine

1   Introduction

The development of membrane computing has provided a rich computational framework for biomolecular and nontraditional computing [1,2]. *Spiking neural P systems* (SN P systems for short) were proposed by Ionescu et al. in 2006 under the influence of using pulse coding information [3]. Their purpose was to establish a new computing model and algorithm under the framework of membrane computing by using some concepts of neurobiology. SN P systems have attracted wide attention from universal scholars since they were put forward, and these systems have become research hotspots in the field of membrane computing. According to the diversity of biological motivation, scholars have proposed several extended models of SN P systems [4–11]. The sequential SN P system based on the number of spikes proposed by Ibarra was one of them [12]. Related scholars have studied the homogeneity, paradigm, and generation language of the system [13–16].

© Springer Nature Singapore Pte Ltd. 2018
J. Qiao et al. (Eds.): BIC-TA 2018, CCIS 951, pp. 94–106, 2018.
https://doi.org/10.1007/978-981-13-2826-8_9

In biological neural networks, when the number of spikes in neurons is excessive, a kind of antimatter will be produced to counteract a certain number of spikes, thus protecting the activity and function of neurons. Similarly, when the number of spikes passing through a synapse is too high, the synapse will inhibit and weaken some of the spikes in order to ensure there is not a large number of spikes entering a neuron at the same time, thereby playing a role in protecting neurons. Inspired by these two biological phenomena, Professor Pan Linqiang introduced anti-spikes in standard SN P systems [17]. There are two ways to generate anti-spikes: by using firing rules and by converting spikes into anti-spikes by inhibitory synapses. In this paper, we study SN P systems with anti-spikes (ASN P systems for short) with the following limitations: (1) there is only one rule for each neuron, (2) no delay or forgetting rules are used, and (3) the min-sequentiality strategy is used, that is, at each step of the calculation, only active neurons (meeting the firing condition) with a minimum number of spikes will fire. If there are multiple neurons that satisfy the conditions at the same time, then one neuron is randomly selected. In this paper, two kinds of ASN P systems are constructed.

In computer science, in order to explore a new computing model, we must first ensure its universality, that is, it needs to be equivalent to a Turing machine. Then, it is considered that the structure of the model can be simplified as much as possible without reducing the computational power and by using fewer computing resources. In this paper, two ASN P systems are verified by simulating a registration machine. We prove the following conclusions: (1) using firing rules of categories (a, a) and $(a, \bar{a})$, ASN P systems based on the min-sequentiality strategy, which produce anti-spikes by firing rules, are universal as both number generators and acceptors. (2) using firing rules of category (a, a), ASN P systems based on the min-sequentiality strategy, which convert spikes into anti-spikes by inhibitory synapses, are universal as both number generators and acceptors.

2 Related Definitions and Concepts

2.1 ASN P Systems Based on the Min-Sequentiality Strategy

We recall the definition of ASN P systems based on the min-sequentiality strategy. In the definition of the systems, the notion of regular expression is used, readers can refer to [18] for the details.

An ASN P system working in the min-sequentiality manner, of degree $m \geq 1$ is a construct of the form

$$\Pi = (O, \sigma_1, \sigma_2, \ldots, \sigma_m, syn, in, out)$$

where

- $O = \{a, \bar{a}\}$ is the alphabet (a is called *spike*, and $\bar{a}$ is called *anti-spike*);
- $\sigma_1, \sigma_2, \ldots, \sigma_m$ are *neurons* of the form $\sigma_i = (n_i, R_i)$ with $1 \leq i \leq m$, where
  (a) $n_i \geq 0$ is the *initial number of spikes* contained in σ_i;

(b) R_i is a finite set of *rules* of the following two forms:

    (1) $E/b^c \rightarrow b'$, where E is a regular expression over $\{a\}$ or over $\{\bar{a}\}$, $b, b' \in O$, and $c \geq 1$;

    (2) $b^s \rightarrow \lambda$, where $b \in O$ and $s \geq 1$, with the restriction that $b^s \notin L(E)$ for any rule $E/b^c \rightarrow b'$ from R_i;

- $syn \subseteq \{1, 2, \ldots, m\} \times \{1, 2, \ldots, m\}$ with $(i, i) \notin syn$ for $1 \leq i \leq m$ (*synapses* between neurons);
- $in, out \in \{1, 2, \ldots, m\}$ indicate the *input* and *output* neurons, respectively.

In the same neuron, a and $\bar{a}$ cannot coexist, they immediately use an annihilation rule $a\bar{a} \rightarrow \lambda$ to cancel each other out. If there are r spikes and s anti-spikes in a neuron, the remaining $r - s(r \geq s)$ spikes or $s - r(s \geq r)$ anti-spikes in the neuron can be obtained by using the annihilation rule $a\bar{a} \rightarrow \lambda$. The annihilation of a and $\bar{a}$ takes no time. The priority of the annihilation rule is higher than that of the firing rule or forgetting rule.

The sequentiality of an ASN P system based on the min-sequentiality strategy is caused by the minimum number of spikes. If there are multiple active neurons at the same time, only the active neurons with a minimum number of spikes can be activated. If there is more than one active neuron with the minimum number of spikes, one of them is selected nondeterministically.

By $N_\alpha^{min} ASNPS(cate_p, Inh)$, we denote the family of all sets of numbers generated or accepted by ASN P systems with at most p categories of spiking rules, and inhibitory synapses, where $\alpha \in \{gen, acc\}$ (gen and acc respectively indicate that the system is working in the generating or accepting mode), min stands for the min-sequentiality, and if inhibitory synapses are not used, the indication of Inh will be removed from the notation.

2.2 Register Machines

In the following sections, we construct two ASN P systems based on the min-sequentiality strategy, one of which uses firing rules to generate anti-spikes while the other converts spikes into anti-spikes by inhibitory synapses. We demonstrate the universality of the two systems in the generating mode and the accepting mode by simulating register machines.

A register machine is a construct $M = (m, H, l_0, l_h, I)$, where m represents the number of registers, H represents the set of instruction labels, l_0 represents the start label, l_h represents the halt label, and I represents the set of instructions. The instructions of the register machine M have three forms:

- $l_i : (\text{ADD}(r), l_j, l_k)$ (the value stored in the register r is added by 1, then the instruction l_j or instruction l_k is randomly selected to execute),
- $l_i : (\text{SUB}(r), l_j, l_k)$ (if the value stored in the register r is not zero, the number is subtracted by 1 before the instruction l_j is executed; if the number stored in the register is zero, the instruction l_k is executed),
- $l_h : \text{HALT}$ (the halt instruction).

A register machine can work in the generating or accepting mode, and it is known that register machines compute all sets of numbers which are Turing computable, hence they characterize NRE (the family of Turing computable sets of numbers) (see, e.g., [19]).

3 ASN P Systems that Use Firing Rules to Generate Anti-spikes

In this section, we prove the universality of ASN P systems based on the min-sequentiality strategy, in which anti-spikes are generated by the firing rules of categories (a, a) and $(a, \bar{a})$. In the proof of the universality, forgetting rules are not used, and there is no delay.

3.1 ASN P Systems Based on Working in Generating Mode

Theorem 1. $NRE = N_{gen}^{min} ASNPS(cate_2)$, where the categories of spiking rules are (a, a) and $(a, \bar{a})$.

Proof. According to Turing-Church's conjecture, $N_{gen}ASNPS(cate_2) \subseteq NRE$, so we have to prove the inclusion relation $NRE \subseteq N_{gen}ASNPS(cate_2)$.

We construct an ASN P system Π based on the min-sequentiality strategy to simulate a register machine $M = (m, H, l_0, l_h, I)$. In initial state, only register 1 is not empty. In the course of calculation, the values in register 1 are only increased and not decreased. System Π is composed of three modules: the addition module, the subtraction module, and the output module, as shown in Figs. 1, 2, 3, respectively. Register r uniquely corresponds to neuron σ_r in system Π. When the number stored in r is $n(n \geq 0)$, then neuron σ_r has $n + 3$ spikes. The instruction label l_i in M uniquely corresponds to the neuron σ_{l_i} in system Π.

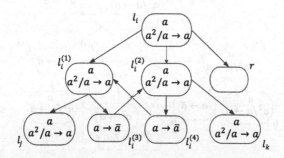

Fig. 1. Addition module of system Π

The addition module simulates the addition instruction $l_i : (\text{ADD}(r), l_j, l_k)$ of M. At step t, the neuron σ_{l_i} receiving one spike reaches the firing condition and sends one spike to each neuron $\sigma_{l_i^{(1)}}$, $\sigma_{l_i^{(2)}}$, and σ_r by rule $a^2/a \to a$. At step $t + 1$, the neuron σ_r receiving one spike simulates the number of register r and is increased by 1. Neurons $\sigma_{l_i^{(1)}}$ and $\sigma_{l_i^{(2)}}$ have two spikes, both of which can be activated. According to the min-sequentiality strategy, system Π randomly selects one of them to fire:

(1) At step $t + 1$, if system Π chooses to fire neuron $\sigma_{l_i^{(1)}}$, then neuron $\sigma_{l_i^{(1)}}$ sends one spike to each neuron $\sigma_{l_i^{(3)}}$ and σ_{l_j}. At step $t + 2$, the number of spikes in neurons $\sigma_{l_i^{(2)}}$, $\sigma_{l_i^{(3)}}$, and σ_{l_j} is 2, 1, and 2, which are active neurons. According to the min-sequentiality strategy, neuron $\sigma_{l_i^{(3)}}$ fires by rule $a \to \bar{a}$, sending one anti-spike to neuron $\sigma_{l_i^{(2)}}$. After one spike is annihilated by the anti-spike, neuron $\sigma_{l_i^{(2)}}$ contains one spike and cannot fire. At step $t + 3$, the only active neuron σ_{l_j} fires. System Π starts to simulate instruction l_j of M.

(2) At step $t + 1$, if system Π chooses to fire neuron $\sigma_{l_i^{(2)}}$, then it sends one spike to each neuron $\sigma_{l_i^{(4)}}$ and σ_{l_k}. At step $t + 2$, neurons $\sigma_{l_i^{(1)}}$, $\sigma_{l_i^{(4)}}$, and σ_{l_k} are active neurons. According to the min-sequentiality strategy, neuron $\sigma_{l_i^{(4)}}$ fires and sends one anti-spike to neuron $\sigma_{l_i^{(1)}}$. After one spike is annihilated by the anti-spike, neuron $\sigma_{l_i^{(1)}}$ contains one spike and cannot fire. At step $t + 3$, neuron σ_{l_k} fires. System Π starts to simulate instruction l_k of M.

Therefore, the addition module shown in Fig. 1 correctly simulates the addition instruction $l_i : (\text{ADD}(r), l_j, l_k)$ of the register machine M.

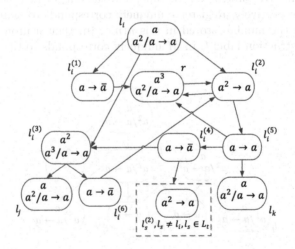

Fig. 2. Subtraction module of system Π

The subtraction module of Fig. 2 simulates the subtraction instruction $l_i :$ $(\text{SUB}(r), l_j, l_k)$ of M. At step t, neuron σ_{l_i} receiving one spike becomes an active neuron and sends one spike to each neuron $\sigma_{l_i^{(1)}}$, $\sigma_{l_i^{(2)}}$, and $\sigma_{l_i^{(3)}}$. At step $t + 1$, neurons $\sigma_{l_i^{(1)}}$, $\sigma_{l_i^{(2)}}$, and $\sigma_{l_i^{(3)}}$ contain 1, 1, and 3 spikes, respectively. Owing to the min-sequentiality, neuron $\sigma_{l_i^{(1)}}$ fires by rule $a \to \bar{a}$ and sends one anti-spike to neuron σ_r. Originally, neuron σ_r has $n + 3(n \geq 0)$ spikes (the number stored in the corresponding register r is n). After one spike is annihilated by the anti-spike, neurons σ_r contains $n + 2$ spikes. According to the number of spikes in neuron σ_r, there are two cases, as follows:

(1) At step $t + 2$, if neuron σ_r has two spikes (the corresponding register r is originally empty, that is, $n = 0$), neuron σ_r fires by rule $a^2/a \to a$ and sends one spike to neuron $\sigma_{l_i^{(2)}}$. At step $t + 3$, neurons $\sigma_{l_i^{(2)}}$ and $\sigma_{l_i^{(3)}}$ contain 2 and 3 spikes, respectively. Neuron $\sigma_{l_i^{(2)}}$ fires by rule $a^2 \to a$ and sends one spike to each neuron $\sigma_{l_i^{(5)}}$ and σ_r. At step $t + 4$, neuron $\sigma_{l_i^{(5)}}$ has one spike and fires by rule $a \to a$, which sends one spike to each neuron $\sigma_{l_i^{(4)}}$, σ_{l_k}, and σ_r. At step $t + 5$, neuron σ_r has 3 spikes, returning to the number of spikes before the subtraction instruction was executed. At the same time, neurons $\sigma_{l_i^{(3)}}$, $\sigma_{l_i^{(4)}}$, and σ_{l_k} contain 3, 1, and 2 spikes, respectively. Neuron $\sigma_{l_i^{(4)}}$ fires by rule $a \to \bar{a}$ and sends one anti-spike to each neuron $\sigma_{l_i^{(3)}}$ and $\sigma_{l_s^{(2)}}$ ($l_s \neq l_i, l_s \in L_t, L_t = \{t | t$ is a subtraction instruction acting on register $r\}$). After one spike is annihilated by the anti-spike, the number of spikes in neurons $\sigma_{l_i^{(3)}}$ and $\sigma_{l_s^{(2)}}$ is restored to the initial value of this simulation, which ensures the correct simulation of the next subtraction instruction. At step $t + 6$, the only active neuron σ_{l_k} fires. System Π starts to simulate instruction l_k of M.

(2) At step $t + 2$, if neuron σ_r has $n + 2$ spikes (the corresponding register r is originally not empty, that is, $n > 0$), since it received an anti-spike from neuron $\sigma_{l_i^{(1)}}$ in the previous step, the number of spikes is subtracted by 1, and the operation corresponding to the number minus 1 stored in the register r has been completed. At this step, neuron $\sigma_{l_i^{(3)}}$ is the only active neuron, which fires by rule $a^3/a \to a$ and sends one spike to each neuron $\sigma_{l_i^{(6)}}$ and σ_{l_j}. At step $t + 3$, neurons $\sigma_{l_i^{(6)}}$ and σ_{l_j} contain 1 and 2 spikes, respectively. Neuron $\sigma_{l_i^{(6)}}$ fires by rule $a \to \bar{a}$ and sends one anti-spike to neuron $\sigma_{l_i^{(2)}}$. This anti-spike cancels a spike of neuron $\sigma_{l_i^{(2)}}$ from neuron σ_{l_i}, and the number of spikes of neuron $\sigma_{l_i^{(2)}}$ recovers to its initial value. At step $t + 4$, the only active neuron σ_{l_j} fires. System Π starts to simulate instruction l_j of M.

Therefore, the subtraction module shown in Fig. 2 correctly simulates the subtraction instruction $l_i : (\text{SUB}(r), l_j, l_k)$ of the register machine M.

When multiple addition and subtraction instructions act on the same register r, the interaction between them is analyzed as follows:

In the addition module shown in Fig. 1, the number of spikes received by neuron σ_r per unit of time is 1, and there is no corresponding firing rule.

Therefore, the addition modules do not affect each other, nor do the addition module and the subtraction module.

For the subtraction module shown in Fig. 2, when multiple subtraction instructions are applied to register r, let $L_t = \{t | t$ is a subtraction instruction acting on $r\}$. When r is not empty, neuron σ_r is not fired, and no spike is sent out. When r is empty, neuron σ_r fires and sends one spike to neuron $\sigma_{l_i^{(2)}}$ in the subtraction module. At the same time, neuron σ_r also sends one spike to the corresponding neuron $\sigma_{l_s^{(2)}}$ $(l_s \neq l_i, l_s \in L_t)$ of other subtraction modules that act on r. Before neuron σ_{l_k} is fired, neuron $\sigma_{l_i^{(4)}}$ will fire and send one anti-spike to neuron $\sigma_{l_s^{(2)}}$. This anti-spike cancels one spike of neuron $\sigma_{l_s^{(2)}}$, restoring the number of spikes to the initial value at the beginning of the simulation. Therefore, there is no interaction between subtraction modules.

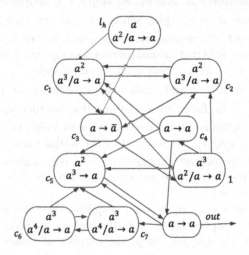

Fig. 3. Output module of system Π

When halt instruction l_h is executed, neurons σ_1 has $n + 3$ spikes (that is, the number stored in register 1 is n). At step t, neuron σ_{l_h} receiving one spike fires and sends one spike to each neuron σ_{c_1} and σ_{c_3}. At step $t + 1$, neurons σ_{c_3} and σ_{c_1} contain 1 and 3 spikes, respectively. Owing to the min-sequentiality, neuron σ_{c_3} fires and sends one anti-spike to each neuron σ_{c_5} and σ_1. After one spike is annihilated by the anti-spike, neurons σ_{c_5} and σ_1 contain 1 and $n + 2$ spikes, respectively. At step $t + 2$, neuron σ_{c_1} fires and sends one spike to each neuron σ_{c_2} and σ_{c_3}.

At step $t + 3$, neuron σ_{c_2} and σ_{c_3} contain 3 and 1 spikes, respectively. Neuron σ_{c_3} fires and sends one anti-spike to each neuron σ_{c_5} and σ_1. After one spike is annihilated by the anti-spike, neurons σ_{c_5} and σ_1 contain 0 and $n + 1$ spikes, respectively. At step $t + 4$, neuron σ_{c_2} fires and sends one spike to each neuron σ_{c_1} and σ_{c_3}, which makes neurons σ_{c_1} and σ_{c3} become active neurons again.

After that, neurons σ_{c_1} or σ_{c_2} will fire alternately with neuron σ_{c_3}. The number of spikes in neurons σ_{c_5} and σ_1 subtracts by 1 for every two steps.

Up to the $t + 2n + 2$ step, neurons σ_{c_5} and σ_1 receive an anti-spike from neuron σ_{c_3}. The number of spikes in neurons σ_{c_5} and σ_1 becomes $1-n$ (a negative number denotes an inverse pulse) and 2, respectively. At this step, when n is an odd number, neurons σ_{c_1} and σ_{c_2} contain 2 and 3 spikes, respectively. When n is an even number, neurons σ_{c_1} and σ_{c_2} contain 3 and 2 spikes, respectively. Neuron σ_1 fires and sends one spike to each neuron σ_{c_1}, σ_{c_2}, σ_{c_4}, and σ_{c_5}. At step $t + 2n + 3$, the number of spikes in neurons σ_{c_1} and σ_{c_2} is 3 and 4 (if n is odd) or 4 and 3 (if n is even), respectively. The number of spikes in neurons σ_{c_4} and σ_{c_5} is 1 and $2-n$, respectively. Neuron σ_{c_4} fires and sends one spike to each neuron σ_{c_1}, σ_{c_2}, σ_{c_5}, and σ_{out}.

At step $t + 2n + 4$, neurons σ_{c_1} and σ_{c_2} contain 4 and 5 spikes (if n is odd) or 5 and 4 spikes (if n is even), respectively. Neither of them can be fired. Neurons σ_{c_5} and σ_{out} contain $3-n$ and 1 spikes, respectively. The output neuron σ_{out} is currently the only active neuron, which sends one spike to each neuron σ_{c_5} and σ_{c_7}. At the same time, neuron σ_{out} sends the first spike to the environment. At step $t + 2n + 5$, neurons σ_{c_5} and σ_{c_7} contain $4 - n$ and 4 spikes, respectively. Neuron σ_{c_7} fires and sends one spike to each neuron σ_{c_5} and σ_{c_6}. At step $t + 2n + 6$, neurons σ_{c_5} and σ_{c_6} contain $5 - n$ and 4 spikes, respectively. Neuron σ_{c_6} fires and sends one spike to each neuron σ_{c_5} and σ_{c_7}. After that, neurons σ_{c_6} and σ_{c_7} will fire alternately. The number of spikes in neuron σ_{c_5} increases by 1 per step.

Up to the $t + 3n + 4$ step, neuron σ_{c_5} has 3 spikes. Neurons σ_{c_6} and σ_{c_7} contain 3 and 4 spikes (if n is odd) or 4 and 3 spikes (if n is even), respectively, Neuron σ_{c_5} preferentially fires, which consumes all 3 spikes and sends a spike to neuron σ_{out}. At step $t + 3n + 5$, neuron σ_{out} has 3 spikes. Neuron σ_{out} fires and sends one spike to each neuron σ_{c_5} and σ_{c_7}. At the same time, neuron σ_{out} sends the second spike to the environment. At the next step, when n is an odd number, neurons σ_{c_6} and σ_{c_7} contain 3 and 5 spikes, respectively. Neurons σ_{c_6} and σ_{c_7} cannot fire, and system Π terminates. When n is an even number, the number of spikes in neurons σ_{c_6} and σ_{c_7} is both 4. System Π will select one to fire indefinitely, and terminate at the next step. The times of the first two spikes sent to the environment by system Π are step $t + 2n + 4$ and step $t + 3n + 5$, which indicate that the number of spikes generated by system Π is $(t + 3n + 5) - (t + 2n + 4) - 1 = n$.

Combined with the above description of the modules shown in Figs. 1, 2, and 3, we can see that ASN P system Π has correctly simulated register machine M. Therefore, the inclusion relation $NRE \subseteq N_{gen}ASNPS(cate_2)$ holds, and Theorem 1 is proved.

3.2   ASN P Systems Based on Working in Accepting Mode

Theorem 2. $NRE = N_{acc}^{min}ASNPS(cate_2)$, *where the categories of spiking rules are* (a, a) *and* $(a, \bar{a})$.

Proof. We construct an ASN P system Π' based on the min-sequentiality strategy to simulate a register machine M. ASNPS Π' consists of the addition module of Fig. 4, the subtraction module as shown in Fig. 2 of Theorem 1, and the input module shown in Fig. 5.

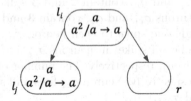

Fig. 4. Deterministic addition module of system Π'

The structure of the deterministic addition module in Fig. 4 is very simple. Neuron σ_{l_i} fires after receiving a spike, and sends a spike to neurons σ_{l_j} and σ_r. In the next step, σ_{l_j} is excited, and the number of spikes in σ_r is increased by 1, that is, the number stored in register r is simulated.

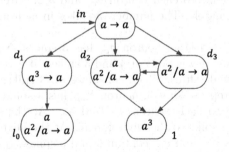

Fig. 5. Input module of system Π'

Initially, neurons σ_{l_0}, σ_{d_1}, σ_{d_2} and σ_1 contain 1, 1, 1, and 3 spikes, respectively. At step t, suppose the input neuron σ_{in} is fired after receiving the first spike from the environment. Neuron σ_{in} sends one spike to each neuron σ_{d_1}, σ_{d_2}, and σ_{d_3}. At step $t+1$, neurons σ_{d_1}, σ_{d_2}, and σ_{d_3} contain 2, 2, and 1 spikes, respectively. Neuron σ_{d_2} fires and sends one spike to each neuron σ_{d_3} and σ_1. At step $t+2$, neuron σ_{d_3} fires and sends one spike to each neuron σ_{d_2} and σ_1. At step $t+3$, neuron σ_{d_2} is the only active neuron in the same state as step $t+1$. After that, neurons σ_{d_2} and σ_{d_3} will fire alternately. The number of spikes in neuron σ_1 increases by 1 per step.

Suppose that neuron σ_{in} receives the second spike at step t. Neurons σ_{in}, σ_{d_1}, and σ_1 contain 1, 2, and $n+2$ spikes, respectively. Neurons σ_{d_2} and σ_{d_3} contain 2 and 1 spikes (if n is odd) or 1 and 2 spikes (if n is even), respectively.

Neuron σ_{in} fires and sends one spike to each neuron σ_{d_1}, σ_{d_2}, and σ_{d_3}. At step $t + n + 1$, neurons σ_{d_1}, σ_{d_2}, and σ_{d_3} contain 3, 3, and 2 spikes or 3, 2, and 3 spikes, respectively. Neurons σ_{d_3} (if n is odd) or neuron σ_{d_2} (if n is even) fires and sends one spike to neuron σ_1. At step $t + n + 2$, neuron σ_1 has $n + 3$ spikes. Neuron σ_{d_1} is the only active neuron, which consumes all three spikes and sends one spike to neuron σ_{l_0}. At step $t + n + 3$, neuron σ_{l_0} fires and starts to simulate instructions l_0 of M. System Π' receives the first two spikes from the environment at step t and step $t+n$, so the number to be received by system Π' is $(t + n) - t = n$.

To sum up, we know that system Π' has correctly simulated the register machine M. Therefore, inclusion relation $NRE \subseteq N_{acc}ASNPS(cate_2)$ holds, and Theorem 2 is proved.

4   ASN P Systems that Convert Spikes into Anti-spikes by Inhibitory Synapses

In this section, no rule can produce an anti-spike in ASN P systems with inhibitory synapses, but there are synapses which transform spikes into anti-spikes. We prove that ASN P systems with inhibitory synapses based on the min-sequentiality strategy are universal as both number generators and acceptors, which are stated as Theorems 3 and 4. In the proof of Theorems 3 and 4, we only provide the modules that the systems consist of, without any explanation about their functioning.

Theorem 3. $NRE = N_{gen}^{min}ASNPS(cate_1, Inh)$, where the category of spiking rules is (a, a).

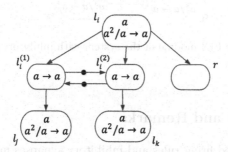

Fig. 6. The ADD module of the system with inhibitory synapses

Proof. The ADD, SUB, FIN modules are shown in Figs. 6, 7 and 8, respectively, where the synapses which convert a into $\bar{a}$ are marked with a "black dot".

Theorem 4. $NRE = N_{acc}^{min}ASNPS(cate_1, Inh)$, where the category of spiking rules is (a, a).

Proof. The INPUT, ADD, SUB modules are shown in Figs. 5, 4 and 7, respectively, where the synapses which change a into $\bar{a}$ are marked with a "black dot".

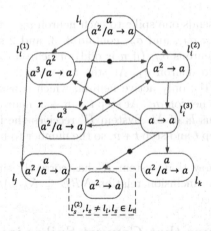

Fig. 7. The SUB module of the system with inhibitory synapses

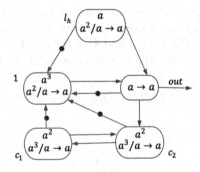

Fig. 8. The FIN module of the system with inhibitory synapses

5 Conclusions and Remarks

In this paper, we used firing rules and inhibitory synapses methods to generate anti-spikes, and constructed corresponding ASN P systems. It was proved that ASN P systems based on the min-sequentiality strategy are universal in both the generating and accepting modes. Only the firing rules of categories (a, a) and $(a, \bar{a})$ were used in the proof of Sect. 3, and only the firing rules of category (a, a) were used in the proof of Sect. 4. No forgetting rules or delays were used.

In [12], the sequentiality of SN P systems is induced by the minimum number of spikes. If at a computation step there is more than one active neuron, then only the neuron(s) containing the minimum number of spikes will be able to fire. There are two sequential strategies: *min-pseudo-sequentiality* (in this case all the neurons containing the minimum number of spikes will fire) and *min-sequentiality* (in this case only one of the neurons containing the minimum number of spikes is chosen non-deterministically). It is interesting to investigate the computational power of ASN P systems based on the min-pseudo-sequentiality.

Acknowledgments. This work was supported by Anhui Provincial Natural Science Foundation (1808085MF173), and Natural Science Key Research Project for Higher Education Institutions of Anhui Province (KJ2017A942).

References

1. Păun, G.: Computing with membranes. J. Comput. Syst. Sci. **61**(1), 108–143 (2000). Oxford University Press, Cambridge (2010)
2. Păun, G.: Membrane Computing - An Introduction. Springer, Berlin (2002). https://doi.org/10.1007/978-3-642-56196-2
3. Ionescu, M., Păun, G., Yokomori, T.: Spiking neural P systems. Fund. Inform. **71**(2–3), 279–308 (2006)
4. Song, T., Pan, L., Păun, G.: Asynchronous spiking neural P systems with local synchronization. Inform. Sci. **219**, 197–207 (2013)
5. Song, T., Pan, L., Păun, G.: Spiking neural P systems with rules on synapses. Theor. Comput. Sci. **529**, 82–95 (2014)
6. Song, B., Pérez-Jiménez, M.J., Pan, L.: An efficient time-free solution to QSAT problem using P systems with proteins on membranes. Inform. Comput. **256**, 287–299 (2017)
7. Song, B., Zhang, C., Pan, L.: Tissue-like P systems with evolutional symport/antiport rules. Inform. Sci. **378**, 177–193 (2017)
8. Wu, T., Zhang, Z., Păun, G., Pan, L.: Cell-like spiking neural P systems. Theor. Comput. Sci. **623**, 180–189 (2016)
9. Wu, T., Zhang, Z., Pan, L.: On languages generated by cell-like spiking neural P systems. IEEE T. NanoBiosci. **15**(5), 455–467 (2016)
10. Pan, L., Păun, G., Zhang, G., Neri, F.: Spiking neural P systems with communication on request. Int. J. Neural Syst. **27**(8), 1750042 (2017). https://doi.org/10.1142/S0129065717500423
11. Pan, L., Wu, T., Su, Y., Vasilakos, A.V.: Cell-like spiking neural P systems with request rules. IEEE T. NanoBiosci. **16**(6), 513–522 (2017)
12. Ibarra, O.H., Păun, A., Rodríguez-Patón, A.: Sequential SNP systems based on min/max spike number. Theor. Comput. Sci. **410**, 2982–2991 (2009)
13. Păun, A., Sidoroff, M.: Sequentiality induced by spike number in SNP systems: small universal machines. In: Gheorghe, M., Păun, G., Rozenberg, G., Salomaa, A., Verlan, S. (eds.) CMC 2011. LNCS, vol. 7184, pp. 333–345. Springer, Heidelberg (2012). https://doi.org/10.1007/978-3-642-28024-5_22
14. Zhang, X., Luo, B., Fang, X., Pan, L.: Sequential spiking neural P systems with exhaustive use of rules. BioSystems **108**(1–3), 52–62 (2012)
15. Zhang, X., Zeng, X., Luo, B., Pan, L.: On some classes of sequential spiking neural P systems. Neural Comput. **26**(5), 974–997 (2014)
16. Jiang, K., Song, T., Pan, L.: Universality of sequential spiking neural P systems based on minimum spike number. Theor. Comput. Sci. **499**, 88–97 (2013)

17. Pan, L., Păun, G.: Spiking neural P systems with anti-spikes. Int. J. Comput. Commun. **4**(3), 273–282 (2009)
18. Rozenberg, G., Salomaa, A. (eds.): Handbook of Formal Languages, vol. 3. Springer, Berlin (1997). https://doi.org/10.1007/978-3-642-59126-6
19. Minsky, M.: Computation - Finite and Infinite Machines. Prentice Hall, Englewood Cliffs (1967)

Solving NP Hard Problems in the Framework of Gene Assembly in Ciliates

Ganbat Ganbaatar, Khuder Altangerel, and Tseren-Onolt Ishdorj[⊠]

Department of Computer Science,
School of Information and Communication Technology,
Mongolia University of Science and Technology,
Ulaanbaatar 21335, Mongolia
{ganbatg,khuder,tseren-onolt}@must.edu.mn

Abstract. Molecular computing [1] is a field with a great potential and fastest growing area of Computer Science. Although some approaches to solve **NP** hard problems were successfully accomplished on DNA strand, only few results of practical use so far. A direction of molecular computing namely Gene assembly in ciliates has been studied actively [3] for a decade. In the present paper, we use a variant of gene assembly computing model of Guided recombination system with only two operations of *insertion* and *deletion* [7] as a decision problem solver. We present our results of parallel algorithms which solve computational hard problems HPP and CSP, in an efficient time.

Keywords: Gene assembly · **NP** hard problems · Parallel complexity

1 Introduction

Computational problems could be classified according to their inherent difficulty and its time necessary to solve the entire problem. In computational complexity theory [2], problems are studied in the next classes: **P** complexity - problems can be solved by a deterministic machine in polynomial time; **NP** complexity - problems can be solved by a non-deterministic machine in polynomial time; **NP**-complete complexity - problems can be solved by a non-deterministic machine in not polynomial time.

Because of the current sequential technology based computing machine's capability, **NP**-complete problems potentially could be solved in time close to exponential order. Currently, scientific community can solve these problems with the construction of parallel computers or supercomputers, which divide and share each part of the problem between all different nodes of the system. This methodology can reduce the computing time close to polynomial, but finally, these solutions require huge number of resources in communications between lots of interconnected nodes, which are normally sequential computers.

In the last three decades, other initiatives have been raised to solve computational hard problems, for example, using organic materials such as DNA

© Springer Nature Singapore Pte Ltd. 2018
J. Qiao et al. (Eds.): BIC-TA 2018, CCIS 951, pp. 107–119, 2018.
https://doi.org/10.1007/978-981-13-2826-8_10

molecules, etc. In 1994, Prof. Adleman [1] did his breakthrough biomolecular experiment to solve an instance of computational hard problem Hamiltonian Path Problem (HPP in short) in an extremely short time. Since then biomolecular and biocellular [10] computing researches have been most active to break Moore's law [9] barrier.

In the field of biomolecular computing, a direction of computing in living cells or gene assembly in ciliates has been studied in [7] and [3], respectively. Ciliates are unicellular organisms with complex nature of the gene rearrangement. Specifically, the DNA in their micronucleus, used in conjugation only, is transformed into shorter molecules used for transcription. This process is called gene assembly. Two main computational models so-called intermolecular model, which allows for operations involving two molecules, while the intramolecular model contains only operations acting on a single molecule have been proposed. Both computing models are proved as powerful as Turing machines, [7] and [5]. Solving computational hard problems by means using these devices has been studied in a number of works, [5,6].

In the present paper, we have explored the efficiency of inter-molecular gene assembly model by solving a couple of well known computational hard problems such as the *Hamiltonian Path Problem*, HPP and the *Closest-string problem*, CSP [8]. The algorithms we used to solve these problems work in a reasonable time by Guided recombination system, [7].

2   Preliminaries and Notation

We assume the reader to be familiar with the basic elements of formal languages, Turing computability [11], computational complexity [2], and molecular computing [3]. We present here only some of the necessary notions and notation.

An *alphabet* is a finite set of symbols (characters), and a word (string) over an alphabet Σ is a finite sequence of letters from Σ; the empty word we denote by λ. The set of all words over an alphabet Σ is denoted by Σ^*. The set of all non-empty words over Σ is denoted as Σ^+, i.e., $\Sigma^+ = \Sigma^* \setminus \{\lambda\}$. The length $|x|$ of a word x is the number of symbols that x contains. The empty word has length 0. If $x = \alpha y \beta$, for some $\alpha, \beta \in \Sigma^*$, we say that y is a *subword* of x and denote it $y \leq x$. The set of all strings x over the alphabet Σ with length $|x| = k$ is denoted Σ^k. We also define circular words over Σ by declaring two words u, v to be equivalent if and only if $u = xy$ and $v = yx$, for some words x, y. We also call u, v conjugates. Then the circular word $\bullet w$ is the equivalence class of w with respect to this relation, for all $w \in \Sigma^*$. The set of all circular words over Σ is denoted by $\Sigma^\bullet$.

A multiset over a finite set V is a mapping $M : V \rightarrow N$, where N is the set of natural numbers. For each $a \in V$ the multiplicity (that is, number of occurrences) of a is the number $M(a)$. The support of a multiset V is the set $supp(M) = \{a \in V \mid M(a) > 0\}$.

A splicing scheme is a pair $R = (\Sigma, \sim)$, where Σ is an alphabet and $\sim$, the pairing relation of the scheme is a relation over $\Sigma^* \Sigma \Sigma^* \times \Sigma^* \Sigma \Sigma^*$. Assume we have two strings x, y and a binary relation between two triples of words $(\alpha, p, \beta) \sim (\alpha', p, \beta')$, such that $x = x'\alpha p\beta x''$ and $y = y'\alpha' p\beta' y''$; then, the strings obtained by the recombination in the context from above are $z_1 = x'\alpha p\beta' y''$ and $z_2 = y'\alpha' p\beta x''$. We consider just the string $z_1 = x'\alpha p\beta' y''$ as the result of the recombination (we call it one-output-recombination), because the string $z_2 = y'\alpha' p\beta x''$, we consider as the result of the one-output-recombination with the respect to the symmetric pair $(\alpha', p, \beta') \sim (\alpha, p, \beta)$.

2.1 NP Hard Problems

In the present work we consider a couple of **NP** hard problems namely *Hamiltonian Path Problem* HPP which is **NP**-complete and *Closest-string problem* CSP. The *Hamiltonian Path Problem* is defined: Let $G = (V, E)$ be a graph with V as the set of nodes and E as the set of edges. G has n nodes. Both nodes b and e are degree one. Then HPP asks whether there is a route in a directed graph from the beginning node b to the ending node e, visiting each node exactly once.

The *Hamming distance* $d(u, v)$ between two strings u and v with $|u| = |v|$ is the number of positions of them in which they differ. Let us define the predicate function $E : A \times A \to \{0, 1\}$ as $E(x, y) = 1$ if and only if $x \neq y$. Thus, we have $d(a, b) = \Sigma_{i=1}^{|a|} E(a_i, b_i)$. For instance, $d(\text{"}CATCC\text{"}, \text{"}CTTGC\text{"}) = 2$.

The *Closest-string problem* is defined as follows: Given a finite set $L = \{w_1, w_2, \ldots, w_n\}$ of strings, with $w_i \in A^m, 1 \leq i \leq n$, find a center-string $c \in A^m$ minimizing l such that, for every string $w_i \in L, d(c, w_i) \leq l$.

Both CSP and HPP are **NP** hard, achieving surprising computational complexity with modest increases in size. This challenge has inspired researchers to broaden the definition of a computer. DNA and/or biological computers such as gene assembly in ciliates have been developed to solve **NP** hard problems.

2.2 Guided Recombination Systems

Let $P = (\Sigma, \sim)$ be a splicing scheme. Then the contextual *intermolecular recombination system* was defined in [7]:

> (del$_p$) $\{x\} \Rightarrow_{\text{del}_p} \{y, z\}$, where $p \in \Sigma, x = upwpv, y = upv, z = \bullet wp$,
> and $u = u'\alpha, w = \beta w' = w''\alpha', v = \beta'v'$, and $(\alpha, p, \beta) \sim (\alpha', p, \beta')$.
> (ins$_p$) $\{x, y\} \Rightarrow_{\text{ins}_p} \{z\}$, where $p \in \Sigma, x = upv, y = \bullet wp, z = upwpv$,
> and $u = u'\alpha, v = \beta v', w = w'\alpha' = \beta'w''$, and $(\alpha, p, \beta) \sim (\alpha', p, \beta')$.

Intermolecular recombination between the linear upv and the circular strand $\bullet wp$ may take place only if the occurrence of p in the linear strand is flanked by α and β and its occurrence in the circular strand is flanked by α' and β'.

Definition 1. *For a splicing scheme* $P = (\Sigma, \sim)$, *we define the set of all contextual gene rearrangement operations under guiding of the splicing scheme* P *as follows* $\tilde{P} = \{\text{ins}_p, \text{del}_p \mid p \in \Sigma\}$.

We now define a guided recombination system that captures the series of dispersed homologous recombination events that take place during scrambled gene rearrangement in ciliates.

Definition 2. *A guided recombination system is a triple* $R = (\Sigma, \sim, t)$ *where* $(\Sigma, \sim)$ *is a splicing scheme, and* $t \in \Sigma^+$ *is a linear string called the axiom.*

A guided recombination system R defines a derivation relation that produces a new multiset from a given multiset of linear and circular strands, as follows. Starting from a "collection" (multiset) of strings with a certain number of available copies of each string, the next multiset is derived from the first one by an intra- or inter-molecular recombination between existing strings. The strands participating in the recombination are "consumed" (their multiplicity decreases by 1) whereas the products of the recombination are added to the multiset (their multiplicity increases by 1).

The guided recombination system is proved to be equivalent to Turing machine.

Theorem 1 ([7]). *Let L be a language over T^* accepted by a Turing machine. Then there exist an alphabet Σ, a sequence $\sigma \in \Sigma^*$, depending on L, and a recombination system R such that a word $w \in L$ iff $\#^6 s_0 w \#^6 \sigma \in L^k(R)$, for some $k \geq 1$.*

We defined acceptance for guided recombination systems in [5] as follows.

Definition 3. *We say a guided recombination system $R = (\Sigma, \sim, t)$ accepts a string w iff there exists $k \geq 1$ such that $w \in L^k(R)$.*

In other words, a guided recombination system accepts a string w if it generates the axiom, when starting with some (sufficient) amount of copies of w. The working places of an applicable operation $\pi \in \tilde{P}$ on a given string is defined.

Definition 4. *Let w be a string and P a splicing scheme. The working places of an operation $\pi \in \tilde{P}$ with respect to a multiset S for w is a set of substrings of w written as $Wp(\pi, w)$ and defined by*

$$Wp(\mathbf{del}_p, w) = \{pw'p \leq w \mid \{upw'pv\} \Rightarrow_{\mathbf{del}_p} \{upv, \bullet w'p\}\},$$
$$Wp(\mathbf{ins}_p, w) = \{upv \leq w \mid \{upv, \bullet w'p\} \Rightarrow_{\mathbf{ins}_p} \{upw'pv\} \text{ for some } \bullet w'p \in S\}.$$

Definition 5. *Let w be a string and P a splicing scheme. The smallest working places of an operation $\pi \in \tilde{P}$ for w is a subset of $Wp(\pi, w)$ defined by $Wp_s(\pi, w) = \{u \in Wp(\pi, w) \mid \text{if } u' \leq u, u' \neq u, \text{then } u' \notin Wp(\pi, w)\}.$*

In each derivation step of a guided recombination system, an operation either `del` or `ins` applies maximally parallel to the pairs of pointers, which are in the splicing relations, in its smallest working places on a linear string [5]. It is possible that two or more smallest working places of different pairs of pointers, to which the operation is applicable in the current step, overlapped or/and include one another. In this case the smallest working places not contradicting each other are chosen non-deterministically for the operation.

We refer reader to [5] for detailed definitions and examples.

Definition 6. *Let R be a guided recombination system. For two multisets S, S' over $\Sigma^* \cup \Sigma^\bullet$, we say that S' derives in non-deterministic, maximally parallel manner from S, denoted $S \Longrightarrow_R^{max} S'$, if one of the following two cases holds:*

(del) there exist $x = u_1 p_1 w_1 p_1 u_2 p_2 w_2 p_2 u_3 \cdots u_n p_n w_n p_n u_{n+1} \in S$,

$y = u_1 p_1 u_2 p_2 \cdots p_n u_{n+1} \in S'$ and $z_i = \bullet p_i w_i \in S'$, for all $1 \leq i \leq n$,

such that $S' = (S \setminus \{x\}) \cup (\{y\} \cup \bigcup_{i=1}^{n} \{z_i\})$ and $p_i w_i p_i \in W p_s(\mathtt{del}_{p_i}, x)$

and for all $1 \leq j \leq n+1$, and $p \in \Sigma$, $W p_s(\mathtt{del}_p, u_j) = \emptyset$.

(ins) there exist $y = \alpha_0 u_1 p_1 u_1' \alpha_1 u_2 p_2 u_2' \alpha_2 \cdots \alpha_{n-1} u_n p_n u_n' \alpha_n \in S$, $z_i = \bullet p_i w_i$,

$z_i \in S', 1 \leq i \leq n$ and $x = u_0 p_1 w_1 p_1 u_2 p_2 w_2 p_2 u_2 \cdots u_{n-1} p_n w_n p_n u_n \in S$,

such that $S' = (S \setminus (\{y\} \cup \bigcup_{i=1}^{n} \{z_i\})) \cup \{x\}$ and $u_i p_i u_i' \in W p_s(\mathtt{ins}_{p_i}, y)$

and for all $0 \leq i \leq n$, and $p \in \Sigma$, $W p_s(\mathtt{ins}_p, \alpha_j) = \emptyset$.

Using the notion of non-deterministic parallel derivation from defined above, we have the corresponding notion of non-deterministic parallel time complexity: each derivation step is replaced by a non-deterministic parallel derivation step.

If in a guided recombination system $R = (\Sigma, \sim, t)$ for some k, those strands which, by repeated recombination with initial and intermediate strands eventually produce the axiom, form the language, then we say that R accepts a string w with non-deterministic maximally parallel time complexity n. Formally, $L^k(R) = \{w \in \Sigma^* \mid \{(w, k)\} \Rightarrow_R^{n, max} T, \text{where } T \subseteq \Sigma^+, t \in T\}$ ((w, k) indicates the fact that the multiplicity of w equals k).

3   Efficiency of Guided Recombination Systems

A possible correspondence between decision problems and languages can be done via an encoding function which transforms an instance of a given decision problem into a string, see, e.g., [7].

Definition 7. *We say that a decision problem X is solved with parallel time complexity $O(t(n))$ by guided recombination systems if there exists a family A of guided recombination systems such that the following condition is satisfied:*

For each instance x of size n of the problem one can effectively construct, with time complexity $O(t(n))$, an encoding $\hat{x}$ and an intermolecular guided recombination system $G(x) \in A$ which accepts $\hat{x}$ with parallel time complexity $O(t(n))$ if and only if the solution to the given instance of the problem is YES.

3.1   Solving the Hamiltonian Path Problem

The Hamiltonian Path Problem, HPP, asks whether there is a route in a directed graph from a beginning node to an ending node, visiting each node exactly once.

Let $G = (V, E)$ be a graph with V as the set of nodes and E as the set of edges. G has n nodes and they are numbered sequentially from 1 to n. The beginning node 1 and the ending node n each have a degree of one.

We now prove a result, namely, that guided recombination systems can uniformly solve HPP with time complexity $O(n \cdot m^2)$ for m edges over n vertices. We say that a solution is uniform if all instances of the same size are solved by the same guided recombination system.

Theorem 2. *For all $m, n \geq 1$, there exists a guided recombination system $G_{(m,n)}$ such that a HPP ϕ with n nodes and m edges is solvable if and only if its encoding $\hat{\phi}$ is accepted by $G_{(m,n)}$. Moreover, $G_{(m,n)}$ and $\hat{\phi}$ can be effectively constructed by a deterministic Turing machine in time $O(n \cdot m)$. Also, $G_{(n,m)}$ decides its acceptance problem in $O(m)$ parallel steps.*

Proof. Let $G = (V, E, b, e)$ be a graph with n vertices and m edges, $V = \{x_1, \ldots, x_n\}$, $E = \{e_1, \ldots, e_m\}$, with a specified beginning vertex b and an ending vertex e. The instance of G (to which the size (m, n) is associated) is encoded in a string, which is built as follows. Each node, x_i, and all its successors, x_j, $((x_i, x_j) \in E, i \neq j)$ are together encoded as a *vertex-string* $v_i = x_i \dagger [y_{i1} y_{i2} \cdots y_{ik_l}]$, $k_l < n$, where $y_{ij} \in \{x_j \mid (x_i, x_j) \in E, i \neq j\}$. Then an instance of HPP (graph) is encoded in a single string: $\phi' = \dagger v_1 \dagger \dagger v_2 \dagger \dagger \cdots \dagger \dagger v_n \dagger$. For each *vertex-string* v_i, we correspond a word $\$_i \langle \dagger \rangle \$_i$. Final *working-place* is constructed by concatenating all vertex-strings, its corresponding words, and some other extra words such as $\$_{n+1} \dagger$ and $\dagger \$_{n+1} \$_{n+2} \$_{n+3}$, and as follows:

$$\hat{\phi} = \$_1 \langle \dagger \rangle \$_1 \$_2 \langle \dagger \rangle \$_2 \cdots \$_n \langle \dagger \rangle \$_n \$_{n+1} \dagger \dagger v_1 \dagger \dagger v_2 \dagger \dagger \cdots \dagger \dagger v_n \dagger \dagger \$_{n+1} \$_{n+2} \$_{n+3}.$$

It is clear that encoding of the string is linear in n. Let us now design a guided recombination system R with input string $\hat{\phi}$ to solve the instance of HPP. $R = (\Sigma, \sim, t)$, where $\Sigma = \{\$_i \mid 1 \leq i \leq n+3\} \cup \{x_i \mid 1 \leq i \leq n\} \cup \{[,], \langle, \rangle\}$, $t = \$_1 \$_2 \cdots \$_{n+2} \$_{n+3}$. The relations $\sim$ over $\Sigma^* \Sigma \Sigma^* \times \Sigma^* \Sigma \Sigma^*$ are defined as follows:

$(\dagger, \dagger, v) \sim (v, \dagger, \dagger)$	(1)	$(\$_1 \langle, \dagger, \lambda) \sim (\langle, \dagger, x_1)$	(5)
$(\$_j \langle, \dagger, \rangle \$_j \$_{j+1}) \sim (v, \dagger, v)$	(2)	$(\langle, \dagger, x_m) \sim (\$_m \langle, \dagger, \lambda)$	(6)
$(\lambda, \$_{m+1}, \dagger^{n+2}) \sim (\dagger^{n+2}, \$_{m+1}, \lambda)$	(3)	$(\lambda, \dagger, [\omega x \psi] \dagger \$_j \$_{j+1}) \sim (], \dagger, \$_j \$_{j+1} \langle \dagger x])$	(7)
$(\langle \dagger, x, \lambda) \sim (\langle \dagger, x, \lambda)$	(4)	$(\langle \dagger x \dagger) \$_{m-1} \$_m \langle \dagger x_m, \dagger, [) \sim (], \dagger, \rangle \$_m \$_{m+1})$	(8)
		$(\dagger), \$_j, \$_{j+1} \$_{j+2} \$_{j+3} \sim (\lambda, \$_j, \dagger)$	(9)

Where $x \in \{x_i \mid 1 \leq i \leq n\}$, $x_1 = b$, $x_n = e$, $v \in \{v_i \mid 1 \leq i \leq n\}$ and $\omega, \psi \in \Sigma^*$. A brief sketch of the algorithm is described in the next steps:

1. All *vertex-strings* are excised from all working places, forming circular strings.
2. All possible paths between n number of nodes are generated by insertion of *vertex-strings* randomly shuffling into auxiliary-words on the working places.
3. Any existing vertex-string repeated in a single working place is eliminated, shortening the working place.
4. Check whether the start node, x_1, and the end node, x_n, are placed in the right positions: $\$_1 \cdots \$_1$ and $\$_n \cdots \$_n$, respectively.

5. For each vertex-string v_j, check whether if its vertex x_j is also contained in the directly previous string v_i's successors of the working place.
6. If all tests (3), (4), (5) have been passed, axiom $\$_1\$_2 \cdots \$_n\$_{n+1}\$_{n+2}\$_{n+3}$ is generated with saying YES.

The solution algorithm scheme mentioned above is illustrated in the diagram Fig. 1. We now prove that R accepts encoding $\hat{\phi}$ if and only if ϕ contains a Hamiltonian path. We will prove it via the following two claims:

Claim 1. If there exists a Hamiltonian path in ϕ, there is a derivation in R that accepts encoding $(\hat{\phi}, k)$ in at most $4n + 5$ parallel steps.

Claim 2. If no Hamiltonian path exists in ϕ, no derivation in R on $(\hat{\phi}, k)$ can yield the axiom t.

Proof of Claim 1: If there exists a solution for ϕ, then there is a sequence $Z = z_1, z_2, \ldots, z_n$, such that $z_j \in V, z_i \neq z_j, 1 \leq i, j \leq n$, and $(z_i, z_{i+1}) \in E, 1 \leq i \leq n - 1$. Let us consider the input string

$$\hat{\phi} = \$_1\langle\dagger\rangle\$_1 \cdots \$_n\langle\dagger\rangle\$_n\$_{n+1}\dagger\dagger v_1\dagger\dagger \cdots \dagger\dagger v_n\dagger\dagger\$_{n+1}\$_{n+2}\$_{n+3}.$$

All vertex-strings from all the copies of working-place are excised by using $\mathtt{del}_\dagger$ in the contexts of relation (1). In fact, we apply n $\mathtt{del}_\dagger$ operations in parallel, giving circular strings $\bullet v_i\dagger$, as well as $\$_1\langle\dagger\rangle\$_1 \cdots \$_n\langle\dagger\rangle\$_n\$_{n+1}\dagger^{n+2}\$_{n+1}\$_{n+2}\$_{n+3}$. We may need to repeat this operation on other copies of $\hat{\phi}$ to obtain sufficient amount of circular strings $\bullet v_i\dagger$, $1 \leq i \leq n$. In the next step, each circular string $\bullet v_i\dagger$ is inserted into auxiliary-words using context of relation (2). This is done in a parallel manner for all vertices. n insertion $\mathtt{ins}_\dagger$ applied, we obtain linear strings as $\$_1\langle\dagger u_1\dagger\rangle\$_1 \cdots \$_n\langle\dagger u_n\dagger\rangle\$_n\$_{n+1}\dagger^{n+2}\$_{n+1}\$_{n+2}\$_{n+3}$, where $u_j \in \{v_i \mid 1 \leq i \leq n\}$, $1 \leq j \leq n$. Meantime, in the context of relation (3) by using $\mathtt{del}_{\$_{n+1}}$, a circular string $\bullet\dagger^{n+2}\$_{n+1}$ is excised: $\$_1\langle\dagger u_1\dagger\rangle\$_1 \cdots \$_n\langle\dagger u_n\dagger\rangle\$_n\$_{n+1}\$_{n+2}\$_{n+3}$. It is important to note that two vertices are linked. This means that a vertex x_r in ith substring $\$_i\langle\dagger x_r\dagger[y_{r1} \cdots y_{rk_r}]\dagger\rangle\$_i$ is contained in the list of linked vertices of the vertex z_{i-1} of $(i-1)$th substring $\$_{i-1}\langle\dagger z_{i-1}\dagger[\omega x_r\psi]\dagger\rangle\$_{i-1}$ as follows:

$$\{\$_1\langle\dagger u_1\dagger\rangle\$_1 \cdots \$_{i-1}\langle\dagger z_{i-1}\dagger[\omega x_r\psi]\dagger\rangle\$_{i-1}\$_i\langle\dagger x_r\dagger[y_{r1} \cdots y_{rk_r}]\dagger\rangle\$_i \cdots$$
$$\$_n\langle\dagger u_n\dagger\rangle\$_n\$_{n+1}\$_{n+2}\$_{n+3}\} \Rightarrow_{\mathtt{del}_\dagger} \{\$_1\langle\dagger u_1\dagger\rangle\$_1 \cdots \$_{i-1}\langle\dagger z_{i-1}\dagger\rangle\$_{i-1}$$
$$\$_i\langle\dagger x_r\dagger[y_{r1} \cdots y_{rk_r}]\dagger\rangle\$_i \cdots \$_n\langle\dagger u_n\dagger\rangle\$_n\$_{n+1}\$_{n+2}\$_{n+3}, \bullet[\omega x_r\psi]\dagger\}.$$

It is clear that neither (4), (5) nor (6) relation are applicable in case there exists a Hamiltonian path as supposed. Now we check whether if all the vertices are formed as a linked list saying that a Hamiltonian path exists. To do that in the context of relation (7) and (8), operation $\mathtt{del}_\dagger$ performs n times, and excises n number of circular strings $\bullet[y_{i1} \cdots y_{ik_i}]\dagger$ thus forming a linear string: $\$_1\langle\dagger z_1\dagger\rangle\$_1 \cdots \$_{n-1}\langle\dagger z_{n-1}\dagger\rangle\$_{n-1}\$_n\langle\dagger z_n\dagger\rangle\$_n\$_{n+1}\$_{n+2}\$_{n+3}$. In the last step of computation, relation (9) is satisfied for deletion. The operation is carried out. So, all substrings containing x_i are excised $\bullet\langle\dagger z_i\dagger\rangle\$_i$, which yields the axiom, and generates as $\$_1\$_2 \cdots \$_n\$_{n+1}\$_{n+2}\$_{n+3}$.

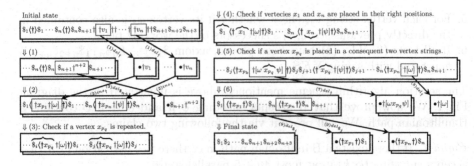

Fig. 1. A graphical illustration of HPP solution scheme.

Proof of Claim 2: In this part of the proof, we show that no axiom is can be generated if no Hamiltonian path exists on the graph. The third step of the proof sketch says that if some vertices appear more than once on the working place, Hamiltonian path does not exist for that working place. If that is the case, substrings between those repeated vertex-strings are eliminated in the context of (4), breaking the working-place on which no further operation applies properly:

$$\{\$_1\langle\dagger u_1\dagger\rangle\$_1\cdots\$_h\langle\dagger x_r\dagger[y_{r1}\cdots y_{rk_r}]\dagger\rangle\$_h\cdots\$_d\langle\dagger x_r\dagger[y_{r1}\cdots y_{rk_r}]\dagger\rangle\$_d\cdots$$
$$\$_n\langle\dagger u_n\dagger\rangle\$_n\$_{n+1}\$_{n+2}\$_{n+3}\}\Rightarrow_{\mathrm{del}_\dagger}\{\$_1\langle\dagger u_1\dagger\rangle\$_1\cdots\$_h\langle\dagger x_r\dagger[y_{r1}\cdots y_{rk_r}]\dagger\rangle$$
$$\$_d\cdots\$_n\langle\dagger u_n\dagger\rangle\$_n\$_{n+1}\$_{n+2}\$_{n+3},\bullet\dagger[y_{r1}\cdots y_{rk_r}]\dagger\rangle\$_h\cdots\$_d\langle\dagger x_r\}.$$

In order for a Hamiltonian path to exist, the beginning vertex, x_1, and the ending vertex, x_n, are supposed to be attached to its corresponding auxiliary-words $\$_1\langle\dagger u_1\dagger\rangle\$_1$ and $\$_n\langle\dagger u_n\dagger\rangle\$_n$, respectively. If that is not the case, relations (5) and (6) allow $\mathrm{del}_\dagger$ operations to be applicable and therefore eliminates the prefix of x_1 and/or suffix of x_n, which again forbids future operations applied to obtain the axiom.

In the next example, because of wrongly placed beginning vertex x_1, deletion operation is performed in the context of relation (5):

$$\{\$_1\langle\dagger x_r\dagger[y_{r1}\cdots y_{rk_r}]\dagger\rangle\$_1\cdots\$_h\langle\dagger x_1\dagger[y_{11}\cdots y_{1k_1}]\dagger\rangle\$_h\cdots$$
$$\$_n\langle\dagger u_n\dagger\rangle\$_n\$_{n+1}\$_{n+2}\$_{n+3}\}\Rightarrow_{\mathrm{del}_\dagger}\{\$_1\langle\dagger x_1\dagger[y_{11}\cdots y_{1k_1}]\dagger\rangle\$_h\cdots$$
$$\$_n\langle\dagger u_n\dagger\rangle\$_n\$_{n+1}\$_{n+2}\$_{n+3},\bullet x_r\dagger[y_{r1}\cdots y_{rk_r}]\dagger\rangle\$_1\cdots\$_h\langle\dagger\}.$$

Similarly, deletion operation will be performed, in case where the ending vertex x_n is placed in a wrong position.

If a link is missing between two vertices, less than $n-1$ edges exist. In the contexts of relations (7) and (8), deletion operation is (mentioned in the *Proof of Claim* 1) applied less than n times because substrings '[ ]' between $\$_j$s remain. There is no relation in which '[ ]' are deleted. It makes no context on the working-place in which relation (9) is satisfied. So, neither insertion nor deletion operations can perform. It claims that the axiom is not generated if no Hamiltonian path exists.

3.2 Solving the Closest String Problem

The Closest-string problem has important applications in computational biology (there is a need to compare and find common features in sequences), as well as in coding theory (the objective is to find sequences of characters that are closest to some given set of strings to determine the best way to encode a set of messages).

An alphabet $A = \{c_1, c_2, \ldots, c_k\}$ is a finite set of elements, called characters, from which strings can be constructed. Each string w is a sequence of m characters $(x_1, \ldots, x_m), x_i \in A$. Given a finite set $W = \{w_1, w_2, \ldots, w_n\}$ of strings, with $w_i \in A^m, 1 \leq i \leq n$, find the center-string $t \in A^m$ and minimize the Hamming distance l such that, for every string $w_i \in W, d(t, w_i) \leq l$.

We now prove a result the guided recombination systems that can uniformly solve CSP with time complexity $O(n \cdot m^3)$.

Theorem 3: *For all $m, n, l \geq 1$, there exists a guided recombination system $Q_{(n,m,l)}$ such that a closest-string problem C with n number of input strings with length m and Hamming distance l is solvable if and only if its encoding ξ is accepted by $Q_{(n,m,l)}$. Moreover, $Q_{(m,m,l)}$ and ξ can be effectively constructed by a deterministic Turing machine in time $O(n \cdot m^2)$. Also, $Q_{(m,n,l)}$ decides its acceptance problem in $O(m)$ parallel steps.*

Proof: Let $C = (A, W, l)$ be a closest-string problem, where $A = \{x_1, \cdots, x_k\}$ is a set of characters and $W = \{w_1, \ldots, w_n\}, w_i = x_{i1} \cdots x_{im}, t_i \in A^m$ is a set of input strings. Also, the Hamming distance is $l \geq 1$. In order to construct a guided recombination system Q which solves CSP, a transformation of the problem CSP to a string is done as shown in the next table. A string a with $|a| = n$ is denoted as $a = a_1 a_2 \cdots a_n = \prod_{i=1}^{n} a_i$.

Input data of C	Encoding of the input in Q
Alphabet: $A = \{x_1, x_2, \cdots, x_k\}$	$A' = \{a_1, a_2, \cdots, a_k\}$, where $a_i = \dagger x_i \dagger$,
Center-string: $u = y_1 y_2 \cdots y_m$	$\rho = \prod_{j=1}^{m} y'_j = \prod_{j=1}^{m}(\#\$_j \dagger \$_j \#)$,
Input strings: $w_i = x_{i1} x_{i2} \ldots x_{im}$	$w'_i = \prod_{j=1}^{m} x'_{ij} = \prod_{j=1}^{m}(\#_i \$_j x_{ij} \$_j \#_i)$,
$W = \{w_i \mid 1 \leq i \leq n\}$	$W' = \{w'_i \mid 1 \leq i \leq n\}$,
Hamming distanse l	$p_i = (0, 1, \ldots, l), p_i = \prod_{j=0}^{l}(\langle \#_i^j \dagger \rangle)$.

For the Hamming distance l, we build a string $p_i = \prod_{j=0}^{l}(\langle \#_i^j \dagger \rangle)$. We attach p_i to each input string as $w'_i p_i$. Then each input string w_i and Hamming distance, l of C, are together encoded in Q as a new input string as $\#_i \dagger w'_i p_i \#_i E$. Moreover, production of all the encoded new input strings form a single string $\sigma = \prod_{i=1}^{n}(E\#_i \dagger w'_i p_i \#_i)$ The production of the encoded characters of the alphabet is denoted as $\mu = \prod_{i=1}^{k} a_i$. Now, the final working place in the new system is constructed as a single *long-string*: $\xi = YE\rho\sigma E\dagger\mu\dagger ES$.

Let us now construct a guided recombination system Q which computes CSP: $Q = (\Sigma, \sim, t)$, where $\Sigma = \{\#_i \mid 1 \leq i \leq n\} \cup \{\$j \mid 1 \leq j \leq m\} \cup A \cup \{Y, E, S, \dagger, \#, \langle, \rangle\}, t = YES$. The relation $\sim$ is defined as follows. Where $1 \leq q \leq l, \psi \in \Sigma^*, \bar{x} \in A \setminus \{x\}, x \in A, 1 \leq i \leq k$.

$$(\dagger, \dagger, x) \sim (x, \dagger, \dagger) \quad (1)$$

$$(\#\$_j, \dagger, \$_j) \sim (x, \dagger, x) \quad (2)$$

$$(\lambda, E, \dagger^{k+2}) \sim (\dagger^{k+2}, E, \lambda) \quad (3)$$

$$(\#\$_j\dagger x\psi, \#_i, \$_j x) \sim (x\$_j\#_i, \#_i, \lambda) \quad (4)$$

$$(\#\$_j\dagger x\psi, \#_i, \$_j\bar{x}) \sim (\bar{x}\$_j, \#_i, \lambda) \quad (5)$$

$$(\#\$_m\dagger x\psi, \#_i, \$_m x) \sim (x\$_m, \#_i, \lambda) \quad (6)$$

$$(\#\$_m\dagger x\psi, \#_i, \#_i\$_m\bar{x}) \sim (\bar{x}\$_m, \#_i, \lambda) \quad (7)$$

$$(E\#_i, \dagger, \#_i^q\langle\rangle) \sim (\langle\#_i^q, \dagger, \rangle) \quad (8)$$

$$(\lambda, E, \#_i\dagger) \sim (\#_i, E, \lambda) \quad (9)$$

$$(Y, E, \#) \sim (\#, E, S) \quad (10)$$

$$\xi = YE\prod_{j=1}^{m}(\#\$_j\dagger\$_j\#)\prod_{i=1}^{n}(E\#_i\dagger w_i'p_i\#_i)E\dagger\prod_{i=1}^{k}\dagger x_i\dagger\dagger ES.$$

A sketch of the non-deterministic algorithm to solve CSP can be described:

1. All alphabetic characters, $a_i = \dagger x_i\dagger$, are excised from the working place, ξ, in a single step forming circular strings, relation (1).

2. Just excised $\bullet x_i\dagger$ strings are inserted in parallel, but are non-deterministically chosen into center-string ρ. We suppose m number of circular strings have been inserted, forming $y_1'y_2'\cdots y_m'$, which we are looking for.

3. Count the Hamming distance between the center-string and each input-string, $d(\rho, w_i')$. It compares each substring $\#\$_j\dagger y_i\dagger\$_j\#$ for characters of center-string with corresponding substring of each input-string w_i'. Delete substring between the underlined pointers $\underline{\#}_i\cdots\underline{\#}_i\#_i$ if those substrings are the same. Otherwise, delete between underlined pointers $\underline{\#}_i\cdots\#_i\underline{\#}_i$, in the context of relation (4)–(7).

4. Count the Hamming distances in Step 3 for each input string. Check if each one is less than the input Hamming distance, $d(\rho, w_i') \leq l, 1 \leq i \leq n$. We check whether if the counted Hamming distance $\#_i\dagger\#_i^k, 1 \leq k \leq m$, for each input string, is found in the encoded Hamming distance p_i, attached to input strings w_i' in the context of relation (8). If that is the case, n number of substrings $E\#_i\rangle, 1 \leq i \leq n$, should be found, which can be checked by relation (9), giving n number of circular strings of type $\bullet E\#_i\dagger\rangle v, v \in \Sigma^*$ which are excised.

5. If the previous step has been accomplished successfully, forming n number of circular strings and only the center-string ρ, remains at the working place, the axiom is generated (10), with the result that there is a solution for CSP.

Due to the page number limit, we had a short explanation of the proof idea. For the sake of the readers, we give an example, below, of how the algorithm works:

Example 1: Let $C = (A, W, l)$ be a CSP. Where $A = \{x, y, z\}, W = \{xyz, zyz, xzz\}$ and the Hamming distance $l = 2$.

Following the proof sketch steps (1)–(5), and the relations (1)–(10), we find a center-string yyz which satisfies the requirement of the Hamming distance of

$d(yyz, w_i) \leq 2$. Each input string $w_i \in W$ is encoded as w_i', and the Hamming distance $l = 2$ is encoded in p_i as follows:

$$w_i' = \#_i \$_1 x \$_1 \#_i \#_i \$_2 y \$_2 \#_i \#_i \$_3 z \$_3 \#_i, p_i = \langle\dagger\rangle\langle\#_i\dagger\rangle\langle\#_i\#_i\dagger\rangle, 1 \leq i \leq 3.$$

We consider the input string $\sigma = E\#_1\dagger w_1' p_1 \#_1 E\#_2\dagger w_2' p_2 \#_2 E\#_3\dagger w_3' p_3 \#_3$. Then working place ξ is constructed following the transformation rule mentioned in Sect. 3: $\xi = YE\#\$_1\dagger\$_1\#\#\$_2\dagger\$_2\#\#\$_3\dagger\$_3\#\sigma E\dagger\dagger x\dagger\dagger y\dagger\dagger z\dagger\dagger ES$. It is important to note that *insertion* and *deletion* operations apply maximally in a parallel manner for the smallest working places. Definitions 5 and 6, through the example.

1. Deletion $\mathtt{del}_\dagger$ applied in the context of relation (1) excising circular strings

$$\{YE\#\$_1\dagger\$_1\#\#\$_2\dagger\$_2\#\#\$_3\dagger\$_3\#\sigma E\dagger\dagger x\dagger\dagger y\dagger\dagger z\dagger\dagger ES\} \Rightarrow_{\mathtt{del}_\dagger}$$
$$\{YE\#\$_1\dagger\$_1\#\#\$_2\dagger\$_2\#\#\$_3\dagger\$_3\#\sigma E\dagger^5 ES, \bullet x\dagger, \bullet y\dagger, \bullet z\dagger\}.$$

2. By insertion operation $\mathtt{ins}_\dagger$, the excised circular strings are inserted into the center-string ρ in relation (2), in the meantime, substring $\dagger^5 E$ is deleted by means relation (3): $\xi = YE\#\$_1\dagger y\dagger\$_1\#\#\$_2\dagger y\dagger\$_2\#\#\$_3\dagger z\dagger\$_3\#\sigma ES$.

3. In the contexts of relations (4), (5), (6), and (7), the Hamming distances for each input strings are counted. Let us start with the relations (4) and (6),

$$\{YE\#\$_1\dagger y\dagger\$_1\#\#\$_2\dagger y\dagger\$_2\#\#\$_3\dagger z\dagger\$_3\#E\#_1\dagger\#_1\$_1 x\$_1\#_1\#_1\$_2 y\$_2\#_1$$
$$\#_1\$_3 z\$_3\#_1 p_1\#_1 E\#_2\dagger\#_2\$_1 z\$_1\#_2\#_2\$_2 y\$_2\#_2\#_2\$_3 z\$_3\#_2 p_2\#_2$$
$$E\#_3\dagger\#_3\$_1 x\$_1\#_3\#_3\$_2 z\$_2\#_3\#_3\$_3 z\$_3\#_3 p_3\#_3 ES\} \Rightarrow_{\mathtt{del}_{\#_i}}$$
$$\{YE\#\$_1\dagger y\dagger\$_1\#\#\$_2\dagger y\dagger\$_2\#\#\$_3\dagger z\dagger\$_3\#E\#_1\dagger\#_1\$_1 x\$_1\#_1 p_1\#_1 E\#_2$$
$$\dagger\#_2\$_1 z\$_1\#_2 p_2\#_2 E\#_3\dagger\#_3\$_1 x\$_1\#_3\#_3\$_2 z\$_2\#_3 p_3\#_3 ES,$$
$$\bullet\#_1\$_2 y\$_2\#_1, \bullet\#_2\$_2 y\$_2\#_2, \bullet\#_1\$_3 z\$_3\#_1, \bullet\#_2\$_3 z\$_3\#_2, \bullet\#_3\$_3 z\$_3\#_3\}.$$

The next operations apply in the contexts of relations (5) and (7),

$$\{YE\#\$_1\dagger y\dagger\$_1\#\#\$_2\dagger y\dagger\$_2\#\#\$_3\dagger z\dagger\$_3\#E\#_1\dagger\#_1\$_1 x\$_1\#_1 p_1\#_1$$
$$E\#_2\dagger\#_2\$_1 z\$_1\#_2 p_2\#_2 E\#_3\dagger\#_3\$_1 x\$_1\#_3\#_3\$_2 z\$_2\#_3 p_3\#_3 ES\} \Rightarrow_{\mathtt{del}_{\#_i}}$$
$$\{YE\#\$_1\dagger y\dagger\$_1\#\#\$_2\dagger y\dagger\$_2\#\#\$_3\dagger z\dagger\$_3\#E\#_1\dagger\underline{\#_1 p_1}\#_1 E\#_2\dagger\underline{\#_2 p_2}\#_2$$
$$E\#_3\dagger\underline{\#_3\#_3 p_3}\#_3 ES, \bullet\$_1 x\$_1\#_1, \bullet\$_1 z\$_1\#_2, \bullet\$_1 x\$_1\#_3, \bullet\$_2 z\$_2\#_3\}.$$

The Hamming distances for each input string and center-string are counted as $d(yyz, xyz) = 1$, $d(yyz, zyz) = 1$, and $d(yyz, xzz) = 2$, respectively, which we see from the number of $\#_i$s in underlined counter substrings ($\underline{\#_1 p_1}$, $\underline{\#_2 p_2}$, $\underline{\#_3\#_3 p_3}$) above.

4. Now, the Hamming distances that were counted, 1, 1, and 2, are checked to see whether if they are less than the given Hamming distance, $l = 2$. In relation (8), the counter strings ($\underline{\#_1 p_1}$, $\underline{\#_2 p_2}$, $\underline{\#_3\#_3 p_3}$) are checked if they

occur in the Hamming distance encoding p_1, p_2, and p_3 respectively.

$\{YE\#\$_1\dagger y\dagger\$_1\#\#\$_2\dagger y\dagger\$_2\#\#\$_3\dagger z\dagger\$_3\#E\#_1\dagger\#_1\langle\dagger\rangle\langle\#_1\dagger\rangle\langle\#_1\#_1\dagger\rangle\#_1$
$E\#_2\dagger\#_2\langle\dagger\rangle\langle\#_2\dagger\rangle\langle\#_2\#_2\dagger\rangle\#_2E\#_3\dagger\#_3\#_3\langle\dagger\rangle\langle\#_3\dagger\rangle\langle\#_3\#_3\dagger\rangle\#_3ES\} \Rightarrow_{del_\dagger}$
$\{YE\#\$_1\dagger y\dagger\$_1\#\#\$_2\dagger y\dagger\$_2\#\#\$_3\dagger z\dagger\$_3\#E\#_1\dagger\rangle\langle\#_1\#_1\dagger\rangle\#_1E\#_2\dagger\rangle\langle\#_2\#_2$
$\dagger\rangle\#_2E\#_3\rangle\#_3ES, \bullet\#_1\langle\dagger\rangle\langle\#_1\dagger, \bullet\#_2\langle\dagger\rangle\langle\#_2\dagger, \bullet\dagger\#_3\#_3\langle\dagger\rangle\langle\#_3\dagger\rangle\langle\#_3\#_3\dagger\}.$

As the result of $del_\dagger$, substrings $E\#_1\dagger\rangle$, $E\#_2\dagger\rangle$, and $E\#_3\dagger\rangle$ are found, which says that all Hamming distances 1, 1, and 2 are $d(yyz, w_i) \leq 2$. Then in relation (9), those circular strings contain the substrings $E\#_i\dagger\rangle$, which are excised by del_E.

$\{YE\#\$_1\dagger y\dagger\$_1\#\#\$_2\dagger y\dagger\$_2\#\#\$_3\dagger z\dagger\$_3\#E\#_1\dagger\rangle\langle\#_1\#_1\dagger\rangle\#_1E\#_2\dagger\rangle\langle\#_2\#_2$
$\dagger\rangle\#_2E\#_3\rangle\#_3ES\} \Rightarrow_{del_E} \{YE\#\$_1\dagger y\dagger\$_1\#\#\$_2\dagger y\dagger\$_2\#\#\$_3\dagger z\dagger\$_3\#ES,$
$\bullet\#_1\dagger\rangle\langle\#_1\#_1\dagger\rangle\#_1E, \bullet\#_2\dagger\rangle\langle\#_2\#_2\dagger\rangle\#_2E, \bullet\#_3\rangle\#_3E\}.$

5. Since all the distances are less than 2, in the context of relation (10), deletion operation del_E is applied, resulting in the axiom *YES*.

$\{YE\#\$_1\dagger y\dagger\$_1\#\#\$_2\dagger y\dagger\$_2\#\#\$_3\dagger z\dagger\$_3\#ES\} \Rightarrow_{del_E}$
$\{YES, \bullet\#\$_1\dagger y\dagger\$_1\#\#\$_2\dagger y\dagger\$_2\#\#\$_3\dagger z\dagger\$_3\#E\}.$

4   Final Remarks

We have presented that computationally hard problems, including *graph* HPP, *string* CSP, and *Boolean logic* SAT [5], can be solved uniformly by the intermolecular gene assembly computing model [7] in an efficient time complexity. This is a proof that other computational hard problems can be attacked such a way. The **PSPACE** problems also have been investigated in [12]. The intramolecular gene assembly model has been proved to be Turing universal [4], but has not got any efficient solution to **NP** and **PSPACE** hard problems.

Acknowledgments. This work has been supported by The Science and Technology Foundation of Mongolia, Research Grants ShUSS-2018/04 and MOST-MECSS2017001. Our thanks to Professor Erdenebaatar Altangerel for his continues support and three anonymous referees for all the suggestions which improved this paper.

References

1. Adleman, L.M.: Molecular computation of solutions to combinatorial problems. Science **266**, 1021–1024 (1994)
2. Carmosino, M.L., Gao, J., Impagliazzo, R., Mihajlin, I., Paturi, R., Schneider, S.: Nondeterministic extensions of the strong exponential time hypothesis and consequences for non-reducibility. In: Proceedings of the 2016 ACM Conference on Innovations in Theoretical Computer Science, Cambridge, Massachusetts, USA, pp. 261–270 (2016)

3. Ehrenfeucht, A., Harju, T., Petre, I., Prescott, D.M., Rozenberg, G.: Computation in Living Cells: Gene Assembly in Ciliates. Springer, Heidelberg (2003). https://doi.org/10.1007/978-3-662-06371-2
4. Ishdorj, T.-O., Petre, I.: Computing through gene assembly. In: Akl, S.G., Calude, C.S., Dinneen, M.J., Rozenberg, G., Wareham, H.T. (eds.) UC 2007. LNCS, vol. 4618, pp. 91–105. Springer, Heidelberg (2007). https://doi.org/10.1007/978-3-540-73554-0_10
5. Ishdorj, T.-O., Loos, R., Petre, I.: Computational efficiency of intermolecular gene assembly. Fundam. Inform. **84**(3–4), 363–373 (2008)
6. Ishdorj, T.-O., Petre, I., Rogojin, V.: Computational power of intramolecular gene assembly. Int. J. Found. Comput. Sci. **18**(5), 1123–1136 (2007)
7. Kari, L., Landweber, L.F.: Computational power of gene rearrangement. In: Winfree, E., Gifford, D.K. (eds.) Proceedings of DNA Based Computers, pp. 207–216. American Mathematical Society (1999)
8. Ma, B., Sun, X.: More efficient algorithms for closest string and substring problems. In: Vingron, M., Wong, L. (eds.) RECOMB 2008. LNCS, vol. 4955, pp. 396–409. Springer, Heidelberg (2008). https://doi.org/10.1007/978-3-540-78839-3_33
9. Moore, E.G.: Cramming more components onto integrated circuits. Electronics **38**(8), 114–118 (1965)
10. Păun, G.: Membrane Computing - An Introduction. Springer, Berlin (2002). https://doi.org/10.1007/978-3-642-56196-2
11. Rozenberg, G., Salomaa, A. (eds.): Handbook of Formal Languages. Springer, Berlin (1997). https://doi.org/10.1007/978-3-642-59126-6
12. Zerjatke, T., Sturm, M.: Solving a PSPACE-complete problem by gene assembly. J. Log. Comput. **23**(4), 897–908 (2013)

A Study of Industrial Structure Optimization Under Economy, Employment and Environment Constraints Based on MOEA

Ruozhu Zhang[✉]

College of Urban and Environmental Sciences,
Peking University, Beijing 100871, China
ruozhuzhang@foxmail.com

Abstract. How to optimize industrial structure to meet coordinated development of economy, society and environment has always been a key issue in research and management. In this paper, an optimization model based on MOEA is proposed to adjust industrial structure to meet the increasing demand. Increasing economy and employment along with reducing carbon emission are the objectives of model, which is solved by one of MOEA, NSGA-II. Jiangsu-Zhejiang-Shanghai is studied as the case. The Pareto fronts of solutions show good convergence and robustness. The optimization methods are compared with each other from operation efficiency and significance which turns out NSAG-II has advantages in studying this issue. Results are also analyzed in different perspective and discussed under Flexible Optimization. The idea of applying MOEA in industrial structure optimization provides a scientific way to promote economic growth and employment along with answering green call for low-carbon life.

1 Introduction

The coordinated development of economy, society and environment emphasizes that economic growth and social development should keep pace with environmental sustainability. How to deal with the relationship among them is a common challenge for its complexity [1]. Research shows that they are all closely related to industrial structure [2]. By industrial structure optimization, economic benefits can be enhanced [3] and social progress can be promoted [4] along with reducing energy conservation [5]. How to deal with optimization, especially in developed regions, has always been a key issue in regional scientific research and government macroeconomic management [6–8].

Industrial structure optimization refers to the rationalization and the upgrading of industrial structure in process of meeting growing needs of society [9,10]. Scholars applied many methods in study of industrial structure optimization, such as the principal component analysis [11], analytic hierarchy process [12], gray relational analysis [13], and data envelopment analysis [14]. Compared

J. Qiao et al. (Eds.): BIC-TA 2018, CCIS 951, pp. 120–132, 2018.
https://doi.org/10.1007/978-981-13-2826-8_11

with above methods, Multi-Objective Evolutionary Algorithm (MOEA) could be a better choice due to its efficiency and science. MOEA is based on evolutionary algorithm which aims to solve multi-objective optimization problem in many areas [15]. Recently some researchers proposed supplementary evolutionary algorithm such as RdEA algorithm [16] and RSEA algorithm [17,18], which enhance the competitiveness of the proposed algorithm in solving many-objective optimization problems. In the application of algorithms, many complex multi-objective optimization problems are well solved. Xu Gongyue [19] applied MOEA to optimize the face-shovel excavator attachment. Wang Xuli [20] used MOEA to optimize transmission planning for the first time. The simulation results illustrated that NSGA-II had better convergence and flexibility which is effective to measure the performance of different objective functions. Zhangrui [21] used MOEA to provide scientific decision for joint operation of cascade reservoirs in Jinsha River. Jianya [22] utilized MOEA for remote sensing image processing. In sum, MOEA has advantages in solving multi-objective problems.

To the author's knowledge, there are few woks focused on multi-objective optimization of regional industrial structure under the economic-social-environmental constraints. Current works are mainly single-objective optimization which focuses on maximizing economic growth or reducing energy conservation. Meanwhile, the existing research optimization is rigid, which takes less consideration of adjusting the optimization results according to economic and social changes. In order to overcome the shortcomings in the current research, a multi-objective optimization model of industrial structure for growth, employment and low-carbon is proposed and NSGA-II is used to solve this problem in this paper.

2   Mathematical Model

2.1   Multi-objective Optimization Model

The multi-objective optimization model to solve the industrial structure adjustment problem under economy, employment and environment constraints is introduced in this section. Firstly, the dimensionless industry sectors x_i are chosen as the design parameters. Secondly, three contradictory goals are utilized as the optimized objectives: to maximize increasing economic growth Y_1, to maximize increasing employment Y_2, and to minimize carbon emissions Y_3. Then the constrains are: industrial added value, employed population, carbon emissions and the thresholds for the employment population, technical input, education investment, and government support investment. The details of the design parameters, constraints, objectives and the settings for NSGA-II are listed in Table.1. In the table, R_0, W_0, and C_0 are the original values of industrial added value, employed population, and carbon emissions, respectively. W_h, T_h, E_h and G_h are the thresholds for the employment population, technical input, education investment, and government support investment, respectively.

Table 1. Optimization model

	Objectives		
Parameter	Y_1	Y_2	Y_3
Target	Max	Max	Min
	Constraints				
Parameter	R	W	C	T	E	G
Constraints	$[0.8R_0,1.2R_0]$	$[W_0,$ Wh] W_h	R_0	E_h	G_h
	Design Parameters	
Parameter	X_i, $i{\in}[1,25]$	
Range	$[0.5,1.5]$	
	NSGA-II parameters settings		
Population size	Number of gernations	crossover probability	crossover distribution index
120	100	0.9	10

2.2   Optimization Solution Algorithm

Nondominated Sorting Genetic Algorithm (NSGA) and the improved version (NSGA-II) are classified as one kind of evolutionary algorithms based on Pareto, of which the main feature is to integrate the Pareto optimal concept into the selection mechanism. The core idea is to divide the evolutionary group into several layers according to the dominant relationship. The first layer is defined as a set of independent individuals of the evolutionary group, while the second one is a set of nondominated individuals after removing the first layer from the evolutionary group. The next layers are obtained like this and so on. The select operation first considers to select the individuals from the first layer according to some strategy, and then select the individuals in the second layer and so on. The operation will end when the group size meets requirements of the new evolutionary group.

NSGA-II is chosen as the optimization algorithm to solve the optimization model. As an improved version of the Nondominated Sorting Genetic Algorithm (NSGA), NSGA-II was proposed by K. Deb and S. Agrawl. It has alleviated all three of the main criticisms of NSGA: high computational complexity of non-dominated sorting, lack of elitism and the need for specifying the sharing parameter. The crowding algorithms and elitism strategy are used to replace the shared function of original algorithm. The improvements help to reduce the computational complexity and time. Two operators are defined to implement this algorithm: density estimation operator (∇_ρ) and crowd comparison operator ($\geq n$). ∇_ρ is used to estimate the population density around one individual, and $\geq n$ is used to form a uniformly distributed Pareto front. The algorithm flow chart is shown in Fig. 1.

2.3   Model Solution

2.3.1   Design Parameters

In this paper, the industrial structure of Jiangsu, Zhejiang and Shanghai are chosen as the test cases and optimized to study the model. 25 industry sectors

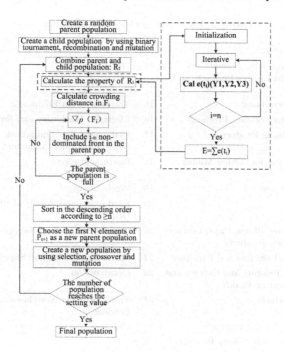

Fig. 1. Flow chart of the NSGA-II

are chosen as design parameters. The data of employees and energy consumption in Jiangsu-Zhejiang-Shanghai comes from the statistical yearbooks of these three regions in 2013. We find that the data in the yearbook is not meticulously categorized which does not correspond to the classification of input-output tables. The industrial Classification in this paper mainly references to Input-Output Table Sector Classification Explanation of China in 2012 and National Economic Industry Classification (GB/T 4754-2002). The industry in the input-output table is firstly subdivided and merged into 25 sectors, and then the data is collected as shown in Table 2. As the input-output table in 2012 is the latest phase of the input-output table, the data is used in this paper.

2.3.2 Targets Calculation Method

The input-output method was first proposed by W. Leontief, an American economist. He established corresponding mathematical models, which meant to reflect the relationships among various sectors (industries) of the economic system. Renowned economists such as Chanari and Kutznitz, applied the input-output method to the study of industrial economy [20]. Since the 1960s, this method has been widely applied to structural analysis and interaction analysis among different regions, and also widely used in the research on resource utilization and environmental protection [21].

Table 2. Industrial sectors classification

No.	Industrial sectors	No.	Industrial sectors
1	Agriculture, Forestry, Animal Husbandry and Fishery Products and Services	14	Metal Products
2	Coal Mining Products	15	Transportation Equipment
3	Oil and Gas Exploration Products	16	Electrical Machinery and Equipment
4	Metal Ore Mining Products	17	Communication Equipment, Computers, and Other Electronic Equipment
5	Non-metallic Pre and Other Mining Products	18	Instrumentation
6	Food and Tobacco	19	Waste Scrap
7	Textiles	20	Production and Supply of Electricity and Heat
8	Textile, Apparel, Shoes, Caps, Leather Down and Their Products	21	Gas Production and Supply
9	Woodworking Products and Furniture	22	Water Production and Supply
10	Papermaking Printing and Culture and Education Sporting Goods	23	Construction
11	Chemical Products	24	Transportation, Warehousing and Postal Services
12	Non-metallic Mineral Products	25	Culture, Sports, and Entertainment
13	Metal Smelting and Rolling Products		

The detailed derivation of the input-output model can be found in Ref. [22]. The basic relationship between input and output is:

$$AX + Y = X \tag{1}$$

Where: X is the total output column vector, Y is the final demand column vector, $A = [\alpha_{ij}]$ is the direct consumption coefficient matrix. $\alpha_{ij} = x_{ij}/x_j$ represents the required input of the ith industry for the unit output of the jth industry.

$$X = (1 - A)^{-1}Y \tag{2}$$

Where $(1 - A)^{-1} = [b^{ij}]$ is the inverse matrix of Leontief.

The direct increase coefficient $R^* = [R^*]$ is defined as $R_d^* = R_d^*/x_i$. R_d is the direct increase value of the ith industry, and x is the total output of the ith industry. The direct employment coefficient W^*, the technology input coefficient T^*, the education input coefficient E^* and he government support coefficient G^* are similarly defined in this paper.

3   Results and Discussion

3.1   Analysis of Convergence and Robustness

3.1.1   Convergence Analysis

To investigate whether the parameter settings of NSGA-II in Table 1 are appropriate or not, the data of Jiangsu is taken as the test case. The initial values of

x_i are all set as 1 and the results of the last 2000 steps of the three objective are plotted in Fig. 2. It can be seen that upper limits of Y_1/Y_{1_0} and Y_2/Y_{2_0} are stable as these two are maximum functions. While the lower limit of Y_3/Y_{3_0} is stable and converged as it is a minimum function. The settings of NSGA-II will be used hereinafter.

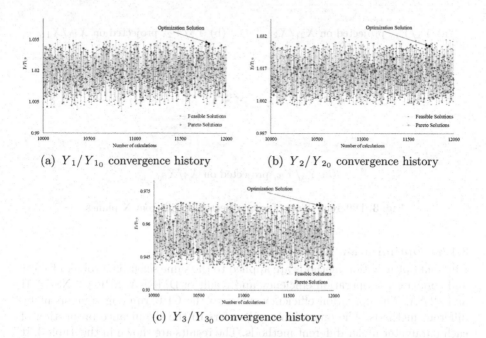

(a) Y_1/Y_{1_0} convergence history   (b) Y_2/Y_{2_0} convergence history

(c) Y_3/Y_{3_0} convergence history

Fig. 2. The convergence process of different optimization goals

3.1.2   Robustness Analysis

Robustness refers to the ability outputs to maintain certain properties under some perturbations of input parameters. In this paper, robustness is used to describe the effect of different initial values on the optimization results. The data of Jiangsu is again taken as the test example. The parameters of NSGA-II are the same in Table 1 and initial values of X_i are randomly setting for three times. The Pareto solutions in these cases of the three dimensionless objectives are projected on three different inputs planes of X_{21}/X_{21_0}, X_{11}/X_{11_0} and X_9/X_{9_0} in Fig. 3.

As can be found from the figure, (1) the variation trend of each objective function is consistent with the positive and negative characteristics of the coefficients. (2) The projections of the different cases on the input planes are almost the same, which reflects that the different initial values will not significantly affect the Pareto fronts.

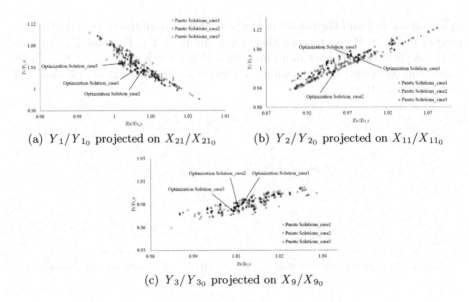

(a) Y_1/Y_{1_0} projected on X_{21}/X_{21_0} (b) Y_2/Y_{2_0} projected on X_{11}/X_{11_0}

(c) Y_3/Y_{3_0} projected on X_9/X_{9_0}

Fig. 3. Different Pareto front projected on different X planes

3.1.3 Optimization Algorithm Comparison

Different optimization methods are applied to the same scientific problem to test and compare the operation efficiency and result of DMOEA, SPRA2, NSGA-II and PESA. The operation efficiency refers to the CPU running time spent by different methods. The operation result refers to the significance proportion of each parameter under different methods. The results are shown in the Table 3. It can be concluded from the table that NSGA-II is the fastest in the same situation, followed by SPEA2 and DMOEA, and the slowest is PESA. The proportion of significance is the same as above. It turns out NSGA-II has advantages in studying this issue.

Table 3. Optimization algorithms comparison

	DMOE	SPEA2	NSGA-II	PESA
Operation time(second)	231.94	111.06	43.03	305.91
Operation result(%)	46.15	57.69	93.59	26.92

3.2 Optimization Results Comparison

3.2.1 Vertical Perspective: Differences Between Current Situation and Targets

Since the 21st century, the industrial structure of Jiangsu-Zhejiang-Shanghai has undergone a marked adjustment, bringing significant economic-social-environmental benefits to the region. According to the optimization result (Table 4), the design parameters, 25 sectors, are divided into five types based on the natural breakpoint classification: Continuous Enhancement (8.4%–12.0%), Moderate Enhancement (3.9%–8.4%), Stability (−2.9%–3.9%), Moderate Reduction (−6.7%–3.9%), Continuous Reduction (−12%–9.7%). 17 sectors in Jiangsu can be expanded, 11 of which are Continuous Enhancement and 4 are Moderate Enhancement and 2 are Continuously Reduced. In Zhejiang 19 sectors can be expanded and 6 need to be reduced. In Shanghai 21 sectors can be expanded and 4 need to be reduced.

After the adjustment of industrial structure according to the optimization result, there is still room for increasing of 3%–4% in economic growth and 2%–4% in employment and a 3% decrease in carbon emissions.

Table 4. Sectoral distribution of industrial structure optimization

Optimization type	Interval	Jiangsu	Zhejiang	Shanghai
Continuous enhancement	8.4%–12%	1, 2, 3, 5,6,7, 8, 12, 17, 19, 24	1, 2, 5, 6, 7, 8, 9, 10, 12, 15, 16, 17, 22, 24, 25	1, 2, 3, 6, 7, 17, 19, 24
Moderate enhancement	3.9%–8.4%	10, 23, 25, 18	5, 8, 9	10, 12, 15, 22
Stability	−2.9%–3.9%	4, 9, 11, 14, 15, 16, 18, 21, 22	4, 14, 19, 21, 23	11, 16, 18, 21, 23, 25
Moderate reduction	−6.7%–3.9%	–	3, 11	4, 14
Continuous reduction	−12%–9.7%	13, 20	13, 20	13, 20

3.2.2 Lateral Perspective: Differences Between Regions

In this section, these three regions are compared with each other to reflect the difference of industrial structure adjustment.

From the optimization results of Jiangsu, it can be seen that there are 8 sectors needing be reduced. They are Metal Ore Mining Products, Woodworking Products and Furniture, Chemical Products, Metal Smelting and Rolling Products, Electrical Machinery and Equipment, Production and Supply of Electricity and Heat, Water Production and Supply, in which Production and Supply of Electricity and Heat has reduced by 12.0%. Other industries has increased by a certain percentage. This industrial structure optimization will achieve the target, namely Jiangsu's total output will increase by 3.42% and employment scale will increase by 3.14%, and carbon emissions will decrease by 3.04%.

From the optimization results of Zhejiang, it can be seen that compared with the adjustment of Jiangsu, Zhejiang has only 6 sectors needing to be reduced. They are Oil and Gas Exploration Products, Chemical Products, Metal Smelting and Rolling Products, Production and Supply of Electricity and Heat, Gas Production and Supply, Water Production and Supply. After optimization, Zhejiang's total output will rise by 3.46% and employment will expand by 4.11% and carbon emissions will decrease by 3.25%. This shows that the status quo of

128   R. Zhang

industrial structure of Zhejiang has more room for improvement than Jiangsu and Shanghai.

From the optimization results of Shanghai, it can be seen that Metal Ore Mining Products, Metal Smelting and Rolling Products, Metal Products, Production and Supply of Electricity and Heat have to be adjusted downward. After optimization, Shanghai's economic growth will increase by 3.32% and employment will increase by 2.63% and carbon emissions will decrease by 3.01%. This shows that the industrial structure of Shanghai is more balanced than that of Jiangsu and Zhejiang. It has a relatively high level of employment and a low degree of carbonization. In the practice, Shanghai can further balance the weights of the three objectives and seek a more reasonable direction of industrial adjustment.

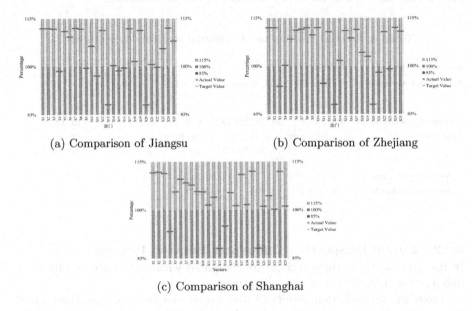

(a) Comparison of Jiangsu

(b) Comparison of Zhejiang

(c) Comparison of Shanghai

Fig. 4. Comparison of the actual value and target value of industrial structure

Comparing the results of industrial optimization in three regions, as shown in Fig. 4 and Table 5, it can be seen that the heavy industry manufacturing sectors such as Metal Smelting and Rolling Products, Production and Supply of Electricity and Heat, have negative effects on the economy-society-environment. The next step in the development of these energy-intensive manufacturing sectors may be industrial upgrading and transformation to increase energy efficiency and reduce environmental pollution. At the same time, the optimized structure shows that the proportion of Agriculture, Forestry, Animal Husbandry and Fishery Products and Services need to increase. This is in contradiction with the land use structure in Jiangsu-Zhejiang-Shanghai. Therefore, the direction of the next improvement of the model can be related to the actual land use status and other factors. Through adjustment of industrial structure, we achieved the goal of maintaining economic growth, expanding employment and reducing carbon emissions. We can promote the efficient and green development of Jiangsu-Zhejiang-Shanghai economies, fully verifying that the optimization of industrial structure has a significant positive effect on the economy-society-environment. It is an important way to achieve the goal of supply-side structural reform.

Table 5. Optimized objectives values

	Y_1/Y_0	Y_2/Y_0	Y_3/Y_0
Jiangsu	1.0342*	1.0314	0.9696*
Zhejiang	1.0346*	1.0411	0.9675
Shanghai	1.0332*	1.0263	0.9699*

4   Flexible Optimization

All along, there is a rigid problem in industrial structure optimization. If the relevant government departments adjust industrial structure in a high frequency, that will no doubt affect the stability of industrial structure and restrict the development of society, economy and environment. Wallace, Mike [23] proposed Flexible Optimization to expand the strain range of urban space and resist more external shocks. Under the comprehensive influence of multiple factors (show in Fig. 5), the dual roles of push and pull have become increasingly prominent. Rigid optimization is difficult to meet the needs of development, and the elastic optimization of the industrial structure has been driven. The concept of Flexible Optimization is proposed in this paper to improve the ability of the industrial structure to respond to uncertain socio-economic development and challenges [24].

Flexible Optimization is achieved followed these steps: (1) determine the design parameters, objective functions, and constraints. (2) Set the priority of the objective function, such as the first-level optimal target, the second-level optimal target, etc. (3) Carry out the multi-objective optimization based on the priority of the objective function; (4) Analysis results. The optimization of industrial structure of Jiangsu-Zhejiang-Shanghai in 2012 are taken as the case to study in this paper. The three objectives, growth, employment, and low-carbon, are prioritized as the first-level respectively to achieve Flexible Optimization in these areas.

From Flexible Optimization results of industrial structure (Table 6), it can be seen that there are differences in the optimization results under the guidance of different optimization-level goals. To a certain extent, these differences are the flexibility of industrial structure optimization. If low-carbon is defined as the first-class optimal target, the carbon emission reduction in Jiangsu-Zhejiang-Shanghai can reach about 6%. There is a 3% adjustment space compared with the reduction of carbon emissions in the comprehensive optimization. This 3%

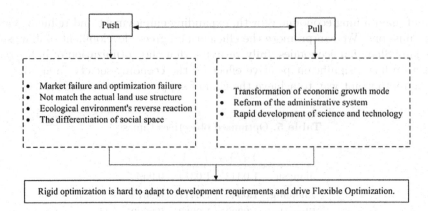

Fig. 5. Feasibility analysis of Flexible Optimization

Table 6. Flexible Optimization of industrial structure

		Comprehensive optimization	First-class optimal target		
			Economic growth	Employment	Low-carbon
Jiangsu	$\Delta Y_1/Y_0$	3.42%	3.53%*	3.43%*	0.23%
	$\Delta Y_2/Y_0$	3.14%	2.85%*	3.15%	0.01%*
	$\Delta Y_3/Y_0$	−3.04%	−3.07%*	-3.01%*	−6.04%*
Zhejiang	$\Delta Y_1/Y_0$	3.46%	3.56%*	3.44%*	0.02%*
	$\Delta Y_2/Y_0$	4.11%	3.92%	4.18%	0.53%
	$\Delta Y_3/Y_0$	−3.25%	−3.05%*	−3.13%	−6.35%
Shanghai	$\Delta Y_1/Y_0$	3.33%	3.39%	3.42%*	0.15%
	$\Delta Y_2/Y_0$	2.63%	2.69%*	2.72%	0.00%
	$\Delta Y_3/Y_0$	−3.01%	−3.05%*	−3.02%*	−5.98%*

Note: * indicates significant at 1% level, and no * indicates significant at 5% level.

can be seen as a decline in the carbon emissions obtained by sacrificing some of the economic growth and employment opportunities. It can also be seen as a hidden carbon emission regulation interval in the face of changes in economic growth patterns, changes in the administrative system, and other socio-economic developments. Flexible Optimization is of great significance in the implementation and management of government departments.

5   Conclusion and Further Discussion

MOEA is applied to optimize the industrial structure in this paper. An optimization model is established to solve the problem of industrial structure adjustment by taking Jiangsu-Zhejiang-Shanghai as the example. 25 different industry sectors are chosen as the design parameters under several certain constraints like industrial added value, employed population, carbon emissions and the thresholds for the employment population, technical input, education investment, and government support investment. Three objectives, including maximizing increasing economic growth and employment and minimizing carbon emissions, are solved by NSGA-II of MOEA. The solution turns out that all the three objectives are optimized in the model. Meanwhile the convergence and robustness of the solution are satisfied. The solutions can converge to almost the same results under different initial input values.

In addition to verifying that MOEA can satisfactorily solve the multi-objective problem, the optimization results show that the existing industrial structure in Jiangsu-Zhejiang-Shanghai is relatively reasonable, but there is still some room for optimization. Specifically, 3%−4% increment of the economic growth, 2%−4% increment of employment scale, and 3% reduction of the carbon emissions can be achieved by the following adjustment: reduce the ratio of resources and energy-dependent sectors, such as Metal Ore Mining Products, Metal Smelting and Rolling Products, Production and Supply of Electricity and Heat, along with increase the ratio of service sectors like Transportation, Warehousing and Postal Services.

Under the concept of Flexible Optimization proposed in this paper, different objectives are given first-level priority to analysis the results. The optimization results can be occurred in a certain interval, which is a buffer against uncertainty and can effectively improve the efficiency of administrative departments, save social resources and form a more reasonable social division of labor.

The idea of applying MOEA in industrial structure of developed regions in China optimization proposed in this paper provides a scientific way to promote economic growth and the employment along with answering the green call for low-carbon development.

References

1. Qin, Q., Li, C.: Analysis on the differences of innovation capabilities of China's high-tech industries based on the Theil entropy and Gini coefficient. AR. Res. Dev. **32**(5), 46–50 (2013)
2. Xiao, H.: Industries strucrure and CO2 emissions in China: evidence from province level data. AR. Res. Dev. **30**(5), 84–92 (2011)
3. Wuyi, Z.: Research on the application of dynamic input-output optimization model. Syst. Eng. **2**, 31–39 (1985)
4. Haiying, W., Suocheng, D., Fei, Y.: Study on the optimizes and adjustment of industry structure subjected to the water resource in drainage areas of the Yellow River. China Popul. Resour. Environ. **13**(2), 82–86 (2003)
5. Yijun, Y., Wei, D.: Research on the optimization of China's industrial structure under the constraint of energy conservation and emission reduction. J. Ind. Technological. Econ. **8**, 53–55 (2008)
6. Dexu, H., Yao, Z.: Effects of China's industrial structure adjustment, object of industrial optimization and policy supporting system. China Ind. Econ. **242**(5), 46–52 (2008)
7. Yan, X., Yao, Y.: Analysis on characteristics of development and spatial distribution of the tertiary sector in Guangzhou. Econ. Geogr. **17**(2), 41–48 (1997)

8. Wang, H., Gu, J.: Effect of industry structure change to regional economic growth: taking Guangxi as an example. AR. Res. Dev. **33**(5), 27–33 (2014)

9. Gang, C., Zheng, R., Yu, D.: An empirical study on the effects of industrial structure on economic growth and fluctuations in China. Econ. Res. J. **46**(5), 4–16 (2011)

10. Chong, P., Chunfeng, L., Li, Y.: Study on the dynamic effects of industrial structure on economic fluctuation. Ind. Econ. Res. **64**(3), 91–100 (2013)

11. Velzquez, E.: An input-output model of water consumption: analyzing inter-sectoral water relationships in Andalusia. Ecol. Econ. **56**, 226–240 (2006)

12. Deb, K., Agrawal, S., Pratap, A., Meyarivan, T.: A fast elitist non-dominated sorting genetic algorithm for multi-objective optimization: NSGA-II. In: Schoenauer, M., et al. (eds.) PPSN 2000. LNCS, vol. 1917, pp. 849–858. Springer, Heidelberg (2000). https://doi.org/10.1007/3-540-45356-3_83

13. Wallace, M.: Flexible planning: a key to the management of multiple innovations. Educ. Manag. Adm. **19**(3), 180–192 (1991)

14. Wei, L., Guicai, L., Yin, X.: Towards muti-dimensional flexibility: the evolution of Shenzhen flexible planning. Urban Plan. Forum **1**, 63–70 (2012)

15. Zheng, J.: Multi-objective Evolutionary Algorithm and its Application. Science Press, Henderson (2007)

16. Xu, G., Ding, H., Sun, Y.: Optimization of face-shovel excavator's attachment based on improved NSGA-II. J. Mech. Eng. **52**(21), 35–43 (2006)

17. Wang, X., Li, S., Chen, H.: Multi-objective and multi-district transmission planning based on NSGA-II and cooperative co-evolutionary algorithm. Proc. CSEE **26**(12), 11–15 (2006)

18. Zhang, R., Zhang, L., Wang, X.: Model and application of multi-objective beneficial dispatch for cascade reservoirs in Jinsha River. J. Sichuan Univ. (Eng. Sci. Ed.) **48**(4), 32–37 (2016)

19. Gong, J., Zhong, Y.: Survey of intelligent optical remote sensing image processing. J. Remote. Sens. **20**(5), 733–747 (2016)

20. Rodrik, D.: One Economics, Many Recipes. Princeton University Press, Princeton (2007)

21. Fan, J., Cao, Z., Liu, X.: On the industrial spatial structure of the Western China. Prog. Geogr. **21**(4), 289–301 (2002)

22. Wenqing, P.: An optimized model for China industry adjustment based on sustainable development. Syst. Eng.-Theory Pract. **22**(7), 23–29 (2002)

DNA Strand Displacement
Based on Nicking Enzyme
for DNA Logic Circuits

Gaiying Wang[1], Zhiyu Wang[2], Xiaoshan Yan[1], and Xiangrong Liu[1(✉)]

[1] School of Information Science and Technology, Xiamen University,
Xiamen 361005, Fujian, China
xrliu@xmu.edu.cn
[2] Key Laboratory of Image Information Processing and Intelligent Control
of Education Ministry of China, School of Automation,
Huazhong University of Science and Technology, Wuhan 430074, Hubei, China
wangzhiyu0471@hust.edu.cn

Abstract. DNA strand displacement is widely used in the construction
of DNA molecule computational models. In this work, nicking enzyme
is used as the input of the logic calculation model for it can cut one
strand of a double-stranded DNA at a specific recognition nucleotide
sequences known as a restriction site. Based on this, a variety of logic
gates are designed and implemented, and a multi-person voting circuit
is constructed.

Keywords: DNA strand displacement · Nicking enzyme
Logic circuit · Multi-person voting circuit

In February 2016, *Nature* Magazine's cover article announced that Moore's
Law was about to expire [1]. In the face of massive information processing,
the pressure of traditional electronic computers has doubled, and people have
gradually turned their attention to new types of computing. DNA computing
is based on the concept that data can be encoded as biological molecules and
can be mathematically or logically manipulated through molecular biological tool
transformations. Due to the natural features such as specificity, high parallelism,
and minimality of DNA molecules, the powerful parallel computing capabilities
and data storage capabilities in the information storage and processing process
[2], DNA molecules have attracted scholars' extensive attention.

In traditional computer designs, microprocessors use logic gates to construct
electronic circuits that can perform Boolean math logic. Similarly, in DNA computing, the use of DNA structures to construct basic logic gates is a prerequisite
for designing molecular computers [3]. DNA is the material basis of biological
inheritance. An important feature of DNA is that DNA strands can form het-
erozygous double-stranded double helixes through base pairing and pairing is
highly specific. This specificity is one of the cornerstones of DNA that can be
used to build logic gates.

© Springer Nature Singapore Pte Ltd. 2018
J. Qiao et al. (Eds.): BIC-TA 2018, CCIS 951, pp. 133–141, 2018.
https://doi.org/10.1007/978-981-13-2826-8_12

Toehold-mediated DNA strand displacement has been widely used to construct DNA devices, including sensors [4–7], machines [8–11], and circuits [12–17], because it enables dynamic control of the displacement reactions. DNA strand displacement technology is the use of molecular hybridization system tends to stabilize the energy level characteristics, by adding different lengths and sequences of input strand to induce the strand displacement reaction, and thus release the process of another DNA strand.

In the traditional strand displacement systems, the toehold and the branch migration domain are covalently connected. However, in large systems with various dynamic interactions, it may be desirable to have a method that allows the reaction to be controlled by adjusting the toehold without having to re-synthesize the DNA sequences. In fact, many efforts have been made to extend the toolbox of the strand displacement techniques, including remote toehold [18], combinatorial displacement [19] and allosteric DNA toehold [20]. Although it is possible to precisely control the toehold by careful design, the pre-exposed toehold is an essential prerequisite to activate further cascade reactions. Therefore, it would be great advantageous to be able to control the generation and removal of toehold dynamically.

In this work, nicking enzymes were introduced to control the generation and removal of toehold in the DNA strand displacement reaction, thereby controlling the entire reaction process. An enzyme-assisted mechanism has been proposed to manipulate DNA strand displacements, where specific nicking enzymes can be programmed to generate or remove pre-designed toehold regions. To prove this mechanism, a protein/DNA-based Boolean operating system that can respond to nicking enzyme regulation was constructed, and the effects of toehold length and other parameters on the circuit were explored to optimize the control effect. To test the scalability of this mechanism for complex applications, a multi-person voting circuit was built based on the toehold-regulating operation system. Through polyacrylamide gel electrophoresis (PAGE), this strategy was proved to be reliable, robust, and qualified to build more complex DNA circuitry.

The experimental details are as follows. Materials. DNA oligonucleotides were PAGE gel-purified and purchased from Sangon Biotech Co., Ltd.(Shanghai, China). Nicking enzyme Nt.BbvCI, Nt.BsmAI, Nb.BtsI and CutSmart buffer were purchased from New England Biolabs Inc. The DNA sequences used in the experiment were designed using NUPACK based on the desired DNA structure. DNA assembly. DNA structures X-Y, B-C, M-N, R and P were generated by mixing corresponding single strands with equal concentrations in $1 \times$ Cutsmart buffer and each of the final concentrations of X-Y, B-C, M-N, R and P and G was $4\,\mu M$. The sample was annealed in a polymerase chain reaction (PCR) thermal cycler to control the temperature from $95\,°C$ to $25\,°C$, wherein $95\,°C$ was maintained for $5\,min$, and the following $65\,°C$, $50\,°C$, $37\,°C$, and $25\,°C$ were maintained for $30\,min$. Catalysis of nicking enzymes. The catalysis of nicking enzymes was performed in $1 \times$ Cutsmart buffer at $25\,°C$. For YES, NOT, AND and NOR gate, the catalysis time was $1\,h$. After catalysis, it took $4\,h$ for strand displacement. Native polyacrylamide gel electrophoresis. Samples were run on

12% native polyacrylamide gel in $1 \times$ TAE buffer at 85 V for 2 h at 4 °C. Gels were scanned with a Fluorchem FC2 gel scanner.

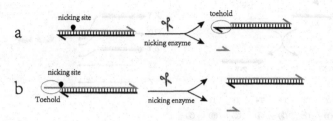

Fig. 1. (a) Toehold generation mechanism. The arrowhead indicates the 3' end. The DNA double strands are completely complementary, the nicking enzyme introduces a nick in the double strand and the left strand dissociates from the double strand to form a toehold. (b) Toehold removal mechanism. The DNA double-stranded structure has a toehold region and is cut after the introduction of the nicking enzyme.

Two toehold-regulating mechanisms are used to control the strand displacement process, including the toehold generation mechanism and the toehold removal mechanism. Nicking enzyme recognizes a specific nucleotide sequence and cleave one strand of double-stranded DNA to create a nick. As shown in Fig. 1a, the starting DNA substrate is completely double-stranded and there is no exposed toehold, so DNA strand displacement cannot occur. When a nick is introduced near the left edge of the orange strand by nicking enzyme, the left portion of the orange strand tends to dissociate from the duplex, resulting in a single-stranded toehold region. The binding capacity of the cleaved region is too weak to remain connected, thereby starting the predesigned downstream strand displacement. The key feature of the toehold generation mechanism is that the new toehold can only be produced after enzyme cleavage and initiate the pre-programmed strand displacement reaction. The toehold removal mechanism is shown in Fig. 1b. The nicking enzyme recognizes and cuts the designated site, eliminating the toehold. In this way, the process of strand displacement is suppressed. Unlike conventional allosteric genetic regulation methods, the nicking enzyme-assisted mechanism proposed here links protein enzymes with specific DNA reactants, thereby enabling enzymes regulation of the entire DNA circuits.

To study the toehold generation mechanism, a basic DNA circuit was produced by using an enzymatic cleavage reaction and DNA strand displacement (Fig. 2a). The circuit consists of three parts, including double-stranded X-Y, single-stranded Z, and nicking enzyme Nt.BbvCI. The strand X is completely complementary to the strand Y, and the strand Z and Y are completely complementary too. In order to clearly observe the experimental results through PAGE, the poly-T was added to both ends of X when the DNA strand was designed. Strand Z cannot displace X without the addition of the nicking enzyme Nt.BbvCI because Y and X are fully complementary. However, once the nicking enzyme Nt.BbvCI is added, the nicking enzyme Nt.BbvCI specifically recognizes the

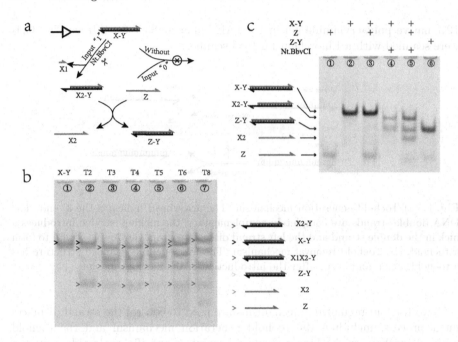

Fig. 2. (a) YES gate schematic based on the toehold generation mechanism. Double-stranded Z-Y and single-stranded X2 are only produced when Nt.BbvCI is present. (b) The effect of the nicking site on the YES gate, where Tx represents the x-nt toehold. (c) Results of the Non-denaturing gel electrophoresis of the YES gate. When Nt.BbvCI was not added, no strand displacement occurred (lane 3), and strand replacement occurred when added (lane 5).

nicking site on the strand X and produces a toehold, and then Z replaces X to form a Z-Y double-stranded structure and a single-stranded X2. Therefore, downstream strand displacement can be triggered only if the nicking enzyme Nt.BbvCI produces a DNA toehold. The toehold generation mechanism consists of two separate steps: In the first step, the nicking enzyme acts to introduce a nick and the toehold is exposed, and in the second step, the strand displacement reaction occurs via the exposed toehold. The length of the toehold is an important parameter for optimizing the reaction and it is necessary to consider the effect on both reaction steps at the same time. Specifically, after the nicking enzyme is introduced, a too long toehold may hinder the separation of the toehold-cover domain, and a too short toehold may reduce the strand displacement efficiency. Therefore, we have designed toeholds of different lengths to screen out the most reactive structures. As shown in the Fig. 2b lane 5, the reaction results are best when the toehold length is 5-nt. As expected, when the toehold length was designed to be 2nt (lane 2), the reaction efficiency decreased sharply and most of the double-stranded X-Y remained undivided. Therefore, the nicking enzyme recognition site is too close to the double-stranded edge to prevent cleavage of the nicking enzyme. When the length of the toehold is increased to 8nt, the strand displacement was also suppressed (lane 6,7), and it is likely that the longer toehold coverage domain was still associated with the complementary strand after cleavage. Therefore, in order to obtain an efficient strand displacement reaction to form a cascade circuit, we chose a 5nt toehold for further experiments.

In order to study the toehold generation mechanism more intuitively, we used PAGE for further experiments. In Fig. 2c lane 3, no strand displacement occurred in the absence of Nt.BbvCI, leaving substrate X-Y and displacement strand Z unreacted. In lane 5, after adding Nt.BbvCI, strand X is cut into X1 and X2, and then X1 is dissociated from X2 to generate toehold on the Y strand. Then, strand Z is bound to X2-Y through the resulting toehold. As expected, a newly generated Z-Y band was clearly observed on lane 5, and no obvious signal was detected in lane 3. This reaction process can be viewed as a protein input YES logic gate. Here, the input is the nicking enzyme Nt.BbvCI and the output is double-stranded Z-Y. In the present of the displacement strand Z the addition of nicking enzyme Nt.BbvCI (input "0") results in a Z-Y double-stranded structure. Without a nicking enzyme (input "0") no Z-Y double-stranded structure is produced.

Using the same method, we constructed the NOT logic gate based on the toehold removal mechanism as shown in Fig. 3a. In the NOT gate, the output always remains the opposite of the input, for example, the True input results in False output. Therefore, if there is a nicking enzyme, we can define the input as True and False if the nicking enzyme does not exist. The output is defined as True if a specific new structure is observed, as False if no specific new structure can be observed. Figure 3b is the corresponding gel electrophoresis result, which is consistent with expectations. Here, Nt.BbvCI is considered as the input of the circuit, and the double-stranded structure B-A is output. As shown in lane 6, when the nicking enzyme Nt.BbvCI was not added, the newly generated B-A

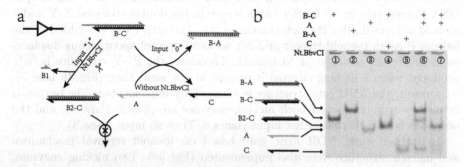

Fig. 3. (a) Schematic of a NOT gate based on the toehold removal mechanism. Double-stranded B-A and single-stranded C are only produced when Nt.BbvCI is not added. (b) Results of Non-denaturing gel electrophoresis of the NOT gate. Strand displacement occurred without addition of Nt.BbvCI (lane 6). In the presence of the nicking enzyme, the toehold will be removed from B-C, thus no further reaction (lane7).

and C bands could be observed obviously. In lane 7, almost no new structure double-stranded B-A was formed after the addition of the nicking enzyme. This is because the toe sequence B1 exposed in the double-stranded structure B-C has been cut off to form the structure B2-C, and this structure cannot undergo strand displacement reaction with the single strand A.

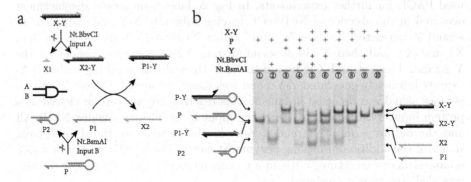

Fig. 4. (a) AND gate schematic based on toehold removal mechanism and toehold generation mechanism. Double-stranded P1-Y and single-stranded X2 are only produced when Nt.BbvCI and Nt.BsmAI are added simultaneously. (b) Results of Non-denaturing gel electrophoresis of the AND gate. Strand displacement occurs when both nicking enzymes are added at the same time (lane 5) and nothing else (lanes 6, 7, 8).

Next, we built a dual-input logic gate. An AND logic gate was first implemented based on the toehold generation mechanism and hairpin DNA structure as shown in Fig. 4a. In the AND gate circuit, the output is generated only when two inputs exist simultaneously. In the experiment, two different nicking enzymes, Nt.BbvCI and Nt.BsmAI were used to act on duplex X-Y and hairpin DNA P, respectively. Nt.BbvCI forms a nick in the double-stranded X-Y and a toehold is formed after the detachment of X1. The area P1 is embedded in the hairpin P as an toehold trigger of X2-Y so as to prevent spontaneous displacement before the addition of Nt.BsmAI. Therefore, the P1-Y structure is only produced when a nicking enzyme is present at the same time (Fig. 4b lane 5). As a result, the AND gate structure is successfully implemented. The output is defined as true only when both nicking enzymes are present (lane 5), and the output is false if there is either input (lanes 6, 7) or no input (lane 8).

In further work, NOR logic gate based on toehold removal mechanism and hairpin structure were also implemented (Fig. 5a). Two nicking enzymes, Nt.BbvCI and Nb.BtsI, act on two substrates, double-stranded M-N and hairpin R, respectively. When no nicking enzyme is added during the reaction, the two substrates will undergo branch migration directly. Based on the exposed toehold, the double-stranded M-N opens the hairpin structure R and complement each other to form a structure with a higher energy level. Next, the other side of the hairpin R will be joined with the detached single-stranded N to form

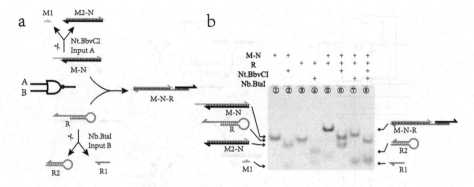

Fig. 5. (a) NOR gate schematic based on toehold removal mechanism and toehold generation mechanism. Triple-stranded M-N-R is formed only when no enzyme is added. (b) Results of Non-denaturing gel electrophoresis of the NOR gate. Strand displacement occurs without any nicking enzyme addition (lane 5) and no strand displacement occurs when at least any of the nicking enzymes are added (lanes 6, 7, 8).

a three-strand structure. The structure M-N-R is considered to be the output of NOR gate circuit. If nicking enzyme Nt.BbvCI is added during the reaction, the toehold M1 originally exposed by the double-stranded M-N will be removed, destroying the downstream reaction conditions (Fig. 5a lane 6,8). Similarly, if Nb.BtsI is added, duplex structure R will be cut and lose the original exposed toehold (Fig. 5a lane 7,8). Therefore, the addition of any nicking enzyme will destroy the necessary conditions for the reaction to take place. Here, the NOR gate is realized.

In order to test the scalability of the system, we designed a multi-input majority voting circuit based on the designed logic gates, in which both the toehold generation mechanism and the toehold removal mechanism were used (Fig. 6a). In this system, three different nicking enzymes were used as system inputs, including the nicking enzymes Nt.BbvCI, Nt.BsmAI, Nb.BtsI. Any one of the double-stranded structures O1-Y, P1-Y, O1-P2 is regarded as an output. If the system has only one input or no input, no output will be generated. When the system has two and three inputs, the condition that triggers the downstream reaction will be met, resulting in an output. Take the input A (Nt.BbvCI) and input B (Nt.BsmAI) as an example, when A and B are both "1", that is, when adding two enzymes at the same time. Nt.BbvCI will cut the X-Y structure to generate X2-Y, Nt.BsmAI will cut the hairpin structure P to generate a single strand P1 that can be replaced with the X2-Y to generate a new structure P1-Y, thus obtaining the expected output. The construction of this complex circuit shows that an enzyme-assisted toehold regulation mechanism can be used to realize high efficiency multi-enzyme circuits reliably.

Here, we have established an enzyme-assisted mechanism to manipulate DNA strand displacements. We nicking enzymes to generate or remove toehold regions that are critical for the strand displacement reaction. It turns out that this reg-

140   G. Wang et al.

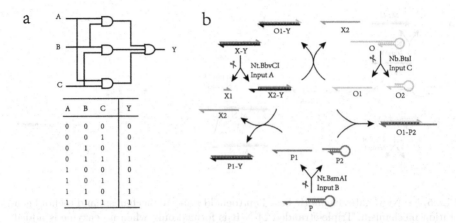

A	B	C	Y
0	0	0	0
0	0	1	0
0	1	0	0
0	1	1	1
1	0	0	0
1	0	1	1
1	1	0	1
1	1	1	1

Fig. 6. (a) Multi-person voting circuit schematic. The output will only be true when the system has two or three inputs. (b) Concrete implementation of a multi-person voting circuit, using both toehold generation mechanisms and toehold removal mechanisms. Only when two or more nicking enzymes are input at the same time will the next-level reaction be triggered, strand displacement will occur, new structures will be generated, and the output of our design will be obtained.

ulation mechanism can be used to build several basic DNA logic circuits. In order to achieve the best performance of the system, we also explored the effect of different toehold lengths. Finally, a multi-person voting circuit was built to test the scalability of logic gates. Compared with previous DNA-based toehold regulatory methods, such as remote toehold, combinatorial displacement and A-toehold, this strategy does not require the initial exposure of the toehold area, thereby greatly reducing the possibility of crosstalk and leakage. Taking into account the above characteristics, this mechanism has many potential applications in the construction of dynamic DNA nanodevices and can be used to construct more complex structures and assemble large programmable structures. Therefore, it is worth noting that the complex nicking enzyme-assisted circuit provides a potential approach for constructing more complex and diverse DNA computing models that can be applied to sensitive and multiple biological sensing and detection.

Acknowledgments. The work was supported by the National Natural Science Foundation of China (Grant Nos. 61472333, 61772441, 61472335), Project of marine economic innovation and development in Xiamen (No. 16PFW034SF02), Natural Science Foundation of the Higher Education Institutions of Fujian Province (No. JZ160400), Natural Science Foundation of Fujian Province (No. 2017J01099), President Fund of Xiamen University (No. 20720170054).

References

1. Waldrop, M.: The chips are down for Moore's law. Nature **530**, 144–147 (2016)
2. Saxena, P., Singh, A., Lalwani, S.: Use of DNA for computation, storage and cryptography of information. Int. J. Innov. Technol. Explor. Eng. (IJITEE) **3**(2), 2278–3075 (2013)
3. Reif, J.H.: Successes and challenges. Science **296**(5567), 478–479 (2002)
4. You, M., Zhu, G., Chen, T., et al.: Programmable and multiparameter DNA-based logic platform for cancer recognition and targeted therapy. J. Am. Chem. Soc. **137**(2), 667–674 (2014)
5. Yang, X., Tang, Y., Mason, S.D., et al.: Enzyme-powered three-dimensional DNA nanomachine for DNA walking, payload release, and biosensing. ACS Nano **10**(2), 2324–2330 (2016)
6. Tang, Y., Lin, Y., Yang, X., et al.: Universal strategy to engineer catalytic DNA hairpin assemblies for protein analysis. Anal. Chem. **87**(16), 8063–8066 (2015)
7. Li, B., Jiang, Y., Chen, X., et al.: Probing spatial organization of DNA strands using enzyme-free hairpin assembly circuits. J. Am. Chem. Soc. **134**(34), 13918–13921 (2012)
8. Peng, H., Li, X.F., Zhang, H., et al.: A microRNA-initiated DNAzyme motor operating in living cells. Nat. Commun. **8**, 14378 (2017)
9. Liu, M., Fu, J., Hejesen, C., et al.: A DNA tweezer-actuated enzyme nanoreactor. Nat. Commun. **4**, 2127 (2013)
10. Gu, H., Chao, J., Xiao, S.J., et al.: A proximity-based programmable DNA nanoscale assembly line. Nature **465**(7295), 202 (2010)
11. Yurke, B., Turberfield, A.J., Mills Jr., A.P., et al.: A DNA-fuelled molecular machine made of DNA. Nature **406**(6796), 605 (2000)
12. Li, W., Zhang, F., Yan, H., et al.: DNA based arithmetic function: a half adder based on DNA strand displacement. Nanoscale **8**(6), 3775–3784 (2016)
13. Li, W., Yang, Y., Yan, H., et al.: Three-input majority logic gate and multiple input logic circuit based on DNA strand displacement. Nano Lett. **13**(6), 2980–2988 (2013)
14. Zhu, J., Zhang, L., Li, T., et al.: Enzyme-free unlabeled DNA logic circuits based on toehold-mediated strand displacement and split G-quadruplex enhanced fluorescence. Adv. Mater. **25**(17), 2440–2444 (2013)
15. Qian, L., Winfree, E.: Scaling up digital circuit computation with DNA strand displacement cascades. Science **332**(6034), 1196–1201 (2011)
16. Qian, L., Winfree, E., Bruck, J.: Neural network computation with DNA strand displacement cascades. Nature **475**(7356), 368 (2011)
17. Seelig, G., Soloveichik, D., Zhang, D.Y., et al.: Enzyme-free nucleic acid logic circuits. Science **314**(5805), 1585–1588 (2006)
18. Genot, A.J., Zhang, D.Y., Bath, J.: Remote toehold: a mechanism for flexible control of DNA hybridization kinetics. J. Am. Chem. Soc. **133**(7), 2177–2182 (2011)
19. Genot, A.J., Bath, J., Turberfield, A.J.: Combinatorial displacement of DNA strands: application to matrix multiplication and weighted sums. Angew. Chem. Int. Ed. **52**(4), 1189–1192 (2013)
20. Yang, X., Tang, Y., Traynor, S.M., et al.: Regulation of DNA strand displacement using an allosteric DNA toehold. J. Am. Chem. Soc. **138**(42), 14076–14082 (2016)

Motor Imaginary EEG Signals Classification Based on Deep Learning

Haoran Wang[1](✉) and Wanying Mo[2]

[1] School of Automation, Harbin Engineering University, Harbin 150000, China
4546672830qq.com
[2] College of Computer Science and Technology, JiLin University,
ChangChun 130000, China

Abstract. Electrocephalogram(EEG) signals classification is an important problem in the field of brain computer interface. There are many EEG signals classification methods, but most of are not very efficient in this problem. Deep learning had been broadly used in image classification and has significant performance in classifying images. This paper proposes a comprehensive spatio-temporal feature classification method based on deep learning. It combines Convolutional Neural Network (CNN) and Long-term Short-term Memory network (LSTM) to the motor imaginary EEG classification. Experimental results show that it can preserve spatial, frequency and temporal features of motor imaginary EEG simultaneously and improves the classification accuracy of EEG signals.

Keywords: Brain computer interface · Motion imaginary
Deep learning · Convolution neural network
Long-term short-term memory

1 Introduction

BCI is a communication way between a brain and a computer. It detects EEG signals generated by brain activity to generate control signals to communicate with some devices. In general, a BCI signal process includes four parts: signal acquisition, feature extraction, pattern recognition (classification), and the output control command [1].

For the feature extraction, many methods had been used to extract the features of EEG signals, including the frequency domain methods such as AR parameter model estimation, wavelet transform and power spectrum analysis [2]; the time domain methods such as zero-crossing point analysis and histogram analysis [3]; the space domain methods such as independent component analysis, common spatial pattern algorithm [4]. After feature extraction, some classifiers will be used to classify the EEG signals, such as the support vector machine, Bayesian classifier, linear discriminant classifier [5]. But different feature extraction and classifiers combination have different classification accuracy, such as

© Springer Nature Singapore Pte Ltd. 2018
J. Qiao et al. (Eds.): BIC-TA 2018, CCIS 951, pp. 142–150, 2018.
https://doi.org/10.1007/978-981-13-2826-8_13

Fourier transform and Fisher classifier, PCA and SVM [6], bandpass filtering and wavelet packet analysis and linear classifier [7], co-space pattern algorithm and SVM [8]. At present, the accuracy of these traditional methods on the classification of EEG of one person generally ranges from 75% to 85%. Many problems exist in these methods. For example, the feature extraction process of EEG is complex and EEG channels selection has influence on the EEG analysis.

In recent years, with the development of machine learning, especially deep learning(DL), some researchers began to use deep learning for the EEG classification. In [9] and [10], convolutional neural network (CNN) was used to identify P300 EEG and visually induced ERP signal, with the accuracy of 95.5% and 92.7%, seperately. The main difference between DL and traditional classification methods is that the DL combines the feature extraction and pattern recognition into one model. At first, it can learn from a large number of samples and then feature extraction and classification can be done automatically and efficiently.

In this paper, we use DL to the EEG of motor imaginary(MI), which is a kind of spontaneous EEG. In [11], it presents a method combining CNN and stack SAE for MI EEG two class classification problem. In [12], it conducted a four-class classification problem using the CNN after arranging the conductive poles. In [13], the original EEG was filtered by a simple method, and the convolution neural network was used to classify the original EEG and obtain the classification accuracy 70%. In [14], the period with obvious characteristic of EEG was chosen at first, then [N, 1] convolution kernel shape was used and got accuracy 88.75%.

At present, most work of using CNN only for single person. In this paper, we adopt two kinds of deep learning methods, CNN and LTSM to recognize EEG. In order to obtain better classification, we integrate multiple persons EEG data to obtain a large data set used to train our model. Since DL is good at classifying graphs. So at first, the common EEG data is converted into a power spectrum graph according to the position of the conducting electrode to preserve its frequency and spatial features. Then, the feature of EEG is extracted by using the CNN algorithm in a way of classifying graphs. The LSTM algorithm is used to extract the time domain features.

2   EEG Classification Based on Deep Learning

2.1   Long Term Short Term Memory Network

LSTM is a variant algorithm based on recurrent networks [15]. The main characteristics is that the neurons in the hidden layers of the LSTM network are connected, and the input of the hidden layer includes not only the output of the input layer but also the output of the hidden layer at the previous moment. This special network structure allows the algorithm to remember previously entered information and apply it to the current output calculation. It emphasizes the importance of time series and has achieved some success in speech recognition and natural language processing. Since EEG is also a time series, it is hypothesized that the EEG features of the subject may be correlated with time when imagining the left and right hand motions. Therefore, this paper apply the LSTM network to the classification of EEG. LSTM network model as shown below:

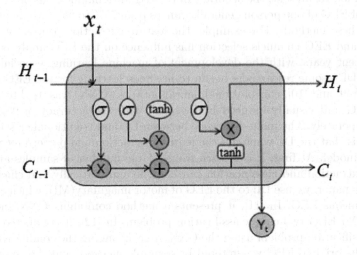

Fig. 1. The structure of LSTM network.

Cell status is the key to LSTM network, which is Ct-1 Ct in Fig. 1, and based on this, a well-designed "gate" is added to remove or add information to the cell state. The LSTM has three gates, the forget gate determines what kind of information to discard; the update gate determines what kind of new information is stored in the cell state; and the output gate determines the output value. The network's forward propagation process is shown in the following Eqs. (1)–(6). This special kind of gate structure is the reason why LSTM is widely used. It solves the problem of gradient diffusion and makes the network remember long-term information at a lower cost.

$$f_t = sigmoid(W_f * [H_{t-1}, X_t] + b_f) \tag{1}$$

$$i_t = sigmoid(W_i * [H_{t-1}, X_t] + b_i) \tag{2}$$

$$C_t = f_t * C_{t-1} + i_t * \tilde{C}_t \tag{3}$$

$$\tilde{C}_t = \tanh(W_c[Ht-1, Xt] + b_c) \tag{4}$$

$$o_t = sigmoid(W_o * [H_{t-1}, X_t] + b_o) \tag{5}$$

$$H_t = o_t * \tanh(Ct) \tag{6}$$

2.2 Convolution Neural Network

The CNN model is applied to the classification of EEG as shown in Fig. 2.

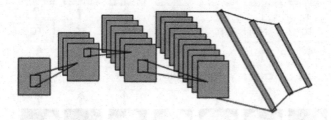

Fig. 2. The structure of Convolutional Neural Network

The forward propagation process of CNN is shown as Eq. (7), where D is the input depth, F is the filter size, $w_{d,m,n}$ represents the weight of the mth row and nth column of the d th layer of the filter. The pooling method includes the average pooling, the maximum pooling and so on. Maximum pooling is more commonly used, which select the maximum value on the pooling filter as the sampled value

$$ai, j = f(\sum_{d=0}^{D-1} \sum_{m=0}^{F-1} \sum_{n=0}^{F-1} w_{d,m,n} x_{d,i+m,j+n} + w_b) \tag{7}$$

2.3 MI EEG Classification

In this section, we design a novel EEG signal processing network structure shown in Fig. 3. First, the cortical EEG voltage signal collected in a certain period of time is converted into an EEG power spectrum map. Based on this step, the two dimensions of the original EEG have different meanings, that is, the horizontal axis along the time direction and the vertical axis along the conductive pole position. Now the horizontal and vertical axis of the EEG graph corresponds to the position where the electrode cap is placed in the cerebral cortex, which completely preserves the spatial characteristics of EEG. The pixels in the EEG power graph correspond to the power spectra among 6.5 Hz to 23 Hz at that location and it preserves the frequency characteristics associated with motor imaginary EEG signals. After all the EEG data are transformed into a series of EEG graphs by time series, these images are input into the CNN network to extract space and frequency features, and then the features extracted by CNN are sequentially input into the LSTM network to extract the timing features of EEG. The advantage of this process is that it combines the features of space, frequency and time domain so that the extracted features are more abundant, especially the complete preservation of the spatial features, which cannot be achieved by using the original EEG data directly as input.

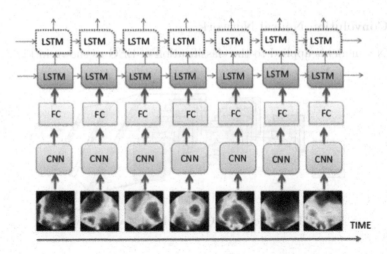

Fig. 3. The structure of model

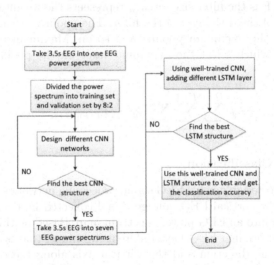

Fig. 4. Flow chart of classifier design

The designing procedure of classifier is shown in Fig. 4. The structure of the CNN is described as below:

First Layer: Using two sets of 32 convolution kernels with shape [3, 3], non-zero-padding mode with stride 1, followed by a maximum pooling layer with window size of [2, 2].

Second Layer: Using two sets of 64 convolution kernels with shape [3, 3], non-zero-padding mode with stride 1, followed by a maximum pooling layer with window size of [2, 2].

Third Layer: Using 128 convolution kernels with shape [3, 3], non-zero-padding mode with stride 1, followed by a maximum pooling layer with window size of [2, 2].

The fourth layer and the fifth layer are two fully connected layer, hidden neurons were 1024 and 80 respectively.

The sixth layer is the Softmax output layer. It uses the Softmax classification function to select a larger probability as a classification result of the input to judge the two categories of left and right. The parameters of the network are set as follows: the learning rate is 0.001 and epoch is 64 and batchsize is 60.

3   Experiment Procedure and Result Analysis

The EEG data set used in the experiment came from the 2005 BCI competition. Five subjects were enrolled in the competition. During the training, batch size is taken as 20, the learning rate is set to 0.01. The number of hidden neurons in LSTM network is 256, the time step is 7, on each step get 80 neurons. The location of the electrodes and the EEG power map converted according to electrode position are shown in Figs. 5 and 6. In order to make the neural network do more fully iterative training, it trains with 1s data length and the data is expanded as shown in Fig. 5. Every 50 points take 1s data in the time dimension and the counts of expanded data for each subject is 1680 with shape of [118, 100]. The data is divided into training set and verification set by 8:2, and for each subject, there are 1344 training set samples and 336 validation sample sets.

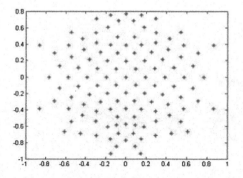

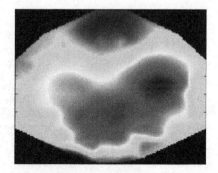

Fig. 5. Pole position map   **Fig. 6.** EEG power graph

There are only 280 samples of one subject after converting the EEG signals to a power graph, the training set is too small to single-network training, so we directly integrated the EEG of different subjects and trained together. The training process is shown as Figs. 7 and 8. In Fig. 7, it shows the loss curves co-trained by 5 subjects. It can be seen that the loss curve on validation set (lower

148   H. Wang and W. Mo

line) is minimized when the iterations is around 20000 steps, and then it starts to have a upward trend, so it can be terminated early in this training process. In Fig. 8, it shows the classification accuracy of the training set and the validation set. It can be seen that the accuracy of the network finally reaches 100% on the training set and reaches about 80% on the validation set. The classification accuracy on the test set of five subjects were 76.78%, 78.57%, 80.36%, 71.43%, 67.86%.

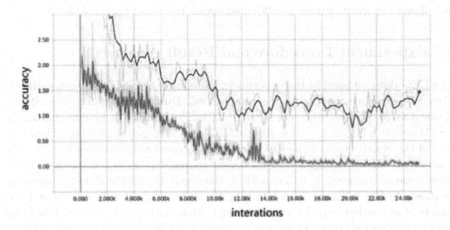

Fig. 7. Loss Curve

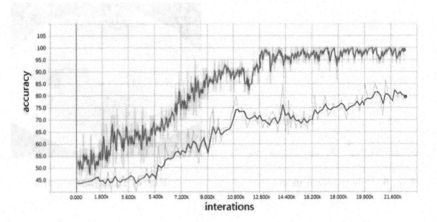

Fig. 8. The accuracy of training and validation set

The above experiments were also done on the EEG data collected by our own laboratory, and the classification accuracy rate is obviously improved. Experiments using 32 conductive poles with frequency of 250 Hz, collected five students' motor imaginary EEG data. The size of training set is 1200, the size of validation set and test set are both 200. The classification accuracy rate of training set and validation set for this group of subjects is shown in Fig. 9 below. Finally, the accuracy of classification of the test set of five students is 90%, 92%, 86%, 88%, 86%, separately. The size of training set for single subject was 720, and the size of the validation set was 72. The classification accuracy of five subjects during training was shown in Fig. 9. The final classification accuracy of each subjects were: 94.44%, 95.83%, 93.06%, 91.66%, 90.28%.

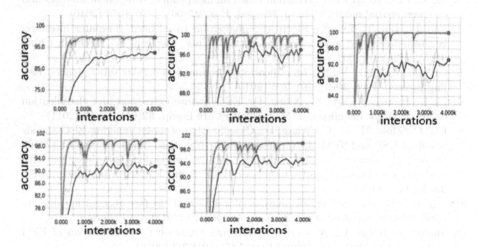

Fig. 9. The classification accuracy rate of training set and validation set of lab data

4   Conclusions

In this paper, a new model based on DL is designed to classify the motor imaginary EEG. In the model, the CNN and LSTM are combined to extract frequency, space and time domain features. The common EEG data set is converted into power maps, CNN is used to extract spatial features from and LSTM is used to extract temporal features. The comprehensive space domain, frequency domain and time domain information overcome the loss of spatial feature from the original EEG. It can preserve the complete spatial features and unifies the two dimensions of EEG signals. Experiment results show that the classification accuracy of multi-subjects has been greatly improved. The proposed method has more robustness and can extract the more general features of MI EEG. In feature, we will improve the model in further and test it on much larger data sets.

References

1. Wang, L.: Based on the motion imaging of brain electrical signal classification and brain-computer interface technology, Hebei University of Technology (2011). (in Chinese)
2. LI, D.: Research on brain-computer interface algorithm based on motion imaging, South China University of Technology (2011). (in Chinese)
3. Wu, X.: Time-frequency analysis and its application in EEG signal analysis, Dalian University of Technology (2005). (in Chinese)
4. Li, X.: EEG-based EEG extraction based on independent component analysis and common spatial model. Chin. J. Biomed. Eng. **27**(06), 1370–1374 (2010)
5. Yao, D., Liu, T., Lei, X.: Electroencephalogram based brain-computer interface: key techniques and application prospect. J. Univ. Electron. Sci. Technol. China **38**(5), 550–554 (2009)
6. Guo, J., Yang, B., Ma, S.: Identification of common molecular subsequences. Beijing Biomed. Eng. **29**(3), 261–265 (2010)
7. Li, L., Huang, S., Wu, X., Xiong, D.: EEG feature extraction and classification based on motor imaginary. J. Med. Health Care Equip. **32**(01), 16–17 (2011)
8. Liu, C., Zhao, H., Li, C., Wang, H.: Classification of motor imaging EEG signals based on CSP and SVM. J. Northeast. Univ. (Nat. Sci.) **31**(8), 1098–1101 (2010)
9. Cecotti, H., Graser, A.: Convolutional neural networks for P300 detection with application to brain-computer interfaces. IEEE Trans. Pattern Anal. Mach. Intell. **33**(3), 433 (2011)
10. Cai, B.: Facility and spatial analysis of single ERP in face recognition and its application to rapid retrieval, Zhejiang University (2015). (in Chinese)
11. Tabar, Y., Halici, U.: A novel deep learning approach for classification of EEG motor imagery signals. J. Neural Eng. **14**(1), 016003 (2016)
12. Walker, I.: Deep convolutional neural networks for brain computer interface using motor imaginary. Thomson Reuters, London (2015)
13. Tang, Z., Zhang, K., Li, C., Sun, S., Huang, Q., Zhang, S.: Identification of common molecularmotion imaginary classification based on deep convolutional neural network and its application in brain control exoskeleton. Chin. J. Comput. **254**, 1–15 (2017)
14. Pfurtscheller, G., Aranibar, A.: Event-related cortical desynchronization detected by power measurements of scalp EEG. Electroencephalogram Clin. Neurophysiol. **42**(6), 817–826 (1977)
15. Kuo, C.: Understanding convolutional neural networks with a mathematical model. J. Vis. Commun. Image Represent. **41**, 406–413 (2016)

DNA Origami Based Computing Model
for the Satisfiability Problem

Zhenqin Yang[1]([✉]), Zhixiang Yin[1], Jianzhong Cui[2], and Jing Yang[1]

[1] School of Mathematics and Big Data, Anhui University of Science and Technology,
Huainan, China
522480882@qq.com
[2] School of Electronic and Information Engineering,
Anhui University of Science and Technology, Huainan 232001, China

Abstract. The satisfiability problem (SAT) is one of the NP-complete problems in the fields of theoretical computer and artificial intelligence, is the core of NP-complete problems. Compared with traditional DNA self-assembly, DNA origami is a new method of DNA self-assembly. We first give a description and the status quo of study of the satisfiability problem, briefly introduce the principle of DNA origami, propose the computing model based on DNA origami to solve the satisfiability problem, and solve an instance with 3 variables, 3 clauses to illustrate the feasibility of the algorithm. The proposed model only uses gel electrophoresis to search the solution to the problem, which is the most reliable biological operation known to date, therefore the proposed model is feasible. At present, the reported results concerning using origami to solve the NP-complete problem is relatively few. Our method is a new attempt to solve the NP- complete problem using biological DNA molecules.

Keywords: The satisfiability problem · DNA self-assembly
DNA origami · Biological operation

1 Introduction

Adleman [1] proposed for the first time in 1994 to solve the NP-complete problem (Hamilton path problem) using DNA molecular to encode the vertices and edges of a given graph, which is a molecular biology tool that is directly applied to solve NP-complete problem. Scientific developments have greatly contributed to the development of molecular biological technology at a rapid speed. In 1995, Lipton [2] solved the SAT problem with contact network G, a more general method of solving NP-complete problems, with faster speed than traditional electronic computers. DNA microchip is then proposed. Michael [3] reported DNA microchip analysis to solve the satisfiability problem and gave a solution to the two-dimensional, 3variables and 4variablesthe SAT problem. In the various models of DNA computing, the initial data pool is usually created, but as the variables increase, the model becomes impossible, due to exponential explosion.

© Springer Nature Singapore Pte Ltd. 2018
J. Qiao et al. (Eds.): BIC-TA 2018, CCIS 951, pp. 151–160, 2018.
https://doi.org/10.1007/978-981-13-2826-8_14

Yang et al. [4] proposed a sticker model of the satisfiability problem that does not need the initial data pool. Due to the complexity of the algorithm, Wang et al. [5] improved the 3-SAT algorithm, which greatly reduced the number of DNA molecules require. The maximum number of DNA strands required is $2^{0.48n}$, when n = 50. In the same year, the new DNA computing algorithm based on ligase chain reaction was presented to solve the SAT problem [6]. The proposed DNA algorithm can solve the SAT problem of the n variable m clause in m steps, and the required computing time is $O(3m + n)$. At this point, more and more scholars are devoted to solving the 3-SAT problem, readers may refer to references [7–13] for other DNA computing models. Li [14] proposed a new DNA computing model based on self-assembly gold nanoparticle probe, which promoted the development of DNA computing in some aspects, in terms of huge parallelism, information density, and easy to operate.

DNA origami was first proposed in 2006 by Rothemund [15]. The so-called DNA origami, is to use the special structure of DNA molecules and the principle of base complementary pairing, long DNA single strand (scaffold strand) of specific areas to be folded, and fixed with DNA short strands (staple strand) to construct the expected structure. Then, Qian Lulu et al. [16] used Rothemund's method to "draw" a map of China using single strands of DNA. In 2008, Andersen [17] designed the logo of the dolphin structure according to DNA origami and could control the activity of its tail. The self-assembly of the gold nanoparticles in the solution to the satisfiability problem due to the linear structure and spacing difficult to control. Yu [18] proposed DNA origami as a template for self-assembly of nanoparticles perfect solved the problem, opened the new door based on self-assembly DNA origami. References [19,20] using DNA origami encoding information, successfully solved the Hamilton path problem and graph coloring problem. Then many scholars devoted themselves to the study of DNA origami, and constructed two-dimensional, three-dimensional nanostructures or graphics, which promoted the development of DNA computing [21–26].

Although there are a variety of study of the SAT problem was fruitful, based on the importance of the problem, the new method for solving it is sure to intrigue the readers' interest. As research progresses, the size and stability of DNA origami structures have been significantly advanced. DNA origami as a new strategy for self-assembly, will play a versatile role in the construction of two-dimensional and three-dimensional nano-assembly structure DNA chips, nanomaterials and surface calculations.

The purpose of this paper was to provide a relative simple DNA computing model to solve the satisfiability problem. Section 1, The definition of the satisfiability problem was given. Section 2, computing model based on the satisfiability problem was presented. It is the basis of using DNA origami to solve the satisfiability problem. Analysis to illustrate the specific operation of solving the satisfiability problem through DNA origami in Sect. 3. Then, complexity analysis of algorithm and conclusion were presented.

2   The Satisfiability Problem

Given a Boolean expression $F = c_1 \wedge c_2 \wedge \ldots \wedge c_m$, where $c_i = x_1 \vee x_2 \vee \ldots \vee x_n$, $x_i (i = 1 \ldots n)$ are Boolean logic variables that represented were assigned 0 or 1, "$\vee$" and "$\wedge$" are called logical "or" and logical "and". For a Boolean expression with n-variables, the problem is to find the existence of one or more sets of variables satisfy each clause in a given instance of the problem, which becomes a satisfiability problem (SAT problem). Obviously, there are 2^n possible Boolean expressions F for n variables.

3   ComputingModel

Basic algorithm

Step 1: Generates all possible solutions for the given problem variable;
Step 2: Eliminates the false solution in each clause and preserves the solution that makes the clause true;
Step 3: Repeat step 2 to eliminate all solutions that make the clause false. The rest is the solution to the satisfiability problem if the given formula is satisfiable.

Biological algorithm

Given the satisfiability problem with n variables and m clause, computing process is as follows:

Step 1: (1) Construct long DNA single strands (scaffold strand). First, 2n kinds of oligonucleotide fragments were synthesized and divided into 2 groups, represented as $x_1, x_1', x_2, x_2', \ldots, x_n, x_n'$. Each variable of long DNA single strands is divided into 3 parts, which are represented as x_i^1, x_i^2, x_i^3 or $x_i^{1'}, x_i^{2'}, x_i^{3'}$, respectively.

(2) Construct short DNA single strands (staple strand). Synthesis of n kinds of short oligonucleotide fragments, represented as $\bar{x}_1, \bar{x}_2, \ldots, \bar{x}_n$. Each short strand is divided into two parts, part 1 is the complement of the base x_i^1 in the first part of $x_1, x_2, \ldots, x_n$, part 2 is the complement of the base x_i^3 in the third part of $x_1, x_2, \ldots, x_n$. Similarly, n kinds of short oligonucleotide fragments $\bar{x}'_1, \bar{x}'_2, \ldots, \bar{x}'_n$ were synthesized. Each short strand is divided into two parts, part 1 is the complement of the base $x_i^{1'}$ in the first part of $\bar{x}'_1, \bar{x}'_2, \ldots, \bar{x}'_n$, part 2 is the complement of the base $x_i^{3'}$ in the third part of $\bar{x}'_1, \bar{x}'_2, \ldots, \bar{x}'_n$.

Step 2: Establish initial data pool. Add $\bar{x}_1$ to the first group of long DNA single strands, for the second group added $\bar{x}_1'$ are formed hairpin structure. The two groups are combined and a DNA strand of length $l + \Delta t$ is selected by gel electrophoresis. Re-divided into two groups, Add $\bar{x}_2$ to the first group of long DNA single strands, for the second group added $\bar{x}_2'$ are formed hairpin structure. The two groups are combined and a DNA strand of length $l + \Delta t$ is selected by gel electrophoresis. Continue until select a length of $l + n\Delta t$ DNA strand, that is, each strand has n hairpin structures, the initial data pool established. (The assignment of the hairpin structure in $x_1, x_2, \ldots, x_n$ is 1, and the assignment of the hairpin structure in $x_1{}', x_2{}', \ldots, x_n{}'$ is 0.)

Step 3: For the clauses of the given formula, a staple strand with corresponding variables is added to the reaction solution in turn. After terminate reaction, the solution of the clause is satisfied if the length is unchanged, and the length of the DNA strand of length $l + n\Delta t$ is separated by gel electrophoresis.

Step 4: Repeat step 2 until all the clauses in the formula are checked to get the solution of the problem (Fig. 1).

Fig. 1. Schematic diagram of reaction

4   An Instance Analysis

The following describes a simple formula $x \wedge (y' \vee z') \wedge (x' \vee y \vee z')$ solution.

Step 1: (1) Construct long DNA single strands (scaffold strand), divided into two groups and represented as x, x', y, y', z, z'. Each long DNA single strand is divided into three parts, which in turn contain 4, 6, and 4 bases.

(2) From the (1), 6 kinds of staple strands are represented as $\bar{x}, \bar{y}, \bar{z}$ and $\bar{x'}, \bar{y'}, \bar{z'}$. Each of the short DNA single strand divided into two parts: the first part is complementary to the first four bases of x, y, z or x', y', z'; the second part is complementary to the last four bases of x, y, z or x', y', z'. (Table 1)

Table 1. Detailed coding diagram

	All DNA sequencs ($5' \to 3'$)	
x : GGCCTAGTCACAGC	y : GCGCAAGTGCTCGA	z : CTAGTGAGACCTCA
x' : ATGATACGCAGCTC	y' : ATAGCTCTAAGGCA	z' : TCGTGCGAAGATCA
$\bar{x}$: GCTGGGCC	$\bar{y}$: TCGAGCGC	$\bar{z}$: TGAGCTAG
$\bar{x'}$: GAGCTCAT	$\bar{y'}$: TGCCCTAT	$\bar{z'}$: TGATACGA

Step 2: Establish initial data pool. Add $\bar{x}$ to the first group of long DNA single strands, for the second group added $x^{'}$ are formed hairpin structure. The two groups are combined and a DNA strand of length $14 + \Delta t$ is selected by gel electrophoresis. Re-divided into two groups, add $\bar{y}$ to the first group of long DNA single strands, for the second group added $\bar{y}^{'}$ are formed hairpin structure. The two groups are combined and a DNA strand of length $14 + 2\Delta t$ is selected by gel electrophoresis. Re-divided into two groups, add $\bar{z}$ to the first group of long DNA single strands, for the second group added $z^{'}$ are formed hairpin structure. The two groups are combined and a DNA strand of length $14 + 3\Delta t$ is selected by gel electrophoresis. (The assignment of the hairpin structure in x, y, z is 1, and the assignment of the hairpin structure in $x^{'}, y^{'}, z^{'}$ is 0. The initial data pool structure shown in Fig. 2.)

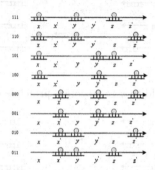

Fig. 2. Initial data pool structure diagram

Step 3: (1) For the first clause, adding $\bar{x}$, staple strand and scaffold strand completely react, the solution of the clause is satisfied if the length is unchanged (Fig. 3). The length of the DNA strand of length $14 + 3\Delta t$ is separated by gel electrophoresis, and the combination of satisfied clauses are (1, 0, 0), (1, 0, 1), (1, 1, 0), (1, 1, 1).

Step 4: (1) For the second clause, the DNA strand separated by step 3 is divided into 3 test tubes. Add $\bar{y}^{'}, z^{'}$, $\bar{y}, z^{'}$, $y^{'}, \bar{z}$ respectively, staple strand and scaffold strand completely react, the solution of the clause is satisfied if the length is unchanged (Figs. 4, 5 and 6).

From Fig. 4 that the combination of satisfied clause 2 is (1, 0, 0), and Fig. 5 shows that the combination of satisfied clause is (1, 0, 1). DNA strands of length $14 + 3\Delta t$ were separated by gel electrophoresis.

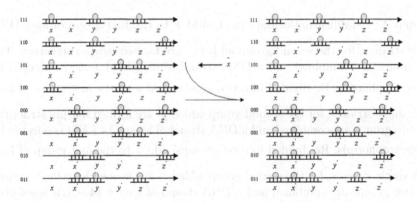

Fig. 3. Add to $\bar{x}$ reaction principle diagram

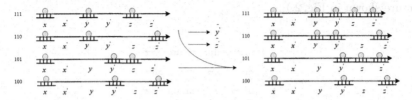

Fig. 4. Add to $\bar{y}', \bar{z}'$ reaction principle diagram

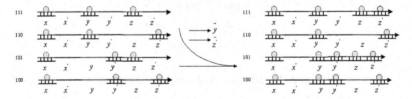

Fig. 5. Add to $\bar{y}, \bar{z}'$ reaction principle diagram

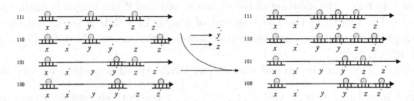

Fig. 6. Add to $\bar{y}', \bar{z}$ reaction principle diagram

Step 5: For the third clause, the DNA strand separated by step 4 is divided into 7 test tubes. Add $\bar{x}',\bar{y}',\bar{z}',\ \bar{x}',\bar{y},\bar{z}',\ \bar{x}',\bar{y},\bar{z},\ \bar{x}',\bar{y}',\bar{z},\ \bar{x},\bar{y},\bar{z},\ \bar{x},\bar{y},\bar{z}',\ \bar{x},\bar{y}',\bar{z}'$, respectively, staple strand and scaffold strand completely react, the solution of the clause is satisfied if the length is unchanged (Figs. 7, 8, 9, 10, 11, 12 and 13).

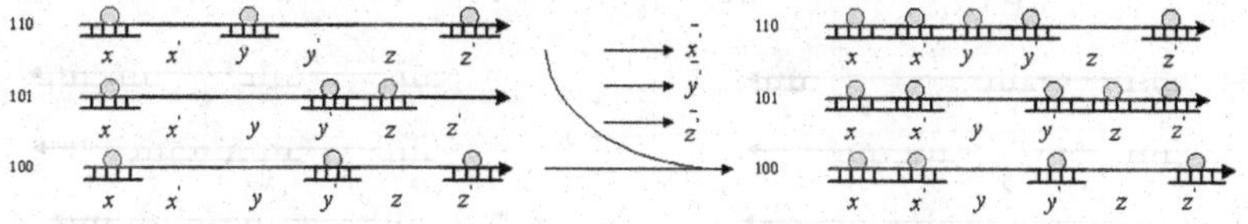

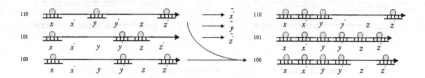

Fig. 7. Add to $\bar{x}',\bar{y}',\bar{z}'$ reaction principle diagram

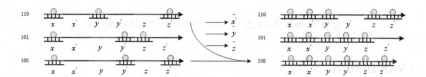

Fig. 8. Add to $\bar{x}',\bar{y},\bar{z}'$ reaction principle diagram

Fig. 9. Add to $\bar{x}',\bar{y},\bar{z}$ reaction principle diagram

From Fig. 12 that the combination of satisfied clause 2 is (1, 1, 0), and Fig. 13 shows that the combination of satisfied clause is (1, 0, 0), Figs. 7, 8, 9, 10 and 11 the combination of non satisfied clauses. DNA strands of length $14+3\Delta t$ were separated by gel electrophoresis.

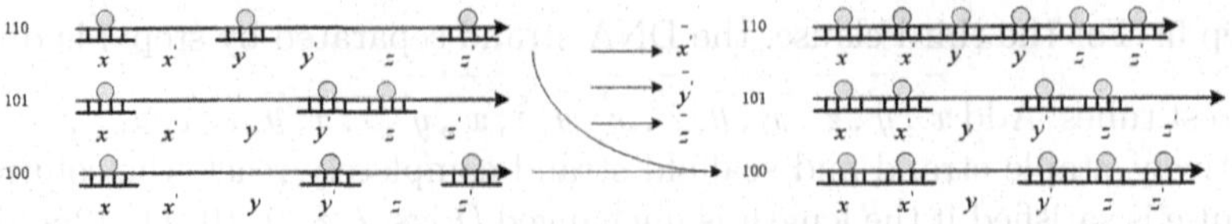

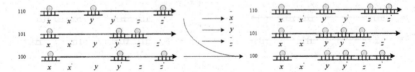

Fig. 10. Add to $\bar{x}', \bar{y}', \bar{z}$ reaction principle diagram

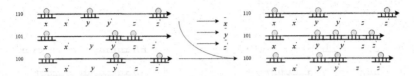

Fig. 11. Add to $\bar{x}, \bar{y}, \bar{z}$ reaction principle diagram

Fig. 12. Add to $\bar{x}, \bar{y}, z'$ reaction principle diagram

Fig. 13. Add to $\bar{x}, \bar{y}', z'$ reaction principle diagram

5   Conclusion

This paper presents a new method to solve the satisfiability problem. Through the related technology of DNA origami, we construct the initial data pool first, using base-pairing principle, long DNA single strand and short DNA single strand hybridize to form hairpin structure, the length is unchanged of the DNA strand in the reaction was separated by gel electrophoresis to obtain a solution to the problem. Successful use of DNA origami addressability, through a simple model to solve the problem. The example given in this paper, we only discuss the conjunctive formula. It is very simple to judge the conjunctive formula of the satisfiability problem. However, we present a novel approach to solving the satisfiability problem using DNA origami. Compared with the previous model to solve the SAT problem, the method is simple, effective and has huge parallelism and the structure is more stable, can be applied to other DNA computing models. Such as DNA self-assembly, three-dimensional DNA structure, DNA chip, molecular beacons, surface calculations, etc. will solve more NP- complete problems, with high application prospects.

Acknowledgement. The author sincerely thanks for the encouragement and advice given by the DNA computing research group, and thanks Professor Yin for his guidance. This research is funded by the National Natural Science Foundation of China; 61672001, 61702008.

References

1. Neidell, N.S.: Amplitude variation with offset. Lead. Edge **5**(3), 47–51 (1986)
2. Li, S.P.: AVO seismic parameter inversion method and its application. China University of Petroleum (2009). (in Chinese)
3. Chen, J.J.: Inversion method of the three AVO parameters. China University of Petroleum (2007). (in Chinese)
4. Wang, L.P.: Prestack AVO non-linear inversion of intelligent optimization algorithm. China University of Geosciences (2015). (in Chinese)
5. Berg, E.: Simple convergent genetic algorithm for inversion of multiparameter data. In: SEG Technical Program Expanded Abstracts 1993, pp. 1126–1128. Society of Exploration Geophysicists (1990)
6. Porsani, M.J.: A combined genetic and linear inversion algorithm for seismic waveform inversion. In: SEG Technical Program Expanded Abstracts 1993, pp. 692–695. Society of Exploration Geophysicists (1993)
7. Mallick, S.: Model-based inversion of amplitude-variations-with-offset data using a genetic algorithm. Geophysics **60**(4), 939–954 (1995)
8. Priezzhev, I.I., Shmaryan, L.E., Bejarano, G.: Nonlinear multitrace seismic inversion using neural network and genetic algorithm. In: 3rd EAGE St. Petersburg International Conference and Exhibition on Geosciences-geosciences: From New Ideas to New Discoveries (2008)
9. Soupios, P., Akca, I., Mpogiatzis, P.: Applications of hybrid genetic algorithms in seismic tomography. J. Appl. Geophys. **75**(3), 479–489 (2011)
10. Bai, J., Xu, Z., Xiao, Y., Xie, T.: Nonlinear hybrid optimization algorithm for seismic impedance inversion. In: Beijing International Geophysical Conference & Exposition 21–24, Beijing, China (2014)
11. Agarwal, A., Sain, K., Shalivahan, S.: Traveltime and constrained AVO inversion using FDR PSO. In: SEG Technical Program Expanded Abstracts 2016, pp. 577–581. Society of Exploration Geophysicists (2016)
12. Sun, S.Z.: PSO non-linear pre-stack inversion method and the application in reservoir prediction. In: SEG Technical Program Expanded Abstracts 2012, pp. 1–5. Society of Exploration Geophysicists (2012)
13. Sun, S.Z., Liu, L.: A numerical study on non-linear AVO inversion using chaotic quantum particle swarm optimization. J. Seismic Explor. **23**(4), 379–392 (2014)
14. Zhou, Y., Nie, Z., Jia, Z.: An improved differential evolution algorithm for nonlinear inversion of earthquake dislocation. Geodesy Geodyn. **5**(4), 49–56 (2014)
15. Gao, Z., Pan, Z., Gao, J.: Multimutation differential evolution algorithm and its application to seismic inversion. IEEE Trans. Geosci. Remote Sens. **54**(6), 3626–3636 (2016)
16. Yin, X.Y., Kong, S.S., Zhang, F.C.: Prestack AVO inversion based on differential evolution algorithm. Oil Geophys. Prospect. **48**(4), 591–596 (2013)

17. Wu, Q.H., Wang, L.P., Zhu, Z.X.: Research of pre-stack AVO elastic parameter inversion problem based on hybrid genetic algorithm. Cluster Comput. **20**(4), 3173–3783 (2017)
18. Wu, Q., Zhu, Z.X., Yan, X.S.: Research on the parameter inversion problem of prestack seismic data based on improved differential evolution algorithm. Cluster Comput. **20**(4), 2881–2890 (2017)
19. De Castro, L.N., Von Zuben, F.J.: Learning and optimization using the clonal selection principle. IEEE Trans. Evol. Comput. **6**(3), 239–251 (2002)
20. Gong, M., Jiao, L., Zhang, L.: Baldwinian learning in clonal selection algorithm for optimization. Inf. Sci. **180**(8), 1218–1236 (2010)
21. Feng, J., Jiao, L.C., Zhang, X.: Bag-of-visual-words based on clonal selection algorithm for SAR image classification. IEEE Geosci. Remote Sens. Lett. **8**(4), 691–695 (2011)
22. Karoum, B., Elbenani, Y.B.: A clonal selection algorithm for the generalized cell formation problem considering machine reliability and alternative routings. Prod. Eng. **2017**(15), 1–12 (2017)
23. Rao, B.S., Vaisakh, K.: Multi-objective adaptive clonal selection algorithm for solving optimal power flow problem with load uncertainty. Int. J. Bio-Inspired Comput. **8**(2), 67 (2016)
24. Swain, R.K., Barisal, A.K., Hota, P.K.: Short-term hydrothermal scheduling using clonal selection algorithm. Int. J. Electr. Power Energy Syst. **33**(3), 647–656 (2011)
25. Chitsaz, H., Amjady, N., Zareipour, H.: Wind power forecast using wavelet neural network trained by improved clonal selection algorithm. Energy Convers. Manage. **89**, 588–598 (2015)
26. Sindhuja, L.S., Padmavathi, G.: Replica node detection using enhanced single Hop detection with clonal selection algorithm in mobile wireless sensor networks. Hindawi Publishing Corp (2016)

DNA 3D Self-assembly Algorithmic Model to Solve Maximum Clique Problem

Jingjing Ma[1($\boxtimes$)] and Wenbin Gao[2]

[1] School of Statistics, Shanxi University of Finance and Economics,
Taiyuan, Shanxi, China
casy@pku.edu.cn
[2] North Automatic Control Technology Institute, Taiyuan, Shanxi, China
8075228804@qq.com

Abstract. Self-assembly reveals the essence of DNA computing, DNA self-assembly is thought to be the best way to make DNA computing transform into computer chip. This paper introduce a method of DNA 3D self-assembly algorithm to solve the Maximum Clique Problem. Firstly, we introduce a non-deterministic algorithm. Then, according to the algorithm we design the types of DNA tiles which the computation needs. Lastly, we demonstrate the self-assembly process and the experimental methods which could get the final result. The computation time is linear, and the number of the distinctive tile types is constant.

Keywords: DNA self-assembly · DNA computing
Maximum Clique Problem · 3D

1 Introduction

Self-assembly process is ubiquitous in nature. Systems form on all scales via self-assembly: atoms self-assemble to form molecules, molecules to form complexes, and stars and planets to form galaxies.

In biological systems, cells are self-assembled by all sorts of biological molecules, meanwhile biological organisms use biochemical approaches to control every molecular and chemical activity, such as the storage and reproduction of genetic information, the control of developmental processes, even the sophisticated computations performed by the nervous system.

Molecular computation is a sort of biochemical algorithm, which finds out the connection between the natural biochemical process and the human process which the electronic microprocessors control electro-mechanical devices. Molecular computation is a new computing method comparing the traditional one, it has two complementary perspectives: using the astounding parallelism of chemistry to solve mathematical problems, such as combinatorial search problems; and using the biochemical algorithms to direct and control molecular processes, such as complex fabrication tasks.

© Springer Nature Singapore Pte Ltd. 2018
J. Qiao et al. (Eds.): BIC-TA 2018, CCIS 951, pp. 161–172, 2018.
https://doi.org/10.1007/978-981-13-2826-8_15

DNA is the genetic material of the most biological organisms, and it is also the carrier of genetic message in itself. Molecular computation uses the massive information storage capacity of DNA and the huge parallelism of biochemical reaction to solve many difficult problems which the traditional computer cannot solve.

DNA computing is a branch of computing which uses DNA, biochemistry, and molecular biology hardware, instead of the traditional silicon-based computer technologies. DNA computing essentially could be divided into three categories: intramolecular, intermolecular and super molecular DNA computing. Takahashi's [1] studies are concerning intramolecular DNA computing, which use only a single DNA molecule. Intramolecular DNA computing is like Adleman's experiments, which are hybridisation of different DNA molecules. Super molecular DNA computing is a process of DNA self-assembly which meanwhile is an algorithm, which is firstly stated by Winfree [2].

Self-assembly reveals the essence of DNA computing, and in a certain extent it avoids the error accumulation caused by the frequent operation in the experimental process, its production is also easy to be analyzed. DNA self-assembly is thought to be the best way to make DNA computing transform into computer chip.

2   3D DNA Nanostructure for Self-assembly

The first work to combine studies of self-assembly with nanotechnology in three dimensions is completed by Kao and Ramachandran [3]. They proposed a general mathematical model for constructing 3D structures from 2D tiles. Their model is a more precise superset of 2D Tile Assembly Model that facilitates building scalable 3D molecules. Under the model, they presented algorithms to build a hollow cube (Fig. 1), which is intuitively one of the simplest 3D structures to construct. They built the 3D structures using the folding technique shown in Fig. 2 and allow construction of all 2D structures possible with the Tile Assembly Model. They are the first to extend nanostructure fabrication to three dimensions.

Their methods are applicable to more complex 2D and 3D nanostructures. But there are some important biological issues. In particular, design of a strong and rigid DNA tile suitable for computation and design of a 3D building block are two important points to increase the feasiblility of 3D self-assembly. Besides the temperature may be further refined and exploited to improve some complexity results and the number of steps needed in the lab.

3   3D DNA Self-assembly Model

Lately Essam Al-Daoud et al. [4] presented a new method to perform the vector and integer multiplication by using the self-assembly of 3D DNA nanostructure. Their method simulates the vector multiplication by using a look up table that represents many pairs of the vectors. The multiplication of each corresponding numbers can be performed by adding the carry and the result in each internal

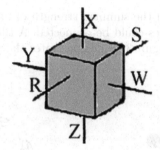

Fig. 1. Hollow cube with six sticky ends

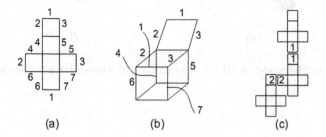

Fig. 2. (a) 2D planar shape that will fold into a box. Each section is formed from many smaller 2D DNA tiles. Edges with the same number have complementary sticky ends exposed so they can hybridize. (b) Folding of the shape in (a) into a box. Here, edges 4, 5, 6, and 7 have all hybridized. Hybridization of edges 2 and 3, whose two complements are now in close proximity, will cause edge 1 to hybridize and form the complete box. (c) Multiple copies of the 2D shape in solution. Copies of the shape can interfere and attach infinitely without control as long as edges have matching sticky ends.

3D tile of the assembled superstructures. The final result can be detected in the first row of the sum layer, where the sum layer uses the sticky ends to accumulate the result from each vertical layer. Their procedure is less energy consumer and can be used at very low cost.

Then Lin [5] invented a 3D DNA self-assembly model to solve the Graph Vertex Coloring problem. The model can simulate a non-deterministic algorithm and solve the problem in linear time:$\Theta(n)$. The number of distinct tiles used in the model is $\Theta(k^2)$, where k is the size of the color set. For the vertex 3-coloring problem, the model requires only 22 types of distinct tiles. We believe that before long this kind of 3D DNA self-assembly algorithm will probably be simulated and executed in lab.

The 3D self-assembly tile is a structure with 6 sticky ends which can assemble in 3D space and is different from the 2D square tile. Its molecular model is as Fig. 3(a). Intuitively, the 3D self-assembly tile is a hexahedron, with each surface represents a direction in the 3D space coordinate system, such as the positive or negative direction of x, y, z axes. The surfaces with sticky ends could connect with each other according to their combining domains. When their adjacent combining domains are matched, and the summed strength of matching domains exceeds τ, the two adjacent surfaces could be connected. A tile's type is decided by its six combining surfaces. Figure 3(b) demonstrates the structure of the abstract hexahedron.

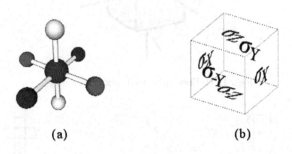

(a)   (b)

Fig. 3. (a) The model of 3D DNA structure. (b) The abstract hexahedron tile.

4   Implementation of DNA 3D Self-assembly Model on Maximum Clique Problem

When we use the DNA self-assembly model to solve the practical problems, firstly we should design a DNA self-assembly system and an algorithm according to the specific problem. The DNA tiles based on the DNA bases' complementary pairing rules according to the specific algorithm we have designed assemble together, when the process of self-assembly finish then we can get the result of the specific problem. For some NP-complete problems such as MCP (Maximum Clique Problem), the massive information storage capacity and the huge parallelism of the biochemistry reaction in the self-assembly process, and the strictness of self-assembly rules can reduce these problems' complexity greatly.

Infra we demonstrate the specific process using the DNA 3D self-assembly model to solve the MCP. MCP can be described as follows:

Suppose G = (V, E) is an undirected graph, V is the set of vertexes and E is the set of edges. The edges of an undirected graph are all disordered pairs of vertexes which usually represented by "()".

If U ∈ V, and ∀ u, v ∈ U, (u, v) ∈ E, so U is called a complete subgraph of G. A complete subgraph of G is called a clique of G, and maximum clique of G is G's maximum complete subgraph.

We take a specific graph for example. Suppose G = (V, E) is an undirected graph, V is the set of vertexes and E is the set of edges (Fig. 4). According to G's adjacent matrix we can get G's adjacent table T_a (Table 1).

In T_a the first line, the first row and the principal diagonal of the table denote the vertexes of the graph, the cells of the below triangle denote the adjacent condition among the vertexes, if two vertexes are connected by an edge then the

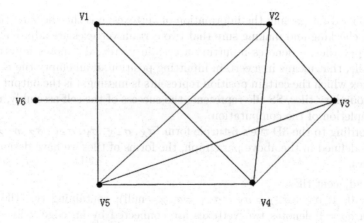

Fig. 4. An undirected graph G

Table 1. Graph G's adjacent table T_a

	1	2	3	4	5	6
1	1					
2	1	2				
3	0	1	3			
4	1	1	1	4		
5	1	1	1	1	5	
6	0	0	1	0	0	6

value of the cell is "1", otherwise it is "0". For example V_1 and V_2 are connected by an edge, so the value of the cell (1,2) is "1".

We define a function $C(i, j)$ to denote the adjacent relation of two vertexes,

$$C(i,j) = \begin{cases} 1, \ if (i,j) \in E \\ 0, \ otherwise \end{cases} \tag{1}$$

The non-deterministic algorithm of the MCP is as below:
maxClique

(1) Random select N_x from V;
(2) Check N_x if all C(i,j)==1; output all kinds N_x to M;
    Else return 1;
(3) inprint the max N_x;

4.1   The Design of the 3D DNA Tiles

Figure 5 demonstrates the tile types we have designed: a is the adjacent tiles, they are used for denoting the adjacent relation of vertexes; b is the passing tiles, they are used for passing the information of vertexes; c is the checking tile, it is used for checking and making sure that two certain vertexes are adjacent; d and e are input tiles, e denotes inputting a certain vertex, d denotes inputting an empty tile, that means in a certain inputting position, if an empty tile is added, the vertex which the certain position represents is missing; f is the output tiles; g is the boundary tiles, SS tile represents the success of the self-assembly, namely the completion of the computation.

According to the 3D tile's 6-turple form $(\sigma_X, \sigma_{-X}, \sigma_Y, \sigma_{-Y}, \sigma_Z, \sigma_{-Z}) \in \Sigma^6$ we have defined in the above paragraph, the forms of tiles we have designed are as follows:

1. The adjacent tiles
   $(\sigma_Z = 0, 1; \sigma_X = \sigma_{-X} = \sigma_Y = \sigma_{-Y} = \sigma_{-Z} = \text{null})$; containing two tile types, when $\sigma_Z = 1$ denotes two vertexes are connected by an edge; while $\sigma_Z = 0$ denotes two vertexes are not adjacent. The adjacent tiles can build different seed configuration according to different graphs. Figure 5a denotes the two tile types, the hexahedron with the symbol "0" on the surface of σ_Z represent the cell with value "0" in the table T_a, while the hexahedron with the symbol "1" on the surface of σ_Z represent the cell with value "1" in the table T_a. The other surfaces of the tiles don't have any symbol.

2. The passing tiles
   $(\sigma_X = \sigma_{-X} = \text{i}, 0; \sigma_Y = \sigma_{-Y} = 0, \text{i}; \sigma_{-Z} = 0, 1; \sigma_Z = \text{OK})$; containing four tile types, they are responsible for passing the information of vertex i to all the possible adjacent vertexes. Figure 5b demonstrates two tile types (other two are left out). The surfaces of σ_{-Z} are symbolized by "0 or 1", the σ_X, σ_{-X} and σ_Y, σ_{-Y} are symbolized respectively by "i or 0"; the surface of σ_Z is symbolized by "OK".

3. The checking tile
   $(\sigma_X = \sigma_{-X} = \text{i}; \sigma_Y = \sigma_{-Y} = \text{j}; \sigma_{-Z} = 1; \sigma_Z = \text{OK})$, containing one tile type, it is responsible for checking and making sure that two certain vertexes i and j are adjacent. Figure 5c demonstrates the checking tile's form, its σ_{-Z} are symbolized by "1", σ_X, σ_{-X} and σ_Y, σ_{-Y} are symbolized respectively by "i" and "j"; σ_Z is denoted by "OK".

4. The input tiles
   Vertex input tile: $(\sigma_X = \sigma_{-X} = \sigma_Y = \sigma_{-Y} = \sigma_Z = \sigma_{-Z} = \text{i})$, containing one tile type, it can input the information of a vertex on a certain inputting position of the seed configuration. Figure 5e demonstrates its form, all of its surfaces are symbolized by "i".
   Empty tile: $(\sigma_X = \sigma_Y = \sigma_Z = 0; \sigma_{-X} = \sigma_{-Y} = \sigma_{-Z} = \text{i})$, it can be inputted in any vertex inputting position of the seed configuration, which means the certain vertex is missing. Figure 5d demonstrates its form, the surfaces of σ_{-X}, σ_{-Y}, σ_{-Z} are all symbolized by "i", the surfaces of σ_X, σ_Y, σ_Z are all symbolized by "0".

5. The output tiles
   $(\sigma_X = \sigma_{-X} = \&; \sigma_Y = \text{null}; \sigma_{-Y} = \text{i}, 0; \sigma_{-Z} = \#; \sigma_Z = \text{null})$; containing four tile types, they are responsible for outputting the last result of the self-assembly. Figure 5f demonstrates two tile types (other two are left out). Their

surfaces of σ_{-Y} are symbolized by "i or 0", the σ_X, σ_{-X} are symbolized by "&", σ_{-Z} is symbolized by "#". In the self-assembly process a set of output tiles are corresponding to a set of input tiles.

6. The boundary tiles
$(\sigma_Z = i, \#; \sigma_X = \sigma_{-X} = \sigma_Y = \sigma_{-Y} = \sigma_{-Z} = \text{null})$, $(\sigma_X = \sigma_Y = i; \sigma_{-X} = \sigma_{-Y} = \sigma_Z = \sigma_{-Z} = \text{null})$, $(\sigma_X = \&; \sigma_{-X} = \sigma_Y = \sigma_{-Y} = \sigma_Z = \sigma_{-Z} = \text{null})$, $(\sigma_X = \sigma_Y = \text{null}; \sigma_{-Z} = \#; \sigma_Z = SS; \sigma_{-X} = \sigma_{-Y} = \&)$, containing five tile types, they can control the growth direction of the self-assembly. Figure 5g demonstrates their forms, the last tile with "#" on σ_{-Z}, "&" on σ_{-X}, σ_{-Y}, and "SS" on σ_Z represents the completion of the self-assembly process.

4.2   Seed Configuration

Figure 6 demonstrates the seed configuration of the self-assembly, it is constructed by the adjacent tiles and the boundary tiles. It contains G's adjacent information, namely when two vertexes are connected by an edge, its value is "1", otherwise is "0". The green lattices denote the inputting positions, and they must be arranged in turn from left to right according to the vertexes' order (Fig. 6b). So in a certain vertex inputting position only the certain vertex can input, others cannot. According to the tiles we have designed (Fig. 5d, e), every inputting position can connect an empty tile (Fig. 5d), which represents a certain vertex is missing, and is denoted by "0".

4.3   The Process of the Self-assembly Process

When the self-assembly start, the seed configuration can assemble with the input tiles (Fig. 5d, e) which represent the graph's vertexes via a non-deterministic self-assembly manner. The first step of the self-assembly process is to form the result non-deterministically. Then check up whether the result is correct or not via the self-assembly process. Only when the correct result is formed the self-assembly process could complete, or we cannot get a successful self-assembly system.

A. The Successful Self-assembly Process

Figure 7a demonstrates the first step, the input tiles demonstrated in Fig. 5d, e are assembled to the seed configuration non-deterministically. Because the inputting positions in the seed configuration are arranged in turn according to the vertexes' order, the input tiles $(\sigma_X = \sigma_{-X} = \sigma_Y = \sigma_{-Y} = \sigma_Z = \sigma_{-Z} = i)$ can only be assembled to the certain position, for example vertex $V_1(\sigma_X = \sigma_{-X} = \sigma_Y = \sigma_{-Y} = \sigma_Z = \sigma_{-Z} = 1)$ can only be assembled to the most left inputting position in the seed configuration. Besides every inputting position in the seed configuration can assemble an empty tile $(\sigma_X = \sigma_Y = \sigma_Z = 0;$ $\sigma_{-X} = \sigma_{-Y} = \sigma_{-Z} = i)$, representing the position misses a vertex, for example in the vertex V_3's position a empty tile $(\sigma_X = \sigma_Y = \sigma_Z = 0; \sigma_{-X} = \sigma_{-Y} = \sigma_{-Z} = 3)$ can be assembled, which means the vertex V_3 is not involved in, we use "0" denotes the missing vertex V_3. Just like this kind of non-deterministically self-assembly process, a result is formed, namely the vertexes set $\{V_1, V_2, V_4, V_5\}$.

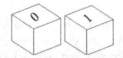

a The adjacent tiles

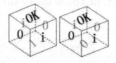

b The passing tiles

c The checking tile

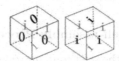

d The empty tile   e The vertex input tile

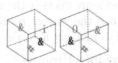

f The output tiles

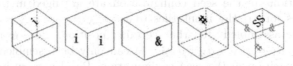

g The boundary tiles

Fig. 5. The basic tile types

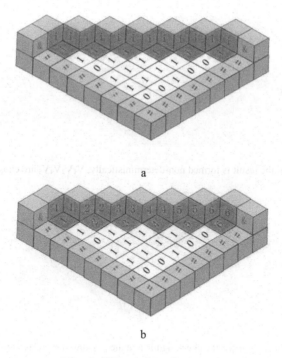

a

b

Fig. 6. The seed configuration

b demonstrates the second step of the self-assembly, it is to check up whether the result is correct or not. This process depends on the checking tiles ($\sigma_X = \sigma_{-X} = $ i; $\sigma_Y = \sigma_{-Y} = $ j; $\sigma_{-Z} = 1$; $\sigma_Z = $ OK) and the passing tiles ($\sigma_X = \sigma_{-X} = $ i, 0; $\sigma_Y = \sigma_{-Y} = $ 0, i; $\sigma_{-Z} = 0$, 1; $\sigma_Z = $ OK). For vertexes V_1, V_2, the check tile ($\sigma_X = \sigma_{-X} = 1$; $\sigma_Y = \sigma_{-Y} = 2$; $\sigma_{-Z} = 1$; $\sigma_Z = $ OK) can be successively assembled to the configuration. For vertexes V_2, V_0, the check tile ($\sigma_X = \sigma_{-X} = 2$; $\sigma_Y = \sigma_{-Y} = 0$; $\sigma_{-Z} = 1$; $\sigma_Z = $ OK) can be successfully assembled to the configuration. Following this manner, the checking tiles can check up all the vertexes' adjacent condition and successfully assemble together.

c demonstrates the step before the self-assembly is completed, the output tiles ($\sigma_X = \sigma_{-X} = $ &; $\sigma_Y = $ null; $\sigma_{-Y} = $ i, 0; $\sigma_{-Z} = $ #; $\sigma_Z = $ null) are assembled to the configuration.

d demonstrates the last step, SS tile ($\sigma_X = \sigma_Y = $ null; $\sigma_{-Z} = $ #; $\sigma_Z = $ SS; $\sigma_{-X} = \sigma_{-Y} = $ &) is assembled to the configuration, which indicates the self-assembly process has complete successfully.

B. The Failed Self-assembly Case

Not all the results formed via non-deterministic self-assembly process are correct, these incorrect results can be detected in a certain step of the self-assembly process. Figure 8 demonstrates a failed self-assembly case. The vertexes set chosen non-deterministically is $\{V_1, V_2, V_3, V_5\}$, the yellow position demonstrates that if existing a tile ($\sigma_X = \sigma_{-X} = 1$; $\sigma_Y = \sigma_{-Y} = 3$; $\sigma_{-Z} = 0$; $\sigma_Z = $ OK) then it

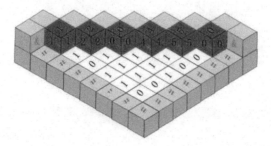

a The first step: the result is formed non-deterministically, $V_1V_2V_4V_5$ are chosen randomly

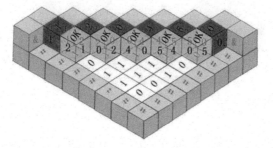

b The following steps: the checking tile and the passing tiles are assembled in.

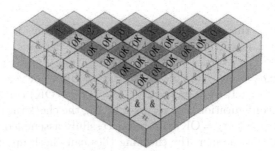

c the step before the self-assembly is completed:the output tiles are assembled in.

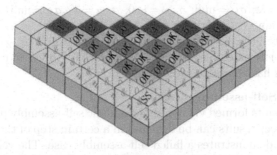

d The last step:the self-assembly process is finished, the SS tile is assembled in.

Fig. 7. The successful self-assembly case

can be assembled to the configuration, the process can proceed, but we didn't design such a tile, that means the two vertexes are not adjacent, the checking tile cannot be assembled to the configuration, the self-assembly process is stopped. This is a failed case, namely the result is not correct.

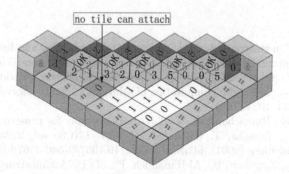

Fig. 8. The failed self-assembly case, the yellow shows the checking tiles cannot attach. (Color figure online)

4.4   The Detecting and Analyzing of the Results

The DNA self-assembly process is a specific biochemistry reaction, when the process is completed, the problem's results exist among the self-assembly systems. We must analyze the successful configuration if we want the correct result of the problem.

In the model we have proposed all the successful configurations are G's clique, while the MCP can be obtained by some experimental techniques of biochemistry and molecular biology. For example, we can firstly separate the successful configuration via fluorescence probe technique and amplify the results via PCR technique, then obtain the DNA strand with the largest molecular mass through gel electrophoresis. After that we could also carry on more accurate analysis to ascertain the vertexes information of the Maximum Clique which the DNA strands encode.

5   Discussion

This paper is using the DNA 3D self-assembly algorithmic model to solve the Maximum Clique Problem. Firstly, we introduce a non-deterministic algorithm. Then, according to the algorithm we design the types of DNA tiles which the computation needs. Lastly, we demonstrate the self-assembly process and the experimental methods which could get the final result. The computation time is linear, and the number of the distinctive tile types is constant.

The model we proposed to solve the Maximum Clique Problem can greatly reduce the computation's complexity, and when the scale of the problem becomes larger, the method is also feasible. Besides the experimental techniques which we use to analyse the results are ripe. As the development of Biological technology, DNA self-assembly algorithm will have more promising applications. Using DNA molecules to make computer chip is under our expectation.

References

1. Winfree, E.: On the computational power of DNA annealing and ligation. In: DNA Based Computers. DIMACS Series in Discrete Mathematics and Theoretical Computer Science, pp. 199–221. American Mathematical Society, Providence (1996)
2. Adleman, L.M.: Molecular computation of solutions to combinatorial problems. Science **266**, 1021–1024 (1994)
3. Ming-Yang, K., Ramachandran, V.: DNA self-assembly for constructing 3D boxes. In: Eades, P., Takaoka, T. (eds.) ISAAC 2001. LNCS, vol. 2223, pp. 429–441. Springer, Heidelberg (2001). https://doi.org/10.1007/3-540-45678-3_37
4. Al-Daoud, E., Zaqaibeh, B., Al-Hanandeh, F.: 3D DNA nanostructures for vector multiplication. Am. J. Sci. Res. **1**, 1450–2223 (2009)
5. Lin, M., Xu, J., et al.: 3D DNA self-assembly model for graph vertex coloring. J. Comput. Theor. Nanosci. **7**, 1246–253 (2010)

Industrial Air Pollution Prediction Using Deep Neural Network

Yu Pengfei[1], He Juanjuan[1], Liu Xiaoming[1], and Zhang Kai[1,2(✉)]

[1] School of Computer Science, Wuhan University of Science and Technology,
Wuhan 430081, People's Republic of China
zhangkai@wust.edu.cn
[2] Hubei Province Key Laboratory of Intelligent Information Processing
and Real-time Industrial System, Wuhan, China

Abstract. In this paper, a deep neural network model is proposed to predict industrial air pollution, such as PM2.5 and PM10. The deep neural network model contains 9 hidden layers, each layer contains 45 neurons. The output of the hidden layer neurons is calculated using the ReLU activation function, which can effectively reduce the gradient elimination effect of the deep neural network. Twelve air pollutant indicators from industrial factories are collected as the input data, such as CO, NO2, O3, and SO2. About 180,000 real industrial air pollution data from Wuhan City are used to train and test the DNN model. Furthermore, the performance of our approach is compared with the SVM and Artificial neural network methods, and the comparison result shows that our algorithm is accurate and competitive with higher prediction accuracy and generalization ability.

Keywords: Industrial air pollution prediction
Deep neural network · PM2.5

1 Introduction

Industrial development has led to serious air pollution and caused smog. The scope and severity of smog have become greater and greater, and people's quality of life have been greatly affected. The main pollutant causing air pollution is PM2.5, and it is also the culprit of haze formation [1]. The prediction algorithm models for PM2.5 concentration include support vector machine(SVM) [2], back-propagation network (BP) [3,4], and genetic neural network(GA_ANN) [5]. Zhao Hong combined genetic algorithm with artificial neural network to improve it, however, the accuracy is low [6]. Yanli Fu predicted the PM2.5 concentration and quality through the establishment of T-S fuzzy neural network and genetic algorithm optimization BP neural network model, the accuracy has improved significantly, but the use of data sets is too small, the model's generalization ability is limited [7]. Until now, Most researchers have mostly focused on BP

© Springer Nature Singapore Pte Ltd. 2018
J. Qiao et al. (Eds.): BIC-TA 2018, CCIS 951, pp. 173–185, 2018.
https://doi.org/10.1007/978-981-13-2826-8_16

and genetic algorithm optimization to establish air pollution quality prediction models, and have not tried deep neural networks [8,9].

With the development of the concept of deep network and deep learning, the neural network has begun to glow a new life [10]. The success of the DNN algorithm has increased the recognition rate of the past by one notch. This paper uses the air quality prediction model established by the deep neural network to effectively extract various factors that affect the concentration of pollutants [11, 12]. This model uses the Adam optimization algorithm and the L2 regularization method [13], and the accuracy of model prediction PM2.5 is much higher than the traditional prediction model [14,15].

2   Data Collection

We have collected hourly concentrations of pollutants in Wuhan from 2016 to 2018a total of 18,000 data. Each piece of data includes CO, CO_24h, NO2, NO2_24h, O3, O3_24h, O3_8h, O3_8h_24h, SO2, SO2_24h, PM10, PM10_24h, PM2.5, PM2.5_24h and AQI. The data is shown in the table below (Table 1):

Table 1. Pollutants dataset

Item	Min	Max	Average
CO	0.1	5.7	1.07
CO_24h	0.1	3.4	1.07
NO2	1	256	49.5
NO2_24h	2	141	49.5
O3	1	406	50.6
O3_24h	3	406	109.1
O3_8h	1	300	49.1
O3_8h_24h	1	300	56.9
SO2	1	229	10.7
SO2_24h	1	44	10.8
PM10	1	1097	94.9
PM10_24h	4	707	93.1
PM2.5	1	414	54.9
PM2.5_24h	1	300	54.7
AQI	8	500	84.4

3 Deep Neural Network Model

3.1 Prediction Models Based Deep Neural Network

This research use a deep neural network to establish the air pollution concentration prediction models. After trial and comparison, the following model was constructed (Fig. 1):

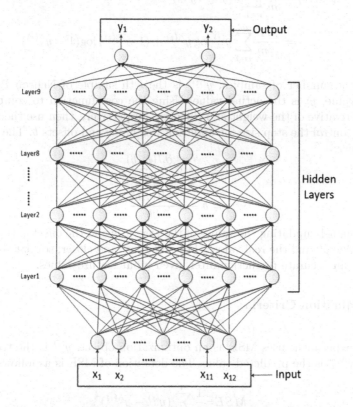

Fig. 1. Deep neural network model.

As shown above, the model sets 9 hidden layers, each layer contains 45 hidden units. The input layer contains 12 cells, and the output layer contains 2 units. Each layer uses the ReLu function. Input feature X is a 12-dimensional vector. The formula is as follows:

$$X = [x_1, x_2, ...x_{11}x_{12}] \tag{1}$$

The input vector consists of CO, CO_24 h, NO2, NO2_24 h, O3, O3_24 h, O3_8 h, O3_8 h_24 h, SO2, SO2_24 h, PM10, PM10_24 h concentration data. The output vector Y is a two-dimensional vector that represents the predicted concentration of PM2.5, PM2.5_24 h. The hidden layer has 9 layers, which are represented as Layer1, Layer2, ..., Layer9.

3.2   Parameter Optimization Process

The algorithm learning process uses a gradient descent method to train each neuron's parameters w and b by minimizing the cost function. For example, in a simple Logistic regression, the cost function can be defined as follows:

$$J(w,b) = \frac{1}{m} \sum_{i=1}^{m} L(y^{\wedge(i)}, y^{(i)})$$

$$= -\frac{1}{m} \sum_{i=1}^{m} y^{(i)} \log y^{\wedge(i)} + (1 - y^{(i)}) \log(1 - y^{\wedge(i)}) \qquad (2)$$

m is the number of samples, $y^{\wedge(i)}$ is the i th sample of Neuron Predicted Output Value, y^i is the actual value. Using the cost function to compute the partial derivative of the weight and the offset respectively, then use the learning rate a to control the step size for updating weights w and offsets b. The formula is as follows:

$$w = w - \alpha \frac{\partial J(w,b)}{\partial w} \qquad (3)$$

$$b = b - \alpha \frac{\partial J(w,b)}{\partial b} \qquad (4)$$

By continuously updating the values of the weight w and the offset b, the neuron output value $y^\wedge$ and the real value y become closer and closer, so that the model can make an accurate prediction after given input feature values.

3.3   Evaluation Criteria

(1) MSE

The experiment uses MSE as an optimization object. $y^{(i)}$ is the true value and $y^{\wedge(i)}$ is the predicted value. The definition of MSE is as follows:

$$MSE = \frac{1}{n} \sum_{i=1}^{n} \left(y^{(i)} - y^{\wedge(i)}\right)^2 \qquad (5)$$

(2) Relative error

To measure the accuracy of forecast results, we use relative errors to determine the accuracy of the forecast results. The formula is as follows:

$$p = \frac{|y - y^\wedge|}{y} * 100 \qquad (6)$$

The experimental definition that p ≤ 10% is excellent results, 10% ≤ p ≤ 30% is accurate results, 30% ≤ p ≤ 50% is poor results, p ≥ 50% is very poor results.

(3) R^2

R^2 is also called Coefficient of determination or Goodness of Fit. The formula is as follows:

$$R^2 = \frac{SSR}{SST} = 1 - SSE/SST \tag{7}$$

SST is the total sum of squares, SSR is the regression sum of squares, and SSE is the error sum of squares. When the goodness of fit R^2 is closer to 1, the higher the reference value is, the better the fit is.

3.4 Training Results

Experiment starts with an unoptimized data set. We choose the Sigmoid function as activation function and try different combinations of hidden layers and hidden units. In each layer, we use the same number of hidden units. Experiment using PM2.5 and PM2.5_24 h as output. Some of the results are shown in the following table (Table 2):

Table 2. Training results

Hidden layer	Nodes of each hidden layer	Training set MSE	Test set MSE	PM2.5 accuracy on testset	PM2.5_24 h accuracy on testset
8	30	0.00872	0.00947	58.3%	59.2%
8	40	0.00704	0.00782	65.3%	67.4%
8	45	0.00513	0.00684	69.5%	72.3%
8	50	0.00516	0.00695	68.9%	72.1%
8	55	0.00685	0.00743	66.6%	68.5%
9	30	0.00767	0.00804	62.4%	65.3%
9	45	0.00641	0.00701	66.9%	69.1%
10	45	0.00515	0.00687	67.9%	70.1%
10	50	0.00472	0.00716	67.4%	70.6%
12	40	0.00545	0.00732	68.1%	71.3%
12	45	0.00538	0.00733	66.5%	70.0%
15	40	0.00562	0.00749	66.7%	69.9%

During the experiment, we found that the model does not fit the data well when there are too few hidden layers and hidden cells. Acceptability decreases when there are too many hidden layers and hidden cells. Training time period is too long when it has excessive training parameters. So the unoptimized models and datasets cannot predict accurately.

4   Improve the Performance of Predict Models

4.1   Dividing the Dataset

In order to ensure that the training set and the test set come from the same distribution, the data is divided into two parts, one part is all the environmental data for 2017 in Wuhan, the other part is pollution data of the monitoring point in Qingshan in 2017.

Due to the complexity of the data, the data in different regions is very different. Therefore, the data set must be filtered. The screening method is as follows:

(1) Remove duplicate data. Data with the same input and different outputs will worsen the performance of the model. Removing these data will speed up the fitting process and improve the prediction accuracy.
(2) Split data by region and time. There are differences in the data in different regions. After the original data set is divided, the training set and the test set will come from the same distribution, which can effectively improve the performance of the model.
(3) Remove too large or too small data. Some data is obviously wrong. Too large or too small will make the network model train in the wrong direction. Removing these erroneous data can effectively improve the performance of the model.

After filtering, the data set is as shown in the following table (Table 3):

Table 3. Dataset partition

Partition	Wuhan	Qingshan
Total data	105000	8699
Training set	95000	6199
Validation set	5000	1250

4.2   Data Normalization

The normalized feature data can speed up the training and convergence of the model. In this experiment, we use the Z-score standardization to normalize the feature. The standardized data conforms to the standard normal distribution, and it conforms to a distribution with a mean of 0 and a standard deviation of 1. Its conversion function is as follows:

$$x = (x - \mu)/\sigma \tag{8}$$

μ is the average of sample data, σ is the standard deviation of sample data. It has been proved by experiments that the Z-score standardization can effectively improve the performance of the prediction model, so this experiment uses this normalization method. Part of the data is normalized as shown in the following table (Table 4):

Table 4. Normalized dataset

AQI	PM2.5	PM10	SO2	NO2	O3	CO
0.147	0.095	0.190	0.153	0.128	0.485	0.156
0.358	0.372	0.475	0.254	0.711	0.091	0.222
0.521	0.541	0.000	0.017	0.154	0.192	0.133
0.295	0.209	0.405	0.237	0.141	0.601	0.200
0.147	0.088	0.190	0.068	0.087	0.540	0.133
0.242	0.155	0.310	0.102	0.228	0.293	0.111

4.3   L2 Regularization

As the number of training increases, the model will perform better on the training set, but the performance on the test set begins to decline. This is called training overfitting. In order to prevent training from overfitting, our experiment uses the L2 regularization method. The formula is as follows:

$$J(w,b) = \frac{1}{m} \sum_{i=1}^{m} L(y^{\wedge(i)}, y^i) + \frac{\lambda}{2m} \sum_{j=1}^{n_x} w_j{}^2 \tag{9}$$

L2 regularization is achieved by adding a regularization term to the cost function. m is the sample size, n_x is the number of samples. L2 regularization is also referred to as weight reduction. The weight becomes smaller, indicating that the complexity of the network is lower and the data fitting is just right.

5   Experimental Results

5.1   Training Results of the Optimized Model

In order to improve the performance of the model, we split the original data set, remove the maximal and minimal erroneous data and remove duplicate data. Then we normalize the data and use Relu function and Adam optimizer to speed up the process of model convergence.

In order to prevent overfitting and improve the prediction accuracy, we have added L2 regularization. Experimental data is shown in the following table (Table 5):

5.2   Evaluation of Training Results

We choose the best training model for analysis and evaluation, it has 9 hidden layers with 45 hidden units on each layer. The decline process of MSE during training is shown in the figure below (Fig. 2):

Table 5. Training results

Hidden layer	Nodes of each hidden layer	Training set MSE	Test set MSE	PM2.5 accuracy on testset	PM2.5_24 h accuracy on testset
7	30	0.00274	0.00597	81.2%	84.0%
7	45	0.00256	0.00575	82.3%	86.4%
8	40	0.00115	0.00467	89.28%	92.5%
9	45	0.00132	0.00372	90.1%	93.3%
10	40	0.00099	0.00421	89.68%	92.8%
12	40	0.00145	0.00732	68.1%	89.3%
12	45	0.00168	0.00733	66.5%	88.9%
15	40	0.00213	0.00749	66.7%	88.4%

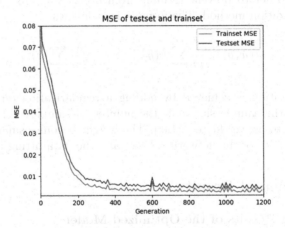

Fig. 2. Descending graph of MSE.

From the descending graph of MSE, it can be found that the model performs well on the training set and the test set. After adding the L2 regularization term, there is no serious over-fitting phenomenon. After 1200 rounds of training, the loss tends to be stable and the result is optimal.

Using the goodness of fit R2 as the evaluation criterion, the experimental results for PM2.5_24 h are shown in the following figure (Fig. 3).

As the picture shows, with the increase of training rounds, the goodness of fit of PM2.5_24 h is continuously approaching 1. This shows that the prediction accuracy is getting higher and higher.

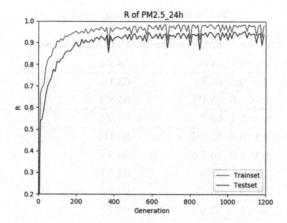

Fig. 3. The goodness of fit of PM2.5_24 h.

To visualize the difference between the forecast result and the original value, we plotted the original value as the abscissa and the predicted value as the ordinate. The closer the scatter distribution is to the straight line y=x, the closer the predicted value is to the true value, and the better the prediction effect of the model. The scatter plot is as follows (Fig. 4):

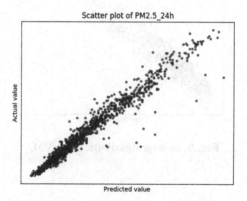

Fig. 4. Scatter distribution of forecast results.

6 Compared with Traditional Methods

6.1 SVM

SVM exhibits many unique advantages in solving small sample, nonlinear and high dimensional pattern recognition. SVM model experimental results are shown in the following table (Table 6):

Table 6. SVM Training results

c	g	PM2.5 accuracy	PM2.5_24h accuracy
1	0.1	54%	56.2%
1	0.5	60%	63.1%
1	1.0	63.1%	65.8%
1	1.4	62%	64.3%
0.1	0.6	55.4%	58.1%
0.1	1.0	56.7%	58.5%
10	1	62%	64.3%
10	2	66.6%	69.2%
5	1	62.8%	65.1%
5	2.5	66.6%	69.2%

The scatter plot of the SVM model is as follows (Fig. 5):

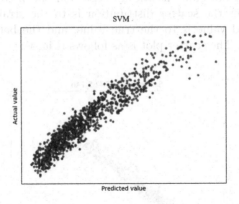

Fig. 5. Scatter distribution of SVM.

6.2   BP Neural Network

Predictive models based on BP neural networks are also common. The BP neural network is mainly composed of three layers: input layer, hidden layer, and output layer. In addition to the neurons in the input layer, each neuron will have a weighted sum of the input values z, and then use the sigmoid function to nonlinearly transform z to get the activation value a.

The BP neural network essentially implements a mapping function from input to output. The mathematical theory proves that the three-layer neural network can approximate any nonlinear continuous function with arbitrary precision. This makes it particularly suitable for solving complex problems, so the BP neural network has strong nonlinear mapping capabilities. The experimental results are shown in the following table (Table 7):

Table 7. BP neural network training results

Nodes of hidden layer	Training set MSE	Test set MSE	PM2.5 accuracy	PM2.5_24 h accuracy
6	0.00874	0.00914	65%	67.1%
7	0.00764	0.00912	67.2%	69.6%
8	0.00808	0.00897	67%	67.3%
9	0.00778	0.00898	65.4%	67.6%
10	0.00808	0.00905	65.2%	66.9%
20	0.00767	0.00879	65.8%	67.2%
30	0.00754	0.00892	65.3%	67.3%
40	0.00755	0.00873	65.4%	66.9%

The scatter plot of the BP neural network model is shown below (Fig. 6):

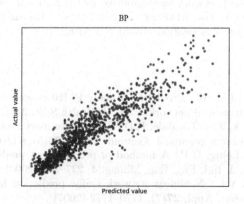

Fig. 6. Scatter distribution of BP.

From the above picture, we find that DNN model performs much better on scatter plots than BP model and SVM model.

6.3   Comparison of Three Models

After several experiments, we chose the optimal parameters of the SVM and BP neural network. The comparison between the traditional model and the deep neural network is shown in the following table (Table 8):

Table 8. SVM training results

Accuracy	SVM	BP	DNN
PM2.5	66.6%	67.3%	90.3%
PM2.5_24 h	69.2%	69.9%	94.2%

7   Conclusion

In this paper, we proposed a deep neural network model to predict industrial air pollutant. About 180,000 real industrial air pollution data from 2016 to 2018 in Wuhan are used to train, validate and test the model. We use ReLU nonlinear activation function instead of the traditional Sigmoid activation function, effectively improve the training speed of the network, eliminating the gradient disappearance or gradient explosion phenomenon. We use the Batch Normalization method to improve the training accuracy and convergence speed of the network. Through the DropOff technology, effectively prevent the depth of the neural network over-fitting, improve the test data prediction accuracy. The performance of our approach is compared with the SVM and BP neural network, and the comparison result shows that our algorithm is accurate and competitive with higher prediction accuracy and generalization ability.

Acknowledgments. This work was supported by the National Natural Science Foundation of China(Grant Nos. 61472293 and 61702383). Research Project of Hubei Provincial Department of Education (Grant No. 2016238).

References

1. Yin, A., Lin, Y., Lin, W.: Prediction of daily PM10 concentration in Guangzhou based on PSO-BP neural network. Chin. J. Health Stat. **3**(5), 763–766 (2016)
2. Yuan, Z., Mattick, J.S., Teasdale, R.D.: SVMtm: support vector machines to predict transmembrane segments. J. Comput. Chem. **25**(5), 632–636 (2004)
3. Yuehong, B.X., Liang, G.P.: A method of product cost prediction based on BP neural networks. J. Ind. Eng. Eng. Manag. **4**, 237–239 (2000)
4. Liu, J., Huang, Y.L.: Nonlinear network traffic prediction based on BP neural network. J. Comput. Appl. **27**(7), 1770–1772 (2007)
5. Cheng, H.: Research on the application of GA-PSO-BP neural network in air pollutant concentration prediction, pp. 138–142 . Huazhong University of Science and Technology (2014)
6. Zhao, H., Liu, A., Wang, W.: Improved air quality prediction model based on GA-ANN. Environ. Sci. Res. **22**(11), 1276–1281 (2009)
7. Fu, Y.: Prediction of PM2.5 mass concentration based on neural network, pp. 98–104. Shaanxi University of Science and Technology (2016)
8. Polson, N.G., Sokolov, V.O.: Deep learning for short-term traffic flow prediction. Transp. Res. Part C Emerg. Technol. **79**(1), 1–17 (2017)
9. Butepage, J., Black, M.J., Kragic, D., et al.: Deep representation learning for human motion prediction and classification. In: IEEE Conference on Computer Vision and Pattern Recognition, pp. 1591–1599. IEEE Computer Society (2017)

10. Wang, J., Gu, Q., Wu, J., et al.: Traffic speed prediction and congestion source exploration: a deep learning method. In: IEEE International Conference on Data Mining, pp. 499–508 (2017)
11. Sun, T., Zhou, B., Lai, L.: Sequence-based prediction of protein protein interaction using a deep-learning algorithm. BMC Bioinform. **18**(1), 277 (2014)
12. Yu, J.X., Yu, J.Q., Wang, X.C.: Highway network scale prediction based on BP neural network. J. Changan Univ. **6**(1), 75–78 (2006)
13. Li, H., et al.: Deep CTR prediction in display advertising. In: ACM on Multimedia Conference, pp. 811–820 (2016)
14. Lei, L.: Application of artificial neural network in air pollution prediction, pp. 35–37. Beijing University of Technology (2007)
15. Lv, Y., Duan, Y., Kang, W.: Traffic flow prediction with big data: a deep learning approach. IEEE Trans. Intell. Transp. Syst. **16**(2), 865–873 (2015)

An Efficient Genetic Algorithm for Solving Constraint Shortest Path Problem Through Specified Vertices

Zhang Kai[1,2], Shao Yunfeng[1], Zhang Zhaozong[1], and Hu Wei[1(✉)]

[1] School of Computer Science, Wuhan University of Science and Technology,
Wuhan 430081, People's Republic of China
14393908@qq.com
[2] Hubei Province Key Laboratory of Intelligent Information Processing and
Real-time Industrial System, Wuhan 430081, China

Abstract. Finding a constraint shortest path which passes through a set of specified vertices is very important for many research areas, such as intelligent transportation systems, emergency rescue, and military planning. In this paper, we propose an efficient genetic algorithm for solving the constraint shortest path problem. Firstly, the Dijkstra algorithm is used to calculate the shortest distance between any two specified vertices. The optimal solution change from the original problem into the Hamilton path problem with the specified vertices. Because the number of specified vertices is much less than the number of vertices for the whole road network, the search space would be reduced exponentially. Secondly, the genetic algorithm is adopted to search for the optimal solution of the Hamilton path problem. Thirdly our algorithm should detect and eliminate the cycle path. Finally, the performance of our algorithm is evaluated by some real-life city road networks and some randomly generated road networks. The computational results show that our algorithm can find the constraint shortest path efficiently and effectively.

Keywords: Genetic algorithm · Shortest path problem
Hamilton path problem

1 Introduction

The shortest path problem is a common problem in the fields of graph theory, operations research, and computer science. Many problems originating from real life can be abstracted as the mathematical model of the shortest path problem. In 1959 Dijkstra proposed a single-source shortest path algorithm with time complexity $O(n^2)$ [1]. In 1962, Floy proposed an arbitrary two-point shortest path algorithm with time complexity $O(n^3)$ [2]. The problem of the shortest path to any two points has been well resolved. However, with the development of geographic information systems, intelligent transportation systems, and Internet communication technologies, solving the shortest path problem with the specified

© Springer Nature Singapore Pte Ltd. 2018
J. Qiao et al. (Eds.): BIC-TA 2018, CCIS 951, pp. 186–197, 2018.
https://doi.org/10.1007/978-981-13-2826-8_17

vertices and the absence of loops has brought new challenges [3–6]. In the areas of navigation systems, public transport inquiries, emergency rescue and logistics transportation, military planning, etc. solving the shortest path problem with a specified apex is an urgent problem to be solved [7–9].

Many scholars at home and abroad have proposed many algorithms to solve the problem of the shortest path to the given vertex. Jia et al. proposed The Middle of the specified node set of shortest path algorithm [10]. Ibaraki proposed two algorithms for dynamic programming and branch-and-bound algorithms to solve the problem, and the branch-and-bound algorithm is more efficient than the dynamic programming algorithm [11]. Nemhauser et al. proposed a generalized permanent label algorithm to solve the shortest path through a specified vertices [12]. Based on the Saksena and Kumar algorithm, Gomes et al. proposed three heuristic hybrid algorithms for solving disjoint shortest paths [13]. Feng et al. proposed a geometric algebraic algorithm to solve the node-constrained shortest path problem [14]. Yao et al. proposed a dynamic pruning search algorithm to solve the shortest path problem that must pass through the vertices set [15]. Xu and Liu used genetic algorithms to solve this problem [16,17]. However, due to need to search for exponential solution space, these algorithms are difficult to efficiently solve large-scale problems. This paper will solve this problem by transforming it into solving the shortest Hamiltonian path problem, which free the calculation of genetic algorithms from large-scale map restrictions. So that the algorithm can narrow the search space and find the shortest path faster in the larger scale graphs.

Firstly, we don't care about the specific path between the specified vertices, but only pay attention to the distance calculated by Dijkstra algorithm between the specified vertices. Secondly, we use the improved genetic algorithm to solve the global optimal combined path of all specified vertices, and use the advantage of swarm intelligence to rapidly search for larger solution space in a short time. Finally restoring the concrete route between the specified vertices to obtain the complete shortest path, at the same time the optimization strategy of eliminating the ring path is also given. We describe the problem to be solved in the Sect. 2 and implement the genetic algorithm in the Sect. 3 while giving the strategy of eliminating the loop. Then we tested and discussed the algorithm in Sect. 4 and summarized it in Sect. 5.

2   Problem Formulation

Given the weighted graph $G = (V, E)$, where V is the set of vertices and E is the set of edges. e_{ij} represents an edge of the vertex v_i to v_j, and c_{ij} represents the weight of the edge e_{ij}. Suppose there are m vertices that must go through is set R, the source point is $s \in R$, the end point is $d \in R$, and P is the path from the source point to the end point, then P is a set of edges $P \subseteq E$. The shortest path problem through the specified vertices can be expressed as follows:

$$Len = \min \sum c_{ij} x_{ij} \qquad (1)$$

$$x_{ij} = \begin{cases} 1, & e_{ij} \in P \\ 0, & e_{ij} \notin P \end{cases} \tag{2}$$

$$\sum x_{ij} - \sum x_{ji} = \begin{cases} 1, & i = s \ and \ \forall j \\ -1, & i = j \ and \ \forall j \\ 0, & i, j \in V - \{s, d\} \end{cases} \tag{3}$$

$$\sum x_{ik} = 1, \ \sum x_{kj} = 1, \ \forall v_k \in R \tag{4}$$

(1) For the objective function, find the shortest distance Len of the path P.
(2) The definition of the decision variable x_{ij}, if there is e_{ij} in the shortest path P, then $x_{ij} = 1$, otherwise $x_{ij} = 0$.
(3) The source s, the end d, the constraint of the middle point, i and j are variables, which can be any vertices in the graph.
(4) The formula is a mandatory constraint, and each specified vertices passes once and only once, i and j are variables, k is a specified vertices.

According to the nature of the city graph, any two vertices v_i and v_j in the graph G are reachable. Therefore, Dijkstra's algorithm can be invoked to find the shortest path of any two specified vertices in the vertex set R. Only concerned with the distance, without considering the specific waypoints between the specified vertices, the problem is transformed into the shortest Hamiltonian problem that requires the vertex set R, as shown in Figs. 1 and 2. After obtaining distance of the specified vertices, the global shortest path is solved by an improved genetic algorithm, at the same time the path is restored and the loop is eliminated.

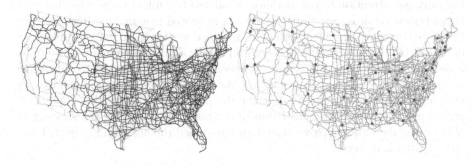

Fig. 1. Calculate the shortest path between any two specified vertices

3 Algorithm Design

The algorithm consists of four main steps, which solve the problem step by step: (1) Calculate the shortest distance between any two specified vertices (2) Calculate the shortest Hamiltonian path that contains only the specified points (3) Restore the complete shortest path (4) Cycle check and eliminate. This algorithm framework is as follows:

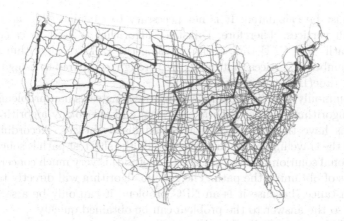

Fig. 2. Calculate the shortest Hamiltonian path between a set of specified vertices

Algorithm 1.

```
Input Graph=(V,E), specified vertices;
Output BestValue;//BestValue is global optimal shortest path
 begin
     Initial:population,P_crossover,P_mutation;
     //P_crossover is crossover probability
     //P_mutation is mutation probability
     Dijkstra(Graph,specified vertices);
     For(i=0;i<Maxnum;i++)  //Max_num is max number of iterations
         Retain elites and random sequences;
         While(new population size<population size)do
             if(fitness>Ram)
             //Ram is a number of 0-1
             //randomly generated by equal probability
                 selection(population);
             End if
         End While
         For(i=0 to population size) do
             If(Ram<P_crossover)
                 crossover(population);
             End if
         End For
         For(i=0 to population size) do
             If(Ram<P_mutation)
                 mutation(population);
             End if
         End For
     setBestValue();  //Set the optimal value
     End for
     Restore full path;
     Cycle replacement;
 end
```

Dijkstra and Floyd's algorithms are very mature shortest path algorithms, in which Dijkstra algorithm's time complexity is $O(n^2)$ and Floyd's algorithm has time complexity $O(n^3)$. In step (1), the shortest distance between specified vertices must be calculated. It is not necessary to calculate the shortest path between all vertices. Therefore, Dijkstra's algorithm is used to calculate the shortest path. The CPU time spent on using the Dijkstra algorithm increases with the number of vertices that must pass through, compared to using the Floyd algorithm, time(Dijkstra) ≤ time(Floyd).

The commonly used methods of solving traveling salesman problems include heuristic algorithms such as genetic algorithm and ant colony algorithm. These calculations have their own advantages and disadvantages. According to the purpose of the traveling salesman problem, only the shortest path is sought, while the traditional solution (such as the greedy method) is very much concerned with the process of obtaining the path. The genetic algorithm will directly target the shortest distance (because it is an NPC problem, it can only be a satisfactory distance), so the answer to the problem can be obtained quickly.

First, Dijkstra algorithm is used to calculate the shortest distance between any two specified vertices in the set R. Second, the genetic algorithm is used to solve the shortest Hamiltonian path and cycle replacement. Finally, restore the full path that contains the specified vertices to determine if the cycle is contained and remove the loop in the shortest path.

3.1   Initialize Population

Any one path containing all necessary vertices can be represented by a randomly arranged sequence from s to d. If a city has m necessary vertices, r_i denotes the ith visited the vertices in sequence, and the path code is shown as follow:

$$X = (r_1, r_2, \ldots, r_i, \ldots, r_m)\, r_i \in R, r_1 = s, r_m = d \tag{5}$$

The algorithm randomly generates n random path sequences based on the initial set of population n. The distance c_{ij} between any two adjacent vertices v_i and v_j in the path can be calculated according to Dijkstra's algorithm.

3.2   Fitness Function

The fitness function is used to evaluate the individuals adaptability to the living environment. This paper designs the fitness function for the purpose of finding the shortest path, which increased chances of survival and reproduction of sequences with smaller sums of path weights in the population. The algorithm chooses the reciprocal of the length of the path as the fitness function value of each individual.

$$Fitness(X) = \frac{1}{Len} = \frac{1}{\sum c_{ij}} \tag{6}$$

3.3   Selection Operation

Selecting operations to simulate the evolutionary process of survival of the fittest, usually based on fitness evaluation functions. Selecting individuals from the population to participate in the evolution process of the next generation. The algorithm uses an elite retention strategy combined with roulette and adjusts the elite retention strategy to ensure the diversity of the population.

First, some candidate solutions with shorter path lengths in the population are reserved. In addition, in order to maintain a certain population diversity, a small number of random sequences are added to the elite retention strategy. The remaining individuals adopt roulette selection algorithm selection, constructing offspring to replace parents and forming new populations. The roulette selection algorithm makes individuals with higher fitness values have the higher probability of selection. Let the scale of the population is n and the fitness of the individual Xi be $F(X_i)$, then the probability $P(X_i)$ is:

$$P(X_i) = \frac{F(X_i)}{\sum\limits_{k=1}^{n} F(X_k)} \tag{7}$$

3.4 Crossover Operation

The crossover operation simulates the process of hybridization of DNA molecules and generates a greater number of new individuals based on the population, expanding the diversity of the population so that the algorithm can search for a wider neighborhood solution space. Parents are cross-computed to get new offspring individuals, that is, through local search to find better offspring than parents.

The algorithm sets the crossover rate $P_{crossover}$ by the user. If the random number P_{random} is less than the crossover rate $P_{crossover}$, the crossover operation is performed. Using a higher crossover rate, the algorithm can generate a greater number of candidate solutions, search for a larger range of solution space, and more likely to find a globally optimal solution. At the same time, setting the crossover rate too high can also lead to the excessive search for some unnecessary solution space, which consumes a lot of computing time. In this paper, an improved crossover operation is used to generate new individuals, that is the generation of offspring by the shortest distance between adjacent specified points, as shown in Fig. 3.

(1) First, randomly select two sequences as parents in a population that satisfies the crossover rate, then randomly select the locus r, and use the locus as a start vertex to search backward or forward in the parent sequence for the next specified vertex.

(2) The r-vertices are located at different positions in the parent's sequence. Assuming a backward search, the r-vertex and its next vertex in the two parents chains are (r, i) (r, j). The distance from r to the next required point i, j, whichever is the smaller distance, is taken as the next required point, and the new vertices is used as the current vertices to find the next vertices, thus forming a new child.

(3) Repeat step 1 and 2 searches to traverse all parent generations that satisfy the crossover rate, generating different children by forward search and backward search and exchange the sequence so that the source point s and the terminal point d will be at the start and end positions. New offspring and individuals retained by elite strategy to constructs new populations.

r
r
P_1
P_2
if $C_{23}<C_{24}$
next r=3
r
r
Search backwards once
O_1

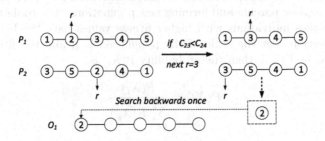

Fig. 3. Crossover operation

3.5 Mutation Operation

The mutation operation simulates gene mutations in individuals in the natural world, mainly to maintain population diversity and prevent the algorithm from falling into a local optimum. This article uses two methods to mutate individuals, as shown in Fig. 4. The algorithm randomly selects one method to generate a new individual sequence and each mutation has a half chance to be selected. The two mutation allows the algorithm search for larger mutation spaces, and the ability to jump out of local optimum is stronger.

Method 1: First, randomly select two intersection points i and j, and then reverse the sequence between two random points i and j to generate a new sequence.

Method 2: Randomly select two intersection points i and j, divide the original sequence into 1, 2, 3 three parts, and then exchange 1, 2 sub-sequences to generate a new sequence.

X_{old} = (4 2 3 1 8 7 6 5 9)
reverse
X_{new} = (4 2 7 8 1 3 6 5 9)
X_{old} = (4 2 3 1 8 7 6 5 9)
① ② ③
X_{new} = (3 1 8 7 4 2 6 5 9)
② ① ③

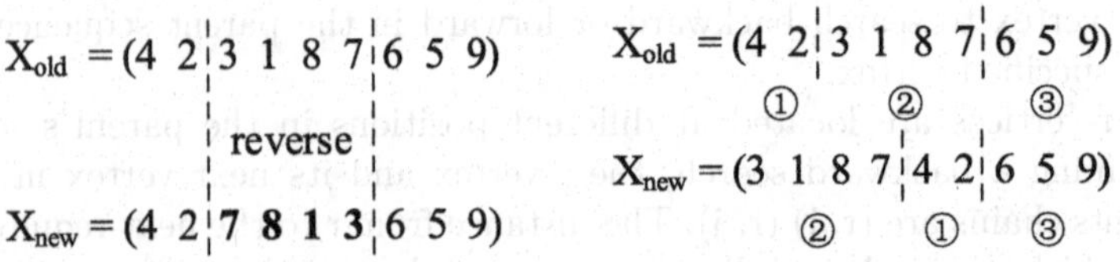

Fig. 4. Two mutation operation of individual sequences

According to the certain probability, the algorithm selects some individuals in the population to mutate and produce new individuals. The algorithm sets the mutation rate $P_{mutation}$ by the user. A 0–1 random number P_{random} generated before each mutation operation. If the random number P_{random} is less than the crossover rate $P_{mutation}$, a mutation operation is performed. If the mutation rate is set too low, It is harder for the algorithm to jump out of local optimum; if the mutation rate is set too high, although diversity is increased, it is possible that there are too many random changes that cause the offspring population to lose its excellent characteristics from its parent. At the same time it make the algorithm not easy to converge.

3.6 Cycle Replacement

After the above genetic algorithm is calculated, the sequence set $R\{r_1, r_2, r_3...r_i\} \subseteq G\{V, E\}$ of the necessary shortest path is obtained, and the elimination loop is performed. The operation steps are as follows:

(1) Find any two adjacent paths with repeated vertices in the sequence R. For example, the necessary sequence of vertices is $\{A, B, C\} \subseteq R$. AB, BC are two sets of sequences containing a large number of ordinary vertices, where the set $D\{d_1, d_2, d_3, ..., d_i\}$ is a repeated link in the sequence of AB and BC routes, that is $(D \subseteq AB) \wedge (D \subseteq BC)$, and the set D is temporarily deleted and saved in the graph G.

(2) Find the new shortest path between AB and BC in the figure and mark it as AB_{new} and BC_{new}. If no new path exists, it means no loop-free path exists and the original path is returned; if a new path is found, the three combinations of $AB_{new} + BC_{new}$, $AB + BC_{new}$, and $AB_{new} + BC$ are saved.

(3) For the new combined path generated in step 2, it is checked whether the ring still remains, and the path with the shortest distance in the combined path is reserved, and steps 1 and 2 are repeated if there is still a ring.

4   Results and Discussion

Experimental environment is that: the system is windows10 with 3.2 GHz i5-4460 CPU, 8 GB memory, and the programming language is java, and JVM is JRE. The experimental data source is divided into two parts. One tests the algorithm through the actual city's Oldenburg road network data graph, and the second is to test the algorithm through four different network graphs generated by the Delaunay triangulation algorithm [18].

The algorithm was tested by the actual city Oldenburg Road Network data map, containing 6105 vertices and 7035 edges. In the roadmap of Oldenburg City, we arbitrarily select 26 specified vertices. We select the path starting vertex S and ending vertex D and the experimental results show that the genetic algorithm takes about 63.614 ms to find the shortest path (Figs. 5 and 6).

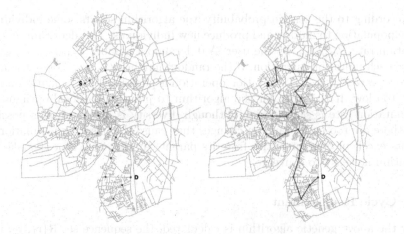

Fig. 5. Specify 26 vertices and calculate Hamiltonian path

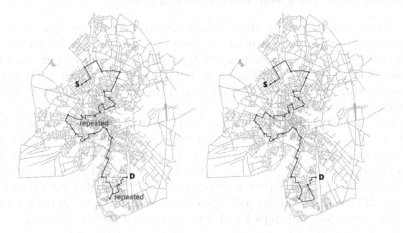

Fig. 6. Restore full path and cycle replacement

The experiment mainly focuses on the computation time and the distance growth caused by the cycle replacement. We uses the Delaunay triangulation algorithm to generate four network maps and the actual city Oldenburg roadmaps to calculate the time efficiency under different number of specified vertices. Randomly generating the specified vertices to test the time required to obtain the shortest path and take the average of the results of 100 experiment (ms) are summarized in Table 1.

In the case of different map sizes, when the number of specified vertices is five, the average time spent by the genetic algorithm is about 1 ms. When the number of required vertices increases to 50, the time spent is about 1.5 s. The scale of time consumed by the genetic algorithm has not increased drastically as the scale of the map has grown. Through analysis, it can be known that the

Table 1. The time (ms) spent at different specified vertices

Graph size (vertices, edges)	5	10	20	50
50, 136	0.59	3.22	38.12	1096.30
238, 692	0.9	3.68	34.41	1111.31
553, 1673	1.07	3.21	37.19	1575.63
907, 2701	1.31	3.93	54.19	1500.85
6105, 7135	1.63	4.83	59.67	1742.38

correlation between the time spent by the genetic algorithm and the size of the network graph is small but it is related to the number of vertices that must be passed. Because when the genetic algorithm is calculated, the input value must be the path length between the vertices, and the genetic algorithm must be the vertex structure sequence, so as the number of specified vertices increases, the time spent by the genetic algorithm to find a shorter route will also increase.

In the elimination loop test, since the first graph in the above four-structure diagram is too small and the cycle has a low probability of occurrence, the 2, 3 and 4 diagrams are taken as the cycle test. The experiment selected 5, 10, 20 and 50 specified vertices test algorithms. These vertices must contain start and end vertices and each group of data is tested 100 times. The detailed data of the fourth map is shown in Table 2.

The analysis shows that the growth rate of the distance tends to be stable with the increase in the number of specified vertices. With the increase of the total distance, the elimination of the loop brings about a decrease in the proportion of distance increase. Statistical test data shows that the ratio of the number of loops and the number of specified vertices in the same route is between 0.1 and 0.2, and the number of loops is less than the number of specified vertices. The elimination of the loop has a distance growth rate of about 0.01 to 0.02 compared to the previous route, and the overall growth rate is small.

The time taken to eliminate the loop is proportional to the number of rings, and the greater the number of rings, the longer it takes to eliminate the loop. In the network map of the same scale, testing different specified points the time taken to eliminate the same number of rings is roughly the same. By eliminating the loop analysis, when the size of the network map increases, the search space will increase and the number of searches will increase. In the process of recalculation, all vertices in the graph except the calculated route are searched, and therefore The time spent for the calculation will vary depending on the scale of the map. The larger the map, the longer it takes. Comparing with the direct use of the genetic algorithm [10], the algorithm proposed in this paper can quickly find the results within 2 s. It is applicable to the case where the map has a large scale and the number of vertices relatively large.

Table 2. Cycle replacement test (907 vertices, 2701 edges)

Different number of specified vertices	Repeat route	Repeat route frequency of occurrence	Distance growth rate	Time spent on eliminating loops (ms)
5	1	0.28	0.013	6.029
10	1	0.37	0.008	4.721
	2	0.03	0.120	10.177
	Sum	0.40	0.016	5.130
20	1	0.37	0.008	4.721
	2	0.17	0.017	9.304
	3	0.01	0.007	11.318
	4	0.01	0.035	18.701
	Sum	0.56	0.011	6.479
50	1	0.35	0.005	4.734
	2	0.3	0.010	9.332
	3	0.09	0.014	12.733
	4	0.05	0.028	18.797
	5	0.01	0.024	25.820
	Sum	0.80	0.009	8.500

5   Conclusion

This paper proposes an efficient algorithm for searching the shortest path through k specified vertices. Firstly, our algorithm adopts the Dijkstra algorithm to calculate the shortest distances between k specified vertices. For any road network with n vertices, the time complexity is $O(kn^2)$. In addition, the genetic algorithm is adopted for solving the Hamiltonian path problem with k specified vertices. The search space is reduced from $O(n!)$ to $O(k!)$. Because k is much less than n, the search space would be reduced exponentially. Furthermore, the cycle path should be detected and eliminated by our algorithm. Lastly, the performance of our algorithm is evaluated by Oldenburg city road network and some randomly generated road networks. The computational results show that our algorithm can find the constraint shortest path efficiently and effectively.

Acknowledgments. This work was supported by the National Natural Science Foundation of China (Grant Nos. 61472293 and 61702383). Research Project of Hubei Provincial Department of Education (Grant No. 2016238).

References

1. Dijkstra, E.W.: A note on two problems in connexion with graphs. Numer. Math. **1**, 269–271 (1959)
2. Floyd, R.W.: Algorithm 97 shortest path. Commun. ACM **5**(6), 345 (1962)
3. Saksena, J.P., Kumar, S.: The routing problem with "K" specified nodes. Oper. Res. **14**(5), 909–913 (1966)
4. Dreyfus, S.E.: An appraisal of some shortest-path algorithms. Oper. Res. **17**(3), 395–412 (1969)
5. Laporte, G., Mercure, H., Norbert, Y.: Optimal tour planning with specified nodes. RAIRO-Oper. Res. **18**(3), 203–210 (1984)
6. Gomes, T., Martins, L., Ferreira, S.: Algorithms for determining a node-disjoint path pair visiting specified nodes. Opt. Switch. Netw. **23**, 189–204 (2017)
7. Bérubé, J.F., Potvin, J.Y., Vaucher, J.: Time-dependent shortest paths through a fixed sequence of nodes: application to a travel planning problem. Comput. Oper. Res. **33**(6), 1838–1856 (2006)
8. Andrade, R.C.: Elementary shortest-paths visiting a given set of nodes. Simpósio Brasileiro de Pesquisa Operacional, 2378–2388 (2013)
9. Andrade, R.C.: New formulations for the elementary shortest-path problem visiting a given set of nodes. Eur. J. Oper. Res. **254**(3), 755–768 (2016)
10. Jia, J., Pan, J.S., Xu, H.R.: The middle of the specified node set of shortest path algorithm. IEEE International Conference on Signal Processing, pp. 1823–1826 (2017)
11. Ibaraki, T.: Algorithms for obtaining shortest paths visiting specified nodes. SIAM Rev. **15**(2), 309–317 (1973)
12. Nemhauser, G.L.: A generalized permanent label setting algorithm for the shortest path between specified nodes. J. Math. Anal. Appl. **38**(2), 328–334 (1972)
13. Gomes, T., Marques, S., Martins, L., et al.: Protected shortest path visiting specified nodes. In: IEEE 7th International Workshop on Reliable Networks Design and Modeling, pp. 120–127 (2015)
14. Feng, L., Yuan, L., Luo, W.: A geometric algebraic algorithm for node-constrained shortest path. Acta Electron. Sin. **5**, 846–851 (2014)
15. Yao, B., Feng, H., Gao, Y., Ma, J., Feng, Y.: Dynamic pruning search algorithm with node sets. Comput. Eng. Appl. 1–8 (2017)
16. Xu, Q., Ke, X.: Research on the shortest path problem model and corresponding genetic algorithm for the mandatory point. Syst. Eng. Electron. **31**(2), 459–462 (2009)
17. Liu, Z., Lin, J., Jin, T.: The shortest path algorithm based on the improved genetic algorithm. Inf. Commun. **2**, 46–48 (2017)
18. Lee, D.T., Schachter, B.J.: Two algorithms for constructing a Delaunay triangulation. Int. J. Comput. Inf. Sci. **9**(3), 219–242 (1980)

An Attribute Reduction P System Based on Rough Set Theory

Ping Guo$^{(\boxtimes)}$ and Junqi Xiang

Colllege of Computer Science, Chongqing University, Chongqing, China
guoping@cqu.edu.cn

Abstract. Attribute reduction is an important issue in rough set theory. Many heuristic algorithms have been proposed to compute the minimal attribute reduction since it is a NP hard problem, while most of them have the drawback to fall into local optimal solution. The other way to solve this problem is based on parallel computing. Membrane computing model is a distributed, maximal parallel and non-deterministic computing model inspired from cell. In this paper, we attempt to solve the attribute reduction problem by membrane computing, and propose a cell-like P system Π_{AR} to compute all exact minimal attribute reductions with $O(m \log n)$ time complexity.

Keywords: Attribute reduction · Rough set · Membrane computing
Cell-like P system

1 Introduction

In the fields of data mining, time consuming has become a big problem with the proliferation of high-dimensional data, especially when the data sets are massive, and the irrelevant attributes have a negative effect on result. So it's significant to reduce some redundant and irrelevant attributes for the subsequent processing.

At present, many attribute reduction methods are based on the rough set theory. Rough set proposed by Pawlak in 1982 [1], is a valid mathematic tool to handle imprecision, uncertainty and vagueness. Recently, rough set theory has been combined with other set theory like soft set theory and fuzzy set theory [2,3]. In rough set theory, attribute reduction is an important issues, while computing minimal attribute reduction is a NP hard problem [4]. So the most common methods to compute the attribute reduction are heuristic algorithms, which depend on attribute significance [5–7]. The main drawback of these heuristic algorithms is that they probably converge to local optimal. Besides, there are other methods to compute attribute reduction in rough set, such as discriminate matrix and information entropy [8–10]. These methods cost time and space to construct the discriminate matrix, or have weak anti-jamming capability.

Membrane computing, also called P system, proposed by Paun in 1998 [11], is a new branch of biological computing inspired from cell model, which has

© Springer Nature Singapore Pte Ltd. 2018
J. Qiao et al. (Eds.): BIC-TA 2018, CCIS 951, pp. 198–212, 2018.
https://doi.org/10.1007/978-981-13-2826-8_18

been widely used in the fields of machine learning, economics, automatic control and so on [12–14]. The current research areas of membrane computing include model research, application research, and realization exploration. With a lot of research on membrane computing model, there are varied kinds of P system model proposed according to different features and mechanisms of cells [15,16]. The application of membrane computing mainly means P system design, which can solve problems by specific P systems [17–20]. And a NP hard problem can be solved in polynomial time by P system, such as Hamiltonian cycle problem [21], TSP problem [22], All-SAT problem [23,24], subset sum problem [25,26] and so on.

Since attribute reduction is a NP hard problem and the common methods have many drawbacks according to above analysis, there are many parallel methods proposed to solve attribute reduction problem [27–30]. In this paper, we proposed a cell-like P system to compute all minimal attribute reductions with $O(mlogn)$ time complexity, where n is the amount of data elements, m is the amount of attributes. With the membrane division feature, all subsets of original attributes can be computed in linear time. The process of computing positive regions is based on membrane creation. The main algorithm is to ensure the positive region invariability, and compute the minimal subsets of original attributes, then these minimal subsets are the minimal attribute reductions.

The remainder of this paper is organized as follows. In Sect. 2, we present the basic concepts about attribute reduction and membrane computing. In Sect. 3, our P system Π_{AR} is proposed and present in detail. Section 4 give an instance of attribute reduction in Π_{AR} to valid the correctness of the rules. The conclusion and future work are included in Sect. 5.

2   Preliminaries

In this section, we first introduce some basic concepts about rough set and attribute reduction, then review some foundations of membrane computing (P system).

2.1   Rough Set and Attribute Reduction

Based on rough set theory, an information system is defined as the 4-tuple:

$$S = (U, A, V, f) \tag{1}$$

where U is a finite nonempty set of objects. A is a finite nonempty set of attributes and if $A = C \cup D$, where C is the condition attributes set, D is the decision attributes set, the information system is called a decision table. V denotes the values of condition attributes. $f\colon U \times A \to V$ is a description function which indicates the attribute values of objects in U.

Definition 1 (*Indiscernible relation*). Given a decision table $S = (U, C \cup D, V, f)$ and a non-empty attribute subset $B \subseteq C$, an indiscernible relation $IND(B)$ can be expressed as [31]:

$$IND(B) = \{(x, y)|f(x, a) = f(y, a), \forall a \in B\} \tag{2}$$

Relation $IND(B)$ divide the U into finite subsets called the equivalence class, according to their values of attribute set B. The subset contains objects with the same attribute value in B, which cause a partition of U, denoted by $U/IND(B)$. The B equivalence class of $x \in U$ is defined as $[x]_B = \{y \in U|(x, y) \in IND(B)\}$.

Definition 2 (*Lower and upper approximation*). Given a decision table $S = (U, C \cup D, V, f)$, $B \subseteq C$, $X \subseteq U$, the lower and upper approximation of X regarding to B can be respectively expressed as [31]:

$$\underline{B}(X) = \{x \in U|[x]_B \in X\} \tag{3}$$

$$\overline{B}(X) = \{x \in U|[x]_B \cap X \neq \phi\} \tag{4}$$

The B-boundary region of X is defined as $BN(X) = \overline{B}(X) - \underline{B}(X)$. The interpretation to these definitions are as follows:

- The lower approximation of a set X with respect to B is the set of all objects, which can be for certain classified as X using B (are certainly X in view of B).
- The upper approximation of a set X with respect to B is the set of all objects, which can be possibly classified as X using B (are possibly X in view of B).
- The boundary region of a set X with respect to B is the set of all objects, which can be neither as X nor as not X using B.

The positive region of D with respect to B is defined as:

$$POS_B(D) = \bigcup_{x \in U/D} \underline{B}(X) \tag{5}$$

Definition 3 (*Attribute reduction*). Given a decision table $S = (U, C \cup D, V, f)$, $B \subseteq C$, B is an attribute reduction if and only if the following two conditions are satisfied [31]:

$$POS_B(D) = POS_C(D) \tag{6}$$

$$\forall a \in B, POS_{B-\{a\}}(D) \neq POS_C(D) \tag{7}$$

The first condition means that the subset B shows the same classification power with original condition attributes set C, and the second condition means that any attribute in B can not be removed to satisfy the first condition.

2.2   Membrane Computing

There are 3 kinds of common P system: cell-like P system, tissue-like P system, and neural-like P system. The proposed attribute reduction P system is based on cell-like P system. A cell-like P system with degree $m(m \geq 1)$ can be defined as the form:

$$\Pi = (O, \mu, \omega_1, \ldots, \omega_m, R_1, \ldots, R_m, \rho_1, \ldots, \rho_m, i_o) \qquad (8)$$

where,

(1) O is the finite and non-empty alphabet of Objects. O is the finite and non-empty multiset over O where λ is empty string and $O^+ = O^* - \{\lambda\}$;

(2) μ is the initial membrane structure, consisting of m membranes, labelled with $1, \ldots, m$;

(3) $\omega_1, \ldots, \omega_m$ are strings over O representing the multisets of objects present in the regions $1, \ldots, m$ of the membrane structure;

(4) $R_1, \ldots, R_m$ are finite sets of evolution rules associated with the regions $1, \ldots, m$ of the membrane structure. The rules in $R_i (1 \leq i \leq m)$ are of the form $U \rightarrow V|_a, k$, with $a \in O, U \in O^+, V = V'$ or $V = V'\delta, V' \in (O \times Tar)^*$, and $Tar = \{here; out; in_j | 1 \leq j \leq m\}$. $here$ means V is left in the same region, out means V goes out of the region, and in_j means V goes to inner membrane j. δ is a special symbol not in O, and it means that the membrane which include it will be dissolved and the content (objects and membranes) in this membrane will be left in the outer one. Object a is a promoter in rule $U \rightarrow V|_a, k$, and this rule can only be applied in the presence of a. Object b is an inhibitor in rule $U \rightarrow V|_{\neg b}, k$, and this rule can only be applied in the absence of b. k is a positive integer which indicates the priority of the rule, and it depends on the precedence relation between the rules in the same membrane. The smaller k is, the higher priority will be.

(5) $\rho_i (1 \leq i \leq m)$ represents the precedence relation between the rules. If $\rho_i = \{a \rightarrow b > c \rightarrow d\}$, both object a and c are available to react, the rule $a \rightarrow b$ will be preferred according to their precedence relation.

(6) i_o is the output region of the system and it saves the final result.

The evolution of the system is based on the application of rules, which follows the basic principles: *Non-determinism* and *Maximal parallelism*. *Non-determinism* means rules will be selected to apply non-deterministically. *Maximal parallelism* means that every membrane evolve independently and in parallel, and every rule in a membrane is applied independently and in parallel. There are membrane division rules and membrane creation rules. The divided and created membranes have the same rule set with original membrane.

3   The Design of P System Π_{AR}

Since attribute reduction is a NP hard problem, membrane computing could be used to solved it. In this section, we propose a cell-like P system Π_{AR}, to computing all minimum attribute reductions with $O(m \log n)$ time complexity. As defined before, n is the amount of elements in data set U, and m is the amount of all conditional attributes in C while D is the decision attributes set.

3.1 The Parallel Algorithm for Computing Minimal Reductions

Preparation. In order to represent the decision table expediently, there are some preparation work to do.

- If the value of an attribute is continuous, it should be discretized appropriately. Without loss of generality, we assume that all attributes are discrete.
- Encode the value of string type to integer type which start from integer 1. For instance, $\{high, normal, low\}$ is the value set of attribute $height$, then the value set will be encoded as $\{1, 2, 3\}$.
- Without loss of generality, we assume that there is one decision attribute.

The Parallel Algorithm. In this paper, the parallel algorithm for computing all minimal attribute reduction is based on positive region invariability. The steps denoted from 1 to 5 of the algorithm is shown as Algorithm 1.

Algorithm 1. Parallel algorithm for all minimal attribute reduction in Π_{AR}

Input: a decision table $S = (U, C \cup D, V, f)$
Output: all minimal reductions of S
1: compute positive region $POS_C(D)$;
2: compute all subsets P_i of condition attribute set C;
3: compute positive regions $POS_{P_i}(D)$ in parallel;
4: if $POS_{P_i}(D) = POS_C(D)$, remain subset P_i; otherwise, reject P_i;
5: compute the minimal $|P_i|$ and output corresponding P_i.

3.2 The Definition of Π_{AR}

According to the previous definition Eq. 8, Π_{AR} can be defined as:

$$\Pi_{AR} = (O, \mu, \omega, R, i_o) \tag{9}$$

where,

(1) O is a finite and non-empty alphabet of objects, it includes:
  - $u_i(i = 1, \ldots, n)$ represent the elements in U.
  - $c_{ijk}(i = 1, \ldots, n; j = 1, \ldots, m)$ indicate the value of the j_{th} attribute of element u_i, k is the encoded value.
  - $z_i, q_i(i = 1, \ldots, m)$ represent the i_{th} condition attribute.
  - $d_{iv}(i = 1, \ldots, n)$ indicate the value of decision attribute of u_i, v is the encoded result from the value of decision attribute of i_{th} data element.
  - λ means empty string.
  - δ means that the current membrane will be dissolved and all objects and membranes in current membrane will be sent out.

Except these objects mentioned above, there are some other objects used to control the process of rule execution in Π_{AR}. And there is no more interpretation about them.

Table 1. Rules of membranes

Membrane	Rules
M	$r_{20}, r_{48} - r_{52}$
A	$r_1 - r_{19}$
B_1	$r_{21} - r_{47}, r_{53}$

(2) $\mu = [[\ ]_A[\ ]_B]_M$ is the initial structure of Π_{AR} as shown in Fig. 1. Membrane A is designed to compute positive region $POS_C(D)$, while membrane B_1 will be divided into 2^m membranes for computing all subsets P_i of condition attribute set C, and in the divided membranes, the positive regions $POS_{P_i}(D)$ will be computed and compared to $POS_C(D)$. So the structure will be changed during the evolution process.

(3) $\omega = \{\omega_M, \omega_A, \omega_{B_1}\}$ indicates the initial objects exist in initial membranes. ω_M is empty, $\omega_A = \{u_i, c_{ijk}, d_{iv}, \beta\}$ and $\omega_{B_1} = \{u_i, c_{ijk}, d_{iv}, \varepsilon, z_i\}$, where $i(i = 1, \ldots, n)$ is the index of data element, $j(j = 1, \ldots, m)$ is the index of condition attribute, v and k are the encoded values. Objects β and ε are only used to control the application of rules.

(4) R is the rule set of Π_{AR} based on the algorithm shown in Algorithm 1. Where $R = R^P \cup R^D \cup R^B \cup R^C \cup R^O$. The rule set R^P is to compute positive region $POS_C(D)$ in membrane A. R^D corresponds to compute all subsets of C by membrane division. R^B is applied to compute the positive regions $POS_{P_i}(D)$ in the created membranes which contain different subsets of C. R^C is the comparison process between $POS_{P_i}(D)$ and $POS_C(D)$. R^O is the rule set to compute the minimal $|P_i|$ and output corresponding minimal reductions P_i.

(5) i_o is the output membrane. In Π_{AR}, the output membranes is the left membranes in membrane M.

The rules of Π_{AR} are shown in Table 1.

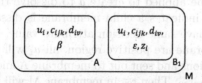

Fig. 1. The initial structure of Π_{AR}

3.3   The Procedure of Π_{AR}

After the preparation work introduced above, the decision table will be represented in Π_{AR} as shown in Fig. 1.

Computing Positive Regions $POS_C(D)$. This part corresponds to step 1 in Algorithm 1 and the rules in this part are included by rule set R^P. The process is as follows:

(1) Partition. In order to compute the positive regions, the elements should be partitioned according to all condition attribute values. By creating different membranes according to different values for this attribute, and regard the value as the index of the created membranes, we can partition the elements to their corresponding membranes according to their values for this attribute.

$$r_1 : c_{ijk}\beta \rightarrow c_{ijk}\gamma_j, 1 \qquad r_7 : t'_k \rightarrow e' e_k[\beta']_k, 3$$

$$r_2 : c_{ijk} \rightarrow t_k c_{ijk}|_{\gamma_j}, 1 \qquad r_8 : u_i c'_{ijk} d_{iv} \rightarrow (u_i d_{iv}, in_k)\sigma_{ik}|_{\gamma_j e_k}, 1$$

$$r_3 : 2t_k \rightarrow t_k, 1 \qquad r_9 : c_{ijk} \rightarrow (c_{ijk}, in_k)|_{\sigma_{ik}}, 1$$

$$r_4 : t_k \rightarrow t'_k|_{\neg t'_k}, 2 \qquad r_{10} : \beta' \rightarrow \beta'', 1$$

$$r_5 : t'_k \rightarrow t_k|_{t_k}, 1 \qquad r_{11} : \beta'' \rightarrow \beta, 1$$

$$r_6 : t'_k \rightarrow t'_k|_{t_j}, 2; j \neq k \quad r_{12} : \beta \rightarrow \omega, 2$$

When Π_{AR} begins, only rule r_1 in membrane A is applied to randomly select a c_{ijk} to react with β and γ_j is created, which means the attribute C_j is selected this time. Rules r_2–r_7 are applied to create membrane k for partition. Object e_k means that membrane k has been created, e' is used to record the number of membranes created in current membrane. The rule r_8 is applied after all membranes are created, and all u_i with d_{iv} will be sent into their corresponding membrane according to c'_{ijk}. Objects σ_{ik} indicates that the i_{th} element has been sent to membrane k. Then the left c_{ijk} are sent into the corresponding membrane by r_9. After r_{11} is applied, if there are still c_{ijk} left, repeat this process from r_1, otherwise, r_{12} will be applied to create ω, which means all attributes have been considered and the partition process is completed.

(2) Computing positive regions. When ω is created in the membrane, rules r_{13}–r_{15} may be applied if there are two elements u_i and u_j in a same membrane, with different values of decision attribute, which means they are not positive regions. Rule r_{15} will be applied to create δ to dissolve this membrane and e'' will be left out which indicates a child membrane is dissolved. If all elements in a same membrane have same decision attribute value, which means that all elements in this membrane are positive region, all u_i will be converted to b_i to denote the positive regions and sent out to membrane A and all child membranes will be dissolved by r_{17}–r_{19}. Then r_{20} in membrane M will be applied to send all b_i to membrane B_1.

$$r_{13} : d_{iv}d_{jz}\omega \rightarrow d_{iv}d_{jz}\tau, 1; i \neq j, y \neq z \quad r_{17} : b_i \rightarrow (b_i, out)b'|_{\neg e'}, 1$$

$$r_{14} : u_i d_{iv} \rightarrow \lambda|_\tau, 1 \qquad\qquad r_{18} : e' e'' \rightarrow \lambda, 1$$

$$r_{15} : \tau \rightarrow e''\delta, 2 \qquad\qquad r_{19} : \omega \rightarrow \omega e''\delta|_{b'\neg e'}, 1$$

$$r_{16} : u_i d_{iv} \rightarrow b_i|_\omega, 2 \qquad\qquad r_{20} : b_i \rightarrow (b_i, in_{B_1}), 1$$

Computing All Subsets P_i of C. This process corresponds to step 2 in Algorithm 1 and the rules is included by rule set R^D. Computing all subsets is based on membrane division. Each division create two membranes and these objects not react will be copied to both created membranes. Every division we consider one attribute left or not. After m times division all subsets of condition attribute set are left in 2^m created membranes.

$$r_{21} : [\varepsilon z_j]_{B_i} \rightarrow [\varepsilon' q_j]_{B_{2i}}[\varepsilon' \varphi_j]_{B_{2i+1}}|_{b_x}, 1 \quad r_{23} : \varepsilon' \rightarrow \varepsilon, 1$$
$$r_{22} : c_{ijk} \rightarrow \lambda|_{\varphi_j}, 1 \qquad\qquad\qquad r_{24} : \varepsilon \rightarrow \beta, 2$$

The rule r_{21} is applied to divide the membrane, z_j denotes attribute C_j, q_j means attribute C_j is left in this created membrane, φ_j means C_j is removed in this created membrane and all c_{ijk} of this attribute will be removed by rule r_{22}. Rule r_{23} is applied for synchronization. Rule r_{24} is applied when all attribute have been considered and all subsets of condition attribute set are created in 2^m created membranes. The object β is created to compute positive regions $POS_{P_i}(D)(P_i \subseteq C)$ in 2^m created membranes.

Computing All Positive Regions $POS_{P_i}(D)$. This process is completed in 2^m membranes which corresponds to step 3 in Algorithm 1 and the rules are included by rule set R^B. This part is similar to computing positive regions in membrane A, while the difference is that the condition attributes are subsets of original condition attribute set.

$r_{25} : c_{ijk}\beta \rightarrow c_{ijk}\gamma_j, 1$

$r_{35} : \beta'' \rightarrow \beta, 1$

$r_{26} : c_{ijk} \rightarrow t_k c'_{ijk}|_{\gamma_j}, 1$

$r_{36} : \beta \rightarrow \omega, 2$

$r_{27} : 2t_k \rightarrow t_k, 1$

$r_{37} : d_{iv}d_{jz}\omega \rightarrow d_{iv}d_{jz}\tau, 1; i \neq j, y \neq z$

$r_{28} : t_k \rightarrow t'_k|_{\neg t'_k}, 2$

$r_{38} : u_i d_{iv} \rightarrow \lambda|_\tau, 1$

$r_{29} : t'_k \rightarrow t_k|_{t_k}, 1$

$r_{39} : \tau \rightarrow e'' \delta, 2$

$r_{30} : t'_k \rightarrow t'_k|_{t_j}, 2; j \neq k$

$r_{40} : u_i d_{iv} \rightarrow a_i|_\omega, 2$

$r_{31} : t'_k \rightarrow e' e_k[\beta']_k, 3$

$r_{41} : a_i \rightarrow (a_i, out)a'|_{\neg e'}, 1$

$r_{32} : u_i c'_{ijk}d_{iv} \rightarrow (u_i d_{iv}, in_k)\sigma_{ik}|_{\gamma_j e_k}, 1$

$r_{42} : e' e'' \rightarrow \lambda, 1$

$r_{33} : c_{ijk} \rightarrow (c_{ijk}, in_k)|_{\sigma_{ik}}, 1$

$r_{43} : \omega \rightarrow \omega e'' \delta|_{a' \neg e'}, 1$

$r_{34} : \beta' \rightarrow \beta'', 1$

Rules r_{25}–r_{36} are applied to partition the elements by condition attribute values. Rules r_{37}–r_{43} are applied to compute the positive regions as introudced in membrane A. The computed positive regions $POS_{P_i}(D)$ are denoted as a_i and will be sent out to membrane B_i to compare with $POS_C(D)$(denoted as b_i).

Comparing Positive Regions and Dissolve Unmatched Membrane. This process corresponds to step 4 in Algorithm 1 and the rules are included by rule set R^C. Rule r_{44} are applied to consume a_i with corresponding b_i. Because $|a_i| \leq |b_i|$, if all a_i are consumed and there are b_i left, it means that $POS_{P_i}(D) \neq POS_C(D)$, r_{45}–r_{46} are applied to dissolve this membrane and the subset P_i is not an attribute reduction. And if there is no b_i left, it means that $POS_{P_i}(D) = POS_C(D)$, the subset P_i is left in this membrane as a candidate reduction.

$$r_{44} : a_i b_i \rightarrow g, 1 \qquad r_{46} : g \rightarrow \lambda \delta|_{g'}, 1$$

$$r_{45} : b_i \rightarrow g'|_\omega, 2$$

Computing $|P_i|(P_i \subseteq C)$ and Output Minimal Attribute Reductions. This process corresponds to step 5 in Algorithm 1 and the rules are included by rule set R^O. Since each left membrane B_i contains a candidate attribute reduction, and the attributes are denoted as q_i. The rule r_{47} is applied to create h_k and send them out, where k is the membrane index and the amount of h_k indicate the amount of attributes in this membrane. Rules r_{48}–r_{50} are applied to consume h_k and the minimal amount h_k will be consumed up first and then r_{51} is applied to create ξ in membrane M and object s into membrane B_k. The object ξ means the minimal subsets have been remarked by sending an object s into the corresponding membrane B_k. The other membranes are sent an object s', which will leads to dissolve operation by Rule r_{53}, and the left membranes remain the minimal attribute reductions denoted as q_i'.

$$r_{47} : [q_i]_{B_k} \rightarrow (h_k, out)q_i'|_{g \neg g'}, 1 \qquad r_{51} : h_k' \rightarrow (s, in_{B_k})\xi|_{\xi}, 2$$

$$r_{48} : 2h_k \rightarrow h_k, 1 \qquad\qquad\qquad r_{52} : h_k' \rightarrow (s', in_{B_k})|_{\xi}, 2$$

$$r_{49} : h_k \rightarrow h_k', 2 \qquad\qquad\qquad r_{53} : s' \rightarrow \lambda \delta, 1$$

$$r_{50} : h_k' \rightarrow h_k|_{\neg h_k}, 1$$

3.4 Analysis for Π_{AR}

In this section, the analysis of Π_{AR} is given. Neither the rule sets nor the initial structure of Π_{AR} will change when dealing with different instances, so Π_{AR} is a uniform P system. Since the n data elements, the m attributes and the values are all denoted by objects in Π_{AR}, so there are $O(mn)$ objects required in Π_{AR}. In P system, a time units is counted by "slices". In a slice, all satisfied rules in each membrane are applied in parallel. The running process of Π_{AR} and the time cost are list as follow:

(1) Cost of Computing $POS_C(D)$. Each time we consider one attribute for partition, and there are m original condition attributes. The time comlexity of every partition is $O(\log n)$ in order to remove redundant t_k. So the time complexity for this step is $O(m \log n)$.
(2) Cost of computing all subsets. Since each division cost 2 slices (r_{21}–r_{23}) and there are m divisions, the total time comlexity is $O(m)$.
(3) Cost of computing $POS_{P_i}(D)$. This process is similar to computing $POS_C(D)$, so the time complexity is $O(m \log n)$.

Table 2. The data set of an instance

Elements	C_1	C_2	C_3	d
u_1	1	1	1	1
u_2	1	1	1	1
u_3	2	2	2	2
u_4	2	2	2	2
u_5	3	3	1	1
u_6	2	2	3	2
u_7	2	2	2	2
u_8	2	3	3	2

(4) Cost of comparison. The comparison is completed in every membrane B_i through the application of rules r_{44}–r_{46}. The time complexity is $O(1)$.

(5) Cost of computing minimal attribute reduction. According to rules r_{47}–r_{53}, the worst case is that the candidate reduction has also m attributes. The time comlexity is $O(\log m)$.

In summary, the total time cost is equal to $O(m \log n)$.

4   Instance

In this section, we present an instance of attribute reduction to show the details of the evolution process in Π_{AR}. The original decision table is showed in Table 2, and the initial objects in Π_{AR} are showed in Fig. 2. In order to show the running process clearly, we omit some intermediate objects in the figures which will not react anymore.

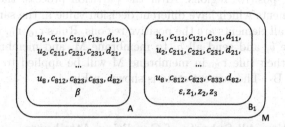

Fig. 2. The initial state of system

4.1   Computing Positive Regions $POS_C(D)$

As introduced before, this process includes two steps:

(1) Partition. In membrane A, suppose c_{332} is selected by r_1 and the γ_3 will be created, which indicates that the attribute C_3 is selected for partition. Then

r_2 is applied to convert all values of $C_3(c_{i3k})$ to c'_{i3k} and create 3 objects of t_1, 3 objects of t_2, 2 objects of t_3. Rules r_3–r_6 are applied to remove redundant t_k and remain only a t'_1, a t'_2, and a t'_3. After that, rule r_7 is applied 3 times parallel to create membrane 1, 2, and 3. Rules r_8–r_9 are applied to send all elements u_i, with their other attribute value c_{ijk} and d_{iv} into corresponding membranes. Then the first partition is completed. In each child membrane, repeat the above process for another attribute for partition. The second partition is shown in Fig. 3. The final partition result is $\{\{u_1, u_2\}, \{u_5\}, \{u_3, u_4, u_7\}, \{u_6, u_8\}\}$.

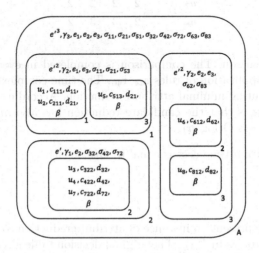

Fig. 3. The second partition

(2) Computing positive regions. After the partition process, there is no more than 2 elements which have different decision value in the same membrane. Therefore, all elements are the positive regions. Rules r_{16}–r_{19} will be applied to generate b_i and send all b_i to membrane M, and membrane A will be dissolved, then rule r_{20} in membrane M will be applied to send all b_i to membrane B_1. The current state is shown in Fig. 4.

4.2 Computing All Subsets of Condition Attributes

In this process, the division rule r_{21} is applied once to randomly select a z_j to react with ε. The created object q_j means this attribute C_j is left in this membrane while φ_j means not left. For this instance, we first select attribute C_2 for division operation, then C_1, finally C_3 is selected as shown in Fig. 5. There are 3 times division and 8 membranes are created which contain all subsets of C. For instance, membrane B_9 contains subset $\{\{C_1, C_2\}\}$.

Fig. 4. The final state of computing $POS_C(D)$

Fig. 5. Select attribute C_3 for division

4.3 Computing All Positive Regions $POS_{P_i}(D)$

For each membrane B_i, compute the positive regions like membrane A. The difference is that the condition attributes in B_i are just a subset of C, and the system compute $POS_{P_i}(D)$ in each membrane. The computed positive regions a_i are sent to B_i and all child membranes in B_i are dissolved like membrane A. The current state is shown in Fig. 6.

4.4 Comparing Positive Regions and Dissolve Unmatched Membranes

Since $POS_{P_i}(D)$ are denoted as a_i and $POS_C(D)$ are computed early as $b_1, \ldots, b_8$, rules r_{44}–r_{46} are applied to compare a_i and b_i, if the positive regions are different, i.e., there are b_i left after the application of r_{44}, g' will be created and leads to dissolve operation for this membrane. The left membranes contain all candidate attribute reductions. The current state is shown in Fig. 7. Membrane B_{11} and B_{15} will be dissolved in next slice by rule r_{46}, and r_{47} will be applied at the same time in other remaining membranes.

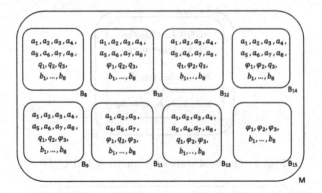

Fig. 6. Computing all positive regions

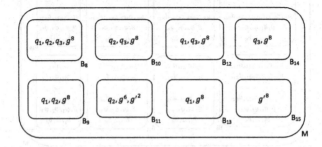

Fig. 7. Comparison of positive regions

4.5 Computing Minimal Attribute Reductions

In the remaining child membranes, rules r_{48}–r_{52} are applied to dissolve the membarnes which are not the minimal attribute reductions. and the final output membranes are B_{13} and B_{14} as shown in Fig. 8. The attribute set $\{C_1\}$ and $\{C_3\}$ are the minimal attribute reductions.

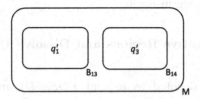

Fig. 8. The final state for output

5 Conclusion

To compute all exact minimal attribute reductions and overcome some limitations of the existing attribute reduction methods, in this paper, a cell-like P system Π_{AR} is proposed which is based on positive invariability in rough set theory. The running process and the time complexity analysis of Π_{AR} is presented in detail. The main contributions of this paper are as follows.

(1) We explore a new way to solve attribute reduction problem. Since attribute reduction is a NP hard problem and membrane computing model is a maximal parallel computing model, we innovate P system to solve this problem.

(2) Most attribute reduction methods are heuristic, so the computed reduction may be local optimal. In our system Π_{AR}, the computed reduction is global optimal.

(3) With the maximal parallelism of membrane computing model, the time complexity of Π_{AR} is only $O(m \log n)$, which is a massive decrease compared with other methods.

(4) The proposed system can compute all minimal attribute reductions rather than only one reduction.

In future works we aim to optimize our system in time complexity, and enable it to handle attribute significance, the relevance between attributes, the missing value of attribute and so on. Besides, we will extend our system for more attribute reduction problems.

References

1. Pawlak, Z., Grzymala-Busse, J., Slowinski, R., Ziarko, W.: Rough sets. Commun. ACM **38**, 88–95 (1995)
2. Feng, F., Li, C., Davvaz, B., Ali, M.I.: Soft sets combined with fuzzy sets and rough sets: a tentative approach. Soft Comput. **14**, 899–911 (2010)
3. He, Q., Wu, C., Chen, D., Zhao, S.: Fuzzy rough set based attribute reduction for information systems with fuzzy decisions. Knowl.-Based Syst. **24**, 689–696 (2011)
4. Pawlak, Z.: Some issues on rough sets. In: Peters, J.F., Skowron, A., Grzymała-Busse, J.W., Kostek, B., Świniarski, R.W., Szczuka, M.S. (eds.) Transactions on Rough Sets I. LNCS, vol. 3100, pp. 1–58. Springer, Heidelberg (2004). https://doi.org/10.1007/978-3-540-27794-1_1
5. Ke, L., Feng, Z., Ren, Z.: An efficient ant colony optimization approach to attribute reduction in rough set theory. Pattern Recognit. Lett. **29**, 1351–1357 (2008)
6. Fang, Y., Liu, Z.H., Min, F.: A PSO algorithm for multi-objective cost-sensitive attribute reduction on numeric data with error ranges. Soft Comput. **21**, 1–17 (2016)
7. Luan, X., Li, Z., Liu, T.: A novel attribute reduction algorithm based on rough set and improved artificial fish swarm algorithm. Neurocomputing **174**, 522–529 (2016)
8. Wei, W., Wu, X., Liang, J., Cui, J., Sun, Y.: Discernibility matrix based incremental attribute reduction for dynamic data. Knowl.-Based Syst. **140**, 142–157 (2018)
9. Konecny, J.: On attribute reduction in concept lattices: methods based on discernibility matrix are outperformed by basic clarification and reduction. Inf. Sci. **415–416**, 199–212 (2017)

10. Hońko, P.: Improving indiscernibility matrix based approach for attribute reduction. In: Ciucci, D., Wang, G., Mitra, S., Wu, W.-Z. (eds.) RSKT 2015. LNCS (LNAI), vol. 9436, pp. 119–128. Springer, Cham (2015). https://doi.org/10.1007/978-3-319-25754-9_11

11. Păun, G.: Membrane Computing: An Introduction. Springer, Berlin (2002). https://doi.org/10.1007/978-3-642-56196-2

12. Păun, G., Păun, R.: Membrane computing and economics: numerical P systems. Fundam. Inform. **73**, 213–227 (2006)

13. Jiang, K., Song, B., Shi, X., Song, T.: An overview of membrane computing. J. Bioinforma. Intell. Control. **1**, 17–26 (2012)

14. Păun, G.: A quick introduction to membrane computing. J. Log. Algebr. Program. **79**, 291–294 (2010)

15. Martín-Vide, C., Păun, G., Pazos, J., Rodríguez-Patón, A.: Tissue P systems. Theor. Comput. Sci. **296**, 295–326 (2003)

16. Song, B., Zhang, C., Pan, L.: Tissue-like P systems with evolutional symport/antiport rules. Inf. Sci. **378**, 177–193 (2017)

17. Wang, B., Chen, L., Cheng, J.: New result on maximum entropy threshold image segmentation based on P system. Optik **163**, 81–85 (2018)

18. Guo, P., Zhang, M., Chen, J.: A family of ant colony P systems. In: He, C., Mo, H., Pan, L., Zhao, Y. (eds.) BIC-TA 2017. CCIS, vol. 791, pp. 175–193. Springer, Singapore (2017). https://doi.org/10.1007/978-981-10-7179-9_14

19. Peng, H., Wang, J., Shi, P., Riscos-Núñez, A., Pérez-Jiménez, M.J.: An automatic clustering algorithm inspired by membrane computing. Pattern Recogn. Lett. **68**, 34–40 (2015)

20. Pavel, A.B., Buiu, C.: Using enzymatic numerical P systems for modeling mobile robot controllers. Nat. Comput. **11**, 387–393 (2012)

21. Guo, P., Dai, Y., Chen, H.: A P system for Hamiltonian cycle problem. Optik **127**, 8461–8468 (2016)

22. Guo, P., Xiang, J., Xie, J., Zheng, J.: A P system for solving all-solutions of TSP. Int. J. Adv. Comput. Sci. Appl. **8** (2017)

23. Guo, P., Zhu, J., Chen, H., Yang, R.: A linear-time solution for all-SAT problem based on P system. Chin. J. Electron. **27**, 367–373 (2018)

24. Song, W., Guo, P., Chen, H.: A solution for all-SAT problem based on P systems. J. Comput. Theor. Nanosci. **13**, 4293–4301 (2016)

25. Song, B., Pérez-Jiménez, M.J., Pan, L.: Efficient solutions to hard computational problems by P systems with symport/antiport rules and membrane division. Biosystems **130**, 51–58 (2015)

26. Song, B., Pan, T.S.L.: A time-free uniform solution to subset sum problem by tissue P systems with cell division. Math. Struct. Comput. Sci. **1**, 1–16 (2015)

27. Chen, H., Li, T., Cai, Y., Luo, C., Fujita, H.: Parallel attribute reduction in dominance-based neighborhood rough set. Inf. Sci. **373**, 351–368 (2016)

28. Liang, B., Zheng, S., Wang, L.: The attribute reduction algorithm based on parallel computing. J. Intell. Fuzzy Syst. **32**, 1867–1875 (2017)

29. Qian, J., Miao, D., Zhang, Z., Yue, X.: Parallel attribute reduction algorithms using MapReduce. Inf. Sci. **279**, 671–690 (2014)

30. Zhang, J., Li, T., Pan, Y.: PLAR: parallel large-scale attribute reduction on cloud systems. Presented at the December (2013)

31. Pawlak, Z.: Rough Sets: Theoretical Aspects of Reasoning about Data. Kluwer Academic Publishers, Dordrecht (1992)

Spatial-Temporal Analysis of Traffic Load Based on User Activity Characteristics in Mobile Cellular Network

Moqin Zhou[1], Xueli Wang[1(✉)], Xing Zhang[2], and Wenbo Wang[2]

[1] School of Science, Beijing University of Posts and Telecommunications,
Beijing 100876, China
wangxl@bupt.edu.cn
[2] Key Laboratory of Universal Wireless Communications,
Ministry of Education Wireless Signal Processing and Network Lab,
Beijing University of Posts and Telecommunications, Beijing 100876, China

Abstract. In this paper, we quantify the interactive pattern between two time series: the number of users (NoU) representing user's activity (UA) and downlink traffic load (DTL) generated from the base station (BS). We model the characteristics of UA, and use K-means clustering algorithm to characterize the hidden spatial association pattern in the wireless cellular system. The results show that (1) there is a strong linear interaction between UA and DTL; (2) the NoU has a strong weekdays and weekends mode. (3) the results of clustering well match the reference scenario information, with the scenario recognition accuracy of 75%. We demonstrate that such approach proposed can identify the scenario of the BSes, which can help us understand the spatial temporal traffic patterns of wireless cellular system.

Keywords: Clustering · Scenario recognition
Spatial temporal analysis · Traffic load · Wireless cellular system

1   Introduction

With the rapid development of wireless network, the scale, dimension and type of traffic data become increasingly complex. It is of great practical significance to optimize the network resource allocation in order to satisfy the user's multiple types of requirements and to understand the spatial association pattern in the wireless cellular system. The users in the cellular wireless network show obvious group behavior in both time domain and spatial domain, which are mainly reflected in the traffic load changes. For example the daily DTL in residential or commercial office scenarios presents a clear day-night living pattern, and the traffic peak is achieved during rush hour in the scenario along the subway line. This paper mainly studies the interactive patterns between the DTL and the UA from the spatial-temporal aspects in the cellular network. It can help us

© Springer Nature Singapore Pte Ltd. 2018
J. Qiao et al. (Eds.): BIC-TA 2018, CCIS 951, pp. 213–222, 2018.
https://doi.org/10.1007/978-981-13-2826-8_19

understand the space-time pattern of the network, so as to realize the dynamic adaptation of network resources, meet the requirements of ultra-high traffic volume density, and achieve the user-centric energy-efficient network purposes.

Many previous works have been done to study the traffic load data in the cellular network system. In terms of statistical feature extraction and modeling, [1] defined the problem of the self-similarity through high-variability in the Ethernet Lan Traffic. [2] proposed a network traffic predictor using multifractal analysis technique. [3] presented modeling and prediction using neural network. [4] used a fractional autoregressive integrated moving average (FARIMA) method to predict traffic load by capturing long-range and short-range dependence in traffic network. [5] described the spatial traffic relationship by using base station social network and made the prediction of spatial traffic in wireless cellular system. Besides, several recent works have taken the traffic patterns of different scenarios into account. Accurate traffic scenario recognition and analysis will lead to more efficient resource management and better quality-of-service provision. The project Earth of the European Union defined typical scenarios based on user's moving speed and base station spacing [6]. The business of different regional types, such as residential area and office, were analyzed systematically in [7], where the network business rules were correlated with the user's behavior. In [8], the authors studied the traffic model of three typical regions including park, campus and central business district and found that the parameters of the model are different from each other. However, the previous work on exploring traffic load data do not study the interactive pattern between the UA and the traffic load.

Different from previous methods, in this paper, we first explore interactive patterns between two time series data: the DTL and the NoU. Then by characterizing the UA, the spatial-temporal association of the BSes is measured by using an unsupervised K-means clustering algorithm. The results show that our proposed method can well identify the scenario information of BS.

2 Model Construction

2.1 Traffic Data

We apply real traffic data from 255 BSes in Hong Kong. For each BS, the data includes two time series: the DTL and the NoU, with a time period of 15 min, spanning 21 days from 2014/02/27 to 2014/03/19, and each BS ID is associated with the GPS coordinates. The geometric locations are shown in Fig. 1, where each point represents a BS. And the data traces are shown in Table 1.

We first give some notation. Let $N = 255$ denote the total number of BSes, $D = 21$ denote the total number of days for dataset, and $T = 4 \times 24 = 96$ be the total number of time points for each day. We use $D_{i,d,t}, U_{i,d,t}$, respectively, to denote the DTL and NoU of BS i at the t time point on day d, where $D_{i,d,t}$ is recorded in mega bytes, and $U_{i,d,t}$ is recorded by the raw count. Let $\overline{D_{d,t}} = \frac{1}{N} \sum_{i=1}^{N} D_{i,d,t}$ and $\overline{U_{d,t}} = \frac{1}{N} \sum_{i=1}^{N} U_{i,d,t}$ denote the average DTL and the average

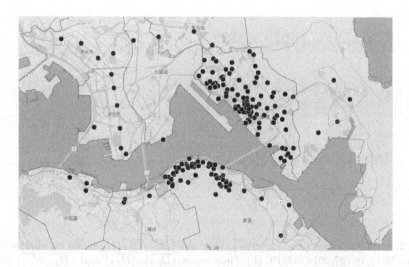

Fig. 1. Geometric locations of the 255 BSes of HongKong.

Table 1. Data traces.

Time	BS ID	DTL (Mbyte)	NoU	Longitude	Latitude
2014/02/27 00:00	BS 1	5.25	92.93	114.15497	22.24843
2014/02/27 00:15	BS 1	2.36	68.42	114.15497	22.24843
......	......	......	......	......	......
2014/03/19 23:45	BS 1	4.36	78.47	114.15497	22.24843
2014/02/27 00:00	BS 2	3.64	29.31	114.16604	22.24875
......	......	......	......	......	......

NoU of 255 BSes at the time point t on day d respectively. Figure 2 shows three time series curves, where the green, red and blue lines are represented $\{\overline{D_{d,t}}\}_{t=1}^T$, $\{\overline{U_{d,t}}\}_{t=1}^T$ and $\{\overline{D_{d,t}}/\overline{U_{d,t}}\}_{t=1}^T$ respectively. From Fig. 2, we can see the following facts:

(1) $\{\overline{D_{d,t}}\}_{t=1}^T$, $\{\overline{U_{d,t}}\}_{t=1}^T$ all have a higher level on weekdays (Monday to Friday) compared with the relatively lower values on weekends (Saturday and Sunday). In particular, there are three peak values each day: 08:45, 13:15 and 18:30.

(2) Although $\{\overline{D_{d,t}}\}_{t=1}^T$ and $\{\overline{U_{d,t}}\}_{t=1}^T$ tend to increase and decrease simultaneously, $\{\overline{D_{d,t}}/\overline{U_{d,t}}\}_{t=1}^T$, meaning the volume of DTL per person consumes varies over time.

(3) Given a time point t, $\{\overline{D_{d,t}}/\overline{U_{d,t}}\}$ can be approximated as a constant.

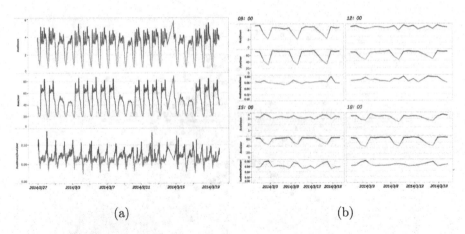

(a)   (b)

Fig. 2. (a) Time series $\{\overline{D_{d,t}}\}_{t=1}^{T}$, $\{\overline{U_{d,t}}\}_{t=1}^{T}$ and $\{\overline{D_{d,t}/U_{d,t}}\}_{t=1}^{T}$ based on all 255 BSes during 2014/02/27-2014/03/19. (b) Time series $\{\overline{D_{d,t}}\}$, $\{\overline{U_{d,t}}\}$ and $\{\overline{D_{d,t}/U_{d,t}}\}$ given time point t=09:00, 12:00, 15:00 and 18:00. (Color figure online)

2.2 Interactive Pattern Modeling

We find out that linear models can offer a good approximation for a variety of BSes. Figure 3 gives the scatter plots of $(D_{i,d,t}, U_{i,d,t})$, for $d = 1, \cdots, D; t = 1, \cdots, T$.

The figure shows that linear regression model can approximate the DTL with respect to the NoU, i.e.,

$$D_{i,d,t} = \alpha_i \cdot U_{i,d,t} + \epsilon_{i,d,t}$$

where α_i can be treated as the volume of DTL per person consumes for BS i, and $\epsilon_{i,d,t}$ is due to measurement errors. However, under the assumption that there is no significant difference of the DTL volume per person consumes the whole day given a BS, the results show that more than half regression models fail to be well interpretative, due to the r^2 of the regression does not exceed 0.5.

Figure 4 shows time curves of α_i of six randomly selected BSes, where red bars denote the NoU and blue lines indicate the evolving time series of α_i given BS i. It can be stated that, as a function of time, α_i fluctuates and does not show a linear trend. That is to say the time-homogeneous assumption for the regression's coefficient may be a strong hypothesis, which therefore motivates us to make a hypothesis test for comparison of several populations under heteroscedasticity.

Many statistical test methods have been proposed to deal with such problem, such as Generalized F-Test [9,10], parametric bootstrap test [11] and Fiducial test based on the idea of Fiducial inference [12,13]. Here the Fiducial test is used to make time-homogeneous test. The results show that more than 93% cases failed to pass the test. Furthermore, Fig. 5 shows a histogram of the distribution of determination coefficient based on 255 BSes, where the x-axis indicates the value of r^2, the bars are presented to count how many values fall into each

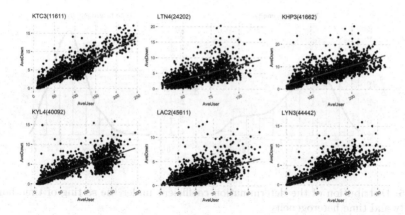

Fig. 3. Graphical illustration of scatter plots for six randomly selected BSes.

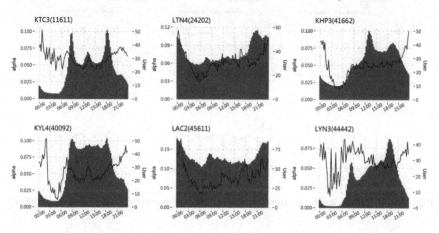

Fig. 4. Graphical illustration of time series $\{\alpha_i\}_{t=1}^{T}$ for six randomly selected BSes. (Color figure online)

interval, and the lines are the corresponding density curve. Obviously the time-heterogeneous assumption has a better performance in terms of the goodness of fit. Hence we put our individual regression coefficient into time-heterogeneous setting, that is, the interactive pattern can be modeled by:

$$D_{i,d,t} = \alpha_{i,t} \cdot U_{i,d,t} + \epsilon_{i,d,t}$$

2.3   User's Activity Modeling

We now explore the characteristics of UA. We observe that NoU has a strong day and night mode. These diurnal patterns differ across weekdays and weekends. Moreover, diurnal pattern and weekend effects of different BSes also vary.

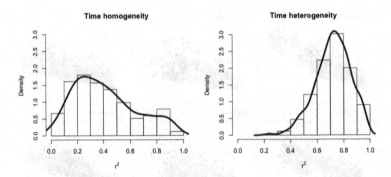

Fig. 5. Distribution of the determination coefficient under the setting of time homogeneity and time heterogeneity.

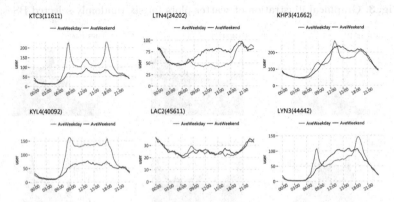

Fig. 6. Individual level for users on weekdays and weekends. (Color figure online)

Figure 6 supports the findings, where the red line denotes the time series of the average NoU within 15 weekdays from 00:00 to 23:45 meanwhile the blue line presents the time series of the average NoU in 3 weekends. It can be seen that BS KTC3(11611) has a larger NoU on average at weekdays. Conversely, BS LTN4(24202) has more NoU over the weekends. And the NoU served by BS LAC2(45611) is not significantly different between weekends and workdays. Then we model UA through a linear regression model, which takes weekend effect into account:

$$U_{i,d,t} = \beta_{i,t}^{(0)} + \beta_{i,t}^{(1)} \mathbb{1}_{d \in H} + \eta_{i,d,t}$$

where H indicates the weekend period (Saturday and Sunday). Here $\beta_{i,t}^{(0)}$ measures the NoU baseline at time point t for BS i, $\beta_{i,t}^{(1)}$ measures the weekend effect, and $\eta_{i,d,t}$ is the random error term.

2.4   Clustering of BSes

We observe that the UA in the same scenario is highly similar in wireless cellular system, such as the NoU will peak for the BSes along the subway at rush hours. In order to explore this property and understand the spatial-temporal association of the BSes, the similarity between two BSes was measured by calculating the Euclidean distance (considering both of DTL and UA patterns), based on the weighted average of the normalized $\{\beta_{i,t}^{(0)}\}, \{\beta_{i,t}^{(1)}\}, \{\alpha_{i,t}\}, t = 1, 2, \cdots, T$. This measure was used as input for a K-means clustering algorithm.

3   Clustering Results

As noted, by applying K-means clustering algorithm, we divided 255 BSes into six categories. Figure 7 shows the average performance of each category in two aspects: NoU baseline $(\beta_t^{(0)})$ and average DTL per user consumes $(\alpha_t), t = 1, 2, \cdots, T$. Different colors indicate different clusters. In Fig. 7(a), Category 3 (dark yellow line) has two peaks corresponds to the rush hours, which suggests the BSes in Category 3 locates around the traffic station, such as subway stations or bus stations; Fig. 7(b) indicates that the average volume of DTL per person consumes in different clusters varies.

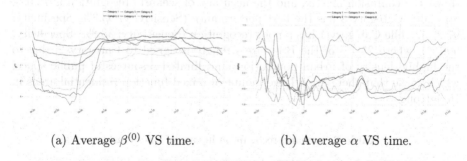

(a) Average $\beta^{(0)}$ VS time.   (b) Average α VS time.

Fig. 7. Results of clustering with average performance for each category. (Color figure online)

In order to better understand the UA patterns in each category and identify the scenario information, we further explore the patterns difference between weekdays and weekends, shown in Fig. 8. The figure clearly shows the findings: (1) there is no significant difference between weekdays (red lines) and weekends (blue lines) in Category 1 and Category 5, however, Category 1 is a little closer to the traffic station because there are two peaks at rush hours of weekdays; (2) the average NoU on weekdays is greater than that on weekends in Category 2 and Category 4, but Category 2 may be more closer to the commercial street and the traffic station because three peaks appear during the weekdays; (3) Category 3 has two peaks during the rush hours of the weekdays; (4) Category 6 presents a

220 M. Zhou et al.

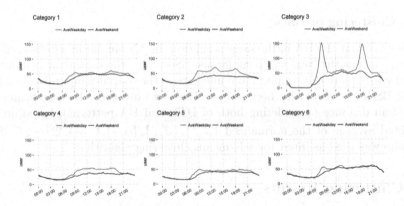

Fig. 8. Clustering results regarding user's activity. (Color figure onilne)

mixed-scene feature that contains not only the three peak on weekdays but also more average NoU over the weekends than any other categories. Moreover, Fig. 9 gives an visualization map of the results with categorical scenarios, where each point means a base station, each icon represents one scenario category. Table 2 provides the summary of what scenario each category corresponds to. Finally, we compare the results of clustering with the reference scenario label. Table 3 shows the confusion matrix, and the accuracy of scenario recognition is 75.0%. Specially, Category 3 has the best performance (Sensitivity: 93.3%, Specificity: 97.2%), while Category 1 has a poor recognition (Sensitivity: 58.8%, Specificity: 90.7%), where 25.4% of the BSes are wrongly assigned to Category 2, due to the highly density of urban population, and limited resources of public space, which cause that there are a large mount of mixed-function residential areas in HongKong.

Table 2. Scenario recognition in case of BSes clusters

Cluster	Scenario
Category 1	Residential District close to station
Category 2	Office District close to commercial street and the station
Category 3	Traffic Station
Category 4	Office District
Category 5	Residential District
Category 6	Mix of Residential and commercial street

Fig. 9. Visualization map of the clustering.

Table 3. Confusion matrix based on six-category scenarios.

		Reference					
		1	2	3	4	5	6
Prediction	1	30	9	0	2	6	1
	2	13	64	2	2	0	0
	3	2	1	28	3	0	0
	4	2	2	0	9	0	0
	5	3	7	0	0	39	1
	6	1	3	0	0	1	13

4   Conclusion

In this paper, a spatial-temporal analysis of DTL based on UA features was explored for the BS scenario recognition. An unsupervised K-means clustering algorithm was considered to reveal the hidden spatial relationships between BSes. The BSes with high degree of similarity would be clustered into the same subgroups. The results of the clustering show that the accuracy of scenario recognition is 75%. It is interesting to highlight that our approach performs well when dealing with an unambiguous scenario, such as Category 3. In fact, it is very common for a BS to locate in a mixed scenario, with a subway station on the left and a commercial or residential area on the right, such as Category 2. Under this situation, the scenario information is too complex to be captured. Therefore we plan to model a curve of DTL as a mixture of people with different levels of factors, such as job and age, to further improve the accuracy of scenario recognition, these are issues we will study in the future.

Acknowledgment. This work was supported by the Key Laboratory of Universal Wireless Communications, Beijing University of Posts and Telecommunications (KFKT-2015103) and National Natural Science Foundation of China (No.11471053).

2

222 M. Zhou et al.

References

1. Willinger, W., Taqqu, M.S., Sherman, R., Wilson, D.V.: Self-similarity through high-variability: statistical analysis of Ethernet LAN traffic at the source level. IEEE/ACM Trans. Netw. **5**(1), 71–86 (1997)
2. Bianchi, G.R., Vieira, F.H.T., Ling, L.L.: A novel network traffic predictor based on multifractal traffic characteristic. In: Global Telecommunications Conference, pp. 680–684. IEEE (2004)
3. Gowrishankar, Satyanarayana, P.S.: Neural network based traffic prediction for wireless data networks. Int. J. Comput. Intell. Syst. **1**(4), 379–389 (2008)
4. Shu, Y., Jin, Z., Zhang, L., Wang, L.: Traffic prediction using FARIMA models. In: IEEE International Conference on Communications, pp. 891–895. IEEE (1999)
5. Yi, Z., Dong, X., Zhang, X., Wang, W.: Spatial traffic prediction for wireless cellular system based on base stations social network. In: IEEE Systems Conference, pp. 1–5. IEEE (2016)
6. The Earth Project: Definition and Parameterization of Reference Systems and Scenarios. Deliverable D2.2. https://www.ict-earth.eu/publications/deliverables/deliverables.html
7. Wang, H., Xu, F., Li, Y., Zhang, P., Jin, D.: Understanding mobile traffic patterns of large scale cellular towers in urban environment. In: Internet Measurement Conference, vol. 25, pp. 225–238. ACM (2015)
8. Wang, S., Zhang, X., Zhang, J., Feng, J., Wang, W., Xin, K.: An approach for spatial-temporal traffic modeling in mobile cellular networks, pp. 203–209 (2017)
9. Watt, S.: Exact statistical methods for data analysis. Technometrics **43**(1), 106–107 (1995)
10. Weerahandi, S.: Size performance of some tests in one-way ANOVA. Commun. Stat.-Simul. Comput. **27**(3), 625–640 (1998)
11. Krishnamoorthy, K., Lu, F., Mathew, T.: A parametric bootstrap approach for anova with unequal variances: fixed and random models. Comput. Stat. Data Anal. **51**(12), 5731–5742 (2007)
12. Fisher, R.A.: The fiducial argument in statistical inference. Ann. Eugen. **6**(4), 391–398 (1935)
13. Eftekhar, S., Sadooghialvandi, M., Kharratikopaei, M.: Testing the equality of several multivariate normal mean vectors under heteroscedasticity: a fiducial approach and an approximate test. Commun. Stat.-Theor. Methods (2017). https://doi.org/10.1080/03610926.2017.1324984

A Simulator for Cell-Like P System

Ping Guo$^{(\boxtimes)}$, Changsheng Quan, and Lian Ye

College of Computer Science, Chongqing University,
Shazhengjie. 174, Chongqing 400044, China
{guoping,quancs,ylredleaf}@cqu.edu.cn

Abstract. Membrane computing is a computational model abstracted from the structure and function of biological cells. Since membrane computing system (also known as P system) was proposed, researchers designed many P systems and P system simulators. However, because of the diversity of evolutionary rules, it is difficult to find suitable simulation tools to implement these P systems. Based on the cell-like P system, this paper proposed a universal P system description language (called UPL) and a universal P system simulator (called UPS). UPL supports the expansion of membrane structural characteristics and the combination of various rule types. UPS can simulate the P system described by UPL. The experimental results verify their effectiveness.

Keywords: P system simulator · Simulation software
P system · Membrane computing model
P system description language

1 Introduction

Membrane computing was proposed by Gh. Păun in 1998 and is one of the branches of natural computing, known as membrane system or P system. Membrane computing has been in rapid growth since Gh. Păun published his first paper entitled Computing with membranes [1] in 2000. After decades of development, computing models, such as cell-like P systems, tissue-like P systems and neural-like P systems, have been formed.

With the deepening of the research on membrane computing theory, some P systems have been designed to solve NP hard problems in polynomial time, such as subset sum [2] and all-set [3]. At the same time, the idea of membrane computing has been applied to many fields such as image processing [4,5], multi-objective optimization [6,7], numerical computation [8] and machine learning [9,10]. In order to validate and simulate these P systems, several P system simulation tools have been developed over the past decade. For example, Spiking Neural P Systems Simulator [11] can be used for the simulation of neural-like P systems; P-Lingua [12,13] as an open source simulation core can simulate many types of P systems including cell-like P system; MeCoSim [14], which is based on P-Lingua Core, has a very friendly interface; the SNP system simulator proposed in [15] can generate a P system transition diagram to help researchers

© Springer Nature Singapore Pte Ltd. 2018
J. Qiao et al. (Eds.): BIC-TA 2018, CCIS 951, pp. 223–235, 2018.
https://doi.org/10.1007/978-981-13-2826-8_20

search invariants; and paper [16] uses GPU to simulate P system, which greatly improves the simulation speed of P system. In addition, a variety of P system simulation tools are also listed in [17].

As membrane computing evolves, researchers continually abstract new concepts and computational mechanisms from cells, presenting new challenges for P system simulation software: How to adapt the simulation software to the diversity of evolutionary rules and the large number of membrane structure characteristics. To solve this problem, a universal cell-like P system simulator (called UPS) is designed to adapt to changes in membrane structure and evolutionary rules. The source files and the program of UPS are licensed under GPL version 3 and can be accessed in [18].

UPL (universal cell-like P system description language) is used by UPS to describe P system models. By dividing rules into conditions and results, UPL can describe any combination of different kinds of supported rules. Furthermore, in UPL, one type of membrane can be defined as a membrane class. Membrane class can be instantiated and inherited. The inherited membrane has all the properties of the original membrane. Meanwhile, new properties can also be increased easily and quickly.

The structure of the rest of this paper is: the research foundation, cell-like P system, is presented in Sect. 2. In the next section, the syntax rules of UPL are introduced by using BNF (Backus-Naur Form). In Sect. 4, UPS, a general purpose software tool for simulating cell-like P systems is proposed, showing its main features. An instance about position-code based **add** membrane is used to show the usage of UPL and UPS in the next section. Finally, in the last section, some conclusions and future work are presented.

2   Cell-Like P System

Cell-like P system is the basic form of P system. This paper's work is based on the cell-like P system. So, this section will briefly introduce the concept of cell-like P system.

2.1   Formal Definition

Cell-like P system is the basic model of P system. Its formal definition is as follows [1]:

$$\Pi = (O, \mu, \omega_1, \omega_2, ..., \omega_m, R_1, R_2, ..., R_m, i_o) \tag{1}$$

- O is the alphabet of system Π, and its elements are known as objects.
- μ is the membrane structure of the system Π, composed of m membranes, and these membranes numbered in turn 1, 2, 3, ..., m, and m is called the degree of system Π.
- ω_i, $1 \leq i \leq$ m, is the initial multiset of objects of the membrane numbered i.
- R_i, $1 \leq i \leq$ m, is a set of evolution rules in the membrane numbered i, whose form will be described in Sect. 2.3.

- $i_o \in$ 1, 2, 3 ..., m is the number of the output membrane, which is used to store the evolutionary result of Π.

The execution of all evolutionary rules on Π satisfies the following three conditions:

- Synchronization: The execution of all evolutionary rules is synchronized, that is, the system has a unified global clock to the whole system timing.
- Nondeterministic: If there is more than one rule compete to execute, it is not certain which rule will be executed.
- Maximum parallelism: All the rules that can be executed in the system should be executed at the same time.

2.2 Membrane Properties

Cell membrane plays an important role in cellular biochemical reactions. It not only divides the cells into different regions to store materials, but also distinguishes cells with different functions. In P system, different membranes can have different objects, rules, and properties.

In studying the evolution of P system, the evolution progress can be restricted, constrained and promoted through some properties like membrane thickness and membrane polarity.

Membrane thickness: The membrane thickness is changed by evolutionary rules to limit object transfer between membranes. Each membrane's thickness is 1 or 2. If the thickness of a membrane is 1, objects can be transported through this membrane; otherwise, objects cannot be exchanged.

Membrane polarity: Membrane polarity is an abstraction of the charged characteristic of a biological cell membrane. There are typically three polarities -, 0 and +. The evolutionary rules change the polarity to accommodate the evolution progress of the membrane. So, membrane polarity is a condition: rules can only be executed when the polarity required by them is the same as the current polarity.

Now the simulation software in membrane computing has less support to membrane properties and does not support the combinations of properties. But, UPS supports known membrane properties and combinations, as well as membrane properties that have not yet been proposed and investigated.

2.3 Rule Types

In membrane computing, the evolutionary rules reflect the functions of the membrane, including the objects evolution and the structures evolution of the membrane. The main rule types in cell-like P system are listed as follows $(u \in O^*, v \in O^*_{tar})$:

(1) $u \to v$

This is the basic rule type for cell-like P system. In this form, u is the multiset on O, and v is the multiset on O_{tar}, where $O_{tar} = O \times TAR$, $TAR = \{here, out\} \cup \{in_j | 1 \leq j \leq m\}$. The elements in TAR are called target instructions, which represent the target membrane.

(2) $u \rightarrow v, p \quad p \in N^+$

This is the form of rules with priority p, and it belongs to the natural numbers set N^+.

(3) $u \rightarrow v | p \quad p \in O$

This is the form of rules with promoter p. Rules with promoters are executed in the presence of the desired promoter only.

(4) $u \rightarrow v | \neg i \quad i \in O$

This is the form of rules with inhibitor i. In contrast to the effect of a promoter, an inhibitor inhibits the execution of a rule.

(5) $u \rightarrow v \tau$

In this form of rules, τ is used to increase the thickness of the membrane. When a membrane has the thickness of 1, the rule increases its thickness to 2.

(6) $u \rightarrow v \delta$

This is the form of rules with δ. The effect of δ and τ is opposite, that is, δ is used to reduce membrane thickness. When the membrane thickness is 0, the membrane will dissolve.

(7) $a \rightarrow [_i u]_i \quad a \in O$

This is the basic form of rules to create a sub-membrane.

(8) $[_h u]_h^{\alpha_1} \rightarrow [_h v]_h^{\alpha_2} \quad \alpha_1, \alpha_2 \in \{+, 0, -\}$

(9) $[_h u \rightarrow v]_h^{\alpha} \quad \alpha \in \{+, 0, -\}$

Both forms (8) and (9) are the forms of rules with membrane polarity. The form (8) changes the membrane polarity from α_1 to α_2 after evolution, while in the form (9), the polarity of the membrane does not change.

In addition to the types of rules already mentioned above, there are many other types of rules in the field of membrane computing. So many kinds of rules have brought a lot of inconvenience to the computer simulation. On the one hand, for new types of rules, it usually needs to modify existing simulation tools or develop new simulation tools. On the other hand, the combination of various types needs to improve the existing simulation tools to obtain good support. For example, in P-Lingua, rules with priority and promoter are not supported. But, UPL can describe these kinds of rules which are a combination of various types. Meanwhile, UPS can simulate the model written in UPL without any modification. What's more, for other not-yet-proposed membrane properties, they also provide good support.

3   UPL: A Cell-Like P System Description Language

The languages used to describe P system models are mainly XML and P-Lingua [12]. XML is universal, but it's too inconvenient to describe P system models. P-Lingua is a language designed for membrane computing and can be used to describe many kinds of P systems, but the separated description of the membrane and its rules is not conducive to the membrane reuse. Most importantly, it does not support the combination of different types of rules.

These problems were solved by UPL. In UPL, a membrane class with certain functions can be defined. To use it, only one statement is required to instantiate an instance of it. Membrane class can also be inherited by another membrane class. And the inherited membrane class not only has all the content of its parent, but also own its own unique content. And, in UPL, the rules are described as two parts which are the condition part and the result part, so that different kinds of rules can be combined to one rule.

Cell-like P system includes five elements: the membrane structure, the object multisets, the evolution rule sets, the alphabet, and the output membrane. Among them, the membrane structure, the object multisets, and the evolution rule sets must be explicitly indicated. But the alphabet and the output membrane can be omitted, because the alphabet can be derived from the initial object multisets and the product of rules, and the output membrane is just used for observation.

3.1   Membrane Representation

The cell-like P system has a nested structure. The nested structure forms a set of distributed computing devices. Just as cells continue to produce new organelles, membranes can continue to produce membranes. By continually producing membranes, the number of membranes increases exponentially. Meanwhile, the computational power also increases exponentially.

The way to describe a membrane in UPL is to define the membranes which have the same rules, the same initial objects, the same attributes, the same submembranes as a membrane class. The definition of a membrane class starts with a keyword "Membrane" and its type name, and ends with its content.

```
<MembraneDefinition> ::= "Membrane" <MembraneType> [ "extends"
 <MembraneType> { "," <MembraneType> } ] "{" <Content> "}"
<MembraneType>::=  <Letters>
<Letters> ::= <Letter> { <Letter> }
<Letter> ::= "a" | "b" |...| "z" | "A" | "B" | ... | "Z"
```

The optional "extends" section indicates the membrane classes which are inherited by this membrane class. Inside the membrane, the initial contents can be declared:

```
<Content>::= { <MemProperty> | <MembraneDeclare> |
 <ObjectDefinition> | <RuleDefinition> }
```

The grammars to define objects and rules will be detailed in Sects. 3.2 and 3.3 respectively.

When declaring a membrane instance, its name and type are needed:

```
<MembraneDeclare>::="Membrane" <MembraneType> <MembraneName>{ "["
 <IntegerDimension> "]" } ( ";" | "{" <Content> "}" )
<MembraneName>::=  <Letters> | <Integer>
<IntegerDimension> ::= <Integer>
<Integer>::= <Digit> { <Digit> }
<Digit>::="0"| "1"| "2"| "3"| "4"| "5"| "6"| "7"| "8"| "9"
```

If the statement ends with a semicolon, it indicates that the membrane is an example of the membrane class. Otherwise, the declared membrane will have more new characteristics than the membrane class it derived from.

The membrane with properties should be given its initial state of properties. If one membrane has more than one properties, they should be separated by commas:

```
<MemProperty>::="Property"<PropertyInit>{ "," <PropertyInit> } ";"
<PropertyInit> ::= <PropertyName> "=" <PropertyValue>
<PropertyName> ::= <Letters>
<PropertyValue> ::= <Letters> | <Integer> | "+" | "-"
```

After all the membrane classes have been defined, the last step for simulation is to use them to build the skin membrane (called "Environment" in UPL). The syntax for defining the skin membrane is as follow:

```
<Environment> ::= "Environment" "{" < Content > "}"
```

3.2   Object Multiset

In a P system, object is the most important information carrier. Often, different objects have different meanings, but the meanings can be similar. These objects with similar meanings are called a class of objects.

A class of objects with n dimensions can be represented as $a_{d_1,d_2,...,d_n}$, where $d_i \in N$ denotes the value of the i-th dimension. UPL provides support for a class of objects.

When defining objects, their names and initial quantities should be given:

```
<ObjectDefinition>::="Object"<ObjectAssign>{","<ObjectAssign>}";"
<ObjectAssign> ::= <ObjectName> { "[" <IntegerDimension> "]" } [
  "^" <ObjectNum> ]
<ObjectName> ::= <Letter> { <Letter> | <Digit> }
<ObjectNum>   ::= <Integer>
```

3.3 Rule Set

In UPL, rule classes are naturally supported, which evolve the object classes:

```
<RuleDefination> ::= "Rule" <RuleName> { "[" <LetterDimension> "]"
  } "=" <ObjectCondition> { <ObjectCondition> } "->" { <Result> }
  [ "|" <OtherCondition> { "&" <OtherCondition> } ] ";"
<RuleName> ::= <Letter> { <Letters> | <Integer> }
<LetterDimension> ::= <Letters>
```

If one rule has at least one dimension, then this rule is used for the evolution of a class of objects. Each dimension in this rule can be used to describe the relationship between the objects.

In UPL, rules are divided into conditions and results. The independence of conditions and results facilitates the addition of new conditions and new results. Meanwhile, it also facilitates the combination of various conditions and results.

There are two categories of conditions: consumptive conditions and nonconsumptive conditions. $\langle ObjectCondition \rangle$ represents a consumptive condition, it will consume a number of objects. The nonconsumptive condition is represented by $\langle OtherCondition \rangle$, which is a constraint on the execution of rules, including promoters, inhibitors, membrane properties, rule priorities, and more.

Object condition needs to specify the name of the consumed object and its quantity (the default quantity is 1 if not specified). If the object consumed belongs to a class of objects, then the object's dimensions also need to be specified:

```
<ObjectCondition> ::= <ObjectName> { "[" <FormulaDimension> "]"
  } [ "^" <ObjectNum> ]
```

The dimension of an object condition can be letters, numbers, or formulas. If it is a letter, then the letter can only be a dimension of the current rule. If it is a formula, it should be a computable formula using dimensions of the current rule as variables and numbers as constants.

```
<FormulaDimension> ::={<LetterDimension>|<Integer>|<Operator>}
<Operator> ::= "+" | "-" | "*" | "/" | "%" | "(" | ")"
```

The definition of ⟨OtherCondition⟩ is as follow:

```
<OtherCondition>::= <PromoterCondition> | <InhibitorCondition>
 | <PriorityCondition>|<BoolCondition>|<MemPropertyCondition>
```

The expression of a promoter condition starts with symbol "@", while a inhibitor condition starts with "!". What follows is their names and dimensions:

```
<PromoterCondition>::= "@"<ObjectName>{"[" <FormulaDimension> "]"}
<InhibitorCondition>::="!"<ObjectName>{"[" <FormulaDimension> "]"}
```

The membrane property condition uses the current properties of the membrane to limit the execution of rules:

```
<MemPropertyCondition>::= "m." <PropertyName> "==" <PropertyValue>
```

The priority condition indicates the priority of this rule, and if no higher priority rule can be executed, the priority condition is satisfied:

```
<PriorityCondition>::="pri" "=" <Priority>
<Priority>::=<Integer>
```

When a rule represents a class of rules, boolean condition can be used to restrict the relationships of the dimensions of this rule. And the boolean condition is satisfied only if the logic relationship of the dimensions of this rule is satisfied:

```
<BoolCondition>::={ <LetterDimension>| <Integer>| <Operator>
 | <LOperator> }
<LOperator>::="&&"| "||" | ">=" | ">" | "==" | "!=" | "<=" | "<"
```

The result of rule execution can be generating objects, changing the properties, dissolving a membrane, or creating a new membrane.

```
<Result>::=<ObjectResult>|<PositionResult>|<MemPropertyResult>|
 <MemDissolveResult>|<MemCreateResult>
<PositionResult>::="(" <ObjectResult> + "," ( "out"|"here"|"in"
 <MembraneName>{ "[" <FormulaDimension> "]" { "."
```

```
<MemPropertyCondition> } ")".)
<ObjectResult>::=<ObjectName> { "[" <FormulaDimension> "]" }
 [ "^" <ObjectNum> ]
<MemPropertyResult>::="m." <PropertyName> "=" <PropertyValue>
<MemDissolveResult>::="m.dissolve"
<MemCreateResult>::="{" (<ObjectResult> | <MemPropertyResult>) "}"
 <MembraneType> [":" <MembraneName> {"[" <FormulaDimension> "]"}]
```

4 UPS: A Cell-Like P System Simulation Software

4.1 Achitecture

UPS consists of several components, such as recognizer, simulater, and user interface.

The sentences which describes a P system will firstly be recognized by the recognizer, and then a skin membrane will be constructed. After that, the skin membrane and its inner sub-membranes will evolve under the control of the simulater. The main function of the simulater is to ensure the synchronization, parallelism and nondeterminism of P system during the execution. User interface will promptly show the status of P system, and the user can control the entire simulation process through the interface.

4.2 Recognizer Design

The function of the recognizer is to recognize the sentence written in UPL and to complete the corresponding action according to the semantic meaning of the sentence. The final result of recognition is a skin membrane. Sentences are identified in the following steps:

(1) Lexical analysis: Recognize the character sequence as a word sequence.
(2) Grammar analysis: Combine the words to get a grammar tree, where the leaf nodes represent terminals, and the non-leaf nodes represent non-terminals.
(3) Semantic analysis: According to the resulting grammar tree, and the semantics of the phrases, do the corresponding actions.

4.3 Simulator Design

As we know, P system is a distributed parallel computing model. Its parallelism is reflected in the parallel membranes and the parallel rules. In order to simulate P system in a serial computer, following measures must be taken to ensure its synchronization, parallelism and nondeterminism:

Synchronization. In simulation, in order to make sure that the execution of the rules is synchronous, the continuous time are divided into time slices, and the rules that can be executed in each time slice must be executed.

Parallelism. When a serial computer simulates the parallelism of membrane computing, all the rules can only be executed one by one. If the rules are not properly executed, the simulation of the whole membrane system will be confused and the result will be biased.

In UPS, the simulator will take the following steps in each time slice to ensure the parallelism:

(1) All rules will be checked if some rules are satisfied.
(2) All the satisfied rules try to fetch all the objects they need, and return the fetched objects if fail.
(3) The rules, which have successfully fetched all the desired objects, set their results according to their number of fetches.

The purpose of the three-step is to prevent the interference between the various steps. For example, the consumption of an object may consume a promoter of one rule, rendering the rule's promoter condition unsatisfied.

Nondeterminism. In step (2) of parallelism, there may be more than one rule that may satisfy the current situation and the sets of the objects that they need to consume are intersected. Therefore, it is necessary to simulate the nondeterminism to solve the problem in a nondeterministic way.

Assuming that the rules which are satisfied belong to set R, the process of simulating nondeterminism is:

(1) Generate random number i, while $i \in \{1, 2, ..., |R|\}$.
(2) Select the i-th rule r_i from R and try to get all the objects it needs.
(3) If fetch successfully, the number of fetches of r_i is increased by 1, and if the fetch fails, the objects that have been fetched this time will be returned and r_i will be removed from R.
(4) Repeat (1) (2) (3) until R is empty.

4.4 User Interface

UPS has also provided an easy-to-use user interface as shown in Fig. 1.

The basic way to import one model into UPS is to import a textual file for each membrane class and a textual file for the skin membrane in the interface. If a number of skin membranes need to be tested, just import them at one-time.

5 Instance

In this section, a position-code based **add** membrane will be described in UPL and simulated by UPS.

5.1 Model

This section will give the definition of the **add** membrane.

Digital Representation. In the add membrane, class object a represents the first operand. In detail, $a_{i,j}$ means that part of the first operand equals to $i \times 10^j$, while $i \in \{0, 1, \ldots, 9\}$, $j \in N^+$. For example, $a_{0,1}$ represents 0, and $a_{8,2}$ represents 800.

And class object b is used to represent the second operand. So as a, $b_{i,j}$ means that part of the second operand equals to $i \times 10^j$, while $i \in \{0, 1, \ldots, 9\}$, $j \in N^+$.

To illustrate the problem briefly, the first operand and the second operand are positive numbers.

Add Membrane. Add membrane is a single membrane. When to add a and b, class object a and b are firstly turned into class object r. And then use the class object r to carry. The rules in add membrane are as follows:

$$r_1 : a_{i,j} \to r_{i,j}\, c \qquad r_2 : b_{i,j} \to r_{i,j}\, c \qquad r_3 : r_{0,j} \to \lambda \qquad r_4 : c \to \lambda$$
$$r_5 : r_{i,j}\, r_{n,j} \to r_{(i+n)/10,\, j+1}\, r_{(i+n)\%10,\, j}\, c \quad (i \neq 0 \, and \, n \neq 0)$$
$$r_6 : d \to e\,|\,\neg c \qquad r_7 : r_{i,j} \to (r_{i,j},\, out)\,|\,e \qquad r_8 : e \to \lambda$$

Simulation Verification. Following steps show how to simulate the model given in this section.

(1) Firstly, define an add membrane class, and then write it to file "AddMembrane.txt".

```
Membrane Add{
    Rule r1[i][j] = a[i][j] -> r[i][j] c;
    Rule r2[i][j] = b[i][j] -> r[i][j] c;
    Rule r3[j] = r[0][j] -> ;
    Rule r4 = c -> ;
    Rule r5[i][j][n] =r[i][j] r[n][j] -> r[(i+n)/10][j+1] r[(i+n)\%10][j] c
        | i!=0 & n!=0;
    Rule r6 = d -> e | !c;
    Rule r7[i][j] = r[i][j] -> (r[i][j] , out) | @e;
    Rule r8 = e -> m.dissolve;
}
```

(2) After that, create an instance of add membrane class in skin membrane, and then place all the objects required for the computation. In the instance, a equals to 123, and b equals to 796. Finally, write the above all to file "instance1.txt".

```
Environment{
    Membrane Add addm{
        Object a[1][2]^1,a[2][1]^1,a[3][0]^1;
        Object b[7][2]^1,b[9][1]^1,b[6][0]^1;
        Object d, c;
    }
}
```

(3) The simulation result is shown in Fig. 1, which equals to 919, and 6 time slices have been used.

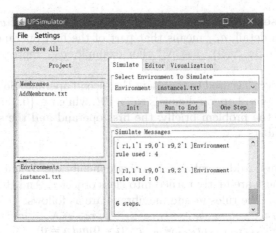

Fig. 1. Simulation result.

6 Conclusions and Future Work

In this paper, we proposed a simulation tool UPS and a general purpose description language UPL for cell-like P system.

There are so many kinds of evolution rules in cell-like P system that makes researchers continually develop their own simulation application to adapt to the diversity of rules. If new characteristics are proposed, huge changes need to be made in their software to adapt to the new characteristics. UPL and UPS solved the problem by dividing the evolution rules into conditions and results. Moreover, the combination of various types of rules can be described and simulated.

However, not all the P system models are supported, like tissue-like P system and neural-like P system and other P system models. These models will be added to UPL in a unified way in the future work. Meanwhile, UPS will provide support to simulate these kinds of P system models.

References

1. Pǎun, G.: Computing with membranes. J. Comput. Syst. Sci. **61**, 108–143 (2000)
2. Song, B., Song, T., Pan, L.: A time-free uniform solution to subset sum problem by tissue P systems with cell division. Math. Struct. Comput. Sci. **27**, 17–32 (2017)
3. Song, W., Guo, P., Chen, H.: A solution for all-SAT problem based on P systems. J. Comput. Theor. Nanosci. **13**, 4293–4301 (2016)
4. Peng, H., Wang, J., Shi, P.: A novel image thresholding method based on membrane computing and fuzzy entropy. J. Intell. Fuzzy Syst. Appl. Eng. Technol. **24**, 229–237 (2013)
5. Díaz-Pernil, D., Berciano, A., PeñA-Cantillana, F., Gutiérrez-Naranjo, M.A.: Segmenting images with gradient-based edge detection using membrane computing. Pattern Recogn. Lett. **34**, 846–855 (2013)
6. Liang, H., He, X., Ning, W., Yi, X.: P systems based multi-objective optimization algorithm. Prog. Nat. Sci.: Mater. Int. **17**, 458–465 (2007)

7. Liu, C., Han, M., Wang, X.Z.: A multi-objective evolutionary algorithm based on membrane systems. In: International Workshop on Advanced Computational Intelligence, pp. 103–109 (2011)
8. Păun, G., Păun, R.: Membrane computing and economics: numerical P systems. Fundamenta Informaticae **73**, 213–227 (2006)
9. Peng, H., Wang, J., Pérez-Jiménez, M.J., Riscos-Núñez, A.: An unsupervised learning algorithm for membrane computing. Inf. Sci. **304**, 80–91 (2015)
10. Cardona, M., Colomer, M.A., Zaragoza, A., Pérez-Jiménez, M.J.: Hierarchical clustering with membrane computing. Comput. Inf. **27**, 497–513 (2012)
11. Cabarle, F.G.C., Adorna, H., Martínez, M.A.: A spiking neural P system simulator based on CUDA. In: Gheorghe, M., Păun, G., Rozenberg, G., Salomaa, A., Verlan, S. (eds.) CMC 2011. LNCS, vol. 7184, pp. 87–103. Springer, Heidelberg (2012). https://doi.org/10.1007/978-3-642-28024-5_8
12. García-Quismondo, M., Gutiérrez-Escudero, R., Pérez-Hurtado, I., Pérez-Jiménez, M.J., Riscos-Núñez, A.: An overview of P-lingua 2.0. In: Păun, G., Pérez-Jiménez, M.J., Riscos-Núñez, A., Rozenberg, G., Salomaa, A. (eds.) WMC 2009. LNCS, vol. 5957, pp. 264–288. Springer, Heidelberg (2010). https://doi.org/10.1007/978-3-642-11467-0_20
13. Pernil, D.D., Hurtado, I.P., Jiménez, M.J.P., Núñez, A.R.: P-lingua: a programming language for membrane computing. In: Algebraic Computing, Soft Computing, and Program Verification, pp. 135–156 (2013)
14. Pérezhurtado, I., Valenciacabrera, L., Pérezjiménez, M.J., Colomer, M.A.: MeCoSim: a general purpose software tool for simulating biological phenomena by means of P systems. In: IEEE Fifth International Conference on Bio-Inspired Computing: Theories and Applications, pp. 637–643 (2010)
15. Gutiérrez-Naranjo, M.A., Pérez-Jiménez, M.J., Ramírez-Martínez, D.: A software tool for verification of spiking neural P systems. Natural Comput. **7**, 485 (2008)
16. Muniyandi, R.C., Maroosi, A.: Enhancing the simulation of membrane system on the GPU for the N-Queens problem. Chin. J. Electron. **24**, 740–743 (2015)
17. Raghavan, S., Chandrasekaran, K.: Tools and simulators for membrane computing- a literature review. In: Gong, M., Pan, L., Song, T., Zhang, G. (eds.) BIC-TA 2016. CCIS, vol. 681, pp. 249–277. Springer, Singapore (2016). https://doi.org/10.1007/978-981-10-3611-8_23
18. The UPSimulator Project. https://github.com/quancs/UPSimulator

Dynamic Multimodal Optimization Using Brain Storm Optimization Algorithms

Shi Cheng[1(✉)], Hui Lu[2], Wu Song[3], Junfeng Chen[4], and Yuhui Shi[5]

[1] School of Computer Science, Shaanxi Normal University, Xi'an 710119, China
cheng@snnu.edu.cn
[2] School of Electronic and Information Engineering, Beihang University,
Beijing 100191, China
mluhui@buaa.edu.cn
[3] School of Information Engineering, Hainan Tropical Ocean University,
Sanya 572000, China
[4] College of IOT Engineering, Hohai University,
Changzhou 213022, China
chen-1997@163.com
[5] Shenzhen Key Lab of Computational Intelligence,
Department of Computer Science and Engineering,
Southern University of Science and Technology, Shenzhen, China
shiyh@sustc.edu.cn

Abstract. Dynamic multimodal optimization (DMO) problem is introduced and solved with brain storm optimization (BSO) algorithms in this paper. A dynamic multimodal optimization problem is defined as an optimization problem with multiple global optima and characteristics of global optima are changed during the search process. The effectiveness of BSO algorithm is validated on a test problem which was constructed based on the dynamic optimization and multimodal optimization. Results show that BSO algorithm is an efficient and robust optimization method for solving dynamic multimodal optimization problems.

Keywords: Brain storm optimization
Dynamic multimodal optimization problem · Swarm intelligence
Developmental swarm intelligence

1 Introduction

Optimization is concerned with finding the optimum feasible solution(s) for a given optimized problem. An optimization problem is a mapping from decision space to objective space. The solutions are searched in the decision space, while the function value (objective) is evaluated in the objective space. For swarm intelligence or evolutionary computation algorithms, the solutions in the search space are represented by individuals in the swarm. The position of an individual is corresponded with decision variables of a solution in the decision space, while

J. Qiao et al. (Eds.): BIC-TA 2018, CCIS 951, pp. 236–245, 2018.
https://doi.org/10.1007/978-981-13-2826-8_21

the fitness value of an individual corresponds with the objective value of the solution in the objective space. Individuals are guided toward the better and better search areas through the cooperation and competition among individuals until some stopping conditions are met.

Many real-world problems could be modeled as optimization problems and solved by using intelligent algorithms. These problems often have several conflicting objectives to be optimized. For example, different factors, which include economic benefits, production efficiency, energy consumption, and environmental protection, need to be optimized simultaneously in the steel production industry.

The brain storm optimization (BSO) algorithm is based on the collective behavior of human being, that is, the brainstorming process [1,2]. The individuals in brain storm optimization are diverging into several clusters. The new individuals are generated based on the mutation of one existing individual or a combination of two individuals. In the original BSO algorithm, the clustering strategy is performed at each iteration. The computational resources are consumed a lot in the clustering operation. Thus, to reduce the computational burden, the clustering strategy needs to be modified. The brain storm optimization in objective space (BSO-OS) algorithm was proposed and the clustering strategy was replaced by a simple elitist strategy based on the fitness values [3,4]. For BSO algorithms, the "good enough" optimum could be obtained through solutions' diverging and converging in the search space. Since the invention of the brain storm optimization algorithm in 2011 [1,2], it has attracted many attentions in the swarm intelligence research community. An analysis of BSO algorithm from the data analytics perspective is introduced in [3]. A comprehensive survey of BSO algorithm was given in [5], and a simple brain storm optimization algorithm with a periodic quantum learning strategy is proposed in [6], just to name a few.

It is often necessary to optimize a series of events in real-world applications in dynamic environments, $i.e.$, an optimization process may contain some changing characteristics [7,8]. The aim of dynamic optimization is to track the moving optima, which indicates that the optima are changed over time. An algorithm should have an ability to track the dynamic optima for dynamic optimization problems. The aim of multimodal optimization is to locate multiple global optima in a single run and maintaining these found optima until the end of a run [9–11]. Two performance criteria could be used to measure the success of search algorithms. One is whether an optimization algorithm could find all desired optima including global and/or local optima, and the other is whether it can maintain multiple candidate solutions stably over a run [11].

Dynamic multimodal optimization (DMO) is a combination of dynamic optimization and multimodal optimization. Multiple global optima are changed during the search process. The aim of solving DMO problems is to track multiple global optima in a single run and to maintain these found optima until the end of a run. Two performance criteria could be used to measure the success of search algorithms. One is whether an optimization algorithm could find all desired optima including global and/or local optima, and the other is the diversity of multiple candidate solutions [11].

The principal contributions presented in this work can be summarized as follow:

- The brain storm optimization algorithms have been utilized in solving the dynamic multimodal optimization problem.
- The analysis on properties of the BSO-OS algorithm to solve dynamic multimodal optimization problems.

The remaining of this paper is organized as follows: In Sect. 2, the basic concepts of BSO algorithms are introduced. Section 3 describes the dynamic multimodal optimization problem with illustrations of a practical example. Section 4 validates the effectiveness of our algorithm. Finally, conclusions are given in Sect. 5.

2   Brain Storm Optimization

The brain storm optimization algorithm is based on the collective behavior of human being, that is, the brainstorming process [1,2]. The individuals (solutions) in BSO are converging into several clusters. The best solution in the population will be kept when the newly generated solution at the same index is not better. The new individual can be generated based on the mutation of one or two individuals in clusters. The exploration ability of algorithm is enhanced when the new individual is generated randomly or generated based on the combination of two individuals in two clusters. While the exploitation ability is enhanced when the new individual is generated close to the best solution founded.

It is simple in concept and easy in implementation for the original BSO algorithm [1,2]. Figure 1 shows the framework of brain storm optimization algorithm. The procedure of BSO algorithm is given in Algorithm 1. There are three strategies in this algorithm: the solution clustering/classification, new individual generation, and selection [12]. The solution clustering and solution classification

---

Algorithm 1. The basic procedure of the brain storm optimization algorithm

---

Initialization: Randomly generate n individuals (potential solutions), and evaluate the n individuals;

while *not find "good enough" solution or not reach the pre-determined maximum number of iterations* **do**

Solution clustering/classification operation: Diverge n individuals into m groups by a clustering/classification algorithm;

New solution generation operation: Select solution(s) from one or two group(s) randomly to generate new individual (solution);

Solution selection operation: Compare the newly generated individual (solution) and the existing individual (solution) with the same individual index; the better one is kept and recorded as the new individual;

Evaluate the n individuals (solutions);

---

strategies are used in the original BSO algorithm and BSO in objective space algorithm, respectively [4].

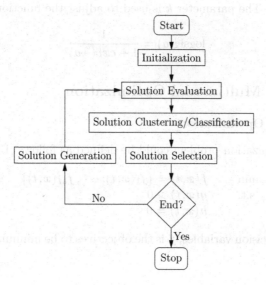

Fig. 1. The framework of brain storm optimization algorithm

In the original BSO algorithm, a lot of the computational resources are spent on the clustering strategy at each iteration. To reduce the computational burden, the brain storm optimization in objective space (BSO-OS) algorithm was proposed, and the clustering strategy was replaced by a simple elitist strategy based on the fitness values [4].

The new individual generation strategy is the major difference between the original BSO and other BSO variant algorithms. Individuals are clustered into several groups in the original BSO algorithm, while different clustering/classification strategies have been utilized in other BSO variants. For example, in the BSO-OS algorithm, individuals are classified into two categories: the elitists and the normals, according to their fitness values.

The new individuals are generated according to the functions (1) and (2).

$$x_{new}^i = x_{old}^i + \xi(t) \times N(\mu, \sigma^2) \tag{1}$$

$$\xi(t) = logsig(\frac{0.5 \times T - t}{k}) \times rand() \tag{2}$$

where x_{new}^i and x_{old}^i are the ith dimension of $\mathbf{x}_{new}$ and $\mathbf{x}_{old}$; rand() is a random function to generate uniformly distributed random numbers in the range $[0, 1)$; and the value $\mathbf{x}_{old}$ is a copy of one individual or a combination of two individuals. The $N(\mu, \sigma^2)$ is a random value that generated with a Gaussian distribution. The parameter T is the maximum number of iterations, t is the current iteration number, k is a coefficient to change logsig() function's slope of the step size function $\xi(t)$, which can be utilized to balance the convergence speed of the algorithm.

A transfer function logsig(a), which is given in Eq. (3), has been deployed in step size Eq. (2). The parameter k is used to adjust the function's slope.

$$\text{logsig}(a) = \frac{1}{1 + exp(-a)} \tag{3}$$

3   Dynamic Multimodal Optimization

3.1   Dynamic Optimization

A dynamic optimization problem could be defined as follows [13,14]:

$$\begin{array}{ll} \min & \boldsymbol{f}(\boldsymbol{x},t) = \{f_1(\boldsymbol{x},t), \cdots, f_M(\boldsymbol{x},t)\} \\ \text{s.t.} & \boldsymbol{g}(\boldsymbol{x},t) > 0 \\ & \boldsymbol{h}(\boldsymbol{x},t) = 0 \end{array} \tag{4}$$

where $\boldsymbol{x}$ is the decision variables; $\boldsymbol{f}$ is the objectives to be minimized with respect to time t.

3.2   Multimodal Optimization

Many optimization algorithms are designed for locating a single global solution. Nevertheless, many real-world problems may have multiple satisfactory solutions exist. The multimodal optimization problem is a function with multiple global/local optimal values [15]. For multimodal optimization, the objective is to locate multiple peaks/optima in a single run [16,17], and to keep these found optima until the end of a run [9–11]. An algorithm on solving multimodal optimization problems should have two kinds of abilities: find global/local optima as many as possible and preserve these found solutions until the end of the search.

3.3   Dynamic Multimodal Problem

A dynamic multimodal optimization problem is a combination of the dynamic optimization problem and multimodal optimization problem. In order to give a simple illustration, an example of a dynamic multimodal optimization problem is as follows.

$$f(x) = |\sin(t \times \pi \times x) - \frac{1}{t \times \pi} \times x| \tag{5}$$

where $x \in [-2, 2]$ and $t \in [\frac{1}{\pi}, \pi]$. The equal maxima function, given in Eq. (5), is an example of the dynamic multimodal optimization problem. From Fig. 2, it can be seen that there are 3, 7, 13 equal optima for Eq. (5) with $t = \frac{\pi}{3}$, $t = \frac{\pi}{2}$, and $t = \pi$, respectively. Figure 2 gives an example of problem with the equal optima, i.e., the value of all optima is equal to 0. The dynamic multimodal optimization problem also could be extended to problems with unequal optima, which will be much harder to solve.

The dynamic multimodal optimization could be applied to real-world problems, for example, nonlinear equation system with time variable. The Eq. (5) could be transferred to the Eq. (6), which has the same optima in range $t \in [\frac{1}{\pi}, \pi]$.

$$\begin{cases} \sin(t \times \pi \times x_1) - x_2 = 0 \\ x_1 - t \times \pi \times x_2 = 0 \end{cases} \tag{6}$$

where $x \in [0, 1]$ and $t \in [\frac{1}{\pi}, \pi]$. The optima in Fig. 2 are converted to the intersections of two curves in Fig. 3. There are 3, 7, 13 optima for Eq. (6) with $t = \frac{\pi}{3}$, $t = \frac{\pi}{2}$, and $t = \pi$, respectively.

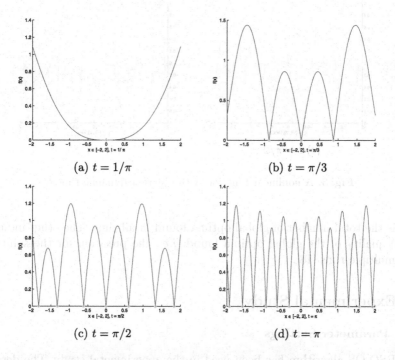

(a) $t = 1/\pi$

(b) $t = \pi/3$

(c) $t = \pi/2$

(d) $t = \pi$

Fig. 2. An example of multimodal function with different dynamic time t.

Unlike the multimodal optimization problems, the uncertainty exists in dynamic multimodal optimization problems. For example, some features of DMO problems are as follows:

1. The number of global optima is changed during the search;
2. The locations of global optima are all/partially changed during the search.

3.4   Performance Criteria

The value and number of found global optima could be used in performance criteria. Two criteria are used to measure the number of found global optima.

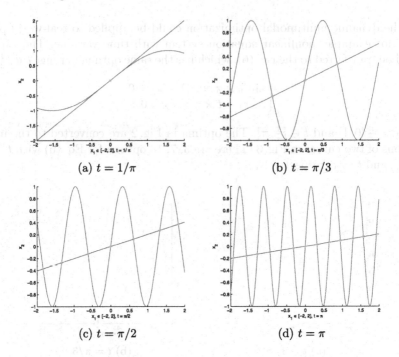

(a) $t = 1/\pi$ (b) $t = \pi/3$

(c) $t = \pi/2$ (d) $t = \pi$

Fig. 3. A nonlinear function with different dynamic time t.

One is the total number of global optima found in all runs. The other indicator is the quality of the global optima found, *i.e.*, the precision for the solutions, over multiple runs [18].

4   Experimental Study

4.1   Parameter Settings

The BSO-OS algorithm has been used in the experimental study. The detailed parameter settings are as follows:

– BSO-OS algorithm: $p_{elitist} = 0.1$, $p_{one} = 0.8$, slope $k = 500$.

4.2   Experimental Results

Figure 4 gives results of BSO-OS algorithm solving a dynamic multimodal optimization problem. It could be seen that the value of the search error is not consistent decreasing because the optima are dynamically changed during the search. The number of global optima found is also changed during the search. To obtain a good performance on this kind of problem, an algorithm should have an ability on tracking and maintaining the global optima found.

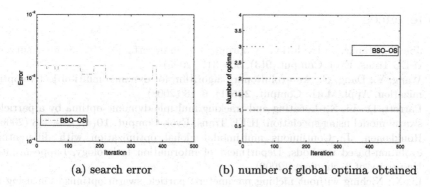

(a) search error   (b) number of global optima obtained

Fig. 4. Results of BSO-OS algorithm solving a dynamic multimodal optimization problem

4.3 Discussion

There are many iterations in the swarm intelligence algorithm, which indicates that massive solutions will be evaluated during the search. For the reason of computing and storage efficiency, there is no algorithm to store all the evaluated solutions. Several representative solutions, such as the local best or personal best solutions in particle swarm optimization algorithm, are used as a memory system for search algorithm [19]. The distribution of solutions is used in BSO algorithms, and there is no explicit memory system of the previous iterations. This memory system will be beneficial when algorithm solves problems in the static environment. However, for problems in the dynamic environment, this memory may mislead the search direction.

Brain storm optimization, more widely, the swarm intelligence algorithms are based on the "trail and error" strategy. More research should be conducted on foundational problems of swarm intelligence. The developmental swarm intelligence algorithm [20] or the unified swarm intelligence algorithms [21] could be an approach to analysis the strength and disadvantages of each algorithm.

5   Conclusion

In this paper, we introduced a new kind of optimization problem, which termed as dynamic multimodal optimization (DMO) problem. The DMO problem is defined as an optimization problem with multiple global optima and the characteristics of global optima are changed during the search process. Brain storm optimization (BSO) algorithm was used to solve the DMO problem. The effectiveness of the BSO algorithm was validated on a test function. Results show that BSO algorithm is an efficient and robust optimization method for solving DMO problems.

Acknowledgments. This work was jointly supported by National Natural Science Foundation of China (No. 61671041, 61773119, 61771297, and 61703256), and the Fundamental Research Funds for the Central Universities under Grant GK201703062.

244   S. Cheng et al.

References

1. Jin, Y., Branke, J.: Evolutionary optimization in uncertain environments-a survey. IEEE Trans. Evol. Comput. **9**(3), 303–317 (2005)
2. Wang, Y., Dang, C.: An evolutionary algorithm for dynamic multi-objective optimization. Appl. Math. Comput. **205**(1), 6–18 (2008)
3. Parrott, D., Li, X.: Locating and tracking multiple dynamic optima by a particle swarm model using speciation. IEEE Trans. Evol. Comput. **10**(4), 440–458 (2006)
4. Rönkkönen, J.: Continuous multimodal global optimization with differential evolution-based methods. Department of information technology, Lappeenranta University of Technology (2009)
5. Li, X.: Niching without niching parameters: particle swarm optimization using a ring topology. IEEE Trans. Evol. Comput. **14**(1), 150–169 (2010)
6. Shi, Y.: Brain storm optimization algorithm. In: Tan, Y., Shi, Y., Chai, Y., Wang, G. (eds.) ICSI 2011. LNCS, vol. 6728, pp. 303–309. Springer, Heidelberg (2011). https://doi.org/10.1007/978-3-642-21515-5_36
7. Shi, Y.: An optimization algorithm based on brainstorming process. Int. J. Swarm Intell. Res. **2**(4), 35–62 (2011)
8. Cheng, S., Qin, Q., Chen, J., Shi, Y.: Brain storm optimization algorithm: a review. Artif. Intell. Rev. **46**(4), 445–458 (2016)
9. Shi, Y.: Brain storm optimization algorithm in objective space. In: Proceedings of 2015 IEEE Congress on Evolutionary Computation, Sendai, Japan, pp. 1227–1234 (2015)
10. Cheng, S., et al.: A comprehensive survey of brain storm optimization algorithms. In: Proceedings of 2017 IEEE Congress on Evolutionary Computation, Donostia, San Sebastián, Spain, pp. 1637–1644 (2017)
11. Song, Z., Peng, J., Li, C., Liu, P.X.: A simple brain storm optimization algorithm with a periodic quantum learning strategy. IEEE Access **6**, 19968–19983 (2017)
12. Cheng, S., Shi, Y., Qin, Q., Gao, S.: Solution clustering analysis in brain storm optimization algorithm. In: Proceedings of The 2013 IEEE Symposium on Swarm Intelligence, Singapore, pp. 111–118 (2013)
13. Goh, C.K., Tan, K.C.: A competitive-cooperative coevolutionary paradigm for dynamic multiobjective optimization. IEEE Trans. Evol. Comput. **13**(1), 103–127 (2009)
14. Jiang, S., Yang, S.: Evolutionary dynamic multiobjective optimization: benchmarks and algorithm comparisons. IEEE Trans. Cybern. **47**(1), 198–211 (2017)
15. Cheng, S., Chen, J., Lei, X., Shi, Y.: Locating multiple optima via developmental swarm intelligence. IEEE Access **6**, 17039–17049 (2018)
16. Qu, B.Y., Liang, J., Suganthan, P.: Niching particle swarm optimization with local search for multi-modal optimization. Inf. Sci. **197**, 131–143 (2012)
17. Qu, B.Y., Suganthan, P., Liang, J.: Differential evolution with neighborhood mutation for multimodal optimization. IEEE Trans. Evol. Comput. **16**(5), 601–614 (2012)
18. Li, X., Engelbrecht, A., Epitropakis, M.G.: Benchmark functions for CEC 2013 special session and competition on niching methods for multimodal function optimization. Evolutionary Computation and Machine Learning Group, RMIT University (2013)

19. Burke, E.K., Hyde, M.R., Kendall, G.: Providing a memory mechanism to enhance the evolutionary design of heuristics. In: Proceedings of 2010 IEEE Congress on Evolutionary Computation, pp. 1–8 (2010)
20. Shi, Y.: Developmental swarm intelligence: developmental learning perspective of swarm intelligence algorithms. Int. J. Swarm Intell. Res. 5(1), 36–54 (2014)
21. Shi, Y.: Unified swarm intelligence algorithms. In: Shi, Y. (ed.) Critical Developments and Applications of Swarm Intelligence, pp. 1–26 (2018)

A Hybrid Replacement Strategy for MOEA/D

Xiaoji Chen[1,2], Chuan Shi[1,2(✉)], Aimin Zhou[1,2], Siyong Xu[1,2], and Bin Wu[1,2]

[1] Beijing Key Lab of Intelligent Telecommunications Software and Multimedia, Beijing University of Posts and Telecommunications, Beijing 100876, China
{chenxiaoji,shichuan,binwu,siyongxu}@bupt.edu.cn
[2] Shanghai Key Laboratory of Multidimensional Information Processing, Department of Computer Science and Technology, East China Normal University, Shanghai 200062, China
amzhou@cs.ecnu.edu.cn

Abstract. In MOEA/D, the replacement strategy plays a key role in balancing diversity and convergence. However, existing adaptive replacement strategies either focus on neighborhood or global replacement strategy, which may have no obvious effects on balance of diversity and convergence in tackling complicated MOPs. In order to overcome this shortcoming, we propose a hybrid mechanism balancing neighborhood and global replacement strategy. In this mechanism, a probability threshold p_t is applied to determine whether to execute a neighborhood or global replacement strategy, which could balance diversity and convergence. Furthermore, we design an offspring generation method to generate the high-quality solution for each subproblem, which can ease mismatch between subproblems and solutions. Based on the classic MOEA/D, we design a new algorithm framework, called MOEA/D-HRS. Compared with other state-of-the-art MOEAs, experimental results show that the proposed algorithm obtains the best performance.

Keywords: Evolutionary algorithm · Multiobjective optimization MOEA/D · Replacement strategy

1 Introduction

Multiobjective optimization problem (MOP) has several objectives to be optimized. Usually, these objectives often conflict with each other, and no single solution can optimize all these objectives at the same time. In General, multiobjective optimization problems (MOPs) can be stated as follows:

$$\min_{s.t\, x \in \Omega} F(x) = (f_1(x), \cdots, f_m(x))^T \tag{1}$$

where Ω is the decision space and $x \in \Omega$ is a decision vector. $F(x)$ consists of m objective functions $f_i : \Omega \rightarrow R, i = 1, \cdots, m$, where R^m is the objective space [1].

© Springer Nature Singapore Pte Ltd. 2018
J. Qiao et al. (Eds.): BIC-TA 2018, CCIS 951, pp. 246–262, 2018.
https://doi.org/10.1007/978-981-13-2826-8_22

Evolutionary algorithms (EAs) are population-based optimization algorithms, which are able to approximate the Pareto front of the MOP by multiple iterations. Because of the advantages of EAs, they are widely used to deal with MOPs. During the past two decades, a large number of multiobjective evolutionary algorithms (MOEAs) have been proposed, which can be roughly classified into three categories [1]: the Pareto domination based approaches [2–5], the indicator based approaches [6–8], and the decomposition based approaches [9,10].

Multiobjective evolutionary algorithm based on decomposition (MOEA/D) is one of the most popular decomposition based MOEAs. In recent years, it has greatly attracted the interest of scientific researchers and thus numbers of MOEA/D variants such as dynamical resource allocation [11,12], enhanced evolutionary operators [10,13–15], preselection [16–19], adaptive control methods [20–24], and matching strategies [25–27], have been designed to further improve the performance of MOEA/D. In these algorithms, most of them use neighborhood replacement strategy. However, neighborhood replacement strategy only replace two neighbor solutions of the current subproblem, which may cause mismatches between solutions and subproblems [27]. Recently, global replacement strategies have become the focus of research. MOEA/D-AGR [27] is the most representative global replacement strategy algorithm. This approach uses DE operator to generate offspring for each subproblem, and assigns each offspring to replace the most suitable subproblem. However, this strategy gradually increases the number of replacement neighbors, although it can achieve better convergence results, but it may lead to a decline in diversity performance [28].

In order to overcome these disadvantages, we propose a novel hybrid mechanism for balancing replacement strategy, and design a new algorithm called MOEA/D-HRS (MOEA/D based on Hybrid Replacement Strategy). In each generation, firstly, we employ nondominated sorting [3], S-metric [4] or hypervolume [44] to measure the fitness value of each solution, and generate multiple temporary solutions. Besides, we generate a small number of Gaussian temporary solutions. In order to make better use of the solution of the corresponding subproblem, we view this solution as a special temporary solution. Second, we employ surrogate model [41] to estimate objective values of each temporary solution, and obtain the optimal one. We generate offspring by employing differential evolution (DE) [34] operator with polynomial mutation [35]. Then, the probability threshold p_t is applied to determine whether an AGR [27] or neighborhood replacement strategy [11–17,19–26] is executed. We conduct large-scale experiments on two test function sets, and compare with other state-of-the-art MOEAs. From the experimental results, we can see that the proposed algorithm has achieved the best results.

The rest of this paper is organized as follows. Section 2 introduces related work. Section 3 describe the details of MOEA/D-HRS. Experimental results of MOEA/D-HRS with other state-of-the-art MOEAs are compared and analyzed in Sect. 4. Section 5 concludes this paper and outlines future research work.

2   Related Work

Recently, a variety of MOEA/D variants have been proposed, which can be summed up into the following five categories.

2.1   Dynamical Resource Allocation

MOEA/D-DRA [11] was proposed based on the fact that different subproblems may have different computational difficulties. With definition and computation of an utility π^i for each subproblem i, its computational efforts are distributed to these subproblems, and thus more computational resources are assigned to the non-convergent subproblems. Another dynamic resource allocation scheme for MOEA/D (MOEA/D-DRA-CMX+SPX) was investigated in [12] to reward the better crossover operator. In this approach, the Simplex Crossover [32] and the Center of Mass Crossover [33] are employed to generate offspring solutions. A crossover is considered to be successful if at least one solution can be replaced to its new generated solution. This means that the more successful crossover operators will be applied to more subproblems than the less successful one.

2.2   Enhanced Evolutionary Operators

For each subproblem, MOEA/D-DE [10] employs differential evolution (DE) [34] operator and polynomial mutation [35] to generate one new trial solution. The DE operator is more efficient than the SBX operator in tackling complex PSs of MOPs. One of the derivative-free optimization methods which named Nelder-Mead simplex (NMS) method was presented in MOEA/D-NMS [15]. This approach integrates the DE operator with the NMS operator to make MOEA/D more effective. The probability threshold p_h is applied to determine the proportion of the utilization of the DE operator, and it assists reproduction to balance the neighborhood exploration and subproblem exploitation so that the PF (PS) calculated by the algorithm closely approximates the real PF (PS) of the MOP.

2.3   Preselection

With the wide application of machine learning algorithms recently, MOEA/D-CPS [16] is commonly used for obtaining offspring solution set as a supervised classification based preselection (CPS). In each generation, a classification model is built according to a set of recorded training data set with either positive or negative labels. Then, a set of candidate offspring solutions are generated and labeled by the classification model, only those with positive labels are kept as the offspring solutions. In MOEA/D-SVM [17], solutions in current population are served as promising training samples, and the solutions in sub-best population are adopted which have been recently discarded for each subproblem as unpromising ones.

2.4   Adaptive Control Methods

An adaptive selection strategy for the neighborhood sizes (NSs) is proposed in ENS-MOEA/D [20] to alleviate the influence of NSs on the performance of MOEA/D. Based on the former successful experiences, different NSs can be adjusted adaptively. The results of the experiment indicate that different MOPs may prefer different settings of NSs. A novel bandit-based adaptive operator selection was presented for MOEA/D (MOEA/D-FRRMAB) in [21]. In this approach, the operator pool was consists of four different DE mutation operators, and the selected probability of different DE operators dynamically calculated by their recent performance. In [22], an adaptive DE for MOPs (ADEMO/D) was reported, which adopts probability matching and adaptive pursuit as two adaptive strategy selection principles. A DE mutation strategy is picked up from a candidates DE pool according to a probability depending on the success rate. In MOEA/D-CDE [24], an adaptive composite operator selection (ACOS) strategy was presented for MOEA/D. Four evolutionary operator pools are used in ACOS and their advantages are combined to provide stronger exploratory capabilities. Regarding each selected operator pool, an online self-adaptation for the parameters tuning is further employed for performance enhancement.

2.5   Matching Strategies

In [25], a stable matching model was proposed for MOEA/D (MOEA/D-STM), assigns each promising solution to a subproblem according to the respective preferences, which keeps good convergence speed and population diversity. Similarly, An improved inter-relationship model was built in MOEA/D-IR [26] to match the solutions and subproblems based on their mutual-preferences. In each generation, this interrelationship is used as a guideline to select the elite solutions to survive as the next parents and balance the convergence and diversity of the search process. In order to overcome mismatch between subproblems and solutions. MOEA/D-AGR [27] proposes a global replacement (GR) strategy for MOEA/D, and also demonstrates that the replacement neighborhood size is critical for controlling the balance between diversity and convergence.

The emphasis of our study lies in conducting in-depth research on replacement strategy, aiming at improving the performance on balance of diversity and convergence.

3   MOEA/D-HRS Algorithm

In this section, firstly, we describe MOEA/D-HRS algorithm framework; then, explain hybrid replacement strategy in detail; finally, introduce the offspring generation method.

3.1   MOEA/D-HRS Framework

It is noteworthy that MOEA/D-AGR [27] uses fixed operators and parameters, only focuses on global replacement while ignores neighborhood replacement, which may be hard to deal with complex MOPs. Therefore, the possible improvements are to generate better offspring and a kind of hybrid adaptive strategy. For the first one, we design an offspring generation method to generate better solution for each subproblem. After that, we set the probability threshold p_t to determine which replacement strategy is to be executed.

Algorithm 1. MOEA/D-HRS

Input: N : population size.
Output: P : final population.
1: initialize $P, F^i, B^i, g^i, z^*, i = 1, \cdots, N$;
2: **while** not terminate **do**
3:     $os = $ **OffspringGeneration**(P);
4:     **for** each $i \in perm(1, \cdots, N)$ **do**
5:         $P = $ **HybridReplaceStrategy**(P, i, os_i);
6:     **end for**
7: **end while**
8: **return** P.

The pseudo-code of the complete MOEA/D-HRS is shown in Algorithm 1. The population is initialized in line 1. In line 3, it generates solution set os by offspring generation method, which is introduced in Subsect. 3.3. In line 5, it executes hybrid replacement strategy and more details about it is shown in Subsect. 3.2.

3.2   Hybrid Replacement Strategy

In order to improve the effectiveness, we simultaneously consider two replacement strategies: (1) neighborhood replacement strategy; (2) global replacement strategy. Meanwhile, we employ a probability threshold p_t to determine which replacement strategy should be executed.

(1) Neighborhood replacement strategy

As introduced in [11–17,19–26], it has been experimentally found that neighborhood replacement strategy has its own advantage in solving different types of MOPs [10,24,27].

The MOEA/D optimizes a number of single objective subproblems at the same time. Each single subproblem i has its current solution x_i. The implementation of the neighborhood replacement strategy is as follow. Each solution has a replacement neighborhood and the number of replacement solutions, which are set in advance. For each current solution x_i to subproblem i, a new solution x_i^{new}

is generated by generation operators by its neighboring solutions, and then x_i^{new} compares with each current solution in the neighborhood of x_i and replaces it if x_i^{new} is better its related subproblem.

(2) Global replacement strategy

MOEA/D-AGR [27] uses global replacement (GR) strategy to update neighborhood information. Global replacement (GR) strategy includes two aspects: one is how to find the most suitable subproblem for x_i^{new}; the other is how to calculate the replacement neighborhood size T_r.

(a) Find the most suitable subproblem for x_i^{new}

In this paper, we also employ the following Tchebycheff approach [42].

$$min \; g^i(x) = g(x|\lambda^i, z^*) = max \left\{ \lambda_j^i |f_j(x) - z_j^*| \right\} \qquad (2)$$

In [27], subproblem j is defined as its most suitable subproblem of current solution x:

$$j = arg \min_{1 \le k \le N} g^k(x) \qquad (3)$$

In this strategy, x_i^{new} is to replace the neighboring solutions of x_j, where x_j is the current solution of the most suitable subproblem for x_i^{new}.

(b) Calculate the replacement neighborhood size T_r

T_r plays an important role in the optimization process. In this strategy, MOEA/D-AGR [27] verifies different optimization stages should set different replacement neighbor sizes. In MOEA/D-AGR, it proposes three calculation methods for replacing neighbors. From the experimental results, the Sigmoid scheme obtains the best performance. Therefore, we also choose Sigmoid scheme as calculation of replacement neighbor size.

$$T_r = \left\lceil \frac{T_{max}}{1 + e^{-20*(\frac{k}{K} - \gamma)}} \right\rceil \qquad (4)$$

where $\lceil . \rceil$ is the ceiling function, T_{max} is the maximal value for T_r, k is the current generation number, K is the maximal generation number and $\gamma \in [0, 1)$ is a control parameter to determine how T_r increases as the search goes.

The process of hybrid replacement strategy is shown in Algorithm 2. In line 1, a probability threshold p_t is used to determine whether to execute a neighborhood or global replacement strategy. If the generated random number is lower than p_t, replacing the neighboring solutions of x_i is executed in line 2. Otherwise, a global replacement strategy should be executed. In line 4, it is used to find replacement subproblem j. Calculating replacement neighborhood T_r is shown in line 5. In line 6, it is used to replace the neighboring solutions of x_j. In line 8, it is used to update best z^*.

Algorithm 2. HybridReplaceStrategy(P, i, os_i)

Input: P : population;
       i : the index of the subproblem;
       os_i : the offspring of the subproblem i.
Output: P : final population.
 1: **if** $rand() < p_t$ **then**
 2:    replace the neighboring solutions of x_i by os_i;
 3: **else**
 4:    find replacement subproblem j by Eq. 3;
 5:    calculate replacement neighborhood T_r by Eq. 4
 6:    replace the neighboring solutions of x_j by os_i;
 7: **end if**
 8: update best z^*;
 9: **return** P.

3.3 Offspring Generation Method

In this subsection, we design an offspring generation method. There are four main tasks we need to solve: (1) How many temporary solutions should be generated; (2) how to define the perturbation radius; (3) how to generate temporary solution set; (4) how to generate offspring for each subproblem. For these issues, we adopt the following strategies:

(1) Calculate the number of temporary solutions and perturbation radius

In FWA [29], FWA-DM [30] and S-MOFWA [31], they use firework to simulate the generation of candidate solutions. Inspired by these algorithms, we use n_i and a_i to represent number and radius, respectively. then, we redesign the equation of the number of temporary solutions and perturbation radius for each subproblem. Finally, we show these contents in Eqs. (5) and (6).

$$n\_i = M_e * \frac{S(x_i) * N + \varepsilon}{\sum_{i=1}^{N}(S(x_i)) + \varepsilon} \tag{5}$$

$$a\_i = \hat{A} * \frac{(S_{max} - S(x_i)) * N + \varepsilon}{\sum_{i=1}^{N}(S_{max} - S(x_i)) + \varepsilon} \tag{6}$$

(2) Generate temporary solution set

In this paper, we dynamically generate two types of temporary solutions, which can improve the probability of generation better offspring. These temporary solutions include: (a) perturbation temporary solutions; (b) Gaussian temporary solutions. In addition, we take x_i as a special temporary solution.

In Algorithm 3, variables d, x_{low} and x_{upp} represent the dimension of x_i, the lower and upper of x_i, respectively. In line 3, it is used to select the perturbation dimension. Inn line 6, it adds an offset to each perturbation dimension. In

---

Algorithm 3. PerturbTS(x_i, n_i, a_i)

Input: x_i : solution of subproblem i;
    n_i : the number of perturbation temporary solutions;
    a_i : perturbation radius.
Output: Y_1 : perturbation temporary solutions.
1:   $x_t = x_i$;
2: **for** $i = 1$ to n_i **do**
3:     $n = ceil(rand * d)$;
4:     $shift = (rand * x_{upp} - x_{low}). * a\_i$;
5:     **for** $k = 1$ to n **do**
6:       $x_t^k = x_i^k + shift$;
7:       **if** $x_t^k < x_{low}^k || x_t^k > x_{upp}^k$ **then**
8:         $x_t^k = x_{low}^k + rem(abs(x_t^k), x_{upp}^k - x_{low}^k)$
9:       **end if**
10:    **end for**
11:    $Y_1 = Y_1 \bigcup \{x_t\}$;
12: **end for**
13: **return** Y_1.

---

lines 7–9, it is used to control each perturbation dimension that cannot exceeds [lower, upper].

In Algorithm 4, line 3 points out that the perturbation dimension is calculated. In line 5, a Gaussian offset is added to perturbation dimension. In lines 7–9, its function is the same as in Algorithm 3.

In order to get the optimal one from these temporary solutions and reduce the cost of real objective values evaluations, we employ the Kriging model [40, 41] to estimate each temporary solution and get the optimal solution.

(3) Generate offspring for each subproblem

In this paper, we employ Eq. 7 to generate offspring solution. Among this equation, os_i is the optimal temporary solution of the ith subproblem, which is obtained in Algorithm 5, t_1 and t_2 are two neighboring subproblems that are randomly selected. The mutation operator is defined as follows:

$$y = os_i + F(x_{t_1} - x_{t_2}) \tag{7}$$

The pseudo-code of the offspring generation method is shown in Algorithm 5. The Kriging model is constructed by the whole population in line 1. Detail of its implementation process is the same as in [40, 41]. In lines 3–7, it employs nondominated sorting [3], S-metric [4] or hypervolume [44] to calculate $S(x_i)$. In lines 8–9, the number of temporary solutions n_i and perturbation radius a_i are calculated for each subproblem, respectively. In line 10, it generates temporary solution set Y for each subproblem. In line 12, it gets the optimal temporary solution. The offspring is generated in line 13.

Algorithm 4. GaussTS(x^i, $gsNum$)

Input: x_i : solution of subproblem i;
    $gsNum$: the number of Gaussian temporary solutions.
Output: Y_2 : Gaussian temporary solutions.
1: $x_t = x_i$;
2: **for** $i = 1$ to $gsNum$ **do**
3:     $n = ceil(rand * d)$;
4:     **for** $k = 1$ to n **do**
5:         $radius = normrnd(x_{low}^k, x_{upp}^k)$;
6:         $x_t^k = x_i^k * radius$;
7:         **if** $x_t^k < x_{low}^k || x_t^k > x_{upp}^k$ **then**
8:             $x_t^k = x_{low}^k + rem(abs(x_t^k), x_{upp}^k - x_{low}^k)$
9:         **end if**
10:     **end for**
11:     $Y_2 = Y_2 \bigcup \{x_t\}$;
12: **end for**
13: **return** Y_2.

4   Experiments

4.1   Test Problems

Two test instance set are adopted to evaluate the performance of MOEA/D-HRS. First, nine test instances named F1-F9 are used [10,27]. In these test instances, most of them are two objectives except F6. Furthermore, the bi-objective or three-objective UF test instances [24] are also adopted as they are characterized by presenting nonconvex, discontinuity, nonuniformity, and the existence of many local PFs (UF5, UF6, UF8-UF10). The detailed characteristics of these test instances are listed in Table 1.

4.2   Comparison Algorithms and Parameter Settings

We compare our proposed algorithm MOEA/D-HRS with NSGA-II [3], IBEA [6], MOEA/D-DE [10], MOEA/D-CPS [16], MOEA/D-MO [43] and MOEA/D-AGR [27]. NSGA-II is a classic MOEA which uses Pareto dominance-based. IBEA is a indicator-based MOEA. MOEA/D-DE is a based on decomposition algorithm. MOEA/D-CPS is a variant of MOEA/D which uses preselection to get offspring. MOEA/D-MO generates three candidate solutions for each subproblem and uses real objective value to evaluation these candidate solutions. MOEA/D-AGR uses global replacement scheme to update population. The parameter settings of these algorithms are the same as in [3,6,10,16,27,43].

The detailed parameter settings are summarized as follows.

(1) For bi-objective instances, the population is set to be 300; and for three-objective instances, the population is set to be 595.

Algorithm 5. OffspringGeneration(P)

Input: P : population.
Output: os : the offspring set.
1: $model = \mathbf{Kriging}(P)$ [40,41];
2: **for** each $i \in perm(1, \cdots, N)$ **do**
3:      **if** $\exists$ *dominated solutions* $\in P$ **then**
4:          calculate $S(x_i)$ by nondominated sorting [3];
5:      **else**
6:          calculate $S(x_i)$ by S-metric [4] or hypervolume [44];
7:      **end if**
8:      calculate number of solutions n_i by Eq. 5;
9:      calculate amplitude a_i by Eq. 6;
10:     $Y = \text{PerturbTS}\ (x_i, n\_i, a\_i) \bigcup \text{GaussTS}\ (x_i, gsNum)$;
11:     $Y = Y \bigcup x_i$;
12:     get los_i by $predictor(Y, model)$;
13:     generate os_i by Eq. 7 and sort;
14: **end for**
15: **return** os.

Table 1. The characteristics of test instances.

Name	n	m	Range	Inter-variable dependencies	Characteristics
F1	30	2	$x_i \epsilon [0,1], 1 \le i \le n$	Nonlinear	Convex, Unimodal
F2	30	2	$x_1 \epsilon [0,1], x_i \epsilon [-1,1], 2 \le i \le n$	Nonlinear	Convex, Multimodal
F3	30	2	$x_1 \epsilon [0,1], x_i \epsilon [-1,1], 2 \le i \le n$	Nonlinear	Convex, Multimodal
F4	30	2	$x_1 \epsilon [0,1], x_i \epsilon [-1,1], 2 \le i \le n$	Nonlinear	Convex, Multimodal
F5	30	2	$x_1 \epsilon [0,1], x_i \epsilon [-1,1], 2 \le i \le n$	Nonlinear	Convex, Multimodal
F6	30	3	$x_1, x_2 \epsilon [0,1], x_i \epsilon [-2,2], 3 \le i \le n$	Nonlinear	Nonconvex, Multimodal
F7	30	2	$x_i \epsilon [0,1], 1 \le i \le n$	Nonlinear	Convex, Multimodal
F8	30	2	$x_i \epsilon [0,1], 1 \le i \le n$	Nonlinear	Convex, Multimodal
F9	30	2	$x_1 \epsilon [0,1], x_i \epsilon [-1,1], 2 \le i \le n$	Nonlinear	Concave, Multimodal
UF1	30	2	$x_1 \epsilon [0,1], x_i \epsilon [-1,1], 2 \le i \le n$	Nonlinear	Convex, Multimodal
UF2	30	2	$x_1 \epsilon [0,1], x_i \epsilon [-1,1], 2 \le i \le n$	Nonlinear	Convex, Multimodal
UF3	30	2	$x_i \epsilon [0,1], 1 \le i \le n$	Nonlinear	Convex, Multimodal
UF4	30	2	$x_1 \epsilon [0,1], x_i \epsilon [-2,2], 2 \le i \le n$	Nonlinear	Concave, Multimodal
UF5	30	2	$x_1 \epsilon [0,1], x_i \epsilon [-1,1], 2 \le i \le n$	Nonlinear	Nonconvex, Multimodal
UF6	30	2	$x_1 \epsilon [0,1], x_i \epsilon [-1,1], 2 \le i \le n$	Nonlinear	Nonconvex, Multimodal
UF7	30	2	$x_1 \epsilon [0,1], x_i \epsilon [-1,1], 2 \le i \le n$	Nonlinear	Convex, Multimodal
UF8	30	3	$x_1, x_2 \epsilon [0,1], x_i \epsilon [-2,2], 3 \le i \le n$	Nonlinear	Nonconvex, Multimodal
UF9	30	3	$x_1, x_2 \epsilon [0,1], x_i \epsilon [-2,2], 3 \le i \le n$	Nonlinear	Nonconvex, Multimodal
UF10	30	3	$x_1, x_2 \epsilon [0,1], x_i \epsilon [-2,2], 3 \le i \le n$	Nonlinear	Nonconvex, Multimodal

(2) All algorithms are run 30 times independently. The maximal number of function evaluations is set to be 150 000 for bi-objective and 297 500 for three-objective instances.

(3) In MOEA/D-HRS, $p_n = 0.9$, the global replacement neighborhood size T_r is set to be in Eq. 4, neighborhood replacement size is set to be 2. The probability threshold $p_t = 0.3$. Similar to [31], the upper number of temporary solutions M_e =20, disturbance amplitude $\hat{A} = (variable.upper[2] - variable.lower[2])/4$, the number of Gaussian temporary solutions $gdNum$ =5.

4.3   Performance Metrics

We use the inverted generational distance (IGD) [16] to assess the performance of the algorithms in our experimental studies. The IGD from P^* to P is defined as

$$IGD(P^*, P) = \frac{\sum_{v \in P^*} d(v, P)}{|P^*|} \qquad (8)$$

where $d(v, P)$ is the minimum Euclidean distance between v and any point in P and $|P^*|$ is the cardinality of P^*. IGD simultaneously measures the diversity and convergence of P. The lower IGD, the better the performance of the algorithm.

In our experiments, for the bi-objective and the three-objective test instances, 500 and 990 points are uniformly distributed to the PF for F1–F9; 1000 and 10 000 points are uniformly distributed to the PF for UF1–UF10.

4.4   Effectiveness Experiment

In this paper, all the algorithms are performed on F1–F9 [10,27] and UF1–UF10 [24]. These algorithms run 30 times independently. The mean IGD and the standard deviation (std) are calculated on each test problem separately. All the statistical results are shown in Tables 2 and 3. In this subsection, we have an in-depth analysis of these experimental results.

(1) Experimental results on F1–F9

Table 2 shows that: (1) MOEA/D-HRS obtains the best performance on most test instances when compared to the other algorithms. In this paper we can not only guarantee the generation of high-quality offspring for each subproblem, but also make good full use of the hybrid mechanism. All of these methods can increase the success rate of the replacement strategy. Moreover, considering two types of strategies is effective for the balance between convergence and diversity. (2) On F5, F6 and F7, MOEA/D-CPS, MOEA/D-MO or MOEA/D-AGR can achieve the best results. F6 has three objectives, F5 and F7 have very complicated PS shape and no algorithm can approximate its PF at the same time. MOEA/D-MO uses the real objective value to generate offspring, it may be more suitable for dealing with three-objective instances. MOEA/D-AGR uses a global replacement scheme and replace to the most suitable subproblems, which fits in dealing with MOPs which contain complicated PS.

Based on the results in Tables 2, we also do some statistical analysis. We apply the Wilcoxon nonparametric statistical test on the algorithms. '$\approx$', $+$ and

Table 2. Comparative results of all the algorithms adopted on F1–F9 regarding IGD.

Instances	Algorithms	NSGA-II	IBEA	MOEA/D-CPS	MOEA/D-DE	MOEA/D-MO	MOEA/D-AGR	MOEA/D-HRS
F1	Mean	1.04E-02	1.05E-02	**1.30E-03**	**1.30E-03**	1.40E-03	**1.30E-03**	1.30E-03
	Std	3.20E-03	2.90E-03	1.16E-05	6.28E-06	1.80E-05	4.76E-06	**4.27E-06**
	Rank	6-	7-	1≈	1≈	5≈	1≈	1
F2	Mean	7.47E-02	9.82E-02	3.80E-03	3.20E-03	4.40E-03	3.50E-03	**2.80E-03**
	Std	1.39E-02	1.12E-02	1.10E-03	4.39E-04	7.24E-04	2.29E-04	**4.76E-05**
	Rank	6-	7-	4-	2-	5-	3-	1
F3	Mean	3.30E-02	4.56E-02	3.40E-03	1.34E-02	3.70E-03	3.70E-03	**2.60E-03**
	Std	1.26E-02	1.04E-02	1.20E-03	2.68E-02	6.62E-04	1.20E-03	**2.62E-04**
	Rank	6-	7-	2-	5-	3-	3-	1
F4	Mean	3.16E-02	4.24E-02	3.80E-03	1.14E-02	4.80E-03	6.70E-03	**2.40E-03**
	Std	6.60E-03	6.70E-03	1.10E-03	1.38E-02	1.20E-03	1.43E-02	**2.50E-04**
	Rank	6-	7-	2-	5-	3-	4-	1
F5	Mean	2.30E-02	3.66E-02	**6.80E-03**	1.10E-02	7.80E-03	1.07E-02	1.08E-02
	Std	5.70E-03	8.70E-03	1.40E-03	2.70E-03	**1.30E-03**	2.80E-03	2.10E-03
	Rank	6-	7-	1+	5-	2+	3≈	4
F6	Mean	1.88E-01	4.49E-01	5.98E-02	5.94E-02	**5.69E-02**	5.73E-02	7.38E-02
	Std	6.86E-02	1.98E-02	8.80E-03	9.80E-03	6.70E-03	8.70E-03	**1.46E-04**
	Rank	6-	7-	4+	3+	1+	2+	5
F7	Mean	2.92E-01	3.51E-01	1.58E-01	2.31E-01	1.14E-01	**7.15E-02**	7.92E-02
	Std	1.17E-01	6.29E-02	9.61E-02	1.35E-01	1.07E-01	8.25E-02	**1.04E-01**
	Rank	6-	7-	4-	5-	3-	1+	2
F8	Mean	1.71E-01	2.64E-01	2.36E-02	2.73E-02	1.30E-02	1.02E-02	**8.00E-03**
	Std	1.62E-02	4.41E-02	2.11E-02	2.37E-02	9.60E-03	6.50E-03	**4.90E-03**
	Rank	6-	7-	4-	5-	3-	2-	1
F9	Mean	1.07E-01	1.16E-01	4.60E-03	5.20E-03	6.30E-03	4.20E-03	**3.60E-03**
	Std	3.34E-02	5.07E-02	8.64E-04	3.10E-03	1.30E-03	1.10E-03	**1.65E-04**
	Rank	6-	7-	3-	4-	5-	2-	1
Rank Sum		54	63	25	35	30	21	17
Final Rank		6	7	3	5	4	2	1
better/worse/similar		0/9/0	0/9/0	2/6/1	1/7/1	2/6/1	2/5/2	/

Table 3. Comparative results of all the algorithms adopted on UF1–UF10 regarding IGD.

Instances	Algorithms	NSGA-II	IBEA	MOEA/D-CPS	MOEA/D-DE	MOEA/D-MO	MOEA/D-AGR	MOEA/D-HRS
UF1	Mean	8.35E-02	1.12E-01	3.70E-03	3.30E-03	4.60E-03	3.40E-03	**2.80E-03**
	Std	2.36E-02	1.81E-02	7.28E-04	6.81E-04	6.20E-04	**1.79E-04**	2.10E-04
	Rank	6-	7-	4-	2-	5-	3-	1
UF2	Mean	2.55E-02	3.79E-02	**7.10E-03**	1.18E-02	8.00E-03	9.70E-03	1.18E-02
	Std	5.60E-03	1.44E-02	**1.20E-03**	3.30E-03	1.20E-03	1.80E-03	**1.91E-04**
	Rank	6-	7-	1+	4≈	2+	3+	4
UF3	Mean	9.81E-02	1.85E-01	1.94E-02	2.58E-02	1.36E-02	9.60E-03	**4.50E-03**
	Std	1.83E-02	2.27E-02	2.17E-02	2.24E-02	8.50E-03	6.40E-03	**2.90E-03**
	Rank	6-	7-	4-	5-	3-	2+	1
UF4	Mean	**4.31E-02**	4.98E-02	5.80E-02	6.53E-02	5.48E-02	6.03E-02	4.59E-02
	Std	**5.28E-04**	3.60E-03	4.70E-03	5.90E-03	5.50E-03	5.00E-03	7.34E-04
	Rank	1+	3-	5-	7-	4-	6-	2
UF5	Mean	2.57E-01	2.46E-01	4.27E-01	4.17E-01	3.90E-01	2.96E-01	**2.33E-01**
	Std	5.03E-02	5.88E-02	9.27E-02	8.56E-02	**7.64E-02**	8.57E-02	8.12E-02
	Rank	3-	2-	7-	6-	5-	4-	1
UF6	Mean	1.70E-01	2.08E-01	1.40E-01	2.06E-01	1.95E-01	1.86E-01	**7.26E-02**
	Std	5.99E-02	5.42E-02	1.52E-01	2.02E-01	2.30E-01	2.02E-01	**5.30E-03**
	Rank	3-	7-	2-	6-	5-	4-	1
UF7	Mean	5.84E-02	2.07E-01	4.70E-03	6.70E-03	5.80E-03	5.00E-03	**3.90E-03**
	Std	7.03E-02	1.45E-01	8.60E-04	3.20E-03	9.47E-04	8.70E-04	**1.52E-04**
	Rank	6-	7-	2-	5-	4-	3-	1
UF8	Mean	1.37E-01	3.50E-01	6.57E-02	**6.00E-02**	6.25E-02	6.55E-02	8.27E-02
	Std	4.71E-02	1.99E-02	9.10E-03	1.03E-02	7.20E-03	**1.07E-03**	1.53E-02
	Rank	6-	7-	4+	1+	2+	3+	5
UF9	Mean	1.28E-01	1.51E-01	4.32E-02	5.33E-02	5.09E-02	7.18E-02	**2.15E-02**
	Std	6.51E-02	5.96E-02	2.55E-02	3.22E-02	3.38E-02	5.34E-02	**3.99E-05**
	Rank	6-	7-	2-	4-	3-	5-	1
UF10	Mean	**2.71E-01**	5.57E-01	6.91E-01	5.52E-01	7.21E-01	4.11E-01	2.84E-01
	Std	**2.36E-02**	3.50E-02	9.13E-02	8.11E-02	1.20E-01	9.59E-02	2.41E-02
	Rank	1+	5-	6-	4-	7-	3-	2
Rank Sum		44	59	37	44	40	36	19
Final Rank		5	7	2	4	3	2	1
better/worse/similar		2/8/0	0/10/0	3/7/0	1/8/1	2/8/0	3/7/0	/

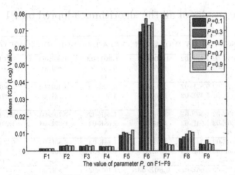

(a) Mean IGD (log) with parameter p_t on F

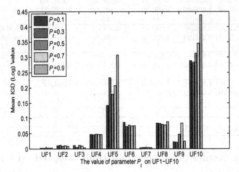

(b) Mean IGD (log) with parameter p_t on UF

Fig. 1. The evolutionary performances of MOEA/D-HRS with different p_t parameter settings

– denote that the algorithm is equal, better, or worse than other algorithms with a 5% significance level. According to the IGD metric, MOEA/D-AGR performs similarly to or is slightly lower than MOEA/D-HRS on nine test instances. Furthermore, the summary result are shown in the last row of Tables 2. From both Wilcoxon nonparametric test and rank values, we can conclude that MOEA/D-HRS performs better than other algorithms although it can not always achieve the best result on a small amount of test instances.

(2) Experimental results on UF1−UF10

Table 3 shows the comparative results of all the algorithms adopted, in which the mean IGD values and the standard deviation (std) from 30 independent runs are listed. These simulation results show that MOEA/D-HRS performs best on most UF instances when compared to the other algorithms. Based on the summary in the last row of Table 3, it is reasonable to conclude that MOEA/D-HRS is better than other algorithms when considering all the UF test instances with respect to IGD. This clearly indicates that the approach we propose enhances the optimization performance of MOEA/D.

4.5 Parameter Analysis

In this subsection, we study the sensitivity parameter of MOEA/D-HRS. Other algorithm's parameters have been adjusted under optimal conditions. There is an important parameter in MOEA/D-HRS, named probability threshold p_t.

We set $p_t = [\,0.1, 0.3, 0.5, 0.7, 0.9\,]$. Figure 1 (a) and (b) show different parameter p_t value get IGD results on two test function sets. As can be seen from Fig. 1 (a) and (b), when $p_t = 0.3$, the number of IGD values (log) obtained in the two test functions is the least, which means that $p_t = 0.3$ can achieve the best performance on most test instances.

5 Conclusion

This paper has proposed a decomposition based multiobjective evolutionary algorithm integrating offspring generation method for the hybrid adaptive strategy. First, we design a offspring generation method, which can generate the high-quality offspring for each subproblem. Then, a probability threshold p_t is applied to determine which replacement strategy should be executed. Compared with the current popular multiobjective evolutionary algorithms, the experimental results show that MOEA/D-HRS has the best performance in most cases. I think there are still some work that could be done in the future: (a) adaptive mating neighborhood size for each subproblem, (b) employ online learning to balance diversity and convergence, and (c) apply this approach to real-world applications.

Acknowledgments. This work is supported in part by the National Natural Science Foundation of China (No. 61375058, 61673397), and the Co-construction Project of Beijing Municipal Commission of Education.

References

1. Zhou, A., Qu, B.Y., Li, H., Zhao, S.Z., Suganthan, P.N., Zhang, Q.: Multiobjective evolutionary algorithms: a survey of the state of the art. Swarm Evol. Comput. **1**(1), 32–49 (2011)
2. Srinivas, N., Deb, K.: Muiltiobjective optimization using nondominated sorting in genetic algorithms. Evol. Comput. **2**(3), 221–248 (1994)
3. Deb, K., Agrawal, S., Pratap, A., Meyarivan, T.: A fast elitist non-dominated sorting genetic algorithm for multi-objective optimization: NSGA-II. In: Schoenauer, M., et al. (eds.) PPSN 2000. LNCS, vol. 1917, pp. 849–858. Springer, Heidelberg (2000). https://doi.org/10.1007/3-540-45356-3_83
4. Zitzler, E., Thiele, L.: Multiobjective optimization using evolutionary algorithms— a comparative case study. In: Eiben, A.E., Bäck, T., Schoenauer, M., Schwefel, H.-P. (eds.) PPSN 1998. LNCS, vol. 1498, pp. 292–301. Springer, Heidelberg (1998). https://doi.org/10.1007/BFb0056872
5. Laumanns, M.: SPEA2: improving the strength Pareto evolutionary algorithm. Eidgenössische Technische Hochschule Zürich (ETH), Institut für Technische Informatik und Kommunikationsnetze (TIK) (2001)

6. Zitzler, E., Künzli, S.: Indicator-based selection in multiobjective search. In: Yao, X., et al. (eds.) PPSN 2004. LNCS, vol. 3242, pp. 832–842. Springer, Heidelberg (2004). https://doi.org/10.1007/978-3-540-30217-9_84

7. Basseur, M., Zitzler, E.: A preliminary study on handling uncertainty in indicator-based multiobjective optimization. In: Rothlauf, F., Branke, J., Cagnoni, S., Costa, E., Cotta, C., Drechsler, R., Lutton, E., Machado, P., Moore, J.H., Romero, J., Smith, G.D., Squillero, G., Takagi, H. (eds.) EvoWorkshops 2006. LNCS, vol. 3907, pp. 727–739. Springer, Heidelberg (2006). https://doi.org/10.1007/11732242_71

8. Bader, J., Zitzler, E.: HypE: an algorithm for fast hypervolume-based many-objective optimization. Evol. Comput. 19(1), 45–76 (2011)

9. Zhang, Q., Li, H.: MOEA/D: a multiobjective evolutionary algorithm based on decomposition. IEEE Trans. Evol. Comput. 11(6), 712–731 (2007)

10. Li, H., Zhang, Q.: Multiobjective optimization problems with complicated pareto sets, MOEA/D and NSGA-II. IEEE Trans. Evol. Comput. 13(2), 284–302 (2009)

11. Zhang, Q., Liu, W., Li, H.: The performance of a new version of MOEA/D on CEC09 unconstrained mop test instances. In: 2009 IEEE Congress on Evolutionary Computation, pp. 203–208. IEEE (2009)

12. Mashwani, W.K., Salhi, A.: A decomposition-based hybrid multiobjective evolutionary algorithm with dynamic resource allocation. Appl. Soft Comput. 12(9), 2765–2780 (2012)

13. Ma, X., et al.: MOEA/D with opposition-based learning for multiobjective optimization problem. Neurocomputing 146, 48–64 (2014)

14. Zhou, A., Zhang, Y., Zhang, G., Gong, W.: On neighborhood exploration and subproblem exploitation in decomposition based multiobjective evolutionary algorithms. In: 2017 IEEE Congress on Evolutionary Computation, pp. 1704–1711. IEEE (2015)

15. Zhang, H., Zhou, A., Zhang, G., Singh, H.K.: Accelerating MOEA/D by Nelder-Mead method. In: 2017 IEEE Congress on Evolutionary Computation, pp. 976–983. IEEE (2017)

16. Zhang, J., Zhou, A., Zhang, G.: A multiobjective evolutionary algorithm based on decomposition and preselection. In: Gong, M., Pan, L., Song, T., Tang, K., Zhang, X. (eds.) BIC-TA 2015. CCIS, vol. 562, pp. 631–642. Springer, Heidelberg (2015). https://doi.org/10.1007/978-3-662-49014-3_56

17. Lin, X., Zhang, Q., Kwong, S.: A decomposition based multiobjective evolutionary algorithm with classification. In: 2016 IEEE Congress on Evolutionary Computation, pp. 3292–3299. IEEE (2016)

18. Zhang, J., Zhou, A., Tang, K., and Zhang, G.: Preselection via classification: a case study on evolutionary multiobjective optimization. arXiv:1708.01146 (2017)

19. Chen, X., Shi, C., Zhou, A., Wu, B ., Cai, Z.: A decomposition based multi objective evolutionary algorithm with semi-supervised classification. In: 2017 IEEE Congress on Evolutionary Computation, pp. 797-804. IEEE (2017)

20. Zhao, S.Z., Suganthan, P.N., Zhang, Q.: Decomposition-based multiobjective evolutionary algorithm with an ensemble of neighborhood sizes. IEEE Trans. Evol. Comput. 16(3), 442–446 (2012)

21. Li, K., Fialho, A., Kwong, S., Zhang, Q.: Adaptive operator selection with bandits for a multiobjective evolutionary algorithm based on decomposition. IEEE Trans. Evol. Comput. 18(1), 114–130 (2014)

22. Venske, S.M., GonçAlves, R.A., Delgado, M.R.: ADEMO/D: multiobjective optimization by an adaptive differential evolution algorithm. Neurocomputing 127(127), 65–77 (2014)

23. Lin, Q., et al.: A novel adaptive control strategy for decomposition-based multiobjective algorithm. Comput. Oper. Res. **78**, 94–107 (2016)
24. Lin, Q., et al.: Adaptive composite operator selection and parameter control for multiobjective evolutionary algorithm. Inf. Sci. **339**, 332–352 (2016)
25. Li, K., Zhang, Q., Kwong, S., Li, M., Wang, R.: Stable matching-based selection in evolutionary multiobjective optimization. IEEE Trans. Evol. Comput. **18**(6), 909–923 (2014)
26. Li, K., Kwong, S., Zhang, Q., Deb, K.: Interrelationship-based selection for decomposition multiobjective optimization. IEEE Trans. Cybern. **45**(10), 2076–2088 (2015)
27. Wang, Z., Zhang, Q., Zhou, A., Gong, M., Jiao, L.: Adaptive replacement strategies for MOEA/D. IEEE Trans. Cybern. **46**(2), 474–486 (2017)
28. Tam, H.H., Leung, M.F., Wang, Z., Ng, S.C., Cheung, C.C., Lui, A.K.: Improved adaptive global replacement scheme for MOEA/D-AGR. In: 2016 IEEE congress on Evolutionary Computation, pp. 2153–2160. IEEE (2016)
29. Tan, Y., Zhu, Y.: Fireworks algorithm for optimization. In: Tan, Y., Shi, Y., Tan, K.C. (eds.) ICSI 2010. LNCS, vol. 6145, pp. 355–364. Springer, Heidelberg (2010). https://doi.org/10.1007/978-3-642-13495-1_44
30. Yu, C., Kelley L., Zheng, S., Tan Y.: Fireworks algorithm with differential mutation for solving the CEC 2014 competition problems. In: 2014 IEEE congress on Evolutionary Computation, pp. 3238–3245. IEEE (2014)
31. Liu, L., Zheng, S., Tan, Y.: S-metric based multi-objective fireworks algorithm. In: IEEE Congress on Evolutionary Computation, pp. 1257–1264 (2015)
32. Cai, Z., Wang, Y.: A multiobjective optimization-based evolutionary algorithm for constrained optimization. IEEE Trans. Evol. Comput. **10**(6), 658–675 (2006)
33. Tsutsui, S., Ghosh, A.: A study on the effect of multi-parent recombination in real coded genetic algorithms. In: IEEE International Conference on Evolutionary Computation Proceedings, IEEE World Congress on Computational Intelligence, pp. 828–833 (1998)
34. Das, S., Suganthan, P.N.: Differential evolution: a survey of the state-of-the-art. IEEE Trans. Evol. Comput. **15**(1), 4–31 (2011)
35. Deb, K., Goyal, M.: A combined genetic adaptive search (GeneAS) for engineering design. Comput. Sci. Inform. **26**, 30–45 (1996)
36. Tizhoosh, H.R.: Opposition-based reinforcement learning. J. Adv. Comput. Intell. Intell. Inform. **10**(4), 578–585 (2006)
37. Vapnik, V.N.: Statistical learning theory. Encycl. Sci. Learn. **41**(4), 3185–3185 (1998)
38. Tanabe, R., Fukunaga, A.: Success-history based parameter adaptation for differential evolution. In: 2013 IEEE Congress on Evolutionary Computation, pp. 71–78. IEEE (2013)
39. Mallipeddi, R., Wu, G., Lee, M., Suganthan, P.N.: Gaussian adaptation based parameter adaptation for differential evolution. In: 2014 IEEE Congress on Evolutionary Computation, pp. 1760–1767. IEEE (2014)
40. Jin, Y.: A comprehensive survey of fitness approximation in evolutionary computation. Soft Comput. **9**(1), 3–12 (2005)
41. You, H., Yang, M., Wang, D., Jia, X.: Kriging model combined with Latin hypercube sampling for surrogate modeling of analog integrated circuit performance. In: International Symposium on Quality of Electronic Design, pp. 554–558. IEEE (2009)
42. Miettinen, K.: Nonlinear Multiobjective Optimization. Kluwer Academic Publishers, Boston (1999)

43. Li, Y., Zhou, A., Zhang, G.: An MOEA/D with multiple differential evolution mutation operators. In: 2014 IEEE Congress on Evolutionary Computation, pp. 397–404. IEEE (2014)
44. Naujoks, B., Beume, N., Emmerich, M.: Multi-objective optimisation using S-metric selection: application to three-dimensional solution spaces. In: 2015 IEEE Congress on Evolutionary Computation, pp. 1282–1289. IEEE (2005)

A Flexible Memristor-Based Neural Network

Junwei Sun[1,2], Gaoyong Han[1,2], and Yanfeng Wang[1,2](✉)

[1] Henan Key Lab of Information-Based Electrical Appliances,
Zhengzhou University of Light Industry, Zhengzhou 450002, China
[2] School of Electrical and Information Engineering,
Zhengzhou University of Light Industry, Zhengzhou 450002, China
yanfengwang@yeah.net

Abstract. Many memristor-based neural network arrays that have been proposed in recent years are simultaneously dealt with all of their signal inputs in signal reception status. Therefore, when a relatively small-scale neural network is implemented with this memristive array, some of the inputs which are not used may cause errors in the result due to the impact of an unexpected signal. In this paper, a flexible memristor-based neural network is proposed. Based on this network, the number of synapses used at work can be flexibly configured according to the required size, thereby improving system performance. The memristor-based neural network is simulated in Pspice to implement two different scales, which proves the feasibility and effectiveness of a flexible memristive neural network.

Keywords: Memristor · Neural network · Circuit
Flexible memristor array

1 Introduction

Memristor was theoretically proposed by Leon Chua in 1971 [1,2], and fabricated by HP in 2008 [3,4]. Since memristor and biological synapse are very similar in characteristics [5–11], many memristor-based neural networks have been implemented [12–20]. A memristive Hopfield neural network was proposed to realize associative memory in [21]. Efficient and self-adaptive in-situ learning was implemented in multilayer memristor neural networks [22]. Fully memristive neural networks were developed for pattern classification with unsupervised learning [23]. A memristor-based artificial neural network was used to predicate house price in [24]. Electronic synapses were used to achieve face classification in [25].

These different memristive neural network architectures can perform different functions, while some of these different functions cannot be implemented on a same memristor array. A specific memristor array architecture can only achieve a specific function of the neural network, so that the memristor chips that have been fabricated cannot be reused, which causes waste of the chips.

In this paper, a memristive neural network structure that is capable of implementing two different scales of neural networks on the same memristor array is

© Springer Nature Singapore Pte Ltd. 2018
J. Qiao et al. (Eds.): BIC-TA 2018, CCIS 951, pp. 263–272, 2018.
https://doi.org/10.1007/978-981-13-2826-8_23

proposed. By using this neural network structure, the number of synapses participating in work can be freely adjusted according to the required neural network scale. When using large-scale memristive neural networks to achieve relatively small-scale tasks, some signal input ports which are not used will be turned off to prevent these ports from receiving unexpected signals, thereby improving system stability. Compared to the previously proposed memristor-based neural networks, the flexible memristor architecture proposed in this paper also enables the reuse of memristor arrays.

This work is presented as follows: in Sect. 2, a decoder for controlling the size of a memristor array is designed. Followed by, two memristive neural networks are used to implement different functions in Sect. 3. In Sect. 4, the ability of the same memristor structure to freely switch between two different functions is demonstrated. Some conclusions are finally obtained in Sect. 5.

2   Controlling Decoder

Since a control module is needed to adjust the size of the memristive neural network according to requirements, the controlling decoder is designed. As shown in Fig. 1, I_0, I_1 are input signals. $I_0 = I_1 = 0$ means that 0 synapse is needed. $I_0 = 0$, $I_1 = 1$ indicate that 1 synapse is needed, and so on. O_1, O_2, O_3 are output signals that decide which synapses are used. The logic circuit composed of D_1, D_2 and D_3 determines the correspondence between I_n and O_n. The truth table is shown in Fig. 1 on the right. When the input signals are $I_0 = I_1 = 0$, the output signals are $O_0 = O_1 = O_2 = 0$. When the input signals are $I_0 = 0$, $I_1 = 1$, the output signals are $O_0 = 1$, $O_1 = O_2 = 0$. When the input signals are $I_0 = 1$, $I_1 = 0$, the output signals are $O_0 = O_1 = 1$, $O_2 = 0$, and so on.

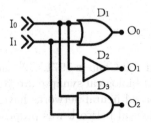

I_0	I_1	O_0	O_1	O_2
0	0	0	0	0
0	1	1	0	0
1	0	1	1	0
1	1	1	1	1

Fig. 1. Controlling decoder and it's truth table. I_0, I_1 are input signals, O_0, O_1, O_2 are output signals. D_1 is an OR gate, D_2 is a BUFFER gate, D_3 is an AND gate.

3   Two Different Sizes of Memristor-Based Neural Networks

3.1   Two-Input Neural Network

As shown in Fig. 2, the two-input memristive neural network is composed of two memristors, three OPAMPs and three resistors. M_1, M_2, R_1 and OP_1 constitute a sum circuit. R_2, R_3 and OP_2 constitute an inverter. The output of OP_2 is

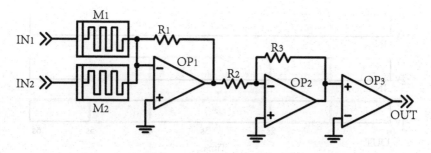

Fig. 2. Two-input neural network. IN_1 and IN_2 are input signals, OUT is output signal, M_1 and M_2 are memristors, R_1, R_2 and R_3 are resistors, OP_1, OP_2 and OP_3 are OPAMPs.

$$OP_2 = (\frac{R_1}{M_1}) * IN_1 + (\frac{R_1}{M_2}) * IN_2 \qquad (1)$$

Let

$$w_1 = \frac{R_1}{M_1} \quad \text{and} \quad w_2 = \frac{R_1}{M_2}$$

$[w_1, w_2]$ represents the row vector of synaptic weights. $[IN_1, IN_2]^T$ represents the column vector of input signals. The Eq. (1) can be rewritten as

$$OP_2 = [w_1, w_2] * [IN_1, IN_2]^T$$

The positive and negative supply voltages of OP_3 are $1v$ and $-1v$, respectively, so that when OP_3 receives a positive voltage, the output is 1, when OP_3 receives a negative voltage, the output is -1. OP_3 can be seen as a neuron, and the activation function is

$$OUT = \begin{cases} 1 & \text{if } OP_2 > 0 \\ -1 & \text{if } OP_2 < 0 \end{cases}$$

A simple classification problem of fruits is implemented by this circuit. The positive and negative threshold voltages of M_1 and M_2 are set to $2v$ and $-2v$, respectively, to avoid changing their memristance values during circuit operation. $R_1 = R_2 = R_3 = 1000\,\Omega$. The synapse weights have been previously trained, so that this circuit can complete the fruits classification task. The memristance of the memristors are changed to $M_1 = 5000\,\Omega$, $M_2 = 2000\,\Omega$. So the row vector of synapse weights is $[w_1, w_2] = [R_1/M_1, R_1/M_2] = [1000/5000, 1000/2000] = [0.2, 0.5]$. For IN_1, 1 means the fruit is round, and -1 means the fruit is oval. For IN_2, 1 means the surface of the fruit is smooth, and -1 means the surface of the fruit is rough. The default value of IN_1 and IN_2 is -1. So $[1, 1]$ means apple and $[1, -1]$ means orange. The output $OUT = 1$ indicates that the result of the classification is apple, and $OUT = -1$ indicates that the result of the classification is orange.

If the object to be judged is apple, the input is $[1,1]$, the output of OP_2 is

$$[w_1, w_2] * [IN_1, IN_2]^T = [0.2, 0.5] * [1, 1]^T = 0.7$$

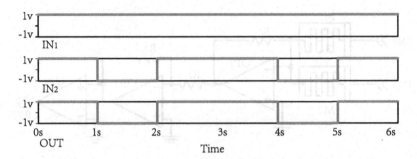

Fig. 3. Simulation result of two-input neural network.

Because $OP_2 = 0.7 > 0$, so $OUT = 1$. The classification result should be apple.

If the object to be judged is orange, the input is $[1, -1]$, the output of OP_2 is

$$[w_1, w_2] * [IN_1, IN_2]^T = [0.2, 0.5] * [1, -1]^T = -0.3$$

Because $OP_2 = -0.3 < 0$, so $OUT = -1$. The classification result should be orange.

Figure 3 shows the simulation results of the circuit, which verify the calculations and prove that this circuit can indeed perform the task of fruits classification.

3.2 Three-Input Neural Network

As shown in Fig. 4, the three-input memristive neural network is composed of three memristors, three OPAMPs and three resistors. M_1, M_2, M_3, R_1 and OP_1 constitute a sum circuit. R_2, R_3 and OP_2 constitute an inverter. The circuit is identical to the circuit shown in Fig. 2 except that it has one more memristor. The output of OP_2 is

$$OP_2 = (\frac{R_1}{M_1}) * IN_1 + (\frac{R_1}{M_2}) * IN_2 + (\frac{R_1}{M_3}) * IN_3 \qquad (2)$$

Let

$$w_1 = \frac{R_1}{M_1} \qquad w_2 = \frac{R_1}{M_2} \quad \text{and} \quad w_3 = \frac{R_1}{M_3}$$

$[w_1, w_2, w_3]$ represents the row vector of synaptic weights, $[IN_1, IN_2, IN_3]^T$ represents the column vector of input signals. The Eq. (2) can be rewritten as

$$OP_2 = [w_1, w_2, w_3] * [IN_1, IN_2, IN_3]^T$$

OP_3 can be seen as a neuron, and the activation function is the same as the function in two-input circuit.

Another simple classification problem of fruits is implemented by the above circuit. The positive and negative threshold voltages of M_1 and M_2 are set

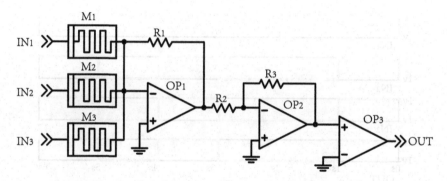

Fig. 4. Three-input neural network. IN_1, IN_2 and IN_3 are input signals, OUT is output signal, M_1, M_2 and M_3 are memristors, R_1, R_2 and R_3 are resistors, OP_1, OP_2 and OP_3 are OPAMPs.

to $2v$ and $-2v$, respectively, to avoid changing their memristance values during circuit operation. $R_1 = R_2 = R_3 = 1000\,\Omega$. The synapse weights have been previously trained, so that this circuit can complete the fruits classification task. The memristance of the memristors are changed to $M_1 = 5000\,\Omega$, $M_2 = 2000\,\Omega$, $M_3 = 1250\,\Omega$. So the row vector of synapse weights is $[w_1, w_2, w_3] = [R_1/M_1, R_1/M_2, R_1/M_3] = [0.2, 0.5, 0.8]$. IN_1 and IN_2 represent the same meaning as two-input circuit in Sect. 3.1. For IN_3, 1 means that the surface has obvious depression, and -1 is just the opposite. So $[1, 1, 1]$ means apple and $[1, -1, -1]$ means orange. Still two kinds of fruits are classified. The output $OUT = 1$ indicates that the result of the classification is apple, and $OUT = -1$ indicates that the result of the classification is orange.

If the object to be judged is apple, the input is $[1,1,1]$, the output of OP_2 is

$$[w_1, w_2, w_3] * [IN_1, IN_2, IN_3]^T = [0.2, 0.5, 0.8] * [1, 1, 1]^T = 1.5$$

Because $OP_2 = 1.5 > 0$, so $OUT = 1$. The classification result should be apple.

If the object to be judged is orange, the input is $[1, -1, -1]$, the output of OP_2 is

$$[w_1, w_2, w_3] * [IN_1, IN_2, IN_3]^T = [0.2, 0.5, 0.8] * [1, -1, -1]^T = -1.1$$

Because $OP_2 = -1.1 < 0$, so $OUT = -1$. The classification result should be orange.

Figure 5 shows the simulation results of the circuit, which verify the calculations and prove that this circuit can indeed perform the task of fruits classification.

3.3 Error Analysis

Here, the unmodified three-input neural network circuit as shown in Fig. 4 is used to implement the classification of the two inputs as described in Sect. 3.1.

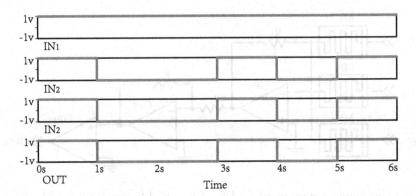

Fig. 5. Simulation result of three-input neural network.

The default value of IN_1, IN_2 and IN_3 is -1. So if IN_3 does not have a clear input signal, the value of IN_3 is -1. If the input is apple, the input vector is $[1,1]$. And at the same time, in fact IN_3 still has signal input which should be -1. The output of OP_2 is

$$[w_1, w_2, w_3] * [IN_1, IN_2, IN_3]^T = [0.2, 0.5, 0.8] * [1, 1, -1]^T = -0.1$$

$OP_2 = -0.1 < 0$, so $OUT = -1$. The calculation results show that apple should be misclassified.

If the input is orange, the input vector is $[1, -1]$. And at the same time, in fact IN_3 still has signal input which should be -1. The output of OP_2 is

$$[w_1, w_2, w_3] * [IN_1, IN_2, IN_3]^T = [0.2, 0.5, 0.8] * [1, -1, -1]^T = -1.1$$

$OP_2 = -1.1 < 0$, so $OUT = -1$. The calculation results show that the classification result should be orange.

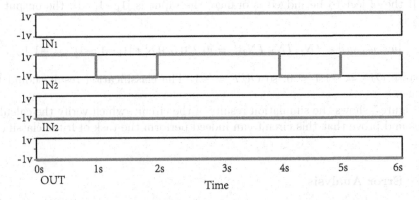

Fig. 6. Simulation results of two-input classification tasks using a three-input circuit.

Figure 6 shows the simulation results of the circuit. It can be seen that when IN_1, $IN_2 = 1$, $OUT = -1$, an error appears in the classification result. Signal -1 from IN_3 is an unexpected interfering signal that participates in subsequent calculations, which affects the accuracy of the output. The circuit simulation results in Fig. 6 verify the calculations and show that the circuit can not achieve the correct classification of fruits.

4 Flexible Memristive Neural Network Architecture

In order to enable the three-input neural network to perform the function of the two-input neural network, and realise the reuse of the memristive neural network, the flexible memristive neural network is designed as Fig. 7. The number of memristive synapses involved in the work can be controlled by controlling the opening or closing of MOSFETs. Memristor and MOSFET are compatible, so this kind of neural network structure can be integrated on the same chip [25]. The threshold voltage of MOSFET used in this circuit is low enough.

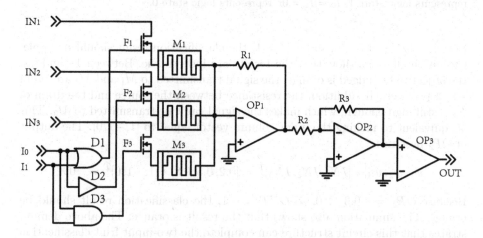

Fig. 7. Flexible memristor-based neural network.

The simulation result is shown in Fig. 8. Starting from 0 s, when $I_0 = 1$, $I_1 = 0$, the outputs of controlling decoder become $O_0 = O_1 = 1$, $O_2 = 0$, this makes the resistance between the source and the drain of F_1 and F_2 very small, and the signal can be transmitted to M_1 and M_2. In addition, the resistance between the source and the drain of F_3 becomes high enough, and the signal can't be transmitted to M_3. At this time, if the object to be judged is apple, the signal transmitted to M_1 and M_2 is 1. Even the default value of IN_3 is -1, the signal transmitted to M_3 is 0. This is equivalent to making the input column vector equal to $[1, 1, 0]$. The output of OP_2 becomes

$$[w_1, w_2, w_3] * [IN_1, IN_2, IN_3]^T = [0.2, 0.5, 0.8] * [1, 1, 0]^T = 0.7$$

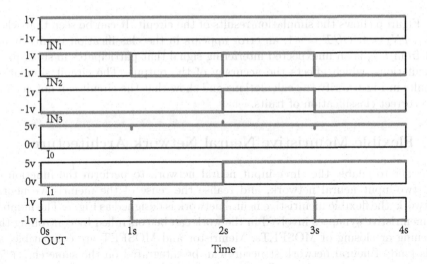

Fig. 8. Simulation result of flexible memristor-based neural network. $I_0 = I_1 = 5v$ represents logic state 1, $I_0 = I_1 = 0v$ represents logic state 0.

Because $OP_2 = 0.7 > 0$, so $OUT = 1$, the classification result should be apple. Circuit simulations show that the results are indeed true. Between 1 s and 2 s, the object to be judged is orange, the signal transmitted to M_1 and M_2 are 1 and -1 respectively. In addition, the resistance between the source and the drain of F_3 is still high enough, which makes the signal can't be transmitted to M_3. This is equivalent to making the input column vector equal to $[1, -1, 0]$. The output of OP_2 becomes

$$[w_1, w_2, w_3] * [IN_1, IN_2, IN_3]^T = [0.2, 0.5, 0.8] * [1, -1, 0]^T = -0.3$$

Because $OP_2 = -0.3 < 0$, so $OUT = -1$, the classification result should be orange. The simulation also shows that the result is orange. The above demonstrates that this circuit structure can complete the two-input fruit classification work. From the end of 2 s, $I_0 = 1$, $I_1 = 1$, $O_0 = O_1 = O_2 = 1$. All of the MOSFETs are open, and the signals come from input ports could be transmitted to memristors. The circuit was changed to a three-input structure. When the input vector is $[1, 1, 1]$, the simulation output is apple, which is consistent with the calculation result. When the input vector is $[1, -1, -1]$, the simulation output is orange, which is also consistent with the calculation result. It can be concluded that the flexible circuit structure is capable of converting between neural networks of different sizes.

5   Conclusion

In this paper, it has been demonstrated errors can occur when performing multiple tasks with the same memristive neural network, and flexible memristor-based neural network has been proposed to achieve different functions by using the same memristive neural network. Different tasks implemented by a same memristive neural networks can enable chip reuse and avoid waste. In the future, our research will focus on achieving flexible switching between more different types of memristive neural networks.

Acknowledgments. The work is supported by the State Key Program of National Natural Science of China (Grant No. 61632002), the National Key R&D Program of China for International S&T Cooperation Projects (No. 2017YFE010 3900), the National Natural Science of China (Grant Nos. 61603348, 61775198, 61603347, 61572446, 61472372), Science and Technology Innovation Talents Henan Province (Grant No. 174200510012), Research Program of Henan Province (Grant Nos. 172102210066, 17A120005, 182102210160), Youth Talent Lifting Project of Henan Province and the Science Foundation of for Doctorate Research of Zhengzhou University of Light Industry (Grant No. 2014BSJJ044).

References

1. Chua, L.O.: Memristor-the missing circuit element. IEEE Trans. Circ. Theory **18**(5), 507–519 (1971)
2. Chua, L.O., Kang, S.M.: Memristive devices and systems. Proc. IEEE **64**(2), 209–223 (1976)
3. Strukov, D.B., Snider, G.S., Stewart, D.R., Williams, R.S.: The missing memristor found. Nature **453**(7191), 80 (2008)
4. Williams, R.S.: How we found the missing memristor. IEEE Spectrum **45**(12), 28–35 (2008)
5. Jo, S.H., Chang, T., Ebong, I., Bhadviya, B.B., Mazumder, P., Lu, W.: Nanoscale memristor device as synapse in neuromorphic systems. Nano Lett. **10**(4), 1297–1301 (2010)
6. Kim, H., Sah, M.P., Yang, C., Roska, T., Chua, L.O.: Neural synaptic weighting with a pulse-based memristor circuit. IEEE Trans. Circ. Syst. I: Regul. Pap. **59**(1), 148–158 (2012)
7. Liu, B., Chen, Y., Wysocki, B., Huang, T.: Reconfigurable neuromorphic computing system with memristor-based synapse design. Neural Process. Lett. **41**(2), 159–167 (2015)
8. Indiveri, G., Linares, B.B., Legenstein, R., Deligeorgis, G., Prodromakis, T.: Integration of nanoscale memristor synapses in neuromorphic computing architectures. Nanotechnology **24**(38), 384010 (2013)
9. Kim, H., Sah, M.P., Yang, C., Roska, T., Chua, L.O.: Memristor bridge synapses. Proc. IEEE **100**(6), 2061–2070 (2012)
10. Sah, M.P., Yang, C., Kim, H., Chua, L.O.: A voltage mode memristor bridge synaptic circuit with memristor emulators. Sensors **12**(3), 3587–3604 (2012)
11. Azghadi, M.R., Linares, B.B., Abbott, D., Leong, P.H.: A hybrid cmos-memristor neuromorphic synapse. IEEE Trans. Biomed. Circ. Syst. **11**(2), 434–445 (2017)
12. Adhikari, S.P., Yang, C., Kim, H., Chua, L.O.: Memristor bridge synapse-based neural network and its learning. IEEE Trans. Neural Netw. Learn. Syst. **23**(9), 1426–1435 (2012)
13. Ebong, I.E., Mazumder, P.: CMOS and memristor-based neural network design for position detection. Proc. IEEE **100**(6), 2050–2060 (2012)

14. Duan, S., Hu, X., Dong, Z., Wang, L., Mazumder, P.: Memristor-based cellular nonlinear/neural network: design, analysis, and applications. IEEE Trans. Neural Netw. Learn. Syst. **26**(6), 1202–1213 (2015)
15. Wang, Z., Wang, X.: A novel memristor-based circuit implementation of full-function Pavlov associative memory accorded with biological feature. IEEE Trans. Circ. Syst. I: Regul. Pap. **65**(7), 2210–2220 (2018)
16. Sheridan, P.M., Cai, F., Du, C., Ma, W., Zhang, Z., Lu, W.D.: Sparse coding with memristor networks. Nat. Nanotechnol. **12**(8), 784 (2017)
17. Wen, S., Huang, T., Zeng, Z., Chen, Y., Li, P.: Circuit design and exponential stabilization of memristive neural networks. Neural Netw. **63**, 48–56 (2015)
18. Yang, J., Wang, L., Wang, Y., Guo, T.: A novel memristive Hopfield neural network with application in associative memory. Neurocomputing **227**, 142–148 (2017)
19. Adam, G.C., Hoskins, B.D., Prezioso, M., Merrikh, B.F., Chakrabarti, B., Strukov, D.B.: 3-D memristor crossbars for analog and neuromorphic computing applications. IEEE Trans. Electron Devices **64**(1), 312–318 (2017)
20. Prezioso, M., Merrikh, B.F., Hoskins, B.D., Adam, G.C., Likharev, K.K., Strukov, D.B.: Training and operation of an integrated neuromorphic network based on metal-oxide memristors. Nature **521**(7550), 61 (2015)
21. Hu, S.G., et al.: Associative memory realized by a reconfigurable memristive Hopfield neural network. Nature Commun. **6**, 7522 (2015)
22. Li, C., et al.: Efficient and self-adaptive in-situ learning in multilayer memristor neural networks. Nature Commun. **9**(1), 2385 (2018)
23. Wang, Z., et al.: Fully memristive neural networks for pattern classification with unsupervised learning. Nat. Electr. **1**(2), 137 (2018)
24. Wang, J.J., et al.: Predicting house price with a memristor-based artificial neural network. IEEE Access **6**, 16523–16528 (2018)
25. Yao, P., et al.: Face classification using electronic synapses. Nature Commun. **8**, 15199 (2017)

A Biogeography-Based Memetic Algorithm for Job-Shop Scheduling

Xue-Qin Lu[1], Yi-Chen Du[1], Xu-Hua Yang[1], and Yu-Jun Zheng[1,2(✉)]

[1] College of Computer Science and Technology,
Zhejiang University of Technology, Hangzhou 310023, China
yujun.zheng@computer.org
[2] Institute of Service Engineering, Hangzhou Normal University,
Hangzhou 311121, China

Abstract. Job shop scheduling problem (JSP) is a well-known combinatorial optimization problem of practical importance, but existing evolutionary algorithms for JSP often face problems of low convergence speed and/or premature convergence. For efficiently solving JSP, this paper proposes a memetic algorithm based on biogeography-based optimization (BBO), named BBMA, which redefines the migration and mutation operators of BBO for JSP, employs a local population topology to suppress premature convergence, and uses a critical-path-based local search operator to enhance the exploitation ability. Numerical experiments on a set of JSP instances show that the proposed BBMA has significantly performance advantage over a number of state-of-the-art evolutionary algorithms.

Keywords: Job-shop scheduling (JSP)
Biogeography-based optimization (BBO) · Memetic algorithm (MA)
Local search

1 Introduction

The job-shop scheduling problem (JSP) is a well-known combinatorial optimization problem that is to schedule a number of jobs on multiple machines in order to optimize one or more certain performance measures such as the total completion time or the makespan [19]. JSP has been extensively studied in the literature, and it is known to be NP-hard in the strong sense when the number of machines exceeds two [6]. Many exact, approximate, and heuristic algorithms have been proposed for JSP. In particular, to obtain satisfactory solutions to large-size JSP instances within an acceptable time, a variety of metaheuristics including genetic algorithms (GAs) [7,16,23], particle swarm optimization (PSO) [5,11,13], differential evolution (DE) [25,28], ant colony optimization (ACO) [8,26], artificial bee colony (ABC) [1], water wave optimization (WWO) [20,29], etc., have been applied to JSP and have shown good performance compared to traditional algorithms. Interested readers can refer to [2] for a survey of recent intelligent algorithms for JSP.

© Springer Nature Singapore Pte Ltd. 2018
J. Qiao et al. (Eds.): BIC-TA 2018, CCIS 951, pp. 273–284, 2018.
https://doi.org/10.1007/978-981-13-2826-8_24

Biogeography-based optimization (BBO) [21] is a metaheuristic algorithm that borrows ideas from island biogeographic evolution for global optimization problem. As most other evolutionary algorithms (EAs), BBO searches for the global optimum in the solution space by continually evolving a population of solutions called habitats. In recent years, BBO and its variants has attracted much attention in the community and has been applied to many real-world optimization problems, which also include various scheduling problems [12, 24, 27, 30].

Nevertheless, a disadvantage of EAs is their slow convergence speed. Memetic algorithms (MAs) are proposed as hybrid EAs that employ local search to accelerate search as well as improve solution quality [17, 18]. In this paper, we propose a biogeography-based memetic algorithm (BBMA), which redefines the migration and mutation operators of BBO for JSP, employs a local population topology to suppress premature convergence, and uses a critical-path-based local search operator to enhance the exploitation ability. Experimental results demonstrate the performance advantage of BBMA over a number of state-of-the-arts on test instances.

In the rest of the paper, Sect. 2 presents the mathematical formulation of JSP, Sect. 3 presents the BBMA for JSP. Section 4 presents the experimental experiments, and finally Sect. 5 concludes with discussion.

2   Problem Formulation

JSP is to schedule n jobs on m machines, where each job has m operations, each of which to be processed by a machine. Note that different jobs can have different processing sequences. For example, in a freighter loading and unloading workshop, an arrived freighter has a sequence of box hanging, box opening, cargo unloading, and box sealing, while a departing freighter has a sequence of box opening, cargo loading, box sealing, and box hanging.

Formally, the inputs to JSP include:

- $J = \{J_1, J_2, ..., J_n\}$, the set of n jobs.
- $M = \{M_1, M_2, ..., M_m\}$, the set of m machines.
- $T_{(n \times m)}$, the job-machine processing time matrix, where each component t_{ij} denotes the processing time of the j-th operation of job J_i.
- $S_{(n \times m)}$, the processing order matrix, where each component s_{ij} denotes the machine on which the j-th operation of job J_i is processed.

The problem needs to determine an execution sequence of jobs for each machine, such that the makespan of all jobs is minimized. The decision variables can be represented as a matrix $X_{(m \times n)}$, where each component x_{jk} denotes the k-th job executed on machine M_j.

Let $C(j, k)$ denote the completion time of k-th job on machine M_j, $i = x_{j,k}$ be the corresponding job index, and p be the index of M_j in the processing sequence of J_i. When $k = 1$ and $p = 1$, J_i is the first job on M_j; when $k = 1$

and $p > 1$, J_i is processed after the previous $(p - 1)$ jobs have been processed on M_j:

$$C(j,1) = \begin{cases} t_{i,1}, & p = 1 \\ C(s_{i,p-1}, i) + t_{i,p}, & p > 1 \end{cases}, \quad j = 1, 2, ..., m \tag{1}$$

When $k > 1$, the job can be processed by M_j only after its previous $(k - 1)$ operations have been processed:

$$C(j,k) = \begin{cases} C(j, k-1) + t_{i,p}, & p = 1 \\ \max\left(C(j, k-1), C(s_{i,p-1}, i)\right) + t_{i,p}, & p > 1 \end{cases}, \quad j = 1, 2, ..., m; k = 2, ..., n \tag{2}$$

And thus the makespan is:

$$C_{\max}(X) = \max_{1 \leq j \leq m} C(j, n) \tag{3}$$

The problem objective is to find a schedule X^* which has minimum makespan among all possible schedules (the set of which is denoted by Π):

$$C_{\max}(X^*) = \min_{X \in \Pi} C_{\max}(X) \tag{4}$$

It is easy to see that the number of all possible solutions of a JSP is $m \times n!$, and the objective function is also computationally expensive. Thus, JSP is a very difficult combinatorial optimization problem.

3 BBMA for JSP

3.1 Biogeography-Based Optimization

BBO [21] is a metaheuristic the mathematics of island biogeography, which shows that the species richness of a habitat can be predicted in terms of such factors as habitat area, immigration rate, and extinction rate [15]. In BBO, each solution is analogous to a habitat, the solution components are analogous to a set of suitability index variables (SIVs), and the fitness of the solution is analogous to the species richness or habitat suitability index (HSI) of the habitat. The central of BBO is the equilibrium theory of biogeography, which indicates that high HSI habitats have high species emigration rates and low HSI habitats have high species immigration rates. Figure 1 illustrates a simple linear migration model, where the immigration rate $\lambda(X)$ and the emigration rate $\mu(X)$ of each habitat X are both functions of the species richness:

$$\lambda(X) = I \cdot \frac{f_{\max} - f(X) + \epsilon}{f_{\max} - f_{\min} + \epsilon} \tag{5}$$

$$\mu(X) = E \cdot \frac{f(X) - f_{\min} + \epsilon}{f_{\max} - f_{\min} + \epsilon} \tag{6}$$

where $f(X)$ is the fitness of X, $f_{\max}$ and $f_{\min}$ are the maximum and minimum fitness among the population, I and E are the maximum possible immigration rate and emigration rate which are typically both set to 1, and ϵ is a small positive number to avoid division-by-zero. There are also some other nonlinear migration models [14].

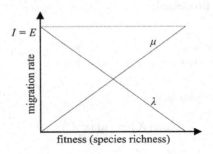

Fig. 1. A linear migration model

BBO has two main operators, migration and mutation. In the original BBO, the migration operator simply migrates an SIV from an emigrating habitat to an immigrating one, and the mutation operator simply resets some SIVs of the solution to random values in the predefined range. However, these operators cannot be directly applied to solutions to JSP. Moreover, in the original BBO, migration can occur between any two habitats in the population, but such a global population topology may easily cause premature convergence [9]. Thus we make the following adaptations in the proposed BBMA in order to efficiently solve JSP.

3.2 Local Population Topology

To overcome the issue of premature convergence in the original BBO, Zheng et al. [31] propose a number of local population topologies, including the ring, square, and random topologies. After testing these topologies for BBMA, we select the local random topology, where each solution is randomly assigned with probably K_N neighbours and K_N is a control parameter. The topology is maintained by an $(N \times N)$-dimensional matrix *Link*, where $Link(i, i') = 1$ indicates that two solutions X_i and $X_{i'}$ are connected and $Link(i, i') = 0$ otherwise ($i, i' = 1, 2, \ldots, N$, and N is the population size).

The local random topology is set as follows: for any two solutions X_i and $X_{i'}$, we use a random function *rand*() to generate a number uniformly distributed between [0,1]; if the number is less than K_N/N, we set $Link(i, i') = 1$, i.e., X_i and $X_{i'}$ become neighbors. In BBMA, migration can only occur between neighbors.

3.3 Migration for JSP

BBMA encodes each solution to JSP as a $(m \times n)$-dimensional matrix, and regards each row (i.e., the job sequence on each machine) as an SIV. When the jth SIV of a solution X (denoted by $X(j)$) is immigrated from an emigrating solution X', BBMA replaces a random subsequence in X with the corresponding subsequence in X', and makes substitution on the remaining components of $X(j)$ to keep it as a permutation of all jobs $\{J_1, J_2, ..., J_n\}$.

Take a JSP instance with six jobs for example. When performing migration from $X'(j) = [1, 3, 5, 6, 4, 2]$ to $X(j) = [1, 2, 3, 4, 5, 6]$, if the subsequence $[3, 5, 6]$ is selected from X', the migration is performed as follows:

1. Replace 2 in $X(j)$ with the first element 3 of the subsequence, and change the original 3 in $X(j)$ to 2.
2. Replace 2 in $X(j)$ with the second element 5 of the subsequence, and change the original 5 in $X(j)$ to 2.
3. Replace 4 in $X(j)$ with the third element 6 of the subsequence, and change the original 6 in $X(j)$ to 4.

The process is illustrated by Fig. 2. After migration we have $X(j) = [1, 3, 5, 6, 2, 4]$, which inherits features from the emigrating solution X'. Since the emigrating solution is selected with a probability in proportional to its emigration (by using a roulette wheel selection method), solutions of higher fitness have more chances to share their features to other solutions.

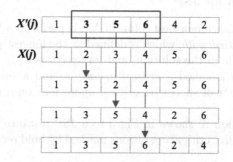

Fig. 2. An example of BBMA migration.

Algorithm 1 presents the BBMA migration procedure.

3.4 Mutation for JSP

The BBMA mutation is also performed on an SIV (i.e., a job sequence) at a time, by swapping two randomly selected jobs in the sequence. Algorithm 2 presents the BBMA mutation procedure, where $\pi(X)$ denotes the mutation rate of X.

Algorithm 1. The BBMA migration on a solution X.

```
1  for j = 1 to n do
2      if rand() < λ(X) then
3          Select a neighbor X′ with a probability in proportional to μ(X′);
4          Let p₁ = rand(1, n/2), p₂ = rand(p₁+1, n);  //subsequence from p₁ to p₂
5          for p = p₁ to p₂ do
6              Let p′ = Indexof(X(j), X(j)(p));
7              X(j)(p′) ← X(j)(p);
8              X(j)(p) ← X′(j)(p);
```

Algorithm 2. The BBMA mutation on a solution X.

```
1  for j = 1 to n do
2      if rand() < π(X) then
3          Let p₁ = rand(1, n);
4          if p₁ < n then
5              Let p₂ = rand(p₁ + 1, n)
6          else
7              Let p₂ = rand(1, n − 1)
8          X(j)(p₁) ↔ X′(j)(p₂);
```

3.5 Local Search for JSP

Whenever BBMA finds a new best solution X^*, it performs a local search around X^* based on the *critical path*, which is defined as the longest path from the start node to the end node in the solution, and its length is $C_{\max}$ [3]. Any operation on the critical path is called a *critical operation*, and a subsequence that has the maximum number of successive critical operations on a machine is called a *critical block*.

Consider a solution X shown in Fig. 3 to a JSP instance with four jobs and three machines, the five critical operations marked by bold rectangular constitute

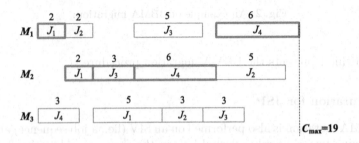

Fig. 3. An example of a schedule and its critical path and operations in JSP.

a critical path. J_1 and J_4 are the two critical blocks on machine M_1, $\{J_1, J_3, J_4\}$ is a critical block on machine M_2, and there is no critical block on M_3.

A critical block has two useful properties [3]:

- Swapping any two jobs in a critical block will not affect the feasibility of scheduling.
- Swapping any two inner operations (except the first and the last operations) will not affect the makespan.

Thus we can limit the local search in a critical block to one of the following three ways:

- Swapping the first and the last operations.
- Moving an inner operation to the first or the last position.
- Moving the first or the last operation into the block.

BBMA uses the last two ways as they have been shown to be more effective than the first one.

For example, for the critical block $\{J_1, J_3, J_4\}$ on machine M_2 in Fig. 3, if we move J_3 to the first position, the makespan of the new schedule is reduced to 18, as shown in Fig. 4.

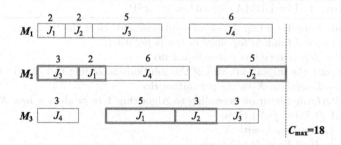

Fig. 4. Changing operations in the critical block on M_2 in Fig. 3.

Algorithm 3 presents the BBMA local search procedure, where the critical path method [4] is employed to find a critical path, $B(p)$ denotes the p-th operation in block B, and $B(1)$ and $B(|B|)$ denote the first and the last operation in B, respectively.

3.6   The Framework of BBMA

Algorithm 4 presents the framework of the BBMA for JSP. Note that we only apply the mutation operator to the worst half of the population, use a uniform mutation rate (set to 0.024) for these solutions. Moreover, if the best solution has not been updated for $\widehat{g}$ consecutive generations (where $\widehat{g}$ is a control parameter), we reset the local population topology to avoid search stagnation.

Algorithm 3. The BBMA local search on a solution X.

---

1 Find the critical path of X using the method in [4];
2 Let $X_{\text{best}} = X$;
3 **for** $i = 1$ *to* m **do**
4   **foreach** *Critical block B in X* **do**
5   **for** $p = 2$ *to* $|B| - 1$ **do**
6   Temporarily move $B(p)$ to $B(1)$;
7   **if** $C_{\max}(X) < C_{\max}(X_{\text{best}})$ **then** $X_{\text{best}} \leftarrow X$;
8   Temporarily move $B(p)$ to $B(|B|)$;
9   **if** $C_{\max}(X) < C_{\max}(X_{\text{best}})$ **then** $X_{\text{best}} \leftarrow X$;
10   Temporarily move $B(1)$ to $B(p)$;
11   **if** $C_{\max}(X) < C_{\max}(X_{\text{best}})$ **then** $X_{\text{best}} \leftarrow X$;
12   Temporarily move $B(|B|)$ to $B(p)$;
13   **if** $C_{\max}(X) < C_{\max}(X_{\text{best}})$ **then** $X_{\text{best}} \leftarrow X$;

14 $X \leftarrow X_{\text{best}}$.

Algorithm 4. The BBMA algorithm for JSP.

---

1 Randomly initialize a population of solutions, and select the best as X^*;
2 Initialize a local random topology of the population;
3 **while** *the stop criterion is not satisfied* **do**
4   Compute the migration rates of the solutions according to Eqs. (5) and (6);
5   **for** *each solution X in the population* **do**
6   Perform migration according to Algorithm 1 to produce a new X';
7   **if** $f(X') < f(X)$ **then**
8   Replace X with X';
9   **if** $f(X) < f(X^*)$ **then**
10                  $X^* \leftarrow X$;
11   perform local search on X;

12   **for** *each solution X in the worst half of the population* **do**
13   Perform mutation according to Algorithm 2 to produce a new X';
14   **if** $f(X') < f(X)$ **then**
15   Replace X with X';
16   **if** $f(X) < f(X^*)$ **then**
17                  $X^* \leftarrow X$;
18   perform local search on X;

19   **if** *X^* has not been updated for $\hat{g}$ consecutive generations* **then**
20   Reset the local random topology of the population;

21 **return** X^*.

---

4   Computational Experiments

To verify the performance of the proposed BBMA, we compare it with the following five popular metaheuristic algorithms for JSP:

- A hybrid GA with local search [7], denoted by HGA.
- A hybrid PSO, simulated annealing (SA) and local search algorithm [13], denoted by HPSO.
- A so-called "best-so-far" ABC algorithm [1].
- A hybrid DE algorithm with local search by parameter perturbation [28], denoted by HDE.
- Another hybrid BBO algorithm [12], denoted by HBBO.

To evaluate the effectiveness of the local population topology of BBMA, we also implement another version of BBMA using the global population topology, denoted by BBMA-G. For BBMA, we set the population size $N = 2\,\text{mn}$, $K_N = 3$, and $\widehat{g} = 6$. The parameters of the other five algorithms are set as suggested in the literature.

The test set consists of 40 JSP instances from [10, 22]. For a fair comparison, the maximum number of iterations is set to 1000 for all algorithms. On each instance, we run each algorithm 20 times, and record the median of the best makespan C^* obtained by the algorithm. For ease of comparison, we use the best relative error (BRE) of C^* to C^b, the best known makespan, as the metric:

$$\text{BRE} = \frac{C^* - C^b}{C^*} \times 100\% \tag{7}$$

The experimental results are presented in Table 1. Among the 40 instances, BBMA and ABC obtain the best known solutions on 38 instances, HDE and HBBO obtain the best known solutions on 34 instances, while HGA and HPSO respectively obtain the best known solutions on 28 and 29 instances. In fact, there are 28 instances on which all the algorithms can always obtain the best known solutions, and on the remaining 12 instances BBMA and ABC have great performance advantages over the other metaheuristic algorithms. In terms of average BRE value, BBMA performs the best, ABC, HDE, and HBBO performs the second to the fourth, while HPSO and HGA are ranked the last two. In summary, BBMA shows competitive performance compared with the other algorithms. As most of the other algorithms also incorporate local search methods, the results demonstrate the effectiveness of the proposed local search procedure based on critical path in BBMA.

Comparing the two BBMA versions, BBMA with the local population topology shows significant performance improvement over BBMA-G, which demonstrates that local random topology can effectively suppress premature convergence by restricting fast information sharing among the whole population. Another observation is that BBMA-G performs slightly worse than HBBO, but BBMA performs much better than HBBO. In fact, we have test the incorporation of local population topology into HBBO, but the resulting algorithm still performs worse than BBMA, which indicates that the proposed BBMA migration

Table 1. The BRE results of the comparative algorithms on test instances

#	$n \times m$	C^b	HGA	HPSO	ABC	HDE	HBBO	BBMA-G	BBMA
LA01	10×5	666	0	0	0	0	0	0	0
LA02	10×5	655	0	0	0	0	0	0	0
LA03	10×5	597	0	0	0	0	0	0	0
LA04	10×5	590	0	0	0	0	0	0	0
LA05	10×5	593	0	0	0	0	0	0	0
LA06	15×5	926	0	0	0	0	0	0	0
LA07	15×5	890	0	0	0	0	0	0	0
LA08	15×5	863	0	0	0	0	0	0	0
LA09	15×5	951	0	0	0	0	0	0	0
LA10	15×5	958	0	0	0	0	0	0	0
LA11	20×5	1222	0	0	0	0	0	0	0
LA12	20×5	1039	0	0	0	0	0	0	0
LA13	20×5	1150	0	0	0	0	0	0	0
LA14	20×5	1292	0	0	0	0	0	0	0
LA15	20×5	1207	0	0	0	0	0	0	0
LA16	10×10	945	0	0	0	0	0	0	0
LA17	10×10	784	0	0	0	0	0	0	0
LA18	10×10	848	0	0	0	0	0	0	0
LA19	10×10	842	0	0	0	0	0	0	0
LA20	10×10	902	0.554	0	0	0	0	0	0
LA21	15×10	1046	0	0	0	0	0	0	0
LA22	15×10	927	0.863	0.539	0	0.539	0	0.863	0
LA23	15×10	1032	0	0	0	0	0	0	0
LA24	15×10	935	1.925	1.604	0	0.642	1.604	0.642	0
LA25	15×10	977	0.921	0.205	0	0	0	0	0
LA26	20×10	1218	0	0	0	0	0	0	0
LA27	20×10	1235	1.700	1.700	0	0	0.324	0	0
LA28	20×10	1216	1.316	0.905	0	0	0	0	0
LA29	20×10	1152	3.819	2.778	1.042	1.823	1.042	1.823	0
LA30	20×10	1355	0	0	0	0	0	0	0
LA31	30×10	1748	0	0	0	0	0	0	0
LA32	30×10	1850	0	0	0	0	0	0	0
LA33	30×10	1719	0	0	0	0	0	0	0
LA34	30×10	1721	0	0	0	0	0	0	0
LA35	30×10	1888	0	0	0	0	0	0	0
LA36	15×15	1268	0.868	1.025	0	0.789	0	0.868	0.789
LA37	15×15	1397	0.787	1.288	0	0	0.787	1.002	0
LA38	15×15	1196	1.923	1.421	0	1.003	1.003	0	0
LA39	15×15	1233	1.054	1.054	0	0	0	0	0
LA40	15×15	1222	1.555	1.473	0.164	0.164	0.245	0.245	0.245
Average			0.432	0.350	0.030	0.124	0.125	0.193	0.026

and mutation operators together with the local population topology contributes as a whole to the improvement of the performance on solving JSP instances.

5   Conclusion and Discussion

This paper proposes a BBMA algorithm for JSP, which redefines the migration and mutation operators for the combinatorial optimization problem, integrates a critical-path-based local search procedure into the framework of BBO to improve the local exploitation ability, and employs a local population topology to suppress premature convergence. Numerical experiments on a set of test instances show that the proposed algorithm has obvious advantage over other five popular metaheuristics. The key ideas of BBMA can be used or extended for many other combinatorial optimization problems. Our ongoing work also includes integrating multiple local search procedures into BBMA to improve the algorithm performance.

Acknowledgements. This work is supported by National Natural Science Foundation (Grant No. 61473263 and 61773348) of China.

References

1. Banharnsakun, A., Sirinaovakul, B., Achalakul, T.: Job shop scheduling with the best-so-far ABC. Eng. Appl. Artif. Intel. **25**(3), 583–593 (2012)
2. Çaliş, B., Bulkan, S.: A research survey: review of AI solution strategies of job shop scheduling problem. J. Intell. Manuf. **26**(5), 961–973 (2015)
3. Chang, Y.L., Matsuo, H., Sullivan, R.: A bottleneck-based beam search for job scheduling in a flexible manufacturing system. Int. J. Prod. Res. **27**, 1949–1961 (1989)
4. Cruz, C.M.A., Frausto, S.J., Ramos, Q.F.: The problem of using the calculation of the critical path to solver instances of the job shop scheduling problem. Int. J. Comput. Intell. ENFORMATIKA **1**(4), 334–337 (2004)
5. Gao, H., Kwong, S., Fan, B., Wang, R.: A hybrid particle-swarm tabu search algorithm for solving job shop scheduling problems. IEEE Trans. Ind. Inf. **10**(4), 2044–2054 (2014)
6. Garey, M.R., Johnson, D.S., Sethi, R.: The complexity of flowshop and jobshop scheduling. Math. Oper. Res. **1**(2), 117–129 (1976)
7. Gonçalves, J.F., Magalhaes, M.J.J., Resende, M.G.: A hybrid genetic algorithm for the job shop scheduling problem. Eur. J. Oper. Res. **167**(1), 77–95 (2005)
8. Huang, K.L., Liao, C.J.: Ant colony optimization combined with taboo search for the job shop scheduling problem. Comput. Oper. Res. **35**(4), 1030–1046 (2008)
9. Kennedy, J.: Small worlds and mega-minds: effects of neighborhood topology on particle swarm performance. In: Proceedings of the 1999 Congress on Evolutionary Computation, vol. 3, pp. 1931–1938 (1999)
10. Lawrence, S.: Supplement to resource constrained project scheduling: an experimental investigation of heuristic scheduling techniques. Energy Proc. **4**(7), 4411–4417 (1984)

11. Lian, Z., Jiao, B., Gu, X.: A similar particle swarm optimization algorithm for job-shop scheduling to minimize makespan. Appl. Math. Comput. **183**(2), 1008–1017 (2006)
12. Lin, J.: A hybrid discrete biogeography-based optimization for the permutation flow-shop scheduling problem. Int. J. Prod. Res. **54**(16), 4805–4814 (2016)
13. Lin, T.L., et al.: An efficient job-shop scheduling algorithm based on particle swarm optimization. Expert Syst. Appl. **37**(3), 2629–2636 (2010)
14. Ma, H.: An analysis of the equilibrium of migration models for biogeography-based optimization. Inform. Sci. **180**(18), 3444–3464 (2010)
15. MacArthur, R., Wilson, E.: The Theory of Biogeography. Princeton University Press, Princeton (1967)
16. Mattfeld, D.C., Bierwirth, C.: An efficient genetic algorithm for job shop scheduling with tardiness objectives. Eur. J. Oper. Res. **155**(3), 616–630 (2004)
17. Moscato, P., Cotta, C.: A gentle introduction to memetic algorithms. In: Glover, F., Kochenberger, G.A. (eds.) Handbook of Metaheuristics, pp. 105–144. Springer, Boston (2003). https://doi.org/10.1007/0-306-48056-5_5
18. Ong, Y.S., Lim, M.H., Zhu, N., Wong, K.W.: Classification of adaptive memetic algorithms: a comparative study. IEEE Trans. Syst. Man Cybern. Part B **36**(1), 141–152 (2006)
19. Pinedo, M.: Scheduling Theory, Algorithms, and Systems, 2nd edn. Prentice Hall, Upper Saddle River (2002)
20. Shao, Z., Pi, D., Shao, W.: A novel discrete water wave optimization algorithm for blocking flow-shop scheduling problem with sequence-dependent setup times. Swarm Evol. Comput. **40**(1), 53–75 (2018)
21. Simon, D.: Biogeography-based optimization. IEEE Trans. Evol. Comput. **12**(6), 702–713 (2008)
22. Storer, R.H., Wu, S.D., Vaccari, R.: New search spaces for sequencing problems with application to job shop scheduling. Manag. Sci. **38**(10), 1495–1509 (1992)
23. Wang, L., Zheng, D.Z.: A modified genetic algorithm for job shop scheduling. Int. J. Adv. Manuf. Technol. **20**(1), 72–76 (2002)
24. Wang, X., Duan, H.: A hybrid biogeography-based optimization algorithm for job shop scheduling problem. Comput. Ind. Eng. **73**(1), 96–114 (2014)
25. Wisittipanich, W., Kachitvichyanukul, V.: Two enhanced differential evolution algorithms for job shop scheduling problems. Int. J. Prod. Res. **50**(10), 2757–2773 (2012)
26. Xing, L.N., Chen, Y.W., Wang, P., Zhao, Q.S., Xiong, J.: A knowledge-based ant colony optimization for flexible job shop scheduling problems. Appl. Soft Comput. **10**(3), 888–896 (2010)
27. Zhang, M.X., Zhang, B., Qian, N.: University course timetabling using a new ecogeography-based optimization algorithm. Natural Comput. **16**(1), 61–74 (2017)
28. Zhang, R., Song, S., Wu, C.: A hybrid differential evolution algorithm for job shop scheduling problems with expected total tardiness criterion. Appl. Soft Comput. **13**(3), 1448–1458 (2013)
29. Zheng, Y.J.: Water wave optimization: a new nature-inspired metaheuristic. Comput. Oper. Res. **55**(1), 1–11 (2015)
30. Zheng, Y.J., Ling, H.F., Shi, H.H., Chen, H.S., Chen, S.Y.: Emergency railway wagon scheduling by hybrid biogeography-based optimization. Comput. Oper. Res. **43**(3), 1–8 (2014)
31. Zheng, Y.J., Ling, H.F., Wu, X.B., Xue, J.Y.: Localized biogeography-based optimization. Soft Comput. **18**(11), 2323–2334 (2014)

Analysing Parameters Leading to Chaotic Dynamics in a Novel Chaotic System

Junwei Sun[1,2], Nan Li[1,2], and Yanfeng Wang[1,2(✉)]

[1] Henan Key Lab of Information-Based Electrical Appliances,
Zhengzhou University of Light Industry, Zhengzhou 450002, China
[2] School of Electrical and Information Engineering,
Zhengzhou University of Light Industry, Zhengzhou 450002, China
{junweisun,yanfengwang}@yeah.net

Abstract. A novel chaotic system of three-dimensional mathematic model is proposed in this paper. According to the changes of system parameters and initial values, the dynamical behaviors of the system are investigated in detail by using the classical dynamical analysis methods, such as Lyapunov exponents, bifurcation diagrams etc. Some abundant dynamical phenomena, such as chaos, transient chaos and period-doubling and so on are observed in numerical simulation by Matlab. The simulation results of Matlab can further prove the feasibility and flexibility of this system.

Keywords: Chaotic system · Dynamical analysis
Lyapunov exponent · Bifurcation diagrams

1 Introduction

During the last two decades, the control and application of nonlinear science have received a great deal of interest among scientists from various research fields. Generally speaking, the main contents of nonlinear science include chaos, fractals and solitons, which is clear that chaos theory is one of the most important achievements of nonlinear science. A nonlinear deterministic system can exhibit chaotic, complex, and unpredictable behaviors, which can be thought as the chaotic system. In the history of chaos, the professor Lorenz has been praised as the father of chaos due to the famous Lorenz system [1]. He has opened a new era of chaos development. After the first chaotic model, the design and research of chaotic system become an important region. Many different chaotic and hyper chaotic systems have been realized in literature which are in order to prove that the solutions are not numerical errors, such as the Geneiso system [2], the memristor-based Henon system [3], the memristor-based Chuas circuit [4], and so on. The chaotic circuits not only have the dynamic behaviors of the classical systems, but also present some complex dynamic behaviors, such as stable equilibria [5], coexisting attractor [6], extreme multi-stability [7], multi hidden attractors [8] and period doubling bifurcation [9–11].

© Springer Nature Singapore Pte Ltd. 2018
J. Qiao et al. (Eds.): BIC-TA 2018, CCIS 951, pp. 285–294, 2018.
https://doi.org/10.1007/978-981-13-2826-8_25

There has been increasing interest in exploiting chaotic dynamics in engineering applications, where some attentions have been focused on effectively creating chaos via simple physical systems, such as electronic circuits [12–15]. Lately, the pursuit of designing circuits to produce chaotic attractors has become a focal point for electronic engineers, not only because of their theoretical interest, but also due to their potential real-world applications [16] in various chaos-based technologies and information systems [17–20]. From the point of view of the circuit design, the chaotic circuit should be able to be implemented with electronic components. Since memristors are not yet commercially available, the dynamical behaviors of the above mentioned classical circuits were investigated only by numerical simulation. Obviously, more and more chaotic systems [21–25] are found to be very necessary.

Based on previous considerations, the idea for developing a new system arose. Specifically, a new chaotic system is proposed starting from the integer-order in this paper. The new system is differ from the tradition chaotic system [2–4], which is sensitive to parameters. It is also observed that the system undergoes an intermittent transition from period directly to chaos. It is shown that in such three-dimensional continuous system, the occurrence of intermittency may indicate a transition from period to chaos not only to chaos, which provides a possible route to chaos. Various nonlinear analysis techniques such as phase portraits, time series, bifurcation diagrams band the spectrum of Lyapunov exponents are exploited to characterize different scenarios to chaos in the new system. A theoretical analysis of its dynamics is illustrated in detail, along with accurate numerical simulations showing chaotic behaviors and oscillations. What's more, by changing the parameter values of the equation, the circuit will produce the different behaviors such as transient chaos, period doubling and so on.

The rest of paper is organized as follows. In Sect. 2, a novel chaotic system is proposed. In Sect. 3, these dynamical properties of the new system are presented and the corresponding effects of the system parameters are analyzed in detail. Finally, some conclusions and suggestions for future work are given in Sect. 4.

2   Mathematical Model and Property of the New System

In this work, a new dynamical equation is given in the system form. On this basis, a simple global observation of the system is carried out by using Lyapunov exponents diagrams, bifurcation diagrams and Matlab phase diagrams.

2.1   Chaotic System Model

The chaotic system is given by

$$
\begin{cases}
\dot{x} = y, \\
\dot{y} = -x + yz(a + by^3), \\
\dot{z} = cy^2 - c,
\end{cases}
\tag{1}
$$

where, x, y and z are three state variables of the chaotic system (1). Based on which the corresponding theoretical analysis and numerical simulations can be conducted. The Lyapunov exponent as a function of time is defined, which is

$$LE = \frac{1}{t_M - t_0} \sum_{k=1}^{M} \ln \frac{L(t_k)}{L(t_{k-1})} \tag{2}$$

$L(t_k)$ represents the distance to the zero point, M is the total number of steps. t_0 is the initial time and t_M is the spent time of M steps. Through the Matlab simulation, the Lyapunov exponent graph of the system (1) is plotted as the following Fig. 1.

Let the system parameters $a = 0.9$, $b = 0.5$, $c = 0.9$, the system (1) is chaotic and displays chaotic attractor under the initial conditions (1.5, −0.1, 0.1). The Lyapunov exponents are $LE_1 > 0$, $LE_2 < 0$ and $LE_3 < 0$ in Fig. 1 and the attractors projection of system (1) in different planes are shown in Fig. 2(a)–(d).

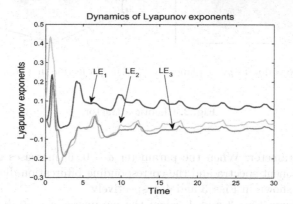

Fig. 1. Lyapunov exponents of chaotic system (1) versus parameter t

3   Dynamics Dependent on Circuit Parameters

Most of chaotic systems can hold chaotic behavior when a chaotic system parameter varies in a certain range. Similar to dynamical analysis of general chaotic circuit, by utilizing the conventional dynamical analysis techniques such as bifurcation diagram, Lyapunov exponent spectra and so on, the dynamical behaviors of the chaotic system (1) are studied under the variation of circuit parameters.

3.1   The Influence of Parameter a

For the system parameters $b = 0.5$, $c = 0.9$ and the initial conditions of the system (1) are $x(0) = 1.5, y(0) = -0.1, z(0) = 0.1$, the circuit parameter a is

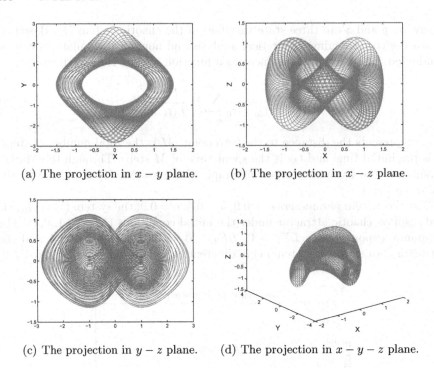

(a) The projection in $x - y$ plane.　　　(b) The projection in $x - z$ plane.

(c) The projection in $y - z$ plane.　　　(d) The projection in $x - y - z$ plane.

Fig. 2. Chaotic attractor.

an varying parameter. When the parameter $a \in [0, 6]$ increases gradually, the Lyapunov exponent spectra and the corresponding bifurcation diagram of state variable a are shown in Figs. 3 and 4, respectively.

Observed from Figs. 3 and 4, when the parameter $a \in [0, 3] \cup [4.2, 6]$, the largest Lyapunov exponent LE_1 is greater than 0 but it is closer to zero in Fig. 3. The system (1) can produce a new chaotic behaviors, which is like periodic oscillation behaviors in Fig. 4. Several from chaotic to periodic windows have been generated within the chaotic region of $a \in [0, 3] \cup [4.2, 6]$. Chaotic orbits and periodic phenomenon are obtained from numerical simulations, as shown in Fig. 4. Also, some further examples of typical points are described in Fig. 5. For example, when a equals to 1, the period-doubling behaviors are observed in Fig. 5(a). However, the dynamics behaviors of the system (1) produce chaotic behaviors for $a = 1.5$ and $a = 5$ in Fig. 5(b) and (d), respectively. With the increase of the parameter $a \in [3, 4.2]$, the largest Lyapunov exponent LE_1 is far greater than 0, the system enters into the chaotic state. In Fig. 5(c), the conclusion can be drawn that the system (1) produces chaotic behaviors. The orbits of this circuit starting from different initial states have different dynamics. In the numerical simulation analysis, the initial states $(1.5, -0.1, 0.1)$ and $(-1.5, 0.1, -0.1)$ are implemented and the trajectories are shown in Fig. 5 by the blue curve and the red curve, respectively.

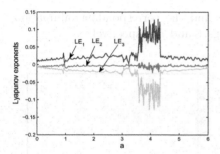

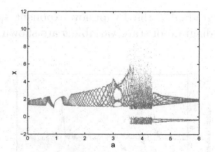

Fig. 3. Lyapunov exponents of chaotic system (1) versus parameter a.

Fig. 4. Bifurcation diagrams of chaotic system (1) versus parameter a.

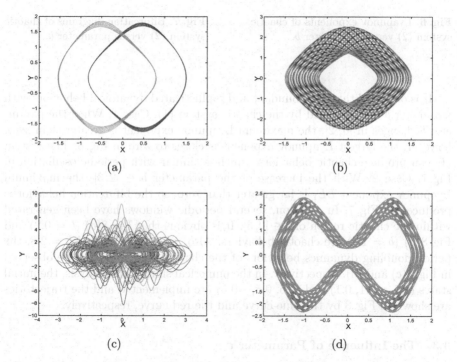

Fig. 5. Phase portrait of system (1) with different circuit parameters (a) $a = 1$, (b) $a = 1.5$, (c) $a = 4$, (d) $a = 5$. (Color figure online)

3.2 The Influence of Parameter b

For the above circuit parameters $a = 0.9$, $c = 0.9$ and the initial conditions of the system (1) are $x(0) = -1.5, y(0) = -0.1, z(0) = 0.1$, the circuit parameter b is an varying parameter. When the parameter b belongs to [0, 3] and increases gradually, the Lyapunov exponent spectra and the corresponding bifurcation diagram of state variable b are shown in Figs. 6 and 7, respectively.

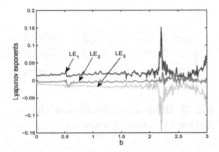

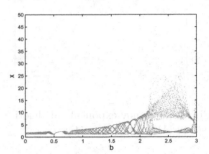

Fig. 6. Lyapunov exponents of chaotic system (2) versus parameter b.

Fig. 7. Bifurcation diagrams of chaotic system (2) versus parameter b.

It is observed that the abundant and sophisticated dynamical behaviors with parameter b are produced by the chaotic system (1). Case 1: When the parameter b changes in $[0, 2]$, the maximum Lyapunov exponent is greater than zero, however, the largest Lyapunov exponent is closer to zero in Fig. 6. The system (1) can produce chaotic behaviors, which is similar with periodic oscillation in Fig. 7. Case 2: With the increase of the parameter $b \in [2, 3]$, the maximum Lyapunov exponent LE_1 is far greater than zero, so the bifurcation behavior is produced in Fig. 7. In addition, several periodic windows have been generated within the chaotic region of $b \in [0, 3]$. It is obvious that Fig. 8(a) ($b = 0.2$) and Fig. 8(b) ($b = 1.4$) are chaotic behaviors. Also, when $b = 1.6$ and $b = 2.8$, the period-doubling dynamics behaviors of the chaotic system (1) can be observed in Fig. 8(c) and (d), respectively. In the numerical simulation analysis, the initial states $(1.5, -0.1, 0.1)$ and $(2.5, 0.5, -0.5)$ are implemented and the trajectories are shown in Fig. 8 by the blue curve and the red curve, respectively.

3.3   The Influence of Parameter c

For the circuit parameters $a = 0.9$, $b = 0.5$ and the initial conditions of the system (1) are $x(0) = 0.9, y(0) = -0.1, z(0) = 0.1$, the circuit parameter c is an varying parameter. When the parameter c belongs to $[0, 6]$ and increases gradually, the Lyapunov exponent spectra and the corresponding bifurcation diagram of state variable c are shown in Figs. 9 and 10, respectively.

By observing the Figs. 9 and 10, it is gained that the largest Lyapunov exponent is from 0 to positive for the parameter c. With the increase of the parameter $c \in [0, 2.4] \cup [3.2, 6]$, the maximum Lyapunov exponent LE_1 is greater than zero in Fig. 9, the system (1) produce chaotic behaviors, which is like period-doubling dynamics behaviors in Fig. 10. It can be seen that there are several periodic

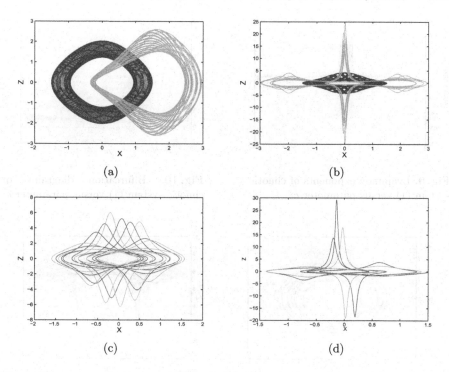

Fig. 8. Phase portrait of system (1) with different circuit parameters (a) $b = 0.2$, (b) $b = 1.4$, (c) $b = 1.6$, (d) $b = 2.8$. (Color figure online)

windows are generated within the region of $c \in [0, 2.4] \cup [3.2, 6]$. For example, when c equals to 6, the system (1) can generate the period-doubling behaviors in Fig. 11(d). The chaotic behaviors can be easily observed in Fig. 11(a) ($c = 0.2$) and Fig. 11(c) ($c = 4.2$), respectively. With the increase of the parameter $c \in [2.4, 3.2]$, the maximum Lyapunov exponent LE_1 is greater than zero in Fig. 9, and the system (1) produce chaotic behaviors in Fig. 11(c) ($c = 2.8$). The initial conditions $(1.5, -0.1, 0.1)$ and $(2, 0.1, 0.2)$ are implemented and the trajectories are shown in Fig. 11 by the red curve and the blue curve, respectively.

Remark 1: Compared the new system with the classical systems [2–4], it can be concluded that the new system is more sensitive to the parameters and initial conditions, and the dynamic behaviors of the system are more abundant. By observing the variables phase graphics, it can be seen clearly that the system have abundant dynamical behaviors under different variables with the same initial conditions or same variables with different initial conditions. Obviously, the different variable values can improve the characteristics of the system and produce more complex trajectory of behaviors.

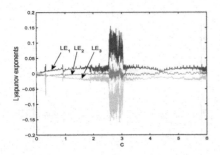

Fig. 9. Lyapunov exponents of chaotic system (1) versus parameter c.

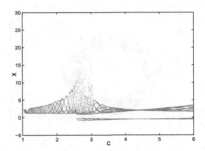

Fig. 10. Bifurcation diagrams of chaotic system (1) versus parameter c.

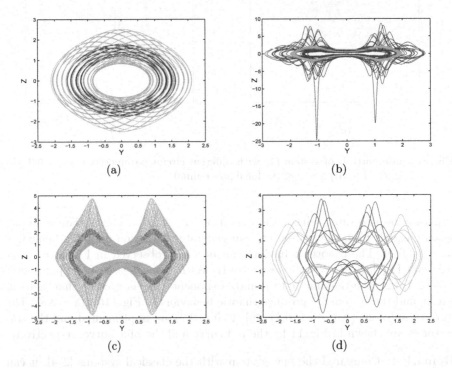

Fig. 11. Phase portrait of system (1) with different circuit parameters (a) $c = 0.2$, (b) $c = 2.8$, (c) $c = 4.2$, (d) $c = 6$. (Color figure online)

4   Conclusion

In this work, a new chaotic system has been proposed. The new system can produce these rich dynamical characteristics. By discussing the parameter variables and the system initial values, we can find the sensitivity of the system to the parameter and initial values, which are the values of the chaotic system. Furthermore, the value of chaotic system can be adjusted or changed to produce different phenomena. States of the chaotic system are sensitive to the initial conditions of the state variables, hence yielding the special phenomena of chaotic and periodic phenomenon. So the chaotic system has broad prospects and great application potential in secure communications and data transmission. The encryption algorithm based on chaotic system is relatively simple, so future work includes exploring the convenience of chaos and designing an more complex algorithm that provides encryption for images or videos.

Acknowledgments. The work is supported by the State Key Program of National Natural Science of China (Grant No. 61632002), the National Key R D Program of China for International S T Cooperation Projects (No. 2017YFE0103900), the National Natural Science of China (Grant Nos. 61603348, 61775198, 61603347, 61572446, 61472372), Science and Technology Innovation Talents Henan Province (Grant No. 174200510012), Research Program of Henan Province (Grant Nos. 172102210066, 17A120005, 182102210160), Youth Talent Lifting Project of Henan Province and the Science Foundation of for Doctorate Research of Zhengzhou University of Light Industry (Grant No. 2014BSJJ044).

References

1. Leonova, G.A., Kuznetsov, N.V., Korzhemanovaa, N.A., Kusakina, D.V.: Lyapunov dimension formula for the global attractor of the Lorenz system. Commun. Nonlinear Sci. Numer. Simul. **41**, 84–103 (2016)
2. Luo, R.Z., Zeng, Y.H.: The control and synchronization of fractional-order Genesiotesi system. Nonlinear Dyn. **88**, 1–11 (2017)
3. Sun, F.Y., Lü, Z.W.: Stability and spatial chaos in 2D Henon system. Appl. Math. Inf. Sci. **10**, 739–746 (2016)
4. Fedele, G., Alfonso, L.D., Pin, G., Parisini, T.: Volterra's kernels-based finite-time parameters estimation of the Chua system. IEEE Proc. **318**, 121–130 (2018)
5. Molaie, M., Jafari, S., Sprott, J.C.: Simple chaotic flows stable equilibrium. Int. J. Bifurcat. Chaos **23**, 1350188 (2013)
6. Zhou, L., Wang, C.H., Zhang, X., Yao, W.: Various attractors, coexisting attractors and antimonotonicity in a simple fourth-order memristive twin-t oscillator. Int. J. Bifurcat. Chaos **28**, 1850050 (2018)
7. Bao, B.C., Xu, Q., Bao, H., Chen, M.: Extreme multistability in a memristive circuit. Electron. Lett. **52**, 1008–1010 (2016)
8. Dudkowski, D., et al.: Hidden attractors in dynamical systems. Phys. Rep. **637**, 1–50 (2016)
9. Bi, Q.S., Ma, R., Zhang, Z.D.: Bifurcation mechanism of the bursting oscillations in periodically excited dynamical system with two time scales. Nonlinear Dyn. **79**, 101–110 (2015)
10. Ngonghala, C.N., Teboh-Ewungkem, M.I., Ngwa, G.A.: Observance of period-doubling bifurcation and chaos in an autonomous ODE model for malaria with vector demography. Theor. Ecol. **9**, 1–15 (2016)
11. Din, Q., Khan, M.A.: Period-doubling bifurcation and chaos control in a discrete-time mosquito model. Comput. Ecol. Softw. **7**, 153–166 (2017)
12. Nakagawa, S., Saito, T.: An RCOTA hysteresis chaos generator. IEEE Trans. Circ. Syst. I Fundam. Theor. Appl. **43**, 1019–1021 (1996)

13. Sprott, J.C.: Simple chaotic systems and circuits. Am. J. Phys. **68**, 758–763 (2000)
14. Ozoguz, S., Elwakil, A., Kennedy, M.P.: Experimental verification of the butterfly attractor in a modified Lorenz system. Inter. J. Bifurcat. Chaos **12**, 1627–1632 (2002)
15. Elwakil, A., Kennedy, M.: Construction of classes of circuit-independent chaotic oscillators using passive-only nonlinear devices. IEEE Trans. Circ. Syst. I: Fundam. Theor. Appl. **48**, 289–307 (2001)
16. Yu, S., Lü, J.H., Tang, W.K.S., Chen, G.: A general multi-scroll Lorenz system family and its realization via digital signal processors. Chaos **16**, 033126 (2006)
17. Farajallah, M., Assad, S.E., Deforges, O.: Fast and secure chaos-based cryptosystem for images. Inter. J. Bifurcat. Chaos **26**, 1650021-1–1650021-21 (2016)
18. Assad, S.E.: Chaos based information hiding and security. IEEE Internet Technol. Secur. Trans. Int. Conf. **7196**, 67–72 (2016)
19. Noshadian, S., Ebrahimzade, A., Kazemitabar, S.J.: Optimizing chaos based image encryption. Multimed. Tools Appli. **1**, 01–22 (2018)
20. Zhao, Y., University, A.: Research on text chaos classification technology based on improved SVM. Modern Electron. Tech. **39**, 39–43 (2016)
21. Jafari, S., Pham, V.T., Moghtadaei, M., Kingni, S.T.: The relationship between chaotic maps and some chaotic systems with hidden attractors. Inter. J. Bifurcat. Chaos **26**, 527–530 (2016)
22. Wang, Q.X., Yu, S.M., Li, C.Q., Lü, J.H., Fang, X.L., Guyeux, C.: Theoretical design and FPGA-based implementation of higher-dimensional digital chaotic systems. IEEE Trans. Circ. Syst. I Regul. Pap. **63**, 401–412 (2016)
23. Li, C.B., Sprott, J.C., Xing, H.Y.: Constructing chaotic systems with conditional symmetry. Nonlinear Dyn. **87**, 1351–1358 (2017)
24. Zhang, W.W., Ran-Chao, W.U.: Dual projective synchronization of fractional-order chaotic systems with a linear controller. Appl. Math. Mech. **37**, 710–717 (2016)
25. Wang, Z.L., Ma, J., Cang, S.J., Wang, Z.H., Chen, Z.Q.: Simplified hyper-chaotic systems generating multi-wing non-equilibrium attractors. Optik Int. J. Light Electr. Opt. **127**, 2424–2431 (2016)

Enhanced Biogeography-Based Optimization for Flow-Shop Scheduling

Yi-Chen Du[1], Min-Xia Zhang[1], Ci-Yun Cai[1], and Yu-Jun Zheng[1,2(✉)]

[1] College of Computer Science and Technology, Zhejiang University of Technology,
Hangzhou 310023, China
yujun.zheng@computer.org
[2] Institute of Service Engineering, Hangzhou Normal University,
Hangzhou 311121, China

Abstract. Flow-shop scheduling problem (FSP) is a well-known NP-hard combinatorial optimization problem that occurs in many practical applications. Traditional algorithms are only capable of solving small-size FSP instances, and thus many metaheuristic algorithms have been proposed for efficiently solving large-size instances. However, most existing algorithms still suffer from low convergence speed and/or premature convergence. In this paper, we propose an enhanced biogeography-based optimization (BBO) algorithm framework for FSP, which uses the largest ranked value representation for solution encoding, employs the NEH method to improve the initial population, and designs a reinsertion local search operator based on the job with the longest waiting time (JLWT) to enhance exploitation ability. We respectively use the original BBO migration, blended migration, hybrid BBO and DE migration, and ecogeography-based migration to implement the framework. Experimental results on test instances demonstrate the effectiveness of the proposed BBO algorithms, among which the ecogeography-based optimization (EBO) algorithm version exhibits the best performance.

Keywords: Flow-shop scheduling problem (FSP)
Biogeography-based optimization (BBO)
Ecogeography-based optimization (EBO) · Local search

1 Introduction

Flow-shop scheduling problem (FSP) is a well-known combinatorial optimization problem which plays a significant role in many practical applications [23]. It is known to be NP-hard when the number of machines is larger than two [5]. Thus, traditional algorithms such as mathematical programming and branch-and-bound [8,18,24,30,40] can only solve small-size or medium-size FSP instances. In recent decades, a number of studies have been conducted on the use of bio-inspired metaheuristics including evolutionary algorithms (EAs) and swarm intelligence algorithms to solve large-size FSP instances. Etiler et al. [2]

© Springer Nature Singapore Pte Ltd. 2018
J. Qiao et al. (Eds.): BIC-TA 2018, CCIS 951, pp. 295–306, 2018.
https://doi.org/10.1007/978-981-13-2826-8_26

develop a genetic algorithm (GA) for FSP, where crossover and mutation operators are similar to that for TSP, and the results show that the performance of GA is better than some well-known exact and approximate heuristic algorithms. Low et al. [15] propose a simulated annealing (SA) algorithm which can restart the search procedure in different regions of the solution space and thus make the solution quality more robust. Onwubolu and Davendra [21] propose a differential evolution (DE) algorithm for FSP, which uses a forward transformation method for transforming integer variables into continuous variables for the internal representation of solution vectors, and its performance is shown to be better than GA. Liao et al. [12] present a discrete particle swarm optimization (PSO) which redefines the particle velocity and movement for FSP and incorporates a local search scheme to improve performance. In [10] Kuo et al. present another PSO algorithm that combines random-key encoding and individual enhancement for solving FSP. Lin [13] proposes a hybrid biogeography-based optimization (BBO) and opposition-based learning method for FSP, which shows better performance than a number of other metaheuristics. Zhao et al. [34] apply the water wave optimization (WWO) metaheuristic [36] to FSP by using a greedy procedure with a changing removing size as the propagation operator and using an insertion-based local search as the breaking operator. Other EAs for FSP can also be found in literature such as [7,17,26,29,35], and interested readers can refer to [6] for a survey of heuristic/metaheuristic algorithms for FSP.

In this paper, we propose a new enhanced BBO algorithm for FSP. The algorithm employs the largest ranked value (LRV) representation for solution encoding, uses the Nawaz-Enscore-Ham (NEH) method [19] to improve the initial population, and designs a reinsertion operator based the longest waiting time to enhance local search. Experiments show that the proposed algorithm outperforms a set of state-of-the-art algorithms on a number of test instances.

The rest of this paper is organized as follows. Section 2 presents the problem formulation, Sect. 3 proposes the enhanced BBO algorithm for FSP, Sect. 4 presents the experimental results, and Sect. 5 concludes.

2   Problem Description

FSP is to schedule n independent jobs $\{J_1, J_2, ..., J_n\}$ on m machines $\{M_1, M_2, ..., M_m\}$. Each job contains exactly m operations. The j-th operation of each job J_i must be executed on the j-th machine, where the execution time t_{ij} is specified $(1 \leq i \leq n; 1 \leq j \leq m)$. No machine can perform more than one operation simultaneously.

The problem needs to decide an execution sequence (permutation) $\pi = \{\pi_1, \pi_2, ..., \pi_n\}$ of the n jobs. Let $C(\pi_i, j)$ denote the completion time of job π_i on machine M_j. For the first machine M_1 we have:

$$C(\pi_1, 1) = t_{\pi_1, 1} \tag{1}$$

$$C(\pi_i, 1) = C(\pi_{i-1}, 1) + t_{\pi_i, 1}, \quad i = 2, ..., n \tag{2}$$

The first job π_1 can be processed on machine M_j immediately after it is completed on machine M_{j-1}:

$$C(\pi_1, j) = C(\pi_1, j - 1) + t_{\pi_1, j}, \quad j = 2, ..., m \tag{3}$$

Each subsequent job π_i can be processed on machine M_j only when the following two conditions are satisfied: (1) The job π_i has been completed on machine M_{j-1}; (2) Its previous job π_{i-1} has been completed on machine M_j. So we have:

$$C(\pi_i, j) = \max\{C(\pi_{i-1}, j), C(\pi_i, j - 1)\} + t_{\pi_i, j}, \quad i = 2, ..., n; j = 2, ..., m \tag{4}$$

Thus the makespan of π is:

$$C_{\max}(\pi) = C(\pi_n, m) \tag{5}$$

The goal of the problem is to find an optimal π^* in the set Π of all possible sequences to minimize the makespan:

$$C_{\max}(\pi^*) = \min_{\pi \in \Pi} C_{\max}(\pi) \tag{6}$$

To improve practicability of FSP, we can pose a due time $d(\pi_i)$ for each job J_i:

$$C(\pi_i, m) \leq d(\pi_i), \quad i = 1, 2, ..., n \tag{7}$$

Using the penalty function method, the objective function (6) can be transformed as follows (where M is a large positive number):

$$f(\pi) = \min \left(C_{\max}(\pi) + M \sum_{i=1}^{n} \max(C(\pi_i, m) - d(\pi_i), 0) \right) \tag{8}$$

3   Enhanced Biogeography-Based Optimization Algorithms for FSP

We propose a new enhanced BBO algorithm for efficiently solving FSP. Initially proposed by Simon [31], BBO is a metaheuristic algorithm borrowing ideas from island biogeographical evolution for optimization problems. In BBO, each solution is analogous to a habitat, the solution fitness is analogous to the habitat suitability index (HSI), and each solution component is analogous to an suitability index variables (SIV). As most other EAs, BBO solves a problem by continually evolving a population of solutions. The distinct features of BBO is that it evolves solutions by mimicking the migration and mutation process in biogeography.

As the initial BBO algorithm cannot directly handle permutation-based solutions, here we adapt the algorithm in the following aspects.

3.1 Solution Encoding and Population Initialization

If directly encoding each FSP solution as a permutation of jobs (or job numbers), we need to design special evolutionary operators to manipulate FSP solutions. Many studies have been done this direction [3]. Here we employ the real number vector encoding, i.e., each solution is encoded as a real number vector. We transform each real number vector to a discrete job permutation based on largest ranked value (LRV) representation [11], where the largest value of the vector is firstly picked as the first order of a job permutation, and then the second largest value is picked as the second one, and so on. In this way, the original evolutionary operators of many EAs (including BBO) can be directly applied.

For example, consider a FSP instance of six jobs, given a solution vector [0.72, 0.65, 0.33, 0.95, 0.23, 0.83], since the largest value is 0.95, the dimension $j = 4$ is picked and assigned a rank value of 1; then, the second largest dimension $j = 6$ is picked and assigned a rank value of 2; by analogy, finally we can obtain the job permutation $\pi = [3, 4, 5, 1, 6, 2]$.

Although most metaheuristics are general-purpose algorithms for a variety of problems, incorporating some problem-specific mechanisms can often improve the problem-solving performance. NEH method [19] is such a problem-specific method, which uses a greedy strategy to construct solution as described in Algorithm 1 .

Algorithm 1. The NEH method [19].

---

1 For each job J_i, compute $T_i = \sum_{j=1}^{n} t_{ij}$, the total processing time on all machines;

2 Sort the job set in increasing order of T_i;

3 Let $k = 2$, take the first two jobs to construct a permutation π that minimizes the makespan;

4 **while** $k < n$ **do**

5   Let $k = k + 1$, take the k-th job, temporarily insert it into all possible k positions in π, and finally select the position which has the minimum makespan to insert the job;

6 **return** π.

NEH method cannot guarantee to find the optimal solution to FSP. Experiments show that, although NEH has good performance on some small-size instances, it does not work well on large-size instances. Nevertheless, the solution obtained by NEH has some useful information that can contribute to the search of other algorithms [3].

Our BBO algorithm for FSP employs NEH in the stage of population initiation. That is, we first use NEH to generate a job sequence π, and then randomly initialize a population of N solutions (real-value vectors), among which randomly select a solution worse than π and replace it with π.

3.2   Migration

The key mechanism of BBO is migration, which is to share information among solutions. In BBO, each solution H_i is analogous to a habitat and is assigned with an immigration rate λ_i and an emigration rate μ_i. Here we calculate the migration rates as follows:

$$\lambda_i = I\frac{f(H_i) - f_{\min} + \epsilon}{f_{\max} - f_{\min} + \epsilon} \tag{9}$$

$$\mu_i = E\frac{f_{\max} - f(H_i) + \epsilon}{f_{\max} - f_{\min} + \epsilon} \tag{10}$$

where $f_{\max}$ and $f_{\min}$ are the maximum and minimum fitness among the population, ϵ is a small positive number to avoid division-by-zero, and I and E are the maximum possible immigration rate and emigration rate which are typically set to 1. In this way, better solutions have higher emigration rates and lower immigration rates, and thus tend to share more information with worse solutions. Figure 1 illustrates the migration model.

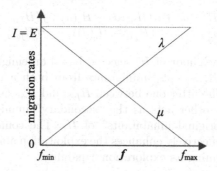

Fig. 1. Illustration of the migration model of BBO.

In the original BBO, at each iteration of the algorithm, each dimension d of each solution H_i has a probability of λ_i to be immigrated and, if so, an emigrating solution H_j is selected with a probability proportional to μ_j, and $H_i(d)$ will be set to $H_j(d)$.

However, the clonal migration operator of the original BBO limits the diversity of the solutions. Ma et al. [16] propose a blended migration operator that mixes each component of an immigrating solution H_i with the corresponding component of the emigrating solution H_j as follows:

$$H_i(d) = \alpha H_i(d) + (1 - \alpha)H_j(d) \tag{11}$$

where α is a real number between [0,1].

Zheng et al. [37,39] equip BBO with a local topology where each solution is only connected to a part of other solutions in the population, and migration can only occur between neighbors. Zheng et al. [37] also propose a hybrid BBO migration and DE mutation operator as follows:

$$H_i(d) = \begin{cases} H_{r_1}(d) + F(H_{r_2}(d) - H_{r_3}(d)), & rand() < c_r \\ H_j(d), & else \end{cases} \tag{12}$$

where r_1, r_2 and r_3 are three mutually distinct random indices of the population, F is the differential weight, c_r is the crossover rate, and $rand()$ generates a random number uniformly distributed between $[0,1]$.

Zheng et al. [38] propose a major improvement of BBO, named ecogeography-based optimization (EBO), which allows both local migration between neighboring solutions and global migration between non-neighboring solutions. Local migration on each dimension d of solution H_i is conducted as follows:

$$H_i(d) = H_i(d) + \alpha(H_{nb}(d) - H_i(d)) \tag{13}$$

where H_{nb} is a neighbor of H_i selected based on emigration rate, and the item $(H_{nb}(d) - H_i(d))$ represents the "ecological differentiation" between the two habitats. The global migration is conducted as follows:

$$H_i(d) = \begin{cases} H_{far}(d) + \alpha(H_{nb}(d) - H_i(d)), & f(H_{far}) \leq f(H_{nb}) \\ H_{nb}(d) + \alpha(H_{far} - H_i(d)), & f(H_{far}) > f(H_{nb}) \end{cases} \tag{14}$$

where H_{far} is a non-neighbor of H_i selected based on emigration rate. That is, in global migration H_i accepts immigrants from both a neighbor H_{nb} and a non-neighbor H_{far}: The fitter one between H_{far} and H_{nb} acts as the "primary" immigrant, while the other acts as the "secondary" immigrant that needs to compete with the "original inhabitants" of H_i. The combination of the two migration operators effectively enhances the exploitation ability of the algorithm without seriously harming its exploration capability.

3.3   Mutation

In the original BBO, the mutation operator simply changes an SIV to a random value in the predefined range. Using the real-number encoding scheme based on LRV, a component is simply mutated to a random value in $[0,1]$, which is equal to change the position of the corresponding job. To improve solution diversity, we add the following two mutation operators:

– Randomly exchanging two components in the solution vector, which is equal to exchange the positions of the corresponding jobs.
– Randomly reversing a subsequence in the solution vector, which is equal to reverse the subsequence of the corresponding jobs.

These three mutations are called basic mutation, exchange mutation, and reverse mutation, respectively.

3.4 Enhancing Local Search

It is known that local search can effectively improve the convergence speed as well as solution quality [9]. We design a reinsert local search based on the job with the longest waiting time (JLWT) to enhance the BBO for FSP. The waiting time τ_{ij} of job π_i on machine M_j is:

$$\tau_{ij} = \min\left(C(\pi_{i-1}, j) - C(\pi_i, j - 1), 0\right) \tag{15}$$

And the total waiting time T_{ij} of job π_i on all machines is:

$$T_{ij} = \sum_{j=2}^{m} \tau_{ij} \tag{16}$$

The local search operator takes the job with maximum T_i from the permutation, temporarily reinserts it into the other $(n-1)$ positions, and replaces the solution with the best one among the $(n-1)$ solutions if it is better than the original solution.

3.5 The Algorithm Framework

Algorithm 2 presents the framework of BBO for FSP. We implement the framework with four versions, using the original BBO migration [31], blended migration [16], Local-DE/BBO migration [37], and ecogeography-based migration [38]. The corresponding algorithm versions are denoted as BBO, B-BBO, LDB, and EBO, respectively.

Algorithm 2. The BBO algorithm for FSP.

---

1 Randomly initialize a population of solutions to the problem, including a
   solution x produced by NEH algorithm;
2 Select the best solution H^* among the population;
3 **while** *the stop condition is not satisfied* **do**
4   Apply the LRV rule to convert each solution to the job permutation, and
     evaluate the objective function of the solution;
5   Calculate the migration rates of the solutions according to Eqs. (9) and (10);
6   **foreach** *solution H in the population* **do**
7   Perform BBO migration on H to produce a new solution H';
8   **if** $f(H') < f(H)$ **then**
9   Replace H with H' in the population;
10   **if** $f(H') < f(H^*$ **then**
11                 $H^* \leftarrow H$;
12   Perform JLWT-based local search on H^*;
13   **else**
14   Randomly select one of the general, exchanging, and reverse
             mutations;
15   Perform the mutation on H';
16 **return** $\mathbf{x}^*$.

---

4   Computational Experiments

We select ten FSP test instances from [27,32], and test the proposed five BBO algorithms with the following four popular algorithms:

- A hybrid BBO algorithm in [33], denoted by HBBO.
- A PSO-based memetic algorithm in [14], denoted by PSOM.
- A hybrid DE algorithm in [25], denoted by HDE.
- A discrete cuckoo search algorithm [1], denoted by CSA.
- A linkage mining in block-based evolutionary algorithm in [7], denoted by LMBEA.

The proposed four BBO versions use the same parameter setting where the population size $N = 50$, the maximum migration rates $I = E = 1$, the maximum mutation rate $\pi_{max} = 0.06$, and the three mutations have the same probability. The parameters of the other four algorithms are set as suggested in their literatures.

For a fair comparison, the maximum number of objective function evaluations is set to 50000 for all algorithms. On each problem instance, we run each algorithm for 30 times with different random seeds, and record the best makespan C_{best}, the worst makespan C_{worst}, and the average makespan C_{avg} over the 30 runs. For ease of comparison, we use the following three metrics based on the best known makespan C^* of each instance to normalize the results:

- BRE: the best relative error with C^*.

$$\text{BRE} = \frac{C_{best} - C^*}{C^*} \times 100\% \qquad (17)$$

- ARE: the average relative error with C^*.

$$\text{ARE} = \frac{C_{avg} - C^*}{C^*} \times 100\% \qquad (18)$$

- WRE: the worst relative error with C^*.

$$\text{WRE} = \frac{C_{worst} - C^*}{C^*} \times 100\% \qquad (19)$$

Table 1 shows the experimental results of the comparative algorithms on the test instances.

As we can see from the results, all the BBO algorithms achieve better results than PSOM, HDE, and CSA, which indicates that the BBO metaheuristic strategy is effective for FSP. LMBEA is one of the most competitive algorithms in the literature, and its performance is better than the original BBO and HBBO, similar to B-BBO, but worse than LDB and EBO. Among the four versions of our BBO algorithm framework, only the original BBO performs worse than HBBO, mainly because its clonal-based migration limits the solution diversity. The other three versions perform much better than HBBO, which demonstrates the effectiveness of the proposed migration, mutation, and local search operators.

Table 1. The experimental results on the benchmark instances of FSP.

Instance	$n \times m$	C^*	Metric	PSOM	HDE	CSA	LMBEA	BBO	HBBO	B-BBO	LDB	EBO
rec01	20*5	1247	BRE	0	0	0	0	0	0	0	0	0
			ARE	$0.144^\dagger$	$0.152^\dagger$	0	0	$0.031^\dagger$	$0.016^\dagger$	0	0	0
			WRE	0.160	0.220	0	0.052	0	0.160	0	0	0
rec07	20*10	1566	BRE	0	0	0	0	0	0	0	0	0
			ARE	$0.986^\dagger$	$0.920^\dagger$	$0.351^\dagger$	$0.270^\dagger$	$0.731^\dagger$	0	$0.322^\dagger$	$0.125^\dagger$	0
			WRE	1.149	1.108	0.833	0.859	0.980	0	0.859	0.813	0
rec13	20*15	1930	BRE	0.259	0.259	0	0	0	0	0	0	0
			ARE	$0.893^\dagger$	$0.705^\dagger$	$0.397^\dagger$	$0.242^\dagger$	$0.509^\dagger$	$0.238^\dagger$	$0.196^\dagger$	$0.167^\dagger$	0
			WRE	1.502	1.719	1.305	0.985	1.502	0.985	1.263	0.985	0
rec19	30*10	2093	BRE	0.430	0.287	0	0	0.287	0.287	0	0	0
			ARE	$1.313^\dagger$	$0.908^\dagger$	$0.198^\dagger$	$0.221^\dagger$	$0.926^\dagger$	$0.401^\dagger$	$0.381^\dagger$	$0.275^\dagger$	0.126
			WRE	2.102	1.899	1.101	0.860	1.753	0.860	0.860	0.860	0.287
rec25	30*15	2513	BRE	0.835	0.676	0	0	0	0	0	0	0
			ARE	$2.085^\dagger$	$1.429^\dagger$	$0.565^\dagger$	$0.311^\dagger$	$0.733^\dagger$	$0.541^\dagger$	$0.480^\dagger$	$0.318^\dagger$	0.133
			WRE	3.233	3.233	1.700	1.050	1.154	1.154	1.154	0.676	0.541
rec31	50*10	3045	BRE	1.510	0.427	0.317	0.193	0.427	0.263	0.263	0	0
			ARE	$2.254^\dagger$	$1.192^\dagger$	$0.406^\dagger$	$0.367^\dagger$	$1.035^\dagger$	$0.450^\dagger$	$0.399^\dagger$	$0.287^\dagger$	0.163
			WRE	2.692	2.108	1.149	1.149	1.510	1.149	1.149	0.427	0.263
rec37	75*20	4951	BRE	2.101	1.697	1.458	1.133	1.697	1.353	1.353	1.133	1.133
			ARE	$3.537^\dagger$	$2.632^\dagger$	$1.898^\dagger$	$1.602^\dagger$	$2.367^\dagger$	$1.759^\dagger$	$1.653^\dagger$	$1.517^\dagger$	1.368
			WRE	4.039	4.039	2.705	2.101	3.860	2.262	2.101	2.101	1.697
ta082	100*20	6183	BRE	1.889	2.011	1.889	1.665	2.033	1.665	1.715	1.459	0.921
			ARE	$2.262^\dagger$	$2.515^\dagger$	$2.079^\dagger$	$1.985^\dagger$	$2.322^\dagger$	$1.927^\dagger$	$1.806^\dagger$	$1.717^\dagger$	1.300
			WRE	2.748	2.794	2.603	2.451	2.603	2.156	2.033	1.908	1.789
ta091	200*10	10862	BRE	2.318	2.209	2.318	2.088	2.318	2.209	2.318	2.100	1.215
			ARE	$3.709^\dagger$	$3.060^\dagger$	$3.137^\dagger$	$2.928^\dagger$	$3.335^\dagger$	$2.825^\dagger$	$2.757^\dagger$	$2.505^\dagger$	1.846
			WRE	5.122	4.393	3.695	3.555	3.830	3.210	3.069	2.758	2.088
ta105	200*20	11259	BRE	3.538	3.620	3.466	3.466	3.499	3.387	3.387	2.996	2.751
			ARE	$4.224^\dagger$	$4.309^\dagger$	$4.103^\dagger$	$3.928^\dagger$	$4.187^\dagger$	$3.679^\dagger$	$3.606^\dagger$	$3.209^\dagger$	3.053
			WRE	5.565	5.299	4.620	4.512	4.870	4.024	3.954	3.618	3.275

Among all nine algorithms, the overall performance of EBO is the best. In particular, CSA, LMBEA, B-BBO, LDE and EBO can obtain the optimal makespan on the first five instances (the BRE values are 0), but only LDE and EBO can do so on the sixth instances. Among the 30 runs, CSA, LMBEA, B-BBO, LDE and EBO always obtain the optimum on rec01 (the VRE values are 0), HBBO and EBO always obtain the optimum on Rec07, and only EBO always obtain the optima on Rec13. This indicates that the proposed mutation operator can effectively improve population diversity in very large solution spaces, and the local search operator enables extensive exploitation around promising solutions to reach the optimum.

Moreover, we conduct paired t-tests between the result of EBO and each of the other algorithms on each instance, and mark a superscript $\dagger$ after the corresponding ARE value if EBO has statistically significant performance improvement over the corresponding algorithms (at 95% confidence level). The results show that EBO is statistically significantly better than PSOM, HDE, and BBO on all the ten test instances, and significantly better than CSA, LMBEA, HBBO,

B-BBO, and LDE on nine instances (except rec01). With increasing instance size, the performance advantages of EBO become more obvious, which demonstrates the good scalability of EBO for solving large-size FSP instances.

5   Conclusion

In this paper, we propose a class of BBO algorithms for efficiently solving FSP. The algorithm framework uses the largest ranked value solution representation, employs the NEH method to improve the initial population, and designs a reinsertion local search operator based on the JLWT to enhance exploitation ability. We implement the framework with four algorithm versions, which use the original BBO migration, blended migration, hybrid BBO and DE migration, and ecogeography-based migration, respectively. Experimental results demonstrate that the BBO algorithms are effective in solving the benchmark FSP instances, and the EBO version exhibits the best performance.

Our ongoing work includes two aspects. The first is to enhance the BBO algorithms by using multiple types of local search operators and developing a dynamic adaptive mechanism for choosing among the operators (like [14] and other memetic algorithms [20,29]). The second is to extend our algorithm framework for more complex versions of FSP, such as hybrid FSP [28], FSP with fuzzy/stochastical processing time [4], and multi-stage FSP [22].

Acknowledgements. This work is supported by National Natural Science Foundation (Grant No. 61473263) and Zhejiang Provincial Natural Science Foundation (Grant No. LY14F030011) of China.

References

1. Dasgupta, P., Das, S.: A discrete inter-species cuckoo search for flowshop scheduling problems. Comput. Oper. Res. **60**, 111–120 (2015)
2. Etiler, O., Toklu, B., Atak, M., Wilson, J.: A genetic algorithm for flow shop scheduling problems. J. Oper. Res. Soc. **55**(8), 830–835 (2004)
3. Framinan, J., Gupta, J., Leisten, R.: A review and classification of heuristics for permutation flow-shop scheduling with makespan objective. J. Oper. Res. Soc. **55**, 1243–1255 (2004)
4. Fu, Y., Ding, J., Wang, H., Wang, J.: Two-objective stochastic flow-shop scheduling with deteriorating and learning effect in Industry 4.0-based manufacturing system. Appl. Soft Comput. **68**, 847–855 (2018)
5. Garey, M.R., Johnson, D.S., Sethi, R.: The complexity of flowshop and jobshop scheduling. Math. Oper. Res. **1**(2), 117–129 (1976)
6. Gupta, U., Kumar, S.: Minimization of weighted sum of total tardiness and make span in no wait flow shop scheduling using different heuristic algorithm: a review. Int. J. Adv. Eng. Sci. **5**(4), 1–10 (2015)
7. Hsu, C.Y., Chang, P.C., Chen, M.H.: A linkage mining in block-based evolutionary algorithm for permutation flowshop scheduling problem. Comput. Ind. Eng. **83**, 159–171 (2015)

8. Karlof, J.K., Wang, W.: Bilevel programming applied to the flow shop scheduling problem. Comput. Oper. Res. **23**(5), 443–451 (1996)
9. Krasnogor, N., Smith, J.: A memetic algorithm with self-adaptive local search: TSP as a case study. In: Proceedings of the 2nd Annual Conference on Genetic and Evolutionary Computation, pp. 987–994. Morgan Kaufmann Publishers Inc. (2000)
10. Kuo, I.H., et al.: An efficient flow-shop scheduling algorithm based on a hybrid particle swarm optimization model. Expert Syst. Appl. **36**(3), 7027–7032 (2009)
11. Liang, J.J., Pan, Q.K., Tiejun, C., Wang, L.: Solving the blocking flow shop scheduling problem by a dynamic multi-swarm particle swarm optimizer. Int. J. Adv. Manuf. Technol. **55**(5), 755–762 (2011)
12. Liao, C.J., Tseng, C.T., Luarn, P.: A discrete version of particle swarm optimization for flowshop scheduling problems. Comput. Oper. Res. **34**(10), 3099–3111 (2007)
13. Lin, J.: A hybrid discrete biogeography-based optimization for the permutation flow-shop scheduling problem. Int. J. Prod. Res. **54**(16), 4805–4814 (2016)
14. Liu, B., Wang, L., Jin, Y.H.: An effective PSO-based memetic algorithm for flow shop scheduling. IEEE Trans. Syst. Man Cybern. Part B **37**(1), 18–27 (2007)
15. Low, C., Yeh, J.Y., Huang, K.I.: A robust simulated annealing heuristic for flow shop scheduling problems. Int. J. Adv. Manuf. Technol. **23**(9–10), 762–767 (2004)
16. Ma, H., Simon, D.: Blended biogeography-based optimization for constrained optimization. Engin. Appl. Artif. Intell. **24**(3), 517–525 (2011)
17. Marichelvam, M.K.: An improved hybrid cuckoo search (IHCS) metaheuristics algorithm for permutation flow shop scheduling problems. Int. J. Bio-Inspired. Comput. **4**(4), 200–205 (2012)
18. Mcmahon, G.B., Burton, P.G.: Flow-shop scheduling with the branch-and-bound method. Oper. Res. **15**(3), 473–481 (1967)
19. Nawaz, M., Enscore, E.E., Ham, I.: A heuristic algorithm for the m-machine, n-job flow-shop sequencing problem. Omega **11**(1), 91–95 (1983)
20. Ong, Y.S., Keane, A.J.: Meta-Lamarckian learning in memetic algorithms. IEEE Trans. Evol. Comput. **8**(2), 99–110 (2004)
21. Onwubolu, G., Davendra, D.: Scheduling flow shops using differential evolution algorithm. Eur. J. Oper. Res. **171**(2), 674–692 (2006)
22. Paternina, A.C.D., Montoya, T.J.R., Acero, D.M.J., Herrera, H.M.C.: Scheduling jobs on a k-stage flexible flow-shop. Ann. Oper. Res. **164**(1), 29–40 (2008)
23. Pinedo, M.: Scheduling Theory, Algorithms, and Systems, 2nd edn. Prentice Hall, Upper Saddle River (2002)
24. Potts, C.N., Baker, K.R.: Flow shop scheduling with lot streaming. Oper. Res. Lett. **8**, 297–303 (1989)
25. Qian, B., Wang, L., Hu, R., Wang, W.L., Huang, D.X., Wang, X.: A hybrid differential evolution method for permutation flow-shop scheduling. Int. J. Adv. Manuf. Technol. **38**(7–8), 757–777 (2008)
26. Rajendran, C., Ziegler, H.: Ant-colony algorithms for permutation flowshop scheduling to minimize makespan/total flowtime of jobs. Euro. J. Oper. Res. **155**(2), 426–438 (2004)
27. Reeves, C.R., Yamada, T.: Genetic algorithms, path relinking, and the flowshop sequencing problem. Evol. Comput. **6**(1), 45–60 (1998)
28. Ruiz, R., Vázquez-Rodríguez, J.A.: The hybrid flow shop scheduling problem. Eur. J. Oper. Res. **205**(1), 1–18 (2010)
29. Santucci, V., Baioletti, M., Milani, A.: Algebraic differential evolution algorithm for the permutation flowshop scheduling problem with total flowtime criterion. IEEE Trans. Evol. Comput. **20**(5), 682–694 (2016)

306   Y.-C. Du et al.

30. Selen, W.J., Hott, D.D.: A mixed-integer goal-programming formulation of the standard flow-shop scheduling problem. J. Oper. Res. Society **37**(12), 1121–1128 (1986)
31. Simon, D.: Biogeography-based optimization. IEEE Trans. Evol. Comput. **12**(6), 702–713 (2008)
32. Taillard, E.: Benchmarks for basic scheduling problems. Euro. J. Oper. Res. **64**(2), 278–285 (1993)
33. Yin, M., Li, X.: A hybrid bio-geography based optimization for permutation flow shop scheduling. Sci. Res. Essays **6**, 2078–2100 (2011)
34. Zhao, F., Liu, H., Zhang, Y., Ma, W., Zhang, C.: A discrete water wave optimization algorithm for no-wait flow shop scheduling problem. Expert Syst. Appl. **91**, 347–363 (2018)
35. Zhao, F., Zhang, J., Wang, J., Zhang, C.: A shuffled complex evolution algorithm with opposition-based learning for a permutation flow shop scheduling problem. Int. J. Comput. Integ. Manuf. **28**(11), 1220–1235 (2015)
36. Zheng, Y.J.: Water wave optimization: a new nature-inspired metaheuristic. Comput. Oper. Res. **55**(1), 1–11 (2015)
37. Zheng, Y.J., Ling, H.F., Wu, X.B., Xue, J.Y.: Localized biogeography-based optimization. Soft Comput. **18**(11), 2323–2334 (2014)
38. Zheng, Y.J., Ling, H.F., Xue, J.Y.: Ecogeography-based optimization: enhancing biogeography-based optimization with ecogeographic barriers and differentiations. Comput. Oper. Res. **50**, 115–127 (2014)
39. Zheng, Y., Wu, X., Ling, H., Chen, S.: A simplified biogeography-based optimization using a ring topology. In: Tan, Y., Shi, Y., Mo, H. (eds.) ICSI 2013. LNCS, vol. 7928, pp. 330–337. Springer, Heidelberg (2013). https://doi.org/10.1007/978-3-642-38703-6_39
40. Ziaee, M., Sadjadi, S.: Mixed binary integer programming formulations for the flow shop scheduling problems. a case study: ISD projects scheduling. Appl. Math. Comput. **185**(1), 218–228 (2007)

A Weighted Bagging LightGBM Model for Potential lncRNA-Disease Association Identification

Xin Chen and Xiangrong Liu[✉]

Department of Computer Science, Xiamen University, Xiamen 361005, China
xrliu@xmu.edu.cn

Abstract. There is increasing evidence that long non-coding RNAs (lncRNAs) are closely related to many human diseases. Developing powerful computational models for potential lncRNA-disease association identification would facilitate biomarker identification and drug discovery for human disease diagnosis, treatment, prognosis and prevention. Now there exist a number of methods specially for this problem based on inductive matrix completion, random walk or classification. In terms of this issue, classification has just come to the fore. Extracting important features from disease network and RNA network, namely network embedding, is the top priority. Moreover, taking the complexity into consideration, genetic algorithm is adopted to tune the hyper-parameters of our network embedding model. Due to a lack of negative samples, we also exploit Positive-Unlabeled (PU) learning to help out. In brief, we propose a weighted bagging lightGBM model for lncRNA-disease association prediction based on network embedding and PU learning.

Keywords: lncRNA-disease association identification
Network embedding · Genetic algorithm · PU learning

1 Introduction

It is commonly accepted that genetic information is included in protein coding genes, which are regarded as the infallible law of molecular biology [1,2]. Hence, RNA is merely thought to be a translator between a DNA sequence and its encoded protein for a considerable long time [3]. However, as the ENCODE project was completed, researchers observed that contrary to only about 1.5% of human genome encoding proteins [4], about 74.7% are transcribed [5]. Growing evidences demonstrate that non-coding RNAs (ncRNAs) are involved in many biological processes. Specially, lncRNAs are critical ncRNAs with the length more than 200 nt [6–8]. A large number of evidences have elucidated that most lncRNAs play significant roles in transcription, translation, splicing, differentiation, epigenetic regulation, immune responses, cell cycle control and so on [9]. Accordingly, mutation and dysregulation of lncRNAs could result in multifarious human diseases, including breast cancer, lung cancer, Alzheimer's disease and others [7].

© Springer Nature Singapore Pte Ltd. 2018
J. Qiao et al. (Eds.): BIC-TA 2018, CCIS 951, pp. 307–314, 2018.
https://doi.org/10.1007/978-981-13-2826-8_27

Though the detailed mechanism of LncRNAs is not extraordinarily explicit, it's generally believed that lncRNAs are conducive to disease diagnosis and treatment. Predicting lncRNA-disease associations is not only helpful in disease therapy, but also of great benefit to figure out biological processes. Of course, computational methods can help to reduce the time and cost of experiments.

LncRNA disease association identification has been intensively investigated. Existing computing methods can be divided into three categories. Methods in the first category identify lncRNA-disease associations based on matrix computation. Chen and Yan [10] used Laplacian regularized least squares to identify possible associations between lncRNAs and diseases based on a semi-supervised learning method LRLSLDA. Methods in the second category use random walk models to identify potential associations. Jie Sun [11] implemented the random walk with restart method on a lncRNA functional similarity network, formulating a global network-based computational framework, RWRLncD, to infer potential human lncRNA-disease associations. Methods in the third category take use of classification model. Lan [12] predicts potential lncRNA-disease associations by using a bagging SVM classifier, LDAP, on the basis of lncRNA similarity and disease similarity.

We put this problem as a classification problem. We utilize a weighted bagging lightGBM method to predict lncRNA-disease association. Firstly, genetic algorithm is employed to obtain an adaptive network embedding model to extract significant features. In addition, according to the characteristics of the corresponding disease and lncRNA in the known associations, samples with unknown lncRNA-disease association are assigned different sampling weights. Lastly, a lightGBM classifier outputs the probability that the samples are positive. The flowchart is shown in Fig. 1.

2   Method

First of all, through our network embedding model, the disease functional similarity network and lncRNA sequence similarity network are effectively represented by lower dimensional vectors. Concatenating these vectors, one sample after another can be acquired, which will be classified via a weighted bagging lightGBM model.

2.1   Network Embedding

Deep neural networks have excellent capability but significant trial and error besides experience is required to achieve good performance. With the depth increasing, the performance of such networks continuously improves [13]. Therefore, developing methods to automatically explore optimal network architectures is urgent and indispensable. The number of layers, choice of activation functions, number of filters in convolutional layers are extremely important in creating deep neural networks [14]. Hence, we pursue genetic algorithm to adjust the parameters of neural network for network embedding according to input data. The key

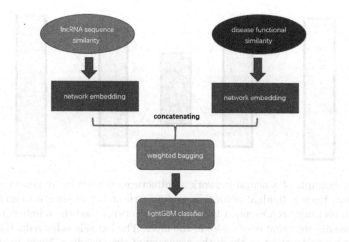

Fig. 1. The flowchart of our method is shown here, including basic steps to predict potential disease-related lncRNAs. We extract informative features from lncRNA sequence similarity network and disease functional similarity network based on network embedding model, respectively. The two extracted parts are spliced together to form the features of the samples. Whether the corresponding disease and lncRNA have an association is deemed as the label of the sample. Then, the train set is obtained by weighted sampling. At last, using a lightGBM classifier trained by these samples predicts potential lncRNA-disease associations.

role of this part is to extract informative features from the disease functional similarity network and lncRNA sequence similarity network.

Graph Convolutional Network (GCN). Based on spectral graph theory and Weisfeiler-Lehman algorithm, GCN is an effective generalization of convolution neural network from the low dimensional regular domain such as image to high dimensional irregular domain like social network, whose computational complexity is linear. GCN are particularly designed for network embedding, especially aiming at irregular grids. Compared with the classical CNN model, GCN reduces to rather trivial operations when applied to regular graphs. It is worth noting that current graph neural network models that apply to arbitrarily structured graphs typically share some drawbacks when applied to regular graphs like grids, chains, fully-connected graphs etc. A localized spectral treatment like in [15], for example, reduces to rotationally symmetric filters and can never imitate the operation of a classical 2D CNN on a grid. In the same way, the Weisfeiler-Lehman algorithm will not converge in regular domain [16]. It is natural that CNN might be thought as an alternative choice right complementary to GCN. Certainly, which kind of model will be chosen depends on the genetic algorithm and the input data.

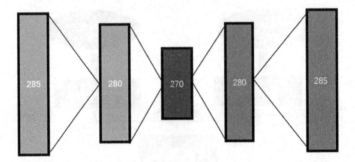

Fig. 2. An example of a neural network architecture encoded by an genetic algorithm chromosome. Each individual network is a symmetric structure similar to an hourglass, where each rectangle represents a layer of neural network and the number in the rectangle represents the number of nodes in the layer. The left side is for reduction and the right is for reconstruction to check the accuracy of the encoding. Right in the middle is what we want.

Genetic Algorithm. In order to avoid the trial-and-error, we choose the genetic algorithm to adjust the number of hidden layer of neural network and the number of hidden layer nodes. We nonlinearly generalize principal components analysis that transforms the original data into a lower dimensional code using a multilayer encoding network and a symmetrical decoding network to reconstruct the data from the code. Initially endowed with random weights, the two networks can be trained together by reducing the gap between the original data and its reconstruction. The required gradients are easily acquired by using the chain rule to backpropagate error which derivatives first through the decoding network and then through the encoding one [17]. Each integrated system is on behalf of an individual in the genetic algorithm. Figure 2 illustrates an example of a neural network architecture encoded by an genetic algorithm chromosome, which looks like an hourglass of symmetric structure. The encoding part consists of random hidden layer number and stochastic node number of every layer, which is guaranteed to gradually decline, while the decoding part is symmetric with the encoding one. Mutations can be obtained by changing the type of network, the number of hidden layers or the number of node of any hidden layer properly. Furthermore, different structures can be explored through hybridization. Eventually, a structure suitable for input data can be acquired after multiple iterations of mutation and hybridization by means of an elite strategy of retaining the individual with the highest fitness.

2.2 Weighted Bagging

Obviously, each of the unlabeled samples has a different probability of being a positive sample. How to delve into existing data deeper? Weighted sampling is a good choice.

Weighted. LncRNA and disease feature vectors obtained from network embedding model are concatenated as features of the sample. Meanwhile, whether the corresponding lncRNA and disease have an association is regarded as the label. Known association are positive samples, samples of unknown association are unlabeled. Our basic assumption is the same as the assumption in previous research that the labeled positive examples are chosen completely randomly from all positive examples [18]. On the basis of this assumption, the formulation three from [18] as illustrated in Fig. 3 can be easily derived.

$$w(x) = p(y = 1|x, s = 0) = \frac{1-c}{c} \frac{p(s = 1|x)}{1 - p(s = 1|x)}$$

Fig. 3. Let x be an example and let y be a binary label. Let s = 1 if the example x is labeled, and let s = 0 if x is unlabeled. Moreover, c is a constant.

Thus the weight that we assign to each unlabeled sample as negative sample is proportional to $1-w(x)$.

Bagging PU Learning. There have been several methods proposed for positive-unlabled (PU) learning. The goal of these methods is to distinguish positive samples (P) and unlabled samples (U). Bootstrap aggregating or bagging is a quite good candidate. Bagging is to use the method of bootstrap resampling to disturb the original data set to train a batch of classifiers and then average the results of these classifiers. The idea seems conceptually simple, which can be applied in many settings and works very well in practice [19]. Bagging can greatly improve performance when there is not much correlation between individual classifiers, especially when the classifier is extremely sensitive to small changes in the training set. Bagging is inspired by [19], which assumes that positive unlabeled learning problems have a particular structure that leads to instability of classifiers while bagging can be used to enhance the performance of instable classifiers [20]. The bagging PU learning is described in Fig. 4. Taking the good performance of lightGBM into account, we use lightGBM model as the basic classifier. In practical, the resampling method can be used to obtain multiple subsamples and establish the final classifier by integrating every lightGBM model, which is responsible for distinguishing the positive sample from each subsample. In the end, the average probabilities of lncRNA-disease associations are outputted by the weighted bagging lightGBM classifier.

3   Experiment

3.1   Leave-One-Out Cross Validation

In order to evaluate the performance of the algorithm, we carried out Leave-one-out Cross Validation (LOOCV). Each positive sample is distributed into

---

INPUT: P, U, K = sampling rate of bootstrap samples, T = number of   bootstraps

OUTPUT : a score s : $U \rightarrow R$

Initialize $\forall x \in U$, $n(x) \leftarrow 0$, $f(x) \leftarrow 0$, $p(x) \leftarrow K * (1 - w(x))$

for t = 1 to T **do**

    Draw a weighted bootstrap sample U_t in U according to p(x).

    Train a classifier f_t to discriminate P against U_t.

    For any $x \in U \setminus U_t$, update:

        $f(x) \leftarrow f(x) + f_t(x)$,

        $n(x) \leftarrow n(x) + 1$

end for

Return $s(x) = f(x)/n(x)$ for $x \in U$

Fig. 4. The bagging PU learning is described in the algorithm above. P and U denote positive samples and unlabeled samples, respectively. K denotes the sampling rate of bootstrap samples. T denotes times of sampling. n(x) is the number of times of unlabeled sample x predicted by a classifier. With each sample x allocated a certain probability p(x), Ut is obtained by each weighted bootstrap sample, which generates a random number for each sample x and if random number is less than p(x), then the sample x will be chosen. The lightGBM is trained to discriminate a positive sample P from the unlabeled random subsample Ut. The aim of resampling method is to induce the variability in the classifiers. In the last, the score of an unlabeled example x, s(x), is obtained by aggregating the predictions of the classifiers trained on subsamples without x.

the validation set in turn. The remaining positive samples and the negative samples obtained from unknown samples are taken as the train set. Evidently, the rest of negative samples are appended to the validation set.

Afterwards, the probabilities of associations between the corresponding lncRNA and disease of each sample are obtained from the average results of LOOCV. All samples are sorted by the prediction results, based on which each sample is successively deemed as positive example and calculate the true positive rate (TPR) and false positive rate (FPR), where TPR is the ratio of the positive samples which are correctly forecasted of all positive samples and FPR is the rate of the mistakenly classified negative samples, respectively. Moreover, the ROC curve is plotted by taking them as horizontal and vertical coordinates. In addition, the area under curve (AUC) value is calculated to assess performance.

3.2   Comparison with Other Methods

We compare our method with the most advanced computational method, LDAP, in terms of the AUC value. LDAP integrated multiple data sources and used the bagging SVM classifier to predict lncRNA-disease associations. On Dataset1, our method obtained an AUC of 0.8021, which is significantly higher than LDAP's 0.6800, indicating that our method can greatly improve the prediction accuracy as shown in Fig. 5(a). On Dataset2, our method with the AUC of 0.8362 also works better than the AUC 0.6851 of LDAP, whose results are shown in Fig. 5(b).

On Dataset3, our approach is much better with AUC of 0.8385 than LDAP's 0.6647, as shown in Fig. 5(c). Overall, our method is more effective than the best of existing methods, which might result from the fact that network embedding model has regarded the mean AUC as the fitness of the individual so that the optimum structure can be acquired through multiple iterations. This kind of result-oriented programming is right suitable for experiments on validation set. In addition, weighted sampling fully excavates the implicit relationship in the data.

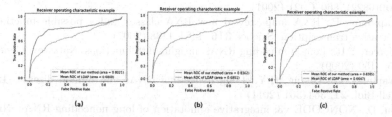

Fig. 5. Comparison with LDAP in terms of the mean AUC value of LOOCV on three datasets respectively. (a) Dataset1 contains 276 lncRNA-disease associations with 112 lncRNAs and 150 diseases. (b) Dataset2 contains 319 lncRNA-disease associations with 131 lncRNAs and 169 diseases. (a) Dataset3 contains 621 lncRNA-disease associations with 285 lncRNAs and 226 diseases.

4   Conclusion

Identification of potential lncRNAs associated with disease plays a key role in the development and progress of serious human disease, which might enlighten biomarker identification and drug design in the diagnosis, treatment and prevention of diseases. In this paper, we propose a weighted bagging lightGBM model based on network embedding and PU learning. Acquiring more lncRNA-disease associations or integrating more bioinformatics data are supposed to greatly improve performance of our model. Our study more or less has a few contributions in predicting lncRNA-disease associations. First, assigning different sampling weights to different unlabeled samples makes information mined more deeply. Second, genetic algorithm can find the most suitable network embedding model for the input data. Undoubtedly, a new train of thought for studying lncRNA-disease relationship is provided. Besides, the parameters of LightGBM are numerous, which have a significant impact on the final result. Furthermore, the universal evaluation criteria just aims at the validation set, so we believe that provided enough time, our results can make noticeable progress. Certainly, if the collaborative effects of different lncRNA-disease pairs are taken into consideration, the final AUC will increase a lot. In the future, We will devote ourself to researching on these fields.

References

1. Crick, F.: General nature of the genetic code for proteins. Nature **192**, 1227–1232 (1961)
2. Yanofsky, C.: Establishing the triplet nature of the genetic code. Cell **128**, 815–C818 (2007)
3. Mattick, J.S., Makunin, I.V.: Non-coding RNA. Hum. Mol. Genet. **15**, R17–R29 (2006)
4. Djebali, S., et al.: (2012)
5. Lander, E.S., et al.: Initial sequencing and analysis of the human genome. Nature **409**(6822), 860–C921 (2001)
6. Kapranov, P.: RNA maps reveal new RNA classes and a possible function for pervasive transcription. Science **316**, 1484–1488 (2007)
7. Mercer, T.R.: Long non-coding RNAs: insights into functions. Nat. Rev. Genet **10**, 155–159 (2009)
8. Wapinski, O., Chang, H.Y.: Long noncoding RNAs and human disease. Trends Cell Biol. **21**, 354–361 (2011)
9. Bu, D.: NONCODE v3: integrative annotation of long noncoding RNAs. Nucleic Acids Res. **40**, 210–215 (2012)
10. Chen, X., Yan, G.Y.: Novel human lncRNA-disease association inference based on lncrna expression profiles. Bioinform. **29**(20), 2617–2624 (2013)
11. Wang, L., He, W., Hao, D., Liu, S., Zhou, M.: Inferring novel lncRNA-disease associations based on a random walk model of a lncRNA functional similarity network. Mol. BioSyst. **10**(8), 2074–2081 (2014)
12. Lan, W., et al.: LDAP: a web server for lncRNA-disease association prediction. Bioinform. **33**(3), 458–460 (2016)
13. Srivastava, R.K., Greff, K., Schmidhuber, J.: Training very deep networks. In: Advances in Neural Information Processing Systems (2015)
14. Emmanuel, D., Bassett, B.A.: EDEN: evolutionary deep networks for efficient machine learning (2017)
15. Michael, D., Xavier, B., Pierre V.: Convolutional neural networks on graphs with fast localized spectral filtering. In: Advances in Neural Information Processing Systems (2016)
16. Thomas, K.: https://tkipf.github.io/graph-convolutional-networks/
17. Hinton, G.E., Salakhutdinov, R.R.: Reducing the dimensionality of data with neural networks. Science **313**(5786), 504–507 (2006)
18. Charles, E., Keith, N.: Learning classifiers from only positive and unlabeled data (KDD). In: Proceedings of the 14th ACM SIGKDD International Conference on Knowledge Discovery and Data Mining, pp. 213–220. ACM (2008)
19. Mordelet, F.: A bagging SVM to learn from positive and unlabeled examples. Pattern Recognit. Lett. **37**, 201–209 (2014)
20. Claesen, M.: A robust ensemble approach to learn from positive and unlabeled data using SVM base models. Neurocomput. **160**, 73–84 (2015)

DroidGene: Detecting Android Malware Using Its Malicious Gene

Yulong Wang[✉] and Hua Zong

State Key Laboratory of Networking and Switching Technology,
Beijing University of Posts and Telecommunications, Beijing, China
{wyl,zonghua}@bupt.edu.cn

Abstract. Android is the most popular smartphone operating system
in the world thanks to its openness, which also attracts many Android
malware writers. It is really a big challenge for the various Android markets to filter out malware accurately and quickly before provisioning a
large number of APPs. Many handcraft feature-based detection solutions
had been proposed for solving this problem. But the malware writers
can always find ways to change the features while maintaining the malware' malicious semantic. Inspired by the findings in biology, we advocate
identifying Android APPs' genes that are responsible for the malicious
behaviors. Based on this idea, we proposed a new method called Droid-
Gene, which treats calling sequences and permissions as DNA, and using
elaborately designed LSTM to find APPs' malicious genes. The result of
experiments on 16,200 Android samples shows that both the accuracy
(99.1%) and the detection time (0.36 s) of DroidGene are superior to the
state-of-the-art method.

Keywords: Android · Malware · Gene · Neural network

1 Introduction

Android is the most popular operating system in the mobile Internet. According
to Garner's report [1], till 2017, the market share of global smart terminals taken
by Android has reached 85.9%. In contrast to iOS, which only allows installing
an APP from Apple's App Store, the openness of Android allows smartphone
vendors to build their own OS based on Android. And Android users can install
APPs from various Android APP markets other than Google Play. For example,
Wandoujia [2], Tencent MyApp [3] and 360 Mobile Assistant [4] are all popular
Android APP markets in China. Android OS's openness boosts the development
and distribution of various kinds of Android APPs, resulting in the prosperous
of the Android ecosystem.

However, the openness of the Android system also provides appealing living
conditions for a large amount of malware. According to the report of Qihoo 360,
one of the famous internet security companies in China, the count of newly found
malware on Android system is 7.573 million in the year of 2017, which amounts

© Springer Nature Singapore Pte Ltd. 2018
J. Qiao et al. (Eds.): BIC-TA 2018, CCIS 951, pp. 315–330, 2018.
https://doi.org/10.1007/978-981-13-2826-8_28

to about 21 thousand new samples each day [5]. Considering most APPs are benign, it is hard, if not impossible, to detect so many malware manually under the constraint of time and cost with Android APP markets. One of the feasible ways is to use an efficient static detection system as the first defense line to filter out the majority of malware quickly and automatically. If some APPs are classified as malware but with low confidence, then a dynamic detection system is employed as the second defense line to re-examine them with in-depth monitoring of their run-time behaviors. If the APP's type is still hard to decide, then a manual inspection by security experts would act as the last defense line. It's not guaranteed that no malware would be left undetected in the end, yet it is a proper balance between security for end-users and cost for Android APP markets. Recently, there emerges many such static and dynamic Android malware detection methods [6–20]. Most of the methods are attempting to find some features of the Android malware and use them as the detection criteria. These features may be URLs or prompt embedded in the APP's reverse-compiled code, or some permission combinations, or API calling sequences. Though these features provide a useful indication of malware, they are becoming more and more unreliable. The main reason is that malware writers can easily understand how the current malware detection methods use these features, thereafter they manage to hide or at least lessen those features while maintaining the majority of its malicious semantic. Therefore, to regain the upper hand of Android malware detection, we need to devise a novel method which relies on the inherent characteristics of the malware which are hard to change (although may also be hard to describe).

Inspired by the findings in biology, we proposed an Android malware detection method called DroidGene based on the idea of genes. It is known that an organism's behavior is significantly influenced by its genes. [21,22]. Whatever appearance the organism may change itself to, its genes would still be the same. So the gene is a trustworthy evidence for characterizing the organism. Similarly, we believe that Android malware also has such genes, which cannot be changed by malware writers as long as they want the APP to keep its malicious semantic. In this paper, we will present the design of DroidGene and prove its effectiveness. The key contributions of our work are: 1. we defined an artificial Android DNA using the appearing sequences of suspicious APIs and permissions in Android APK; 2. we used the Word2Vector encoding scheme to enhance the representation of the API related artificial DNAs; 3. we constructed a multilayer bidirectional LSTM neural network with a dense attention mechanism to learn the malicious gene; 4. the experimental results show our method is better than previous static methods in terms of both accuracy and speed.

The rest of the paper is organized as follows. Section 2 overviews the existing works on the problem of Android malware detection. Section 3 presents detailed design of DroidGene including the mapping of the molecule, DNA, and gene to Android concepts. Then we provide an experimental evaluation of DroidGene in Sect. 4. Finally, Sect. 5 concludes the whole paper and describes the next step work.

2   Related Works

The problem of Android malware detection has been researched intensively in recent years. According to whether the samples under detection are required to run or not, these method can be categoried as static methods [6–15] and dynamic methods [16–20]. In order to clearify easily confused metrics used for evaluating these methods, we summarized the definitions of each metric in Table 1 and Eqs. 1, 2, 3 and 4.

Table 1. True conditions and predicted conditions [33]

	True condition positive	True condition negative
Predicted condition positive	True positive (tp)	False positive (fp)
Predicted condition negative	False negative (fn)	True negative (tn)

$$Precision = \frac{tp}{tp + fp} \tag{1}$$

$$DetectionRate = Recall = \frac{tp}{tp + fn} \tag{2}$$

$$Accuracy = \frac{tp + tn}{tp + tn + fp + fn} \tag{3}$$

$$F1 = 2 \times \frac{Precision \times Recall}{Precision + Recall} \tag{4}$$

Static methods are suitable for detecting a large number of samples within a short period of time. Since the detection object is the APK file of the suspected Android APP, and all of the potential features used for detection can be readily read from the reverse-compiled code of the APK file, static methods can quickly accomplish detection tasks. The differences between various static methods are the selected features and the decision procedures using these features. Earlier methods use easy-to-get features, such as permissions declared in the AndroidManifest.xml file of the APK. Su et al. [23] collect sets of permissions from Andoird malware and benign APPs separately. Exploiting the fact that some permissions appear more frequently in malware than in benign APPs, they categorize APPs into five malicious levels according to the weighted ratio of these permissions. But permission-based methods are not accurate enough since the correlation between permissions and malicious behaviors is not strong. Thus, more recent methods use Dalvik bytecode as the source of features. Dalvik bytecode has rich semantics since it contains classes, methods and instruments. The classes can be used to infer the APP's behavior. A detailed analysis of methods and instruments can generate the APP's control flow and data flow, which are very helpful for predicting dangerous actions such as privacy leaking and misuse of telephone services [24], as well as eliminating the influence of obfuscations used by malware for detection evasion [25]. DroidLegacy [26] uses APIs appearing in the bytecodes as features and reaches a 93.0% detection rate (a.k.a recall).

DroidMiner [9] uses both called APIs and call graphs as detection features and improves the detection rate to 95.3%. DroidAPIMiner [6] is more aggressive, which uses permissions declared in the AndroidManifest.xml file as well as the information on called APIs and called packages from bytecodes to determine the type of the given APP sample. Such a broad coverage of features leads to an amazing detecting rate of 99.0%. But the accuracy of the detection drops from 98.0% (DroidLegacy [26]) to 92.0% (DroidMiner [9]). Although DroidAPIMiner [6] doesn't provide its accuracy figure, it is expected to be even lower due to the tradeoff between recall and accuracy.

While static methods tried to mine more useful detection features, some features are hard to get or to measure precisely by inspecting the static contents of Android APKs. One of such features is resource consumption. Some methods [16–18] collect figures of Android system resources (e.g. CPU utilities, memory consumptions, network traffic pattern, battery usage and system calls) and use them to detect malware. Another kind of such features is the APPs' dynamic behaviors, especially those caused by run-time loaded codes. Yan et al. [19] implemented DroidScope based on Android source codes. DroidScope is an Android malware dynamic monitoring system, which can monitor the API usage on three levels including hardware, system and Dalvik virtual machine. It can collect the APP's behaviors on both the native code level and the Java level, and can implement various security policies. Dynamic detection methods can usually produce more accurate results than static methods but suffer from low detection speed, since the APPs under detection are required to run in a controlled environment to monitor its dynamic outputs. Some researchers attempt to combine the advantages of static and dynamic methods. Spreitzenbarth et al. [27] implemented a smartphone sandbox system that records API calling information, and combined it with features collected through static methods, then used machine learning to detect malware. MADAM [14] is a host-based malware detection system, which includes four levels: kernel, application, user and software library. It retrieves features such as system call, suspect API calling and suspect operations such as SMS sending through dynamic analysis, and takes static features such as permissions, metadata and market information as the supplement of dynamic features to decide whether an APP is a malware.

With more features utilized by various static and dynamic methods, the increasing trend of Android malware hasn't stopped. The main reason is that all of the above features are handcrafted. Although the handcrafted features have clear semantics and are easy to use in malware detection, they are potentially easy to be disguised by a smart malware writer. And there is no guaranteed coverage of malicious features. There are always be new malware whose inherent features are not included in the current feature set used for detection. So researchers begin to use machine learning, especially deep learning to acquire features deep inside the malware. For example, Saxe et al. [28] proposed to use the reverse-compiled code of Android APP to retrieve contextual byte features, PE import features, string 2D histogram features and PE metadata features and feed these features to DNN to classify the APPs under detection. Yuan et al. [29] used 200 features, including statically retrieved permissions, sensitive APIs and dynamically observed specific operation features, as the input of a neural network for malware detection. Some methods treat reverse-compiled codes of Android APPs as text and adopt NLP technology for malware detection [30, 31]. These methods use n-gram scheme to encode the bytecodes of APPs and employ KNN to determine malware. Since deep learning achieved great success in the field of image processing, some researchers attempt to transform malware detection problem to image classification problem so as to filter out Android malware. L. Nataraj et al. [32] proposed to transform the binary form of Android APP bytecodes to gray image and use image classification methods based on deep learning to complete the task of malware detection indirectly.

With new Android malware rapidly emerging, it is preferred to employ a fast and accurate detection method as the first defense line on the Android market. This criteria makes some slow methods, such as DroidMiner [9] (19.8 s), DroidSIFT [11] (175.8 s), RevealDroid [13] (95.2 s) and DroidNative [7] (26.87 s) unsuitable for this situation. For those fast methods, such as Drebin [10] (0.75 s) and R2-D2 [15] (0.5 s), the accuracy needs improvement.

To improve accuracy while decreasing detection time, we need to capture the minimum and most reliable features of Android malware. Put it another way, we need to identify the gene of Android malware. Ki et al. [20] had tried this idea on PC. They utilized the DNA sequence matching algorithm to detect the API sequences in PC malware and claimed an amazing performance with a precision of 100% and a recall of 99.8%. We reached nearly the same performance with a different mechanism on Android malware and outperforms the previously published static Android malware detection methods.

3   DroidGene

Before designing a malware detection method, we want to ask ourselves: what makes an APP a malware? The malware, like benign APPs, are just some execution codes calling some APIs of the Android OS and requesting some permissions granted by the OS. None of these APIs or permissions are malicious by itself. So where does the malicious semantic come from?

If we jump out of the Android malware detection problem and take a look at some phenomenon in biology, we can get some insight into this problem. According to the findings in the field of *behavior genetics*, which is a field of scientific research that uses genetic methods to investigate the nature and origins of individual differences in behavior, nearly all researched behaviors are under significant degrees of genetic influence [21]. And we also know that a gene is a sequence of DNA or RNA that codes for a molecule that has a function [22]. But it is not the molecules or DNA/RNA that determine the living organism's behaviors, similarly, neither does the APIs and permissions or whatever basic elements of an Android APP determine the malicious semantic of the APP. It is the gene that determined it. But what is the malware gene of an Android APP?

We solve the problem by proposing a novel method called DroidGene. We borrowed the ideas from *behavior genetics* to find the gene of Android malware. The mapping from the organism's gene to the Android's gene is shown in Table 2.

Table 2. Mapping from Organism's Gene to Android APP's Gene

Organism	Android APP
Molecule	Suspicous API
DNA	Call flow segment, permissions
Gene	A vector representing Android's malicous semantic

3.1 Android Molecule

First of all, DroidGene needs to select which *molecules* are the basic building blocks of Android APPs' *genes*. Although constant strings like URLs (which could be the Web address of the command and control server) or prompts (which may be specific to an Android malware) are obvious selections and can help detect some Android malware, we don't take them into consideration. The reason is that these strings are just the appearance of an APP, and can be easily changed without losing the malicious function of the malware. Instead, DroidGene chooses suspicious APIs to be the *molecues*. The rationale behind this decision is two folded. The first one is that a malicious function is still a function, thus has to call APIs provided by the Android OS. So APIs must play a role, though not directly, in the provision of malicious semantic. The second reason is that existing research works (e.g. [6,9,23,26]) had demonstrated that some APIs do appear more in malware than other APIs, which make them good indications of Android malware. The suspicious APIs used in DroidGene are defined as follows.

Definition 1. *Suspicious API, a_i, is one of the Android APIs that satisfies one of the following conditions:*
1. a_i's appearing frequency f_m in malware and appearing frequency f_b in benign satisfy: $f_m - f_b \geq \delta, \delta \in \mathbb{R}^+$;
2. a_i's function is more likely to be used abusely by malware according to an analysis of security experts.
$A = \{a_i | i = 1, 2, ..., N\}$ is the set of Suspicious API. N is the count of suspicious APIs.

For example, the Android APIs *getAllMessagesFromSim*, *getWifiState* and *sendTextMessage* are classified as suspicious APIs according to Definition 1. Their malicious semantics are relatively obvious because an Android malware can steal a user's privacy from his/her SIM card and send it to a C&C server when network access is available. Other suspicious APIs' malicious semantics may not be apparent, but they can still be picked out using the first condition in Definition 1 with a proper δ value. Note that too small a δ value may produce too many suspicious APIs from a base set of nearly 30 thousand Android APIs and may lead to severe over-fitting.

3.2   Android DNA

With the above *molecules*, DroidGene has to combine them in a meaningful form to represent suspicious malicious behaviors. Note that a suspicious API by itself doesn't contain any malicious semantic, it's the way of using these APIs that matters. Based on this observation, we define the concept of *suspicious movement*.

Definition 2. *A suspicious movement, s_i, is the name of the user-defined function that contains suspicious APIs directly or indirectly.*

Let S denote the set of suspicious movements. For example, $S = \{F_a, F_b, F_c\}$, in which the function body of F_a doesn't contain any suspicious API, but contains F_b that calls suspicious APIs. Thus F_a is also a suspicious movement. To get the semantic of a suspicious movement (since the user-defined name is not trustworthy), we need to extract the malicious pattern from the function body of the suspicious movement. Thus we define the concept of *suspicious action*.

Definition 3. *A suspicious action of a suspicious movement s_i, $A(s_i)$, is an ordered multiset of the orderly appeared names of suspicious APIs, suspicious movements and conditional branch statements in its function body.*

For example, $A(F_c) = \{API_a, F_b, API_a, API_b, F_b, F_a\}$ is the suspicious action of suspicious movement F_c. Now we can define the first type of Android APP's DNA.

Definition 4. *An Android APP's API DNA is the ordered union of all suspicious actions in an Android APP in the order of their appearances in the APK file.*

The procedure of retrieving an Android APP's API DNA is shown in Algorithm 1. The main work of Algorithm 1 is illustrated in Fig. 1. DroidGene compresses the reverse-compiled code of an APK in such a way that all of the benign codes are stripped off while all suspicious codes remain in their original order. Note that we also keep the conditional branch statements. The reason is two-fold. Firstly, conditional branch statements may contain information on the execution order of suspicious APIs or functions. And their number is usually much less than that of other statements, thus brings in little burden for the latter machine learning process. Secondly, some malware adds more conditional branch statements on purpose to complicate the call graph in order to evade detections. In this case, the abnormally large amount of conditional branch statements may contribute to the malware's detection.

The second type of Android APP DNA is Android permissions. Since there is no sequential relationship between different permissions and the count of all possible permissions are small, we treat it using a simple way, just use the One-Hot scheme to encode permissions.

Definition 5. *An Android APP's Permission DNA is an One-Hot encoding of the requested permissions in an Android APP APK.*

Algorithm 1. Generating Android APP's API DNA

    Input : Android APK
    Output: Android DNA D

1 Let S be the reverse-complied code of the Android APK
    `/* initialize the set of suspicious movements                    */`
2 **foreach** *API w in S* **do**
3   **if** *w satisfies definition 1* **then**
4         $\tilde{W} \leftarrow w$;
5   **end**
6 **end**
7 $M \leftarrow \tilde{W}$;
8 $D \leftarrow \varnothing$;
9 Generate call graph G from S;
    `/* find all suspicious movements                                   */`
10 **foreach** *edge $< f_i, f_j >$ in G* **do**
11   **if** $f_j \in \tilde{W}$ **then**
12         $\tilde{W} \leftarrow f_i$;
13   **end**
14 **end**
15 Let B be a set of names of conditional branch statements of Android;
    `/* find suspicious actions                                         */`
16 **foreach** *token t in S* **do**
17   **if** $t \in M$ *or* $t \in B$ **then**
18         $D \leftarrow t$;
19   **end**
20 **end**

3.3 Android Gene

Now we are ready to find the Android malware's gene responsible for its malicious behavior. To this end, we suggest learning the gene using machine learning technology instead of identifying it manually. Although manually defined genes have explicit physical meaning, it will suffer from being evaded by new malware finely crafted to hide this kind of gene. The downside of deep learning is that the reason for its effectiveness is usually hard to understand. But we can exploit this fact to counter the evasion of detection. If the gene of Android malware is learned from a large number of samples, the gene's reliability can be guaranteed as it is enhanced by continuously incoming samples. In this way, we find an effective method that is hard to evade for detecting Android malware.

Inputs of Learning. Based on this idea, DroidGene learns Android genes using a dedicated LSTM neural network. In order to use LSTM, we need first to encode Android APP's API DNA, which is a vector of texts (i.e. API names, function names and conditional branch statement names), into a vector of numbers. We choose Word2Vector to be the encoder for two reasons. Firstly, Word2Vector is

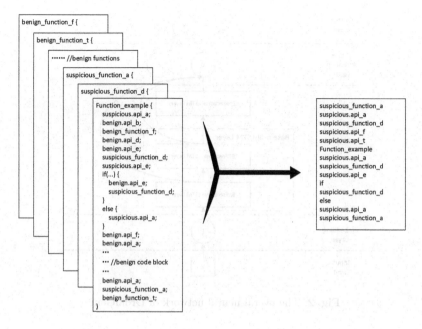

Fig. 1. Illustration of getting API DNA from an android APK

able to assimilate suspicious APIs with similar usage patterns. Among malicious behaviors in Android malware, many are very similar. For example, there are two malicious behaviors. The first one is: the user sends SMS → malware sniffs SMS → saves it to a local file → sends the file to a C&C server. The second one is: the user sends SMS → malware sniffs the destination number of SMS → saves it to a local file → sends the file to a C&C server. Both of the above behaviors enable the malware to acquire SMS related information. Even though the acquired information is not identical, these behaviors are similar in essence. Therefore, DroidGene aims to represent similar suspicious APIs with closer numeric vectors, so as to simplify the input data and speed up the training process. Secondly, Word2Vector helps to weaken the impact of user-defined function names. Two literally different user-defined functions may call suspicious APIs with similar sequences. So the *suspicious actions* of these two functions have almost the same malicious behavior. If we encode them with almost the same vector, it would cost less computation during the training process.

Structure of the Neural Network. The structure of the neural network used in DroidGene is show in Fig. 2. The Word2Vector encoded API DNAs are fed to a multi-layered bidirectional LSTM neural network, whose output undergoes a layer of dense attention. And in the dense attention layer, the permission DNAs are added to compute the final result.

DroidGene uses bidirectional LSTM neural network as the foundation. The *suspicious movements* in the input may have two different orders. The first is

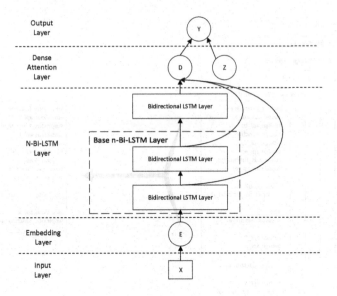

Fig. 2. The overal neural network of DroidGene

the front-to-end writing order for all *suspicious movements*. The second is a backward occurrence order that happens to some of the *suspicious movements* (e.g. those caused by back jumping of conditional branch statements). Thus, compared to uni-directional LSTM, bidirectional LSTM would learn more relationships between data so as to better provide for determination (as confirmed in Fig. 3). Specifically, the detailed structure of bidirectional LSTM used by Droid-Gene is shown in Fig. 3. In order to make full use of the output of the LSTM neural units, we propose a *dense* attention mechanism (see Fig. 4), which utilizes all of the output of every bidirectional LSTM neural unit at each time point. Specifically, the layer of dense attention connects the output of each layer of bidirectional LSTM together and sends the results to a fully connected layer to reduce the dimension. The dense attention mechanism not only takes the output of the last layer of bidirectional LSTM as input, but also takes previous LSTM layers' outputs into consideration to obtain a more comprehensive result. What's more, the dense attention mechanism solves the gradient disappearing problem caused by multiple layers of the LSTM to some extent.

Since each Android APP may contain different numbers of *DNA*, while the input of the neural network must have a fixed length, we take 256, which is the 70th percentile of the numbers of all possible *DNAs* in the trained Android samples, as the length of the input vector. All *DNA* vectors will either be truncated or padded with zeroes to fit this window. We also set the dimension used by Word2Vector to 250. Each layer of the bidirectional LSTM contains 256 hidden neural units. Each attention layer in the dense attention layer (see Fig. 4) contains 1000 hidden neural units. And the fully-connected layer in the dense attention layer contains 1000 hidden neural units. We also utilized a 0.3 dropout mechanism to prevent over-fitting.

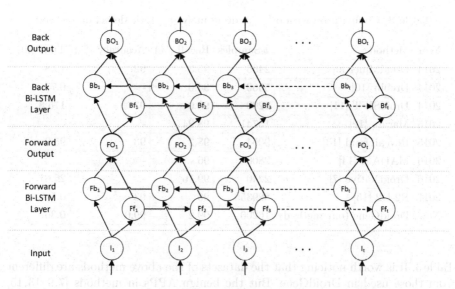

Fig. 3. The structure of the bidirectional LSTM of DroidGene

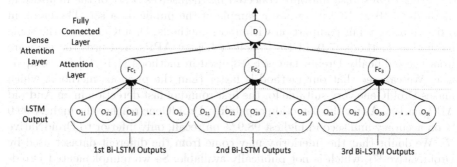

Fig. 4. The structure of bidirectional LSTM of DroidGene

4 Experiments

In this section, we will evaluate the effectiveness of DroidGene. We collected 16,200 Android samples, which includes 5,560 malware from the publically available Drebin Dataset [10]. The remaining samples are benign APPs collected from Android APP market WanDouJia [2], which covers journey, finance, video, social network, shopping, music, photo, news and games. In order to ensure, to the best of our efforts, that these samples are benign, we submitted them to Virus Total [34]. And only samples with no positive detection results from all of the 61 virus engines in Virus Total are considered benign. In this way, we got 10,640 benign samples.

We compared the effectiveness of DroidGene with other Android malware static detection methods published in recent years, the results are shown in

Table 3. Comparision with other android malware static detection methods

Year	Method	#Samples	Recall (%)	Accuracy (%)	Time (s)
2014	DroidMiner [9]	2466	95.3	92	19.8
2014	Drebin [10]	5560	94.0	-	0.75
2014	DroidSIFT [11]	2200	98.0	93	175.8
2015	Marvin [12]	15741	98.24	-	-
2015	RevealDroid [13]	9054	98.2	93	95.2
2016	MADAM [14]	2800	96	-	-
2016	DroidNative [7]	2240	99.16	-	26.87
2017	R2-D2 [15]	829356	96	93	0.5
Now	DroidGene (our method)	16200	99.2	99.0	0.36

Table 3. It is worth noticing that the datasets of the above methods are different
from those used in DroidGene. But the benign APPs in methods [7,9–13,15]
are collected by themselves and are different from each other. Meanwhile, methods [9,12,15] also use malware collected by themselves. Part of the malware in
methods [7,10,11,13,14] contain a sample of the public data set. Therefore, in
order to make a fair comparison with above methods, DroidGene uses the same
method as methods [7,9–13,15] to collect benign APPs, and uses the malware
from the publically Drebin Dataset [10] used in methods [7,10,13] for comparison. We can see that our method is faster than the previous methods, which
makes DroidGene very suitable for the first round of fast detection in an Android
APP market. As for the detection capability, DroidGene reaches the highest 99.0
% on accuracy and second highest 98.9 % on recall, only inferior to DroidNative
[7]. We doubt that the inferiority may come from the different dataset used by
DroidNative [7], which is not publically available. So we reimplemented Droid-
Native [7] and performed the evaluation on our dataset. The results are shown in
Table 4. We can see that our method has a better performance than DroidNative
[7] with the same dataset.

Table 4. Comparision with DroidNative on Our Dataset

Method	Recall (%)	Accuracy (%)	F1 (%)	Hardware	Time (s)
DroidNative [7]	98.9	95.6	97.2	CPU E5-2660	20.89
DroidGene (our method)	99.2	99.0	99.1	GPU Tesla K80	0.36

We also evaluated the performance of variant encoding and neural network
designs for retrieving the Android gene to validate the design in Sect. 3.3. The
results are shown in Table 5, in which L, D, A and DA means layer, direction,
attention and dense attention respectively. For example, 3L2D+DA means 3-
layer-bidirectional LSTM with dense attention mechanism.

Table 5. Comparision of variant designs of gene retriving scheme

Encoding	LSTM	Perm.	Precision (%)	Recall (%)	F1 (%)	Accuracy (%)	Time (s)
One-hot	1L1D	No	89.2	91.3	90.2	89.1	0.37
Word2Vector	1L1D	No	96.4	96.0	96.2	96.0	0.24
	1L2D	No	98.0	97.0	97.5	97.3	0.26
	2L2D	No	98.1	98.0	98.0	98.0	0.29
	3L2D	No	98.0	98.2	98.1	98.1	0.31
	4L2D	No	97.5	97.5	97.5	97.5	0.36
	2L2D+A	No	99.1	97.4	98.4	98.3	0.33
	3L2D+A	No	98.5	98.2	98.5	98.5	0.36
	4L2D+A	No	98.9	97.3	98.1	98.1	0.39
	2L2D+DA	No	99.1	98.3	98.6	98.6	0.33
	2L2D+DA	Yes	99.1	98.5	98.7	98.7	0.34
	3L2D+DA	No	99.2	98.7	98.9	99.0	0.36
	3L2D+DA	Yes	99.2	99.0	99.1	99.1	0.36
	4L2D+DA	No	99.0	98.8	98.9	98.9	0.41
	4L2D+DA	Yes	99.0	98.9	98.9	98.9	0.42

It can be seen in Table 5 that, choosing Word2Vecor instead of One-Hot makes the accuracy of DroidGene increase from 89.1% to 96.0% with about 7% improvement. And it also decreases detection time from 0.37 s to 0.24 s with a 35.14% reduction. The improvements show that Word2Vector is a key selection in the design of DroidGene. We can also find that bidirectional LSTM does gain more knowledge on the relations between *suspicious movements*, thus improving accuracy by about 1.3% (from 96.0% to 97.3%). An appearance effort for further increasing the accuracy of the LSTM network is to add more layers to the LSTM. Yet too much layers will lead to over-fitting and decrease the accuracy, as shown in rows 4–6 in Table 5. We found that for DroidGene, a layer number of three is the proper setting. And this decision is confirmed in rows 9,14 and 15 of Table 5. Since adding more layers than three only causes more detection time, we need to find other ways to further improve the performance of detection. Instead of feeding the output from the last time point of LSTM to its next layer, we use the attention mechanism to take the LSTM's outputs from each time point and feed them to the next layer. The experimental results show that it did improve the accuracy by about 0.4%. Encoughed by this result, we invented a new attention mechanism called the dense attention mechanism as described in Sect. 3.3, and got a even better performance with about 0.5% improvement on accuracy. Finally, we also took permissions into consideration, and obtained an amazing 99.1% accuracy with only 0.36 s of detection time.

5   Conclusion

Rapidly filtering out Android malware with a high accuracy is critical for maintaining the reputation of Android APP markets. Nevertheless, the openness of the Android system makes this task very challenging since malware writers can always find ways to hide the detection features while preserving the malware's malicious semantics. We want to stop this cat-and-mouse game by finding inherent unremovable features of Android malware. Inspired by the findings in biology, we managed to define the DNA of Android APP and learned its genes using a finely designed LSTM neural network. The experimental evaluation of our method shows a promising result, both in accuracy and detection time. Our future work would focus on the proper interface of DroidGene with other complementary methods such as native code detection and dynamic detection.

Acknowledgments. The work was supported in part by the National High-tech R&D Program of China (863 Program) (2015AA017201) and National Key Research and Development Program of China (2016QY01W0200). The authors are very grateful to the anonymous viewers of this paper.

References

1. Gartner, Gartner Says Worldwide Sales of Smartphones Recorded First Ever Decline During the Fourth Quarter of 2017, 22 February 2018. https://www.gartner.com/newsroom/id/3859963
2. Wandoujia. https://www.wandoujia.com/
3. Tencent MyApp. http://Android.myapp.com/
4. Mobile Assistant. http://zhushou.360.cn/
5. Qihoo 360, 2017 Android Malware Report, 01 March 2018. http://blogs.360.cn/360mobile/2018/03/01/review_Android_malware_of_2017
6. Aafer, Y., Du, W., Yin, H.: DroidAPIMiner: mining API-level features for robust malware detection in android. In: Zia, T., Zomaya, A., Varadharajan, V., Mao, M. (eds.) SecureComm 2013. LNICST, vol. 127, pp. 86–103. Springer, Cham (2013). https://doi.org/10.1007/978-3-319-04283-1_6
7. Alam, S., Qu, Z., Riley, R.: DroidNative: automating and optimizing detection of Android native code malware variants. Comput. Secur. **65**, 230–246 (2016)
8. Enck, W., Ongtang, M., Mcdaniel, P.: On lightweight mobile phone application certification. In: ACM Conference on Computer and Communications Security, pp. 35–245. ACM (2009)
9. Yang, C., Xu, Z., Gu, G., Yegneswaran, V., Porras, P.: DroidMiner: automated mining and characterization of fine-grained malicious behaviors in android applications. In: Kutyłowski, M., Vaidya, J. (eds.) ESORICS 2014. LNCS, vol. 8712, pp. 163–182. Springer, Cham (2014). https://doi.org/10.1007/978-3-319-11203-9_10
10. Arp, D., Spreitzenbarth, M., Hbner, M., et al.: DREBIN: effective and explainable detection of android malware in your pocket. In: Proceedings of the 2018 International Conference on Computing and Artificial Intelligence, pp. 35–40. ACM (2018)
11. Zhang, M., Duan, Y., Yin, H., et al.: Semantics-aware android malware classification using weighted contextual API dependency graphs. In: ACM SIGSAC Conference on Computer & Communications Security, pp. 1105–1116. ACM (2014)
12. Lindorfer, M., Neugschwandtner, M., Platzer, C.: MARVIN: efficient and comprehensive mobile app classification through static and dynamic analysis. In: Computer Software and Applications Conference, pp. 422–433. IEEE (2015)
13. Garcia, J., Hammad, M., Sam, M.: Lightweight, obfuscation-resilient detection and family identification of android malware. ACM Trans. Softw. Eng. Methodol. **26**(3), 11 (2018)

14. Saracino, A., Sgandurra, D., Dini, G.: MADAM: effective and efficient behavior-based android malware detection and prevention. IEEE Trans. Dependable Secur. Comput. **15**(1), 83–97 (2018)
15. Huang, H.D., Kao, H.Y: ColoR-inspired Convolutional NeuRal Network (CNN)-based AndroiD Malware Detections. arXiv preprint arXiv:1705.04448 (2017)
16. Shabtai, A., Kanonov, U., Elovici, Y., et al.: Andromaly: a behavioral malware detection framework for Android devices. J. Intell. Inf. Syst. **38**(1), 161–190 (2012)
17. Reina, A., Fattori, A., Cavallaro, L.: A system call-centric analysis and stimulation technique to automatically reconstruct Android malware behaviors. In: Proceedings of the 6th European Workshop on System Security (EuroSec), pp. 1–6. ACM (2013)
18. Damopoulos, D., Kambourakis, G., Portokalidis, G.: The best of both worlds: a framework for the synergistic operation of host and cloud anomaly-based IDS for smartphones. In: Proceedings of the Seventh European Workshop on System Security, pp. 1–6. ACM (2014)
19. Yan, L.K., Yin, H.: DroidScope: seamlessly reconstructing the OS and Dalvik semantic views for dynamic android malware analysis. In: Proceedings of the 21st USENIX Conference on Security symposium, pp. 569–584. USENIX Association (2013)
20. Ki, Y., Kim, E., Kim, H.K.: A novel approach to detect malware based on API call sequence analysis. Int. J. Distrib. Sens. Netw. **11**(6), 659101 (2015)
21. Wikipedia, Behavioural genetics, 25 June 2018. https://en.wikipedia.org/wiki/Behavioural_genetics
22. Wikipedia, Gene, 23 June 2018. https://en.wikipedia.org/wiki/Gene
23. Su, M.Y., Chang, W.C.: Permission-based malware detection mechanisms for smart phones. In: 2014 International Conference on Information Networking, pp. 449–453. IEEE (2014)
24. Michael, G., Zhou, Y., Zhang, Q., et al.: RiskRanker: scalable and accurate zero-day android malware detection. In: The 10th International Conference on Mobile Systems, Applications and Services, pp. 281–294. ACM (2012)
25. Wognsen, E.R., Karlsen, H.S., Olesen, M.C.: Formalisation and analysis of Dalvik bytecode. Sci. Comput. Program. **92**(6), 25–55 (2014)
26. Deshotels, L., Notani, V., Lakhotia, A.: DroidLegacy: automated familial classification of android malware. In: ACM SIGPLAN on Program Protection and Reverse Engineering Workshop, pp. 1–12. ACM (2014)
27. Spreitzenbarth, M., Schreck, T., Echtler, F., et al.: Mobile-Sandbox: combining static and dynamic analysis with machine-learning techniques. Int. J. Inf. Secur. **14**(2), 141–153 (2015)
28. Saxe, J., Berlin, K.: Deep neural network based malware detection using two dimensional binary program features. In: International Conference on Malicious and Unwanted Software, pp. 11–20. IEEE (2015)
29. Yuan, Z., Lu, Y., Wang, Z., et al.: Droid-Sec: deep learning in Android malware detection. ACM SIGCOMM Comput. Commun. Rev. **44**(4), 371–372 (2014)
30. Abou A.T., Cercone, N., Keselj, V., et al.: N-gram-based detection of new malicious code. In: International Computer Software and Applications Conference - Workshops and FAST Abstracts. IEEE Computer Society, pp. 41–42 (2004)
31. Reddy, D.K.S., Pujari, A.K.: N-gram analysis for computer virus detection. J. Comput. Virol. **2**(3), 231–239 (2006)

32. Nataraj, L., Karthikeyan, S., Jacob, G., et al.: Malware images: visualization and automatic classification. In: Proceedings of the 8th International Symposium on Visualization for Cyber Security, pp. 1–7. ACM (2011)
33. Wikipedia, Precision and recall, 12 June 2018. https://en.wikipedia.org/wiki/Precision_and_recall
34. Virus Total. https://www.virustotal.com/#/home/

Visualize and Compress Single Logo Recognition Neural Network

Yulong Wang[(✉)] and Haoxin Zhang

State Key Laboratory of Networking and Switching Technology,
Beijing University of Posts and Telecommunications, Beijing, China
{wyl,csj}@bupt.edu.cn

Abstract. Logo recognition by Convolutional Neural Networks (CNNs) on a smartphone requires the network to be both accurate and small. In our previous work [1], we proposed the accompanying dataset method for single logo recognition to increase the recall and precision of the target logo recognition. However, the reason why it works was unclear, thus it was hard to compress the network while maintaining the same accuracy. In this paper, we use DeconvNet [9] to visualize our network's feature maps and propose a metric to analyze them quantitatively. Finally, we obtain a better understanding of the influences in the network brought by accompanying datasets. Under its guidance, an effective way to compress the network is devised by us. The experiments show that we can reduce the size of the neural network's first layer by 30% while only lower the recall and precision by 0.014 and 0.01. The training time is also saved by 40% due to the network compression.

Keywords: Logo recognition · Visualization
Convolutional neural network · AlexNet · Accompanying dataset

1 Introduction

Convolutional neural networks are widely used in image recognition. The precision is getting higher and higher. In the 2017 ImageNet competition, the champion team reached a precision of 97.749 [3]. However, the cost comes from the deeper and deeper layers of the network, the increasing number of convolution kernels, and the increasingly complex models. For example, the latest ResNet has 1001 layers [4]. And in 2016 ImageNet competition, the champion team made 1207 layers with the best performance [5]. Generally, when we want to improve the precision of recognition, we can get started from the following aspects: optimizing the network model, increasing the number of network layers, feature screening, and data enhancement. For the logo recognition application at a resource-limited device, such as a smartphone, data enhancement, and model optimization are preferred methods. In our previous work, we proposed a method of data enhancement called accompanying dataset to increase the recognition performance by using the shape context algorithm [1].

© Springer Nature Singapore Pte Ltd. 2018
J. Qiao et al. (Eds.): BIC-TA 2018, CCIS 951, pp. 331–342, 2018.
https://doi.org/10.1007/978-981-13-2826-8_29

When performing single logo recognition, we want our model to have a strong preference for the target logo's image. Thus, the precision of the target class is highly demanded while other classes do not matter. The accompanying dataset mechanism is helpful to achieve this goal. We can make the target image class as the positive sample. The negative sample is the image class found by the shape context algorithm with a similarity degree of the target class of about 80% [1]. Then we perform two-class training. This negative sample is called *accompanying dataset*. The aim of the accompanying dataset is not to classify itself, but to promote the training of the target logo. Our previous experiments [1] show that the results with different accompanying datasets vary greatly. However, it was not clear what changes in the neural network brought by the accompanying dataset lead to the better recognition performance. So, in this paper, we attempt to investigate them and use the finding to optimize the neural network in size.

In this paper, we choose AlexNet [2] to train the logo recognition neural network and DeconvNet [9] to visualize the network. AlexNet is a widely used network structure. Compared to the aforementioned large neural networks, its structure is simpler with only eight layers. Although its performance is inferior to those of the most recent CNNs such as GoogLeNet [18], ResNet [4], etc. its linear structure makes it easy to visualize different convolution layers and is easier to train. We pre-trained decomposing elements of loges and obtained pre-trained features which can be used to calculate the quality of learned features. The key contributions of this paper are 1. it presents the visual analysis on the effects of accompanying datasets on AlexNet-based logo recognition neural network; 2. an effective optimization method for reducing the size of the logo recognition neural network is proposed; 3. the experiments are carried out for validating the optimization method.

The remainder of this paper is organized as follows. In Sect. 2, we summarized recent research works on neural network visualization and network compression. In Sect. 3, we described the proposed method of visualization analysis in detail. In Sect. 4, we presented and discussed the experimental results about network compression. Finally, we conclude our work in Sect. 5.

2   Related Works

Neural network visualization has been a hotspot in the field of deep learning. In general, a neural network is like a black-box structure. It is difficult for us to understand why it works or fails. Neural network visualization attempts to interpret the network either by outputting feature maps in the middle of the network or through network-processed images. Erhan et al. [7] proposed Activation Maximization to explain traditional neural networks. It can visualize the preferred input of neurons in each neural network layer. The preferred input can indicate the features that the neuron has learned. These learned features will be represented by a comprehensive input pattern that can maximize the activation of neurons. To synthesize such an input pattern, each pixel of the CNN input will be iteratively changed to maximize the activation of neurons. Mahendran et al. [8] proposed Network Inversion, which is based on multiple neuron activations to illustrate the integrated feature maps learned by each CNN layer, revealing the internal characteristics of the CNN network on the network layer level. Network Inversion reconstructs the input image from the original image in the feature map of a particular layer, which reveals the image information saved by that layer. In contrast, Zeiler et al. [9] proposed a method based on deconvolution neural network. This method utilizes the DeconvNet framework [20] to map feature maps directly to image dimensions, so as to find image patterns in the original input image that is activated by a specific neuron. Through direct mapping, DeconvNet can highlight which patterns in the input image activate specific neurons, thereby directly linking the meaning of neurons and input images. We also use DeconvNet to visualize our CNN model.

Works on compressing CNNs are getting more and more attraction. Wang et al. [10] composed CNN in the frequency domain. They regarded convolution kernels as images and divided them to common parts shared with each other and individual private parts. Lots of common parts were discarded then to produce a high compression. Luo et al. [11] proposed an entropy-based method to asses the convolution kernels' importance. Then they dropped several unimportant kernels to get a smaller CNN model. The method mainly focused on reducing the size of intermediate activations. Guo et al. [12] compressed CNNs through knowledge distillation. They used a composed network including a teacher network which is trained to generate soft labels with better classification feasibility and a student network with simple architectures which uses the soft label to compress model complexity. Hu et al. [13] simply removed inner ReLU functions within each convolutional block to compress the network. They didn't keep the balance of accuracy and speed. Hu et al. [14] and Li et al. [15] were both combining the CNNs and the traditional method. They used the traditional method to replace some evaluation of CNNs to speed up the training. Different from the standard neural networks, the combined networks got better performance and shorter time. Mitani et al. [16] proposed a technique that compresses the intermediate data and aggregates common computation in AlexNet for video recognition. They evaluated the size of communication and recognition ratio, which had a trade-off. But they did not take the computationally expensive into account. Although the above methods can compress a neural network while maintaining high precision, they are failed to provide the visualized causes for the optimization, which is important for deeply understanding the compression mechanism.

Evaluating model performance by visualizing the intermediate features of CNN learning is effective, and network redundancy can also be avoided. The most similar work to ours is the work of Xie et al. [17]. Their ideas of adjusting the network through visualization are consistent with us. The difference is that they cut the layer's redundancy by visualizing the last convolution layer of the network, while we compare the first convolution layer of the network with the pre-trained filters (details are shown in Sect. 3.2). We choose this strategy because the lower layer of a CNN learns more detailed features than higher layers, which is helpful to capture the subtle impacts of the different accompanying dataset.

3   Network Visualization

3.1   Accompanying Dataset

In our previous work, we found that the recognition recall reaches the highest value when the similarity between the target logo and the accompanying dataset is about 80%. The experimental results in paper [1] are shown in Fig. 1.

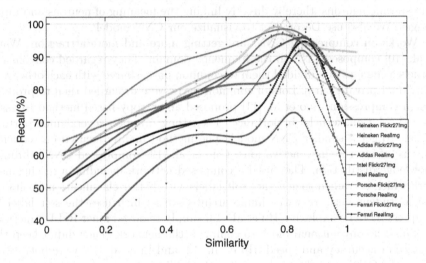

Fig. 1. Correlation between similarity and recall [1], in which Flickr27Img is public logo dataset FlickrLogos-27 [19], and RealImg is a logo dataset collected by the authors.

It can be seen that for different logos, training with an accompanying dataset of 80% similarity can obtain the highest recognition recall. When the similarity is lower or higher than 80%, the recall values will decrease proportionally. In this paper, we visualize the network by DeconvNet [9] to help us intuitively understand what the accompanying dataset mechanism does. A DeconvNet can be thought of as a CNN that uses the same operations (e.g. filtering, pooling) but in a reverse order (see the specific steps and principles in literature [9]).

We choose the same target logos as the ones used in our previous work [1] for comparison. Each target logo image is trained for five times with five different accompanying datasets who have different similarities to the target logo. Then we use DeconvNet to get the visualization result of the convolution kernels' feature maps of the first layer of the trained AlexNet. Taking Adidas as an example, the kernels' feature maps we obtained are shown in the Fig. 2. There are 96 convolution kernels of the first convolution layer of the trained AlexNet [2]. Figure 2 shows the 96 feature maps of the input image after these convolution operations.

Fig. 2. Visualized feature map of the first layer of the trained AlexNet when feeding an adidas logo image

3.2 Pre-trained Features

Note that a CNN model relies on the learned features to classify the images. For example, assume that one class can be perfectly identified by five distinct features, as shown in Fig. 3(a). We use five shapes to represent the different features and expect our trained AlexNet to accurately learn these features (red crosses in Fig. 3(a) represent learned features). So ideally, we only need five convolution kernels in this case. But the chance to pinpoint these real features with exactly the same amount of neurons is usually very low due to the large searching space. Thus, the reality is more like Fig. 3(b), in which we use a lot of convolution kernels (see red crosses in Fig. 3(b)) to increase the chance that most of the real features would be covered by the learned features. These convolution kernels may eventually approximate the real features (see the red crosses near the diamond and circle in Fig. 3(b)). Under-fitting occurs when the features learned by the convolution kernel are far from the real features (see the red cross near the pentagram and triangle in Fig. 3(b)). Over-fitting occurs when a large number of learned features are clustered at a position where there is no one real feature (see the red crosses near the lower left corner in Fig. 3(b)). If we know all the real features of the target logo in advance, optimizing our network will be very easy. But this is impossible obviously.

However, for the logo recognition problem, we can guess parts of the real features according to the nature of logos. The logo is a special type of image, which is usually composed of some common basic shapes such as circles, triangles,

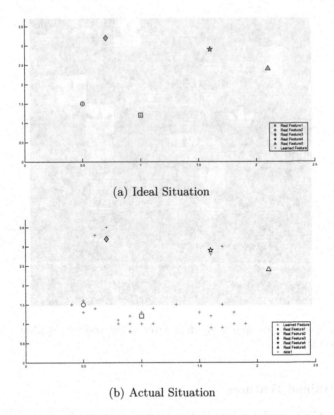

(a) Ideal Situation

(b) Actual Situation

Fig. 3. The relationship between real features and learned features (Color figure online)

bars, and letters. Therefore, we can grasp these features in advance, and use them as a measurement for the quality of the set of learned features. Take Adidas as an example. All Adidas logo images contain basic shapes that are similar to triangles or bars. There are even some letters including a, d, i, and s. We proposed to use these basic shapes to pre-train a corresponding neural network for classifying each basic shape. The convolution kernels of the pre-trained model will be used as reference filters for a specific shape. Although we cannot know the whole set of real features of Adidas logo, we can use the pre-trained features to measure the quality of the learned features under the assumption that learned feature sets that contain more pre-trained features are better than less. This assumption is rationale in that the features are learned from the whole searching space with a uniform distributed initial position. Thus each real feature can be learned with the same possibility. If a model can learn more known real features, it suggests that the model's learning capability is more powerful, thus is usually able to learn more unknown real features. With help of visualization, we calculated the similarity between learned feature maps and pre-trained feature maps as the similarity between learned features and real features.

3.3 Metric for Measuring Learned Features' Quality

It is not accurate to only regard the similarity between the learned features and the pre-trained features as the metric of features' quality. Consider the situation in Fig. 4.

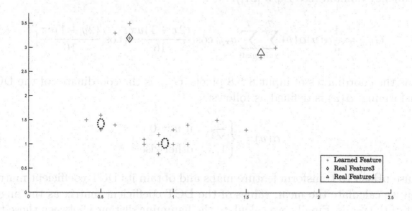

Fig. 4. Missing features (Color figure online)

Diamonds and pentagrams represent the pre-trained features. We regard these two pre-trained features as the real features to measure the quality of learned features. The red crosses represent the distribution of the learned features. It can be seen that there are a lot of red crosses at the bottom of the picture, but they are far from the two real features. This suggests that the model may miss some real features during pre-training, which is usually unavoidable since we cannot know all of the real features in advance. For the trained model, the convolution kernel may learn these features, which will gather around some unknown real features (see the dotted circles in Fig. 4). In this case, if only considering the similarities between them and the pre-trained features, then they will be judged as the bad-quality features. So we use the Eq. 1 to calculate the metric.

$$m_p = \frac{\frac{1}{n}\sum_{i=0}^{n} D(F_i, f_p)}{\sum_{j=0}^{C} N(f_j, f_p)} \tag{1}$$

in which, m_p denotes the metric value of the pth learned features, n denotes the number of pre-trained features, F_i denotes the ith pre-trained feature map, f_p denotes the pth learned feature map. $N(f_j, f_p)$ is defined as follows:

$$N(f_j, f_p) = \begin{cases} 1, & \text{if } D(f_j, f_p) < \frac{1}{C}\sum_{i=0}^{C} D(f_i, f_p) \\ 0, & \text{otherwise} \end{cases} \tag{2}$$

which denotes the number of learned features whose distance with the pth learned features is less than the average mutual distance among C learned features. $D(f_i, f_p)$ is the hash distance of f_i and f_p, which is calculated using Perceptual hash algorithm (pHash) [6]. pHash uses the DCT (Discrete Cosine Transform [21]) to obtain the low-frequency component of an image. DCT is an image compression algorithm used for lossy compression of images (including still images and moving images). It transforms an image from a pixel domain to a frequency domain (see Eq. 3 [21]).

$$G_{u,v} = \frac{1}{4}\alpha(u)\alpha(v) \sum_{x=0}^{7} \sum_{y=0}^{7} g_{x,y} \cos[\frac{(2x+1)u\pi}{16}] \cos[\frac{(2y+1)v\pi}{16}] \qquad (3)$$

$g_{x,y}$ is the coordinates of input 8 * 8 pixels. $G_{x,y}$ is the coordinates of the DCT transforming. $\alpha(u)$ is defined as follows:

$$\alpha(u) = \begin{cases} \frac{1}{\sqrt{2}}, & \text{if } u = 0 \\ 1, & \text{otherwise} \end{cases} \qquad (4)$$

We use pHash to transform feature maps and obtain its DCT coefficient matrix. Then we calculate the mean values of the DCT coefficient matrix as the fingerprint of the maps. Finally, we calculate the hamming distance between these two maps using their fingerprints. The detailed process is shown in Algorithm 1.

A lower metric value indicates a higher quality of the learned feature. It can be seen from Eq. 1 that the metric value will decrease when the distance between the learned features and the pre-trained features becomes shorter. In this case, the learned features are more likely to cover the real features that are represented by the pre-trained features. The metric value will also decrease when there are more learned features around the measured learned feature. In this case, the measured learned feature is more likely to cover an unknown real feature. By calculating the metric of 96 convolution kernels in the AlexNet's first layer, we obtained results shown in Fig. 5. We selected five accompanying datasets with different similarity to Adidas and got the five lines in Fig. 5. It can be seen that the convolution kernel has the highest metric value when the accompanying dataset whose similarity is 80% is used for model training. This result is consistent with Fig. 1, which shows that the quantitative metric defined in Eq. 1 is able to explain the accompanying dataset mechanism.

4 Network Compression

Based on the results of network visualization, we have taken the following measures to optimize the network. Take Adidas's image as an example, we optimized the network in which Adidas's best accompanying dataset (the one making Adidas recognition precision reach the highest) is used in the model training. We calculated the metrics of the 96 convolution kernels in AlexNet's first layer according to Eq. 1, and list them in the ascending order. Convolution kernels with metrics at the end of the list are of low quality. We re-trained the network by removing the convolution kernels from the last 10%, 20%, ..., up to 50%

Algorithm 1. Calculate Hamming Distance Between Two Logo Images

---

Input   : $image_A$ and $image_B$
Output: hamming distance D
/* Calculating the hamming distance of two images using pHash
  algorithm   */
1 Resize $image_A$ and $image_B$ to 32×32;
2 Turn $image_A$ and $image_B$ to grayscale images;
3 Calculate two images' DCT coefficient matrix A and B and their average
   values $\bar{a}$ and $\bar{b}$;
4 **foreach** *value a_i in A* **do**
5 | **if** $a_i \geq \bar{a}$ **then**
6 | | $a_i \leftarrow 1$;
7 | **end**
8 | **else**
9 | | $a_i \leftarrow 0$;
10 | **end**
11 **end**
12 **foreach** *value b_i in B* **do**
13 | **if** $b_i \geq \bar{b}$ **then**
14 | | $b_i \leftarrow 1$;
15 | **end**
16 | **else**
17 | | $b_i \leftarrow 0$;
18 | **end**
19 **end**
20 Transform A and B into two series P and Q, the length of series is n;
21 $D \leftarrow 0$;
22 $i \leftarrow 1$;
23 **while** $i \leq n$ **do**
24 | **if** $P_i \neq Q_i$ **then**
25 | | $D \leftarrow D+1$;
26 | **end**
27 **end**
28 **return** D

---

of the list. Then we calculated the network's recall and precision and recorded
the training time (the time when the value of the loss function drops to 5). The
comparison between the new networks and the original network are shown in
Table 1.

It can be seen that after compressing the network's first layer by 30%, the
network's recognition precision only decreased slightly (1% for the best accompanying dataset) but it still has remained at a high level (89%). And the training
time has reduced by nearly 40%. Too much compression may significantly harm
the precision and recall of the model and lead to more training time, as shown in
the case of 40% and 50% compression. The increase of the training time in 40%
and 50% compression is because the network drops too many convolution kernels

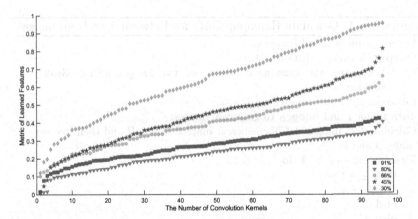

Fig. 5. The metric values of learned features for adidas using accompanying datasets with different similarities

Table 1. Effects of Compression

Similarity (%)	Network	Recall (%)	Precision (%)	Training time (min.)
91	Original	91.3	88.0	15
	10% Compression	90.7	87.2	13
	20% Compression	90.6	87.2	10
	30% Compression	**90.2**	**86.6**	**9**
	40% Compression	88.3	85.3	11
	50% Compression	86.2	85.1	15
80	Original	94.2	90.0	15
	10% Compression	93.5	89.6	13
	20% Compression	93.2	89.2	12
	30% Compression	**92.8**	**89.0**	**10**
	40% Compression	90.5	87.6	11
	50% Compression	90.3	87.6	14
66	Original	84.1	77.6	17
	10% Compression	82.5	74.4	13
	20% Compression	81.5	74.0	11
	30% Compression	80.3	73.5	10
	40% Compression	78.5	72.4	12
	50% Compression	72.1	72.9	16

to converge in a short time. Therefore, the last 30% of convolution kernels in the list are the proper set of kernels that should be abandon with high priority. We can use this finding to compress the neural network and save training time while maintaining a comparable recognition performance.

5   Conclusion

We utilized DeconvNet to visually analyzed the mechanism of the accompanying dataset scheme and designed a quantitative metric for measuring the quality of learned features of the first layer of the AlexNet. By using the pre-trained features that are trained from decomposing elements of loges, we obtain the references for representing real features, which can be used to calculate the quality of learned features. We utilized the result of the analysis to compress the AlexNet model for logo recognition, which can compress 30% of the convolutional kernels in the first layer and save 40% training time while only decreasing the recall and precision by 0.014 and 0.01 respectively. This promising result means that our model is more suitable for resource-limited terminals such as a smartphone for logo recognition without having to send the recognition task to the remote server, thus would obtain a more appropriate user experience. In our next step work, we would refine the metric so as to further compress the network while maintaining a high recognition performance.

Acknowledgments. The work was supported in part by the National High-tech R&D Program of China (863 Program) (2015AA017201) and National Key Research and Development Program of China (2016QY01W0200). The authors are very grateful to the anonymous viewers of this paper.

References

1. Wang, Y., Yang, W., Zhang, H.: Deep learning single logo recognition with data enhancement by shape context. In: The 2018 International Joint Conference on Neural Networks (2018)
2. Krizhevsky, A., Sutskever, I., Hinton, G.E.: ImageNet recognition with deep convolutional neural networks. In: Advances in Neural Information Processing Systems, pp. 1097–1105 (2012)
3. Hu, J., Shen, L., Sun, G.: Squeeze-and-excitation networks. arXiv preprint arXiv:1709.01507 (2017)
4. He, K., Zhang, X., Ren, S., Sun, J.: Identity mappings in deep residual networks. In: Leibe, B., Matas, J., Sebe, N., Welling, M. (eds.) ECCV 2016. LNCS, vol. 9908, pp. 630–645. Springer, Cham (2016). https://doi.org/10.1007/978-3-319-46493-0_38
5. Zhang, X., Li, Z., Loy, C.C., Lin, D.: PolyNet: a pursuit of structural diversity in very deep networks. In: 2017 IEEE Conference on Computer Vision and Pattern Recognition, pp. 3900–3908. IEEE (2017)
6. Yang, B., Gu, F., Niu, X.: Block mean value based image perceptual hashing. In: International Conference on Intelligent Information Hiding and Multimedia Signal Processing, pp. 167–172. IEEE (2006)
7. Erhan, D., Bengio, Y., Courville, A., Vincent, P.: Visualizing higher-layer features of a deep network. Univ. Montr. **1341**(3), 1 (2009)
8. Mahendran, A., Vedaldi, A.: Understanding deep image representations by inverting them. In: Proceedings of the IEEE Conference on Computer Vision and Pattern Recognition, pp. 5188–5196. IEEE (2015)

9. Zeiler, M.D., Fergus, R.: Visualizing and understanding convolutional networks. In: Fleet, D., Pajdla, T., Schiele, B., Tuytelaars, T. (eds.) ECCV 2014. LNCS, vol. 8689, pp. 818–833. Springer, Cham (2014). https://doi.org/10.1007/978-3-319-10590-1_53

10. Wang, Y., Xu, C., Xu, C., Tao, D.: Packing convolutional neural networks in the frequency domain. IEEE Trans. Pattern Anal. Mach. Intell. (2018). https://doi.org/10.1109/TPAMI.2018.2857824

11. Luo, J., Wu, J.: An entropy-based pruning method for CNN compression. arXiv preprint arXiv:1706.05791 (2017)

12. Guo, J., Zhou, B., Zeng, X., Freyberg, Z., Xu, M.: Model compression for faster structural separation of macromolecules captured by Cellular Electron Cryo-Tomography. In: International Conference Image Analysis and Recognition, pp. 144–152. ACM (2018)

13. Hu, J., He, K., Hopcroft, J.E., Zhang, Y.: Deep compression on convolutional neural network for artistic style transfer. In: Du, D., Li, L., Zhu, E., He, K. (eds.) NCTCS 2017. CCIS, vol. 768, pp. 157–166. Springer, Singapore (2017). https://doi.org/10.1007/978-981-10-6893-5_12

14. Hu, J., Li, M., Xia, C., Zhang, Y.: Combine traditional compression method with convolutional neural networks. In: Proceedings of the IEEE Conference on Computer Vision and Pattern Recognition Workshops, pp. 2563–2566. IEEE (2018)

15. Li, M., Hu, J., Xia, C., Zhang, Y.: An implementation of picture compression with a CNN-based Auto-encoder. In: Proceedings of the IEEE Conference on Computer Vision and Pattern Recognition Workshops, pp. 2543–2546. IEEE (2018)

16. Mitani, T., Fukuoka, H., Hiraga, Y., Nakada, T., Nakashima, Y.: Compression and aggregation for optimizing information transmission in distributed CNN. In: 2017 Fifth International Symposium on Computing and Networking, pp. 112–118. CANDAR (2017)

17. Xie, X., Han, X., Liao, Q., Shi, G.: Visualization and pruning of SSD with the base network VGG16. In: Proceedings of the 2017 International Conference on Deep Learning Technologies, pp. 90–94. ACM (2017)

18. Szegedy, C., et al.: Going deeper with convolutions. In: Proceedings of the IEEE Conference on Computer Vision and Pattern Recognition, pp. 1–9. IEEE (2015)

19. Kalantidis, Y., Pueyo, L., Trevisiol, M., van Zwol, R., Avrithis, Y.: Scalable triangulation-based logo recognition. In: Proceedings of ACM International Conference on Multimedia Retrieval (ICMR 2011), Trento Italy (2011)

20. Zeiler, M.D., Taylor, G.W., Fergus, R.: Adaptive deconvolutional networks for mid and high level feature learning. In: 2011 IEEE International Conference on Computer Vision (ICCV), pp. 2018–2025. IEEE (2011)

21. Ahmed, N., Natarajan, T., Rao, K.R.: Discrete cosine transform. IEEE Trans. Comput. 100(1), 90–93 (1974)

Water Wave Optimization for Artificial Neural Network Parameter and Structure Optimization

Xiao-Han Zhou[1], Zhi-Ge Xu[1], Min-Xia Zhang[1], and Yu-Jun Zheng[1,2(✉)]

[1] College of Computer Science and Technology, Zhejiang University of Technology,
Hangzhou 310023, China
seanzxhan@gmail.com, xuzhige@foxmail.com, zmx@zjut.edu.cn,
yujun.zheng@computer.org
[2] Institute of Service Engineering, Hangzhou Normal University,
Hangzhou 311121, China

Abstract. Artificial neural networks (ANNs) have powerful function approximation and pattern classification capabilities, but their performance is greatly affected by structural design and parameter selection. Traditional training methods have drawbacks including long training time, over-fitting, premature convergence, etc. Evolutionary optimization algorithms have provided an effective tool for ANN parameter optimization, but simultaneously optimizing ANN structure and parameters remains a difficult problem. This paper adapts a relatively new evolutionary algorithm, water wave optimization (WWO), for both structure design and parameter selection for ANNs. The algorithm uses a variable-dimensional solution representation, and designs new propagation, refraction, and breaking operators to effectively evolve solutions towards the optimum or near-optima. Computational experiments show that the WWO algorithm exhibits significant performance advantages over other popular evolutionary algorithms including genetic algorithm, particle swarm optimization, and biogeography-based optimization, for ANN structure and parameter optimization.

Keywords: Artificial neural networks (ANNs)
Evolutionary neural networks · Parameter selection · Structural design
Water wave optimization (WWO)

1 Introduction

Since the original work of McCulloch and Pitts [8] in the 1940s, artificial neural networks (ANNs) have become an active research field in artificial intelligence. Nevertheless, the performance of ANNs is seriously affected by the selection of their structures and parameters. Traditional training methods, such as the back-propagation (BP) algorithm [3], have drawbacks such as long training time, over-fitting, and premature convergence. To overcome these disadvantages, a number

© Springer Nature Singapore Pte Ltd. 2018
J. Qiao et al. (Eds.): BIC-TA 2018, CCIS 951, pp. 343–354, 2018.
https://doi.org/10.1007/978-981-13-2826-8_30

of heuristic optimization algorithms, in particular bio-inspired evolutionary algorithms, have been applied to and shown good performance on ANN training [10]. Essentially, the problem of selecting parameters (including neuron biases and connection weights) for an ANN can be regarded as a high-dimensional global optimization problem [14], for which metaheuristic algorithms including genetic algorithms (GA) [13], evolutionary programming (EP) [12], particle swarm optimization (PSO) [9,15], biogeography-based optimization (BBO) [16], etc., can efficiently explore the search space.

Nevertheless, simultaneously optimizing the structure and parameters of an ANN is much more complex. Lam et al. [6] use an improved GA to tune ANN structure and parameters, where number of hidden nodes starts from a small number and will continue to increase if the fitness is not acceptable. However, such a tuning method is very time-consuming. Kiranyaz et al. [5] propose a multi-dimensional PSO algorithm that removes the necessity of fixing the dimension in advance and thus enables encoding both network structure and parameters into particles. Das et al. [2] propose another PSO algorithm for ANN training, where the number of layers and neurons are also regarded as parameters encoded into particles, but this also makes the search space extremely huge and thus degrades the algorithm performance. Salama and Abdelbar [11] propose an ant colony optimization (ACO) algorithm to learn ANN structure, where the number of hidden neurons is determined by pruning the maximally connected network structure, but it does not simultaneously optimize the structure and parameters. In general, simultaneously optimizing ANN structure and parameters remains a quite difficult optimization problem.

In this paper, we propose a new water wave optimization (WWO) algorithm for ANN structure and parameters optimization. The algorithm uses a variable-dimensional solution representation to encode both structure configurations and neuron/connection parameters, and efficiently explore the huge solution space based on adapted propagation, refraction, and breaking operators. Computational experiments show that the WWO algorithm exhibits competitive performance on ANN parameter & structure optimization compared to other popular metaheuristics.

In the rest of this paper, Sect. 2 describes the problems of ANN structural design and parameter selection. Section 3 proposes the WWO algorithm. Section 4 presents the computational experiments, and finally Sect. 5 concludes.

2   ANN Parameter and Structure Optimization

An ANN is a collection of simple computational units (called neurons) interlinked by a systems of weighted connections to model complex relationships between input and output variables. ANN provides a powerful model that can learn any kind of continuous nonlinear mapping [4]. ANN training is an optimization task for determining the optimal network structure and parameters to minimize the deviations of the network outputs and the expected outputs over training samples.

2.1   The Problem of ANN Parameter Optimization

In this paper we focus on the most widely-used feedforward neural networks, where each layer contains a set of artificial neurons that can only be connected to the neurons of the next layer. However, it is not difficult to extend our approach for other types of ANNs. In a feedforward ANN, each neuron in the input layer directly accepts an input, while each neuron j in the hidden or output layer accepts a set of inputs x_{ij} from the neurons of the previous layer and produces an output y_j as follows:

$$y_j = \phi(\sum_{i=1}^{m} w_{ij}x_{ij} - \theta_j) \tag{1}$$

where m is the number of inputs, w_{ij} is the connection weight of ith input, θ_j is the threshold of the neuron, and ϕ is the activation function which typically uses the Sigmoid function or the hyperbolic tangent function.

Once the structure of the network has been (manually) determined, we need to tune the parameters including all neuron biases θ_i and all connection weights w_{ij}, such that the actual output of the ANN on the training set is as close as possible to the expected output. Suppose that the training set has N samples, the input-output pair of each sample is $(\boldsymbol{x}_i, \boldsymbol{y}_i)$, the output of the ANN for $\boldsymbol{x}_i$ is $\boldsymbol{o}_i$, the ANN training is to minimize the root mean square error (RMSE) between the actually outputs and the expected outputs:

$$\min \text{RMSE} = \sqrt{\frac{1}{N}\sum_{i=1}^{N} \|\boldsymbol{y}_i - \boldsymbol{o}_i\|^2} \tag{2}$$

Thus the ANN training problem can be regarded as a high-dimensional optimization problem. Typically, the values of biases and weights can be limited in the range of $[0,1]$ or $[-1,1]$. For example, for a typical three-layer feedforward ANN, let n_1, n_2, and n_3 be the number of neurons in the input layer, the hidden layer, and the output layer, respectively, the problem dimension is $(n_1 n_2 + n_2 n_3 + n_1 + n_2 + n_3)$.

2.2   The Problem of ANN Structure Optimization

The above problem assumes that the ANN structure has been fixed, and only neuron biases and connection weights are to be optimized. However, ANN performance also heavily depends on its structure. When the input-output scheme of an ANN is known, we need to determine the number of neurons in each hidden layer. For example, for a three-layer ANN, if the number n_2 of neurons in the hidden layer is too small, the computing power of the ANN will be limited, and the training will be easily trapped in local optima; on the contrary, if n_2 is too large, the training time will be prolonged, and the training results are more likely to be over-fitting. However, in traditional approaches the number of neurons is determined mainly based on experiences, which often leads to inappropriate structural design.

Therefore, it is reasonable to simultaneously optimize the structure and parameters of ANN. For a three-layer ANN, the number n_2 of neurons in the hidden layer should be an additional decision variable to be optimized. Empirically, the value range of n_2 can be set as follows:

$$\log_2 n_1 \leq n_2 \leq \sqrt{n_1 + n_3} + 10 \tag{3}$$

Besides the minimization of RMSE on the training set, we also expect that n_2 can be as small as possible in order to simplify the network structure, and thus we can set the objective function as follows:

$$\min f = w \cdot \text{RMSE} + (1 - w)\frac{n_2}{n_1 + n_3 + \sqrt{n_1 + n_3} + 10} \tag{4}$$

where w represents the weight of RMSE in the objective function, and its value is typically between 0.6 and 0.9.

By analogy, for a K-layer ANN, we need to determine $(K - 2)$ additional decision variables, i.e., $n_2, n_3, \ldots, n_{K-1}$ the objective function as follows:

$$\min f = w \cdot \text{RMSE} + (1 - w)\frac{n_2 + n_3 + \cdots + n_{K-1}}{n_2^{\text{U}} + n_3^{\text{U}} + \cdots + n_{K-1}^{\text{U}}} \tag{5}$$

where n_k^{U} denotes the upper limit of the number of neurons in the k-th layer.

Although structural design itself adds only a small number of decision variables, it makes the number of other bias and weight parameters variable, and thus makes the integrated ANN structure and parameter optimization problem become a variable-dimensional optimization problem that is much more difficult to solve.

3 A New WWO Algorithm for ANN Parameter and Structure Optimization

In this paper we propose a new WWO algorithm for ANN optimization. WWO [18] is a relatively new metaheuristic that takes inspiration from shallow water wave models for optimization, where each solution X is analogous to a wave. The higher (lower) the energy or fitness of the wave, the smaller (larger) the wavelength λ_X, and the smaller (larger) the range it explores, as shown in Fig. 1. In this way, the algorithm can achieve a good dynamic balance between diversification and intensification.

3.1 WWO for ANN Parameter Optimization

The original WWO uses three operators, named propagation, refraction, and breaking, for searching in high-dimensional continuous solution space, and thus can directly apply to the ANN parameter optimization problem.

Propagation of a solution X is done by shifting each dimension d of X as follows (where function *rand* produces a random number uniformly distributed

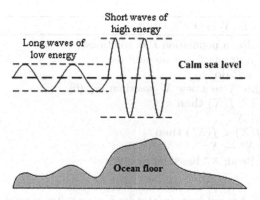

Fig. 1. Illustration of wave propagation in shallow water.

in the given range, and $L(d)$ is the length of the dth dimension of the search space):

$$X'(d) = X(d) + \lambda_X \cdot rand(-1, 1) \cdot L(d) \tag{6}$$

All wavelengths are initially set to 0.5, and then updated after each generation as follows:

$$\lambda_X = \lambda_X \cdot \alpha^{-(f(X)-f_{\min}+\epsilon)/(f_{\max}-f_{\min}+\epsilon)} \tag{7}$$

where $f_{\max}$ and $f_{\min}$ are respectively the maximum and minimum fitness values among the population, α is the wavelength reduction coefficient set to 1.0026, and ϵ is a very small number to avoid division-by-zero.

Remark 1. f in Eq. (7) denotes the fitness function. For a problem minimizing an objective function as Eqs. (4) or (5), the numerator of the exponential term in Eq. (7) can be replaced by $-(f_{\max} - f(X) + \epsilon)$.

Refraction replaces a wave X losing energy (i.e., having not been improved after several generations) with a new wave generated at a random position between the old wave and the best known solution X^*:

$$X'(d) = \mathcal{N}\left(\frac{X^*(d) + X(d)}{2}, \frac{|X^*(d) - X(d)|}{2}\right) \tag{8}$$

where $\mathcal{N}(\mu, \sigma)$ generates a Gaussian random number with mean μ and standard deviation σ.

Breaking breaks any newly found best wave X^* into several solitary waves, each of which moves a small distance from X^* at a random direction:

$$X'(d) = X^*(d) + \mathcal{N}(0, 1) \cdot \beta L(d) \tag{9}$$

where β is the breaking coefficient. The best solitary wave, if better than X^*, will replace X^* in the population.

Algorithm 1 presents the framework of WWO. If the number of neuron biases and connection weights is n, each solution to the ANN parameter optimization problem is an n-dimensional real-valued vector.

Algorithm 1. The WWO algorithm.

1 Randomly initialize a population P of solutions;
2 **while** *the stop criterion is not satisfied* **do**
3   **foreach** $X \in P$ **do**
4   Propagate X to a new X' based on Eq. (6);
5   **if** $f(X') < f(X)$ **then**
6           $X \leftarrow X'$;
7   **if** $f(X) < f(X^*)$ **then**
8              $X^* \leftarrow X$;
9   Break X^* based on Eq. (9);
10   **else**
11   **if** *X has not been updated for* $\widehat{g}$ *consecutive generations* **then**
12   Refract X to a new X' based on Eq. (8);
13   Update the wavelengths based on Eq. (7);
14 **return** X^*.

3.2 WWO for ANN Structure and Parameter Optimization

When simultaneously optimizing ANN structure and parameters, we use a variable-dimensional solution representation. For a K-layer ANN, the number of hidden layers is $(K - 2)$, and each solution to the ANN structure & parameter optimization problem consists of two parts:

- The first part has $(K - 2)$ integer components $\{n_2, n_3, \ldots, n_{K-1}\}$, each representing the number of neurons in the corresponding hidden layer.
- The second part has $\left(\sum_{i=1}^{K} n_i\right) + \left(\sum_{i=1}^{K-1} n_i n_{i+1}\right)$ real-valued components, each representing a bias or a connection weight.

When propagating a variable-dimensional solution X, we first modify the first $(K - 2)$ components according to the standard propagation operation (6) and round the results into the nearest integers. For each integer component n_k, its value change can be divided into the following three cases:

Case 1. The updated $n'_k = n_k$, which will not affect other real-valued components, and these components are also updated according to the standard propagation operation (6).

Case 2. $n'_k < n_k$, which indicates that the number of neurons decreases. Those real-valued components related to the remaining neurons are updated according to Eq. (6), and the other real-valued components related to the removed neurons are also removed.

Case 3. $n'_k > n_k$, which indicates that the number of neurons increases. Those real-valued components related to the original neurons are updated according to Eq. (6), and those new real-valued components related to the new neurons are randomly generated within the predefined range.

When refracting a stationary solution X based on the best known solution X^*, for each dimension k of the first $(K-2)$ integer components we also have three cases:

Case 1. $X(k) = X^*(k)$, for which the standard refraction operation (8) is directly applied.

Case 2. $X(k) > X^*(k)$, for which we set the refracted $X'(k)$ to a Gaussian random value between $[X^*(k), X(k)]$. For each corresponding real-valued dimension d in both X and X^*, the refracted values is set according to Eq. (8); for each corresponding real-valued dimension d in X but not in X^*, the refracted values is set to a Gaussian random value with mean $X(d)$ and standard deviation 0.5.

Case 3. $X(k) < X^*(k)$, for which we set the refracted $X'(k)$ be a Gaussian random value within $[X(k), X^*(k)]$. For each corresponding real-valued dimension d in both X and X^*, the refracted values is set according to Eq. (8); for each corresponding real-valued dimension d in X^* but not in X, the refracted value is set to a Gaussian random value with mean $X^*(d)$ and standard deviation 0.5.

When breaking a newly found best solution X^*, if the selected dimension d is a real-valued dimension, the standard breaking operation (9) is directly applied. If the selected dimension d is among the first $(K-2)$ integer dimensions, the breaking is done by one of the following two ways:

Case 1. $n_k = n_k - 1$, i.e., a neuron is removed from the k-th layer, and those real-valued dimensions related to the removed neuron are also removed.

Case 2. $n_k = n_k + 1$, i.e., a new neuron is added to the k-th layer, and those new real-valued components related to the new neuron are first randomly generated and then updated by applying the back-propagation algorithm.

By adapting the three operators of WWO, the algorithm can effectively solve the ANN structure & parameter optimization problem.

4   Computation Experiments

We respectively test the algorithm's performance on ANN parameter optimization, one-hidden-layer ANN structure & parameter optimization, and two hidden-layer ANN structure & parameter optimization. For ANN parameter optimization, the training task is to classify three categories of wines according to 13 attributes including alcohol content, acidity, color, etc. Accordingly, the input dimension is 13 and the output dimension is one. The number of neurons in the hidden layer is empirically set to $(13+1)/2 = 7$. The test set is the WINE dataset from the UCI Repository [1], which contains 178 samples. The experiment is divided into three groups, where the ratio of training set size to test set size is set to 2:3, 3:2, and 4:1, respectively. The proposed algorithm is compared with the traditional BP algorithm and four evolutionary learning algorithms, including GA [7], PSO [15], BBO [16], and EBO [19], and their performance is evaluated in terms of the average classification accuracy, i.e., the percentage of the number of samples that are correctly classified. The BP algorithm is run once, while each metaheuristic algorithm is run for 20 times.

Table 1 presents the classification results of the algorithms for ANN parameter optimization, where the maximum/mean classification accuracies among the algorithms are shown in bold. As we can see from the results, the performance of GA is not always better than the traditional BP algorithm: on the first group, both the maximum and the mean accuracies of GA are smaller than BP; on the second and the third groups, the maximum accuracies of GA are larger than BP, but the mean accuracies of GA are smaller. Thus, the adoption of GA for ANN parameter optimization achieves little performance improvement, mainly because the crossover and mutation operations of GA easily lead to premature convergence. However, the other four metaheuristic algorithms show significant performance improvement over BP. On the first group, both EBO and WWO obtain the best maximum accuracy, and EBO obtains the best mean accuracy. On the second and the third groups, both the maximum and the mean accuracies of WWO are the best among all algorithms. In particular, on the third group, the ANN optimized by WWO is able to correctly classify all the 36 test samples. The results demonstrate that, even only for optimizing ANN parameters, the proposed WWO shows competitive performance on the test problem.

Table 1. Classification accuracies of three-layer ANNs trained by the algorithms for parameter optimization.

Group	Metrics	BP	GA	PSO	BBO	EBO	WWO
2:3	Max	84.11	83.18	92.52	88.79	**96.26**	96.26
	Min	84.11	79.44	90.65	82.24	94.39	92.52
	Mean	84.11	81.33	91.67	85.2	**95.13**	94.96
	Std	–	1.88	0.9	2.12	1.02	1.49
3:2	Max	84.27	84.87	93.28	89.08	**97.48**	97.48
	Min	84.27	80.67	91.60	84.87	94.96	96.64
	Mean	84.27	83.15	92.35	87.11	96.29	**96.95**
	Std	–	2.06	0.89	2.33	1.15	0.89
4:1	Max	77.78	83.33	94.44	88.89	97.22	**100.00**
	Min	77.78	75.00	94.44	80.56	97.22	97.22
	Mean	77.78	80.78	94.44	82.9	97.22	**98.05**
	Std	–	3.2	0	3.16	0	1.27

However, the improvement of ANN training effects is usually at the expense of training time. Table 2 compares the training time of the algorithms. As we can see, the BP algorithm uses the least training time, and the five evolutionary algorithms consume much more time. Thus, we can use evolutionary learning for

ANN to achieve a much higher accuracy, if the training time is affordable. Among the five evolutionary algorithms, PSO consumes the least training time, and WWO consumes the second least. Given its advantage in classification accuracy, WWO is the most preferable algorithm for evolutionary learning.

Table 2. The training time (in seconds) of the algorithms for ANN parameter optimization.

Group	BP	GA	PSO	BBO	EBO	WWO
2:3	0.61	7.93	6.30	7.88	7.28	6.96
3:2	1.08	9.82	7.13	9.55	8.35	7.78
4:1	1.59	10.50	9.07	11.20	9.10	9.40
Average	1.09	9.42	7.50	9.54	8.24	8.05

The test of one-hidden-layer ANN structure & parameter optimization is also conducted on the WINE dataset and uses three groups as described above, except that the number of neurons in the hidden layer is also optimized by the algorithms. The proposed algorithm is compared with GA [7], PSO [2], and BBO and EBO which also encode the number of neurons as a solution component [20]. Table 3 presents the classification results of the algorithms for ANN structure & parameter optimization. The results show that EBO and WWO also achieve the much better classification accuracies than the other three algorithms. Compared to Table 1, we can see that for GA and BBO, the classification accuracies obtained by optimizing both network structure and parameters are even worse than that are obtained by only optimizing parameters. This is because the inclusion of the structure parameter greatly enlarges the solution space, and GA and BBO cannot efficiently explore such a large solution space. The other three algorithms show much better performance as they can find better network structures (if exist) than the structure set based on experience. In particular, as a major upgrade of BBO, EBO exhibits significant performance improvement over the original BBO, because the combination of global migration and local migration in EBO ha much higher exploration ability than the original clonal migration in BBO [19]. In this experimental part, both EBO and WWO can find the optimal number of neuron in the hidden layer, and they reach the same accuracies on the second and the third groups, while WWO performs slightly better than EBO on the first group.

The test of two hidden-layer ANN structure & parameter optimization is conducted on an airline passenger dataset from [17]. The task is to identify suspicious terrorists from normal passengers. The input dimension is around 7000, and thus using a single hidden layer is not sufficient for such a high-dimensional problem. The number of samples in the dataset is huge, and for convenience we conduct three groups of experiment which take 1000, 3000, and 6000 samples, respectively. The number of positive samples is 162 in all three groups. The five metaheuristics are the same as used in the second group. Table 4 present

Table 3. Classification accuracies of three-layer ANNs trained by the algorithms for structure & parameter optimization.

Group	Metrics	GA	PSO	BBO	EBO	WWO
2:3	Max	84.11	94.39	86.92	96.26	**98.13**
	Min	79.44	93.46	83.18	96.26	96.26
	Mean	81.70	93.69	84.89	96.26	**96.65**
	Std	2.01	0.71	1.61	0	0.88
3:2	Max	84.87	94.12	88.24	**97.48**	**97.48**
	Min	82.35	90.76	85.71	97.48	97.48
	Mean	83.60	92.23	86.86	**97.48**	**97.48**
	Std	1.12	1.55	1.22	0.91	0
4:1	Max	80.56	97.22	88.89	**100**	**100**
	Min	77.78	97.22	77.78	100	100
	Mean	79.32	97.22	81.38	**100**	**100**
	Std	2.05	0	5.16	0	0

the experimental results. On this much more complex problem, the performance of GA is still the worst, and its accuracies are quite unstable among different runs. On the last group, the mean accuracies of GA and BBO are below 50% and cannot be acceptable in practice. The performance of EBO is much higher than GA, PSO, and BBO, but obviously worse than WWO. In summary, WWO exhibits significant performance advantages over all other four algorithms, and

Table 4. Classification accuracies of four-layer ANNs trained by the algorithms for structure & parameter optimization.

Group	Metrics	GA	PSO	BBO	EBO	WWO
#1	Max	70.50	73.70	69.80	79.70	**82.20**
	Min	53.20	65.80	61.10	75.10	78.00
	Mean	61.55	69.63	65.50	77.02	**79.31**
	Std	7.36	2.93	3.51	2.11	1.56
#2	Max	58.90	67.67	62.53	71.30	**74.80**
	Min	49.63	60.27	57.80	66.56	70.17
	Mean	54.21	63.39	59.91	69.03	**72.23**
	Std	4.55	3.02	1.96	2.76	2.60
#3	Max	47.53	56.57	50.13	63.20	**65.10**
	Min	39.50	51.23	46.60	57.93	60.60
	Mean	42.66	53.09	48.12	60.11	**62.39**
	Std	3.84	2.05	1.80	2.51	2.37

it uniquely obtains the best maximum and mean classification accuracies on all three groups. This demonstrates that the proposed WWO algorithm is quite efficient for complex ANN training problems.

5 Conclusion

This paper proposes a new WWO algorithm for ANN structure and parameter optimization. The algorithm uses a variable-dimensional solution representation, and proposes new propagation, refraction, and breaking operators to effectively evolve variable-dimensional solutions towards the optimum or near-optima. Computational experiments show that the WWO algorithm exhibits competitive performance on ANN parameter & structure optimization compared to some other popular evolutionary algorithms. Our ongoing work is to adapt the algorithm for more complex ANN types, including recurrent neural networks, neuro-fuzzy systems, and deep neural networks.

Acknowledgements. This work is supported by National Natural Science Foundation (Grant No. 61473263) and Zhejiang Provincial Natural Science Foundation (Grant No. LY14F030011) of China.

References

1. Blake, C.L., Merz, C.J.: UCI repository of machine learning databases (1998). http://www.ics.uci.edu/~mlearn/MLRepository.html
2. Das, G., Pattnaik, P.K., Padhy, S.K.: Artificial neural network trained by particle swarm optimization for non-linear channel equalization. Expert Syst. Appl. **41**(7), 3491–3496 (2014)
3. Hopfield, J.J.: Neural networks and physical systems with emergent collective computational abilities. Proc. Nat. Acad. Sci. **79**, 2554–2558 (1982)
4. Hornik, K.: Approximation capabilities of multilayer feedforward networks. Neural Netw. **4**(2), 251–257 (1991)
5. Kiranyaz, S., Ince, T., Yildirim, A., Gabbouj, M.: Evolutionary artificial neural networks by multi-dimensional particle swarm optimization. Neural Netw. **22**(10), 1448–1462 (2009)
6. Lam, H.K., Ling, S.H., Leung, F.H.F., Tam, P.K.S.: Tuning of the structure and parameters of neural network using an improved genetic algorithm. In: The 27th Annual Conference of the IEEE Industrial Electronics Society, vol. 1, pp. 25–30. IEEE (2001)
7. Leung, F.H.F., Lam, H.K., Ling, S.H., Tam, P.K.S.: Tuning of the structure and parameters of a neural network using an improved genetic algorithm. IEEE Trans. Neural Netw. **14**, 79–88 (2003)
8. McCulloch, W.S., Pitts, W.H.: A logical calculus for the ideas immanent in nervous activity. Bull. Math. Biophys. **5**, 115–133 (1943)
9. Mendes, R., Cortez, P., Rocha, M., Neves, J.: Particle swarms for feedforward neural network training. In: International Joint Conference on Neural Networks, pp. 1895–1899. IEEE (2002)

10. Ojha, V.K., Abraham, A., Snášel, V.: Metaheuristic design of feedforward neural networks: a review of two decades of research. Eng. Appl. Artif. Intell. **60**, 97–116 (2017)
11. Salama, K.M., Abdelbar, A.M.: Learning neural network structures with ant colony algorithms. Swarm Intell. **9**(4), 229–265 (2015)
12. Sarkar, M., Yegnanarayana, B.: Feedforward neural networks configuration using evolutionary programming. In: International Conference on Neural Networks, pp. 438–443. IEEE (1997)
13. Whitley, D., Starkweather, T., Bogart, C.: Genetic algorithms and neural networks: optimizing connections and connectivity. Parall. Comput. **14**(3), 347–361 (1990)
14. Yao, X.: A review of evolutionary artificial neural networks. Int. J. Intell. Syst. **8**(4), 539–567 (1993)
15. Zhang, J.R., Zhang, J., Lok, T.M., Lyu, M.R.: A hybrid particle swarm optimization-back-propagation algorithm for feedforward neural network training. Appl. Math. Comput. **185**(2), 1026–1037 (2007)
16. Zhang, Y., Phillips, P., Wang, S., Ji, G., Yang, J., Wu, J.: Fruit classification by biogeography-based optimization and feedforward neural network. Expert Syst. **33**(3), 239–253 (2016)
17. Zheng, Y.J., Sheng, W.G., Sun, X.M., Chen, S.Y.: Airline passenger profiling based on fuzzy deep machine learning. IEEE Trans. Neural Netw. Learn. Syst. **28**(12), 2911–2923 (2017)
18. Zheng, Y.J.: Water wave optimization: a new nature-inspired metaheuristic. Comput. Oper. Res. **55**(1), 1–11 (2015)
19. Zheng, Y.J., Ling, H.F., Xue, J.Y.: Ecogeography-based optimization: enhancing biogeography-based optimization with ecogeographic barriers and differentiations. Comput. Oper. Res. **50**, 115–127 (2014)
20. Zheng, Y., Chen, S., Zhang, M.: Biogeography-Based Optimization: Algorithms and Applications. Science Press (2016)

Adaptive Recombination Operator Selection in Push and Pull Search for Solving Constrained Single-Objective Optimization Problems

Zhun Fan$^{(\boxtimes)}$, Zhaojun Wang, Yi Fang, Wenji Li, Yutong Yuan,
and Xinchao Bian

Department of Electronic Engineering, Shantou University, Shantou 515063,
Guangdong, China
zfan@stu.edu.cn

Abstract. This paper proposes an adaptive method to select recombination operators, including differential evolution (DE) operators and polynomial operators. Moreover, a push and pull search (PPS) method is used to handle constrained single-objective optimization problems (CSOPs). The PPS has two search stages—the push stage and the pull stage. In the push stage, a CSOP is optimized without considering constraints. In the pull stage, the CSOP is optimized with an improved epsilon constraint-handling method. In this paper, twenty-eight CSOPs are used to test the performance of the proposed adaptive GA with the PPS method (AGA-PPS). AGA-PPS is compared with three other differential evolution algorithms, including LSHADE44+IDE, LSHADE44 and UDE. The experimental results indicate that the proposed AGA-PPS is significantly better than other compared algorithms on the twenty-eight CSOPsq.

Keywords: Adaptive recombination operator selection
Constrained single-objective optimization
Constraint-handling technique · Push-pull search

1 Introduction

Many real-parameter single-objective optimization problems have constraints [1,2]. In general, a constrained single-objective optimization problem can be defined as follows:

$$\text{minimize } f(\mathbf{x}), \ \mathbf{x} = (x_1, \ldots, x_D) \in S \tag{1}$$
$$\text{subject to} \quad g_i(x) \geq 0, i = 1, \ldots, q$$
$$h_j(x) = 0, j = 1, \ldots, p$$

© Springer Nature Singapore Pte Ltd. 2018
J. Qiao et al. (Eds.): BIC-TA 2018, CCIS 951, pp. 355–367, 2018.
https://doi.org/10.1007/978-981-13-2826-8_31

where $f(\mathbf{x})$ is the objective function. $\mathbf{x}$ is a decision vector. x_i is the i-th variable of $\mathbf{x}$. $S = \prod_{i=1}^{D}[L_i, \ U_i]$ is the decision space, where L_i and the U_i are the lower and the upper bounds of x_i. $g_i(\mathbf{x})$ denotes the i-th inequality constraint, and $h_j(\mathbf{x})$ denotes j-th equality constraint.

In order to evaluate the constraint violation of a solution $\mathbf{x}$, the overall constraint violation method is adopted, which summaries all constraints into a scalar value $\phi(\mathbf{x})$, as follows:

$$\phi(\mathbf{x}) = \sum_{i=1}^{q} \max(g_i(\mathbf{x}), 0) + \sum_{j=1}^{p} \max(|h_j(\mathbf{x})| - \sigma, 0) \qquad (2)$$

In this paper, σ is set to 0.0001 as suggested in [3]. If $\phi(\mathbf{x}) = 0$, the $\mathbf{x}$ is a feasible solution. Otherwise it is an infeasible solution.

At present, the Constraint-handling Technique based on evolutionary algorithm can be divided into the following two categories: Penalty Function Based Methods and Multi-objective Based Methods. For example: Le Riche et al. [4] proposed a segregated genetic algorithm (SGGA), It contains two values of the penalty parameter, SGGA permits to balance the inuence of the two penalty parameters. Huang et al. [5] proposed a novel method co-evolutionary differential evolution (CDE), two kinds of populations are used in CDE, In the population denotes a set of penalty factors, and in another kind of populations denotes a decision solution. Surry and Radcliffe [6] proposed COMOGA, that is, the single-objective constrained optimization problem is considered as a constraint satisfaction problem or a single-object unconstrained optimization problem.

As a representative heuristic algorithm, generic algorithm (GA) [16] can be used to optimize real-parameter SOPs. A typical example of GA is differential evolution algorithm (DE). There are many different variants of DE. For example, FADE [7], jDE [8], JADE [9], CoDE [10], SHADE [11], L-SHADE [12], L-SHADE44 [13] and so on. FADE [7] sets the DE parameters by using the fuzzy logic control. jDE [8] updates the DE parameters with different probabilities. JADE [9] proposes a current-to-$p$best/1 with an external archive, a greedy mutation operator. It adaptively updates its parameters in each generations. CoDE [10] applies several groups of suitable parameter settings to the DE. SHADE [11] proposes an adaptive technique of parameter settings by using successful historic memories. L-SHADE [12] is an improved version of SHADE, which reduces the population size linearly during the evolutionary process. As an variant of L-SHADE, L-SHADE44 [13] proposes a strategy to select four different kinds of DE operators adaptively.

However, in some circumstance, the diversity of a population may be lost by only adopting DE operators. A polynomial operator proposed in [17] can be used to enhance the diversity of a population.

To solve CSOPs, an efficient constraint-handling method should be applied [14,18]. ϵ constrained method [15] is a representative constraint-handling method, which can be concluded as the following three rules:

1. When the constraint violations of two individuals are both lower than or equal to ϵ, the individual with the lower objective value is better than the other.

2. When the constraint violations of two individuals are the same, the individual with a lower objective value is better than the other.
3. When at least one constraint violation of two individuals is larger than ϵ, the individual with a lower constraint violation is better than the other.

In this paper, we propose a GA with an adaptive recombination operator selection (AGA) method and a PPS constraint-handling method, namely AGA-PPS.

The rest of this paper is organized as follows. Section 2 introduces some related work. Section 3 introduces the proposed method AGA-PPS. Section 4 shows the experimental results of AGA-PPS and other three DE algorithms (LSHADE44+IDE, LSHADE44 and UDE) on 28 test instances. Section 5 gives the conclusion.

2   Adaptive Recombination Operator Selection

2.1   Successful History Based DE Parameter Settings

In SHADE [11], a method of adaption parameter setting is proposed. For each individual $\mathbf{x}_i$, $i = 1, \ldots, N$, its matching parameters F_i and CR_i are generated according to successful historic memories M_F and M_{CR} with H cells, respectively. A pointer k is used to record the memories. k is initially set to 0. At the beginning of each generation, two sets S_F and S_{CR} are both set as $\emptyset$, which stores the successful parameter pair $\{F_i, CR_i\}$ for each individual $\mathbf{x}_i$, $i = 1, \ldots, N$. At the end of each generation, if S_F is not empty, the k will be increased by 1. If the value of k is larger than H, k will be reset as 1. The adaption factors m_F and m_{CR} are calculated by Eq. (3)–(8), which are stored into the k-th cell of memories M_F and M_{CR}, respectively.

$$m_F = mean_{WL}(S_F) \text{ if } S_F \neq \emptyset \tag{3}$$

$$m_{CR} = mean_{WA}(S_{CR}) \text{ if } S_{CR} \neq \emptyset \tag{4}$$

$$mean_{WL}(S_F) = \frac{\sum_{t_1=1}^{|S_F|} \omega_{t_1} F_{t_1}^2}{\sum_{t_2=1}^{|S_F|} \omega_{t_2} F_{t_2}} \tag{5}$$

$$mean_{WA}(S_{CR}) = \sum_{t=1}^{|S_{CR}|} \omega_t CR_t \tag{6}$$

$$\omega_t = \frac{\Delta func_t}{\sum_{u=1}^{|S_{CR}|} \Delta func_u} \tag{7}$$

$$\Delta func_t = |func(\mathbf{x}_t) - func(\mathbf{y}_t)| \tag{8}$$

In Eq. (8), $func(\cdot) = f(\cdot)$ when $\phi(\mathbf{x}_t) = \phi(\mathbf{y}_t)$ and $f(\mathbf{x}_t) > f(\mathbf{y}_t)$. $func(\cdot) = \phi(\cdot)$ when $\phi(\mathbf{x}) > \phi(\mathbf{y})$. Where $f(\cdot)$ and $\phi(\cdot)$ are objective function and the constraint violation according to Eqs. (1) and (2).

Before performing the DE operators for $\mathbf{x}_i$, the parameter pair $\{F_i, CR_i\}$ is generated by a Cauchy (Normal) distribution of mean $\mu_{F_i}(\mu_{CR_i})$ and a standard deviation σ. The means μ_{F_i} and μ_{CR_i} are generated as follows:

$$F_i = randc_i(\mu_F, 0.1) \tag{9}$$
$$CR_i = randn_i(\mu_{CR}, 0.1) \tag{10}$$

where $randc_i(\mu, \sigma)(randn_i(\mu, \sigma))$ denotes a value generated by a Cauchy (Normal) distribution. When the memories M_F and M_{CR} are both empty, the values of μ_F and μ_{CR} are set as 0.5. Otherwise, an integer r_i is uniformly selected from $[1, H]$, which means the r_i-th pair of values in M_F and M_{CR} will be selected as the means. These values should fall in $[0, 1]$. Otherwise, Eqs. (9) and (10) will be repeated until the pair $\{F_i, CR_i\}$ falls in $[0,1]$.

2.2 Competing Strategy for Selecting DE Operators

In real world, many optimization problems can be seen as black-box problems. Without prior knowledge of problems, it is hard to select a suitable DE strategy. To enhance the robust of an algorithm, various kinds of strategies for selecting DE operators can be used [13].

At the beginning of the evolutionary process, each DE operator has the same probability to be used. This probability is q_l, and q_l is equal to $1/K$. Where K is the number of DE operators. When a DE operator generates a successful trial vector, the probability of each DE operator will be updated as follows:

$$q_l = \frac{n_l + n_0}{\sum_{k=1}^K (n_k) + n_0} \tag{11}$$

where n_l is the successful number of the l-th DE operator, and $n_0 > 0$ is a constant, which is used to smooth the influence of each DE operator. When one of the probabilities is less than a threshold δ, each q_l and n_l is reset as $1/K$ and 0, respectively.

In this paper, four kinds of DE operators are used. They are DE/current-to-pbest/1/Bin (with archive), DE/current-to-pbest/1/Bin (without archive), DE/randr1/1/Bin and DE/current-to-randr1/1/Bin.

2.3 Local Convergence Detection

To detect the status of population, we define a convergence parameter C as follows:

$$C(G) = \frac{f(\mathbf{x}_{i,G}) - f(\mathbf{x}_{j,G-L})}{f(\mathbf{x}_{j,G-L}) - f(\mathbf{x}_{k,G-2L})} \tag{12}$$

where G is current generation and L is a positive integer defined by users, and $L < 0.5G$. $i = \arg_i \min f(\mathbf{x}_{i,G})$, $j = \arg_j \min f(\mathbf{x}_{j,G-L})$ and $k = \arg_k \min f(\mathbf{x}_{k,G-2L})$ are the indexes of the best solutions in different generations.

We initialize the flag f_{local} to zero, which means the population is not locally convergent. If $f_{local} = 1$, it means that the population is locally convergent. With a given threshold η, the f_{local} is updated at end of each generation as follows:

$$f_{local}(G) = \begin{cases} 0, \text{ if } C(G) > \eta \\ 1, \text{ if } C(G) \leq \eta \end{cases} \tag{13}$$

When $f_{local} = 1$, the polynomial operator [17] will perform for each individual after the DE operator.

3   The Proposed Method

In this paper, we propose a GA with an adaptive recombination operator selection (AGA) method and a PPS constraint-handling method, namely AGA-PPS. The details are as following:

1. The GA uses the framework of SHADE [13] to perform the DE operators with the adaption parameter technique. At the beginning of each generation, the status of the current population is detected. If the population is considered to be locally convergent, the polynomial operator will be performed to each individual after the DE operators. Otherwise, each individual is only performed by the DE operators.
2. The PPS method has two stages to handle the constraints. In the first stage, the algorithm optimizes the CSOPs without considering constraints. When the status of population is considered to be locally convergent, the improved epsilon method, which controls the ϵ according to the feasible rate of the current population (fr), will be applied to the algorithm until the stopping criteria are met, which can help to accelerate the convergence of the population and escape from the local optima.

As a variant of epsilon constrained method, the PPS firstly sets the value of ϵ to be infinity, which makes the algorithm optimize a CSOP without considering constraints in the push stage. When f_{local} becomes 0 at the first time, the algorithm optimizes the CSOP in the pull stage, and then an improved ϵ constrained method will be executed.

To balance the evolutionary search of the population between feasible and infeasible regions, an improved ϵ setting approach is suggested as follows:

$$\epsilon(k) = \begin{cases} \textbf{Rule1}(if\ f_{push} = 1) : \infty \\ \textbf{Rule2}(if\ f_{push} = 0 \wedge r_k < \alpha \wedge FEs < T_c) : \epsilon(k-1)(1 - \frac{FEs}{T_c})^{cp} \\ \textbf{Rule3}(if\ f_{push} = 0 \wedge r_k \geq \alpha \wedge FEs < T_c) : (1+\tau)\phi_{max} \\ \textbf{Rule4}(otherwise) : 0 \end{cases} \tag{14}$$

where f_{push} is the pushing flag initialized as 1. r_k is the proportion of feasible solutions in the generation k. FEs is the number of objective function evaluations (FEs). T_c is a controlled objective function evaluations, which is set according to Eq. (15). ϵ will be set to 0 when FEs reaches to T_c. cp and τ are two parameters to control the decreasing and the increasing speed of ϵ. α is a threshold defined by users. When f_{push} becomes 1, the value of ϵ begins to change. When $r_k \geq \alpha$, it means that the number of feasible solutions in the population is enough, and ϵ tends to increase in order to allow more infeasible solutions to have chances to stay in the population. When $r_k < \alpha$, the ϵ tends to decrease, which tends to search for feasible solutions.

$$T_c = FEs_c + 0.8(MaxFEs - FEs_c) \qquad (15)$$

where $MaxFEs$ is the maximal FEs and FEs_c is the FEs when the $f_{local} = 1$ at the first time.

In this paper, the PPS method is embedded in the adaptive GA (AGA-PPS), which is devoted to solve CSOPs, and the pseudo-code of AGA-PPS is shown in Algorithm 1. The best solution $\mathbf{x}_{best}$ updated by each evaluation is the optimal result.

4   Experimental Study

All 28 test instances defined in the report [3] are optimized by the proposed AGA-PPS in this paper. Each instance is a single-objective optimization problem with some inequality or equality constraints. Twenty-five independent runs are carried out for each problem at each kind of dimension levels ($D = 30, 50,$). The maximal FEs is set as $20000D$. The experimental results are shown in Tables 1, 2 and 3. As defined in [3], 'Mean' and 'std' in tables respectively denote the mean value and the standard deviation of the objective during the 25 runs.

4.1   Experimental Settings

The parameter settings are listed as follows:

(1) Population size: $N = 5D$.
(2) The length of historic memory: $H = 10$.
(3) Parameters of strategy for selecting DE operators: $K = 4$, $n_0 = 2$, $\delta = 0.05$.
(4) DE/current-to-$p$best/1 parameter: $p = 0.2$.
(5) The size of external archive: $N_A = 2.5N$
(6) Parameters of IEpsilon: $cp = 2$, $\eta = 0.01$, $\alpha = 0.5$, $\tau = 0.1$, $L = 5$.

4.2   Comparison Among AGA-PPS and Three DE Algorithms

We compare AGA-PPS with three algorithms in 30 and 50 dimensions. Three algorithms are LSHADE44+IDE [19], LSHADE44 [13] and UDE [20]. All the experimental results of these three algorithms come from the official website of CEC2018.

Algorithm 1: AGA-PPS
Input:

A CSOP and a stopping criterion.

N, N_A: the sizes of population and external archive.

cp, L, η, T_c, α, τ: parameters of PPS.

H: the length of the historic memory.

n_0, δ: parameters of strategy competition.

Output: The best solution $\mathbf{x}_{best}$.
Step 1: Initialization:

a) Set probabilities $q_l = 1/4 \; for \; l = 1, 2, 3, 4$.
b) Set counts $n_l = 0 \; for \; l = 1, 2, 3, 4$.
c) Generate a population $P = \{\mathbf{x}_1, ..., \mathbf{x}_N\}$.
d) Evaluate $f(\mathbf{x}_i)$ and $\phi(\mathbf{x}_i)$, $i = 1, ..., N$. Get the maximal constraint violations ϕ_{max}.
e) Set $\epsilon = \infty$. Set $f_{local} = 0$, $f_{push} = 1$.

Step 2: Population update
For $i = 1, \ldots, N$, do

a) Choose the lth strategy according to the $q_l, l = 1, 2, 3, 4$.
b) Generate DE parameters F_i and CR_i according to the memories M_F and M_{CR}.
c) **If** $f_{local} = 0$ **then** perform the selected DE strategy to generate a trial vector $\mathbf{y}_i$.
d) **Else** perform the selected DE strategy and polynomial operator to generate a trial vector $\mathbf{y}_i$.
e) Evaluate $f(\mathbf{y}_i)$ and $\phi(\mathbf{y}_i)$, update $\mathbf{x}_{best}$ and ϕ_{max}.
f) **If** $max(\phi(\mathbf{y}_i) - \epsilon, 0) < max(\phi(\mathbf{x}_i) - \epsilon, 0)$ **then**
    1) replace $\mathbf{x}_i$ with $\mathbf{y}_i$,
    2) $n_l = n_l + 1$, update $q_s, s = 1, 2, 3, 4$ according to Eq (11),
    3) store $|\phi(\mathbf{x}_i) - \phi(\mathbf{y}_i)|$, store F_i and CR_i.
g) **ElseIf** $max(\phi(\mathbf{y}_i) - \epsilon, 0) = max(\phi(\mathbf{x}_i) - \epsilon, 0) \land f(\mathbf{y}_i) < f(\mathbf{x}_i)$ **then**
    1) insert $\mathbf{x}_i$ to the archive A, replace $\mathbf{x}_i$ with $\mathbf{y}_i$.
    2) $n_l = n_l + 1$, update $q_s, s = 1, 2, 3, 4$ according to Eq (11),
    3) store $|f(\mathbf{x}_i) - f(\mathbf{y}_i)|$, store F_i and CR_i.

Step 3: Memories update
Update M_F and M_{CR} for each strategy.
Step 4: Convergence status update
Update f_{local}, T_c, and f_{push} according to Eq (13), (15).
Step 5: Epsilon update
If $f_{push} = 0$, **then**

a) Get the proportion of feasible solutions r_k in the current generation k.
b) **If** $r_k < \alpha \land FEs < T_c$ **then**
    $\epsilon = \epsilon(1 - FEs/T_c)^{cp}$,
c) **ElseIf** $r_k \geq \alpha \land FEs < T_c$ **then**
    $\epsilon = (1 + \tau)\phi_{max}$,
d) **ElseIf** $FEs \geq T_c$ **then**
    $\epsilon = 0$.

Step 6: Termination
If stopping criteria are satisfied, output the best solution $\mathbf{x}_{best}$. Otherwise, go to **Step 2**.

Tables 1 and 3 show the results of mean values of the four single-objective constrained optimization algorithms applying to 28 constraint problems after 25 independent runs implemented in each problem at each kind of dimension levels ($D = 30$, 50). According to the Friedman aligned test, AGA-PPS achieves the highest ranking among the four single-objective constrained optimization algorithms. The p values calculated by the statistics of the Friedman aligned test are 3.61923E−05, 1.02665E−05, and 1.49E−05 for $D = 30$, 50, which reveals the difference among the four algorithms. To compare the statistical difference between the AGA-PPS and other three algorithms, we perform a series of post-hoc tests. Since each adjusted p value in Tables 2 and 4, is less than the preset significant level 0.05, To control the Family-Wise Error Rate (FWER), a set of post-hoc procedures are used as suggested in [21]. we can conclude that AGA-PPS is significantly better than the other three algorithms in the performance of mean value of the objective.

The experimental results in Tables 1 and 3 indicate that AGA-PPS significantly outperforms other three algorithms on C01, C02, C16, C18, C21 and C27 test problems. We analyze the possible reason for C01 test problem. In Fig. 1, the blue area is the objective function and the red area is the constraint function. AGA-PPS can find unconstrained optimal solutions in the push stage, and the unconstrained optimal solutions are the very feasible solutions.

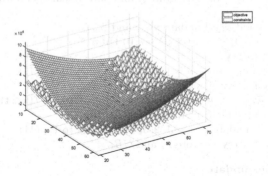

Fig. 1. The C01 test problem. (Color figure online)

Table 1. The mean value and the standard deviation of the objective during the 25 runs on the test instances C01 - C28 with $D = 30$.

Test instances		AGA-PPS	LSHADE44+IDE	LSHADE44	UDE
C01	Mean	7.10E−29	3.37E−11	1.02E−21	2.21E−15
	Std	4.23E−29	4.11E−11	4.87E−21	7.08E−15
C02	Mean	6.27E−29	1.77E−11	2.86E−21	1.17E−14
	Std	4.24E−29	2.52E−11	9.27E−21	3.65E−14
C03	Mean	1.08E+03	1.13E+07	1.12E+06	8.59E+01
	Std	4.16E+02	4.60E+06	1.95E+06	22.89161
C04	Mean	2.19E+01	1.39E+01	1.97E+01	8.45E+01
	Std	3.87E+00	0.778232	0.540477	23.64712

(*continued*)

Table 1. (*continued*)

Test instances		AGA-PPS	LSHADE44+IDE	LSHADE44	UDE
C05	Mean	6.47E−28	1.30E−16	4.25E−03	7.22E+00
	Std	9.26E−28	7.82E−17	0.004395	1.065887
C06	Mean	4.09E+02	5.67E+03	3.96E+03	3.28E+02
	Std	5.59E+01	1031.592	722.409	105.1588
C07	Mean	−2.21E+02	−1.02E+01	−5.55E+01	−4.11E+02
	Std	6.65E+01	96.7726	108.028	225.5643
C08	Mean	−2.84E−04	−2.40E−04	−2.80E−04	−2.40E−04
	Std	3.56E−09	4.05E−05	5.77E−10	4.94E−05
C09	Mean	−2.67E−03	−2.67E−03	−2.67E−03	−2.67E−03
	Std	8.85E−19	5.44E−09	1.33E−18	3.32E−16
C10	Mean	−1.03E−04	−9.00E−05	−1.00E−04	−9.12E−05
	Std	4.25E−09	8.64E−06	4.76E−10	1.79E−05
C11	Mean	−3.04E+02	−8.55E−01	−8.75E−01	−2.70E+01
	Std	3.06E+02	0.096998	0.109523	4.755493
C12	Mean	3.98E+00	6.07E+00	4.00E+00	1.57E+01
	Std	4.26E−04	2.839335	0.013465	8.832025
C13	Mean	1.29E+01	3.27E+01	5.03E+01	9.64E+01
	Std	3.02E+01	39.16682	13.6338	129.0651
C14	Mean	1.45E+00	1.93E+00	1.86E+00	1.59E+00
	Std	6.09E−02	0.046647	0.044671	0.193245
C15	Mean	2.73E+00	1.29E+01	1.92E+01	9.27E+00
	Std	1.38E+00	1.539043	3.61396	2.22144
C16	Mean	0	1.56E+02	1.54E+02	8.92E+00
	Std	0	13.61105	15.3015	3.066072
C17	Mean	1.21E+00	1.03E+00	1.00E+00	1.03E+00
	Std	3.17E−01	0.005842	0.018234	0.002783
C18	Mean	3.66E+01	7.54E+03	9.13E+03	9.84E+03
	Std	1.39E−01	5261.00831	6634.57	3779.395
C19	Mean	0	1.28E−03	1.08E−03	1.97E+00
	Std	0	0.000399	0.00094	3.515707
C20	Mean	4.38E+00	2.92E+00	3.55E+00	4.00E+00
	Std	6.63E−01	0.31498	0.221087	1.064174
C21	Mean	9.37E+00	2.77E+01	2.28E+01	1.25E+01
	Std	6.49E+00	9.187089	8.98664	8.474046
C22	Mean	1.84E+02	1.18E+03	3.24E+03	2.21E+02
	Std	2.09E+02	2023.388	3173.81	181.7431
C23	Mean	1.43E+00	1.91E+00	1.86E+00	1.50E+00
	Std	4.48E−02	0.05499	0.060907	0.117495
C24	Mean	3.36E+00	1.42E+01	1.22E+01	9.27E+00
	Std	1.50E+00	1.369376	1.04194	1.28255
C25	Mean	1.83E+01	1.48E+02	1.47E+02	1.59E+01
	Std	7.25E+00	13.87661	12.7452	3.636656
C26	Mean	9.05E−01	1.03E+00	1.00E+00	1.03E+00
	Std	1.92E−01	0.0018	0.021067	0.005126
C27	Mean	3.71E+01	4.16E+04	3.19E+04	3.07E+04
	Std	1.83E+00	19984.77	11319.9	13370.99
C28	Mean	4.94E+01	1.55E+02	1.51E+02	6.50E+01
	Std	2.17E+01	19.07424	20.4233	19.27773
Friedman aligned test		3.13E+01	7.03E+01	7.01E+01	5.43E+01

Table 2. Adjusted p-values for the Friedman Aligned test in terms of mean metric (AGA-PPS is the control method and $D = 30$).

Friedman aligned	Unadjusted	Bonferroni	Holm	Hochberg	Hommel	Holland	Rom	Finner	Li
LSHADE44 +IDE	0.000007	0.000022	0.000022	0.000016	0.000014	0.000022	0.000016	0.000022	0.000007
LSHADE44	0.000008	0.000023	0.000022	0.000016	0.000016	0.000022	0.000016	0.000022	0.000008
UDE	0.008149	0.024448	0.008149	0.008149	0.008149	0.008149	0.008149	0.008149	0.008149

Table 3. Results obtained for $D = 50$, all results for C01–C28.

Test Instances		AGA-PPS	LSHADE44+IDE	LSHADE44	UDE
C01	Mean	6.76E−25	1.21E−03	9.80E−19	6.77E−04
	Std	8.43E−25	0.000758	1.88E−18	0.000977
C02	Mean	1.01E−24	8.25E−04	2.70E−17	2.89E−04
	Std	3.71E−24	0.0007	7.75E−17	0.00033
C03	Mean	5.44E+03	4.14E+07	3.54E+06	3.41E+02
	Std	1.40E+03	1.36E+07	5.08E+06	115.2714
C04	Mean	1.40E+02	1.40E+01	1.48E+02	1.61E+02
	Std	2.67E+01	0.986834	7.4323	27.97972
C05	Mean	1.29E−19	4.31E−09	2.11E+01	3.19E+01
	Std	3.98E−19	1.05E−08	0.379687	3.211975
C06	Mean	8.16E+02	8.99E+03	7.41E+03	6.56E+02
	Std	8.44E+01	1064.459	1203.89	224.7076
C07	Mean	−1.89E+02	−3.65E+01	−3.94E+01	−6.73E+02
	Std	9.48E+01	121.0128	160.717	244.2575
C08	Mean	−1.17E−04	2.96E−04	−1.30E−04	1.62E−03
	Std	3.21E−05	7.59E−05	2.33E−07	0.00079
C09	Mean	−2.04E−03	−1.56E−03	−2.04E−03	−2.04E−03
	Std	1.94E−09	0.000235	1.33E−18	5.84E−11
C10	Mean	−4.75E−05	9.36E−05	−4.82E−05	6.06E−05
	Std	1.33E−06	3.77E−05	8.10E−08	4.70E−05
C11	Mean	−2.59E+03	−7.30E−01	−1.19E+00	−9.48E+01
	Std	3.64E+02	3.298387	2.44299	46.61275
C12	Mean	6.63E+00	7.36E+00	5.20E+01	1.25E+01
	Std	4.07E+00	2.860924	20.8675	5.861807
C13	Mean	6.34E+01	9.14E+01	6.50E+02	1.37E+03
	Std	5.42E+01	24.87958	101.664	416.8811

(continued)

Table 3. (*continued*)

Test Instances		AGA-PPS	LSHADE44+IDE	LSHADE44	UDE
C14	Mean	1.17E+00	1.49E+00	1.41E+00	1.29E+00
	Std	8.75E−02	0.029674	0.029579	0.09744
C15	Mean	5.25E+00	1.45E+01	1.78E+01	1.17E+01
	Std	1.26E+00	1.652444	2.99689	1.428187
C16	Mean	6.28E−02	2.72E+02	2.72E+02	1.26E+01
	Std	3.14E−01	17.73679	18.4244	7.25E−15
C17	Mean	1.01E+00	1.05E+00	1.04E+00	1.05E+00
	Std	2.75E−01	0.000586	0.005574	0.001564
C18	Mean	3.66E+01	2.00E+04	2.05E+04	3.40E+04
	Std	3.74E−01	6831.056	7214.01	9621.109
C19	Mean	0	3.54E−02	6.66E−02	6.42E+00
	Std	0	0.019309991	0.038894	7.264131
C20	Mean	1.03E+01	5.63E+00	8.12E+00	7.85E+00
	Std	6.01E−01	0.293081	0.299347	1.640922
C21	Mean	6.62E+00	6.28E+01	6.53E+01	7.64E+00
	Std	3.77E+00	1.433125	2.04016	4.221377
C22	Mean	4.12E+03	1.13E+04	1.45E+04	4.09E+03
	Std	6.42E+03	6028.40364	7731.5	3048.246
C23	Mean	1.15E+00	1.44E+00	1.42E+00	1.26E+00
	Std	3.99E−02	0.029772	0.031323	0.077029
C24	Mean	5.50E+00	1.56E+01	1.43E+01	1.14E+01
	Std	9.07E−01	1.570784	1.28254	1.381348
C25	Mean	5.30E+01	2.65E+02	2.53E+02	2.34E+01
	Std	1.67E+01	20.04611	16.8844	7.592
C26	Mean	9.91E−01	1.05E+00	1.04E+00	1.05E+00
	Std	1.50E−01	0.00346	0.003285	0.003759
C27	Mean	4.07E+01	7.60E+04	8.40E+04	1.09E+05
	Std	1.93E+01	2.03E+04	28825.7	18819.77
C28	Mean	1.39E+02	2.74E+02	2.67E+02	1.33E+02
	Std	3.65E+01	18.77917	17.8361	21.89726
Friedman aligned test		3.21E+01	6.94E+01	7.47E+01	4.98E+01

Table 4. Adjusted p-values for the Friedman Aligned test in terms of mean value of the objective (AGA-PPS is the control method and $D = 50$).

Friedman Aligned	Unadjusted	Bonferroni	Holm	Hochberg	Hommel	Holland	Rom	Finner	Li
LSHADE44 +IDE	0.000001	0.000003	0.000003	0.000003	0.000003	0.000003	0.000003	0.000003	0.000001
LSHADE44	0.000017	0.000052	0.000034	0.000034	0.000034	0.000034	0.000034	0.000026	0.000018
UDE	0.0425	0.127499	0.0425	0.0425	0.0425	0.0425	0.0425	0.0425	0.0425

5 Conclusion

The paper proposes a method to adaptively select the operators according to current convergence status of population, which can prevent the population from being trapped into local optimal. Moreover, the paper also proposes a novel PPS method for solving CSOPs. It divides the search process in two stages, which can help to accelerate the convergence of population and maintain a good balance of searching between feasible and infeasible regions. The proposed AGA-PPS and other three DEs (LSHADE44+IDE, LSHADE44 and UDE) are tested on the CEC2017 benchmarks with 30 and 50 dimensions. The experimental results show that AGA-PPS is significantly better than other three DEs, which manifests that AGA-PPS is a quite competitive algorithm for solving these CSOPs.

References

1. Floudas, C.A., Pardalos, P.M.: A Collection of Test Problems for Constrained Global Optimization Algorithms. LNCS, vol. 455. Springer, Heidelberg (1990). https://doi.org/10.1007/3-540-53032-0
2. Gen, M., Cheng, R.: Genetic Algorithms and Engineering Optimization. Wiley, Hoboken (2000)
3. Mallipeddi, R., Suganthan, P.N.: Problem definitions and evaluation criteria for the CEC 2017 Competition on Constrained Real-Parameter Optimization. In: Nation University of Defense Technology, Changsha, Hunan, PA China and Kyungpook National University, Daegu, South Korea and Nanyang Technological University, Singapore, Techical report (2016)
4. Le, R.R.G., Knopf, L.C., Haftka, R.T.: A segregated genetic algorithm for constrained structural optimization. In: International Conference on Genetic Algorithms, pp. 558–565. Morgan Kaufmann Publishers Inc. (1995)
5. Huang, F., Wang, L., He, Q.: An effective co-evolutionary differential evolution for constrained optimization. Appl. Math. Comput. **186**(1), 340–356 (2007)
6. Surry, P.D., Radcliffe, N.J.: The COMOGA method: constrained optimisation by multi-objective genetic algorithms. Control Cybern. **26**(3), 391–412 (1997)
7. Lampinen, J.: A fuzzy adaptive differential evolution algorithm. Soft Comput. **9**(6), 448–462 (2005)
8. Brest, J., Greiner, S., Boskovic, B., Mernik, M., Zumer, V.: Self-adapting control parameters in differential evolution: a comparative study on numerical benchmark problems. IEEE Trans. Evol. Comput. **10**(6), 646–657 (2006)
9. Zhang, J., Sanderson, A.C.: JADE: adaptive differential evolution with optional external archive. IEEE Trans. Evol. Comput. **13**(5), 945–958 (2009)
10. Wang, Y., Cai, Z., Zhang, Q.: Differential evolution with composite trial vector generation strategies and control parameters. IEEE Trans. Evol. Comput. **15**(1), 55–66 (2011)
11. Tanabe, R., Fukunaga, A.: Success-history based parameter adaptation for Differential Evolution. In: 2013 IEEE Congress on Evolutionary Computation, pp. 71–78. IEEE (2013)
12. Tanabe, R., Fukunaga, A.S.: Improving the search performance of SHADE using linear population size reduction. In: 2014 IEEE Congress on Evolutionary Computation, pp. 1658–1665. IEEE (2014)

13. Polkov, R.: L-SHADE with competing strategies applied to constrained optimization. In: 2014 IEEE Congress on Evolutionary Computation, pp. 1683–1689. IEEE (2017)
14. Jordehi, A.R.: A review on constraint handling strategies in particle swarm optimisation. Neural Comput. **26**(6), 1265–1275 (2015)
15. Takahama, T., Sakai, S., Iwane, N.: Solving nonlinear constrained optimization problems by the ε constrained differential evolution. In: IEEE International Conference on Systems, Man and Cybernetics, pp. 2322–2327. IEEE (2006)
16. Holland, J.H.: Genetic algorithms. Sci. Am. **267**(1), 66–73 (1992)
17. Deb, K., Goyal, M.: A combined genetic adaptive search (GeneAS) for engineering design. Comput. Sci. Inform. **26**, 30–45 (1996)
18. Coello, C.A.C.: Theoretical and numerical constraint-handling techniques used with evolutionary algorithms: a survey of the state of the art. Comput. Methods Appl. Mech. Eng. **191**(11–12), 1245–1287 (2002)
19. Tvrdik, J., Polakova, R.: A simple framework for constrained problems with application of L-SHADE44 and IDE. In: 2017 IEEE Congress on Evolutionary Computation, pp. 1436–1443. IEEE (2017)
20. Trivedi, A.: A unified differential evolution algorithm for constrained optimization problems. In: 2017 IEEE Congress on Evolutionary Computation, pp. 1231–1238. IEEE (2017)
21. Derrac, J., Garcia, S., Molina, D., Herrera, F.: A practical tutorial on the use of nonparametric statistical tests as a methodology for comparing evolutionary and swarm intelligence algorithms. Swarm Evol. Comput. **1**(1), 3–18 (2011)

DeepPort: Detect Low Speed Port Scan Using Convolutional Neural Network

Yulong Wang[(✉)] and Jiuchao Zhang

State Key Laboratory of Networking and Switching Technology,
Beijing University of Posts and Telecommunications, Beijing, China
{wyl,zhangjiuchao}@bupt.edu.cn

Abstract. Port scanning is a widely used technology in reconnaissance, which aims to determine remotely the running services on the target TCP/UDP ports. Current research works have achieved acceptable performance for detection of conventional port scanning, which use hand-crafted features such as packets receiving rate, count of requesting ports and packets arriving time distribution. However, advanced attacks such as APT usually employ low-speed scans to lower the risk of exposure. Nevertheless, it is a challenge to precisely detect a low-speed scan since it has much coarser features that are hard to be matched by the current approaches. We propose a novel method DeepPort to solve this problem. DeepPort filters out a majority of normal packets using their well-defined features. Thereafter, DeepPort detects port scans using learned features using a dedicated Convolutional Neural Network (CNN) that is trained from real scanning packets under various time interval configurations. The experiments carried in our campus network show that DeepPort can detect 10 class of low-speed scans with a precision of 97.4% and a recall of 96.9%.

Keywords: Port scanning · Deep learning
Convolutional neural network · Nmap

1 Introduction

In recent years, cyberattacks become more and more sophisticated with the advances of defending technologies. Especially, to lower the risk of an attack, an adversary would try his/her best to hide their activities during the attack. Reconnaissance, as the first phase in the cyber kill chain [1], is used for adversaries to collect useful information (e.g. alive hosts, hosts' OS and services) about the target. During the reconnaissance phase, port scanning is one of the most effective technologies utilized by adversaries for active internal footprinting [2]. Therefore, a stealth port scanning is appealing for sophisticated attacks such as APT [3]. Although other strategies exist for stealth port scanning to evade an IDS, stretching time interval of port scanning is a simple-to-employ and effective strategy for adversaries. This kind of port scanning, a.k.a low speed port scan or LSPS, becomes the major threat to corporates' internal networks.

© Springer Nature Singapore Pte Ltd. 2018
J. Qiao et al. (Eds.): BIC-TA 2018, CCIS 951, pp. 368–379, 2018.
https://doi.org/10.1007/978-981-13-2826-8_32

However, detecting LSPS on-line is a challenging task. In a LSPS, very few scanning packets are interleaved with a large amount of normal packets within a short time window. Since the packet sending rate of a LSPS is usually lower than the threshold of flooding detection, rating-based schemes such as Giotis et al. [4] and Khamphakdee et al. [5] are not applicable in this scenario. On the other hand, the strategy of delayed packet sending in LSPS significantly changes the packets' sending time distribution, thus the schemes based on scanning traffic waveform [6] is ineffective for LSPS. Other researchers [7,8] use neural networks to learn the detection rules using handcrafted features as inputs. But these handcrafted features are unreliable when detecting LSPS.

We proposed a novel scheme named DeepPort to eliminate the aforementioned shortcomings. DeepPort is a two-stage solution. In the first stage, DeepPort washes the raw data to get rid of most of normal packets. Since most normal packets conform to a well-known pattern (e.g. a complete three handshake of TCP), it is relatively easier to filter them out. For the fewer normal packets that are hard to pick out, DeepPort just left them to the second stage and utilize CNN to diminish their influences. In the second stage, DeepPort uses a finely design CNN that is trained using real LSPS packets to examine the packet stream from the first stage for suspicious scanning packets. The key contributions of our work are 1. DeepPort is the first scheme using learned features to detect LSPS; 2. DeepPort is an on-line scheme that can achieve a high detection performance; 3. We carry out experiments in a campus network with real LSPS to evaluate the effectiveness of DeepPort.

The remainder of the paper is organized as follow: Sect. 2 overviews the background knowledge and the existing work related to our work. Section 3 describes the problem description that we try to solve. Section 4 presents the detailed design of DeepPort. Then we provide the experimental evaluation of DeepPort in Sect. 5. Finally, Sect. 6 concludes the whole paper and describes the next step work.

2   Related Works

The key for detecting a port scan is to find a set of features that can effectively discriminate scanning packets from normal packets. According to the count of features they select or construct, current approaches can be grouped into three categories: simple feature based, combined features based and abstract features based.

The simple feature-based approaches utilize only one or two features for port scanning detection. For example, Giotis et al. [4] use the entropy of accessed IP address and TCP/UDP ports as the metric for detecting anomaly on the distribution of ports and IP addresses in a short period of time. With a proper threshold, this approach performs well in conventional port scanning activities that cause a sharp increase in the volume of network traffic. However, a proper threshold value is hard to decide since the counts of ports and IP addresses vibrate with the provision/deletion of services and joining/leaving of mobile end-hosts such as laptops. What's more, very few of the delayed sent scanning packets in LSPS, if any, will fall in a short detection time window, thus this method is infeasible for detecting LSPS.

The combined features based approaches utilize a series of basic features to determine the appearance of a port scanning. Bou-Harb et al. [6] model the port scanning traffic waveform using the Detrended Fluctuation Analysis (DFA) [9]. In contrast to the approach proposed by Giotis et al. [4], they use DFA to characterize the distribution (instead of expectation) of packets' count on arrival time. This kind of feature extraction allows them to obtain a more detailed detection result that not only indicates the appearance of a port scanning but also identifies the type of port scanning among 10 classes. However, this approach assumes the scanning packets to be sent at their normal speed without any dedicated delay. This assumption does not hold when a LSPS is conducted by a smart adversary who adds additional delays for port scanning to hide his/her malicious activities. Also, the large amount of normal packets may cause severe impacts on the network traffic waveform, which are not solved in the approach. Khamphakdee et al. [5] propose to detect network probe attack through a set of basic features based rules for matching data packets traffic, but their approach is prone to generate a lot of false alerts and achieve low accuracy.

The abstract features based approaches attempt to get high-level features that are tolerable to minor distortion of basic features. Radford et al. [7] use Long-Short-Term Memory (LSTM) to capture the temporal relationship among network flows. According to the anomaly of the temporal relationship, this approach may detect a port scanning activity. But they use traffic log data as input, which makes them an off-line detection scheme. And the precision of detection is low with the highest ROC of 0.84. Shone et al. [8] propose a probe detection approach that uses a nonsymmetric deep autoencoder (NDAE) for unsupervised feature learning and a deep learning classification model based on stacked NDAEs. The proposed approach achieves very promising results on the benchmark KDD Cup'99 [10] and NSL-KDD datasets [11]. But this approach is not dedicated for LSPS since it depends on a fixed detection time window.

To the best of our investigation, there is not a published approach that is dedicated for LSPS and achieves practically acceptable performance. Our approach attempts to achieve this goal by picking out suspicious packets then classifying them with a well-trained convolutional neural network.

3   Problem Description

Port scanning is a process that sends finely crafted requests to a range of service ports on target hosts and listens to the response which indicates the port status that is helpful for determining the host status, operating system and other information. There are many tools that can perform a port scanning. Some dedicated tools include Nmap [12], Xprobe2 [13] and hping3 [14]. Nmap supports various types of port scanning. For example, in TCP SYN scanning, Nmap sends a TCP SYN packet for a connection request to a service port on the target host, the port is determined to be open if a TCP ACK packet is received, and the target port is determined to be closed if a TCP RST packet is received. Port scanning doesn't compromise the system directly, but it can help an adversary find the vulnerability to exploit. Therefore, port scanning is always considered as the primary stage of a typical network attack.

Usually, port scanning is expected to be completed as soon as possible. After all, even in a small local network with one block of Class C IP addresses assigned, there are over 16 million ports that are potentially needed for scanning. To speed up the process of port scanning, an adversary may launch multiple scanning for different IP addresses and ports simultaneously. The downside of this strategy is that the volume feature of the port scanning can be easily identified by existing detection approaches [4].

In order to hide the volume feature from an IDS/IPS, adversaries tend to lower the speed of scanning packets sending. As long as the speed of a port scanning is endurable for the adversaries, e.g. an APT attack is allowed to gather the valid information about target hosts or networks for weeks before launching an exploitation, then such a low speed port scan is one of the appropriate options for adversaries.

Therefore, according to the sending speed of packets, port scans can be classified as conventional port scan and low speed port scan (LSPS). In general, a conventional port scan for a host can complete in less than a minute, while the time for LSPS is uncertain, depending on the value of the scan-delay parameter set by the adversary. However, the upper bound time for LSPS is constrained by two factors: the stationary of the target hosts and the time limitation of the attack. The stationary of the target hosts ensures that the collected information is still valid when it is used for attacking. Although servers may keep running for a long time, end-hosts' status are more easily changed over time. Also, the security policies of the target network may also affect the sensed status of the target hosts. So, adversaries are discouraged to perform a port scanning for a long time. The time limitation of the attack may also prohibit the adversary to spend too much time on port scannings.

Therefore, the problem to be solved in this paper is: detecting low speed port scan in an on-line way, whose scanning speed is lower than conventional port scanning but higher than several hours per host. We believe this upper bound of scanning speed reaches the limit of enduring of most adversaries.

4   DeepPort

Unlike a conventional port scanning that usually results in sharp increasement of network traffic and diversity of ports, LSPS nearly doesn't lead to network traffic changes. The traffic of LSPS is hidden in the large volume of normal network traffic. And there is no difference between a single normal packet and a port scanning packet since both conform to the same network protocol, so it's very difficult to detect LSPS.

The key idea of DeepPort is to firstly filter out a majority of normal network traffic using normal network traffic features. Then DeepPort classifies the left suspicious network traffic through a dedicated CNN model that is trained beforehand. This strategy would be helpful for reducing the difficulty of detecting LSPS. Thus DeepPort is a two-stage method that comprises of the filtering stage and the detection stage.

In the filtering stage, DeepPort filters out normal packets mainly using the TCP connection information. A TCP connection is established using the three-way handshake mechanism. Initially, a client sends a TCP SYN packet to a server requesting for a TCP connection. If the server accepts the connection request, it responds by sending back a TCP SYN-ACK packet. Finally, the client replies with a TCP ACK packet to complete the TCP connection establishment. If the server doesn't accept the connection request, it responds by sending back a TCP RST packet. The TCP connection is closed by either side by sending TCP FIN packet. In contrast to a normal TCP connection, a TCP scanning process adopts a semi-connected scan which does not establish a TCP connection. At the port scanning phase, an adversary sends a TCP SYN packet to a victim's port and observe the victim's response. If the adversary receives a TCP SYN-ACK packet, then the scanned port is open. In this case the adversary replies immediately with a TCP RST packet to abandon the connection. If the adversary receives a TCP RST packet, then it implies that the scanned port is closed. This is the typical process of a single port scanning. A whole port scanning may involves thousands of single port scanning. Therefore, the length of every flow is less than 3 packets, so we treat flows longer than 3 packets as normal traffic and filter them out. Other rules for filtering out normal packets can be easily adopted by DeepPort.

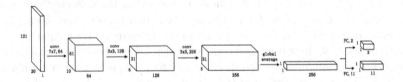

Fig. 1. LSPS detection model architecture

In the detection stage, DeepPort requires a pre-trained CNN model. We designed a neural network to learn features directly from raw network traffic. We choose CNN model as our base components for the proposed LSPS detection model. The architecture of the LSPS detection model consists of 3 convolutional layers and one single fully-connected softmax output layer. Batch normalization (BN) and rectified linear activation are applied after each convolutional layer. In addition, LSPS detection model performs global average pooling on the output of the last convolutional layer to produce the input of fully-connected layer. A softmax function takes the output of fully-connected layer and products the probability of probe action. The model's architecture is shown in Fig. 1, in which Conv 7×7, 64 means convolution with 7×7 kernel, 64 output channels, stride 2 is applied in the first and second Conv-layer, and the stride of the third Conv-layer is 1.

The softmax function takes an n-dimensional vector of real numbers and transforms it into a vector of real number in range $(0, 1)$ which add up to 1, as shown in

$$p_i = \frac{e^{a_i}}{\sum_{k=1}^{N} e^{a_k}}, \tag{1}$$

in which p_i presents the probability of the data sample whose label is i, a_i is the output value of the LSPS detection model, and N is the count of classes. In our experiment in Sect. 5, N is set to 2 or 11.

The loss function of the LSPS detection model is

$$L = -\frac{1}{N} \sum_{i=1}^{N} y_i \log p_i, \tag{2}$$

in which N is the number of data samples, y is the truth label of a data sample whose value is either 0 or 1, p is the output value of the LSPS detection model which present the probability of a data sample being a port scanning traffic. This loss function measures the probability error in classifying the traffic samples. The LSPS detection model is trained to minimize the loss function by end-to-end.

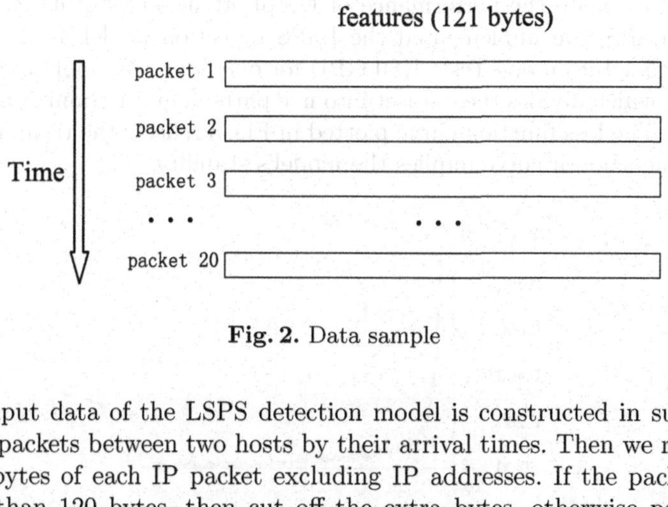

Fig. 2. Data sample

The input data of the LSPS detection model is constructed in such a way. We order packets between two hosts by their arrival times. Then we remain the first 120 bytes of each IP packet excluding IP addresses. If the packet length is longer than 120 bytes, then cut off the extra bytes, otherwise pad it with zeros to 120 bytes. In a LSPS, the time interval of port scanning packets is an important feature. So we append the time interval of port scanning packets at the end of the above 120 bytes. We treat each group of 20 packets as a data sample. Finally, a data sample contains 20 consecutive packets, each of which consists of 121 features, as shown in Fig. 2.

5   Experiment

In this section, we will evaluate the performance of DeepPort and compare Deep-Port with other ralated works.

5.1 Evaluation and Results

Most researchers evaluate their machine-learning based approaches on probe attacks on KDD datasets [10,11], which consists of many manually selected features for each flow. However, DeepPort requires raw traffic as inputs. Thus the public datasets such as KDD do not meet our requirements. We collected real traffic in our campus network for several days, during which we launch LSPS using Nmap [12], which is one of the most widely used scanning tools. The nmap scanning parameters are set as in Table 1. Our collected dataset contains 16497 malicious samples and 754 normal samples.

Table 1. Nmap scanning parameters

Scan techniques	-sA, -sF, -sN, -sO, -sR, -sS, -sT, -sU, -sW, -sX
OS detection	-O, –osscan-guess
Timing and performance	scan-delay, –max rate
Firewall/IDS evasion and spoofing	-f, –data-string, –data-length, –ttl

We will evaluate the performance of DeepPort in terms of its capability of detecting LSPS. We implemented the LSPS detection model using tensorflow [15] and trained it on one Tesla K80 GPU for one hour. We apply 5 folds cross-validation, which divides the dataset into five parts: four for training and one for validation. The loss function curve plotted in Fig. 3 reflects the training process, in which the smooth curve implies the model's stability.

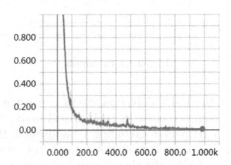

Fig. 3. Training process of loss function

We consider two kinds of detection requirements: the binary one and the multi-class one. The former only tells whether there is some kind of LSPS occurring, while the latter one further tells the specific LSPS classes.

For the first detection requirements, we construct the LSPS detection model as a binary classifier, whose performance is depicted with Receiver Operating Characteristic (ROC) [16] plots in Fig. 4. ROC plot depicts the diagnostic ability of a binary classifier system when its discrimination threshold varies. ROC plot is created by plotting the true positive rate (TPR) against the false positive rate (FPR) at various threshold settings. The diagonal line $x = y$ represents the random classifier, if the observed curve in a ROC plot falls along line x = y, the model is assessed to perform no better than a random chance. The best possible predicting method would yield a point in the upper left corner or coordinate (0, 1). The Area Under the Curve (AUC) is the value obtained by integrating over the ROC curve. The range of AUC is [0, 1]. An AUC of 1 indicates the best classifier while an AUC of 0.5 indicates a random classifier. Thus, all efficient model should attain AUC values in the range [0.5, 1]. So we select AUC as the metric for measuring the LSPS detection model's performance. As seen in Fig. 4, we find that the model's AUC reaches 0.9977 which is close to the best theoretical value. Therefore, the proposed LSPS detection model can perfectly satisfy the first requirement of LSPS detection.

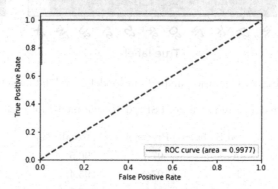

Fig. 4. ROC plot for the LSPS detection model

For the second type of requirement, we constructed the LSPS detection model as an eleven-class classifier. We use the confusion map on validation set to show the performance of the proposed model, as seen in Fig. 5. In this figure, columns present the count distribution of predict labels for a true label, and rows present the count distribution of true labels for a predict label. We can see that the proposed model has a strong capability for classifying multi-class LSPS.

We also use the precision and recall metric to quantitatively measure the classification performance of the proposed model. The calculation formula as follows:

$$Precision_i = \frac{M_{ii}}{\sum_j M_{ji}} \tag{3}$$

$$Recal_i = \frac{M_{ii}}{\sum_j M_{ij}} \tag{4}$$

M_{ij} is the total number of samples whose truth label is i and predicted label is j. The results is listed in Table 2. It is worth noting that the precision for normal

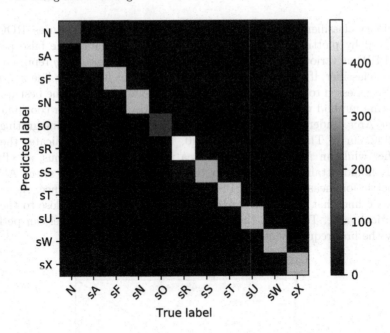

Fig. 5. Confusion map of our model on validation set

Table 2. Precision and recall of LSPS detection model for each LSPS class

LSPS classes	Precision (%)	Recall (%)
sA	97.1	96.5
sF	97.4	95.4
sN	95.3	97.9
sO	97.8	94.7
sR	95.3	97.4
sS	96.0	93.5
sT	98.9	98.9
sU	98.3	99.1
sW	96.7	97.6
sX	98.2	97.6
Normal	100.0	97.7
Mean	97.4	96.9

traffic is 100% which implies no port scanning traffic was determined as normal traffic, meaning no port scanning packets can evade the detection.

Overall, for either type of LSPS detection, DeepPort can obtain promising results which are appealing for a security critical local network.

5.2   Comparison with Related Works

We also compare the performance of our DeepPort with the state-of-the-art method in [6].

Refinement. In [6], the authors model the port scanning traffic waveform using the DFA. The output of the DFA procedure is a relationship $F(n)$, the average fluctuation as a function of window size n. Typically, $F(n)$ will increase with the window size n. A linear relationship on a log-log graph indicates the presence of scaling, statistical self-affinity expressed as $F(n) \sim n^\alpha$. The scaling exponent α is calculated as the slope of a straight line fit to the log-log graph of n against $F(n)$ using least-squares. They compute scaling exponent α of each traffic waveform generated by 10 cyber scanning techniques, and divide the port scanning into three categories based on the range of α ($\alpha < 0.5$, $0.5 < \alpha < 1$ and $\alpha > 1$), while DeepPort could detect precisely ten categories. Therefore, DeepPort has more detailed detections for port scanning.

Table 3. DFA results in our experimental environment

Cyber scanning technique	Scaling exponent (elias)	Scaling exponent (ours)
TCP SYN scan	0.57	0.88
TCP connect() scan	0.87	0.92
FIN scan	0.31	0.91
Xmas scan	0.30	0.95
Null scan	0.37	0.94
UDP scan	0.66	0.96
IP protocol scan	1.13	0.59
ACK scan	0.44	0.99
Window scan	1.24	0.97
RPC scan	1.31	0.93

Robustness. Bou-Harb et al. [6] detects port scanning through traffic waveform. Intuitively, this method is susceptible to the network environment and the speed of sending packets. We implement this method in our network environment. As seen in Table 3, in our experimental environment, there are no obvious discrimination among scaling exponent α of ten cyber scanning techniques, which means that we could not determine effectively the kind of port scanning through the scaling exponent α. Therefore, Bou-Herb's method fails to work in our network environment. DeepPort detects port scanning based packet sequence which is independent of delay of sending packets and network environment, and the experimental results above show that DeepPort is more robust.

6   Conclusion

We proposed a CNN-based low speed port scan detection approach, which can both determine the existing of LSPS and their specific classes with a high accuracy. DeepPort makes the LSPS traffic more significant by filtering out most normal packets and grouping the left suspicious packets by the pairs of source and destination IP addresses. DeepPort also uses CNN to capture the complex features containing sequential and interval information. DeepPort is also insensitive for a long port scanning interval by aggregating a proper number of suspicious packets other than depending on a fixed time window. All of the above designing decisions make DeepPort a suitable solution for LSPS detection. Our experiments based on real data in a campus local network validate the effectiveness of DeepPort. For future work, we plan to extend our work to other types of probe attack such as low speed OS and version detection.

Acknowledgments. The work was supported in part by the National High-tech R & D Program of China (863 Program) (2015AA017201) and National Key Research and Development Program of China (2016QY01W0200). The authors are very grateful to the anonymous viewers of this paper.

References

1. Okhravi, H., et al.: Survey of Cyber Moving Targets Second Edition, Lincoln Laboratory Massachusetts Institute of Technology Technical Report 1228 (2018)
2. PTES Technical Guidelines. http://www.pentest-standard.org/index.php/PTES_Technical_Guidelines
3. Chen, P., Desmet, L., Huygens, C.: A study on advanced persistent threats. In: De Decker, B., Zúquete, A. (eds.) CMS 2014. LNCS, vol. 8735, pp. 63–72. Springer, Heidelberg (2014). https://doi.org/10.1007/978-3-662-44885-4_5
4. Giotis, K., Argyropoulos, C., Androulidakis, G., Kalogeras, D., Maglaris, V.: Combining OpenFlow and sFlow for an effective and scalable anomaly detection and mitigation mechanism on SDN environments. Comput. Netw. **62**, 122–136 (2014)
5. Khamphakdee, N., Benjamas, N., Saiyod, S.: Improving intrusion detection system based on snort rules for network probe attack detection. In: 2nd International Conference on Information and Communication Technology (ICoICT), pp. 69–74. IEEE Press, New York (2014)
6. Bou-Harb, E., Debbabi, M., Assi, C.: A statistical approach for fingerprinting probing activities. In: 2013 International Conference on Availability, Reliability and Security, pp. 21–30. IEEE Press, New York (2013)
7. Benjamin, J.R., Leonardo, M.A., Antonio, J.T., Jim, A.S.: Network traffic anomaly detection using recurrent neural networks (2018). CoRR: https://arxiv.org/abs/1803.10769
8. Shone, N., Ngoc, T.N., Phai, V.D., Shi, Q.: A deep learning approach to network intrusion detection. IEEE Trans. Emerg. Top. Comput. Intell. **2**, 41–50 (2018)
9. Peng, C.K., Buldyrev, S.V., Havlin, S., Simons, M., Stanley, H.E., Goldberger, A.L.: Mosaic organization of dna nucleotides. Phys. Rev. E. **49**, 1685–1689 (1994)
10. KDD Cup'99 dataset. http://kdd.ics.uci.edu/databases/kddcup99/kddcup99.html
11. NSL-KDD dataset. http://www.unb.ca/cic/datasets/nsl.html

12. Lyon, G.F.: Nmap Network Scanning: The Official Nmap Project Guide to Network Discovery and Security Scanning. Insecure (2009)
13. Arkin, O., Yarochkin, F.: Xprobe v2.0: A "Fuzzy" Approach to Remote Active Operating System Fingerprinting. www.xprobe2.org
14. hping3. http://www.hping.org/
15. Google, Tensorflow. https://www.tensorflow.org/
16. Fawcett, T.: An introduction to ROC analysis. Pattern Recogn. Lett. **27**, 861–874 (2006)

A Dual-Population-Based Local Search for Solving Multiobjective Traveling Salesman Problem

Mi Hu[1,2], Xinye Cai[1,2,3(✉)], and Zhun Fan[4]

[1] College of Computer Science and Technology,
Nanjing University of Aeronautics and Astronautics, Nanjing 210016, Jiangsu,
People's Republic of China
xinye@nuaa.edu.cn
[2] Collaborative Innovation Center of Novel Software Technology and
Industrialization, Nanjing 210023, People's Republic of China
[3] Information Technology Research Base of Civil Aviation Administration of China,
Civil Aviation University of China, Tianjin 300300, People's Republic of China
[4] Department of Electronic Engineering, School of Engineering, Shantou University,
Shantou 515063, Guangdong, People's Republic of China

Abstract. The decomposition-based algorithms, such as MOEA/D, transform a multiobjective optimization problem into a number of single-objective optimization subproblems and solve them in a collaborative manner. It is a natural framework for using single-objective local search for solving combinatorial multiobjective optimization problems. However, the performance of the decomposition-based algorithms strongly depends on the shape of PFs. For this purpose, this paper proposed a dual-population-based local search in MOEA/D framework (DP-MOEA/D-LS) to address the multiobjective traveling salesman problem. Two populations using different sets of direction vectors and different decomposition approaches cooperate with each other for achieving appropriate balance between the convergence and diversity. The experimental results show that DP-MOEA/D-LS significantly outperforms the compared algorithms (MOEA/D-LS (WS, TCH, PBI and iPBI)) on all the test instances.

Keywords: Combinatorial multiobjective optimization
Traveling salesman problem · Local search · Decomposition
Dual-population

1 Introduction

Many real-world optimization problems involve the simultaneous optimization of multiple conflicting objectives. They are usually known as the multiobjective optimization problems (MOPs). Among them, the combinatorial MOPs (CMOPs), such as the multiobjective traveling salesman problem (MOTSP) [1–4], have attracted a great amount of attention over the decades. MOTSP is

© Springer Nature Singapore Pte Ltd. 2018
J. Qiao et al. (Eds.): BIC-TA 2018, CCIS 951, pp. 380–388, 2018.
https://doi.org/10.1007/978-981-13-2826-8_33

usually $\mathcal{NP}$-hard thus the exact methods are not suitable for tackling them even for the single-objective ones.

The multiobjective evolutionary algorithm based on decomposition (MOEA/D) [5] has become a popular framework for MOPs. MOEA/D decomposes a MOP into a number of single-objective subproblems with aggregated functions and each subproblem can be solved by a single-objective heuristic in a collaborative way. In addition, local search (LS) plays a key role on solving single-objective combinatorial optimization problems [6]. It is natural to apply it to MOEA/D framework for CMOPs. However, MOEA/D may fail to obtain a well-distributed Pareto front (PF) approximation due to the following two reasons [7]. First, MOEA/D with a single decomposition method (e.g., Weighted Sum (WS), Tchebycheff (TCH) or Penalty-based Boundary Intersection (PBI)) tends to be very sensitive to the shapes of PFs. Second, in MOEA/D, the same solution is very likely to associate with multiple subproblems, which may lead to the loss of diversity [8]. An inverted PBI (iPBI) has been proposed to tackle MOPs with extremely convex PFs in [9] but the use of it still needs to assume the convexity of PFs. More recently, two sets of prefixed direction vectors have been adopted in MOEA/D to address MOPs with both convex and concave PFs [10]. Since the direction vectors are prefixed throughout the whole process of the algorithm, it is less flexible to the shape of the PFs.

To address the above issues for CMOPs, this paper proposed a dual-population-based local search algorithm and incorporated it into MOEA/D framework. The proposed algorithm, called DP-MOEA/D-LS, adopts two populations using different decomposition methods. The cooperations between the dual population can effectively work well with local search heuristics for CMOPs.

2   Background

2.1   Combinatorial Multiobjective Optimization

In MOPs and CMOPs, the set of all the Pareto-optimal solutions is called the *Pareto set (PS)* and the corresponding set of all the Pareto-optimal objective vectors is the *Pareto front (PF)* [11].

The *ideal* and *nadir point (objective vectors)* can be used to define the ranges of PFs. The ideal objective vector $\mathbf{z}^* = (z_1^*, \ldots, z_m^*)^T$ can be calculated by

$$z_j^* = \min_{\mathbf{x} \in \Omega} f_j(\mathbf{x}), \ j \in \{1, \ldots, m\} \tag{1}$$

where m is the number of objectives.

The nadir objective vector $\mathbf{z}^{nad} = (z_1^{nad}, \ldots, z_m^{nad})^T$ can be calculated by

$$z_j^{nad} = \max_{\mathbf{x} \in PS} f_j(\mathbf{x}), \ j \in \{1, \ldots, m\}. \tag{2}$$

2.2   Decomposition Methods

Two decomposition methods are adopted in this paper, which are the Weighted Sum (WS) and inverted Penalty-based Boundary Intersection (iPBI) approach [9]. They are defined as follows.

Let $\boldsymbol{\lambda}^i = (\lambda_1^i, \ldots, \lambda_m^i)^T$ be a direction vector for i^{th} subproblem, where $\lambda_j^i \geq 0, j \in 1, \ldots, m$ and $\sum_{j=1}^m \lambda_j^i = 1$.

1. **Weighted Sum (WS) Approach:** The ith subproblem is defined as

$$\text{minimize} \quad g^{ws}(\mathbf{x}|\boldsymbol{\lambda}^i) = \sum_{j=1}^m \lambda_j^i f_j(\mathbf{x})$$

$$\text{subject to} \quad \mathbf{x} \in \Omega. \tag{3}$$

2. **Inverted Penalty-based Boundary Intersection (iPBI) Approach:** This approach is a variant of PBI. The ith subproblem is defined as

$$\text{maximize} \quad g^{ipbi}(\mathbf{x}|\boldsymbol{\lambda}^i, \mathbf{z}^{nad}) = d_1^i - \theta d_2^i,$$
$$d_1^i = (\mathbf{z}^{nad} - \mathbf{F}(\mathbf{x}))^T \cdot \boldsymbol{\lambda}^i / ||\boldsymbol{\lambda}^i||,$$
$$d_2^i = ||\mathbf{z}^{nad} - \mathbf{F}(\mathbf{x}) - (\boldsymbol{\lambda}^i / ||\boldsymbol{\lambda}^i||) \cdot d_1^i|| \tag{4}$$
$$\text{subject to} \quad \mathbf{x} \in \Omega.$$

3   The Main Framework of DP-MOEA/D-LS

Algorithm 1 presents the general framework of DP-MOEA/D-LS. Two populations (e.g. P and Q) are maintained throughout the whole process of the algorithm. The first population P, adopts WS with a set of uniformly predefined direction vectors (the number of it is set to approximate $\frac{N}{2}$), while the second population Q adopts iPBI, whose direction vectors are updated with P. In addition, two populations interact by updating each other. In DP-MOEA/D-LS, the goal of the first population P using WS with fixed direction vectors is to achieve

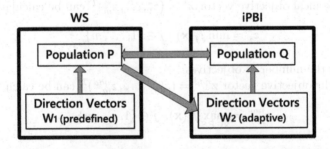

Fig. 1. The framework of two populations in DP-MOEA/D-LS.

fast convergence[1]; while the second population Q using iPBI with the dynamic direction vectors aims for the complementarily diverse solutions based on the first population P. The cooperation of two populations in DP-MOEA/D-LS has been illustrated in Fig. 1.

Local search (LS) heuristic plays a key role on the framework for generating new individuals. For one particular subproblem, LS maintains one candidate solution and iteratively improves it by exploring its neighbors in the search space. During the optimization process, the current solution is replaced by its better neighbor.

Algorithm 1: Main Framework of DP-MOEA/D-LS

Input:
- A MOP;
- A stoping criterion;
- N: The population size;
- $W : \{\lambda^1, \lambda^2, ..., \lambda^{\frac{N}{2}}\}$, the direction vectors set.

Output: Approximated pareto-optimal front PF.

1   *Initialize $P : \{x^1, x^2, ..., x^{\frac{N}{2}}\}$;*
2   *Update the ideal point z^* based on Eq. (1);*
3   *Set $Q := \varnothing$;*
4   **while** *termination criterion is not fulfilled* **do**
5   *Do local search on population P with the ideal point z^*;*
6   *Update z^* based on Eq. (1) and z^{nad} based on Eq. (2);*
7   *$Q \leftarrow$ UPDATESUBPS(z^{nad}, P, Q, N);*
8   *Do local search on population Q with the nadir point z^{nad};*
9   *Update the population P with the individuals gotten from population Q;*
10 **end**
11 **return** *Nondominated solutions in $P \bigcup Q$;*

Algorithm 2 shows how the second population is updated. After a circle of local search for the first population is done, the subroutine will update the second population according to the current obtained individuals. First, all the individuals in P are put together to indicate the distribution of solutions. Given the fixed size of the total populations N, then we can get the size of the second population size L according to N and the size of P. The primary motivation of this algorithm is to get direction vectors in the area where there are sparse solutions. Aiming to this, some clustering methods are integrated to avoid the direction vectors in crowding areas. In set P, every element is connected to its nearest neighbor[2] which can be seen as a set of graphs and union-find algorithm [12] partitions P into a number of disjoint subsets which we can see as the clusters

---

[1] In practice, WS is about 10 times faster than TCH and PBI in the same condition for solving 100 cities of MOTSP. However, it usually get less solutions.
[2] We set every individual to link to another individual with minimal euclidean distance.

(denoted as set C). It is worth to note that the union-find algorithm can be replaced by other clustering techniques. After that, the centroids of those clusters among which the direction vectors are inserted between a pair of them could be calculated. If the number of clusters is not sufficient which means that the number of direction vectors got from every pair of all the clusters is less that L, one individual in P is randomly chosen to be as a new cluster until the condition is satisfied. All the point pairs are extracted from the centroids of clusters C. All point pairs' middle points are stored in an array V and their euclidean distances are stored in an array D accordingly. Beginning from elements in V which has the least distance, direction vectors are inserted with regard to the nadir point. Then the individuals in population P and Q are associated with each direction vector according to Eq. (4) to form a new population Q on which the local search is conducted next.

Algorithm 2: Update Collaborative Subproblems (UPDATESUBPS)

Input:
  - z^{nad} : The nadir point;
  - Population P;
  - Population Q;
  - N: The population size.

Output: New population Q.

1 $L := N - |P|$;

2 $C \leftarrow$ UNIONFIND(P);// Applying the union find algorithm to find the clusters C in P.

3 $\{u^1, ..., u^k\} \leftarrow centroid(C)$;

4 **while** $\binom{2}{k} \leq L$ **do**
  // If there are not enough clusters.

5 $\quad$ *Randomly choose one solution x from P;*

6 $\quad$ $\{u^1, ..., u^{k+1}\} := \{u^1, ..., u^k\} \bigcup \{x\}$;

7 $\quad$ $k := k + 1$;

8 **end**

9 *All point pairs got from set $\{u^1, ..., u^k\}$ and their middle point coordinates and euclidean distances are stored in array $V : [v^1, ..., v^{\binom{2}{k}}]$ and $D : [d_1, ..., d_{\binom{2}{k}}]$;*

10 $[D, I] \leftarrow$ SORT(D); // I stores the index of direction vectors after sorting D.

11 $VL := V[\ I[1 : L]\ ]$;

12 $W := \varnothing$;

13 **foreach** $v \in VL$ **do**

14 $\quad$ $\lambda := z^{nad} - v$;

15 $\quad$ $W := W \bigcup \{\lambda\}$;

16 **end**

17 $Q \leftarrow$ ASSOCIATION(W, $P \bigcup Q$, z^{nad}); // Associate the direction vectors with individuals according to Eq. (4) to form a new population.

18 **return** Q;

---

4   Experimental Studies and Discussions

DP-MOEA/D-LS is compared with four decomposition-based algorithms which are three classical decomposition approaches incorporated in the framework of MOEA/D (WS, TCH and PBI) and iPBI (one variation of PBI which adopts nadir point as its reference point).

Nine MOTSP test instances[3] are used in our experimental study. For the parameter settings, all the population size is set as 300 and for DP-MOEA/D-LS, the first population size is 150 for bi-objective TSP and 153 for the tri-objective ones for the sake of uniformly designed direction vectors. The penalty factor θ is set to 5.0 in MOEA/D-LS(PBI) as suggested in [5] meanwhile we choose 1.0 for penalty factor θ in MOEA/D-LS(iPBI) and DP-MOEA/D-LS. The well-known 2-opt neighborhood [13] is adopted for the neighborhood search in local search. The maximal number of iterations is set to 100 for bi-objective problems and 200 for tri-objective ones. Each algorithm is conducted 31 times independently for each instance and for each run the algorithm will stop when no more new individuals will be generated.

Table 1. Mean and standard deviation values of normalized HV obtained by DP-MOEA/D-LS and four comparison algorithms

Instance		DP-MOEA/D-LS	MOEA/D-LS			
			WS	TCH	PBI	iPBI
ClusterAB100	mean	9.491E-01	9.419E-01⁻	9.476E-01⁻	9.252E-01⁻	9.414E-01⁻
	std	1.42E-03	1.81E-03	1.73E-03	3.14E-03	4.35E-03
ClusterAB300	mean	9.750E-01	9.647E-01⁻	9.587E-01⁻	9.413E-01⁻	9.589E-01⁻
	std	1.91E-03	2.08E-03	2.58E-03	3.06E-03	2.11E-03
euclidAB100	mean	7.966E-01	7.769E-01⁻	7.949E-01⁻	7.862E-01⁻	7.903E-01⁻
	std	1.53E-03	3.31E-03	1.76E-03	3.12E-03	2.80E-03
euclidAB300	mean	9.128E-01	9.017E-01⁻	8.957E-01⁻	8.851E-01⁻	8.930E-01⁻
	std	1.59E-03	2.01E-03	1.38E-03	2.49E-03	2.60E-03
kroAB100	mean	8.697E-01	8.575E-01⁻	8.681E-01⁻	8.538E-01⁻	8.632E-01⁻
	std	2.33E-03	2.81E-03	1.70E-03	3.49E-03	4.16E-03
kroAB200	mean	9.742E-01	9.656E-01⁻	9.599E-01⁻	9.522E-01⁻	9.613E-01⁻
	std	1.66E-03	2.08E-03	1.98E-03	4.01E-03	3.84E-03
kroAB300	mean	9.482E-01	9.393E-01⁻	9.302E-01⁻	9.179E-01⁻	9.288E-01⁻
	std	1.63E-03	1.73E-03	1.29E-03	1.68E-03	2.47E-03
euclidABC100	mean	6.682E-01	6.642E-01⁻	6.508E-01⁻	6.156E-01⁻	6.324E-01⁻
	std	1.76E-03	1.35E-03	1.64E-03	3.05E-03	2.80E-03
kroABC100	mean	7.671E-01	7.653E-01⁻	7.472E-01⁻	7.064E-01⁻	7.349E-01⁻
	std	1.45E-03	1.51E-03	1.49E-03	3.78E-03	2.68E-03

'+', '−' and '≈' indicate that the result is significantly better, significantly worse and statistically similar to that of DP-MOEA/D-LS on this test instance, respectively (wilcoxon's rank sum test at the 0.05 significance level). The best HV values are highlighted with gray background.

---

[3] Files are downloaded from https://sites.google.com/site/thibautlust/research/. They have the nominating rule as follows, for example, "kroABC100" means that the instance is "kro" with 100 cities and three objectives ('A', 'B' and 'C').

Table 2. Comparisons of DP-MOEA/D-LS with MOEA/D-LS (WS, TCH, PBI and iPBI) in terms of C-metric

Instance	MOEA/D-LS (WS)		MOEA/D-LS (TCH)		MOEA/D-LS (PBI)		MOEA/D-LS (iPBI)	
	C(A, B)	C(B, A)	C(A, B)	C(B, A)	C(A, B)	C(B, A)	C(A, B)	C(B, A)
ClusterAB100	**70.91**	13.15	27.29	**48.86**	**48.86**	26.30	31.66	**43.02**
ClusterAB300	**78.11**	14.89	**38.40**	27.17	**63.53**	21.44	**59.85**	23.24
euclidAB100	**95.22**	1.11	**53.47**	37.30	**67.74**	21.27	**60.71**	20.48
euclidAB300	**82.47**	8.58	**54.39**	19.09	**88.62**	7.33	**46.30**	33.20
kroAB100	**84.67**	6.40	**46.52**	39.52	**49.44**	28.64	**55.06**	36.00
kroAB200	**87.67**	6.32	**44.35**	27.12	**52.31**	30.12	**51.61**	30.78
kroAB300	**86.60**	8.60	**40.13**	28.57	**94.12**	2.04	**66.49**	16.18
euclidABC100	14.07	**29.10**	**64.70**	2.63	**64.51**	5.33	**99.68**	0.00
kroABC100	13.70	**28.86**	**68.29**	2.36	**59.71**	3.93	**97.31**	0.02

A corresponds to DP-MOEA/D-LS; B: corresponds to the compared algorithm; The relatively better C-metric values are in bold typeface.

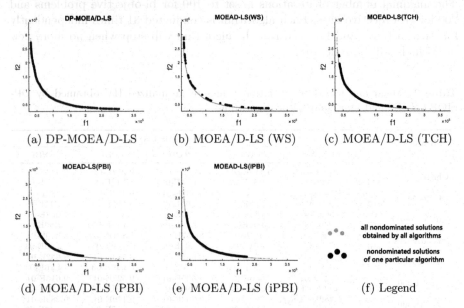

(a) DP-MOEA/D-LS   (b) MOEA/D-LS (WS)   (c) MOEA/D-LS (TCH)

(d) MOEA/D-LS (PBI)   (e) MOEA/D-LS (iPBI)   (f) Legend

Fig. 2. The nondominated solutions obtained by five algorithms in the run with the median HV value on kroAB200.

The performance of five algorithms are presented in Table 1 in terms of HV value [14] and in Table 2 in terms of C-metric [14] respectively. DP-MOEA/D-LS significantly outperforms other algorithms in terms of HV value and is better on most of the instances in terms of C-metric except for "ClusterAB100", "euclidABC100" and "kroABC100". It can be observed from Table 1 that DP-MOEA/D-LS significantly outperforms other algorithms on all nine mTSP instances in terms of HV value. Apart from the numerical results on two indicators, the visible approximate PFs of "kroAB200" test instance is illustrated in Fig. 2. All the nondominated solutions gained by all the algorithms and all

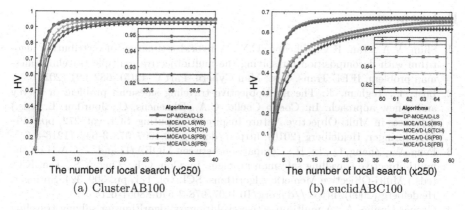

(a) ClusterAB100   (b) euclidABC100

Fig. 3. The mean normalized HV values versus the number of local search times obtained by five algorithms over 31 runs.

the 31 runs are scattered in red as the reference. It can be seen clearly that the solution set obtained by DP-MOEA/D-LS are most widely and uniformly distributed. The solution sets obtained by MOEA/D-LS (WS) are widely but unevenly distributed. The solution sets obtained by MOEA/D-LS (TCH, PBI and iPBI) are uniformly but narrowly distributed. In addition, the convergence plots among all the five algorithms over "ClusterAB100" and "euclidABC100" are illustrated in Fig. 3a and b. It can be observed that DP-MOEA/D-LS converges very fast and always achieves the best final performance in terms of HV. Over all, the proposed algorithm DP-MOEA/D-LS shows the best performance.

5   Conclusion

In this paper, we propose a dual-population-based local search in MOEA/D framework named as DP-MOEA/D-LS. DP-MOEA/D-LS is designed to attain good solutions along with an enhanced effective and efficient performance. It is compared with four decomposition based MOEAs on MOTSP test suites. The experimental results show that the overall performance of DP-MOEA/D-LS outperforms all the compared algorithms.

Acknowledgement. This work was supported in part by the National Natural Science Foundation of China (NSFC) under grant 61300159 and 61732006, by the Natural Science Foundation of Jiangsu Province of China under grant SBK2018022017, by China Postdoctoral Science Foundation under grant 2015M571751, by Open Project Foundation of Information Technology Research Base of Civil Aviation Administration of China under grant CAAC-ITRB-201703, by Open Project Foundation of the Guangdong Key Laboratory of Digital signal and Image Processing under grant 2017GDDSIPL-05 and by the Fundamental Research Funds for the Central Universities under grant NS2017070.

References

1. Shim, V.A., Tan, K.C., Cheong, C.Y.: A hybrid estimation of distribution algorithm with decomposition for solving the multiobjective multiple traveling salesman problem. IEEE Trans. Syst. Man Cybern. Part C **42**(5), 682–691 (2012)
2. Lust, T., Teghem, J.: The multiobjective traveling salesman problem: a survey and a new approach. In: Coello Coello, C.A., Dhaenens, C., Jourdan, L. (eds.) Advances in Multi-Objective Nature Inspired Computing. SCI, vol. 272, pp. 119–141. Springer, Heidelberg (2010). https://doi.org/10.1007/978-3-642-11218-8_6
3. Peng, W., Zhang, Q., Li, H.: Comparison between MOEA/D and NSGA-II on the multi-objective travelling salesman problem. In: Goh, C.K., Ong, Y.S., Tan, K.C. (eds.) Multi-Objective Memetic Algorithms. SCI, vol. 171, pp. 309–324. Springer, Heidelberg (2009). https://doi.org/10.1007/978-3-540-88051-6_14
4. Gaspar-Cunha, A.: A multi-objective evolutionary algorithm for solving traveling salesman problems: application to the design of polymer extruders. In: Ribeiro, B., Albrecht, R.F., Dobnikar, A., Pearson, D.W., Steele, N.C. (eds.) Adaptive and Natural Computing Algorithms (Coimbra, Portugal), pp. 189–193. Springer, Heidelberg (2005). https://doi.org/10.1007/3-211-27389-1_45
5. Zhang, Q., Li, H.: MOEA/D: a multiobjective evolutionary algorithm based on decomposition. IEEE Trans. Evol. Comput. **11**, 712–731 (2007)
6. Ke, L., Zhang, Q., Battiti, R.: Hybridization of decomposition and local search for multiobjective optimization. IEEE Trans. Cybern. **44**(10), 1808–1820 (2014)
7. Cai, X., Mei, Z., Fan, Z., Zhang, Q.: A constrained decomposition approach with grids for evolutionary multiobjective optimization. IEEE Trans. Evol. Comput. **22**(4), 564–577 (2017)
8. Wang, L., Zhang, Q., Zhou, A., Gong, M., Jiao, L.: Constrained subproblems in a decomposition-based multiobjective evolutionary algorithm. IEEE Trans. Evol. Comput. **20**(3), 475–480 (2016)
9. Sato, H.: Analysis of inverted PBI and comparison with other scalarizing functions in decomposition based moeas. J. Heuristics **21**(6), 819–849 (2015)
10. Wang, Z., Zhang, Q., Li, H., Ishibuchi, H., Jiao, L.: On the use of two reference points in decomposition based multiobjective evolutionary algorithms. Swarm Evol. Comput. **34**, 89–102 (2017)
11. Miettinen, K.: Nonlinear Multiobjective Optimization. International Series in Operations Research and Management Science, vol. 12. Kluwer Academic Publishers, Dordrecht (1999)
12. Sedgewick, R., Wayne, K.: Algorithms. Addison-Wesley Professional, Boston (2011)
13. Borges, P.C., Hansen, M.P.: A basis for future successes in multiobjective combinatorial optimization. Technical report IMM-REP-1998-8, Institute of Mathematical Modelling, Technical University of Denmark (1998)
14. Zitzler, E., Thiele, L.: Multiobjective evolutionary algorithms: a comparative case study and the strength pareto approach. IEEE Trans. Evol. Comput. **3**, 257–271 (1999)

A Cone Decomposition Many-Objective Evolutionary Algorithm with Adaptive Direction Penalized Distance

Weiqin Ying[1(✉)], Yali Deng[1], Yu Wu[2], Yuehong Xie[1], Zhenyu Wang[1], and Zhiyi Lin[3]

[1] School of Software Engineering, South China University of Technology,
Guangzhou 510006, China
yingweiqin@scut.edu.cn
[2] School of Computer Science and Educational Software, Guangzhou University,
Guangzhou 510006, China
wuyu@gzhu.edu.cn
[3] School of Computers, Guangdong University of Technology,
Guangzhou 510006, China

Abstract. The effectiveness of most of the existing decomposition-based multi-objective evolutionary algorithms (MOEAs) is yet to be heightened for many-objective optimization problems (MaOPs). In this paper, a cone decomposition evolutionary algorithm (CDEA) is proposed to extend decomposition-based MOEAs to MaOPs more effectively. In CDEA, a cone decomposition strategy is introduced to overcome potential troubles in decomposition-based MOEAs by decomposing a MaOP into several subproblems and associating each of them with a unique cone subregion. Then, a scalarization approach of adaptive direction penalized distance is designed to emphasize boundary subproblems and guarantee the full spread of the final obtained front. The proposed algorithm is compared with three decomposition-based MOEAs on unconstrained benchmark MaOPs with 5 to 10 objectives. Empirical results demonstrate the superior solution quality of CDEA.

Keywords: Many-objective optimization · Evolutionary algorithms
Decomposition · Scalarization approach · Pareto front

1 Introduction

Many real-life business and engineering applications can be naturally modeled as multi-objective optimization problems (MOPs) [1], which optimize multiple and often competing objectives simultaneously. More specifically, a MOP can be formulated as follows:

$$minimize \quad \mathbf{F}(\mathbf{x}) = (f_1(\mathbf{x}), f_2(\mathbf{x}), \cdots, f_m(\mathbf{x}))^T$$
$$subject\ to \quad \mathbf{x} \in \Omega \tag{1}$$

© Springer Nature Singapore Pte Ltd. 2018
J. Qiao et al. (Eds.): BIC-TA 2018, CCIS 951, pp. 389–400, 2018.
https://doi.org/10.1007/978-981-13-2826-8_34

where $\mathbf{x} = (x_1, x_2, \cdots, x_n) \in \Omega$ denotes the decision vector, $\mathbf{F}(\mathbf{x}) \in \mathbb{R}^m$ is the objective vector, $\mathbf{F} : \Omega \to \mathbb{R}^m$ constitutes m objective functions, Ω and $\mathbb{R}^m$ represent the decision space and objective space respectively. Furthermore, MOPs involving four or more objectives are generally referred as many-objective optimization problems (MaOPs) [2]. Because of the intrinsic conflicting nature of the objectives, it is generally impossible to find a single solution to optimize all objectives simultaneously. Instead, a set of non-dominated trade-off solutions can be achieved in terms of a Pareto set (PS) [3].

Evolutionary algorithms are population-based stochastic search approaches that are particularly suitable for solving MOPs because their inherent parallelism enables them to find a set of non-dominated solutions in a single run [4], instead of multiple separate runs as in the case of traditional techniques. For this reason, a number of multi-objective optimization evolutionary algorithms (MOEAs) have been developed over the last two decades [1]. According to their different selection strategies, the majority of existing MOEAs can be classified into three categories: dominance-based MOEAs, indicator-based MOEAs, and decomposition-based MOEAs. The high performance of these MOEAs has been verified on 2- or 3-objective optimization problems.

However, as the number of objectives increases, dominance-based MOEAs and indicator-based MOEAs will face some challenges that can lead to performance degradation, including the operational efficiency, selection pressure, and maintenance of uniform distributions. In contrast, decomposition-based MOEAs can better overcome these challenges on MaOPs thanks to their inherent advantages. First, as one of the most representative decomposition-based MOEAs, the multi-objective evolutionary algorithm based on decomposition (MOEA/D) [4] only needs to compare every offspring with the solutions of its T neighbor subproblems instead of the expensive non-dominated checking and hypervolume calculation. Hence, MOEA/D has a low complexity of $O(mTN)$ for one generation of evolution. Second, decomposition-based MOEAs utilize scalarization approaches as the selection criterion. In these methods, the selection pressure is hardly affected by the mutually non-dominated characteristic of MaOPs. Moreover, evenly spaced weight vectors in decomposition-based MOEAs can systematically and intrinsically maintain a uniform distribution of the population, even in high-dimensional objective spaces.

Furthermore, the selection operators in decomposition-based MOEAs play a vital role in balancing the population diversity and convergence in the search process, but the original selection operator in MOEA/D may cause some potential troubles that may mislead to the replacement of unsuitable subproblems and cause the population diversity or convergence performance to deteriorate for some complicated optimization problems. To enhance the selection scheme when dealing with complicated optimization problems, several improved selection schemes have been proposed. MOEA/D-DE [5] uses n_r instead of neighborhood size T to limit the maximum number of solutions replaced by one offspring. It further introduces a DE operator to generate new offsprings. MOEA/D-CD and MOEA/D-ACD [4] introduce a constrained decomposition approach to reduce the improvement region of each subproblem. Both strategies in MOEA/D-DE and MOEA/D-CD aim to reduce the chance that a solution has many copies in the population, hence maintaining the population diversity. MOEA/D-GR and MOEA/D-AGR [6] adopt a global replacement scheme for selection in MOEA/D that finds the most appropriate subproblem according to the objective functions first and then updates its neighbor subproblems using the offspring as in the original MOEA/D. This scheme can reduce the case of updating unsuitable subproblems. In addition, some other decomposition-based MOEAs like CAEA [7] and CHEA [8] were proposed to overcome the potential troubles existing in MOEA/D as well as to improve the efficiency of MOEAs. However, these MOEAs are designed mainly for MOPs with two or three objectives and have difficulty in effectively handling the mentioned potential troubles for MaOPs. Moreover, for MaOPs whose Pareto fronts have extremely small slopes at the boundary region, the traditional scalarization approaches such as Tchebycheff (TCH), penalty boundary intersection (PBI), and angle penalized distance (APD) [9] for decomposition-based MOEAs are unable to preserve solutions at the boundary region.

In this paper, a cone decomposition evolutionary algorithm (CDEA) is proposed to handle the mentioned potential troubles and heighten the performances of decomposition-based MOEAs for solving MaOPs. In addition, a scalarization approach of adaptive direction penalized distance (ADPD) is designed to utilize an adaptive direction-based penalty factor to emphasize boundary reference directions. The rest of this paper is organized as follows. The main ideas and the procedure of the proposed CDEA are described in Sect. 2. Next, Sect. 3 presents empirical results of CDEA and three decomposition-based MOEAs on unconstrained benchmark MaOPs. Finally, the conclusion is given in Sect. 4.

2   Cone Decomposition Evolutionary Algorithm

In this section, the main ideas of CDEA, including the cone decomposition strategy and the ADPD scalarization approach, as well as the procedure of CDEA, are introduced in detail respectively.

2.1   Cone Decomposition

In MOEA/D, a MOP is partitioned into a series of subproblems. In this paper, a strategy of cone decomposition is introduced to decompose the MOP more thoroughly. First, we introduce an observation vector in Definition 1. According to this definition, all solutions can be projected onto a hyperplane $\sum_{i=1}^{m} f_i' = 1$, called an observation hyperplane, and the origin of this hyperplane's coordinate system is moved to the ideal point $\mathbf{z}^{ide}$. In fact, observation vector $V(\mathbf{x})$ represents the direction of solution $\mathbf{x}$.

Definition 1 (Observation vector). *The observation vector for any solution* $\mathbf{x}$ *is* $V(\mathbf{x}) = (v_1, v_2, \cdots, v_m)$, *where* $v_i = \frac{f_i(\mathbf{x}) - \mathbf{z}_i^{ide}}{\sum_{j=1}^{m}(f_j(\mathbf{x}) - \mathbf{z}_j^{ide})}$, $i \in [1, \cdots, m]$.

Like most of the decomposition-based MOEAs [4,7,8], a set of uniformly distributed direction vectors is also required in CDEA. These vectors are called the reference directions in this paper. First, a systematic approach developed from Das and Dennis's method [10] is used to generate the reference directions $D = \{\lambda^1, \cdots, \lambda^N\}$ when $m < 7$, where $N = C_{H+m-1}^{m-1}$. The uniformly distributed direction vectors are sampled from a unit simplex on the observation hyperplane $\sum_{i=1}^m f_i' = 1$ by using this method. As discussed in [3], when $m \geq 7$, the number of reference directions generated by Das and Dennis's method grows sharply and is a computational burden for MOEAs. Therefore, a two-layer generation method in [3] is adopted to generate reference directions in this case.

In our proposed algorithm CDEA, objective space Φ is divided into N cone subregions corresponding to the direction vectors. Further, the cone subregion Φ^i (corresponding to λ^i) can be defined as follows:

$$\Phi^i = \left\{ \mathbf{F}(\mathbf{x}) \in \mathbb{R}^m | d(V(\mathbf{x}), \lambda^i) \leq d(V(\mathbf{x}), \lambda^j) \right\} \qquad (2)$$

where $j \in [1, \cdots, m] \setminus \{i\}$, $\mathbf{x} \in \Omega$ and $d(V(\mathbf{x}, \lambda^j))$ represent the Euclidean distance between the observation vector of solution $\mathbf{x}$ and reference direction vector λ^j. Figure 1 depicts an illustration of cone subregions in the intuitive case of 3-dimensional objective space. A total of 10 direction vectors are evenly distributed on the observation hyperplane, which leads to a uniform decomposition of 10 cone subregions. The observation vector $V(\mathbf{x})$ of solution $\mathbf{x}$ belonging to the cone subregion Φ^k is closer to its corresponding direction vector λ^k than any other cone subregion. Furthermore, all half-lines from the ideal point $\mathbf{z}^{ide}$ towards all points (observation vectors) in the observation hyperplane that are closer to direction vector λ^k in objective space constitute a cone subregion, as indicated by the shaped cone shown in Fig. 1.

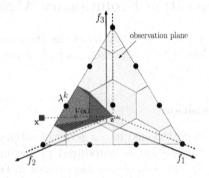

Fig. 1. Illustration of cone subregions in the intuitive case of 3-dimensional objective space.

To consider computing efficiency, a special data structure, multidimensional binary search tree, also called a KD-tree [11] where K is the dimensionality of the objective space, is utilized for indexing the corresponding cone subregion of a certain solution based on the rule in Eq. (2). The KD-tree, built according to the set of reference directions, is used to store the distribution information of the reference directions. Hence, we can identify the cone subregion Φ^k that a certain solution $\mathbf{x}$ belongs to by searching for the nearest direction vector λ^k to observation vector $V(\mathbf{x})$ based on the Euclidean distance. The simplified computation of the observation vector and the efficiency of the KD-tree can save a substantial amount of computing time.

Using the cone decomposition strategy introduced above, a MOP is divided into a set of subproblems and each subproblem is associated with a reference direction vector. Also, the proposed algorithm, CDEA, assigns a certain cone subregion in the objective space for each subproblem with the same corresponding direction vector. This restricts every solution to a certain subregion, which, together with the CDEA update scheme, enables it to overcome the two potential troubles.

2.2 Adaptive Direction Penalized Distance

The aim of solving each cone subproblem in CDEA is to find a solution closest to the ideal point along the associated direction vector in its cone subregion. To meet this criterion, which consists of two subcriteria, the convergence criterion and directivity criterion, scalarization is needed to balance them. In this paper, a scalarization approach of adaptive direction penalized distance, referred as ADPD, is designed to evaluate the fitness value of a solution with respect to a direction vector. The ADPD can be formulated as follows:

$$
\begin{aligned}
minimize \quad & g^{ADPD}(\mathbf{x}|\lambda^i, \mathbf{z}^{ide}) = D_c^i \left(1.0 + \alpha \cdot \beta \cdot D_d^i\right) \\
subject\ to \quad & \mathbf{x} \in \Omega^i \\
& D_c^i = \|F(\mathbf{x}) - \mathbf{z}^{ide}\| \\
& D_d^i = \frac{\|V(\mathbf{x}) - \lambda^i\|}{d_0} \\
& \alpha = \sum_{j=1}^{m} \frac{1}{\lambda_j^i}, \ \beta = m \cdot \left(\frac{t}{t_{max}}\right)^{\gamma}
\end{aligned}
\tag{3}
$$

where D_c^i is the convergence criterion, which evaluates the closeness of the candidate solution to ideal point $\mathbf{z}^{ide}$, D_d^i is the directivity criterion, which means the distance between the observation vector $V(\mathbf{x})$ of the candidate solution $\mathbf{x}$ and reference direction vector λ^i, and α and β represent two adaptive penalty factors based on direction and stage, respectively. In addition, d_0 in D_d^i is the average of the minimum distance between each predefined reference direction and the other directions.

Within the stage-based adaptive penalty factor β, m is the number of objectives, t is the current number of generations, t_{max} is the predefined maximum number of generations, and γ is a user defined parameter controlling the changing rate of the penalty factor. The benefit of using the sum of reciprocals of components of the reference direction vector in the penalty factor α is that the penalty factor can emphasize boundary reference directions to guarantee the full spread of the final obtained Pareto set. Using this penalty function, $t \ll t_{max}$ in the early stage of the search process, and then $\beta \approx 0$, and thus $g^{ADPD} \approx D_c^i$ achieved, which means that the ADPD approach applies a high selection pressure on the convergence to push the population towards the Pareto front. While in the late stage of the search process, with the value of t approaching t_{max}, the influence of D_d^i will be gradually accumulated to exert selection pressure on the diversity to generate well distributed candidate solutions.

Algorithm 1: CDEA Framework

> **Input**: T: the neighborhood size; m: the number of objectives; H_1: the parameter for generating reference directions in the boundary layer; H_2: the parameter for generating reference directions in the inner layer; δ: the probability of selecting parent solutions locally.
> **Output**: $\tilde{P}^*$: An approximation to the PS.
> 1 Generate one layer or two layers of reference directions $\Lambda = \{\lambda^1, \cdots, \lambda^N\}$ with parameters H_1 and H_2 for $m < 7$ and $m \geq 7$, respectively;
> 2 Initialize T neighbor indexes $B^i = \{j_1, j_2, \cdots, j_T\}$ for each reference direction $\lambda^i \in \Lambda$, where $\lambda^{j_1}, \lambda^{j_2}, \cdots, \lambda^{j_T}$ are the T closest reference directions to λ^i;
> 3 $I \leftarrow$ `BuildKDTree`(Λ);
> 4 Create N initial solutions $P' = \{\mathbf{y}^1, \mathbf{y}^2, \cdots, \mathbf{y}^N\}$ by uniformly randomly sampling from the decision space Ω ;
> 5 Initialize the ideal point $\mathbf{z}^{ide} = (z_1^{ide}, z_2^{ide}, \cdots, z_m^{ide})$ where $z_j^{ide} = \min_{\mathbf{y} \in P'} f_j(\mathbf{y})$;
> 6 Get a population $P = \{\lambda^1.\mathbf{x}, \lambda^2.\mathbf{x}, \cdots, \lambda^N.\mathbf{x}\}$ associated with subproblems by assigning each solution in the population to the nearest reference direction;
>   `// main loop`
> 7 **while** *the termination criterion is not met* **do**
> 8   **for** $i \in [1, \cdots, N]$ **do** `// for each subproblem`
> 9   Choose some mating parents pp randomly;
> 10   Generate an offspring $\mathbf{y}$ by applying recombination and mutation operators to the selected parents pp ;
> 11   Apply $\mathbf{y}$ to update the current ideal point $\mathbf{z}^{ide}$;
> 12 $P, U \leftarrow$ `ConeUpdate`$(\mathbf{y}, \mathbf{z}^{ide}, P, \Lambda, I)$;
> 13   **end**
> 14 **end**
> 15 Obtain an approximate to the PS, $\tilde{P}^*$, by removing all the dominated solutions from the final population P ;
> 16 **return** $\tilde{P}^*$

Note that the major difference between the ADPD and the traditional approach such as TCH, PBI and APD is that the adaptive direction-based penalty factor in ADPD considers the distribution of the reference directions and adaptively emphasizes the boundary reference directions. Hence, the boundary subproblems in ADPD have the greater penalty factors which are very conducive to achieving the more complete spread of solutions for some complex MaOPs.

2.3 Framework of CDEA

Algorithm 1 presents the framework of CDEA. First, the initialization procedure of CDEA is presented in Lines 1–6. Then, the code in Lines 9–10 generate an offspring. Next, the offspring is used to update the current population in Lines 11–12. Finally, after meeting the termination criterion, the final population is returned after all the dominated solutions have been removed. The implementation details of the cone update scheme in CDEA are explained in the following subsection.

2.4 Cone Update Scheme

Algorithm 2: Cone Update Procedure of Subproblem (ConeUpdate)

Input: $\mathbf{y}$: an offspring solution for update; $\mathbf{z}^{ide}$: the current ideal point; P: the current population; Λ: the set of reference directions; I: the KD-tree; B: the index set of neighbor reference directions.

Output: P: the population after update; U: a sign records whether the population is updated.

1 $U \leftarrow False$;
2 $k \leftarrow$ QueryKDTree $(V(\mathbf{y}, \mathbf{z}^{ide}), I)$;
3 $\mathbf{y}' \leftarrow \lambda^k.\mathbf{x}$;
4 $k' \leftarrow$ QueryKDTree $(V(\mathbf{y}', \mathbf{z}^{ide}), I)$;
5 **if** $k' == k$ **then** // in place
6   **if** $g^{ADPD}(\mathbf{y}|\lambda^k, \mathbf{z}^{ide}) < g^{ADPD}(\mathbf{y}'|\lambda^k, \mathbf{z}^{ide})$ **then**
7           $\lambda^k.\mathbf{x} \leftarrow \mathbf{y}$;
8           $U \leftarrow True$;
9   **end**
10 **else** // out of place, recursive mode
11      $\lambda^k.\mathbf{x} \leftarrow \mathbf{y}$;
12      $U \leftarrow True$;
13      $P, \_ \leftarrow$ ConeUpdate $(\mathbf{y}', \mathbf{z}^{ide}, P, \Lambda, I)$;
14 **end**
15 **return** P, U

According to the cone decomposition strategy and the ADPD scalarization approach, a cone update scheme whose pseudocode is presented in Algorithm 2, is further designed to update the current population with a new solution. Only the stored solution $\mathbf{y}'$ in the population currently associated with cone subregion Φ^k to which the new solution $\mathbf{y}$ corresponds based on the cone decomposition strategy is allowed to be compared and updated by $\mathbf{y}$. This is the main concept of this scheme.

Further, if the comparison solution $\mathbf{y}'$ is in place (Line 5), which means that $\mathbf{y}'$ lies exactly in the cone subregion Φ^k it is currently associated with, then the better of the stored and new solutions is chosen to store in the population according to the scalar ADPD function. If the comparison solution is out of place (Line 10), this stored solution is directly replaced by the new one. Specifically, a recursive mode (Line 13) is introduced in this scheme to increase its stability. The process to call the cone update operation recursively is only conducted when the comparison solution is out of place and the discarded solution in this case is regarded as a new solution.

3   Experiments and Analysis

In this section, the performance of the proposed CDEA is verified by empirical experiments. The parameter settings in the experiment are given in this section first, followed by an analysis of the experimental results.

3.1   Parameter Settings

In this paper, empirical experiments were conducted on 3 benchmark test problems taken from one widely used DTLZ test suite [12], i.e., DTLZ3, DTLZ4 and Convex_DTLZ2, to compare the proposed CDEA with three state-of-the-art decomposition-based MOEAs, MOEA/D, MOEA/D-AGR and MOEA/D-ACD. For each test problem, objective numbers varying from 5 to 10, i.e., $m \in \{5, 8, 10\}$, are considered. As suggested in [12], the number of decision variables was set as $n = m + k - 1$ for all DTLZ test problems, where $k = 10$. All of the algorithms above are implemented on JMetal, a Java-based framework for multi-objective optimization. In our experiments, each algorithm is performed 30 times on each test problem independently and the hypervolume (HV) is used as the performance indicator to make empirical comparisons between the obtained results.

Several parameters of all four comparison algorithms considered in this paper are summarized as follows. For the objective numbers of 5, 8 and 10, H_1 and H_2 are set to (6, 0), (3, 2) and (3, 2) respectively. Correspondingly, the population size is 210, 156 and 275 respectively. In this paper, the predefined maximal number of generations are used as the termination criterion. Specifically, with the objective number varying from 5 to 10, the maximal numbers of generations are set to (1000, 1000, 1500) for DTLZ3, (1000, 1250, 2000) for DTLZ4, and (750, 2000, 4000) for Convex_DTLZ2, respectively. The SBX recombination operator was adopted in all comparison algorithms with a crossover probability $p_c = 1.0$ and a distribution index $\eta_c = 30$. A polynomial mutation with distribution index $\eta_m = 20$ was used for each algorithm and the mutation probability was $p_m = \frac{1}{n}$. In addition, the neighborhood size and the penalty parameter of PBI are set as $T = 20$ and $\theta = 5.0$, respectively. Specifically, instead of the Tchebycheff approach, the PBI approach is also utilized as the decomposition approach in MOEA/D-AGR and MOEA/D-ACD.

Table 1. The statistical results (best, median and worst) of the HV values obtained by four comparing algorithms on DTLZ3, DTLZ4, Convex_DTLZ2

Test Instance	m	MOEA/D	MOEA/D-ACD	MOEA/D-AGR	CDEA
DTLZ3	5	$0.81165_{(4)}$	$0.81233_{(2)}$	$0.81211_{(3)}$	$0.81260_{(1)}$
		$0.80986_{(4)}$	$0.81062_{(2)}$	$0.81007_{(3)}$	$0.81225_{(1)}$
		$0.80609_{(4)}$	$0.80671_{(2)}$	$0.80662_{(3)}$	$0.80903_{(1)}$
	8	$0.92464_{(1)}$	$0.92111_{(4)}$	$0.92272_{(3)}$	$0.92398_{(2)}$
		$0.91909_{(3)}$	$0.91459_{(4)}$	$0.92085_{(2)}$	$0.92258_{(1)}$
		$0.13242_{(4)}$	$0.90552_{(3)}$	$0.91384_{(1)}$	$0.90556_{(2)}$
	10	$0.97021_{(1)}$	$0.96957_{(4)}$	$0.96973_{(2)}$	$0.96972_{(3)}$
		$0.96982_{(1)}$	$0.96894_{(4)}$	$0.96952_{(3)}$	$0.96969_{(2)}$
		$0.96721_{(3)}$	$0.96670_{(4)}$	$0.96896_{(2)}$	$0.96920_{(1)}$
DTLZ4	5	$0.81264_{(2)}$	$0.81264_{(2)}$	$0.81264_{(2)}$	$0.81266_{(1)}$
		$0.71395_{(4)}$	$0.81264_{(2)}$	$0.81264_{(2)}$	$0.81265_{(1)}$
		$0.54384_{(4)}$	$0.81263_{(3)}$	$0.81264_{(2)}$	$0.81265_{(1)}$
	8	$0.92412_{(1)}$	$0.92408_{(3)}$	$0.92408_{(3)}$	$0.92409_{(2)}$
		$0.84752_{(4)}$	$0.92407_{(1)}$	$0.92407_{(1)}$	$0.92407_{(1)}$
		$0.76648_{(4)}$	$0.92405_{(2)}$	$0.92405_{(2)}$	$0.92406_{(1)}$
	10	$0.96990_{(2)}$	$0.96990_{(2)}$	$0.96990_{(2)}$	$0.97001_{(1)}$
		$0.93755_{(4)}$	$0.96989_{(2)}$	$0.96989_{(2)}$	$0.97000_{(1)}$
		$0.84618_{(4)}$	$0.96988_{(2)}$	$0.96988_{(2)}$	$0.96999_{(1)}$
Convex_DTLZ2	5	$0.99277_{(4)}$	$0.99451_{(2)}$	$0.99447_{(3)}$	$0.99933_{(1)}$
		$0.99018_{(4)}$	$0.99100_{(3)}$	$0.99195_{(2)}$	$0.99932_{(1)}$
		$0.98790_{(4)}$	$0.98921_{(3)}$	$0.99013_{(2)}$	$0.99932_{(1)}$
	8	$0.97660_{(4)}$	$0.98049_{(3)}$	$0.98051_{(2)}$	$0.99999_{(1)}$
		$0.97348_{(4)}$	$0.97421_{(3)}$	$0.97669_{(2)}$	$0.99999_{(1)}$
		$0.97193_{(4)}$	$0.97272_{(3)}$	$0.97334_{(2)}$	$0.99999_{(1)}$
	10	$0.97055_{(4)}$	$0.97340_{(3)}$	$0.97344_{(2)}$	$0.99999_{(1)}$
		$0.96954_{(4)}$	$0.96992_{(3)}$	$0.97120_{(2)}$	$0.99999_{(1)}$
		$0.96915_{(3)}$	$0.96908_{(4)}$	$0.96998_{(2)}$	$0.99999_{(1)}$

3.2 Quality Analysis

To evaluate the performance of the proposed CDEA on MaOPs, the HV indicator was used to assess the quality of solutions obtained by all four algorithms. Especially, the best, median and worst HV results obtained by four comparing algorithms on each test instance are listed in Table 1. Here, the values of all comparison algorithms are ordered and the rank of each value is indicated as a subscript, where the best results are indicated by a dark gray background as well as a bold font, and the second best is only indicated by a light gray background.

First, we compare CDEA with MOEA/D and its two variants MOEA/D-ACD and MOEA/D-AGR by investigating the solution quality of the results of these four decomposition-based MOEAs on the DTLZ3 and DTLZ4 test instances. As shown by the results of HV in Table 1, CDEA and MOEA/D-AGR outperform MOEA/D on most of the DTLZ3 and DTLZ4 test instances. Since DTLZ3 and DTLZ4 are designed to contain local optima and have a biased density in the search space, respectively, both make it challenging for MOEAs to maintain good distributions of solutions. Overall, with the help of the cone decomposition strategy, CDEA is the best decomposition-based MOEA of these

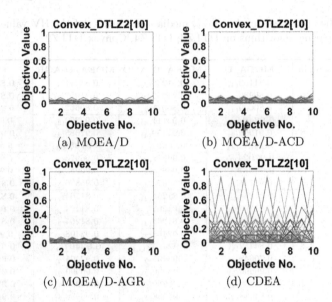

Fig. 2. Parallel coordinates of nondominated fronts with the median HV value obtained, respectively, by four comparing algorithms on 10-objective Convex_DTLZ2.

four comparison algorithms for the DTLZ3 and DTLZ4 test instances, as it has the best results for 13 out of 18 comparisons on the DTLZ3 and DTLZ4 test instances in Table 1.

Then, we compare these four decomposition-based MOEAs on the Convex_DTLZ2 test instance which is a modification of DTLZ2, whose Pareto front is $f_m(\mathbf{x}^*) + \sum_{i=1}^{m-1} \sqrt{f_i(\mathbf{x}^*)} = 1$. The design of Convex_DTLZ2 aims to reveal an ability of handling MaOPs with convex Pareto fronts. Due to the shape of Convex_DTLZ2, the HV results in Table 1 are similar, but CDEA has better results with respect to the other three algorithms. For a more intuitive view, Fig. 2 further plots the parallel coordinates of nondominated fronts with the median HV values obtained by each of four comparing algorithms on the 10-objective Convex_DTLZ2 test instance. It can be observed from Fig. 2 that CDEA achieves a nondominated front with a wider spread whose maximum value for each objective nearly comes up to 1.0, while the other three comparisons can only converge to very narrow Pareto fronts. It can be inferred that the distributions of Pareto fronts obtained by CDEA are obviously more complete than those of the others. The good performance of CDEA on Convex_DTLZ2 is mainly owing to the use of the scalarization approach of ADPD which adaptively emphasizes the boundary subproblems.

In summary, CDEA performs the best among all four comparison algorithms for handling MaOPs by achieving the best HV values for 22 out of 27 in comparison with the other algorithms in Table 1.

4 Conclusion

In this paper, the CDEA algorithm was proposed to extend the decomposition-based MOEAs to handle MaOPs effectively. First, a cone decomposition strategy in CDEA decomposes a MaOP into a set of cone subproblems. Each cone subproblem is assigned a unique cone subregion corresponding to its reference direction in the objective space. Moreover, an ADPD scalarization approach is designed to balance the convergence and directivity in each subproblem and adaptively emphasize the boundary subproblems. As a result, CDEA overcomes the potential troubles existing in the original MOEA/D well. The performance of CDEA was investigated on several unconstrained benchmark DTLZ test problems with 5 to 10 objectives. Empirical results demonstrate that the proposed CDEA performs very well at maintaining the population convergence and diversity for most of the test instances when compared with three decomposition-based MOEAs.

In the future, we are interested in investigating the performance of CDEA for a wider range of MaOPs, such as those with complicated Pareto set shapes and constrained MaOPs.

Acknowledgments. This work was supported partially by the Natural Science Foundation of Guangdong Province, China, under Grants 2015A030313204, 2017A030310013, and 2018A030313389, in part by the Fundamental Research Funds for the Central Universities, SCUT, under Grant 2017MS043, in part by the Pearl River S&T Nova Program of Guangzhou under Grant 2014J2200052, in part by the National Natural Science Foundation of China under Grants 61203310 and 61503087, in part by the Major Research and Development Program for Industrial Technology of Guangzhou City under Grant 201802010025, and in part by the Platform Development Program for Innovation and Entrepreneurship at Colleges in Guangzhou under Grant 2019PT103.

References

1. Zhang, J., Xing, L.: A survey of multiobjective evolutionary algorithms. In: 2017 IEEE International Conference on Computational Science and Engineering (CSE) and IEEE International Conference on Embedded and Ubiquitous Computing (EUC), vol. 1, pp. 93–100 (2017)
2. Maltese, J., Ombuki-Berman, B.M., Engelbrecht, A.P.: A scalability study of many-objective optimization algorithms. IEEE Trans. Evol. Comput. **22**, 79–96 (2018)
3. Li, K., Deb, K., Zhang, Q., Kwong, S.: An evolutionary many-objective optimization algorithm based on dominance and decomposition. IEEE Trans. Evol. Comput. **19**, 694–716 (2015)
4. Wang, L., Zhang, Q., Zhou, A., Gong, M., Jiao, L.: Constrained subproblems in a decomposition-based multiobjective evolutionary algorithm. IEEE Trans. Evol. Comput. **20**, 475–480 (2016)
5. Li, H., Zhang, Q.: Multiobjective optimization problems with complicated pareto sets, MOEA/D and NSGA-II. IEEE Trans. Evol. Comput. **13**, 284–302 (2009)
6. Wang, Z., Zhang, Q., Zhou, A., Gong, M., Jiao, L.: Adaptive replacement strategies for MOEA/D. IEEE Trans. Cybern. **46**, 474–486 (2016)

7. Ying, W., Xu, X., Feng, Y., Wu, Y.: An efficient conical area evolutionary algorithm for bi-objective optimization. IEICE Trans. Fund. Electron. Commun. Comput. Sci. **95**, 1420–1425 (2012)
8. Ying, W., Xie, Y., Xu, X., Wu, Y., Xu, A., Wang, Z.: An efficient and universal conical hypervolume evolutionary algorithm in three or higher dimensional objective space. IEICE Trans. Fund. Electron. Commun. Comput. Sci. **98**, 2330–2335 (2015)
9. Cheng, R., Jin, Y., Olhofer, M., Sendhoff, B.: A reference vector guided evolutionary algorithm for many-objective optimization. IEEE Trans. Evol. Comput. **20**, 773–791 (2016)
10. Das, I., Dennis, J.E.: Normal-boundary intersection: a new method for generating the pareto surface in nonlinear multicriteria optimization problems. SIAM J. Optim. **8**, 631–657 (1998)
11. Bentley, J.L.: Multidimensional binary search trees used for associative searching. Commun. ACM **18**, 509–517 (1975)
12. Deb, K., Thiele, L., Laumanns, M., Zitzler, E.: Scalable test problems for evolutionary multiobjective optimization. In: Abraham, A., Jain, L., Goldberg, R. (eds.) Evolutionary Multiobjective Optimization, pp. 105–145. Springer, London (2005). https://doi.org/10.1007/1-84628-137-7_6

Origin Illusion, Elitist Selection and Contraction Guidance

Rui Li[1(✉)], Guangzhi Xu[1,2], Xinchao Zhao[1], and Dunwei Gong[3]

[1] School of Science, Beijing University of Posts and Telecommunications,
Beijing 100876, China
[2] Automation School, Beijing University of Posts and Telecommunications,
Beijing 100876, China
[3] School of Information and Electrical Engineering,
China University of Mining and Technology, Xuzhou 221116, China
zmdsn@126.com

Abstract. Most of existing swarm intelligence (SI) algorithms is modeling based on natural phenomena. Firstly, different from the previous practices, this paper constructs a mathematical model based on the traditional optimization algorithms. To simplify this model, a new algorithm Linear Transformation and Elitist Selection algorithm (LTES) is proposed. Experiment shows that the algorithm has origin illusion phenomenon. Then, this paper observes origin illusion phenomenon for the population-based optimization algorithm, and experiments shows that crossover operator is an effective way for LTES' origin illusion problem. Finally, another algorithm Contraction and Guidance Algorithm (CGA) is proposed to prove that elitist selection is not necessary. The experimental results show that both algorithms are effective.

Keywords: Origin illusion · Elitist selection · Crossover
Contraction and guidance

1 Introduction

In the past decades, many population-based swarm intelligence (SI) algorithms have been proposed. These algorithms have shown great success in dealing with optimization problems in various application fields. The famous SI algorithms are particle swarm optimization (PSO) [1,2] and ant colony optimization (ACO) [3,4]. The great successes of PSO and ACO for solving optimization problems greatly push the SI developments forward. Algorithms inspired by collective biologic behavior of bee [5,6], glowworm [7], fish school [8], firefly [9], cuckoo [10], krill herd [11,12], bacteria [13], bat [14] are proposed. Almost all of these algorithms are adopted variform elitist selection.

By the observing and modeling of the cooperative swarm behavior of living creatures, artificial systems, researchers try to understand these mechanisms and use them to design new algorithms. Different from the usual way, this article

© Springer Nature Singapore Pte Ltd. 2018
J. Qiao et al. (Eds.): BIC-TA 2018, CCIS 951, pp. 401–410, 2018.
https://doi.org/10.1007/978-981-13-2826-8_35

hopes to look at it from a mathematical perspective. Following the traditional optimization method, a general mathematical model is given. Then an algorithm constructed in the simplest case.

This paper is organized as follows. Origin illusion problem is proposed, analyzed and fundamentally solved with crossover operation in Sect. 2. In Sect. 2.1 a model is constructed and an algorithm is designed based on the model. Origin Illusion problem is indicated in Sect. 2.2. Convergence analysis of the new algorithm is presented in Sect. 2.3. The concept of origin illusion is further explained in Sect. 2.4. In Sect. 3, Contraction and Guidance Algorithm is proposed. Experimental verifications are given in Sect. 4. Concluding remarks are drawn in Sect. 5.

2   Origin Illusion Problem and Crossover

In this section a simple algorithm linear transformation and elitist selection algorithm (LTES) based on population is proposed. Experiment shows that origin illusion problem occurs in this algorithm. After discussing about this phenomenon, crossover operator is used to solve the origin illusion problem. Then a mathematical explanation is given.

2.1   A Simple Algorithm

Each population algorithm in each iteration can be presented as follow.

$$Swarm^{t+1} = \mathcal{A}(Swarm^t)$$

$Swarm^t = (x_1^t, x_2^t, \ldots, x_{PopSize}^t)$ is the swarm at the t-th iteration and $x_i^t \in \Omega^n \subseteq R^n$. $Swarm^{t+1} = (x_1^{t+1}, x_2^{t+1}, \ldots, x_{PopSize}^{t+1})$ is the swarm at the $t+1$-th iteration $x_i^{t+1} \Omega^n \subseteq R^n$. $\mathcal{A}$ represents all operations that generate new populations of a give algorithm. Ω^n is the search space and R^n is the $n-$dimension Euclidean space.

However, as we know, $\mathcal{A}$ is usually quite complicate for most of the existing algorithms. But in this paper the simplest case will be considered. The simplest $\mathcal{A}$ is sure to be a linear transformation, which means that $\mathcal{A}$ is a matrix and $\mathcal{A} \in R^{n*n}$. But only $\mathcal{A}$ is not enough to construct an algorithm. Elitist selection is used to drive and complete the algorithm. Elitist selection is adopted obviously or implicitly in most of the existing algorithms. In this paper, both concepts are considered and one simple algorithmic model is constructed as Algorithm 1.

2.2   Origin Illusion Problem

Some functions are solved with Algorithm 1 and the results are presented in Table 1. When all functions are not shifted, the minimum objective function values are zero and the optimal solutions locate at origin point, experiments show that Algorithm 1 can find the optimal solutions for all those functions. But

---

Algorithm 1. Linear transformation and elitist selection algorithm (LTES)

Input: n is the dimension of x, $[xmin_j, xmax_j]$ is the range of x_j
Initialize:

1: $t = 0$
2: **for all** $i \in \{1, 2, \ldots, PopSize\}$ **do**
3:    **for all** $j \in \{1, 2, \ldots, n\}$ **do**
4:       $swarm_{j,i}^0 = xmin_j + rand(0,1) * (xmax_j - xmin_j)$
5:    **end for**
6: **end for**
7: $fvalue^t \Leftarrow$ fitness calculation

Main Loop:

   while $FES \leq maxFES$ **do**
      $t = t + 1$
      1) Generate new population:
      $S_b^t \Leftarrow$ the best $\lfloor \frac{PopSize}{4} \rfloor$ of $swarm^t$
      $S_w^t \Leftarrow$ the worst $\lfloor \frac{PopSize}{4} \rfloor$ of $swarm^t$
      $A = S_b^t * pinv(S_w^t)$, pinv() is the pseudo-inverse operators, $A \in R^{n*n}$
      $newswarm^t = A * swarm^t$
      2) Fitness calculation:
      $fvnew^t \Leftarrow$ fitness calculation, $FES = FES + PopSize$
      3) Elitist Selection:
      for all $i \in \{1, 2, \ldots, PopSize\}$ **do**
         if $fvnew_i^t \leq fvalue_i^t$ **then**
            $swarm_i^{t+1} := newswarm_i^t$
            $fvalue_i^{t+1} := fvnew_i^t$
         else
            $swarm_i^{t+1} := swarm_i^t$
            $fvalue_i^{t+1} := fvalue_i^t$
         end if
      end for
   end while

---

the performance of the same algorithm appears a sudden deteriorate when those functions became shifted.

Observed from the phenomenon, the definition of origin illusion is descriptively given as follows in this paper. **Origin illusion** is a phenomenon that population based algorithm performs well in those problems whose optimal solutions are the origin point. However, the performance of the same algorithm deteriorates obviously in those problems whose optimal solutions are not the origin point. Those algorithms, which have origin illusion phenomenon, maybe simply regarded as excellent or bad algorithms. But lot of works still deserve to do to understand and deal with this phenomenon. In the next subsection the possible reasons for this phenomenon will be discussed.

Table 1. Result on unshifted and shifted functions

	Unshifted LTES	Shifted LTES	Unshifted LTXES	Shifted LTXES
$f_1 = \sum_{i=1}^{D} x_i^2$	0	24427.3	2.24E$-$124	1.67E$-$11
$f_2 = \sum_{i=1}^{D} |x_i| + \prod_{i=1}^{D} |x_i|$	1.18E$-$300	1.57E$+$11	6.72E$-$69	1.70E$-$05
$f_3 = \sum_{i=1}^{D} \left(\sum_{j=1}^{i} x_j \right)^2$	0	231208.4	1.50E$-$23	8.37E$-$05
$f_4 = \sum_{i=1}^{D} (\lfloor x_i + 0.5 \rfloor)^2$	0	30175.6	0	0.8

The optimal solution of Shifted Functions is moved to $(50, 50, \ldots, 50)$

2.3 Phenomenon Analysis

As shown in the Table 1, LTES has origin illusion phenomenon. Experiments and mathematical analysis can help to understand the reason of this phenomenon. When solving the problem whose optimal solution is the origin, LTES without elitist selection tends to converge to **0** at the beginning decades. It will shake repeatedly after a certain degree of individual aggregation. LTES with elitist selection converges to **0** in a rapid rate for the same situation. This observation shows that the elitist selection operation enables the algorithm to avoid the latter impact and thus has the ability to converge to a point. Experiments show that LTES can converge to a point when solving shifted problems. Based on the above analysis, we discuss the cause of origin illusion.

For Those Problems Whose Optimal Solution Is Origin Point
Take problem (1) as an example

$$min \ f(x) = \sum_{i=1}^{n} x_i^2 \tag{1}$$

Suppose the algorithm has a central tendency, that is, the distance from the origin will gradually decrease. Defined as

$$\frac{1}{popsize} \sum_{i=1}^{popsize} d(x^i(t+1), 0) \leq \frac{1}{popsize} \sum_{i=1}^{popsize} d(x^i(t), 0) \tag{2}$$

in which $x^i(t+1) \in swarm(t+1), x^i(t) \in swarm(t)$. Then, the algorithm converges to the origin more quickly, that is, the existence of the best sequence of every generation $\{g_{best}(t)\} \rightarrow 0$, when $t \rightarrow \infty$. Due to the elitist selection, it is easy to see that

$$f(g_{best}(t)) \geq f(g_{best}(t+1)).$$

According to the expression of problem (1) we have

$$|g_{best}(t)| \geq |g_{best}(t+1)|.$$

Denoting $x_1 = g_{best}(t),\ x_2 = g_{best}(t+1)$

$$|f(x_1) - f(x_2)| = |(x_1 - x_2)(x_1 + x_2)| \leq |x_1 + x_2||x_1 - x_2|$$

because $L = |g_{best}(0) + g_{best}(1)| > 0$, then $|f(x_1) - f(x_2)| \leq L|x_1 - x_2|$ satisfies the Lipschitz condition and converges to the origin point. However, the conclusion may not be so clear for other functions.

According to the experiment and analysis, LTES tends to converge to the origin and the selection operation accelerates this tendency for the unshifted functions. Therefore, LTES can converge to **0** at a very high speed. But for the shifted functions, the linear transformation tends to converge to **0**, and the elitist selection tends to the optimal points. Both operations conflict each other and cannot uniformly approach to the optimal solution when the optimal points are **not** 0.

2.4   Crossover and Origin Illusion

$$min\ f(x) = \sum_{i=1}^{n}(x_i - 50)^2 \tag{3}$$

Problem Eq. (3) is taken as an example. When the variance of LTES $D(x^{LTES} - x^*)$ is computed, it is very large according to the above analysis. It not only means the result is bad, but also means there is no effective combination of components. In order to improve the performance of LTES, a simple crossover operator is adopted here as Eq. (4).

$$swarm_{j,i}^{t+1} = r_{j,i} * newswarm_{j,i}^{t} + (1 - r_{j,i}) * swarm_{j,i}^{t},$$
$$r_{j,i} = rand(0,1), i \in \{1, 2, \ldots, popsize\}, j \in \{1, 2, \ldots, n\} \tag{4}$$

The new Algorithm 2 is followed.

The comparison experimental results are presented as the last two columns of Table 1. LTXES's excellent performance shows that there is no origin illusion phenomenon in LTXES. As for LTXES, crossover is not important for convergence, but it is very important for the quality of solution. It concludes that crossover can reduce the conflict between both operations and can make them work together harmoniously observed from the results of the previous section and the discussion.

3   Contraction and Guidance Algorithm

This hypothesis in Eq. (2) is usually hard to judge whether it is satisfied for a given algorithm. At the same time, operator's effect can't be described accurately. In this section, a new algorithm satisfying the hypothesis is proposed. On the other hand, as shown in Sect. 2, the selection operation can lead the algorithm to the optimal solution. Therefore, another guidance operator can be used to replace the selection operator, which means that elitist selection can be replaced. Elitist selection is not a necessary component which is different from the existing algorithms.

Firstly, an operator that naturally satisfies the convergence conditions are adopted. Let $k \in (0,1)$, the $swarm^{t+1} = k * swarm^t$ will converge to origin point. Convergence rate is

$$Q_1 = \limsup \frac{\|x_{t+1} - x^*\|_2}{\|x_t - x^*\|_2} = k$$

where x^* is the true optimal solution of problem. Due to $k \in (0,1)$, $\{swarm^t\}$ is Q-linear converging to $\mathbf{0}$. Considering that the optimal solution is not always the origin, a certain amount of offset is given in each iteration.

$$\begin{aligned} swarm_i^{t+1} &= \bar{S} + k * (swarm_i^t - \bar{S}) \\ &= k * swarm_i^t + (1-k) * \bar{S}, k \in (0,1) \end{aligned} \tag{5}$$

$\bar{S}$ is the mean vector of best $\lfloor \frac{PopSize}{2} \rfloor$ of $swarm^t$. $swarm_i^t$ and $swarm_i^{t+1}$ denote the i-th solution at the t-th and $(t+1)$-th iteration respectively. According to Eq. (5) $\{swarm^t\}$ is Q-linear converging to a unknown point.

A guidance operator as Eq. (6) is used to lead swarm to a better position, in which S_b^t is the best $\lfloor \frac{PopSize}{4} \rfloor$ of $warm^t$, S_w^t is the worst $\lfloor \frac{PopSize}{4} \rfloor$ of $swarm^t$.

$$\begin{aligned} S_G &= S_b^t - S_w^t \\ swarm &= swarm + S_G \end{aligned} \tag{6}$$

Crossover is required, but any kind of elitist selection is not necessary in this algorithm. This phenomenon is not common in existing algorithms. The proposed complete algorithmic framework is shown as Algorithm 3.

Algorithm 2. Linear transformation, Crossover and elitist selection algorithm (LTXES)

Input: n is the dimension of x, $[xmin_j, xmax_j]$ is the range of x_j
Initialize: The same as algorithm 1
Main Loop:
  while $FES \leq maxFES$ do
    $t = t+1$
    1) **Generate new population:** same as algorithm 1
    2) **CrossOver:**
    for all $i \in \{1,2,\ldots,PopSize\}$ do
      for all $j \in \{1,2,\ldots,n\}$ do
        $r = rand(0,1)$;
        $newswarm_{j,i}^t = r * newswarm_{j,i}^t + (1-r) * swarm_{j,i}^t$
      end for
    end for
    3) **Fitness calculation:** same as algorithm 1
    3) **Elitist Selection:** same as algorithm 1
  end while

Algorithm 3. Contraction and Guidance Algorithm (CGA)

Input: n is the dimension of x,$[xmin_j,\ xmax_j]$ is the range of x_j, $\rho=0.99$
Initialize: same as algorithm 1
Main Loop:
  while $FES \leq maxFES$ **do**
    $t = t + 1$
    1) Generate new population:
    1.1) Contraction:
    $\bar{S} \Leftarrow$ the mean of best $\lfloor \frac{PopSize}{2} \rfloor$ of $swarm^t$
    $newswarm = \rho * swarm + (1 - \rho) * \bar{S}$
    1.2) Guidance:
    $S_b^t \Leftarrow$ the best $\lfloor \frac{PopSize}{4} \rfloor$ of $swarm^t$
    $S_w^t \Leftarrow$ the worst $\lfloor \frac{PopSize}{4} \rfloor$ of $swarm^t$
    $S_G = S_b^t - S_w^t$
    $newswarm = newswarm + S_G$;
    2) CrossOver: same as algorithm 2
    3) Fitness calculation: same as algorithm 1
    4) Update swarm: $swarm^{t+1} := newswarm^t$
  end while

Contraction and guidance is segmented in this algorithm. Contraction means that the algorithm converges naturally, and guidance means that the operator can guide the group to a better position. If the contraction and the guidance are inherent, algorithm is sure to have a satisfied performance. Once contraction and guidance are separated, researchers can focus on how to guide a group rather than on convergence.

4   Comprehensive Evaluation

Benchmark functions of IEEE CEC 2015 [17] competition benchmarks are used to verify the effectiveness of the algorithm in this paper.

4.1   Experimental Setup

Several parameters are set as follows. The dimension of benchmark function is 30. All the algorithms are performed 30 independent runs on each benchmark; The final mean best results are recorded with 300 000 function evaluations. Population size is 100 for all algorithms. Some existing algorithms PSO [1], bRGA [18], DE/rand/1 [19] are compared with the new algorithms to determine the validity.

4.2   Experimental Results and Analysis

The comparison results are shown in Table 2. The simulation results show that both algorithms are effective.

Observed from experimental comparison, LTXES performs pretty well on 8 functions which is the best among its competitors, especially in some shifted simple problems.

CGA is more suitable for solving simple multimodal functions and composition functions of them. This shows that local optimal solutions can be ignored by guidance operator of CGA. It further illustrates the advantages of statistical methods in algorithm operation.

Table 2. The mean value of 30 times run in CEC2015

	LTXES	CGA	PSO	DErand1	bRGA
f1	**855473.11**	141325155.67	4407500.24	25704647.91	1409869.79
f2	**2608.58**	82445.57	55721.43	30378.27	31641.63
f3	320.40	**320.00**	320.06	320.92	320.01
f4	444.97	**435.06**	544.80	556.45	555.02
f5	3162.44	**1921.77**	4030.63	6803.13	4079.57
f6	**165519.43**	35808163.68	263506.13	1315756.66	234191.50
f7	712.11	723.77	715.99	**710.39**	720.32
f8	84410.94	18928613.99	115431.37	205749.37	**47836.59**
f9	**1002.68**	1010.50	1005.84	1003.07	1034.32
f10	**139843.72**	40864179.45	371322.24	451915.53	260061.07
f11	1945.49	1673.31	2068.38	**1535.02**	2007.93
f12	**1305.90**	1311.22	1311.29	1307.07	1308.52
f13	1422.67	1444.62	1427.83	**1421.84**	1809.43
f14	**10010.61**	20983.79	36602.39	34235.95	23875.05
f15	**1600.00**	**1600.00**	1609.10	**1600.00**	1600.04

Parameters in PSO: $w = 1/(2*\log(2))$, $c1 = c2 = 0.5 + \log(2)$
Parameters in GA: pCrossover = 0.8, pMuation = 0.1
Parameters in DE: $F \sim N(0.5, 0.3)$,CR = 0.9

5   Conclusion

Origin illusion phenomenon is common in population based optimization algorithm. This article has carried on the observation and the suggestion to this. Origin illusion is a phenomenon that one algorithm performs wellon those problems whose optimal solutions are the origin point. However, its performance deteriorates obviously on those problems which optimal solutions are not the origin point. Based on linear transformation LTES is proposed in this paper. Experiments show that crossover operation can overcome the illusion of origin effectively and improve the performance of LTES. An attempt is made to give a mathematical explanation of the convergence of the LTES algorithm. The analysis shows that elitist selection can provide certain convergence ability, and make sure the algorithm has the ability to advance to the optimal solution. In order to divide the two ability of elitist selection, based on the empirical comparison and analysis CGA is proposed which can meet all requirements of Eq. (2). The performance of CGA shows that contraction and guidance can be divided and that elitist selection is not necessary. In the future, more works will explore what type of crossover operations can overcome the origin illusion, and how to improve the guidance operator of CGA.

Acknowledgement. This research is supported by National Natural Science Foundation of China (61375066, 71772060).

References

1. Kennedy, J., Eberhart, R.C.: Particle swarm optimization. In: Proceedings of IEEE International Conference on Neural Networks, vol. 4, pp. 1942–1948 (1995)
2. Bonyadi, M.R., Michalewicz, Z.: Particle swarm optimization for single objective continuous space problems: a review. Evol. Comput. **25**(1), 1–54 (2017)
3. Dorigo, M., Maniezzo, V., Colorni, A.: Ant system: optimization by a colony of cooperating agents. IEEE Trans. Syst. Man Cybern. Part B: Cybern. **26**(1), 29–41 (1996)
4. Wei, X., Fan, J., Wang, T., et al.: Efficient application scheduling in mobile cloud computing based on MAX–MIN ant system. Soft Comput. - Fus. Found. Methodol. Appl. **20**(7), 2611–2625 (2016)
5. Karaboga, D.: An idea based on honey bee swarm for numerical optimization. Technical report-tr06. Erciyes University, Engineering Faculty, Computer Engineering Department (2005)
6. Gao, K.Z., Suganthan, P.N., Pan, Q.K., et al.: An improved artificial bee colony algorithm for flexible job-shop scheduling problem with fuzzy processing time. Expert Syst. Appl. **65**(C), 52–67 (2016)
7. Krishnanand, K.N., Ghose, D.: Glowworm swarm optimization for simultaneous capture of multiple local optima of multimodal functions. Swarm Intell. **3**(2), 87–124 (2009)
8. Filho, C.J.A.B., de Lima Neto, F.B., Lins, A.J.C.C., Nascimento, A.I.S., Lima, M.P.: Fish school search. In: Chiong, R. (ed.) Nature-Inspired Algorithms for Optimisation. SCI, vol. 193, pp. 261–277. Springer, Heidelberg (2009). https://doi.org/10.1007/978-3-642-00267-0_9
9. Łukasik, S., Żak, S.: Firefly algorithm for continuous constrained optimization tasks. In: Nguyen, N.T., Kowalczyk, R., Chen, S.-M. (eds.) ICCCI 2009. LNCS, vol. 5796, pp. 97–106. Springer, Heidelberg (2009). https://doi.org/10.1007/978-3-642-04441-0_8
10. Yang, X.S., Deb, S.: Cuckoo search via Levy flights. In: Mathematics, pp. 210–214 (2010)
11. Gandomi, A.H., Alavi, A.H.: Krill Herd: a new bio-inspired optimization algorithm. Commun. Nonlinear Sci. Numer. Simul. **17**(12), 4831–4845 (2012)
12. Wang, G.G., Deb, S., Gandomi, A.H, et al.: A hybrid PBIL-based Krill Herd algorithm. In: International Symposium on Computational and Business Intelligence, pp. 39–44 (2016)

13. Shi, Y.: Brain storm optimization algorithm. In: Tan, Y., Shi, Y., Chai, Y., Wang, G. (eds.) ICSI 2011. LNCS, vol. 6728, pp. 303–309. Springer, Heidelberg (2011). https://doi.org/10.1007/978-3-642-21515-5_36

14. Yang, X.S.: A new metaheuristic bat-inspired algorithm. Comput. Knowl. Technol. **284**, 65–74 (2010)

15. Shah-Hosseini, H.: The intelligent water drops algorithm: a nature-inspired swarm-based optimization algorithm. Int. J. Bio-Inspir. Comput. **1**(2), 71–79 (2009)

16. Tan, Y., Zhu, Y.: Fireworks algorithm for optimization. In: Tan, Y., Shi, Y., Tan, K.C. (eds.) ICSI 2010. LNCS, vol. 6145, pp. 355–364. Springer, Heidelberg (2010). https://doi.org/10.1007/978-3-642-13495-1_44

17. Liang, J.J., Qu, B.Y., Suganthan, P.N.: Problem definitions and evaluation criteria for the CEC 2015 competition on learning-based real-parameter single objective optimization (2014)

18. Yoon, J.H., Shoemaker, C.A.: Improved real-coded GA for groundwater bioremediation. J. Comput. Civ. Eng. **15**(3), 224–231 (2001)

19. Storn, R., Price, K.: Differential evolution - a simple and efficient heuristic for global optimization over continuous space. J. Glob. Optim. **11**(4), 341–359 (1997)

A Multi Ant System Based Hybrid Heuristic Algorithm for Vehicle Routing Problem with Service Time Customization

Yuan Wang and Lining Xing[✉]

College of Systems Engineering, National University of Defense Technology,
Changsha, People's Republic of China
Xinglining@gmail.com

Abstract. This paper addresses the Vehicle Routing Problem with Service Time Customization (VRPTW-STC), which is an extension of the classic Vehicle Routing Problem with Time Window (VRPTW). In VRPTW-STC, the decision maker tries to find an optimum solution with the smallest fleet size, the lowest travelling distance as well as the largest total service time of all customers. The objective to enlarge each customer's service time obviously conflicts with the need of reducing both changeable and fixed transport costs, i.e. travelling distance and fleet size. At the same time, the routing plan must meet the time window constraint and the vehicle capacity constraint. To solve this problem, we designed a Multi Ant System (MAS) based hybrid heuristic algorithm inspired by to decompose a multi-objective problem into several single objective ones. Then, Ant Colony Optimization (ACO) algorithms are applied to every single-objective problem. A unique global best solution is maintained to record the current best solution. The global best solution will be updated when a new feasible solution found by any ACO dominate current global best solution. Several local search algorithms are also incorporated into MAS to help improve the solution quality. Solomon's benchmark tests are used to test the effectiveness of the proposed algorithm. The computation experiment results show that our proposed MAS based hybrid heuristic algorithm performs better than typical existing algorithms.

Keywords: Vehicle routing problem with time window
Multi ant system · Local search · Heuristic

1 Introduction

In this paper, we propose a new extension of VRPTW problem called VRPTW-STC. The VRPTW-STC has a new problem objective: maximization of the total service time. This problem objective is combined with two classic problem objectives, namely minimization of the fleet size and minimization of the total travelling distance. The VRPTW-STC is different from the formal VRPTW in

© Springer Nature Singapore Pte Ltd. 2018
J. Qiao et al. (Eds.): BIC-TA 2018, CCIS 951, pp. 411–422, 2018.
https://doi.org/10.1007/978-981-13-2826-8_36

that the service time of each customer can be decided by the decision maker. To give a detailed description of the VRPTW-STC, we consider the scenario of a Chinese express delivery company. In this scenario, we suppose that there is an express delivery company A who wants to collect packages from n blocks and take them to its package warehouse. In each of the n blocks, the company has a service office that collects packages from all its customers in the block. The company also has at most m delivery people (where m is normally far less than n) who collect packages from all the service offices. Thus, for the company manager, he or she has three things to decide in the service plan of company A: how many delivery people the company must use, the service route of each delivery person and the waiting time at each service office. The importance of deciding the waiting time at each service office is that a delivery person can visit more service offices on each route when the waiting time at each service office is less yet the delivery person can collect more packages when the waiting time at each service office is longer. For example, if a delivery person's waiting time at an office of a university is from 9:00 a.m. to 9:30 a.m., the students who have classes at this time must choose another express company with a different service time. Company A will thus lose some of its potential customers. Meanwhile, the waiting time at each service office cannot be extended too long considering the service time windows of other offices and the time that a delivery person must spend travelling.

To the best of our knowledge, there is no existing literature on this kind of problem. However, there is much literature on the vehicle routing problem (VRP) and its variants that studies VRP with uncertainty. [1] and [2] for instance, studied the vehicle routing problem with soft time window, where the constraint of time window can be broken with a price of a low profit. [3] and [4] introduced the fuzzy time window concept to the VRPTW. In the fuzzy vehicle routing problem with time window, the time at which the service provider chooses to start a service affects the service profit. The vehicle routing problem with stochastic demands is another problem including customer requirement uncertainty that deals with the uncertainty of the cargo demand delivered to each customer. Excellent studies on this problem were conducted by [5] and [6]. The vehicle routing problem with fuzzy travel time is another kind of customer uncertainty problem in which the travel time from one customer to another is uncertain. This kind of problem is normally connected to a delivery problem based on real-world traffic conditions. This problem was studied by [7–9]. The time-dependent vehicle routing problem is another uncertainty problem. The time-dependent factors include the travel speed ([10,11]), path choice ([12]) and fuel consumption ([13] and [14]). Finally, the uncertainty of depots is another uncertainty. In a study on this problem conducted by ([15]), the original locations of depots are uncertain. The decision maker must first allocate the original depot locations before route planning.

The present paper employs an ACO algorithm called the multi-ant system (MAS). The MAS algorithm was first proposed by [16], who pointed out that the original ACO algorithm can be a more elaborate and efficient computational paradigm. The MAS is basically a cooperative system in which several ant colony systems work independently to find their own best solutions. In the MAS, a multi-objective optimization problem is divided into several single objective optimization problems in which the objectives of other problems are the problem constraints, and each single objective optimization problem is assigned to a certain ant system.

Four local search strategies are implemented to improve the algorithm's performance. A heuristics-based method is designed to help choose customers that can be given more service time. Benchmark instances extended from Solomons 100 benchmark tests are used to test the performance of the proposed MAS-based heuristics. Experimental results show that in most test instances, the proposed MAS-based algorithm has better performances.

The remainder of the paper is organized as follows. Section 2 describes the problem model in detail; Sect. 3 presents the main structure of our hybrid MAS algorithm and local search procedures; Sect. 4 presents numerical computational results; and Sect. 5 presents conclusions and future research directions.

2   Problem Model

A general VRPTW model can be described as (a) an undirected graph $G = (N, E)$ that includes a set of nodes N and a set of edges E; (b) a depot d that includes the location and number of vehicles at the depot and; (c) a customer set $\{n_i \in \mathbf{N} | i = 1, 2, 3 \cdots N\}$ that includes the customer locations, the demand information and preference service time window of each customer; (d) a set of edges $\{e_{ij} \in \mathbf{E} | i, j = 0, 1, 2, 3 \cdots N, i \neq j\}$ that correlates with the travelling cost c_{ij} that correlates with the travelling cost i to j; (e) a vehicle set $\{v_k \in \mathbf{K} | k = 1, 2, 3 \cdots K\}$ that includes the capacity information q_k of v_k; (f) an objective set $\{f_l(x) \in \mathbf{O} | l = 1, 2, 3 \cdots O\}$.

In our model, the decision making factors are:

$x_{ijk} = \{0, 1\}$, which takes a value of zero if there is no arc from node i to node j, and 1 otherwise;

$i \neq j, i, j \in \{0, 1, 2 \cdots N\}$, where i or $j = 0$ indicates the depot node;

w_i denoting the waiting time at node i; and

st_i denoting the service start time for customer i.

The parameters are:

K denoting the total number of vehicles;

N denoting the total number of customers;

c_{ij} denoting the cost incurred on arc from node i to node j;

t_{ij} denoting the travelling time cost from node i to node j;

m_i denoting the demand at node i;

q_k denoting the capacity of vehicle k;

e_i denoting the earliest arrival time at node i;

l_i denoting the latest arrival time at node i;

f_i denoting the service time at node i; and

fm_i denoting the minimum service time at node i.

The optimization objective are:

$$Minimize \sum_{k=1}^{K} \sum_{i=0}^{N} \sum_{j=0}^{J} c_{ij} x_{ijk} \qquad (1)$$

$$Minimize \sum_{k=1}^{K} \sum_{j=1}^{J} x_{0jk} \qquad (2)$$

$$Maximize \sum_{i=1}^{N} f_i \qquad (3)$$

subject to:

$$\sum_{k=1}^{K} \sum_{j=1}^{J} x_{ijk} \leq K, \, for \, i = 0 \qquad (4)$$

$$\sum_{j=1}^{J} x_{ijk} = \sum_{j=1}^{J} x_{jik}, \, for \, i = 0 \, and \, k \in \{1,2,3 \cdots K\} \qquad (5)$$

$$\sum_{j=0,j\neq i}^{N} \sum_{k=1}^{K} x_{ijk} = 1, \, for \, i = \{1,2,3 \cdots N\} \qquad (6)$$

$$\sum_{i=0,i\neq j}^{N} \sum_{k=1}^{K} x_{ijk} = 1, \, for \, i = \{1,2,3 \cdots N\} \qquad (7)$$

$$\sum_{i=0}^{N} \sum_{j=0,j\neq i}^{N} x_{ijk} m_i \leq q_k, \, for \, k = \{1,2,3, \cdots K\} \qquad (8)$$

$$f_i \geq fm_i, \, for \, i \in \{1,2,3, \cdots N\} \qquad (9)$$

$$st_i \geq e_i \, for \, i \in \{1,2,3, \cdots N\} \qquad (10)$$

$$st_i + f_i \leq l_i, \, for \, i \in \{1,2,3, \cdots N\} \qquad (11)$$

$$st_i + f_i + t_{ij} + w_j = st_j, \, for \, any \, arc \, ij \, in \, a \, service \, plan. \qquad (12)$$

This model considers three objectives: (a) minimization of the fleet size (b) minimization of the travelling cost and (c) maximization of the service time. Constraints considered in the model are as follows. Constraint (4) ensures the total number of used vehicles does not exceed the fleet size. Constraints (5) ensure that the travelling route of a vehicle starts and finishes at the depot node. Constraints (6) and (7) together ensure that each customer is visited by any of the used vehicles exactly once. Constraint (8) ensures that for any vehicle used, the total demand allocated to it must not exceed the vehicle's capacity. Constraint (9) ensures that the service time of each customer i exceeds the minimum required service time of customer i must exceed the minimum required service time of customer i; Constraints (10) and (11) together ensure that the service offered to any customer starts and ends in the service time window exactly; Constraints (12) ensures the finish time and the starting time of the customers following each other are related to each other with the travel time between them.

3   Hybrid MAS Algorithm

The proposed MAS-based heuristics consists of three parts: an MAS procedure that deals with the search for the global solution of the VRPTW-STC; a local search procedure that deals with the improvement of solutions found by the MAS; and a heuristic-based procedure that is responsible for choosing customer nodes to which extra service time is added. The upper-level algorithm structure is shown in Fig. 1.

The detailed description of proposed MAS algorithm is as follow.

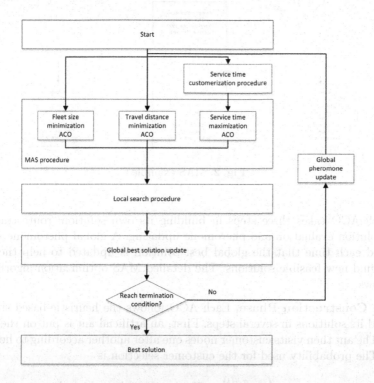

Fig. 1. Algorithm structure

3.1 MAS Procedure

In the MAS procedure, there are three independently running ACO algorithms: the fleet size minimization ACO algorithm, travelling cost minimization ACO algorithm and service time maximization ACO algorithm. The objectives of these three ACOs coincide with the original problem objectives of the VRPTW-STC. A global best solution is maintained to record the current best solution found by any of these three ACOs. At the beginning of the three ACOs, each algorithm first checks the global best solution. Parts of the global best solution become constraints of the ACO problems. By solving the original problem with extra constraints, the ACOs find new feasible solutions. Each time that the global best solution is found, all three ACOs stop to update their own problem constraints. An example is shown in Fig. 2. In this example, the current best global solution is a fleet size of 20, a total travelling distance of 1000, and a total service time of 500.

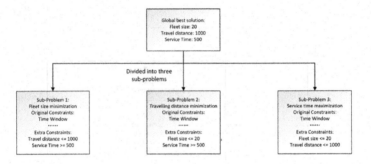

Fig. 2. MAS example

Each ACO takes three steps in building its own solution: route construction, solution evaluation and pheromone updating. A global pheromone map is updated each time that the global best solution is updated to help the three ACOs find new feasible solutions. The detailed MAS optimization algorithm is as follows.

Route Construction Phase. Each ACO follows the heuristic-based strategy to build its solutions in several steps. First, an artificial ant is put on the depot node. The ant then visits customer nodes one after another according to heuristic roles. The probability used for the customer selection is

$$p_{ij}^k(t) = \begin{cases} \dfrac{\sigma_{ij}(t)}{\sum_{l=1}^{N}\sigma_{il}(t)}, & \text{if } j \text{ is visited by vehicle } k \\ 0, & \text{otherwise} \end{cases} \tag{13}$$

where $p_{ij}^k(t)$ is the probability that vehicle k departs from node i and visited node j at time t. $\sigma_{ij}(t)$ is a heuristic factor expressed by

$$\sigma_{ij}(t) = \left(\frac{c_{ij}}{\sum_{l=1}^{N} c_{il}}\right)^{\alpha} \times \left(\frac{\tau_{ij}(t)}{\sum_{l=1}^{N} \tau_{ij}(t)}\right)^{\beta} \tag{14}$$

where $\tau_{ij}(t)$ is the pheromone left on the arc ij at time t. α and β are factors that control the importance of the heuristic factor and pheromone factor. At the beginning of the algorithm, all $\tau_{ij}(t)$ are equal to 1.

When no more customers can be inserted onto this route, the ant returns to the depot node, and the customer set is then checked. If there is no unvisited customer, then a new feasible solution is generated. If there are unvisited customers left and the number of used vehicles is no larger than the total number of vehicles, a new ant will be put on the depot node and a new route built; otherwise, for the travelling cost minimization ACO, this solution will be discarded.

Local Pheromone Updating Phase. Two pheromone update strategies are used to enhance both the space searching ability and cost minimization ability of the MACS solution. For the travelling cost minimization ACO, each time that a feasible solution is found, the pheromone is updated as

$$\tau_{ij}(t+1) = (1 - \rho)\tau_{ij}(t) + \rho\tau_0, for\ arc\ ij\ in\ solution\ t+1 \tag{15}$$

where the factor ρ is the pheromone evaluation rate and the factor τ_0 is the pheromone deposit on arc ij when arc ij is visited by any vehicle.

Because the vehicle minimization ACO and service time maximization ACO must have a greater ability to find a global solution and they find mostly infeasible solutions, a global searching enhancement strategy is applied to these two ACOs. We also apply this strategy to the travelling cost minimization ACO to accelerate the convergence speed when an infeasible solution is found. The strategy is expressed as

$$\tau_{ij}(t+1) = (1 - \rho)\tau_{ij}(t) - \rho\tau_0, for\ arc\ ij\ in\ solution\ t+1 \tag{16}$$

Each time that an infeasible solution is found, equation (15) is applied to reduce the pheromone deposited by τ_0 on each arc ij in this solution. Using this strategy, all arcs in the infeasible solution are less likely to be chosen in the next iteration.

Global Pheromone Updating Phase. A global pheromone information matrix is maintained to help the MACS system get better solutions. Each time the global feasible solution is found, the global pheromone information is updated according to

$$G\tau_{ij}(t+1) = (1 - \rho)G\tau_{ij}(t) + \rho G\tau_0, for\ arc\ ij\ in\ solution\ t+1 \tag{17}$$

where $G\tau_{ij}(t)$ is the global pheromone deposited on arc ij at time $t+1$, and $G\tau_0$ is the global pheromone deposit factor.

To maximize the total service time, a service time maximization procedure is applied each time a feasible solution is found by the service time maximization

ACO. This procedure uses a probability-based strategy to help find a longer total service time. When a feasible solution is found, this procedure is used to select customer nodes to which extra service time et_0 is added. To obtain the probability of any customer being selected, we first introduce a factor called the time window overlapping rate, which is closely related to the total overlapping of one customer's service time window with the windows of other customers (Fig. 3).

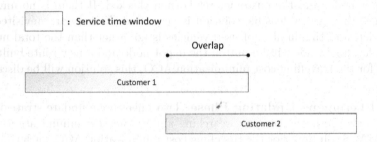

Fig. 3. Example of time window overlap

According to our experience, the service time window is more expandable when the overlapping rate is relatively low. This conclusion seems reasonable. The customer's time window overlapping rate is expressed as

$$Or_i = \frac{f_i + \sum_{j\neq i, j=1}^{j\in N} Ol_j}{l_i - e_i} \tag{18}$$

where Or_i is the time window overlapping rate of customer i, and Or_j is the length of the overlapping time window of any customer j relative to customer i. Using Or_i, the probability that customer i is chosen in the service time maximization procedure is defined as

$$pa_i = \frac{\frac{1}{Or_i}}{\sum_{j=1}^{j\in N} Or_i} \tag{19}$$

where pa_i is the probability that customer i is chosen for the addition of extra service time et_0.

3.2 Local Search Algorithm

We apply four local search algorithms: the widely implemented 2-opt algorithm, 3-opt algorithm, and two algorithms called node exchange algorithm and route relinking algorithm, to improve the solution of the MAS. Additionally, an insertion-based heuristic [17] is used to repair the infeasible solution generated during the node exchange and path relinking procedures. The node exchange algorithm and route relinking algorithm details are as follows (Figs. 4 and 5).

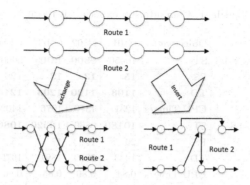

Fig. 4. Node exchange strategy

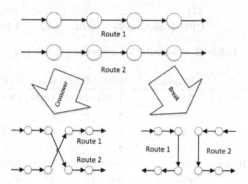

Fig. 5. Path breaking and relinking

4 Computational Experiments

In our experiment, a subset of Solomon's classic 100 benchmark problems was chosen to test the performance of the proposed MAS-LS algorithm. Solomon's benchmark problems were named on the basis of the rules that test designers use to create a benchmark test. It is noted that some of Solomon's benchmark instances are not suitable for testing the present problem; e.g., problems R101 and R107 have a time window length of only 10 for each customer and, therefore, no more service time can be added to any customer. Additionally, because the total service time window differs from one instance to another (e.g., the total time window of instance R108 is 230 while that of instance C103 is 1236), we used different values of et_0 to ensure that our algorithms get better results. We used an et_0 of 10 at each time and for those have large total time window, we used a et_0 of 10 at each time for those instances that have a short time window, and an et_0 of 20 at each time for those instances that have a long total time window. The computational experiment result are as follows (Tables 1, 2 and 3).

Table 1. Computation experiment result 1

	Objective	C101	C102	C103	C104
MACS-LS	ST	10050	**9900**	10100	9600
	FS	**15**	**13**	**13**	**12**
	TD	**1103**	**1120**	**1203**	**1214**
	CPU Time/s	1231	1370	1076	1402
HG-LS	ST	**10180**	9860	**10320**	**10800**
	FS	20	18	17	15
	TD	1933	2039	1891	1675
	CPU Time/s	0.84	0.86	0.85	0.85
HRG-LS	ST	9490	9530	9690	9590
	FS	21	18	16	13
	TD	2227	2213	1983	1692
	CPU Time/s	0.99	1.01	1.22	1.13

Table 2. Computation experiment result 2

	Objective	R202	R203	R111	R112
MACS-LS	ST	**1900**	**1600**	**1800**	**1300**
	FS	**8**	**8**	20	12
	TD	**1582**	**1401**	**1493**	**1192**
	CPU Time/s	849	1892	512	455
HG-LS	ST	1890	1540	1280	**1300**
	FS	9.6	9	12	**8**
	TD	1744	1624	1619	1278
	CPU Time/s	0.87	0.86	0.9	0.9
HRG-LS	ST	1430	1570	1250	1290
	FS	9	8.1	**11.3**	8
	TD	1873	1685	1667	1375
	CPU Time/s	0.92	1.14	0.72	0.79

Table 3. Computation experiment result 3

	Objective	RC102	RC103	RC104	RC105
MACS-LS	ST	**1500**	**1300**	**1400**	**1300**
	FS	18	16	14	22
	TD	**2211**	**1660**	**1567**	**2211**
	CPU Time/s	598	524	458	565
HG-LS	ST	1170	1260	1380	1220
	FS	**13**	**13**	**10**	**15**
	TD	2339	2039	1574	2678
	CPU Time/s	0.85	0.85	0.94	0.92
HRG-LS	ST	1390	1310	1390	1260
	FS	14.8	13.2	10.2	15.7
	TD	2506	2270	1770	2709
	CPU Time/s	1.04	0.86	1.05	0.78

The following findings are obtained from the detailed experimental results.

(a) From the experiment results we can infer that the MAS-LS algorithm obtains 3 best results (C102, R202 and R203), which means that the solutions contain the largest service time, lowest travelling distance and smallest fleet size in the problem set. (b) The MAS-LS algorithm has different performances in instances that have different problem characteristics. In C series instances, the MAS-LS algorithm gets solutions that have smaller fleet size and lower travelling distances than the solutions obtained by HG-LS and HRG-LS. And in R and RC series instances, the MAS-LS algorithm gets solutions that have longer total service time and lower travelling distances.

5   Conclusion

This paper investigated a special VRPTW called the VRPTW-STC. This problem, which is inspired by a large number of real-world applications, is an extension of the classical VRPTW. The VRPTW-STC is worth studying because of the complexity and value of practical applications in real-world industry. We proposed a hybrid MAS algorithm with local search strategies, called the MAS-LS algorithm, to get optimized solutions. We tested our algorithm with instances generated from classical VRPTW benchmark tests. Computational results showed that our method performed better than comparison algorithms, especially in terms of reducing the travelling distance and increasing the total service time.

Acknowledgments. This work is supported by the National Natural Science Foundation of China (Grant numbers: 71701203, 71690233).

References

1. Calvete, H.I., Galé, C., Oliveros, M.J., Sánchez-Valverde, B.: A goal programming approach to vehicle routing problems with soft time windows. Eur. J. Oper. Res. **177**(3), 1720–1733 (2007)
2. Beheshti, A.K., Hejazi, S.R.: A novel hybrid column generation-metaheuristic approach for the vehicle routing problem with general soft time window. Inf. Sci. **316**(C), 598–615 (2015)
3. Lin, J.J.: A GA-based multi-objective decision making for optimal vehicle transportation. J. Inf. Sci. Eng. **24**(1), 237–260 (2008)
4. Gupta, R., Singh, B., Pandey, D.: Multi-objective fuzzy vehicle routing problem: a case study. Int. J. Contemp. Math. Sci. **5**(29), 1439–1454 (2010)
5. Gupta, A., Nagarajan, V., Ravi, R.: Approximation algorithms for VRP with stochastic demands. Oper. Res. **60**(1), 123–127 (2012)
6. Shukla, N., Choudhary, A.K., Prakash, P.K.S., Fernandes, K.J., Tiwari, M.K.: Algorithm portfolios for logistics optimization considering stochastic demands and mobility allowance. Int. J. Prod. Econ. **141**(1), 146–166 (2013)
7. Peng, J., Shang, G., Liu, H.: A hybrid intelligent algorithm for vehicle routing models with fuzzy travel times. Computational Intelligence. LNCS (LNAI), vol. 4114, pp. 965–976. Springer, Heidelberg (2006). https://doi.org/10.1007/978-3-540-37275-2_122

8. Sarhadi, H., Ghoseiri, K.: An ant colony system approach for fuzzy traveling sales-man problem with time windows. Int. J. Adv. Manuf. Technol. **50**(9–12), 1203–1215 (2010)
9. Zarandi, M.F., Hemmati, A.: Capacitated location-routing problem with time windows under uncertainty. Knowl.-Based Syst. **37**(2), 480–489 (2013)
10. Wen, L., Eglese, R.: Minimum cost VRP with time-dependent speed data and congestion charge. Comput. Oper. Res. **56**, 41–50 (2015)
11. Kok, A.L., Hans, E.W., Schutten, J.M.J.: Vehicle routing under time-dependent travel times: the impact of congestion avoidance. Comput. Oper. Res. **39**(5), 910–918 (2012)
12. Kuo, Y.: Using simulated annealing to minimize fuel consumption for the time-dependent vehicle routing problem. Comput. Ind. Eng. **59**(1), 157–165 (2010)
13. Hooshmand, F., Mirhassani, S.A.: Time dependent green VRP with alternative fuel powered vehicles. Energy Syst. (2018). https://doi.org/10.1007/s12667-018-0283-y
14. Huang, Y., Zhao, L., Woensel, T.V., Gross, J.P.: Time-dependent vehicle routing problem with path flexibility. Transp. Res. Part B Methodol. **95**, 169–195 (2017)
15. Ray, S., Soeanu, A., Berger, J., Debbabi, M.: The multi-depot split-delivery vehicle routing problem: model and solution algorithm. Knowl.-Based Syst. **71**(1), 238–265 (2014)
16. Dorigo, M., Gambardella, L.M.: Ant colony system: a cooperative learning app-roach to the traveling salesman problem. IEEE Trans. Evol. Comput. **1**(1), 53–66 (1997)
17. Solomon, M.M.: Algorithms for the vehicle routing and scheduling problems with time window constraints. Oper. Res. **35**(2), 254–265 (1987)

Model Predictive Control of Data Center Temperature Based on CFD

Gang Peng[1,2,3], Chenyang Zhou[1,2,3], and Siming Wang[1,2,3(✉)]

[1] School of Automation, Huazhong University of Science and Technology,
Wuhan 430074, China
penggang@hust.edu.cn, zcyxyz@163.com,
1627508303@qq.com
[2] Shenzhen Institute of Huazhong University of Science and Technology,
Shenzhen 518060, China
[3] State Key Laboratory of Air-Conditioning Equipment and System Energy
Conservation, Zhuhai 519070, China

Abstract. This paper presents the MPC (Model Predictive Control) method based on CFD (Computational Fluid Dynamics), aiming to optimize the temperature control of the data center. The paper establishes the three-dimensional physical model of the data center according to the boundary conditions, gets the unit step function response of the input and output temperature by the steady and unsteady simulation solution, then gets the mathematical model of data center temperature by system identification. The MPC simulation experiment is carried out, compared with the traditional PID control, resulting in that MPC has better control quality and has great application values on the temperature control of the data center.

Keywords: CFD · MPC · System identification · Room temperature

1 Introduction

With the advent of the period of big data, many telecom companies and IT companies have built large-scale data centers. In order to keep the temperature of the data center stable, air conditioners usually work in constant temperature cooling mode for a long time. This extensive management method will result in great waste of energy, and increase the cost of business. Therefore, optimizing the temperature control of the data center will bring great social and business benefits. For researching the temperature control methods of the data center, we need to collect a large number of real-time temperature data to establish the mathematical model of data center temperature. This method requires the installation of many sensors and other hardware facilities indoors, which is difficult to implement in practice. Besides, it is hard to collect accurate data because of hysteresis of indoor temperature. Meanwhile, temperature control methods of the data center are mainly the traditional PID control, which has the disadvantages of large overshoot and slow response. In view of the above defects or improvement requirement, this study introduces a method for modeling and controlling the data center temperature, aiming to solve the problem of establishing a data center

© Springer Nature Singapore Pte Ltd. 2018
J. Qiao et al. (Eds.): BIC-TA 2018, CCIS 951, pp. 423–433, 2018.
https://doi.org/10.1007/978-981-13-2826-8_37

temperature mathematic model and improve the poor control quality of traditional control method.

This study takes a method of CFD to simulate the indoor temperature field, which does not need to deploy sensors. Based on the boundary conditions, a temperature field model of the data center is established, and a large amount of temperature data is obtained. Then, the temperature mathematic model of the data center is established by system identification and the temperature control of the data center is implemented by using MPC. MPC is one of the advanced control methods successfully applied to industrial control. It has the advantages of high precision and strong robustness, and it can overcome the disadvantages of large overshoot and slow response of traditional PID control in the air-conditioning system. MPC has lower requirements on the accuracy of the system model, and the rolling optimization strategy is used instead of the global one-time optimization, which can overcome the influence of the system model mismatch and external disturbance [1–3].

The main contributions of this paper can be summarized as follows:

(1) This study takes a method of CFD to simulate the temperature field of the data center and obtain temperature data, which does not need to deploy many sensors.
(2) The advantages of MPC in the temperature control of the data center are discussed compared with the traditional PID control method.

2   CFD Modeling

Fluent is pervasive CFD software, and contains rich and advanced physical models, which can simulate the indoor flow field [4]. In this study, the steady state model of data center temperature is first established as initial condition, and then unsteady solution (dynamic process) is performed. Next, the outlet temperature of the air conditioner is increased by one unit, and the curve of data center temperature with time is obtained, that is, the unit step response curve, and the dynamic model is established.

2.1   Steady State Model

The 3D model of 40 m × 15 m × 3 m data center is established by Gambit software. The data center has 6 surfaces, including 5 rows of server racks and 10 air-conditioning vents that can independently control temperature and wind speed. The calculation domain is divided by the type of TGrid in the Tet/Hybird element to obtain unstructured tetrahedron mesh. The mesh spacing is set to 500 mm, and the sum of grid cells is 92,943, as shown in Fig. 1. The boundary type is setting as shown in Table 1, and air conditioned blow angle is 45°.

Fluent is used to read the established data center model mesh file, and the standard k-ε turbulence model is used. The equations have the following form [5].

$$\frac{\partial(\rho k)}{\partial t} + \frac{\partial(\rho k u_i)}{\partial x_i} = \frac{\partial}{\partial x_j}\left[\left(\mu + \frac{\mu_t}{\sigma_k}\right)\frac{\partial k}{\partial x_j}\right] + G_k - \rho\varepsilon \qquad (1)$$

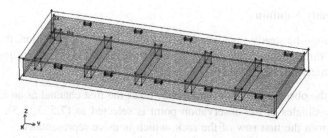

Fig. 1. Meshing of data center model

Table 1. Sets of boundary type

Boundary	Type	Item	Value
Air	Fluid	Materials	Air
Air-conditioning vents	Velocity-inlet	Speed (m/s)	4
		Temperature (K)	292
		Angle (°)	45
Server rack	Wall	Heat flux (w/m²)	200
Wall	Wall	Heat flux (w/m²)	0

$$\frac{\partial(\rho k)}{\partial t} + \frac{\partial(\rho \varepsilon u_i)}{\partial x_i} = \frac{\partial}{\partial x_j}\left[\left(\mu + \frac{\mu_t}{\sigma_\varepsilon}\right)\frac{\partial \varepsilon}{\partial x_j}\right] + \frac{C_{1\varepsilon}\varepsilon}{k}G_k - C_{2\varepsilon}\frac{\rho\varepsilon^2}{k} \tag{2}$$

where $C_{1\varepsilon}$, $C_{2\varepsilon}$ is the constant obtained from the experiment. $C_{1\varepsilon} = 1.44$, $C_{2\varepsilon} = 1.92$. μ_t is the turbulent viscosity coefficient, $\mu_t = \rho C_\mu \frac{k^2}{\varepsilon}$. C_μ is the empirical constant. G_k is the generating term of turbulent kinetic energy.

The semi-implicit algorithm of SIMPLE is used to solve the equations, and the model reached the convergence state after 137 iterations. Temperature field of the data center in the 1.5 m above the ground is shown in Fig. 2.

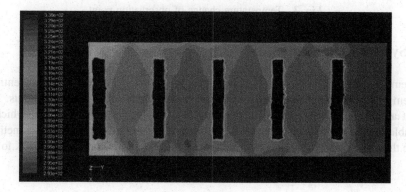

Fig. 2. Temperature field of the data center in the 1.5 m above the ground

2.2   Unsteady Solution

The model after the steady-state solution is taken as the initial condition, that is, the air-conditioned outlet temperature is 292 K. Then the model is solved in unsteady state. The main process is as follows [6].

(1) Select the observation point: This study takes the first channel as an example, and the coordinates of the observation point is selected as (7.5, 3, 1.5), that is, 1 m away from the first row of the rack, which is more representative;

(2) Modify the boundary conditions: temperature of 10 air conditioners is increased from 292 K to 293 K;

(3) Modify options of Solver: the option in Time is changed from Steady to Unsteady, that is, the unsteady solution;

(4) Set Time Step Size to 1 s, the number of steps to 900, the maximum number of iterations per step to 10, and start the iterative calculation.

The system reaches the convergence state after 900 s. The temperature curve of the selected observation point with time is shown in Fig. 3, and the horizontal axis and the vertical axis respectively represent time (s) and temperature (K). The observation point data is saved as the recognition set.

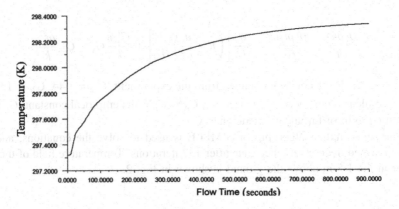

Fig. 3. Temperature change of observation point

3 System Identification

System identification is the process of determining a system equivalent to an identified system in a given type of system, based on observations of inputs and outputs. The input and output of the system in this study is a single measurable value, which is suitable for the mathematical model of the system by using the step response method. Take the observation point data collected changes. The unit is converted from K to °C.

The identification is processed by using System Identification Toolbox of MATLAB, which can process discrete time-domain signals and use least squares to identify them [7]. In this identification method, the structure of the model is given first, and the optimal parameters of the system model are determined under the framework of the structure. In this study, ARX, ARMAX, first-order pure lag system and second-order pure lag system model are used to fit the step response curve respectively. The parameters of each model are adjusted respectively, and a group of parameters with the best fitting degree are selected. Fitting curves of four models are shown in Fig. 4.

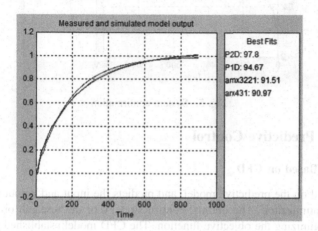

Fig. 4. System identification

Comparing the four models, we can see that the second-order pure lag system model has the highest fitting degree to the system, reaching 97.8%. Its transfer function has the form

$$G(s) = \frac{K_p}{(T_{p1} \cdot s + 1)(T_{p2} \cdot s + 1)} e^{-T_d s} \tag{3}$$

where $K_p = 1.0341$, $T_{p1} = 253.57$, $T_{p2} = 32.282$, $T_d = 1$.

Depending upon the same method, the air outlet temperature of air conditioning is reduced from 293 K to 292 K. Take the input and output changes to obtain the cooling unit step response data, as the validation set. The second-order pure lag system model is fitted with validation set curve fitting, and the fitting degree is up to 95.7%, as shown in Fig. 5. This shows that the mathematical model obtained by the identification is accurate and effective. Based on this, the control method of data center temperature can be studied.

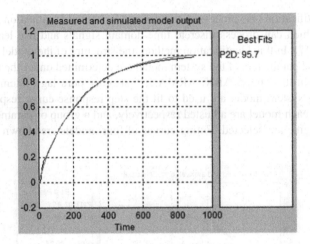

Fig. 5. System confirmation

4   Model Predictive Control

4.1   MPC Based on CFD

MPC is based on the predictive model, and predicts the input and output of the model by rolling optimization. The optimal control strategy of the research object is determined by optimizing the objective function. The CFD model established has an error, and the model structure and the choice of parameters in the system identification process also affects the accuracy of the model. However, MPC is robust and does not require a high-precision system model. Rolling optimization, rather than a one-time global optimization, can make up for uncertainty problems caused by system model mismatch and external interference.

The theory of MPC based on CFD is shown in Fig. 6. First, the system CFD model is established according to the boundary conditions. Then the steady-state and unsteady-state simulation experiments are performed to obtain the unit step response curve of input and output. The mathematical model of the system is established by the system identification method. Finally, MPC algorithm is used to obtain the control input sequence.

In this study, the second-order pure lag system is used as the predictive model to perform rolling time domain optimization and feedback correction. The objective function usually takes the form of a quadratic function of prediction output and reference trajectory error which is as follows [8]:

$$J(k) = \lambda_1 \sum_{j=1}^{N_p} (\hat{y}(k+j|k) - y_r(k+j))^2$$
$$+ \lambda_2 \sum_{j=1}^{N_c} (\Delta u(k+j-1))^2$$

$$(4)$$

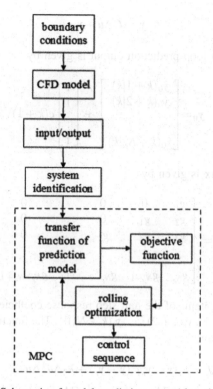

Fig. 6. Schematic of model predictive control based on CFD

where $\hat{y}(k+j|k)$ is the process output of j steps in the future predicted on the basis of information available at time k, $y_r(k+j)$ is the sequence of the reference signal. λ_1 is weighting coefficient for the output error. λ_2 is weighting coefficient for control. N_p is prediction horizon, N_c is control horizon, and $N_p > N_c$. $\Delta u(k+j-1)$ is the sequence of the future control increments that have to be calculated.

$$\Delta u(k+j-1) = \begin{cases} u(k) - u(k-1) & (j=1) \\ u(k+j-1) - u(k+j-2) & (j=2,3,\cdots,N_c) \end{cases} \tag{5}$$

The role of the reference trajectory is to let the output smoothly reach the actual set point $y(k)$ to avoid excessive changes in the control input. The reference trajectory is given as:

$$\begin{cases} y_r(k) = y(k) \\ y_r(k+j) = \alpha \cdot y_r(k+j-1) + (1-\alpha) \cdot y(k+j) \end{cases} \tag{6}$$

Suppose that the output of the model (predictor) is as follows.

$$\hat{y} = G\Delta u + y_0 \tag{7}$$

where the system open loop prediction output is given by

$$y_0 = \begin{bmatrix} \hat{y}_0(k+1|k) \\ \hat{y}_0(k+2|k) \\ \vdots \\ \hat{y}_0(k+N_p|k) \end{bmatrix} + \begin{bmatrix} 1 \\ 1 \\ \vdots \\ 1 \end{bmatrix} e(k+1) \tag{8}$$

And dynamic matrix is given by

$$G = \begin{bmatrix} g_1 & 0 & 0 & \cdots & 0 \\ g_2 & g_1 & 0 & \cdots & 0 \\ g_3 & g_2 & g_1 & \cdots & 0 \\ \vdots & \vdots & \vdots & \ddots & \vdots \\ g_{N_p} & g_{N_p-1} & g_{N_p-2} & \cdots & g_{N_p-N_c+1} \end{bmatrix} \tag{9}$$

where g_i is the first N_p items of the unit step response coefficient.

Define $y_r = [y_r(k+1), y_r(k+2), \ldots, y_r(k+N_p)]^T$, The function (4) can be modified to the matrix form below

$$\begin{aligned} J &= \lambda_1(\hat{y} - y_r)^T(\hat{y} - y_r) + \lambda_2\Delta u^T\Delta u \\ &= \lambda_1(G\Delta u + y_0 - y_r)^T(G\Delta u + y_0 - y_r) \\ &\quad + \lambda_2\Delta u^T\Delta u \end{aligned} \tag{10}$$

The solution can be found by setting the partial derivative of J with respect to Δu as zero and yields:

$$\Delta u = (G^TG + \lambda_2 I)^{-1}G^T\lambda_1(y_r - y_0) \tag{11}$$

In the process of rolling optimization, the first element of the resulting vector is then applied as the increment of the manipulated variable. Then, the control sequence can be obtained.

4.2 MPC Simulation Experiment

MPC simulation experiment of this system is carried out by using MPC Toolbox of MATLAB. When N_p is larger, the system is more stable, but its dynamic response is softer. When N_c is larger, the control is more sensitive, but the system is less stable and less robust, and the computational complexity of the matrix inversion can be increased. The parameters of MPC controller are set as follows: $N_p = 20$, $N_c = 2$; the control interval is set to 10 s; the weighting coefficient for the output error is set to 1 and the weighting coefficient for control is set to 0; to make the input change softly, the rate

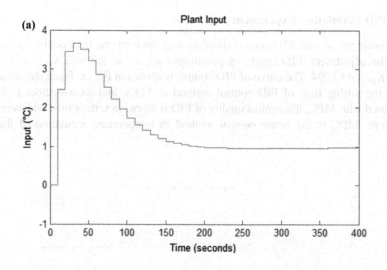

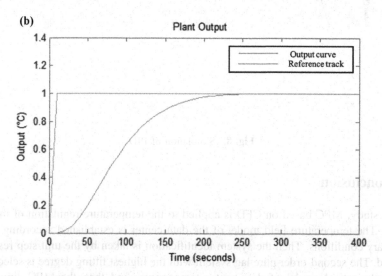

Fig. 7. (a). Input sequence, (b). Output temperature curve

weight is set to 0.2 and the input constraints is set as $-4 \leq \Delta u \leq 4$. The simulation result is shown in Fig. 7.

It can be seen from the simulation curve that the setting time of MPC is 230 s, and there are not overshoot and steady-state error, and the change of control is accurate and rapid. The control effect is well and can meet requirements of data center temperature regulation.

4.3   PID Simulation Experiment

To compare the results, PID control simulation of the temperature model is carried out. After the adjustment, PID controller parameters are set as follows: $K_P = 4.485$, $K_I = 0.02$, $K_D = 43.1594$. The curve of PID control is shown in Fig. 8. From the simulation curve, the setting time of PID control method is 325 s, and its overshoot is 5.62%. Compared with MPC, the control quality of PID is worse in setting time and overshoot. Therefore, MPC is the better control method in temperature regulation of the data center.

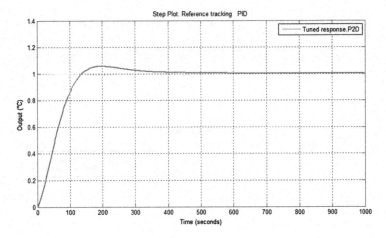

Fig. 8. Simulation of PID

5   Conclusion

In this study, MPC based on CFD is applied to the temperature regulation of the data center. The temperature field model of the data center is established according to the boundary conditions. Then the system identification is taken by the unit step response method. The second-order pure lag system with the highest fitting degree is selected as the mathematical model of data center temperature, and then the MPC simulation experiment of this system is carried out. This control method changes the extensive management mode of long-term constant temperature refrigeration. MPC adopts the rolling optimization strategy, which does not require a high-precision system model and can overcome the problems of system model mismatch and external disturbance. Compared with the traditional PID control, MPC has faster response and less over-shoot, and has obvious advantages in the comprehensive control quality.

The main shortcoming of this study is that only one observation point is selected in the process of CFD modeling and the role of CFD was not fully utilized. There remain some problems to be studied in future research.

Acknowledgments. This paper was supported by foundation research project No. JCYJ20150730103208405 of Shenzhen Science and Technology Innovation Committee, and open research project of State Key Laboratory of Air-conditioning Equipment and System Energy Conservation, China.

References

1. Desta, T.Z., Janssens, K.: CFD for model-based controller development. Build. Environ. **39** (6), 621–633 (2004)
2. Li, S., Cui, X., Wang, G., et al.: Simulation for model-based generalized predictive control of air-conditioning room temperature. Build. Energy Environ. **22**(6), 23–26 (2003)
3. Zhou, W., Li, Y., Wang, X.: Model predictive control of air temperature in greenhouse based on CFD unsteady model. Trans. Chin. Soc. Agric. Mach. **45**(12), 335–340 (2014)
4. Liu, Z., Zhao, Y.: Fluent character functions and application for indoor temperature computation. Appl. Electron. Tech. **37**(7), 48–50 (2011)
5. Cheng, X.: Predication and CFD modeling for greenhouse microclimates temporospatial distributions. Jiangsu University (2011)
6. Han, Z., Wang, J., Lan, X.: FLUENT: Example and application of fluid engineering simulation calculation. Beijing Institute of Technology Press (2010)
7. Sun, Q., Jin, Z., Mao, Y., et al.: System identification of refrigerating system transfer function by partition step-response. Vac. Cryogenics **5**, 307–310 (2015)
8. Bobal, V., Kubalcik, M., Dostal, P., et al.: Adaptive predictive control of time-delay systems. Comput. Math Appl. **66**(2), 165–176 (2013)

Computer System for Designing Musical Expressiveness in an Automatic Music Composition Process

Michele Della Ventura[✉]

Department of Technology, Music Academy "Studio Musica", Treviso, Italy
dellaventura.michele@tin.it

Abstract. Artificial Intelligent Systems have shown great potential in the musical domain. One task in which these techniques have shown special promise is in the automatic music composition. This article describes the development of an algorithm for designing musical expressiveness for a tonal melody generated by computer. The method employed is based on a model of self-recognition of the harmonic structures contained in the melody and, by means of the "harmonic function" carried by every single one of these, provides useful information for the dynamics. The article is intended to demonstrate the effectiveness of the method by applying it to some (tonal) musical pieces of the 18th and of the 19th century. At the same time it is going to indicate ways to improve the method.

Keywords: Artificial intelligence · Functional harmony
Musical expressiveness

1 Introduction

An attempt was made to create (using a computer), with the current Artificial Intelligence (AI) techniques, a music (melody) that could be appreciated by people [1]. One of the fundamental aspects to this respect derives from the concept of "musical expressiveness" [2]. it is an added value to a melody, that renders it pleasant and interesting to listen to.

Musical expressiveness is closely tied to the concept of musical interpretation that the executant achieves during his/her own performance [3]. The sounds are all played with the same intensity and the various elements inherent to the musical phrase are highlighted with different sonorities (forte, piano, crescendo, diminuendo, accents, sforzato...). This interpretation, though, is not defined by the executant based on personal taste: in some cases the indications on the dynamics are already specified in the score, but in other cases they are absent. In this latter case, the musician does not leave it to chance, but performs based on the analysis of the score [4, 5]: it is actually in the very score that the "hidden" indications of the composer may be identified. This explains why various executants can achieve a similar interpretation of the same piece.

The dynamics of a piece may be built by analyzing the harmonic functions (derived from the Functional Harmony theory) that the composer used when writing a phrase

© Springer Nature Singapore Pte Ltd. 2018
J. Qiao et al. (Eds.): BIC-TA 2018, CCIS 951, pp. 434–443, 2018.
https://doi.org/10.1007/978-981-13-2826-8_38

[6]: these functions allow highlighting (with different intensities indeed) fundamental elements of a musical phrase, such as for instance a cadence, an ostinato or a change of tonality (modulation) [7].

This article will present an algorithm able to investigate the musical expressiveness of a musical piece, by reading the score on its symbolic level. Instead of manually modeling the expressiveness, the algorithm identifies the harmonic functions and based on the them it provides indications for the dynamics by means of graphic representation. The concept of expressiveness is then analyzed from the standpoint of musical dynamics and not from the interpretative standpoint, which allows using elements such as the accelerando, the ritardando, the rubato and so on; moreover, the rhythm is not taken into consideration.

This paper is structured as follows. We start by reviewing background and related work in Sect. 2. The theory of Functional Harmony is described in Sect. 3. The Harmonic Operator is described in Sect. 4. We discuss the methods and initial results in Sect. 5. Section 6 contains the conclusions.

2 Background and Related Works

Musical expressiveness is an important research theme within the context of artificial intelligence and it was studied from various perspectives.

Approaches to this problem were based on a statistical analysis [8, 9], on mathematical models [10] or on analysis by synthesis [11, 12, 13]. They are usually empirical methods, which allow obtaining results expressed by numbers, therefore easy to analyze. All these approaches have an algorithm created by a person who conceived a mathematical model able to seize the musical expressiveness elements of a performance.

Another interesting approach is the one based on inductive learning of the rules [14, 15, 16, 17]: instead of manually creating a model for the recognition of the elements related to musical expressiveness, the computer must automatically discover these elements through certain learning rules.

Each of these studies provided important contributions to research thanks to the different perspectives that were used: all the studies formalized mathematically the various observation points.

This article presents an article that, drawing inspiration from the preceding studies, has the objective of identifying the musical dynamics of a melody. Unlike the aforementioned studies that are based on the analysis of an execution, the algorithm tries to define the musical expressiveness on the basis of a musical grammar which is reflected in the functional harmony. The algorithm created for such purpose has the task of reading a certain melody on its symbolic level (this is why scores in MIDI format were used, without any indication on dynamics); to identify the harmonic structures (through a melody segmentation process) and the corresponding harmonic functions (see paragraph 3); finally, to render in graphic format a diagram related to the musical dynamics to apply to the melody.

The effectiveness of the method was tested by analyzing piano pieces of the 18th and of the 19th century, the results of which were compared with the scores reviewed by important musicians.

These results allow applying this method to the algorithms for the automatic generation of a tonal melody so as to render it pleasant and interesting.

3 Functional Harmony

In the Functional Harmony the objective, on the one hand is to identify a sound, a chord or a succession of chords, the "intrinsic sound value" assumed with respect to a certain reference system [18]: the tonality. For instance the *D-F#-A* chord represents the tonic chord in the tonal system of D major or of dominant with respect to the tonal system of G major or G minor.

On the other hand, the Functional Harmony allows highlighting the capacity of a sound, chord or succession of chords, to establish organic relations with other sounds, chords or successions of chords of the same tonal system [19, 20].

From this it ensues that in the functional harmony there are the following fundamental principles.

- The chords are made up of single sounds of the tonal system to which they belong (Fig. 1).

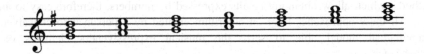

Fig. 1. Chords on the degrees of the G major scale.

- The degrees of the scale (therefore of a tonal system) belong to a specific harmonic function: *harmonic function* of tonic (T) (I degree), subdominant (S) (IV degree) and dominant (D) (V degree) [18]. The three harmonic functions of I, IV and V degree are called main because they are linked by a relation based on the interval of the perfect 5th that separates the keynotes of the three corresponding chords; the chords relating to the rest of degrees on the scale are considered "representatives" of the I, IV and V degree (with which there is an affinity of the third - two sounds in common - because the 3rd is actually the interval that regulates the distance between the respective keynotes) and secondary harmonic functions rest with it (Fig. 2).
- Every degree of the scale has its own resolution tendency based on its own harmonic functions [18, 20]. It follows that all the chords will have a harmonic function of relaxation or of tonal center T, or of tension towards such center D, or of breakaway from it S (Fig. 3).

It is important to note that the resolution of the chords may even not follow the diagram of Fig. 3 [18]: this means that one function of tonic may resolve towards a

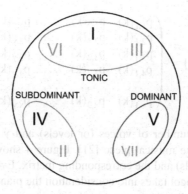

Fig. 2. Degrees of the scale grouped per harmonic function.

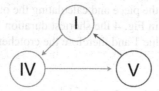

Fig. 3. Resolution tendency of the chords based on the harmonic function.

function of dominant without necessarily passing through a function of subdominant or one function of subdominant may resolve to a function of tonic without passing through a function of dominant.

The identification of these harmonic functions allow the executant to have an image of the character of the piece so as to better define the field of dynamics.

4 Functional Harmony Operator

The identification of the harmonic functions, indispensable to describe the dynamics of a score, is performed by the FHO (Functional Harmony Operator) Harmonic Operator created for the occasion.

Initially the score of a musical piece in MIDI format is read. This protocol allows having various voices of the melody divided into levels and it entails the identification of the pitch and of the duration of a sound in numerical form.

A monodic score may therefore be represented as a sequence S_m of N notes n_i indexed on the basis of the appearance order i:

$$S_m = (n_i)_{i \in [0, N-1]}$$

A polyphonic score may be considered as the overlapping of two or more monodic sequences S_{m1}, S_{m2}, ... which may be represented by a matrix $P_{x,y}$

$$P(k) = \begin{pmatrix} p_{1,1}(k) & p_{1,2}(k) & \cdots & p_{1,y}(k) \\ p_{2,1}(k) & p_{2,2}(k) & \cdots & p_{2,y}(k) \\ p_{3,1}(k) & p_{3,2}(k) & \cdots & p_{3,y}(k) \\ p_{4,1}(k) & p_{4,2}(k) & \cdots & p_{4,y}(k) \\ \cdots & \cdots & \cdots & \cdots \\ p_{x,1}(k) & p_{x,2}(k) & \cdots & p_{x,y}(k) \end{pmatrix}$$

where x represents the number of voices (or levels) and y the number of rhythmic movements existing in the musical piece [21]. Figure 4 shows a polyphonic musical segment (4 voices or levels) and the corresponding matrix. Every sound is identified by a number: the MIDI protocol takes into consideration the pianoforte keyboard (because it is the instrument with the maximum sound extension) and it assigns to the lowest note (A), the value 1 and to every subsequent sound an increasing value (A# = 2, B = 3, C = 4, etc.). Every sound has its own duration which is defined considering the shortest duration existing in the piece and calculating the other durations proportionally [22]. In the example shown in Fig. 4 the shortest duration is represented by the quaver ( ) which will assume the value 1 and therefore the crotchet will assume the value 2 ( ).

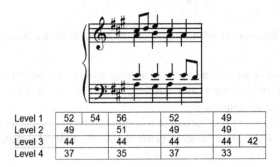

Level 1	52	54	56	52		49	
Level 2	49		51	49		49	
Level 3	44		44	44		44	42
Level 4	37		35	37		33	

Fig. 4. Score representation matrix.

The next stage of the score reading entails the recognition of the tonalities to identify the tonal systems to which the sounds belong (see paragraph 3). This is done by identifying the *characteristic notes*, i.e. the notes for which the two tonalities are different, the one that is left and the one to which modulation occurs [19, 23].

At this point, for every single rhythmic movement, the sounds that make up a chord are identified (keeping in mind that the sounds must be distant from each other by a third interval) and the sounds which are extraneous to the harmony must be eliminated (Fig. 5) [24].

Finally, FHO identifies for each chord the harmonic function (T, S, D) associated to it (based on the pertaining tonal system), so as to have for each movement a functional indication to be used for the definition of the dynamics (Fig. 6) [24, 25].

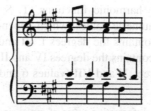

Fig. 5. Simplification of the score by eliminating the notes which are extraneous to a harmony.

Fig. 6. Tonal functions of the chords.

5   Obtained Results

The developed algorithm has the objective of defining the dynamics (expressiveness) of a musical piece considering only the harmonic functions contained in it. As such, the system may be applied only to tonal musical pieces and it may be an important help for the systems of automatic creation of tonal melodies: currently one of the most interesting fields within the context of artificial intelligence in the music field.

Input parameters are not necessary for the elaboration: the algorithm reads the initial musical notes and it defines automatically the first tonal system, and after that, with every change of the characteristic notes it defines a new tonal system. This score segmentation process (for the identification of the modulations) does not impose any limit to the dimensions of the score representative matrix, which will be instead dimensioned for every reading of the piece, on the basis of its intrinsic characteristics (number of voices, number of sounds, number of movements or rhythmic divisions).

The initial tests were carried out on a set of musical segments of various lengths, specifically selected, in order to verify the "validity" of the analysis. Then, entire scores were taken into consideration, so as to compare them with scores that had been already reviewed by important musicians, in order to verify the validity of the method.

The results of the analysis are indicated in an isometric diagram which compares the harmonic function of every single chord with the harmonic function of rest expressed by T which represents the chord of the reference tonal system and with respect to which the comparisons and classifications may be made: otherwise, every single chord may not provide any information.

Table 1 shows the three harmonic functions (T, S, D) every single one being identified by an interval of numeric values, which depends on the number of degrees contained in it: function T contains the degrees I, III and VI (therefore the values go from 1, 2 and 3), function S contains the degrees IV and II (values 4 and 5) and, finally, function D contains the degrees V and VII (values 6 and 7).

Table 1. Information value of every single chord.

T	S	D
1 2 3	4 5	6 7
I III VI	II IV	V VII

Figure 7 proposes a musical segment with the corresponding graphic analysis.

In the upper part of the diagram colors are used to represent the various brackets of information of the harmonic functions of the single chords, while the lower part of the diagram shows the information of the single Tonic chord (to which the comparison is made). The color representing a certain bracket will have a darker or a clearer tone based on whether the value of a harmonic function is of a major (D) or of a minor (S) tension. If the chord has a T function the diagram will contain a column having only the color of the corresponding information bracket (green). If, instead, the chord has an S or D function the color within the column changes by fading out, passing from the color of the preceding value to the color of the value representing the tonal function. The larger the color difference, the greater the musical tension expressed in the phrase and, therefore, the higher the sound intensity. Following the gradualness of the color fad-out it is possible to create:

• a "crescendo", in case the transition is from green (T) to orange (S) or to red (D); this effect is represented by the graphic symbol < the length of which varies based on the fade-out duration;
• a "diminuendo", in case the transition goes from red (D) or orange (S) to green (T); this effect is represented by the graphic symbol > the length of which varies based on the fade-out duration;
• an "accento" or "appoggiato", in case a transition occurs in succession from T–D–T (green-red-green): the "accento" or "appoggiato" would be on the harmonic function D (see Fig. 7, bar 3, second movement); this effect is represented by the graphic symbol "-".

On the basis of this information the algorithm then proposes a dynamics to apply to the piece (see Fig. 7).

Fig. 7. Mendelssohn "Songs without words" n.6 op.19: functional analysis. (Color figure online)

6 Conclusions and Discussion

This article presented an algorithm for designing musical expressiveness for a tonal melody generated by computer. The model is based on the concept of "harmonic function" derived from the theory of De la Motte, which allows drawing a graphic diagram representing the sound intensity and, therefore, the evolution of the musical dynamics (or musical expressiveness). Thus, the proposed method observes both the musical grammar related to the succession of harmonies and the musical phrase syntax.

The results allow the use of the method not only to render a computer-generated melody creative, but also to comment on the existing music. In other words the method may have implications on the musical analysis and, therefore, represent a means of support for the teaching activity: a tool to stimulate the recovery of not-fully-acquired abilities or as simple tool of consultation and support to the explanation of the teacher.

It can be noticed that musical expressiveness is an interesting topic for scientific investigation and for technology research. A future study might target a combined analysis of the harmonic structure and of the rhythm of the computer-generated melody in order to give major coherence to the musical phrase.

References

1. Miranda, E.R., Biles, J.A.: Evolutionary Computer Music. Springer, London (2007). https://doi.org/10.1007/978-1-84628-600-1
2. Canazza, S., De Poli, G., Drioli, C., Rodà, A., Vidolin, A.: Modeling and control of expressiveness in music performance. Proc. IEEE **92**(4), 686–701 (2004)
3. Minsky, M.L., Laske, O.: A conversation with Marvin Minsky. AI Mag. **13**(3), 31–45 (1992)
4. Nielsen, R.: Musical forms. Bongiovanni Editore (1961)
5. Baroni, M., Jacoboni, C., Dal Monte, R.: The music rules, EDT/SidM (1999)
6. de la Motte, D.: Manuale di armonia. Bärenreiter (1976)
7. Ames, C.: The Markov process as a compositional model: a survey and tutorial. Leonardo **22** (2), 175–187 (1989)
8. Amatriain, X., Bonada, J., Loscos, A., Arcos, J., Verfaille, V.: Content-based transformation. J. New Music Res. **32**(1), 95–114 (2003)
9. Bresin, R., Battel, G.U.: Articulation strategies in expressive piano performance analysis of legato, staccato, and repeated notes in performances of the andante movement of Mozart's sonata in g major (k 545). J. New Music Res. **29**(3), 211–224 (2000)
10. Todd, N.: The dynamics of dynamics: a model of musical expression. J. Acoust. Soc. Am. **91**, 3540 (1992)
11. Friberg, A.: A Quantitative Rule System for Musical Performance, PhD thesis, KTH, Sweden (1995)
12. Grachten, M., Widmer, G.: Linear basis models for prediction and analysis of musical expression. J. New Music Res. **41**(4), 311–322 (2012)
13. Rodà, A., Canazza, S., De Poli, G.: Clustering affective qualities of classical music: beyond the valencearousal plane. IEEE Trans. Affect. Comput. **5**(4), 364–376 (2014)
14. Ramirez, R., Hazan, A.: Rule induction for expressive music performance modeling. In: ECML Workshop Advances in Inductive Rule Learning, September 2004
15. Ramirez, R., Maestre, E., Serra, X.: A rule-base evolutionary approach to music performance modeling. IEEE Trans. Evol. Comput. **16**(1), 96–107 (2012)
16. Clark, P., Boswell, R.: Rule induction with CN2: some recent improvements. In: Kodratoff, Y. (ed.) EWSL 1991. LNCS, vol. 482, pp. 151–163. Springer, Heidelberg (1991). https://doi.org/10.1007/BFb0017011
17. Lindgren, T., Boström, H.: Classification with intersecting rules. In: Cesa-Bianchi, N., Numao, M., Reischuk, R. (eds.) ALT 2002. LNCS (LNAI), vol. 2533, pp. 395–402. Springer, Heidelberg (2002). https://doi.org/10.1007/3-540-36169-3_31
18. de la Motte, D.: Manuale di armonia. Bärenreiter (1976)

19. Coltro, B.: Lezioni di armonia complementare. Zanibon (1979)
20. Schonber, A.: Theory of Harmony. University of California Press, Berkeley (1983)
21. Della Ventura, M.: Toward an analysis of polyphonic music in the textual symbolic segmentation. In: Proceedings of the 2nd International Conference on Computer, Digital Communications and Computing (ICDCC 2013), Brasov, Romania (2013)
22. Della Ventura, M.: Rhythm analysis of the "Sonorous Continuum" and conjoint evaluation of the musical entropy. In: Proceedings of the 13th International Conference on Acoustics & Music: Theory & Applications (AMTA 2012), Iasi, Romania, pp. 16–21 (2012)
23. Bent, I.: Analysis. Macmillan Publishers LTD, London (1980)
24. Della Ventura, M.: Automatic tonal music composition using functional harmony. In: Agarwal, N., Xu, K., Osgood, N. (eds.) SBP 2015. LNCS, vol. 9021, pp. 290–295. Springer, Cham (2015). https://doi.org/10.1007/978-3-319-16268-3_32
25. Martin, B., Hanna, P., Robine, M., Ferraro, P.: Structural analysis of harmonic features using string matching techniques ISMIR (2012)

A Hybrid Dynamic Population Genetic Algorithm for Multi-satellite and Multi-station Mission Planning System

Yan-Jie Song, Xin Ma, Zhong-Shan Zhang[✉], Li-Ning Xing,
and Ying-Wu Chen

College of Systems Engineering, National University of Defense Technology,
Changsha 410073, Hunan, China
zszhang@nudt.edu.cn

Abstract. Satellite is an important space platform today. Achieving reasonable satellite management control greatly affects the development of the aerospace field. Multi-satellite and multi-station mission planning system was proposed to achieve control of satellite resources. In the system, planning algorithms are particularly important, so we proposed a mathematical model for the mission planning of multi-satellite and multi-ground station. Then, we proposed a hybrid dynamic population genetic algorithm (HDPGA) for satellite mission planning. In this algorithm, the large-population size is used for global optimization and the small-population size is used for local improvements. Additionally, the mission planning algorithm (MPA) is used to arrange the mission sequence on the ground station time window. We designed multiple sets of experiments to verify the effect of HDPGA. The results show that our proposed algorithm can meet the needs of the planning system. At the same time, HDPGA is better than the other four algorithms.

Keywords: Hybrid dynamic population genetic algorithm
Multi-satellite & Multi-station mission planning system
Mission planning algorithm · Bio-inspired computing

1 Introduction

Satellite is a spacecraft that uses spaceborne sensors to complete various space missions. It has unique advantages such as wide coverage, long running time, no limitation of national borders and airspace, and no need to consider personnel safety. It is mainly divided into remote sensing satellites, navigation satellites, and communications. Remote sensing satellites are responsible for obtaining ground image data from space. Navigation satellites enable global positioning and communications satellites provide support for ground communications. At present, satellites have played an important role in many fields such as disaster prevention, environmental protection, urban planning, agriculture, and meteorology, and have also received great attention from countries in the world.

The satellite control work is mainly carried out by satellite ground stations. The number of satellites has always been on the rise, but the number of satellite ground

© Springer Nature Singapore Pte Ltd. 2018
J. Qiao et al. (Eds.): BIC-TA 2018, CCIS 951, pp. 444–453, 2018.
https://doi.org/10.1007/978-981-13-2826-8_39

stations is limited. This means that there is a conflict between missions and satellite resources. The establishment of an effective multi-satellite and multi-ground station control model has important implications for ensuring that satellites break through the bottleneck of resource constraints and complete as many tasks as possible.

Intelligent optimization algorithms such as simulated annealing (SA), tabu search (TS), and genetic algorithm (GA) show strong ability in solving combinatorial optimization problems. These algorithms also have many applications in the field of imaging satellite mission planning. [1] used tabu search to obtain good results in the SPOT-5 satellite's planning. [2] used the step-by-step algorithm composed of greedy algorithm and tabu search algorithm to research the data transfer problem of the "Mars Express" rover. [3] used the tabu search algorithm to solve the single satellite orbit planning problem within a single orbit. By inserting, removing, and replacing tasks and tasks in pairs, six neighborhood structures are constructed. In the search process, certain time window constraints are allowed to be violated. Penalty parameters are added when time window violations are violated, and continuous differentiation is used. [4] considered the single-space mission planning problem as a single-machine scheduling problem with time window constraints, and the machine preparation time is related to the order between tasks. Using the Lagrangian relaxation method, the main problem is decomposed into several sub-problems, and solved by linear programming techniques. The United States Air Force Institute of Technology first conducted research on the application of genetic algorithms in mission planning of imaging satellites [5]. [6] introduced a task execution decision variable and a task execution position decision variable in the population evolution process of genetic algorithm, combined with priority-based greedy algorithm (Priority Dispatch) and Look Ahead technology, and accelerated the search speed. [7] introduced domain knowledge into the evolutionary algorithm and used explicit and tacit knowledge to deal with the static and dynamic constraints in the satellite imaging process. This solved the task planning problem of a constellation of 25 satellites. [8] designed a heuristic search algorithm based on greedy rules for task scheduling of ASTER (Application Sheet Train Evolutionary Reengineering) systems. The scheduling goal of the algorithm is to maximize the benefits of completing the task (the sum of the priorities). [9] proposed a tabu search algorithm that is mixed with the system search to solve agile satellite scheduling problems involving stereo and time window constraints. [10] discussed the first agile satellite scheduling problem for environmental and disaster monitoring and forecasting in China. They proposed a nonlinear model of the problem and developed a heuristic approach to avoiding conflicts, limiting backtracking, and downloading on-demand features. At the same time, a decision support system based on models and heuristics was also provided. [11] proposed an improved genetic algorithm based on Hybrid Dynamic Variation (HDM) and applied it to multiple satellite task planning. Experiments show that the algorithm has a high calculation speed and reliability.

The structure of this article is as follows. In the second part, we will give a mathematical description of multi-satellite and multi-ground station mission planning problems. After that, the Hybrid dynamic population genetic algorithm (HDPGA) will be introduced in detail in the third part. The fourth part will use experiments to verify the effectiveness of the algorithm. The conclusions of the study will be given in the last part of this article.

2 Problem Description

Our goal is to solve the satellite mission planning problem of multi-satellite and multi-ground stations. This is a complex problem with a typical engineering background that we need to turn into an easy-to-solve scientific problem. In this section, based on the analysis of the problem, the mathematical model, the corresponding assumptions and constraints will be given. First, we describe the background of the scientific problem of the problem. After that, the mathematical model will be proposed.

The mission planning of multi-satellite and multi-ground station involves several satellites, each of which has a fixed operational status. At the same time, each ground station also exists in a fixed geographical location. The limitation of the fixed parameters makes the time for the satellites to pass through the satellite earth station in one day is limited. This time range is called the visible time window. The mission planning problem for multi-ground station with multi-satellite is to schedule tasks that maximize the total tasks' revenue as much as possible within the time window.

In order to facilitate the establishment of models and problem solving, we make the following assumptions:

1. Only consider mission planning. The hardware conditions of satellites and ground stations can meet the mission planning requirements.
2. Our planning is limited to a certain time frame, and the subsequent mission planning follows the method proposed by us.
3. Once each task is executed, it cannot be terminated.
4. Each task is only considered to be executed once in the time range, and no repeated execution will occur.

A task set T containing M tasks, each task t includes an earliest begin time et, a latest end time lt, a task duration d, and a successful execution of the task can obtain the task profit of p. There are N available time window sets TW, each of which has an available time window tw, where there is an earliest visible time evt and a latest visible time lvt. Due to the satellite and ground station antenna capabilities, after the completion of a task, other tasks cannot be immediately started, and task transition times of tr are required. In the same way, the ground station antenna cannot start performing tasks immediately after the earliest satellites are visible, and it needs to go through a state adjustment time of at.

In addition, we also propose a decision variable x_i. When x_i is 0, the task is not executed; 1 means that the task will be executed.

Our objective function follows the evaluation criteria commonly used in satellite mission planning studies. The goal of planning is to maximize the benefits of the task sequence. The model is expressed as follows:

$$\max f(x) = \sum\nolimits_{j=1}^{M} p_i x_i \tag{1}$$

The constraints of multi-satellite and multi-station mission planning:

1. The actual start time of the task *ast*, needs to be adjusted after the satellite passes through:

$$et + at \leq ast \tag{2}$$

2. The start time of the task needs to be within the available time window of the ground station;

$$evt \leq ast \tag{3}$$

3. The task needs to be completed within the minimum time of the mission and the time window of the ground station;

$$ast + d \leq \min\{lt, lvt\} \tag{4}$$

4. There can be no overlap between the two tasks;

$$ast_i + d_i \leq ast_{i+1} \tag{5}$$

5. The task can only be executed once at most;

$$x_i \leq 1 (i \in T) \tag{6}$$

The mission planning problem of multi-satellite and multi-ground station is an NP-Hard problem. The number of constraints and tasks make it impossible for an exact solution algorithm to obtain an optimal solution when the problem size increases to a certain extent. The use of heuristic algorithms can't be proved to be able to reach the optimal solution, but it can obtain satisfactory results and guide the task planning in practical projects.

3 Method

As an effective bionic optimization algorithm, GA algorithm is widely used in various fields, but the traditional GA algorithm is difficult to balance both efficiency and effect [12, 13]. The Hybrid Dynamic Population Genetic Algorithm (HDPGA) proposed by us adopts the rule of dynamic adjustment of the number of individuals in the population, and it improves the speed of solution while ensuring the quality of the solution. In this section, we will first introduce the mission planning algorithm (MPA) algorithm. After that, the HDPGA algorithm flow will be introduced in detail.

3.1 Mission Planning Algorithm (MPA)

Mission planning algorithm (MPA) is used to select a given set of tasks in order to select their execution location in the ground station available time window. MPA will place each satellite mission at the earliest place where it can begin execution. The distribution of tasks can be made more compact with this improvement. The MPA pseudo code is as follows:

Algorithm 1: Mission planning algorithm (MPA)

```
Input Tasks Sequence T, Available Time Windows ATW
Output Solution S
For each task t in T
  Select the most forward location(t)
  Check constraint(t)
  If No Conflict
    S ← Generate plan(t)
  Else
    Turn to next task
  End If
End For
Return S
```

In the MPA, follow the principle of task scheduling, use **Select the most forward location** to select the location where the task can start execution, and then use **Check constraint** to ensure that the task can meet all the constraints presented in the previous section. If the constraints can be met, then arrange the task in the planning plan, otherwise, consider the next task.

3.2 Hybrid Dynamic Population Genetic Algorithm (HDPGA)

Hybrid dynamic population genetic algorithm (HDPGA) is an improved GA algorithm that introduces dynamic changes in the population scale and adapts to the optimization effect of the algorithm. In the initial optimization phase, a large number of individuals are used to achieve a rapid improvement solution [14–16]. If HDPGA does not improve for several generations of population fitness, the population size will be reduced locally for local optimization. In the local optimization process, if there is no improvement in several generations of fitness, the algorithm will return to the global optimization stage. We introduce an adaptive threshold function to make the algorithm no longer jump out of the local optimization process after entering the local optimization from global optimizations. Instead, the local optimization method is used to continuously improve the quality of the solution. The specific flow of the dynamic population operator is as follows:

```
Dynamic Population Operator
Initialize global population pop_gol, local population pop_loc, glob-
al no improvement generation Gen, local no improvement genera-
tion Gen_loc, adaptive threshold at, adjustment times count
Calculate no improvement generation
If no improvement generation > Gen
    pop= pop_loc
End If
Calculate no improvement generation in new population
If no improvement generation in new population > Gen_loc
    If count < at
        pop= pop_gol
        count= count +1
    End If
End If
```

Coding: We use real-coded methods, where the numbers indicate the location of the task in the initial given sequence.

Selection: The selection operation uses the roulette method to determine the selection operation in the genetic operation based on the fitness ratio of each individual in the population in the population.

Crossover: Crossover in HDPGA is performed using the recombination of two gene segments in an individual. Through the recombination of the two gene segments, the diversity of individuals in the population is increased while the original genetic characteristics in the individual are maintained.

Mutation: mutations are performed on two alleles in an individual. When mutating, the two alleles in the individual are swapped to create new individuals.

Stop Criterion: The HDPGA stop criterion is set such that after the number of iterations of the algorithm reaches the preset maximum number, the algorithm no longer iterates and outputs the final result.

The HDPGA algorithm proposed by us improves the optimization efficiency in the local search process through the mechanism of population update. At the same time, the frequency of local optimization and global optimization is set in the algorithm to prevent continuous global search and make the algorithm converge slowly.

4   Experimental Analysis

Experimental environment: The proposed algorithms are implemented by Matlab2017a on a desktop with Core I7-7700 3.6 GHz CPU, 8 GB memory, and Windows 7 operating system.

Experimental Example: Our experimental example involves different types of satellites and globally distributed satellite ground stations. The task scales were 50, 100, 150, 200, 250, and 300 tasks respectively. We set two scenarios separately for each task size.

Evaluation Indicators: We mainly consider two indicators, one is the total mission profit of the objective function, and the other is the completion rate of the mission

(MCR). These two aspects are two aspects that need to be considered in practical engineering applications. More task execution can improve the utilization rate of equipment, and the level of overall return of tasks reflects the value that can be brought by task execution.

Satellite Orbital Parameters: The experiments are based on several LEO satellites and HEO satellites in China. The initial orbital parameters of one of the satellites are given. The locations of satellites in space are characterized by six orbital parameters: the length of the semi-major axis (LSA), eccentricity (E), inclination (I), argument of perigee (AP), right ascension of the ascending node (RAAN), and mean anomaly (MA). The initial orbital parameters for the satellite are presented in Table 1.

Table 1. Satellite parameters

Parameter	LSA	E	I	AP	RAAN	MA
Value	7141701.7	0.000627	98.5964	95.5069	342.307	125.2658

Contrast Algorithm: We have chosen four heuristic algorithms commonly used in satellite mission planning as comparison algorithms: Duration First Algorithm, Start Time First Algorithm, Task Benefit First Algorithm, and Average Task Revenue First Algorithm. These four algorithms focus on different task characteristics, task's time or profit and so on.

We conducted experimental tests on the eight scenarios in the example, and the results are shown in Table 2.

Table 2. Experiment results for different task sizes

Problems	HDPGA		DPA		TPA		PPA		APPA	
	Profit	MCR	Profit	MCR	Profit	MCR	Profit	MCR	Profit	MCR
50-1	**894**	**1**	569	0.94	591	0.96	585	0.94	569	0.94
50-2	**922**	**1**	543	0.94	582	0.98	597	0.98	576	0.96
100-1	**1247**	**0.98**	1120	0.95	1178	0.97	1178	0.97	1163	0.94
100-2	**1298**	**0.98**	1151	0.95	1179	0.95	1164	0.93	1157	0.93
150-1	**1662**	**0.96**	1513	0.9067	1601	0.9467	1603	0.9267	1551	0.9
150-2	**1667**	**0.9267**	1554	0.9067	1596	0.92	1609	0.9067	1560	0.9
200-1	**2297**	**0.915**	2162	0.9	2208	0.9	2198	0.87	2203	0.895
200-2	**2452**	**0.9**	2270	0.885	2389	**0.915**	2419	0.88	2313	0.87

It can be seen from the experimental results that when the number of tasks is 50, the HDPGA can realize that all tasks are successfully planned, while the maximum completion rate of the other four heuristic algorithms can only reach 96%. When the scale of the task rises from 50 to 100, the proportion of tasks that cannot be successfully executed increases with the number of tasks and constraints. The rate of increase in the level of mission revenue has also slowed. At this point TPA and PPA achieved the same task completion rate.

After that, the scale of the task continued to increase to 150, 200 tasks. HDPGA still maintained a very good performance under the declining task completion rate. While the performance of the other four algorithms varies greatly in different scenarios, TPA performs better than the other three heuristic algorithms. When the experimental scenario is 200-2, the TPA algorithm has a 91.5% completion rate of the task, which is 1.5% higher than our proposed algorithm, and the task revenue does not exceed HDPGA.

Then, we designed a second experiment to further increase the task size to 250, 300 tasks. The result is shown in Fig. 1.

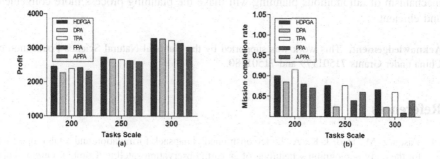

Fig. 1. The result of large-scale tasks

From the experimental results of large-scale tasks, we can see that the gap between our proposed HDPGA and the other four heuristic algorithms has increased. This is due to the fact that the genetic algorithm has an advantage in individuals when the number of genes increases to a certain extent. When the number of tasks is 250, 300, the tasks that can be successfully completed in the HDPGA planning result do not exceed 90%. In the case of 250 tasks, the mission completion rate of the DPA is the lowest; in the case of 300 tasks, the mission completion rate of the PPA is the lowest.

On the whole, HDPGA, which we put forward, can achieve good planning results, whether in the case of small-scale tasks, medium-scale tasks, or large-scale tasks. The algorithm has achieved good performance in terms of both task revenue and task completion rate. It can be seen that our algorithm is more effective when the task scale is relatively large. In the other four heuristics algorithm, DPA is the best way to plan for results.

5   Conclusion

The mission planning system of multi-satellite and multi-ground station can effectively realize satellite management and control. This paper establishes a mathematical model for the mission planning of multi-satellite and multi-ground station and analyzes the assumptions and constraints of the model. We proposed a mission planning algorithm (MPA) for the scheduling of missions on the ground station time window. Later, a hybrid dynamic population genetic algorithm (HDPGA) was used to optimize the task sequence. The dynamic population adjustment is used to adjust the local optimization process and the global optimization process.

Then, we designed several scenarios to test the effectiveness of HDPGA. From the experimental results, we can see that in the experiments of small-scale missions, medium-scale missions, and large-scale missions, the proposed algorithm has a very good performance in terms of both task revenue and task completion rate, which can meet the needs of system applications.

In our further work, we will conduct a study of planning system design. Further increasing the speed of planning scheme generation and ensuring the missions profit is also of great significance for engineering applications. In addition, research on the mechanism of autonomous planning will make the planning process more convenient and efficient.

Acknowledgement. This work was supported by the National Natural Science Foundation of China under Grants 71501179 and 71501180.

References

1. Vasquez, M., Hao, J.-K.: A "logic-constrained" knapsack formulation and a tabu algorithm for the daily photograph scheduling of an earth observation satellite. Comput. Optim. Appl. **20**(2), 137–157 (2001)
2. Angelo, O., Amedeo, C., Nicola, P., Gabriella, C.: Scheduling downlink operations in Mars-express. In: Proceedings of the 3rd NASA Workshop on Planning and Scheduling, Huston (2002)
3. Cordeau, J.-F., Laporte, G.: Maximizing the value of an earth observation satellite orbit. J. Oper. Res. Soc. **56**(8), 962–968 (2005)
4. Lin, W.C., Liao, D.Y., Liu, C.Y., Lee, Y.Y.: Daily imaging scheduling of an earth observation satellite. IEEE Trans. Syst. Man Cybern.-Part A: Syst. Hum. **35**(2), 213–223 (2005)
5. Parish, D.A.: A genetic algorithms approach to automating satellite range scheduling. Master's thesis, Air Force Institute of Technology (1994)
6. Wolfe, W.J., Sorensen, S.E.: Three scheduling algorithms applied to the earth observing systems domain. Manage. Sci. **46**(1), 148–168 (2000)
7. Bonissone, P.P., Subbu, R., Eklund, N., Kiehl, T.R.: Evolutionary algorithms + domain knowledge = real-world evolutionary computation. IEEE Trans. Evol. Comput. **10**(3), 256–280 (2006)
8. Muraoka, H., et al.: Aster observation scheduling algorithm. In: International Symposium Space Mission Operations and Ground Data Systems (2010)
9. Habet, D., Vasquez, M., Vimont, Y.: Bounding the optimum for the problem of scheduling the photographs of an agile earth observing satellite. Comput. Optim. Appl. **47**(2), 307–333 (2010)
10. Wang, P., Reinelt, G., Gao, P., Tan, Y.: A model, a heuristic and a decision support system to solve the scheduling problem of an earth observing satellite constellation. Comput. Ind. Eng. **61**(2), 322–335 (2011)
11. Zheng, Z., Guo, J., Gill, E.: Swarm satellite mission scheduling and planning using hybrid dynamic mutation genetic algorithm. Acta Astronaut. **137**, 243–253 (2017)

12. Ho, W., Ho, G.T.S., Ji, P., Lau, H.C.W.: A hybrid genetic algorithm for the multi-depot vehicle routing problem. Eng. Appl. Artif. Intell. **21**(4), 548–557 (2008)
13. Bortfeldt, A.: A genetic algorithm for the two-dimensional strip packing problem with rectangular pieces. Eur. J. Oper. Res. **16**(6), 814–837 (2009)
14. Salido, M.A., Escamilla, J., Giret, A., Barber, F.: A genetic algorithm for energy-efficiency in job-shop scheduling. Int. J. Adv. Manuf. Technol. **85**(5–8), 1303–1314 (2016)
15. Rashid, M.A., Khatib, F., Hoque, M.T., Sattar, A.: An enhanced genetic algorithm for ab initio protein structure prediction. IEEE Trans. Evol. Comput. **20**(4), 627–644 (2016)
16. Hartmann, S.: A competitive genetic algorithm for resource-constrained project scheduling. Naval Res. Logist. **45**(7), 733–750 (2015)

An 8 to 3 Priority Encoder Based on DNA Strand Displacement

Mingliang Wang$^{(\boxtimes)}$ and Bo Bi

School of Mathematics and Statistics, Northeast Petroleum University,
Daqing, Heilongjiang, People's Republic of China
bibo@nepu.edu.cn

Abstract. DNA strand displacement is a recently emerging technology which is widely used in constructing logic circuit, building a bio-chemical computer and etc. A bio-chemical 8 to 3 priority encoder based on DNA strand displacement technology which is the basic unit of a bio-chemical computer is introduced in this paper. The proposed encoder is verified by the simulation using programming language Visual DSD. Simulation results further confirm that the DNA strand displacement technology is a promising method which could be implemented in bio-chemical circuit and computers.

Keywords: Priority encoder · Visual DSD · DNA strand displacement
Logic circuit

1 Introduction

In recent years, there are many attempts to the implementation of new computing models, in which DNA computing models is one of the most important one since Adleman proposed the new computing models in reference [1]. DNA computing has been a hot field of theoretical computer science in recent years, because of the natural advantage of DNA as the nano-scale engineering material for constructing DNA molecule device, logic circuit, and DNA reaction networks. Moreover, DNA computing models have its advantages of solving NP hard computational problems. Y Hao et al. describe a sequence dependent rotary DNA device in reference [2] which is controlled by hybridization technology. Qian et al. proposed a DNA logic circuit which could implement the computation of square root in reference [3], and reported that the logic gate could be the element of more complex circuit. Wei et al. raised a simple easy strategy in reference [4] that could control nanorods and nanowires on the surface of DNA network. Shi et al. reported a new sub-tile strategy which could easily create whole families of programmable tiles in reference [5]. Liu et al. [6] summarized the progress on DNA devices and further discussed the evolutional processes to find the further direction. Lu et al. [7] reported an emerging application of DNAzymes and aptamers which could combine functional DNA biology with nanotechnology. Moreover, DNA computing models are applied to solve NP hard problems, Lipton [8] conducted a DNA experiment to solve the famous SAT problem.

DNA strand displacement technology is an emerging mechanism of DNA assembly which has attracted lots of attention from the scholars and scientists. Lee et al. [9] firstly conducted an experiment which could successfully observe the DNA branch migration and the process of DNA strand displacement. Seeling et al. [10] firstly constructed the simple logic gates with DNA strand displacement method. Soloveichik et al. [11] made a research on time complexity of DSD-based logic circuits. Winfree et al. [12] focused on the kinetics control of DNA toehold exchange. Qian et al. [13] proposed a simple DNA gate motif which could be used to construct complex logic circuit. Qian et al. [14] constructed a brain like neural network with DNA strand displacement using dual-rail logic and the motif in [13]. Qian [3] used the DNA gate motif in [13] to build a DSD-based circuit that can compute the square root of four bit binary number.

DNA strand displacement technology can be used in genetic testing and other detection studies. Rinaudo et al. [15] constructed a universal RNAi-based logic evaluator that operated in mammalian cells which could implement general Boolean logic to make decisions based on endogenous molecular inputs. Xie et al. [16] proposed a RNA exchange experiment which expanded the utility of RNAi computing and pointed toward the possibility of using strand exchange in a native biological setting. DNA strand displacement can also be applied to catalyze the hybridization which would make the DNA reaction network more effective. Yurke et al. [17] reported a new catalyst to catalyze the hybridization which could be the basis of a strategy for using DNA as a fuel to drive free-running artificial molecular machines. Seeling et al. [18] reported a metastable DNA fuel and a corresponding DNA catalyst which could improve upon the original hybridization-based catalyst system. Song et al. [21–23] reported solutions to several problems using P systems.

Coding is the process that information changes from a formalization to another. It is the basic logic function of the computer and has been widely used in computer, sensing and communication. During the process computers change the data into the form they could understand in order to work normally. Computers will implement the encoding function through the basic logic component-encoder. Thus, encoder is a key logic component of computers. When a DNA computer will be constructed, the basic logic encoder should be constructed firstly. In this paper, an 8 to 3 priority encoder which allows for multi-input signals at the same time is proposed in this paper. It is an improved one from 74HC148 which could implement the same function with a simpler structure. A simulation is made by Visual DSD which confirms the prospect of DNA Strand displacement.

2   Modeling

Qian et al. [14] proposed the seesaw gate motif which could be used as a unit of a more complex computing system and attracted the attentions from scholars all over the world. In reference [3], Qian et al. used the DNA gate motif to construct a seesaw circuit which could implement the computation of the square root of 4 bit binary numbers. Wang et al. [19] constructed a full adder using the seesaw gate motif. Qian et al. [13] constructed a brain like neural network using seesaw gate motif. Most of these scientists focused on computing function of DNA strand technology. However, as an important function of computers, coding has been ignored until now. An 8 to 3 encoder, a basic logic component of a computer which implements coding function for

8 bit binary number converted into 3 bit binary number, is not yet be implemented for the bio-chemical computer because the formal logic gate could not implement such a large circuit and few materials could be used in these circuit. Thus, a method based on seesaw gate motif is proposed to implement the basic component 8 to 3 priority encoder in this paper.

An ordinary encoder has a disadvantage that it will appear mistakes when multi-signals are input into it. To solve this problem, priority encoder is designed which allows for multi-inputs at the same time. The priority of the input signals will be set during the design of the encoder. When there are multi-inputs, the encoder will implement the encoding of the high-level signal, and the low-level signal does not work. The priority encoder in this paper is an 8 to 3 priority encoder which could implement the transformation of 8-bit binary code into 3-bit binary code. A novel method is used in the design of the circuit. Comparing with the traditional priority encoder, the four NOT gate in the internal layer of the circuits were omitted and the inverters of all the outputs were omitted which could reduce the scale of the whole circuit. The Boolean equation of the 8 to 3 priority encoder is as following:

$$A_2 = (I_4 + I_5 + I_6 + I_7) * EI \tag{1}$$

$$A_1 = (I_2 I_4 I_5 + I_3 I_4 I_5 + I_6 + I_7) * EI \tag{2}$$

$$A_0 = (I_2 I_4 I_6 + I_3 I_4 I_6 + I_5 I_6 + I_7) * EI \tag{3}$$

where EI is the enable input, the switch of the encoder, A_i is the output signal of the encoder, and I_i is the input signal of the encoder. When the enable input EI = 1, all the outputs will stay at high potential; and when the enable input EI = 0, the encoder could do encoding work normally. The priority of the inputs I0–I7 which determines the priority of the ranking of encoding is decreasing. The Boolean equation of output of enable input is as following:

$$EO = I_0 I_1 I_2 I_3 I_4 I_5 I_6 I_7 * EI \tag{4}$$

When EI and all the inputs is at a high potential state, the output of enable input will at high potential state which indicates there is no code input into the encoder; when EO = 0, namely it is at low potential state, which indicates that the encoder could work normally. However, with no code input into it. The Boolean equation of the expended priority encoding output is:

$$Gs = (I_0 + I_1 + I_2 + I_3 + I_4 + I_5 + I_6 + I_7) * EI \tag{5}$$

The equation above means that when one of the inputs is at low level potential state and EI = 0, the expended priority encoding output Gs = 0, which indicates the encoder could work normally and there is code input into it.

Figure 1 is the digital circuit of the 8 to 3 priority circuit which is an improved one based on the exits chip 74HC148. The four NOT gate in the internal layer of the circuits were omitted and the inverters of all the outputs were also omitted. Thus, the scale of the whole circuit is reduced. In Fig. 1, I0–I7 are the inputs signals of the priority encoder; S is the enable input of the priority encoder; YS is the enable output of the priority encoder; YEX is the expanded priority encoding output of the priority encoder. A0–A2 are the outputs of the priority encoder. A bio-chemical logic circuit is constructed which could implement the encoding function. However, the bio-chemical NOT gate will output false signals when the input signal is a logic zero. Thus, the digital circuit of the 8 to 3 priority encoder will be changed into a dual-rail circuit to solve the false output problem.

A dual-rail logic will make all the signals in the circuit changed into two complementary code, for instance, I0 will be changed into I_0^0 and I_0^1.

Figure 2 is the dual-rail circuit of the 8 to 3 priority encoder which is transformed from the digital circuit in Fig. 1. The dual-rail logic solve the problem that the NOT gate will send a false output when a logic "0" is input into the gate by uses AND-OR logic instead of NOT gate. The dual-rail circuit uses a pair of AND-OR gate to replace NOT gate in the circuit. It has an advantage of that the NOT gate in the circuit, however, the scale of the circuit will be twice of that of the original digital circuit.

Reference [14] proposed a simple DNA gate motif-seesaw gate motif which is referred in this paper to construct the 8 to 3 priority encoder. The seesaw reactions are the reaction which is based on toehold mediate reactions.

Figure 3 is the seesaw circuit of the 8 to 3 priority encoder. In the seesaw circuit, there are three pairs of seesaw AND-OR logic gate which are the basic unit of the 8 to 3 encoder introduced in this paper. The three pairs of seesaw AND-OR logic gate are 2 input seesaw gate, 3 input seesaw gate and 4 input seesaw gate. All of the gates contain seesaw AND gate and seesaw OR gate. These seesaw gates constitute the whole seesaw circuit which implement the function of the 8 to 3 priority encoder.

In this section, an 8 to 3 encoder based on seesaw gate motif with DNA strand displacement technology is constructed in detail. Seesaw gate motif is used in constructing the circuit of the 8 to 3 priority encoder. Comparing with other DNA displacement cascades circuit, seesaw gate motif could be applied to various molecular events as inputs and outputs. The simple structure of the seesaw gate motif makes it easily to build up a more complex computing system.

3   Modeling

An 8 to 3 priority encoder based on DNA strand displacement technology is modeled foregoing. The diagram of seesaw gate will be introduced and a simulation will be made by Microsoft software package Visual DSD [20]. Visual DSD is a design and analysis tool for DNA circuit based on DNA strand displacement technology which could compiles DNA molecules into a set of chemical reactions and then simulate the system dynamics with a stochastic simulator or a deterministic simulator which could forms and solves the system dynamic ODEs. Moreover, a reachable state space analysis could be implemented with the DSD tool.

A pair of seesaw logic gate could perform the AND-OR logic which is sufficient for universal Boolean computation. The seesaw gate motif has three steps of reactions which are seesawing, threshold and reporting. The threshold gate is associated with a

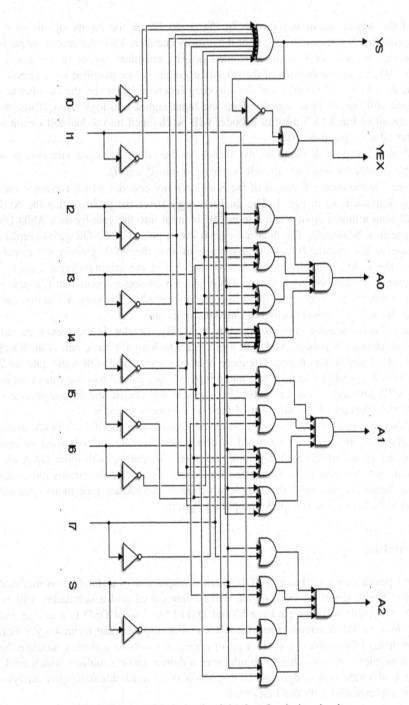

Fig. 1. Digital circuit of the 8 to 3 priority circuit

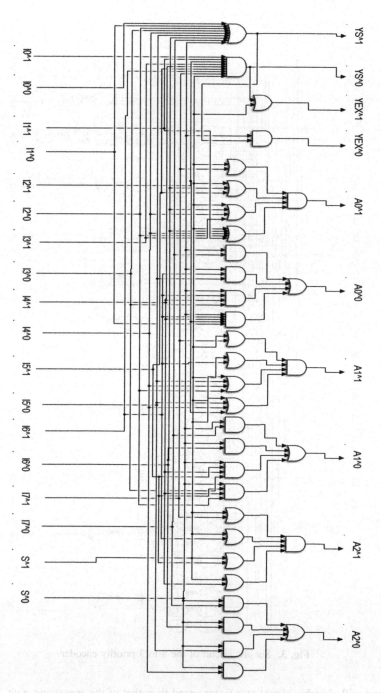

Fig. 2. Dual-rail circuit of the 8 to 3 priority encoder

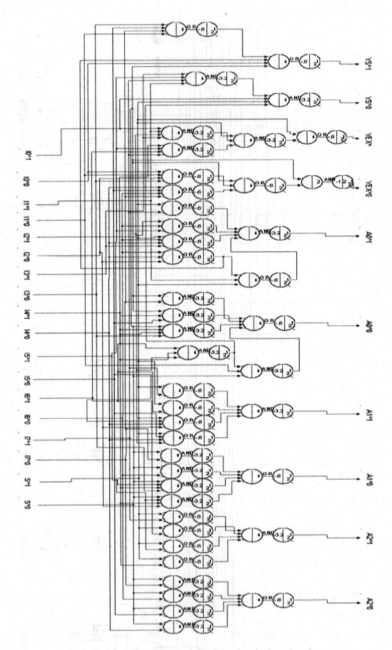

Fig. 3. Seesaw circuit of the 8 to 3 priority encoder

gate and will absorb a signal at a faster speed than that of the seesawing gate. Finally, the signal will react with the reporter strand.

The seesawing gate [14] is presented with a two side node which is connected by one or more wires each other. Each wire is a DNA strand with special sequence which is called signal wire that is either positive or negative. A variety of seesaw gates constitute a complex circuit which could implement complex logic function.

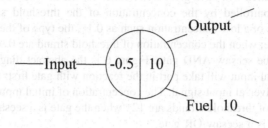

Fig. 4. Abstract diagram of seesaw gate

Figure 4 is the abstract diagram of seesaw gate in which the number indicates the initial concentrations of the inputs. The concentration of threshold gate is negative because that the function of threshold gate is to absorb corresponding signal strands. In Fig. 4, the concentration of input signal is 1*, the concentration of threshold is 0.5*, the concentration of output signal is 10*, the concentration of fuel strand is 10*.

The structure of the input and output signals have a similar structure. They have a universal toehold and different left and right side of the strands. Figure 5 is the structure of the initial input signal of a seesaw gate is a pair of complementary signals which have a universal right side of the strands. The universal right side of the input signal will react with the gate reactant which could exchange a universal input signal that will take part in the next steps of reaction. The right side of the universal input signal and the left side of the output signal have a same structure which makes it could react with a gate: output strand and unbind the output signal. It is the same structure that of the right side of the output signal and the left side of the reporter which makes the reporter reacts with the output signal. The similar structure of the input and output signals insures the presentence of the cascade reaction. The process of a seesaw gate will be introduced in detail in the next section.

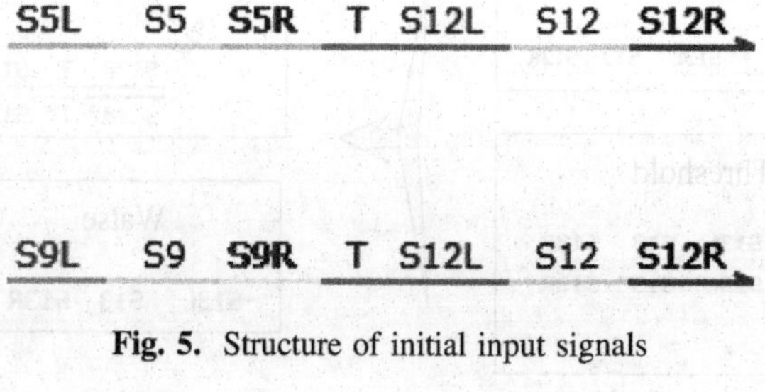

S5L   S5   S5R   T   S12L   S12   S12R

S9L   S9   S9R   T   S12L   S12   S12R

Fig. 5. Structure of initial input signals

3.1   Threshold Reactions

The first step of a seesaw gate reaction is threshold reaction which could generate a universal signal which will have great significance for the next reactions. The type of a seesaw gate is controlled by the concentration of the threshold strand. When the threshold strand is of a low concentration such as 0.1*, the type of the seesaw gate will be seesaw OR gate; when the concentration of threshold strand are 0.9*, the type of the seesaw gate will be seesaw AND gate. Figure 6 is the abstract diagram of threshold reaction. The initial input will take part in the reaction with gate first: fuel strand which will generate a universal input signal. The concentration of initial input signals are 20*, the concentration of threshold strands are 12* when the gate is a seesaw AND gate and 6* when the gate is a seesaw OR gate.

3.2   Fuel Circle

Fuel will be added into solution in order to keep the system run continuously. The universal signal strands which are generated during the process of threshold reactions will react with gate: output strand which will generate output strands and the fuel will react with the input: gate strand which constructs a circle and continuously generates

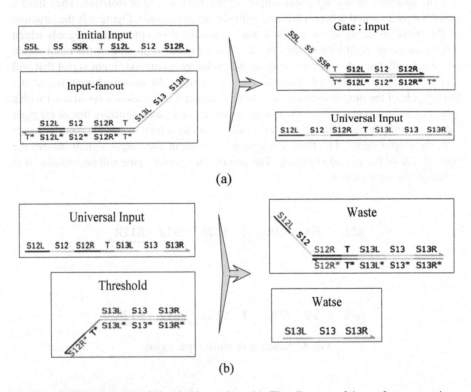

(a)

(b)

Fig. 6. Abstract diagram of threshold reaction. (a) The diagram of input fanout reactions. (b) The diagram of threshold reactions.

initial input signals which makes the system continued. Figure 7 is the abstract diagram of fuel circle. The concentration of the gate: output strand is 10*; the concentration of the universal input is 8* when the gate is a seesaw AND gate; the concentration of the universal input is 14* when the gate is a seesaw OR gate. The universal input first reacts with gate: output signal which will generate gate: input signal and output strand. Because of the lack of universal input, fuel strand will be added into solution to react with gate: input signal which will generate universal input and negative gate: fuel strand. Then, the system could continuously run. The final concentration of output signal will be 10* because that the concentration of gate: output signal is 10*.

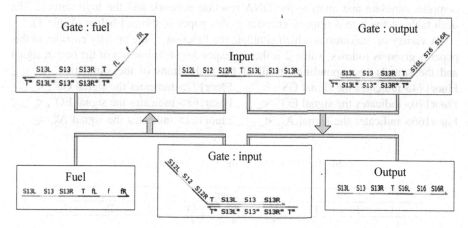

Fig. 7. Abstract diagram of fuel circle

3.3 Fluorescence Reaction

The final step of the seesaw gate is florescence reaction which will generate output signal with florescent label that could report the result of circuit. Figure 8 is the abstract diagram of florescence reaction. The output signal strand which is displaced during the fuel circle will react with florescence and generate a florescent output signal which could report the result of whole circuit. The concentration of output signal is 10*, thus, there will be 10* final florescent output signal.

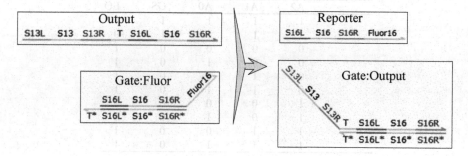

Fig. 8. Abstract diagram of florescence reaction

In this section, a kinetics simulation is made for a 2 inputs 1 output seesaw AND gate by Visual DSD which is a Microsoft package for strand displacement cascade simulation. It will be the basic module of the 8 to 3 priority encoder in this paper. Further simulation will be done in next section.

4   Experimental Result

In this section, a simulation of the 8 to 3 priority encoder which is designed in this paper will be made by a Microsoft programming language Visual DSD which could compile, simulate and analyze the DNA reaction network and the logic circuit. The truth table of the 8 to 3 priority encoder in this paper is showed below (Table 1).

A variety of realizations which simulate the function of the priority encoder in this paper is given as follows. Table 2 is the corresponding relationship of the output signal and the strands corresponding. In all of the realizations of the simulation, <_ _ _ Fluor174> indicates the signal GS^1, <_ _ _ Fluor172> indicates the signal GS^0, <_ _ _ Fluor170> indicates the signal EO^1, <_ _ _ Fluor168> indicates the signal EO^0, <_ _ _ Fluor166> indicates the signal A_2^1, <_ _ _ Fluor164> indicates the signal A_2^0, <_ _ _

Table 1. Truth table of the 8 to 3 priority encoder

Input								
EI	I0	I1	I2	I3	I4	I5	I6	I7
1	*	*	*	*	*	*	*	*
0	1	1	1	1	1	1	1	1
0	*	*	*	*	*	*	*	0
0	*	*	*	*	*	*	0	1
0	*	*	*	*	*	0	1	1
0	*	*	*	*	0	1	1	1
0	*	*	*	0	1	1	1	1
0	*	*	0	1	1	1	1	1
0	*	0	1	1	1	1	1	1
0	0	1	1	1	1	1	1	1

Output				
A2	A1	A0	GS	EO
1	1	1	1	1
1	1	1	1	0
0	0	0	0	1
0	0	1	0	1
0	1	0	0	1
0	1	1	0	1
1	0	0	0	1
1	0	1	0	1
1	1	0	0	1
1	1	1	0	1

Fluor162> indicates the signal A_1^1, <_ _ _ Fluor160> indicates the signal A_1^0, <_ _ _ Fluor158> indicates the signal A_0^1, <_ _ _ Fluor156> indicates the signal A_0^0.

In all realizations, the threshold of 2 input seesaw AND gate is 1.2*, the threshold of 3 input seesaw AND gate is 2.2*, the threshold of 4 input seesaw AND gate is 3.2*; the threshold of all seesaw OR gate are 0.6*. The threshold of fuel is 2*.

Table 2. Output signals and the corresponding strands

Output	Strand	Output	Strand
GS^1	<_ _ _ Fluor174>	A_2^0	<_ _ _ Fluor164>
GS^0	<_ _ _ Fluor172>	A_1^1	<_ _ _ Fluor162>
EO^1	<_ _ _ Fluor170>	A_1^0	<_ _ _ Fluor160>
EO^0	<_ _ _ Fluor168>	A_0^1	<_ _ _ Fluor158>
A_2^1	<_ _ _ Fluor166>	A_0^0	<_ _ _ Fluor156>

Figure 9 is the simulation result which shows the realization when EI = 1. According to the function of the encoder, when the enable input EI = 1 the encoder could not work normally and all the output value will be 1. In Fig. 9, obviously, <_ _ _ Fluor174>, <_ _ _ Fluor170>, <_ _ _ Fluor166>, <_ _ _ Fluor162>, <_ _ _ Fluor158> are all of high level concentration which indicates that all the output signals are logic one.

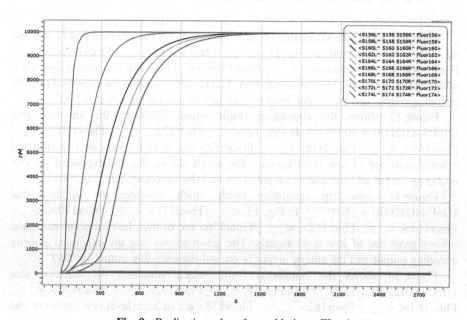

Fig. 9. Realization when the enable input EI = 1

According to the function of 8 to 3 priority encoder, when EI = 0 and all the input are 1, only the enable output EO = 0 and all the output else will be 1 which means that the switch of the encoder is on and there is no code input into it. In Fig. 10, <_ _ _ Fluor174>, <_ _ _ Fluor168>, <_ _ _ Fluor166>, <_ _ _ Fluor162>, <_ _ _ Fluor158> are of high level concentration which means that the switch is on and there is no signal input into it.

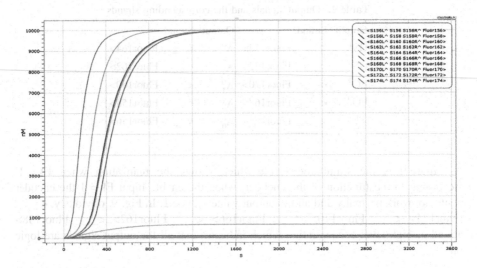

Fig. 10. Realization when the enable input EI = 0 and all the inputs else is 1

Figure 11 shows the simulation result which simulates the situation that I7 = 0 and all other inputs are zero. In Fig. 11, <_ _ _ Fluor172>, <_ _ _ Fluor170>, <_ _ _ Fluor164>, <_ _ _ Fluor160>, <_ _ _ Fluor156> are of high level concentration, when other signals are of low level concentration. The results show that the expended priority encoding output and the enable output is on and the encoding output is "000".

Figure 12 shows the simulation result which simulates the situation that I7I6I5I4I3I2I1I0 = 10******. In Fig. 12, <_ _ _ Fluor172>, <_ _ _ Fluor170>, <_ _ _ Fluor164>, <_ _ _ Fluor160>, <_ _ _ Fluor158> are of high level concentration and other signals are of low level signals. The result shows that the expended priority encoding output and the enable output is on and the encoding output is "001".

Figure 13 shows the simulation result which simulates the situation that I7I6I5I4I3I2I1I0 = 110*****. In Fig. 13, <_ _ _ Fluor172>, <_ _ _ Fluor170>, <_ _ _ Fluor164>, <_ _ _ Fluor162>, <_ _ _ Fluor156> are of high level concentration and other signals are of low level signals. The result shows that the expended priority encoding output and the enable output is on and the encoding output is "010".

Figure 14 shows the simulation result which simulates the situation that I7I6I5I4I3I2I1I0 = 1110****. In Fig. 14, <_ _ _ Fluor172>, <_ _ _ Fluor170>, <_ _ _ Fluor164>, <_ _ _ Fluor162>, <_ _ _ Fluor158> are of high level concentration and

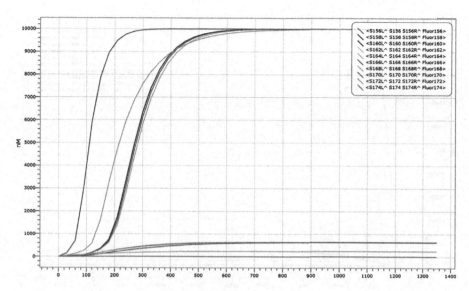

Fig. 11. Realization when I7 = 0

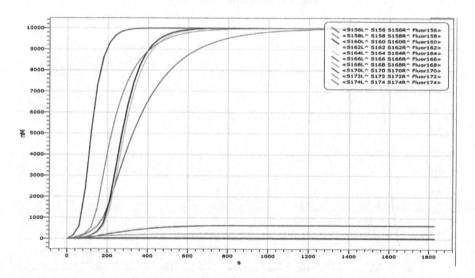

Fig. 12. Realization when I6 = 0

other signals are of low level signals. The result shows that the expended priority encoding output and the enable output is on and the encoding output is "011".

Figure 15 shows the simulation result which simulates the situation that I7I6I5I4I3I2I1I0 = 11110***. In Fig. 15, <_ _ _ Fluor172>, <_ _ _ Fluor170>, <_ _ _ Fluor166>, <_ _ _ Fluor160>, <_ _ _ Fluor156> are of high level concentration and other signals are of low level signals. The result shows that the expended priority encoding output and the enable output is on and the encoding output is "100".

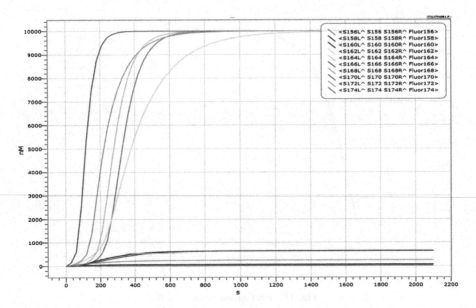

Fig. 13. Realization when I5 = 0

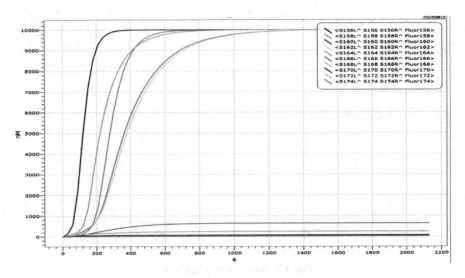

Fig. 14. Realization when I4 = 0

Figure 16 shows the simulation result which simulates the situation that I7I6I5I4I3I2I1I0 = 111110**. In Fig. 16, <_ _ _ Fluor172>, <_ _ _ Fluor170>, <_ _ _ Fluor166>, <_ _ _ Fluor160>, <_ _ _ Fluor156> are of high level concentration and other signals are of low level signals. The result shows that the expended priority encoding output and the enable output is on and the encoding output is "101".

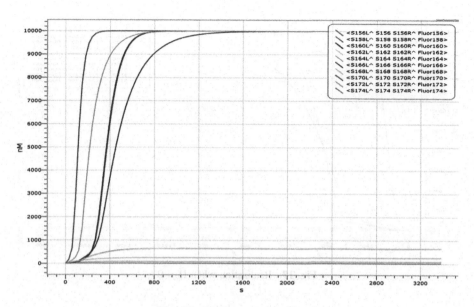

Fig. 15. Realization when I3 = 0

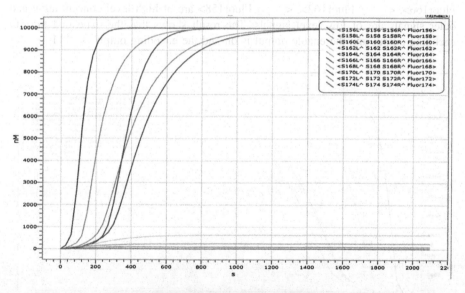

Fig. 16. Realization when I2 = 0

Figure 17 shows the simulation result which simulates the situation that I7I6I5I4I3I2I1I0 = 1111110*. In Fig. 17, <_ _ _ Fluor172>, <_ _ _ Fluor170>, <_ _ _ Fluor166>, <_ _ _ Fluor162>, <_ _ _ Fluor156> are of high level concentration and other signals are of low level signals. The result shows that the expended priority encoding output and the enable output is on and the encoding output is "110".

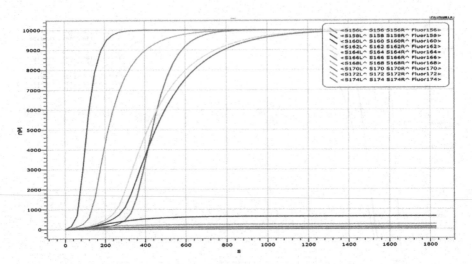

Fig. 17. Realization when I1 = 0

Figure 18 shows the simulation result which simulates the situation that I7I6I5I4I3I2I1I0 = 11111110. In Fig. 18, <_ _ _ Fluor172>, <_ _ _ Fluor170>, <_ _ _ Fluor166>, <_ _ _ Fluor162>, <_ _ _ Fluor158> are of high level concentration and other signals are of low level signals. The result shows that the expended priority encoding output and the enable output is on and the encoding output is "111".

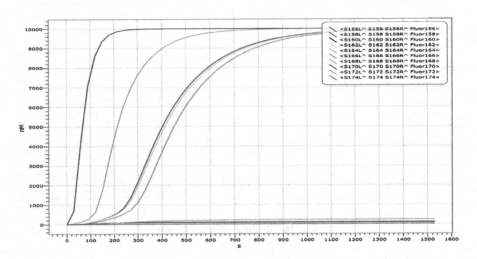

Fig. 18. Realization when I0 = 0

Summarizing the 10 realizations above, the 8 to 3 priority encoder could correctly implement logic function of coding. For instance, in Fig. 15, the input signal is

I7I6I5I4I3I2I1I0 = 11110*** and the output signal is 100 which shows the same result corresponds to the truth table. For other realizations, correct results correspond to the truth table are obtained. All the simulation results show that the method in this paper can correctly implement coding function. Besides, when the input is I7I6I5I4I3I2I1I0 = 1110****, the output is 101. It means when I5 holds the highest priority, the encoder will encode with the input I5, which indicates that the priority encoder in this paper also implements priority coding when multi-inputs is input into it.

5 Conclusion

An 8 to 3 priority encoder which could implement the encoding of 8-bit binary code into 3-bit binary code is proposed in this paper, and a simulation of the encoder was made by the programming language Visual DSD. Results showed the promising prospect of DNA strand displacement technology as a mechanism to construct bio-chemical circuit. The implementation of the priority encoder based on dual-rail logic and seesaw gate motif is of important significance that the encoder is basic and widely used logic unit in computer. However, the dual-rail logic has its disadvantage that it is a larger scale circuit which would reduce the efficiency of circuit. In the future, the design of a much simpler module for constructing large scale logic circuit will be the key point of DNA strand displacement technology.

References

1. Adleman, L.M.: Molecular computation of solutions to combinatorial problems. Science **266** (5187), 1021–1024 (1994)
2. Yan, H., Zhang, X., Shen, Z., Seeman, N.C.: A robust DNA mechanical device controlled by hybridization topology. Nature **415**(6867), 62–65 (2002)
3. Qian, L., Winfree, E.: Scaling up digital circuit computation with DNA strand displacement cascades. Science **332**(6034), 1196 (2011)
4. Wei, G., Zhou, H., Liu, Z., Song, Y., Sun, L.: One-step synthesis of silver nanoparticles, nanorods, and nanowires on the surface of DNA network. J. Phys. Chem. B **109**(18), 8738–8743 (2005)
5. Shi, X., Lu, W., Wang, Z., Pan, L., Cui, G., Xu, J.: Programmable DNA tile self-assembly using a hierarchical sub-tile strategy. Nanotechnology **25**(7), 188–194 (2014)
6. Liu, H., Liu, D.: DNA nanomachines and their functional evolution. Chem. Commun. **19** (35), 2625–2636 (2009)
7. Lu, Y., Liu, J.: Functional DNA nanotechnology: emerging applications of DNAzymes and aptamers. Curr. Opin. Biotechnol. **17**(6), 580–588 (2006)
8. Lipton, R.J.: DNA solution of hard computational problems. Science **268**(5210), 542–545 (1995)
9. Lee, C.S., Davis, R.W., Davidson, N.: A physical study by electron microscopy of the terminally reptitious, circularly permuted DNA from the coliphage particles of Escherichia coli. J. Mol. Biol. **15**(48), 1–22 (1970)
10. Seelig, G., Soloveichik, D., Zhang, D.Y., Wifree, E.: Enzyme-free nucleic acid logic circuits. Science **314**(5805), 1585–1588 (2006)

11. Seelig, G., Soloveichik, D.: Time-complexity of multilayered DNA strand displacement circuits. In: Deaton, R., Suyama, A. (eds.) DNA 2009. LNCS, vol. 5877, pp. 144–153. Springer, Heidelberg (2009). https://doi.org/10.1007/978-3-642-10604-0_15
12. Zhang, D.Y., Winfree, E.: Control of DNA strand displacement kinetics using toehold exchange. J. Am. Chem. Soc. 131(47), 17303–17314 (2009)
13. Qian, L., Winfree, E., Bruck, J.: Neural network computation with DNA strand displacement cascades. Nature 475(7536), 368–372 (2011)
14. Qian, L., Winfree, E.: A simple DNA gate motif for synthesizing large-scale circuits. In: Goel, A., Simmel, Friedrich C., Sosík, P. (eds.) DNA 2008. LNCS, vol. 5347, pp. 70–89. Springer, Heidelberg (2009). https://doi.org/10.1007/978-3-642-03076-5_7
15. Rinaudo, K., Bleris, L., Maddamsetti, R., Subramanian, S., Weiss, R.: A universal RNAi-based logic evaluator that operates in mammalian cells. Nat. Biotechnol. 25(7), 795–801 (2007)
16. Xie, Z., John, L.S., Leonidas, B., Yaakov, B.: Logic integration of mRNA signals by an RNAi-based molecular computer. Nucleic Acids Res. 38(8), 2692–2701 (2010)
17. Turberfield, A.J., Mitchell, J.C., Yurke, B., Mills, A.P., Blakey, M.L.: DNA fuel for free-running nanomachines. Phys. Rev. Lett. 90(11), 118102 (2003)
18. Seelig, G., Bernard, Y., Winfree, E.: Catalyzed relaxation of a metastable DNA fuel. J. Am. Chem. Soc. 128(37), 12211–12220 (2006)
19. Wang, Y., Tian, G., Hou, H., Ye, M., Cui, G.: Simple logic computation based on the DNA strand displacement. J. Comput. Theor. Nanosci. 11(9), 1975–1982 (2014)
20. Lakin, M.R., Youssef, S., Polo, F., Emomott, S., Phillips, A.: Visual DSD: a design and analysis tool for DNA strand displacement systems. Bioinformatics 27(22), 3211–3213 (2011)
21. Song, B., Song, T., Pan, L.: A time-free uniform solution to subset sum problem by tissue P systems with cell division. Math. Struct. Comput. Sci. 27(1), 17–32 (2017)
22. Song, B., Pérez-Jiménez, M.J., Pan, L.: An efficient time-free solution to QSAT problem using P systems with proteins on membranes. Inf. Comput. 256, 287–299 (2017)
23. Song, B., Zhang, C., Pan, L.: Tissue-like P systems with evolutional symport/antiport rules. Inf. Sci. 378, 177–193 (2017)

Multifunctional Biosensor Logic Gates Based on Graphene Oxide

Luhui Wang[1], Yingying Zhang[2], Yani Wei[1], and Yafei Dong[1,2(✉)]

[1] College of Life Sciences, Shannxi Normal University, Xi'an 710119, China
dongyf@snnu.edu.cn
[2] College of Computer Sciences, Shannxi Normal University,
Xi'an 710119, China

Abstract. In this paper, a biological sensing model based on graphene oxide is proposed. A YES gate and a AND gate are constructed by using the ability of graphene oxide to adsorb single strand and quench fluorescence. The biosensor we designed can be used not only as a logical element, but also to detect a specific target DNA. Then, taking YES gate as an example, orthogonal experiments, condition optimization and target selective detection are carried out to demonstrate the practical significance of the sensing model designed. In subsequent experiments, we will design more complex logic components on this basis and try to apply them to practice.

Keywords: Graphene oxide · Biosensor · Logic gate

1 Introduction

1.1 Biosensor

With the further development of science and the in-depth study of various disciplines, we have found some difficult problems can not be solved perfectly only on the single subject. Therefore, the concept of interdisciplinary and the way of research have emerged. As a typical representative of cross disciplines, DNA computing is a new computing technology combining computer science, biology, mathematics, chemistry and other disciplines. Compared with the traditional electronic computer, biological computing has the advantages of high parallel processing speed and high molecular parallelism, which has received extensive attention and rapid development. In recent years [1], DNA computing has become the focus and hotspot of cutting-edge scientific research with its strong information storage capacity and low loss. Today, its research process has only been in the past twenty years, but biocomputing has made some progress in theoretical research and application [2]. Biosensors, as a platform for applying the theory of biological computing to practice, are particularly important in researching and discussing, and researchers have come up with numerous of new insights in this field.

1.2   Graphene

Graphene, as a new type of nano material, has been applied in gas sensors, aerospace and photosensitive elements. The graphene based composite has become a field of graphene applications because of its excellent performance in energy storage, liquid crystal devices, electronic devices, sensing materials and catalyst carriers. At present, the in-depth study of graphene composites is becoming more mature [3], but its application in biosensing has not been widely studied. Graphene has many special properties in biosensor. For example, it can selectively adsorb DNA single strand by π-π accumulation, quench the fluorescence of single strand by fluorescence co energy transfer, protect the DNA by absorbing single strand and avoiding enzyme digestion [4–6], and on the other hand, graphene can be combined with other nanomaterials to have peroxidase activity [3, 7, 8]. By combining the special properties of this kind with the design of biosensors, it is expected to put forward more convenient, quick and convenient biological calculation models based on graphene. On the other hand, the development of such biosensors, in addition to providing new ideas for the development of biological computing, is of great significance to the diagnosis of disease and the construction of drug carrying systems.

1.3   Strand Displacement

Since Watson Crick discovered DNA double helix molecules, DNA strand displacement technology has been applied to many biological studies. Because more complementary bases can make the double stranded structure more stable, we can make more complementary bases strands displacement the strands with less complementary bases and form strand replacement processes. Based on strand replacement and base complementary pairing, multiple DNA strands can form complex structures or complicate complementarity processes [2, 9]. Reasonable design of such structures and processes can provide a variety of convenient, fast and sensitive biosensing platforms.

1.4   Fluorescence Labeling Technique

The fluorescent substance is a kind of material which can be illuminated by laser. It is stimulated by laser stimulation and then retreats and emit light from the low energy level of the ground state to the high energy level of the excited state. Fluorescence labeling technology uses the characteristic of fluorescent substance to play a role. It can connect the fluorescent group through covalent modification to a group to be measured, and transfer out some information to be detected by the change of its fluorescence to achieve the purpose of detection [10, 11]. Compared with other detection methods, fluorescence labeling technology has many advantages [12, 13], including stable structure, high efficiency, high efficiency, and many tools, so it is widely used in the detection of bacteria, virus and living cells in biomedicine.

1.5 Molecular Beacon

Molecular beacon is a fluorescent labeled oligonucleotide strand. There are three parts generally: (1) loop area: 15–30 nucleotides that can be specifically combined with target molecules; (2) Stem regions: generally composed of 5–8 base pairs that can occur reversible dissociation; (3) fluorophores and quenching groups: the two ends of molecular beacons are labeled with fluorophores and quenching groups respectively. When there is no target molecule, the fluorescence of the molecular beacon and the quencher group are very close, and the fluorescence is quenched. After binding to the target molecule, the spatial configuration of the molecular beacon is changed, resulting in fluorescence recovery [14]. Because of its high specificity and sensitivity, molecular beacon technology has been widely used in clinical diagnosis, gene detection, environmental monitoring, living cell imaging, gene chip and biosensors [15].

1.6 Logic Gate

Traditional computer data analysis and processing mainly rely on thousands of logic gate components. Logic gates are the basis for building computers. Traditional logic gates include AND, NAND, OR, NOR, XOR, NXOR, INH, NINH and so on. They can convert the input electronic signals into binary signals and construct threshold and logical conversion to binary signals. The signals above the threshold value are defined as 1, and the signals below threshold values are defined as 0 [16]. Similarly, building a DNA computer first needs to design and build simple molecular logic gates and connect the relationships between these logical gates into a more complex logic loop [17]. Therefore, building molecular logic gates with multiple functions is the most important part of building molecular computers. Nowadays, many scientists also focus on applying some characteristics of the DNA strand to the application of logic gates to environmental monitoring, forensic identification, medical diagnosis, food detection and so on [6, 18–21].It not only satisfies the purpose of constructing various logic gates [22], but also can make up for the loopholes of present detection methods.

2 Experiment

2.1 Materials and Instrument

All DNA were purchased from Sangon Biotechnology Co. Ltd (Shanghai, China) and purified by PAGE and ULTRAPAGE, their sequences are listed in Table 1. All DNA sequence (100 µM) were obtained in ultrapure water as stock solution.

GO was purchased from Nanjing XFNANO Materials Tech Inc (Nanjing, China) and suspended in water via sonication.

Tris, 6*loading buffer and agarose were bought from Xi'an JingBo Bio-Technique Co. ammonium persulfate and stain all were bought from Sigma-Aldrich Co. LLC. 10 * TAE/Mg $^{2+}$ buffer (48.4 g Tris base, 26.75 g Mg(CH$_3$COOH)$_2$, 20 ml 0.5 mol/L EDTA, 1L, pH 8.0) and the 500 mL storage liquor of acrylamide at the concentration of 40% (217 g acrylamide and 8 g N,N'-Methylenebisacrylamide), Stain-All were purchased from AAT Bioquest inc.

In this study, we choose to label substrates with fluorophore TAMRA, and the fluorescent results are obtained using a fluorescent scanning spectrometer for TAMRA at 542 nm excitation and 568 nm emission by EnSpire ELIASA from PerkinElmer USA.

2.2 DNA Sequence

See Table 1.

Table 1. The DNA strand-sequences in the experiment

Single-strand	Strand-sequence
Target	5'-GACATTCATCACGCTCAATCACTACTT-3'
H1	5'-AAGTAGTGATTGAGCGTGATGAATGTC-3'
HH1	5'-AAGTAGTGATTGAGCGTGATGAATGTCACTACTTCAACTCGC ATTCATCACGCTCAATC-3'
HH2	5'-TGATGAATGCGAGTTGAAGTAGTGACATTCATCACGCTCAAT CACTACTTCAACTCGCA-3'

3 Principle

In this paper, we have designed two complementary double strands, in which the strand to be detected is named Target, and its complementary single strand is named H1, with TAMRA fluorescent group is marked at its 5' end. As graphene oxide (GO) can adsorb single strand and quenching fluorescence, in the absence of Target, GO adsorbs single strand H1, and the fluorescence of H1 is quenched by fluorescence co energy transfer, the fluorescence of H1 is low and the output is 0. In the presence of Target, Target and H1 are combined to form double helix structure, the fluorescence of H1 far away from graphene oxide surface, and the system has strong fluorescence and the output is 1. This sensor can be used to detect specific DNA sequences, and it is also a simple YES logic gate. The reaction principle is shown in Fig. 1A, and the true value table is shown in Fig. 1B.

On this basis, we design a stem ring structure HH1 and the other stem ring structure HH2 with TAMRA fluorescent group at its 5' end, taking HH1 and Target as the two inputs. In the presence of Target and HH1, Target can open the stem part of HH1, and the part of the stem that the HH1 is opened can open the stem part of HH2, thus HH1 and HH2 form a double stranded structure, then releasing the Target and keep it circulating. At this time, the double strand is far away from the GO, the fluorescence intensity of the system is high and the output is 1. When there is only one input or no input, the structure of the stem ring of HH2 can not be opened, and the part of the HH2 ring is adsorbed by GO, the fluorescent group is close to GO and the fluorescence quenching is quenched, thus the fluorescence value of the system is low and the output is 0. The reaction principle is shown in Fig. 2A, and the true value table is shown in Fig. 2B.

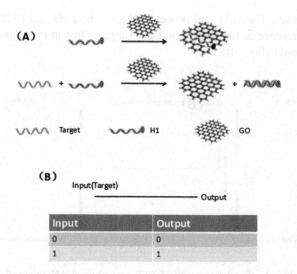

Fig. 1. YES logic gate schematic diagram (A). The true value table (B).

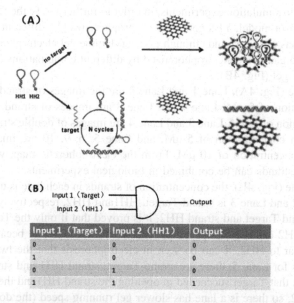

Fig. 2. AND logic gate schematic diagram (A). The true value table (B).

4 Results and Discussion

4.1 Feasibility Analysis

We carry out NUPACK simulation on the designed strand, preliminary verify its binding ability. As you can see from the Fig. 3, in the YES gate, H1 and Target can be perfectly combined (Fig. 3A), and in the AND gate, the HH1 and HH2 form a double strand in the presence of two inputs, and the Target is free in the solution, as same as the expected result (Fig. 3B).

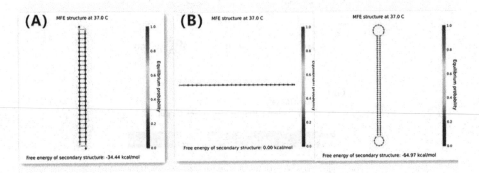

Fig. 3. Simulation result of YES gate (A) and AND gate (B)

In addition to simulation experiments, in order to further verify the feasibility of the designed biosensor model, YES gate were electrophoretized by different concentrations and combinations of two strands though polyacrylamide gel electrophoresis (Fig. 4A). Similarly, AND gate were electrophoretized by different combinations of three strands though agarose gel (Fig. 4B).

In YES gate (Fig. 4A), Lane 1 and Lane 2 are the images of strand H1and Target with concentration of 5 μM, Lane 7 and Lane 8 are images of strand H1 and Target with concentration of 1 μM. Lane 3 and Lane 4 are images of double strands formed by H1 and T with concentration of 5 μM, and Lane 5, 6, 9, 10 are images of double strands with concentration of 10 μM. From the electrophoretic map, we demonstrate that H1 and T strands can be combined in biological experiments.

In AND gate (Fig. 4B), the concentration of strands in each lane is uniform 10 μM. Lane 1, Lane 2 and Lane 3 is strand Target, HH1and HH2, respectively. Lane 4 is the mixture of strand Target and strand HH2, it is proved that if only the Target exists, the stem part of HH2 can not be opened to form double strands, but because the lane of Target is similar to HH2, it can be seen in electrophoresis that the two strands were overlapped. As for Lane 5, there are strand Target, strand HH1 and strand HH2 here, and we can see that Target succeeded in opening the strand HH1and then HH1 opened the strand HH2, so there is a lane has slower gel running speed (the double strands of HH1and HH2) because of its bigger molecular weight. And because the strand Target can be recycled, free in the solution, it has another lane with a smaller molecular weight and faster gel running speed. Lane 6 is the mixture of strand HH1 and strand HH2, from the graph, we can see that the strands HH1 and HH2 will open partially without Target, but the amount of double strands is less than the presence of Target, therefore, in subsequent experiments, we need to improve the experimental method or set the appropriate threshold.

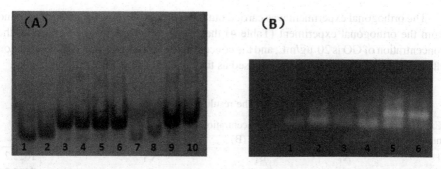

Fig. 4. Polyacrylamide gel electrophoresis of YES gate (A) and agarose electrophoresis of AND gate (B)

4.2   Orthonormal Preliminary Optimization

The optimization in this paper is taken as an example of YES gate.

In the initial stage of the experiment, we designed three factors and three levels of orthogonal experiments, preliminarily verified the feasibility of the experiment and obtained the general optimization conditions. The table of factors is as follows in Tables 2 and 3.

Table 2. Level of factor

Factor	Reaction time (A)	Concentration of GO (B)	Concentration of target (C)
1	60 min	20 µg/ml	50 nM
2	90 min	40 µg/ml	100 nM
3	120 min	60 µg/ml	150 nM

Table 3. Test orthogonal table

Experiment number	Reaction time (A)	Concentration of GO (B)	Concentration of target (C)
1	A_1	B_1	C_1
2	A_1	B_2	C_3
3	A_1	B_3	C_2
4	A_2	B_1	C_3
5	A_2	B_2	C_2
6	A_2	B_3	C_1
7	A_3	B_1	C_2
8	A_3	B_2	C_1
9	A_3	B_3	C_3

The orthogonal experiment was carried out three times to reduce the error. It is found from the orthogonal experiment (Table 4) that when the reaction time is 60 min, the concentration of GO is 20 µg/mL, and the concentration of Target is 150 nM, the reaction effect is best, so these conditions are used as the constant of the further optimization.

Table 4. The result of orthogonal

Experiment number	Reaction time (A)	Concentration of GO (B)	Concentration of target (C)	ΔF
1	A_1	B_1	C_1	1622.2
2	A_1	B_2	C_3	7494.2
3	A_1	B_3	C_2	3773.2
4	A_2	B_1	C_3	4461.2
5	A_2	B_2	C_2	3540
6	A_2	B_3	C_1	2033.2
7	A_3	B_1	C_2	3407
8	A_3	B_2	C_1	2010
9	A_3	B_3	C_3	6340.2
K_1	12889.6	9490.4	5665.4	
K_2	10034.4	13044.2	10720.2	
K_3	11757.2	12146.6	18295.6	
k_1	4296.5	3163.5	1888.5	
k_2	3344.8	4348.1	3573.4	
k_3	3919.1	4048.9	6098.5	
R	574.3	1184.6	4210.1	

4.3   Condition Optimization

Optimization of the concentration of GO, it is found that when the concentration of GO is too low, the fluorescence of single strand H1 can not be quenched well and the background fluorescence is too large. When H1 and Target form a double strand, the value of the fluorescence recovery is not obvious. When the concentration of GO is too high, the fluorescence of the double strand of H1 and Target will also be quenched. Therefore, the optimum concentration of GO is 30 µg/mL (Fig. 5A), and the fluorescence intensity is the largest.

The reaction temperature is optimized. It is found that the experimental results are best when the experimental temperature is 35 °C (Fig. 5B), but the change of fluorescence intensity is also stable at other temperatures, which proves that the sensor is not affected by the temperature change, but it can play a better role at 35 °C.

The reaction time is optimized. It is found that when the reaction time is 60 min (Fig. 5C), the effect is the best. The double strand can not be well formed when the reaction time is too short, and the time of reaction too long will result in the decay of the fluorescence value.

The H1 concentration was optimized and the optimum concentration of H1 was 125 nM (Fig. 5D). When the concentration of H1 is too small, the initial fluorescence value is low, the change of fluorescence is small, the experimental results are not obvious, while the high concentration of H1 can not be well combined with Target, and the chance of contact with GO increases, which leads to the decrease of fluorescence.

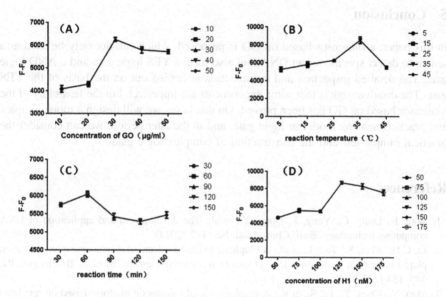

Fig. 5. Condition optimization. Optimization of the concentration of GO (A). Optimization of reaction temperature (B). Optimization of reaction time (C). Optimization of the concentration of H1

In the experiment of target concentration selectivity, it can be seen that when the target concentration is 0 to 250 nM, the target concentration has a good linear relationship with the change of fluorescence (Fig. 6). It can predict that the sensor has a good linear relationship in a larger range, and the minimum concentration of 10 nM

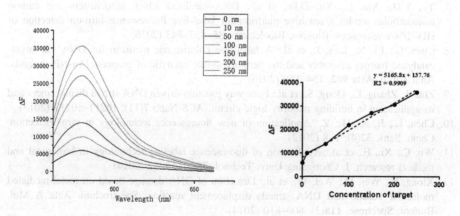

Fig. 6. Concentration selectivity for different targets and the linear relationship between target concentration and fluorescence intensity

used in this experiment is not the test limit of the experiment, and the follow-up will continue to be carried out the verification.

5 Conclusion

In this paper, a biosensor based on GO is proposed, which can not only be used as a sensor to detect specific target DNA, but also form a YES logic gate and a AND logic gate. The detailed inspection and optimization is carried out on the basis of the YES gate. The disadvantage is that some experiments are imperfect, but the feasibility of the biosensor based on GO has been proved. On this basis, we will design a more complex and practical sensing model or logic gate, and in the later period, we can consider the practical sample test and the construction of complex logic gates.

References

1. Wan, F., Dong, C., Yang, J., Dong, Y., et al.: The development and application of DNA computing technology. Bull. Chin. Acad. Sci. 1–7 (2014)
2. Li, C.H., Xiao, X., Tao, J., et al.: A graphene oxide-based strand displacement amplification platform for ricin detection using aptamer as recognition element. Biosens. Bioelectron. **91**, 149–154 (2017)
3. Mao, Y., Chen, Y., Li, S., et al.: A graphene-based biosensing platform based on regulated release of an aptameric DNA biosensor. Sensors **15**(11), 28244–28256 (2015)
4. Wang, L., Tian, J., Huang, Y., et al.: Homogenous fluorescence polarization assay for the DNA of HIV A T7 by exploiting exonuclease-assisted quadratic recycling amplification and the strong interaction between graphene oxide and ssDNA. Microchim. Acta **183**(7), 2147–2153 (2016)
5. Luo, F., Xi, Q., Jiang, J.H., et al.: Graphene oxide based DNA nanoswitches as a programmable pH-responsive biosensor. Anal. Methods **8**(38), 6982–6985 (2016)
6. Zhou, C., Liu, D., Wu, C., et al.: Integration of DNA and graphene oxide for the construction of various advanced logic circuits. Nanoscale **8**(40), 17524–17531 (2016)
7. Ye, Y.D., Xia, L., Xu, D.D., et al.: DNA-stabilized silver nanoclusters and carbon nanoparticles oxide: a sensitive platform for label-free fluorescence turn-on detection of HIV-DNA sequences. Biosens. Bioelectron. **85**, 837–843 (2016)
8. Chen, C., Li, N., Lan, J., et al.: A label-free colorimetric platform for DNA via target-catalyzed hairpin assembly and the peroxidase-like catalytic of graphene/Au-NPs hybrids. Anal. Chim. Acta **902**, 154–159 (2016)
9. Zhu, J., Zhang, L., Dong, S., et al.: Four-way junction-driven DNA strand displacement and its application in building majority logic circuit. ACS Nano **7**(11), 10211–10217 (2013)
10. Chen, L., Ji, X., He, Z.: Application of new fluorescence technology in virus detection. Chem. Sens. **32**(4), 1–8 (2012)
11. Wu, C., Xu, F., et al.: Application of fluorescence labeling technology in biological and medical research. J. Chongqing Univ. Technol. **28**(5), 55–62 (2014)
12. Xiong, Y., Wei, M., Wei, W., et al.: Detection of DNA damage based on metal-mediated molecular beacon and DNA strands displacement reaction. Spectrochim. Acta A Mol. Biomol. Spectrosc. **118**(2), 806–810 (2014)

13. Zhang, L., Bluhm, A.M., Chen, K.J., et al.: Performance of nano-assembly logic gates with a DNA multi-hairpin motif. Nanoscale **9**(4), 1709–1720 (2017)
14. Li, X., Guo, J., Zhai, Q., et al.: Ultrasensitive electrochemical biosensor for specific detection of DNA based on molecular beacon mediated circular strand displacement polymerization and hyperbranched rolling circle amplification. Anal. Chim. Acta **934**, 52–58 (2016)
15. Adinolfi, B., Pellegrino, M., Giannetti, A., et al.: Molecular beacon-decorated polymethyl-methacrylate core-shell fluorescent nanoparticles for the detection of survivin mRNA in human cancer cells. Biosens. Bioelectron. **88**, 15–24 (2016)
16. Desilva, A.P., Mcclenaghan, N.D.: Molecular-scale logic gates. Cheminform **10**(3), 574–586 (2004)
17. Reif, J.H.: Successes and challenges. Science **296**(5567), 478–479 (2002)
18. Patel, P.D.: (Bio) sensors for measurement of analytes implicated in food safety: a review. Trends Anal. Chem. **21**(2), 96–115 (2002)
19. Bagni, G., Osella, D., Sturchio, E., et al.: Deoxyribonucleic acid (DNA) biosensors for environmental risk assessment and drug studies. Anal. Chim. Acta **573–574**(1), 81 (2006)
20. Wang, J.: Electrochemical biosensors: towards point-of-care cancer diagnostics. Biosens. Bioelectron. **21**(10), 1887–1892 (2006)
21. Bond, J.W.: Value of DNA evidence in detecting crime. J. Forensic Sci. **52**(1), 128–136 (2007)
22. Cheng, N., Zhu, P., Xu, Y., et al.: High-sensitivity assay for Hg (II) and Ag (I) ion detection: a new class of droplet digital PCR logic gates for an intelligent DNA calculator. Biosens. Bioelectron. **84**, 1–6 (2016)

Medium and Long-Term Forecasting Method of China's Power Load Based on SaDE-SVM Algorithm

Yuansheng Huang, Lijun Zhang, Mengshu Shi[✉], Shijian Liu, and Siyuan Xu

North China Electric Power University, Baoding 071003, China
1083861219@qq.com

Abstract. Medium and long-term power load forecasting is the basis for power system planning and construction. This paper builds a prediction model based on SaDE-SVM algorithm. In order to reduce its selection problem of excessive large-scale hyperplane parameters, improve global optimization ability of traditional SVM, and further improve the prediction accuracy of SVM, the SaDE-SVM optimization algorithm is proposed. This algorithm optimizes the training process of traditional SVM based on adaptive differential evolution algorithm. The results of the medium and long-term forecasting for China's power load show that the improved SaDE-SVM algorithm has good adaptability, robustness, fast convergence rate, and high accuracy for multi-influencing factors prediction model with less data volume, and is applicable to relevant medium and long-term forecasts.

Keywords: SaDE-SVM algorithm
Medium and long-term power load forecasting · Econometrics

1 Introduction

Medium and long-term power load forecasting plays an important role in power planning and construction, saving investment, ensuring social economy operations, and improving the operating efficiency of power enterprises. Therefore, the establishment of scientific forecasting methods has always been concerned by people. At present, medium and long-term load forecasting methods are roughly divided into three categories: traditional forecasting models, Single intelligent algorithm forecasting models, and combined predictive optimization models [16, 19, 21, 22]. Traditional forecasting models include econometric models [6–10], trend extrapolation, regression analysis, time series prediction [14], and grey prediction [11, 12].

The prediction methods based on machine learning include artificial neural networks [13, 15], support vector machines [17, 18], wavelet analysis, genetic algorithms [22], etc. Geem established a multiple linear regression model and BPNN model to predict South Korea's transportation energy load. The prediction results prove that the prediction error of BPNN model is lower than that of multiple linear regression model [1].

The predictive optimization model mainly uses intelligent algorithms for parameter optimization or algorithm architecture optimization of traditional and deep learning

© Springer Nature Singapore Pte Ltd. 2018
J. Qiao et al. (Eds.): BIC-TA 2018, CCIS 951, pp. 484–495, 2018.
https://doi.org/10.1007/978-981-13-2826-8_42

algorithms, based on which a new combined forecasting model is established. Xia, Wang and McMenemy used artificial neural networks for VI design of short-, medium-, and long-term load forecasting. The results show that the prediction model RBFNN has high accuracy and stability [3]. Ekonomou used artificial neural networks to predict energy consumption in Greece and tested several possible architectures through building a multilayer perceptron model (MLP) to select one with the best generalization capability [4]. De Felice, Alessandri and Catalano conducted a correlation analysis on the effect of the seasonal climate factor, air temperature, on power load, and established linear and nonlinear models to predict medium-term electricity demand in Italy [5].

The traditional forecasting model has higher requirements on the sample size, and is insensitive to the uncertainty factors and the abnormal data. Therefore, the forecasting accuracy is low when encountering small sample data. Among some existing single intelligent algorithm prediction models, although grey system prediction, neural network, SVM, etc. can perform small sample forecasting, the parameters of grey system prediction have a great influence on the prediction error, and it is not applicable to the forecasting of internal mechanisms; The scope of application of neural network is limited, it is difficult to accurately analyze various performance indicators, its training time is long, and it is easy to fall into local extremum; And for SVM, when the training set is large, there will be problems as slow training speed, complicated algorithm, and low efficiency occur.

This paper aims at medium and long-term power load forecasting, and uses the econometric model to select per capita GDP, population, energy supply structure, and technological advances in the whole society as influencing factors to predict. In terms of prediction methods, aiming at the problem of traditional SVM for slow training of large-scale data, and further improving its global optimization ability and prediction accuracy, an adaptive differential evolution algorithm is introduced.

2   Algorithm Overview

2.1   SVM

The basic idea of the Support Vector Machine is based on Mercer's theorem, transforms the input space into a high-dimensional feature space through appropriate nonlinear transformation, now that finding Linear regression optimal hyperplane equals to solving convex programming problems, through which we seek the global optimal solution. On the basis of the Structural Risk Minimization (SRM) principle, Support Vector Machine (SVM) is a small sample statistical learning theory based on the principle of Vapnik-Chervonenkis (VC) dimension.

Let the sample set be $\left\{ (x_1, y_1), (x_2, y_2), \ldots, \{(x_l, y_l)\} \in (x \times y)^l, x_i \in x \subset R^n \right\}$ as input vector, $y_i \in y \subset R$ as output. The input variables in this paper are the influencing factors mentioned below, and the output variables are the per capita electrical load.

When the sample set satisfies the linear relationship, the problem boils down to the following optimization problem:

$$\min \frac{1}{2}\|\omega\|^2 + C\sum_{i}^{l}(\zeta_i + \zeta_i^*)$$

$$s.t. (\omega \cdot x_i) + b - y_i \le \zeta_i^* + \varepsilon, i = 1, 2, \ldots, l \tag{1}$$
$$y - (\omega \cdot x_i) - b \le \zeta_i + \varepsilon, i = 1, 2, \ldots, l$$
$$\zeta_i, \zeta_i^* \ge 0, i = 1, 2, \ldots, l$$

When the data set cannot achieve linear regression, the original data set is passed through a nonlinear mapping $\varphi(x)$, inferred to the high-dimensional feature space and achieve linear regression in high-dimensional feature space. The inner product operation on the high-dimensional feature space can be defined as a core function: $k(x_i, x_j) = \varphi(x_i) \cdot \varphi(x_j)$.

Now we only need to perform the core function operation on the original low-dimensional space, the constraint expression is as follows:

$$\min \frac{1}{2}\sum_{i,j=1}^{l}(a_i^* - a_i)(a_j^* - a_j)K(x_i, x_j) + \varepsilon \sum_{i=1}^{l}(a_i^* + a_i) - \sum_{i=1}^{l}y_i(a_i^* - a_i)$$

$$s.t. \sum_{i}^{l}(a_i - a_i^*) = 0 \tag{2}$$
$$0 \le a_i \le C; 0 \le a_i^* \le C$$

We now get the optimal solution: $\bar{a} = (\bar{a}_1, \bar{a}_1^*, \ldots, \bar{a}_l, \bar{a}_l^*)^T$

Calculated

$$\bar{b} = y_j - \sum_{i=1}^{l}(\bar{a}_i^* - \bar{a}_i)^* K(x_i, x_j) + \varepsilon \tag{3}$$

The regression decision function is:

$$f(x) = \sum_{i=1}^{l}(\bar{a}_i^* - \bar{a}_i)K(x_i \cdot x) + \bar{b} \tag{4}$$

2.2 Adaptive Differential Evolution Algorithm

Differential Evolution algorithm (DE) is an efficient global optimization algorithm. In the optimization process of the DE algorithm, firstly, it selects two individuals from the parent individuals to perform vector difference to generate differential vectors. Secondly, it selects another individual and a differential vector to generate an experimental individual. Thirdly, it conducts cross-operations for the parent individuals and their corresponding experimental individuals to generate new offspring individuals. Finally, a selection operation is performed between the parent and offspring individuals, and the eligible individuals are saved to the next generation. The standard DE algorithm includes 4 steps, the details of each step are as follows:

(1) Initialization
In this article, *DE* algorithm adopts real number coding method. In this step, we first initialize the parameters including population size N, gene dimension D, variation factor (also known as scaling factor) F, crossover rate CR, as well as range of values for each gene $[U_{min}, U_{max}]$. We then randomly initialize the population as shown in formula (5):

$$x_{ij} = U_{min} + rand \times (U_{max} - U_{min})$$ (5)

In formula (5), $i = 1, 2, \ldots, N$, $j = 1, 2, \ldots, D$, *rand* is a random number that is uniformly distributed.

(2) Mutation
For each target vector x_i^G, $i = 1, 2, \ldots, N$, the standard DE algorithm will generate a corresponding variation vector according to formula (6):

$$v_i^{G+1} = x_{r_1}^G + F \times (x_{r_2}^G - x_{r_3}^G)$$ (6)

In formula (6), individual serial number r_1, r_2 and r_3 is randomly selected and is different from each other, and from the number of the target individual i, so the population size $N \geq 4$.

(3) Crossover
Through formula (7), the crossover operation generates an experimental individual:

$$u_{ij}^{G+1} = \begin{cases} v_{ij}^{G+1}, & if : r(j) \leq CR; or, j = rn(i) \\ x_{ij}^G, & else \end{cases}$$ (7)

In formula (7), $r(j)$ is a random number that obeys $[0, 1]$ even distribution, j indicates the number of the gene is j, the range of crossover rate CR is $[0, 1]$, which is usually set by the user. $rn(i) \in [1, 2, \ldots, D]$ is the index of randomly selected gene dimensions, its function is ensuring that at least one dimensional variable of the experimental individual is obtained from the mutant individual. We can learn from formula (7) that, smaller CR gets, better the global search operates.

(4) Selection
DE adopts so called "greedy" search strategy. It competes each target individual x_i^G with its corresponding individual u_i^{G+1}, compares the adaptability value, only when the adaptability value of the experimental individual u_i^{G+1} is better than the target individual x_i^G, u_i^{G+1} can be chosen as offspring individual. Otherwise, x_i^G will be chosen as offspring individual. Take the minimization optimization as an example, the selection operation is as shown in formula (8), $f(.)$ is an adaptability function, like cost function and error prediction function.

$$x_i^{G+1} = \begin{cases} u_i^{G+1}, & if : f(u_i^{G+1}) < f(x_i^G) \\ x_i^G, & else \end{cases}$$ (8)

For the differential evolution algorithm, there are shortcomings such as precocious convergence and massive deviation form ideal optimal value. As a result, a stochastic adaptive differential evolution algorithm is proposed. The algorithm uses a mutation operation based on a random selection strategy followed by a small probability disturbance, the mutation factor and the crossover probability are adaptively manipulated to meet the requirements of the different stages of the algorithm. Adaptive differential evolution algorithms include ADE and SaDE. The ADE algorithm only uses adaptive mutation factors. The SaDE algorithm introduces adaptive crossover factors on the basis of ADE.

(1) Adaptive Mutation Factor

Mutation factor F determines the scale of the differential vector. Larger the F gets, lower the search efficiency of DE algorithm and poorer global search result are induced. But if F gets too small, population diversity is reduced and DE algorithm produces premature results. So, in this article, we introduce adaptive mutation factor as shown in formula (9). The characteristic of this adaptive mutation factor is that the initial variation factor of the algorithm is large, which ensures the diversity of the population, with the increase of the number of iterations, F becomes smaller, and a smaller variation factor at the later stage of the algorithm can retain better individuals.

$$F = F_{\min} + (F_{\max} - F_{\min}) \times e^{1 - \frac{GenM}{GenM - G + 1}} \tag{9}$$

In this formula, $F_{\min}$ is the minimum variation factor, $F_{\max}$ is the maximum variation factor, $GenM$ is the maximum number of iterations, G is the current number of iterations.

(2) Adaptive Crossover Factor

With the increase of the number of iterations, the crossover rate of the crossover factor also changes dynamically. The initial large crossover factor ensures the global scope of the variation, and the later smaller crossover rate pays more attention to the local convergence. The design of the adaptive crossover factor is shown in formula (10):

$$CR = CR_{\max} - \frac{G(CR_{\max} - CR_{\min})}{GenM} \tag{10}$$

In this formula, $CR_{\min}$ is the minimum value of cross parameter, $CR_{\max}$ is the Maximum value of cross parameter.

2.3   SaDE-SVM Algorithm

The SaDE-SVM algorithm is structured as follows: Adaptive SaDE algorithm is used to globally pre-optimize the penalty parameter c of the SVM and the parameter g of the core function. The optimal penalty parameter c and the parameter g of the core function are assigned to the SVM as the initial c and g, then the SVM training is conducted. In the adaptive DE algorithm, each iteration gets the optimal values of c and g and the output value of the SVM under this parameter $\hat{y}_t, t = (1, 2, \ldots, k)$, k is the number of neural network output samples, The Mean Squared-sum Error (MSE) of the target output value and the actual output value is used as the adaptability function of the population. So, the adaptability of individual $i(i = 1, 2, 3, \ldots, N)$ is shown as formula (11):

$$f_i = \frac{\sum_{t=1}^{k} (\hat{y}_t - y_t)^2}{k} \tag{11}$$

Among which, y_t is the target output of SVM. The process of the SaDE-SVM algorithm is shown in Fig. 1.

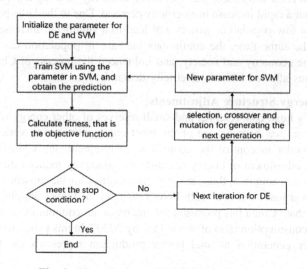

Fig. 1. Flow diagram of SaDE-SVM algorithm

3 Research on Influencing Factors of Medium and Long-Term Power Load of China

3.1 Influencing Factors Selection

(See Table 1).

Table 1. Variable symbols and explanations

Symbol	Explanation	Unit
EC	Per capita electricity consumption	kwh/person
GDP	GDP	Yuan/ person
PP	Population	Ten thousand people
ES	Energy structure	–
STP	Science and technology progress	Pieces

490   Y. Huang et al.

GDP Per Capita
GDP is the sum of all final products and services produced in the economy of a country or region in a given period of time. As a basic industry for social and economic development, the power industry is also driven by the economy while promoting economic development. When GDP growth slows down, the growth trend of electricity consumption in the region will slow down; when GDP grows rapidly, the electricity consumption in the region will increase sharply, that is, there is a stable and significant positive relationship between GDP and electricity consumption.

Population
The population is the most basic factor of social economy. The rapid population growth will bring about a rapid increase in electricity demand. Due to the large population base in China, even low population growth will lead to a significant increase in electricity demand. At the same time, the continuous increase in population has exerted great pressure on the economy and society, and influenced the process of China's modernization and thus affected China's electricity demand.

Electrical Energy Structure Adjustments
Due to China's huge coal reserves and small reserves of other energy sources such as oil and gas, coal has become one of the most energy-consuming varieties in China. However, in order to control the ecological environment, the Chinese government reinforced the adjustment of energy structure and gradually reduced the proportion of coal in energy consumption, thus creating opportunities for the growth of medium and long-term power load. China's "13th Five-Year Plan for Power Supply" (2016–2020) clearly states that "China has promised the international community to achieve a non-fossil energy consumption ratio of about 15% by 2020". In this paper, the proportion of thermal power generation to total power production represents the power energy structure.

$$\text{Energy structure} = \frac{\text{Electricity consumption}}{\text{Total energy consumption}} \times 100\% \qquad (12)$$

Technology Drivers
The scientific and technological progress of the whole society, on the one hand, has an obvious effect on improving the efficiency of electricity consumption in the whole society; on the other hand, with the advancement of science and technology, China's competitiveness in the international arena will gradually increase, so as to continue to explore the international market, promote the growth of economic aggregates, and drive the growth of power load. It can be seen from the data analysis in recent years that technological advancement still has a driving effect on the power load.

3.2 Cointegration Test of Variables

The research object of cointegration theory is to find an equilibrium relationship in two or more non-stationary time series, which is mainly applied to the economic system where the short-term dynamic relationship is susceptible to random disturbance, and the long-term relationship is subject to economic equilibrium.

As shown in Table 2, "None" denotes the null hypothesis that there is no cointegration relationship, the trace statistic of this hypothesized is 139.9497, but the critical value of 0.05 is 60.06141. That is, the trace statistic is larger than the critical value. Therefore, the result does not support the null hypothesis, indicating there is at least one cointegration relationship. Then, "At most 1*" represents the null hypothesis that there is at most one cointegration relationship, the trace statistic of this hypothesized is 80.78266, but the critical value of 0.05 is 40.17493. Therefore this finding does not support the null hypothesis, revealing there is at least one cointegration relationship. Similarly, it can be seen that there are four cointegration relationships. Max-eigenvalue test and trace test results are consistent. The result suggests that Per capita electricity consumption and its four influencing factors respectively maintain long-term equilibrium relationships.

Table 2. Johansen Cointegration Test

Hypothesized no. of CE(s)	Eigenvalue	Trace statistic	0.05 Critical value	Prob.**
None*	0.975226	139.9497	60.06141	0.0000
At most 1*	0.888939	80.78266	40.17493	0.0000
At most 2	0.805613	45.61991	24.27596	0.0000
At most 3	0.676749	19.41341	12.32090	0.0028
At most 4	0.080581	1.344210	4.129906	0.2880
Trace test indicates 4 cointegration at the 0.05 level				
None*	0.975226	59.16706	30.43961	0.0000
At most 1*	0.888939	35.16276	24.15921	0.0011
At most 2	0.805613	26.20650	17.79730	0.0022
At most 3	0.676749	18.06920	11.22480	0.0027
At most 4	0.080581	1.344210	4.129906	0.2880
Max-eigenvalue test indicates 4 cointegration at the 0.05 level				

4 China Power Load Forecasting Model Based on SaDE-SVM Algorithm

This paper selects the per capita electricity consumption of China from 2000 to 2017 for training prediction, and introduces the influencing factors mentioned above, including data of 2000–2013 for training set data and those of 2014–2017 for predicted value data.

4.1 Traditional Forecasting Model

Using multiple linear regression, the variables are linearly fitted. By establishing multiple linear regression, the following model is obtained (Fig. 2).

$$EC = 0.0956 \times PP + 0.1148 \times GDP - 2372 * ES - 0.00005212 \times STP - 11710 \quad (13)$$

4.2 Single Intelligent Algorithm Forecasting Model

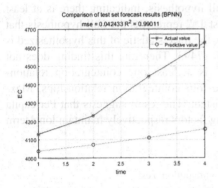

Fig. 2. Comparison chart of BPNN forecasting results

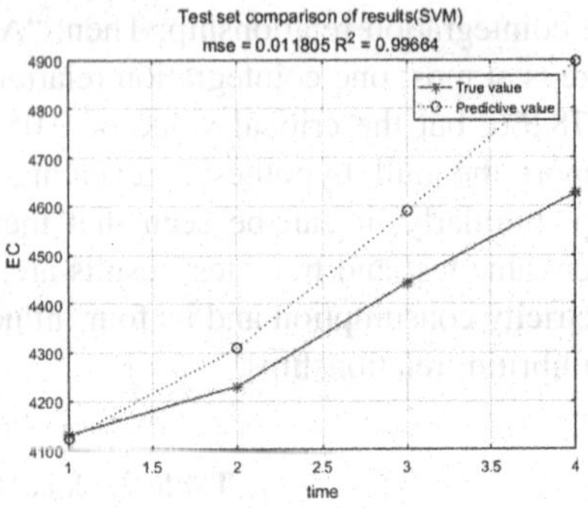

Fig. 3. SVM forecasting results

The Fig. 3. shows the error between the predicted and true values of BP neural network. As is shown in Fig. 3 after training, the optimal parameters of the SVM are obtained. C is 0.2500, and g is 0.00097656.

4.3 Based on SaDE-SVM Algorithm Model

As is shown in Fig. 4, after training, the optimal parameters of SVM based on SaDE are obtained. C is 5.5913, g is 56.1356.

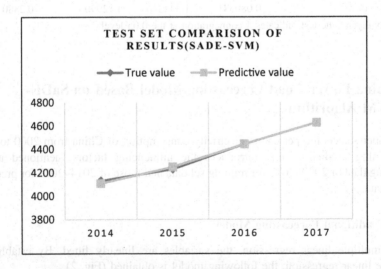

Fig. 4. Comparison chart of SaDE-SVM forecasting results

4.4   Comparative Analysis

As can be seen from the Table 3, among the four methods, BPNN has the largest error rate, followed by the traditional multiple linear regression. This also proves that for the method of machine learning, once the parameters setting is not suitable, the result is rather worse than the traditional prediction method. SVM has better forecasting performance than BPNN, but its prediction error rate is significantly higher than SaDE-SVM. Therefore, the improved SaDE-SVM is significantly better than other algorithms in terms of forecasting accuracy.

Table 3. Comparison of forecasting results of four methods

Year	Actual value	Multiple linear regression		BPNN		SVM		SaDE-SVM	
		Predictive value	Error rate	Predictive value	Error rate	Predictive value	Error rate	Predictive value	Error rate
2014	4130.4	4244.7	2.77%	4038.2	−2.23%	4122.5	−0.2%	4107.5	−0.55%
2015	4229.9	4451.2	5.23%	4071.8	−3.74%	4309.5	1.88%	4248.8	0.45%
2016	4442.4	4696.0	5.71%	4110.2	−7.48%	4589.4	3.31%	4442.5	0.002%
2017	4625.5	5077.7	9.78%	4158.0	−10.1%	4895.3	5.83%	4625.5	0.00%
Average error		5.98%		−6.02%		2.80%		−0.02%	

The forecasting results in Fig. 5 show that among the four prediction methods, the SSE of other methods show a gradual increasing trend with the increase of the year. This indicates that they have large errors for long-term forecasting. The SSE of improved SaDE-SVM has smaller and smaller value with time, indicating that the improved algorithm has higher accuracy for medium and long-term forecasting.

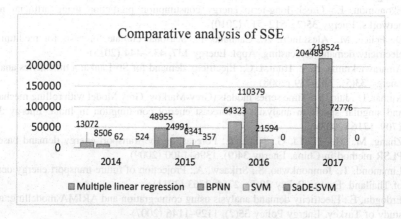

Fig. 5. SSE comparison chart of four methods

5   Conclusion

In order to further verify the factors that affect the per capita electricity consumption, in addition to the traditional GDP and population factors, this paper introduces the power supply structure and the social science and technology development level indicator, analyze electrical energy consumption from both ends of supply and demand. Using econometric methods to further verify the cointegration among variables. The SaDE model is used to improve the SVM based on Gaussian kernel function, and the developed model is used for medium and long-term power load forecasting in China.

The following conclusions are drawn from the research results of this paper:

(1) The SaDE-based optimization algorithm proposed in this paper is superior to the traditional prediction method and single machine learning method in accuracy.
(2) At the application level, the SaDE-SVM algorithm proposed in this paper is superior to linear regression, BPNN and SVM in short-term prediction, and it has superior effect on medium and long-term prediction.

In the future, the research will further deepen and expand the application field on the basis of further improvement of the algorithm.

References

1. Geem, Z.W.: Transport energy demand modeling of South Korea using artificial neural network. Energy Policy **39**(8), 4644–4650 (2011)
2. Yu, S., Wei, Y.M., Wang, K.: A PSO–GA optimal model to estimate primary energy demand of China. Energy Policy **42**(2), 329–340 (2012)
3. Xia, C., Wang, J., Mcmenemy, K.: Short, medium and long term load forecasting model and virtual load forecaster based on radial basis function neural networks. Int. J. Electr. Power Energy Syst. **32**(7), 743–750 (2010)
4. Ekonomou, L.: Greek long-term energy consumption prediction using artificial neural networks. Energy **35**(2), 512–517 (2010)
5. De Felice, M., Alessandri, A., Catalano, F.: Seasonal climate forecasts for medium-term electricity demand forecasting. Appl. Energy **137**, 435–444 (2015)
6. Amarawickrama, H.A., Hunt, L.C.: Electricity demand for Sri Lanka: a time series analysis. Energy **33**(5), 724–739 (2008)
7. Kumar, U., Jain, V.: Time series models (Grey-Markov, Grey Model with rolling mechanism and singular spectrum analysis) to forecast energy consumption in India. Energy **35**(4), 1709–1716 (2008)
8. Zhang, M., Mu, H., Li, G., Ning, Y.: Forecasting the transport energy demand based on PLSR method in China. Energy **34**(9), 1396–1400 (2009)
9. Limanond, T., Jomnonkwao, S., Srikaew, A.: Projection of future transport energy demand of Thailand. Energy Policy **39**(5), 2754–2763 (2011)
10. Erdogdu, E.: Electricity demand analysis using cointegration and ARIMA modelling: a case study of Turkey. Energy Policy **35**(2), 1129–1146 (2007)
11. Akay, D., Atak, M.: Grey prediction with rolling mechanism for electricity demand forecasting of Turkey. Energy **32**(9), 1670–1675 (2007)
12. Pi, D., Liu, J., Qin, X.: A grey prediction approach to forecasting energy demand in China. Energy Sour. **32**(16), 1517–1528 (2010)

13. Cadenas, E., Rivera, W.: Short term wind speed forecasting in Laventa, Oaxaca, Mxico, using artificial neural networks. Renew. Energy **34**(1), 274–278 (2009)
14. Cancelo, J.R., Espasa, A., Grafe, R.: Forecasting the electricity load from one day to one week ahead for the Spanish system operator. Int. J. Forecast. **24**(4), 588–602 (2008)
15. Escriv-Escriv, G., Alvarez-Bel, C., Roldn-Blay, C., Alczar-Ortega, M.: New artificial neural network prediction method for electrical consumption forecasting based on building end-uses. Energy Build. **43**(11), 3112–3119 (2011)
16. Lydia, M., Selvakumar, A.I., Kumar, S.S., Kumar, G.E.P.: Advanced algorithms for wind turbine power curve modeling. IEEE Trans. Sustain. Energy **4**(3), 827–835 (2013)
17. Sun, W., Liang, Y.: Research of least squares support vector regression based on differential evolution algorithm in short-term load forecasting model. J. Renew. Sustain. Energy **6**(5), 110 (2014)
18. Wang, J., Li, L., Niu, D., Tan, Z.: An annual load forecasting model based on support vector regression with differential evolution algorithm. Appl. Energy **94**(6), 65–70 (2012)
19. Xiao, L., Shao, W., Wang, C., Zhang, K., Lu, H.: Research and application of a hybrid model based on multi-objective optimization for electrical load forecasting. Applied Energy **180**(C), 213–233 (2016)
20. Han, Z., Li, Z.: Analysis of economic comparison between China and the United States. J. Quant. Tech. Econ. **31**(7), 115–133 (2014)
21. Amjady, N., Daraeepour, A.: Midterm demand prediction of electrical power systems using a new hybrid forecast technique. IEEE Trans. Power Syst. **26**(2), 755–765 (2011)
22. Wu, Q., Peng, C.: A hybrid BAG-SA optimal approach to estimate energy demand of China. Energy **120**, 985–995 (2016)

Coupling PSO-GPR Based Medium and Long Term Load Forecasting in Beijing

Yuansheng Huang, Jianjun Hu, Yaqian Cai[(⊠)], and Lei Yang

North China Electric Power University, Baoding, Hebei, China
Yqcai1996@163.com

Abstract. Establishing a scientific and reasonable mid- and long-term power load forecasting method is the premise of power industry planning and construction. This paper constructs a hybrid electric load forecasting model based on Gaussian process (GPR) and particle swarm optimization (PSO). The paper uses the PSO algorithm to optimize the parameters in the co-variance function, and uses the modified parameters as the initial value to train the power load in the GPR model. Under the Bayesian framework, the parameters in the co-variance function are again optimized. Finally, the trained GPR model is used to predict the power load, and the results are compared with the auto-regressive integral moving average model and the exponential smoothing model. The verification results show that the hybrid electric load forecasting model based on Gaussian process (GPR) and particle swarm optimization (PSO) has good stability and higher prediction accuracy, and is suitable for medium and long-term electric load forecasting.

Keywords: Artificial intelligence · Gaussian process regression
Particle swarm algorithm · Beijing · Power load forecast
Neural network training

1 Introduction

Constantly improving the accuracy of medium and long-term power load forecasting is an eternal issue in power planning and construction. Because the power industry is the foundation of the national economy, and its production cannot meet the needs of society, it will restrict the stable development of the economy and society. The power industry is a capital-intensive industry, and its investment requires a large amount of capital. Therefore, excessive investment will inevitably produce huge waste. To this end, people have been studying the medium and long-term power load forecasting methods.

Traditional methods of load forecasting include time-series methods and regression analysis. The most typical representation of the time series method is the ARMA (AR, MA) model proposed by Box-Jenkins and its derived model. This method uses the power load data as a chronological time series, uses the power load as a random variable, establishes or selects a suitable mathematical model to describe the statistical law of the power load change process, and establishes a complete mathematical expression. Forecast the future load [1]. The regression analysis method is to analyze the variable

© Springer Nature Singapore Pte Ltd. 2018
J. Qiao et al. (Eds.): BIC-TA 2018, CCIS 951, pp. 496–507, 2018.
https://doi.org/10.1007/978-981-13-2826-8_43

observation data, find the quantitative relationship between the influencing factors and the load, establish the regression equation and use this method to predict [2].

Modern load forecasting methods are widely used in expert system method, artificial neural network method, gray system theory, wavelet analysis method and so on. The expert system method is to sum up a large amount of expert knowledge into the system to summarize and use the software program to design a knowledge processing system that can make intelligent decisions after reasoning [3]; artificial neural network was introduced by DCPark et al. The model introduces a mathematical mathematical model that imitates the behavioral characteristics of animal neural networks through the introduction of load forecasting [4]. The Grey system theory was first proposed by Professor Deng Julong of our country in 1982. The gray prediction method is mainly to accumulate historical data. Generating, accumulating generation, average value generation and other technical processes are transformed into new series with stronger regularity, and a new series of models is established to predict the model [5]. The wavelet analysis and prediction method is a time domain-frequency domain analysis method. It can automatically adjust the sampling density according to the signal frequency, and is good at capturing and focusing analysis of weak, singular or abrupt signals [6]. The support vector machine prediction method was proposed and developed by Vapnk et al. in the 1990s Machine learning algorithms. The algorithm focuses on the principle of structural risk minimization. The main idea is to use the inner product function to define the nonlinear transformation, transform the input space into high-dimensional space, find the nonlinear relationship between input variables and output variables in the space, and finally realize the actual risk. The minimization [7] combined forecasting method is to combine multiple forecasting methods and assign certain weights to multiple forecasting methods according to certain principles. Finally, the optimal predictive model combination with the smallest co-variance is obtained [8].

The classical load forecasting technique has a poor prediction effect on sudden and random disturbances. For example, when the load changes at a special time point such as a major festival, the performance has certain limitations. Although the modern theoretical prediction model has been greatly developed, the prediction accuracy has been greatly improved, but there are still many shortcomings. If the expert system method does not have the ability to self-learn, in order to ensure the richness of the model, it is necessary to add new models to the expert system on a regular basis; the adaptability of the artificial neural network is poor and cannot be directly copied to another system; the gray in the grey system theory The research limit value is difficult to define and is still under study. The training efficiency and prediction effect of wavelet analysis prediction method have a great relationship with the initial setting of key parameters. There is no good initial parameter selection method at present; support vector machine prediction method When the number of samples is large, the calculation is time-consuming and takes up a large amount of memory; the combined prediction method does not substantially improve the fitting result of the load-influencing factors.

In view of the shortcomings of the previous load forecasting model, the Gaussian process (GPR) and particle swarm (PSO) hybrid electric load forecasting model adopted in this paper are based on the randomness of the factors affecting the electric load. The power load forecasting is carried out, and the prediction accuracy is greatly improved by optimizing the parameters multiple times. The empirical analysis shows that the Gaussian process (GPR) and particle swarm optimization (PSO) hybrid electric load forecasting model not only have higher prediction accuracy, but also increase the elasticity of prediction.

2 Method

The results shown in this paper first obtain preliminary prediction results through Gaussian Process Regression (GPR), then obtain the optimal value through the initial value of the particle swarm optimization (POS) parameter, and finally input the new data into the GPR model to obtain the final prediction result. The results show that the accuracy of the prediction after optimization is significantly improved, indicating that this is a mature bionic algorithm.

2.1 Gaussian Process Regression (GPR)

GPR is a powerful probabilistic modeling tool. Gaussian process is also called normal stochastic process. It is a universal and important random process in the world. The noise in the communication channel is usually a kind of Gaussian process, so it is also called Gaussian noise. In layman's terms, the random process is observed at any time. If the probability distribution of random variables satisfies the Gaussian distribution, this random process is a Gaussian process. It can be used to define the prior distribution of the hidden function in the hierarchical Bayesian model. It can also be directly inferred in the function space by estimating the posterior distribution. Compared with the neural network and support vector machine method, Gaussian process regression has the advantages of easy implementation, hyper-parametric adaptive acquisition and output of probability significance. The Gaussian regression process has developed rapidly at home and abroad, and has achieved remarkable results. This is inseparable from its advantages of easy integration with predictive control, adaptive control, and deviation filtering.

First, GPR establishes a priori function of the model in the form of a probability distribution, and then performs a transformation from a priori function to a posterior function based on the Bayesian framework, and at the same time can calculate the "hyper-parameter" of the kernel function. However, the selection of the SVM kernel function. Usually based on empirical values or cross-validation. The training process based on training data is a process of selecting parameters, which is one of the advantages of the Gaussian model. The basic principle of Bayesian optimization is to treat the hyper-parametric search as an optimization problem. The expected process of the high-level parameter (hyper-parametric) inferred function is treated as a regression process. The deviation principle provides an order for the calculation. The unified framework of human conviction makes the Gaussian regression model with Gaussian noise easy to calculate, and the model can be flexibly adjusted.

Where $m(x)$ and $k(x, x'|\theta)$ represent the mean and co-variance functions, and are the parameters of the observation model and the co-variance function, respectively. The reason that the co-variance function plays an important role in Gaussian process regression is that it can reflect the a priori assumption of the hidden function. GP is a set of arbitrary random variables with a joint Gaussian distribution whose properties are determined by the mean function and the co-variance function. GPR can choose different co-variance functions such as Square Index (SE), Rational Quadratic (RQ), and Matern's co-variance function. In this article, we use (SE):

$$k(x_i, x_j|\theta) = \sigma_{se}^2 \exp\left(\sum_{k=1}^d \frac{(x_{ik} - x_{jk})^2}{2l_k^2}\right) \tag{1}$$

$\theta = \{\sigma_{se}^2, 1_1, \cdots 1_k\}$ containing all the parameters. σ_{se}^2 is a measure of the total variance of the implicit function. l is a scale parameter that controls the degree of reduction associated with an increase in the input dimension.

Considering noise, we can build a general model of a Gaussian process:

$$y_i = f(x_i) + \varepsilon_i, i = 1, \cdots, n \tag{2}$$

$\varepsilon \sim N(0, \sigma^2)$ and $f(x)$ follow the prior distribution of the Gaussian process. Assuming that the hidden function is a mapping of the new input variable to the predicted value, the joint Gaussian distribution between the hidden variables and is:

$$\begin{bmatrix} y \\ \bar{f} \end{bmatrix} \sim N\left(0, \begin{bmatrix} K_{ff} + \sigma^2 I & K_{f\bar{f}} \\ K_{\bar{f}f} & K_{\bar{f}\bar{f}} \end{bmatrix}\right) \tag{3}$$

$K_{f\bar{f}} = k(x, \bar{x}|\theta)$ and $K_{\bar{f}\bar{f}} = k(\bar{x}, \bar{x}|\theta)$
The resulting conditional distribution:

$$\bar{f}|y, x, \bar{x} \sim N(m(\bar{x}|\theta), \text{cov}(\bar{f})) \tag{4}$$

Among them, the average function is:

$$m(\bar{x}|\theta) = k(x, x|\theta)(K_{ff} + \sigma_n^2 I)^{-1} y \tag{5}$$

The co-variance function is:

$$\text{cov}(\bar{f}) = k(\bar{x}, \bar{x}'|\theta) - k(\bar{x}, x|\theta)(K_{ff} + \sigma_n^2 I)^{-1} k(x, \bar{x}'|\theta) \tag{6}$$

2.2 Particle Swarm Optimization (PSO)

In the particle swarm optimization algorithm, the entity is abstracted as a particle. The initial value of the system is a set of random particles (a set of random solutions), and the optimal solution is obtained through iteration. The position of the particle is the solution to the problem. The particle searches for the optimal particle in the solution space. Therefore, the best solution is to find the position of the updated particle, specifically, how to update the particle position so that the algorithm converges faster and more accurately. To the optimal solution. If the current position of the i is better than its historical optimal position, update it to p_i. In addition, the historically optimal position of the entire group is $p_g = (p_{g1}, p_{g2}, \cdots, p_{gd})$. Then update the i dimension value j with the following two formulas $(1 \leq j \leq d)$:

$$v_{ij} = v_{ij} + c_1 \cdot rand() \cdot (p_{ij} - x_{ij}) + c_2 \cdot rand() \cdot (p_{gj} - x_{gj}) \qquad (7)$$

$$x_{ij} = x_{ij} + v_{ij} \qquad (8)$$

Among them, c_1, c_2 are non-negative constants, which make the particles have the ability to self-summary and learn the best individual in the population, and can be closer to their historical optimal position and global optimal position. $rand()$ Is a random number between $[0, 1]$. In addition, the speed of particle motion is limited between $[v_{min}, v_{max}]$. The PSO process is as follows:

Step 1, Initialization: Position and velocity of randomly generated particles in D-dimensional space; Step 2, Position Assessment: Evaluate each particle using a constructed positional objective function; Step 3, Update historical best position and global optimum of particle Location: Compared with the historical location's optimal value, if the location evaluation value is better than the historical optimal value of the particle, then the current location is used to replace the historic optimal location of the particle; if compared with the global optimum, if the current evaluation value is superior For the global optimal value of the group, the global value is replaced with the current value; Step 4, update the position and velocity of the particles by the above formula; Step 5, the cycle termination condition: execute the second to fourth steps for each particle cycle until the cycle termination condition is satisfied. The loop termination condition is similar to the genetic algorithm, it is an iteration number or a good fitness value.

2.3   Construction of PSO-GPR Combined Forecasting Model

The prediction process of the model is divided into three stages: In the first stage, a general model of the Gaussian process regression process is established according to the Gaussian process regression theory, and the PSO is used to optimize the Gaussian process's two-parameter co-variance functions σ2 and l to get close The initial value of the optimal value parameter; In the second stage, we use the initial value of the first stage GPR model and parameters to train the data, and use the Bayesian theory to optimize the hyper-parameter. After the first-order particle swarm optimization, the initial values of the parameters are close to the optimal values, the optimization process can be completed quickly, and it is not easy to fall into the local optimum. In the third stage, the new data is input into the GPR model to obtain the final prediction results.

3 Empirical Analysis

Taking Beijing's urban population, per capital living area, proportion of tertiary industry, and resident's consumption index as the sample data from 1995 to 2009, Beijing's electric load data from 2010 to 2014 was used as test data of this model to verify the forecast results. Accuracy.

3.1 Electric Load

The electricity load for each year of 1995–2014 in Beijing is shown in Table 1.

Table 1. Electricity load for 1995–2014.

Year	1995	1996	1997	1998	1999	2000	2001	2002	2003	2004
Electricity load/100 million kwh	222.6	244.4	263.6	276.2	297.3	331.8	346.4	384.2	414.8	451.7
Year	2005	2006	2007	2008	2009	2010	2011	2012	2013	2014
Electricity load/100 million kwh	570.5	618.9	667.0	689.7	739.1	809.9	821.7	874.3	913.1	937.0

Using MATLAB to make the line graph of Beijing's year and electricity load is shown in Fig. 1.

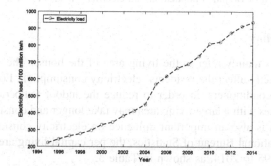

Fig. 1. The line graph of Beijing's year and electricity load.

3.2 Population Factors

When the total population of the society changes, the total electricity consumption of the society will also change; for a family, when the household population increases, the demand for electricity will also change. Therefore, whether it is from the macro level or the micro level, the population will have an impact on electricity consumption. By referring to the relevant information, the urban population in Beijing from 1995 to 2014 is shown in Table 2.

Table 2. Urban population in Beijing, 1995–2014.

Year	1995	1996	1997	1998	1999	2000	2001	2002	2003	2004
Urban population/ 10,000 people	696.9	709.7	722.7	733.7	747.2	760.7	780.1	806.9	830.8	854.7
Year	2005	2006	2007	2008	2009	2010	2011	2012	2013	2014
Urban population/ 10,000 people	880.2	905.4	929.0	950.7	971.9	989.5	1013.8	1039.3	1065.0	1089.8

Using MATLAB to make the line graph of Beijing's year, urban population and electricity load is shown in Fig. 2.

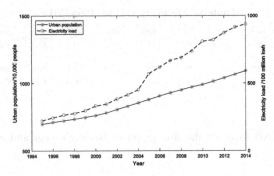

Fig. 2. Line graph of Beijing's population and electricity load for years, towns and cities.

3.3 Living Factors

Residential factors mainly refer to the living area of the house. The size of the living area will also directly affect the residents' electricity consumption. For example, when residents use air conditioners, in order to reduce the indoor temperature to the same temperature, houses with a large living area may take longer and consume more power, so the living area is also an important influence on electricity consumption. Through the data of the National Bureau of Statistics, the per capital living area of Beijing was obtained from 1995 to 2014, as shown in Table 3.

Table 3. Per capital living area of Beijing in 1995–2014.

Year	1995	1996	1997	1998	1999	2000	2001	2002	2003	2004
Per capital living area/m^2	9.03	9.33	9.66	10.03	10.63	11.15	11.64	11.93	12.20	19.09
Year	2005	2006	2007	2008	2009	2010	2011	2012	2013	2014
Per capital living area/m^2	19.45	20.00	20.30	21.56	21.61	19.49	29.40	29.26	31.31	31.54

Using MATLAB to make the line graph of Beijing's year, per capital living area and electric load is shown in Fig. 3.

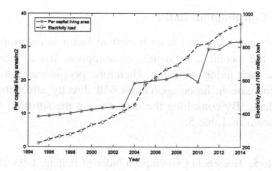

Fig. 3. Line chart of Beijing's year, per capital living area and electric load.

3.4   The Ratio of Three Production

The proportion of tertiary industry is the ratio of the tertiary industry to the GDP. The proportion of the three industries is an important indicator of the type and structure of economic development. At the same time, the proportion of the three industries is also an important factor affecting electricity consumption. In general, the higher the ratio of tertiary industry to production, the better the national economic development level. Therefore, the proportion of three production will also have a certain impact on the power load. According to the data from the National Bureau of Statistics, Beijing's tertiary industry accounted for in the period from 1995 to 2014, as shown in Table 4.

Table 4. Proportion of three production in Beijing from 1995–2014.

Year	1995	1996	1997	1998	1999	2000	2001	2002	2003	2004
Three production ratio/%	0.50	0.52	0.55	0.57	0.57	0.58	0.61	0.62	0.62	0.60
Year	2005	2006	2007	2008	2009	2010	2011	2012	2013	2014
Three production ratio/%	0.69	0.71	0.72	0.73	0.76	0.75	0.76	0.76	0.77	0.78

Using MATLAB to make the line graph of the year of Beijing, the proportion of three productions, and the electricity load shown in Fig. 4.

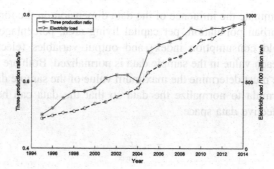

Fig. 4. Line chart of the percentage of Beijing's vintage, the proportion of three productions, and the electricity load.

3.5 Household Consumption Index

The household consumption index is an important factor in determining the needs of residents. When the people's resident's consumption index increases, they will appropriately raise their living standards. Therefore, people may purchase more home appliances. The increase in home appliances will directly affect the electricity consumption of residents. By consulting the data, we got the situation in Beijing during 1995–2014, as shown in Table 5.

Table 5. Household Consumption Index of Beijing, 1995–2014.

Year	1995	1996	1997	1998	1999	2000	2001	2002	2003	2004
Household consumption index/%	117.9	111.6	105.3	102.4	100.6	103.5	103.1	98.2	100.2	101
Year	2005	2006	2007	2008	2009	2010	2011	2012	2013	2014
Household consumption index/%	101.5	100.9	102.4	105.1	98.5	102.4	105.6	103.3	103.3	101.6

Using MATLAB to make the line graph of Beijing's year, resident's consumption index and electricity load shown in Fig. 5.

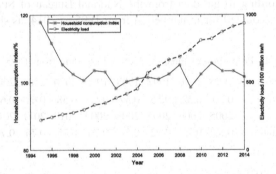

Fig. 5. Line chart of Beijing's year, residents' consumption index and electricity load.

In order to eliminate the influence of the data dimension on the forecast results, the input variables (urban population, per capital living area, percentage of tertiary production, household consumption index) and output variables (electricity load) are normalized, and each value in the sample data is normalized. Both are in the range of 5 of $[0, 1]$. First, we must determine the maximum value of the sample data, and then use the following formula to normalize the data so that the data can be uniformly distributed in the effective data space.

$$z = \frac{y_i}{y_{max}} \qquad (9)$$

$y_{\max}$ indicates the maximum value of the sample data. After the prediction process is finished, because the predicted values obtained are normalized, it is necessary to perform anti-normalization in order to predict the authenticity of the experiment.

It is also very important to choose a reasonable evaluation indicator to evaluate the prediction effect. In this article, the following two indicators are used to test the forecast results:

$$\sigma_{MAPE} = \frac{1}{N} \sum_{i=1}^{N} \frac{|\bar{y}(i) - y(i)|}{y(i)} \tag{10}$$

$$\sigma_{RMSE} = \sqrt{\frac{1}{N} \sum_{i=1}^{N} (\bar{y}(i) - y(i))^2} \tag{11}$$

σ_{MAPE} absolute percentage error; σ_{RMSE} root mean square error; $\bar{y}(i)$ predicted value; $y(i)$ true value.

Based on the data from 1995–2014 Beijing electric power load, using PSO-GPR model and GPR model as data, the regression model of Gaussian process is used to obtain a corresponding ground-penetrating radar prediction model. In the Gaussian process prediction model, the most important parameter is the two parameters of the co-variance function. In the GPR prediction model, these two parameters are set to 120 and 10 respectively, and then Bayesian theory is used to optimize the parameters in the training process. However, the optimal value of the two parameters of the co-variance function is away from the initial value (120, 10).

Therefore, in the combined prediction model, the PSO algorithm is used to optimize the parameters of the two co-variance functions and parameters, so as to obtain the optimal initial value (21.5, 200) relative to the initial value of the GPR prediction model. Then, the Bayesian is used. The theory again optimizes the parameters, which will increase the accuracy of the prediction.

The Gaussian process regression of the kernel function is SE, which is a square exponential co-variance function. In the PSO algorithm, the particle range is [1, 100], the population size is 50, and the maximum number of iterations is 100. Due to the fitness of the PSO optimization algorithm used in this paper. The function is a function of minimizing fitness, so root mean square error RMSE is used as a fitness function. The results are shown in Table 6.

Table 6. Predicted values of different models.

Year	Actual value	Predictive value			
		PSO-GPR	GPR	ARIMA	ES
2010	809.9	740.23	496.61	824.34	738.78
2011	821.7	833.93	562.20	955.67	740.19
2012	874.3	843.30	562.20	1144.41	740.23
2013	913.1	899.52	580.94	1402.99	740.23
2014	937.0	918.26	590.31	1744.94	740.23

The energy consumption prediction errors in Table 6 are analyzed using evaluation indicators. The results are shown in Table 7. It can be seen that the error based on the PSO-GPR combined forecasting model is the smallest, the average absolute error is 11.85, the root mean square error is 87.75, and the model prediction accuracy is obviously improved.

Table 7. Prediction error analysis.

Error	PSO-GPR	GPR	ARIMA	ES
RMSE	36.06	314.14	428.53	140.20
MAPE	3.54%	44.84%	37.77%	14.79%

4   Conclusion

With the rapid growth of power load, accurate and reliable medium and long-term power load forecasting methods and technologies are urgently needed. Due to various environmental factors, it is difficult to predict the electrical load with a single model. This paper proposes a hybrid prediction method based on the concept of hybrid prediction, which integrates the concepts of PSO and GPR.

First of all, the PSO algorithm has the characteristics of few parameters and easy implementation. The generalization ability of the Gaussian process can be improved by particle swarm optimization of Gaussian process parameters. The application of coupled PSO-GPR in energy time series prediction has probabilistic significance and can meet the needs of prediction.

Second, different kernel functions have different effects on machine learning and predictability, but the difference is small. In this article, the SE kernel function is chosen. The experimental results show that PSO has better prediction accuracy after optimizing the parameters of GPR kernel function. After the Gaussian process particle swarm optimization algorithm, the initial and local optimization problems and the determination of the model parameters are solved. Therefore, the combined prediction model based on PSO-GPR has good application value in power load forecasting.

References

1. Wang, X., Liu, S., Yan, L., Wang, N.: Energy consumption forecast based on coupling PSO-GPR. In: International Conference on Economics, Social Science, Arts, Education and Management Engineering (2017)
2. Felice, M.D., Alessandri, A., Catalano, F.: Seasonal climate forecasts for medium-term electricity demand forecasting. Appl. Energy **137**, 435–444 (2015)
3. Lee, Y.S., Tong, L.I.: Forecasting energy consumption using a grey model improved by incorporating genetic programming. Energy Convers. Manag. **52**(1), 147–152 (2011)
4. Xu, C., Liu, B.G., Liu, K.Y., Guo, J.Q.: Intelligent analysis model of landslide displacement time series based on coupling PSO-GPR. Rock Soil Mech. **32**(6), 1669–1675 (2011)

5. He, Y., He, Z., Zhang, D.: A study on prediction of customer churn in fixed communication network based on data mining. In: International Conference on Fuzzy Systems and Knowledge Discovery, pp. 92–94 (2009)
6. Chen, H., Zhou, D.: A forecast of gross energy consumption in china based on GM(1,1) model. Min. Res. Dev. **3**, 029 (2007)
7. Liang, N., Zhang, J.G.: China's total energy consume forecasting based on grey-RBF neural network. J. Jiamusi Univ. **2**, 029 (2008)
8. Zhang, X., Fan, Y.I.: Boiler soot-blowing optimal control system based on statistical forecast of power load. Power & Energy (2015)

Nonlinear Finite-Element Analysis of Offshore Platform Impact Load Based on Two-Stage PLS-RBF Neural Network

Shibo Zhou and Wenjun Zhang$^{(\boxtimes)}$

Navigation College, Dalian Maritime University, Dalian 116026, China
shibodmu@163.com, 18018901293@163.com

Abstract. Feature selection is a vital step in many machine learning and data mining tasks. Feature selection can reduce the dimensionality, speed up the learning process, and improve the performance of the learning models. Most of the existing feature selection methods try to find the best feature subset according to a pre-defined feature evaluation criterion. However, in many real-world datasets, there may exist many global or local optimal feature subsets, especially in the high-dimensional datasets. Classical feature selection methods can only obtain one optimal feature subset in a run of the algorithm and they cannot locate multiple optimal solutions. Therefore, this paper considers feature selection as a multimodal optimization problem and proposes a novel feature selection method which integrates the barebones particle swarm optimization (BBPSO) and a neighborhood search strategy. BBPSO is a simple but powerful variant of PSO. The neighborhood search strategy can form several steady sub-swarms in the population and each sub-swarm aims at finding one optimal feature subset. The proposed approach is compared with four PSO based feature selection methods on eight UCI datasets. Experimental results show that the proposed approach can produce superior feature subsets over the comparative methods.

Keywords: Dropped objects · Impact angle · ANSYS/LS-DYNA
PLS-RBF neural network · Risk assessment

1 Introduction

Dropped objects have been identified as a potential hazard in a variety of offshore operational activities. An estimated 10% of facilities and thousands of medical treatment and lost-time injuries are caused by dropped objects. The partial impact may cause deck structure and deck equipment damaged, in serious cases, the sequence may lead to the oil and gas leaks, casualties and huge economics losses. Although it is strongly recommended by international organizations to reference the operation guideline and rules in offshore industry, most engineers have difficulty in establishing or putting forward a more reliable and effective estimating method of risk value. The prevention and safety assessment of dropped objects are an important component of safeguarding personal, property and the environment [1]. To mitigate such catastrophes, this paper is evolving towards a methodology based on the two-stage PLS-RBF

© Springer Nature Singapore Pte Ltd. 2018
J. Qiao et al. (Eds.): BIC-TA 2018, CCIS 951, pp. 508–517, 2018.
https://doi.org/10.1007/978-981-13-2826-8_44

neural network which applied on risk analysis of offshore dropped objects. In recent years. Several studies have proposed relevant analysis method in the field of offshore risk assessment. Md. Rokan Uddin Kawsar, Samy Adly Youssef have proposed a probabilistic methodology to establish risk reduction strategy in offshore oil and gas industry and assess meticulous safety measurements [2]. Bai and Bai suggested the probability and consequences of the failure of subsea pipelines from different types of impact and investigated the prediction of risk and acceptance criteria to establish an optimal plan for inspection. Yeong and Thomas [3] have introduced an algorithm to compute a reasonable probability of structural failure.

The Two-stage PLS-RBF network combines the structural features of RBF neural networks with advantages of PLS regression method, Using PLS regression method to find the connection matrix of hidden layer response matrix and output matrix, the RBF neural network based on PLS regression. This study conducted a numerical simulation of dropped tubular based on the real offshore platform with nonlinear finite element analysis ANSYS/LS-DYNA. In one side, the numerical simulation method is used to address structural integrity in case of impact scenario at different impact angle. The computational and statistical analysis involves the impact consequences and likely to predict the probability of unexpected dropped accidents and the extent of the damage. This paper discussed the consequences of an impact failure of offshore platform deck structures and assesses the potential dropping risk analysis process to life, assets and environment from an offshore loading and unloading facility.

As the number of simulations is limited, the present simulation circumstances cannot cover all the conditions which would occur in the real world. The fitting can also be difficult if the number of simulation circumstances is small. Under such circumstances, the fitting accuracy is important for applications of impact result, such as risk assessment and safety precaution. The booming of computational approaches, such as fuzzy inference system and neural networks, has also gained much popularity in areas of naval architecture [4] and marine engineering [8]. They played an important role for system identification [9], prediction and control [10], attributing their merits such as nonlinearity, adaptivity, and satisfactory fault tolerant ability caused by its parallel processing mechanism. They also provide new tools for nonlinear mapping and interpolation. In our study, the custom fitting method of polynomial and intelligent method of PLS-RBF networks is both applied for nonlinear fitting and the results are compared and analyzed.

2 Methodology

2.1 Statistics of Dropped Objects

A dropped object is defined as an object, with the potential to cause death, injury or equipment/environmental damage, which falls from its previous static position under its own weight. The Lifting activities with possibility of dropped objects are mainly from the following three conditions:

(1) objects lifting between supply vessel and platform/rig
(2) objects lifting between platform/rig and subsea installation
(3) objects lifting internally on the platform, but with potential for objects to drop into the sea.

From statistical data, the potential dropped objects can be classified into several types generally, as listed in Table 1.

Table 1. Dropped object classification

No.	Description	Weight in air (tonnes)	Typical objects
1	Flat/long shaped	<2	Drill collar/casing, scaffolding
2		2–8	Drill collar/casing
3		>8	Dill riser, crane boom
4	Box/round shaped	<2	container (food, space parts), basket, crane, block
5		2–8	container (space parts), basket, crane test block
6		>8	container (equipment), basket
7	Box/round shaped	>>8	Massive objects as BOP, Pipe reel, etc.

2.2 Analysis Method of Impact Problem

The interaction of offshore platform structure and dropped objects is a typical impact problem, which is a complicated problem because of the high nonlinearity involved. The commonly used and effective calculation approach for this kind of collision problem is FE method.

$$M\ddot{X}(t) + C\dot{X}(t) + KX(t) = F^E(t) \tag{1}$$

In this equation, M and C are the mass matrix of the system, respectively. K is the stiffness matrix that takes into account the constitutive relations of the system material elements. $\ddot{X}(t)$ is the acceleration vector at time t. Gravitational acceleration is generally considered when involved dropping problem. $\dot{X}(t)$ is the velocity vector at time t. $X(t)$ is displacement vector. $F^E(t)$ is the external load matrix.

If $F^I(t) = C\dot{X}(t) + KX(t)$, the collision equation can be rewritten as:

$$M\ddot{X}(t) = F^E(t) - F^I(t)$$

In LS-DYNA display kinetic analysis take the Central difference method, each node in the collision system ends at the time of n, so the acceleration vector expression at time t_n is:

$$\ddot{X}(t_n) = M^{-1}\left\{M\ddot{X}(t_n)\right\} = M^{-1}\left\{F^E(t_n) - F^I(t_n)\right\}$$

According to the basic idea of the center difference method, we can get the node velocity vector and displacement vector at time t_{n+1}

$$\ddot{X}_{t+\frac{\Delta t}{2}} = \dot{X}_{t-\frac{\Delta t}{2}} + (\Delta t_{t+\Delta\frac{\Delta t}{2}} + \Delta t_{t-\frac{\Delta t}{2}})/2$$

$$X_{t+\Delta t} = \dot{X}_t + \Delta t_{t+\frac{\Delta t}{2}} + \dot{X}_{t+\frac{\Delta t}{2}}\Delta t_{t+\frac{\Delta t}{2}}$$

For the dynamic problem, explicit algorithm is very suitable for solving large matrix equations. Since the explicit algorithm does not require matrix transposition and iteration, all its nonlinear are included in the internal force vector, so within the same time step, explicit algorithm are more efficient than implicit algorithm [5].

3 Nonlinear Fem Numerical Analysis

3.1 ANSYS/LS-DYNA

ANSYS/LS-DYNA is the most commonly used explicit simulation program, capable of simulating the response of materials to short periods of severe loading. Its many elements, contact formulations, material models and other controls can be used to simulate complex models with control over all the details of the problem. ANSYS LS-DYNA has a vast array of capabilities to simulate extreme deformation problems using its explicit solver. Engineers can tackle simulations involving material failure and look at how the failure progresses through a part or through a system. Models with large amounts of parts or surfaces interacting with each other are also easily handled, and the interactions and load passing between complex behaviors are modeled accurately. Using computers with higher numbers of CPU cores can drastically reduce solution times [6].

3.2 Working Condition Design

On the basis of the drilling platform, based on the real offshore platform deck, a typical finite element model with stiffeners was built in the geometry of ANSYS. This study concerns an offshore platform 200 m long and 140 m wide, the thickness is 3.8 cm. the width of the transverse section is 3.1 m. the elastic of all components is E = 210 Gpa, passion ratio is $\mu = 0.3$, The density is p = 7850 kg/m^3. The drill risers fell from 10 m, the length is 1000 cm. According to Table 1, OD is 325.55 mm, ID is 200 mm, initial vertical velocity is 8 m/s, gravitational acceleration is 9.81 m/s^2. Several typical dropped risers with different impact angle are simplified as tubular shaped and the parameter are listed in Table 2 (Fig. 1).

Table 2. Simulation experiment design

Condition	Shape	Dimension (mm)	Height of fall (m)	Velocity (m/s)	Mass (t)	Elastic modulus	Density (kg/m3)	Angle (°)	Length (m)	Poisson ratio
PIPE-0	Riser	OD = 325.55 ID = 200	5	8	8.1362	2.10E+11	7850	0	10	0.3
PIPE-10	Riser	OD = 325.55 ID = 200	5	8	8.1362	2.10E+11	7850	10	10	0.3
PIPE-20	Riser	OD = 325.55 ID = 200	5	8	8.1362	2.10E+11	7850	20	10	0.3
PIPE-30	Riser	OD = 325.55 ID = 200	5	8	8.1362	2.10E+11	7850	30	10	0.3
PIPE-40	Riser	OD = 325.55 ID = 200	5	8	8.1362	2.10E+11	7850	40	10	0.3
PIPE-50	Riser	OD = 325.55 ID = 200	5	8	8.1362	2.10E+11	7850	50	10	0.3
PIPE-60	Riser	OD = 325.55 ID = 200	5	8	8.1362	2.10E+11	7850	60	10	0.3
PIPE-70	Riser	OD = 325.55 ID = 200	5	8	8.1362	2.10E+11	7850	70	10	0.3
PIPE-80	Riser	OD = 325.55 ID = 200	5	8	8.1362	2.10E+11	7850	80	10	0.3
PIPE-90	Riser	OD = 325.55 ID = 200	5	8	8.1362	2.10E+11	7850	90	10	0.3

3.3 Numerical Simulation of Dropped Objects

An offshore platform with superstructure and crane is taken for the parametric numerical experiment of dynamic responses of the platform deck and dropped object using ANSYS/LS-DYNA. The Fig. 2 has been chosen as a source of perspective model of the offshore platform deck structure. The analytical and numerical evaluation of the dropped object will be completed at the view of reference demonstrate.

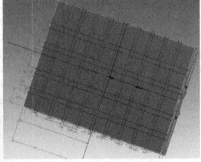

Fig. 1. The 3D structural model view of upper platform

Fig. 2. Structural model of upper deck impact area

Mesh generation is one of the most critical aspects of the simulation. Too many cells may result in long solver runs, and few may lead to inaccurate results. Therefore, the meshing is one of the most important sets in the problem simulation (Figs. 3, 4 and 5).

Fig. 3. The finite element model of dropped riser at impact angle 60°

Fig. 4. The finite element model of dropped riser at impact angle 90°

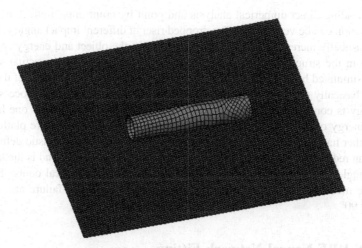

Fig. 5. The meshing impact area of dropped riser and platform deck

3.4 Numerical Simulation Results

To evaluate the consequence of the impact on the platform deck material and its behavior, the result of the total deformation, equivalent stress, and equivalent elastic strain is considered. Through explicit dynamic analysis, the deformation diagram and the force diagram of the platform deck are obtained. The calculation results show that there are two processes for the collision between the dropped riser and the deck. The first process is a depression or breaks in the deck after impact. The second process is the damage caused by the second impact. The impact angle of the dropped object significantly influences the deformation and structural properties. Different impact angles will produce different impact forces on the deck, creating depressions of different depths. The Figs. 6 and 7 shows the stress cloud at the impact angle of 60° and 90°.

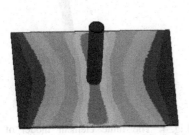

Fig. 6. The stress distribution clouds at an impact angle of 90°

Fig. 7. The stress distribution clouds at an impact angle of 60°

The leading direct numerical analysis and point by point impact effect area on the basic reaction can be verified [5]. The dropped riser at different impact angle is the local strain drastically increase while the kinetic energy in the object and energy engrossing limit are in the structure can't change. Figures 6 and 7 displays the actual structural damage simulated by ANSYS/LS-DYNA. It can be seen that the damage of the impact is local, basically concentrated in the impact area. During the impact process, part of the energy is converted into the kinetic energy of the platform. On the one hand, the impact energy of the object is relatively small compared to the offshore platform, and on the other hand, the overall performance of the platform is good elastic deformation, which can reduce the structural damage of the object. The overall trend is the larger the impact angle, the longer the collision time and the deeper the local dents. The local dents are most large at the impact angle of 80°. Deck structure failure at a collision angle of 90°.

4   PLS-RBF Neural Network Fitting

Fitting analysis of the simulation results, try to find out the relationship between the impact results and the impact angle. Regression analysis is a conventional mathematical statistical method that deals with the statistical correlation of variables. Regression analysis mainly solves the following problems:

(1) Determine whether there is a correlation between variables, if any, find the appropriate mathematical expression between them.
(2) Depending on the value of one or several variables, the value of the other variable is predicted or controlled and it is possible to know what the accuracy of such a prediction or control can achieve (Fig. 8).

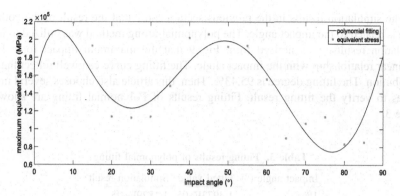

Fig. 8. The relationship between maximum equivalent stress and impact angle based on polynomial fitting

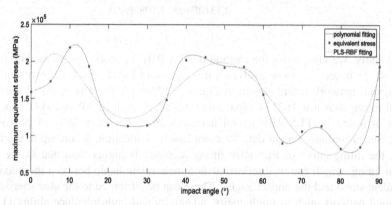

Fig. 9. Fitting of mapping between stress and impact angle based on polynomial fitting and PLS-RBF fitting

Based on the selected resulting damage indices in terms of the maximum plastic strain, it is observed that the length of Z-direction is more influential in the computed damages at the impact angle 80° compared to other impact angles. A multi nonlinear regression model for the structural response can be established using the computed structural damage values described in the previous section. The regression model meets quite nicely the trend of the actual structural responses. A structural Elastic Strain curve is created, which provides the exceedances probability of a damaged state for the offshore deck structure protection system at each level of impact angle [4]. For the entire collision system, the total energy is supplied by the initial kinetic energy of the falling object; the quality and speed of the falling object determine the initial kinetic energy of the falling object. In determining the impact force of the process, the perspective of falling objects is also an important factor cannot be ignored.

The simulation results in the previous section show that the result of the collision force is related to the impact angle. The polynomial fitting method was utilized to fit the simulation results. It is noticed from Fig. 9 that the maximum impact force has a nonlinear relationship with the impact angle. The fitting curve can well reflect the data distribution. The fitting degree is 95.43%. Then, this article also chooses several impact angles to verify the fitting result. Fitting results of Polynomial fitting are shown in Table 3.

Table 3. Fitting results of polynomial fitting

Impact angle (°)	Fitted value	Simulation result
18	1.3973E+05	1.1829E+05
26	1.2862E+05	1.0198E+05
35	1.621E+05	1.9441E+05
58	1.5702E+05	1.7208E+05
75	2.1310E+05	1.1983E+05

Similarly, we also verify the method of PLS-RBF network algorithm. The impact angle of 35° is selected to be analyzed. It is shown in Table 3 that, the result of PLS-RBF neural network fitting shown in Fig. 9 is 173884 MPa. The result of the Polynomial fitting shown is 162114 Mpa. The simulation result of 35° is 19441 Mpa. The results of fitting by PLS-RBF neural networks are better than those of polynomial fitting. Select multiple sets of data for comparison verification, according to the fitting result, the fitting curve of PLS-RBF fitting accuracy is higher than that of the polynomial fitting, which can well reflect the nonlinear relationship between the maximum equivalent stress and the impact angles. These can be attributed to the characteristics of the neural network such as nonlinearity, adaptivity and fault tolerance ability [11].

5   Conclusions

The objective of this paper is to introduce an algorithm for offshore dropped objects risk assessment. Combine the structural features of the RBF neural network with the advantages of the PLS regression method, Get more accurate and reliable analysis results. And the algorithm has a very fast convergence speed. Applying this method to the field of marine platform risk assessment, the analysis may give the designer some useful information on the area where the maximum impact frequency occurs so that the loading and unloading works can be more careful operated. In particular, a structural reliability-based on analysis will be utilized for evaluating the failure probability given the impact. Simulation results of dropped objects demonstrated the feasibility and effectiveness of the proposed learning algorithm.

References

1. Arabzadeh, H., Zeinoddini, M.: Dynamic response of pressurized submarine pipelines subjected to transverse impact loads. Proc. Eng. **14**, 648–655 (2011)
2. Kawsar, M.R.U., Youssef, S.A., Faisal, M., et al.: Assessment of dropped object risk on corroded subsea pipeline. Ocean Eng. **106**, 329–340 (2015)
3. Bai, Y., Bai, Q.: Subsea Pipeline Integrity and Risk Management. Gulf Professional Publishing, Waltham (2014)
4. Yin, J.C., Perakis, A.N., Wang, N.: A real-time ship roll motion prediction using wavelet transform and variable RBF network. Ocean Eng. **160**, 10–19 (2018)
5. Janine, B., Coetsee, W.J.: Safety climate dimensions as predictors for risk behavior. Accid. Anal. Prev. **55**, 256–264 (2013)
6. Mazzola, A.: A probabilistic methodology for the assessment of safety from dropped loads in offshore engineering. Risk Anal. **20**, 327–338 (2000)
7. Chen, S., Cowan, C.F.N., Grant, P.M.: Orthogonal least squares learning algorithm for radial basis function networks. IEEE Trans. Neural Netw. **2**(2), 302–309 (1991)
8. Yin, J.C., Wang, N., Perakis, A.N.: A real-time sequential ship roll prediction scheme based on adaptive sliding data window. IEEE Trans. Syst. Man Cybern.: Syst. (2017). https://doi.org/10.1109/tsmc.2017.2735995
9. Wang, N., Sun, J.C., Er, M.J.: Tracking-error-based universal adaptive fuzzy control for output tracking of nonlinear systems with completely unknown dynamics. IEEE Trans. Fuzzy Syst. **26**(2), 869–883 (2018)
10. Wang, N., Sun, Z., Zheng, Z.J., Zhao, H.: Finite-time sideslip observer based adaptive fuzzy path following control of underactuated marine vehicles with time-varying large sideslip. Int. J. Fuzzy Syst. **20**(6), 1767–1778 (2018)
11. Sun, L.P., Ma, G., Nie, C.Y., Wang, Z.H.: The simulation of dropped objects on the offshore structure. Adv. Mater. Res. **339**, 553–556 (2011)

Author Index

Ahmad, Wasim   II-360
Ahn, Chang Wook   II-388, II-397, II-477
Altangerel, Khuder   I-107

Bai, Shuai   II-178
Bi, Bo   I-454
Bian, Xinchao   I-355

Cai, Ci-Yun   I-295
Cai, Xinye   I-380
Cai, Yaqian   I-496
Chen, Jiaqi   II-415
Chen, Jie   I-12
Chen, Jinsong   II-316, II-435
Chen, Junfeng   I-236
Chen, Li   II-296
Chen, Xiaoji   I-246
Chen, Xin   I-307
Chen, Ying-Wu   I-444
Chen, Zhichuan   II-296
Chen, Zhihua   II-63
Cheng, Jian   II-178
Cheng, Shi   I-236
Cheong, Yun-Gyung   II-477
Choi, Tae Jong   II-477
Cong, Xuwen   II-201
Cui, Guangzhao   II-226
Cui, Jianzhong   I-151, II-55
Cui, Yang   II-351

Deng, Yali   I-389
Ding, Rui   I-24
Dong, Hongbin   I-24
Dong, Yafei   I-473
Du, Yi-Chen   I-273, I-295

Fan, Yuanyuan   I-60
Fan, Zhun   I-355, I-380
Fang, Wangsheng   II-457
Fang, Xianwen   II-72
Fang, Yi   I-355
Feng, Xianbin   I-24

Ganbaatar, Ganbat   I-107
Gang, Yusen   II-178

Gao, Chong   II-72
Gao, Hai-rong   II-308
Gao, Wenbin   I-161
Geng, Shuang   II-360
Gong, Dunwei   I-401, II-188, II-415
Guan, Jing   I-82
Guo, Miao   I-12
Guo, Ping   I-198, I-223
Guo, Yi-nan   II-178

Han, Gaoyong   I-263
He, Chun-lin   II-308
He, Jun   I-24
Hu, Jianjun   I-496
Hu, Long   II-1
Hu, Mi   I-380
Hu, Zhongdong   II-457
Huang, An   II-63
Huang, Chun   II-13, II-129, II-162, II-287
Huang, Weidong   II-351
Huang, Yifeng   II-377
Huang, Yuansheng   I-1, I-36, I-48, I-484,
   I-496
Hussain, Safdar   II-360

Ishdorj, Tseren-Onolt   I-107

Jafar, Rana Muhammad Sohail   II-360
Jia, Shiyu   II-1
Jiang, Keqin   I-94
Jie, Wang   II-264
Juanjuan, He   I-173

Kai, Zhang   I-173, I-186
Kim, Jun Suk   II-397

Lei, Heng   I-82
Li, Chao   II-466
Li, Chen   II-23
Li, Jing   II-31
Li, Juan   II-446
Li, Li   I-94
Li, Lijie   I-24
Li, Meng   II-13

Li, Nan   I-285
Li, Rui   I-401, II-415, II-426
Li, Wang   II-252
Li, Wenji   I-355
Li, Xingmei   II-415
Li, Yan   II-118
Li, Yanyue   II-23
Li, Yuan-Xiang   II-446
Li, Yuanyuan   II-104
Li, Zehua   II-138
Li, Zheng   I-60
Lin, Qiuzhen   II-188
Lin, Zhiyi   I-389
Liu, Hongwei   II-118
Liu, Huan   II-316, II-328
Liu, Hui   I-1
Liu, Jia   II-239, II-435
Liu, Jie   I-70
Liu, Lei   II-239, II-328
Liu, Qianying   II-316, II-435
Liu, Shijian   I-48, I-484
Liu, Shuaichen   II-118
Liu, Xiangrong   I-133, I-307
Lu, Hui   I-236
Lu, Xue-Qin   I-273
Lv, Aolong   II-129

Ma, Jingjing   I-161
Ma, Xin   I-444
Mei, Lin   I-70
Mo, Wanying   I-142

Ni, Yudong   II-104
Ning, Ding   II-252
Niu, Ben   II-201, II-296, II-328
Niu, Ying   II-213

Park, Dongju   II-388
Peng, Chao   II-188
Peng, Gang   I-423, II-95
Pengfei, Yu   I-173

Qi, Huaqing   II-1
Qiang, Xiaoli   II-63
Qiu, Chenye   II-42
Qu, Rong   II-201, II-296
Quan, Changsheng   I-223

Shen, Lei   I-36
Shen, Yindong   II-104
Shi, Chuan   I-246

Shi, Hongyi   II-152
Shi, Mengshu   I-484
Shi, Yuhui   I-236
Song, Feng   II-338
Song, Wu   I-236
Song, Yan-Jie   I-444
Sun, Junwei   I-263, I-285, II-13, II-129,
    II-275, II-287

Tan, Yihua   II-405
Tang, Ke   I-60
Tang, Zhen   II-55

Ventura, Michele Della   I-434

Wan, Xing   II-338
Wang, Bin   II-72, II-83
Wang, Chunlu   II-152
Wang, Dongwei   II-178
Wang, Gaiying   I-133
Wang, Haoran   I-142
Wang, Hong   II-328, II-360
Wang, Hongwei   I-48
Wang, Jun   II-316, II-435
Wang, Lingfei   II-213, II-226, II-466
Wang, Luhui   I-473
Wang, Min   II-95
Wang, Mingliang   I-454
Wang, Shengsheng   I-70
Wang, Siming   I-423
Wang, Wenbo   I-213
Wang, Xueli   I-213
Wang, Yanfeng   I-263, I-285, II-13, II-129,
    II-162, II-213, II-275, II-287
Wang, Yipeng   I-12
Wang, Yuan   I-411
Wang, Yulong   I-315, I-331, I-368, II-377
Wang, Zhaojun   I-355
Wang, Zhenyu   I-389
Wang, Zhiyu   I-133
Wei, Hu   I-186
Wei, Teng   II-252
Wei, Xiaopeng   II-83
Wei, Yani   I-473
Wu, Bin   I-246
Wu, Xiuli   II-31
Wu, Yu   I-389
Wu, Zhi   II-377

Xiang, Junqi   I-198
Xiao, Lu   II-239, II-316

Xiaoming, Liu   I-173
Xiaoxiao, Ren   II-264
Xie, Haibo   II-138
Xie, Yuehong   I-389
Xin, Bin   I-12
Xing, Lining   I-411
Xing, Li-Ning   I-444
Xing, Shanshan   II-83
Xu, Guangzhi   I-401, II-426
Xu, Siyong   I-246
Xu, Siyuan   I-484
Xu, Zhi-Ge   I-343

Yan, Pei   II-405
Yan, Peng   II-264
Yan, Xiaoshan   I-133
Yan, Xuesong   I-60
Yang, Chen   II-239
Yang, Geng   II-457
Yang, Jing   I-151, II-55
Yang, Lei   I-496
Yang, Ming   I-82
Yang, Xu-Hua   I-273
Yang, Yu   II-1
Yang, Zhenqin   I-151
Yang, Zuhuang   II-95
Ye, Lian   I-223
Yin, Zhixiang   I-151, II-55, II-72
Ying, Weiqin   I-389
Yixuan, Qiao   II-264
Yu, Mingzhu   II-201, II-296
Yu, Xiaodong   I-24
Yuan, Guodong   II-287
Yuan, Yutong   I-355
Yue, Zhao   II-252
Yunfeng, Shao   I-186

Zhang, Haoxin   I-331
Zhang, Heping   II-1
Zhang, Jiuchao   I-368
Zhang, Lijun   I-484
Zhang, Min-Xia   I-295, I-343
Zhang, Qiang   II-55, II-72, II-83
Zhang, Ruozhu   I-120
Zhang, Wenjun   I-508, II-118, II-138
Zhang, Xing   I-213
Zhang, Xuncai   II-213, II-226, II-466
Zhang, Xu-tao   II-308
Zhang, Yingying   I-473
Zhang, Yong   II-308
Zhang, Zhong-Shan   I-444
Zhang, Zhou   II-1
Zhao, Xinchao   I-401, II-152, II-188, II-415,
    II-426
Zhao, Xingtong   II-275
Zhaozong, Zhang   I-186
Zhen, Yiting   II-1
Zheng, Yu-Jun   I-273, I-295, I-343
Zheng, Zhonglong   II-83
Zhou, Aimin   I-246
Zhou, Changjun   II-72, II-83
Zhou, Chenyang   I-423
Zhou, Hangyu   II-466
Zhou, Kang   II-1
Zhou, Moqin   I-213
Zhou, Qinglei   II-162
Zhou, Shibo   I-508
Zhou, Xiao-Han   I-343
Zhou, Yalan   II-23
Zhou, Zheng   II-213, II-226, II-466
Zong, Hua   I-315
Zou, Jie   II-446
Zuo, Lulu   II-239
Zuo, Xingquan   II-42, II-152, II-338

Printed in the United States
By Bookmasters